Niuatoputapu

View northward from the central ridge to the leeward coastline and lagoon of Niuatoputapu, with Tafahi Island in the distance.

Niuatoputapu

The Prehistory of a Polynesian Chiefdom

Patrick Vinton Kirch

Thomas Burke Memorial
Washington State Museum
Monograph No. 5

Burke Museum
Seattle

Thomas Burke Memorial Washington State Museum Monographs

1. *Northwest Coast Indian Art: An Analysis of Form,*
   by Bill Holm
2. *Edward S. Curtis in the Land of the War Canoes: A Pioneer Cinematographer in the Pacific Northwest,*
   by Bill Holm
3. *Smoky-Top: The Art and Times of Willie Seaweed,*
   by Bill Holm and George Irving Quimby
4. *Spirit and Ancestor: A Century of Northwest Coast Indian Art at the Burke Museum,*
   by Bill Holm with photographs by Eduardo Calderón
5. *Niuatoputapu: The Prehistory of a Polynesian Chiefdom,*
   by Patrick Vinton Kirch

Printed and bound by the Department of Printing, University of Washington, Seattle, United States of America

Library of Congress Cataloging-in-Publication Data

Kirch, Patrick Vinton.
Niuatoputapu: the prehistory of a Polynesian chiefdom.

(Thomas Burke Memorial Washington State Museum monograph; 5)
Bibliography: p.
1. Man, Prehistoric—Tonga—Niuatoputapu Island. 2. Polynesians—Antiquities.
3. Niuatoputapu Island (Tonga)—Antiquities. 4. Tonga—Antiquities.
I. Title. II. Series: Monograph (Thomas Burke Memorial Washington State Museum; 5)
GN875.T6K57 1988 573.3'0996 88-7482
ISBN 0-929598-01-6

Burke Museum Publications

Cover: "A Fiatooka, or Morai, in Tongataboo," engraving by W. Ellis based on a drawing by J. Webber made during the third voyage of Captain James Cook.

Koau e Niua teke vaka
Tala ki Tonga ke tapu e vaha.

I am Niua which resists vessels
Tell Tonga the sea is forbidden (to her)

Gifford, *Tongan Place Names*

CONTENTS

	Page
Preface	*viii*
CHAPTER ONE. INTRODUCTION	1
Western Polynesia: Background to the Research	2
Language Subgrouping in Western Polynesia	4
The Archaeological Sequences	6
Niuatoputapu and the Tongan Maritime Chiefdom	8
Design of the Research	13
CHAPTER TWO. THE SETTING	16
Geology and Geomorphology	20
Resources of the Island	23
Principal Biotopes	26
Environment and Subsistence: The Ethnographic Baseline	27
The Agricultural System	30
Marine Exploitation	34
CHAPTER THREE. THE ARCHAEOLOGICAL LANDSCAPE	37
Survey: Background and Methods	37
Settlement Pattern Components	38
Occupation Deposits	38
Architectural Sites	41
Mounds and Platforms	44
Terraces	63
Fermentation Pits	63
Upright Stones	69
Site Distribution and Settlement Patterns	69
Extra-Areal Comparisons	76
CHAPTER FOUR. ARCHAEOLOGICAL EXCAVATIONS	79
Excavation Methods and Sampling Considerations	79
The Ceramic Sites	81
Geomorphological Considerations	81
Lolokoka Excavations (Site NT–90)	82
Loto'aa Excavations (Site NT–100)	94
Pome'e-Nahau Excavations (Site NT–93)	101
Ha'afisi Excavations (Site NT–91)	111
Holoiafu Excavations (Site NT–113)	112
Tu'afonua Excavations (Site NT–129)	114
Hihifo Excavations (Site NT–163)	115
Excavations at Other Ceramic Zone Sites	115
Aceramic Occupation Sites	116
Niutoua Excavations (Site NT–125)	116
Hihifo Transect Excavations (Site NT–163)	122
Matavai Village Excavations (Site NT–110)	122
Architectural Sites	124
Funga'ana Mound (Site NT–139)	124
Hihifo Burial Mound (Site NT–150)	125
Houmafakalele Complex (Sites NT–52, –54, –55, –164 through –169)	127

Page

Chronology of the Sites 138
Radiocarbon Dating 138
Hydration-Rind Dating of Volcanic Glass Flakes 142
Site Correlations 144

CHAPTER FIVE. MATERIAL CULTURE AND TECHNOLOGICAL CHANGE 145

Ceramics 145
The Ceramic Sample 145
Body Sherd Analysis 148
Diagnostic Sherd Analysis 156
Analysis of Decoration 167
The Lapita Decorative System 175
Probable Fijian Sherds 181
Extra-Areal Comparisons 182
Adzes 189
Stone Adzes 192
Shell Adzes 198
Fishing Gear 204
Ornaments 206
Food Preparation Equipment 208
Manufacturing Tools 211
Flaked Stone 212
Miscellaneous Artifacts 218
Historic Period Artifacts 218

CHAPTER SIX. FAUNAL ANALYSIS AND SUBSISTENCE PATTERNS. 219

The Vertebrate Sample 219
Mammals 221
Birds 221
Reptiles 221
Fish 221
Molluscs 225
Terrestrial Gastropods 233
Changing Subsistence Patterns 235
Niuatoputapu Subsistence in Regional Perspective 236

CHAPTER SEVEN. SYNTHESIS. 239

The Niuatoputapu Sequence 239
The Lolokoka Phase (1400/1200–500 B.C.) 241
The Pome'e Phase (500 B.C.–A.D. 800) 242
The Niutoua Phase (A.D. 800–1550) 243
The Houmafakalele Phase (A.D. 1550–1830) 244
Niuatoputapu and Western Polynesian Prehistory 244
The Dynamic Environment 247
Development of the Production System 250
Changing Configurations of Long-Distance Exchange 253
Niuatoputapu and the Tongan Maritime Chiefdom 258

REFERENCES CITED. 261

APPENDICES. 270

Appendix A. Archaeological Sites of Niuatoputapu Island 270
Appendix B. Temper Sands in Sherds from Niuatoputapu Excavations in Tonga (W. R. Dickinson) 274
Appendix C. Archaeological Investigations on Tafahi Island (Tom Dye) 278

PREFACE

THE 1976 BISHOP MUSEUM TONGAN EXPEDITION to Vava'u, Niuatoputapu, Tafahi, and Niuafo'ou was the second field phase of a research program, under my direction, focusing on the ethnoarchaeological study of Western Polynesian settlement and subsistence systems. An earlier phase in 1974 had concentrated on the islands of Futuna and 'Uvea (Kirch 1975a, 1976, 1978b, 1981), and my original plans were to return to Futuna for intensive work in 1976. Finding that island closed to researchers by the local French authorities, I chose instead to turn my attention to the little-known northern islands of the Tongan archipelago. One month was spent in Vava'u on our way to the main objective, Niuatoputapu, and the results of a study of burial monuments in Vava'u have been published elsewhere (Kirch 1980a). Seven months were devoted to intensive work on Niuatoputapu, both archaeological and ethnoecological. Preliminary accounts of the archaeological results, as well as analysis of ethnographic and ecological data, have already been published (Kirch 1978b, 1979; Kirch and Dye 1979; Dye 1983; St. John 1977). At the close of the expedition my assistant, Thomas Dye, carried out a brief reconnaissance of Tafahi Island (see appendix C, this volume), and proceeded to Niuafo'ou, where he both conducted a reconnaissance archaeological survey and extended our knowledge of the Niuafo'ou dialect (Dye 1980).

Although various aspects of the 1976 Tongan Expedition have been summarized in separate reports, and while some of the key archaeological findings have been incorporated in synthetic papers and monographs (e.g. Kirch 1979, 1980b, 1982a, 1984a), publication of a definitive archaeological monograph on Niuatoputapu prehistory has been delayed much longer than was originally planned. The lack of final site reports for many of the key archaeological localities in Oceania is one of the lamentable aspects of prehistoric research in this region (one need only list such important excavations as South Point, Nualolo Kai, Hane, Maupiti, Sarah's Gulley, or Ile de Pins to gain an idea of the problem). It is therefore with some relief that the following account of the Niuatoputapu work has, even after more than a decade, been brought to its proper conclusion. I hope not to appear overly pedantic in stressing my view that the publication of complete excavation reports is essential if many of the current issues of Oceanic prehistory are to be satisfactorily resolved.

The Tongan Expedition was carried out under the auspices of the Bernice P. Bishop Museum of Honolulu, and received the support of both the Director, Roland W. Force, and the Chairman of Anthropology, Yosihiko Sinoto. The National Science Foundation funded the project through Grant No. BNS 76–04782, and provided additional supplementary support in 1977 for specialized laboratory analysis of finds (BNS 76–04782–A01).

I owe a special debt of gratitude to the Tongan government of H. M. Taufa'ahau Tupou IV, and particularly to the Prime Minister and Cabinet members for granting permission to conduct research in the kingdom. The Honorable Tofa Tuita, Mr. Jack Reichelman, and Mr. Busby Kautoke of the Prime Minister's Office in Nuku'alofa were especially helpful in making initial arrangements, as was Mr. Vainga Palu of the Ministry of Works. Among the Nuku'alofa business community, Mr. Adolph Johanson, Mr. Dan Bohart, Mr. Leo Abbott, and Mr. Ross Chapman offered assistance in preparing and equipping the expedition. Mr. Mikio Filitonga, of Burns Phillip South Seas Co., and Mr. Pau Hekeheke, of the Pacific Navigation Company, expedited matters in Vava'u, and kept us well supplied on remote Niuatoputapu. The Ministry of Lands and Survey in Nuku'alofa kindly supplied maps of the islands, and subsequently gave permission to use the excellent aerial photographs of Niuatoputapu taken by the British Directorate of Overseas Surveys.

On Niuatoputapu Island, our first and foremost thanks go to Mr. Nikolasi Fonua, Magistrate and *Fakafofonga Pule'anga,* who officially greeted us on the Falehau wharf the first day, befriended us, gently counseled us in the intricacies of Tongan custom and lore, and aided our work in countless ways. Taniele Loholoho and his family lent us their house and looked after our daily needs, and along with our neighbors Sione Holikimafua Hoa and Piula Hoa became our fast friends and helpers. The *kau hou'eiki* or chiefs of Niuatoputapu, and particularly Fuimaono Leonaitasi, Telai Halapua, and Lapuka, helped to clear away any obstacles to our work, and offered their friendship. The ultimate success of our work was, of course, due to our splendid archaeological crew, fondly named "Kulo" (pottery): Viliami 'Ofa Halapua (foreman), Sione Usa Ngahe, Mosese Falala, Lufusi Vea Tokolahi, Sione Vakapuna Musu, Peni Latou Tafea, Vili Talikiha'apai, Setiveni Uasi, Lino 'Atelea, Loketi Vaoahi, and Taniele Selui–*malo 'aupito ho'omou ngaue.*

Thomas Dye was an excellent field assistant throughout the course of the expedition: cheerful, energetic, and ever willing to engage in stimulating arguments over details of field strategy or the interpretation of evidence. His own research on fishing and language has added greatly to the results of the project.

In the subsequent analyses of materials and preparation of the results for publication many individuals have contributed their time or expertise. Mrs. Karla Kishinami supervised most of the tedious cataloguing and laboratory work throughout 1977–78. Dr. Harold St. John kindly identified the botanical vouchers collected by the expedition, while Dr. Jack Randall, Dr. Dennis Devaney, and Mrs. Ann Fielding assisted in the identification of marine biological specimens. Dr. Carl Christensen determined both terrestrial and marine molluscs. The vertebrate faunal remains were sorted and identified by Dr. Alan C. Ziegler, and additional analysis of the avifaunal bones was provided by Dr. David Steadman. Chert samples were submitted for X-ray diffraction analysis by Dr. Graeme Ward. Mr. Terry Hunt photographed ceramic samples under the SEM, and also performed grain-size analysis of sediment samples. Prof. William R. Dickinson kindly sectioned and examined pottery samples for temper composition, and his results were further extended by Mr. Thomas Dye. The superb line drawings of artifacts are by Mrs. Joyce Kokuban, while Mr. Eric Komori and Mr. Terry Hunt produced some of the charts and graphs. Laboratory photography was by Mr. Peter Gilpin.

During the final stages of preparation of this monograph in Seattle, I was assisted by Mr. Terry Hunt, who gave most of the manuscript a critical reading, by Prof. Robin Wright, who unraveled the electronic complexities of converting CP/M files to Macintosh files, and by Ms. Elzelina Callis, Ms. Christine Kleinke, and Ms. Catherine Dooley, who corrected and retyped portions of the text. Dr. Susan Libonati-Barnes edited the text, and Ms. Margaret Davidson assisted in production. I am especially grateful to Ms. Kleinke who handled the computer formatting of text.

P. V. Kirch
13 May 1987

CHAPTER ONE

INTRODUCTION

IN THE OPENING DECADES OF THE SEVENTEENTH CENTURY, the "Great South Sea" remained a shadowy void on the maps of European cartographers—a space to be filled in with sea monsters and imaginary lands. Barely a century had passed since Magellan rounded the tip of South America; it would be two more centuries before Cook dispelled the notion of a great southern continent, Terra Australis. The Dutch, however, were already beginning to expand their commercial interests in the East Indies, and there was much speculation about the possibilities of "new passages, harbours, or lands" to be found in the trackless South Sea. In 1615 two Dutch ships, the *Eendracht* and the *Hoorn,* under the command of Jacob Le Maire and Willem Schouten, set sail from Holland, the *Eendracht* entering the Pacific in January 1616.

On the 9th of May, "...about noone we saw a sayle...comming out of the south" (Schouten 1619:36). This proved to be a "ship...made of 2 long faire Canoes with a good space betweene them" (1619:37) with a sail of mats, almost certainly a Tongan double-hulled *tongiaki,* perhaps bound for Samoa. The canoe was a harbinger of land, for on the 10th "after breakefast, we saw very high land on backeboord, lying Southeast and by south, about eight leagues from us" (1619:38). The Dutchmen were unable to make land that day, but during the night saw several canoes illuminated by fires on their decks, near the island. By morning, the *Eendracht* was close enough to distinguish two islands separated by a channel (fig. 1). The higher island, they observed, was "full of trees, most *Cocos* trees, therefore we called it Cocos Island. The other island is much longer, but lower, lying East and West" (1619:39). Before departing, they would name it Traitors Island in memory of an attack by canoes from there (1619:44–45).

For three days the Dutch stood offshore, conducting a brisk trade in coconuts and other produce, and while they did not land, Schouten's journal provides the first written account of Tafahi and Niuatoputapu, northern outliers of the Tongan archipelago. The islanders were clearly rich in vegetable produce, and eager to exchange this for "nayles and beades, whereof they were very desirous" (1619:40). So desirous, indeed, that the Tongans looked "round about upon the nayles and bolts of the shippe, thinking to pull them out and to steale them away, but they were to fast in the wood" (1619:41). After first sending a messenger with a "young black wilde hog" as a present, the "king" of Niuatoputapu visited the *Eendracht* in a "great shippe with a sayle...with at least thirtie five Canoes to accompany him. This king was by his men called *'Latou'"* (1619:42). The generally amicable relations between Dutch and Tongans were shattered on the morning of the 13th, when more than 23 double-hulled and 45 smaller outrigger canoes surrounded the *Eendracht* for an attack coordinated by the "Latou." European firepower prevailed, allowing the Dutch to hoist anchor and escape again on their westward voyage.

Schouten and Le Maire were the first Europeans to venture into the archipelagoes of Western Polynesia, a region which had been inhabited by Oceanic peoples for

Figure 1. Cocos (Tafahi) and Verraders (Niuatoputapu) Islands as seen by the Dutch explorers Willem Schouten and Jacob Le Maire in April, 1616. (From Villiers 1906, pl. 24.)

three millennia. The Dutchmen's fleeting visit was not without significance for Polynesian ethnology, for a word list made by Le Maire (Kern 1948) was among the critical evidence used as early as 1706 by Hadrian Reland to infer a linguistic relationship with Malay and Javanese, and "a former common language extending from Madagascar to Cocos Island," (i.e., the first definition of the Malayo-Polynesian or Austronesian language family; Biggs 1971:467). Not until the last three decades, however, has the prehistory of this region become the subject of intense scholarly study. Like a mirror of Le Maire's first efforts, recent studies have again proven the significance of Western Polynesia for understanding the prehistory of the vast eastern Pacific.

WESTERN POLYNESIA: BACKGROUND TO THE RESEARCH

Western Polynesia is generally defined as the large archipelagoes of Tonga and Samoa, along with several more isolated islands including Rotuma, 'Uvea, Futuna and Alofi, Niuafo'ou, Niuatoputapu and Tafahi, and Niue (fig. 2). For reasons shortly to be made clear, I also include within this geographical region the extensive Fijian archipelago. Originally proposed by Burrows (1939), the distinction between Western and Eastern Polynesia reflects a basic culture-historical sequence of settlement and cultural differentiation. Stratigraphic excavations, beginning with Gifford's pioneering Fijian work (1951), have demonstrated that Western Polynesia was the first region within the vast Polynesian Triangle to have been settled. The founding populations in Western Polynesia can be linked, in turn, to the older and more widespread Lapita Cultural Complex (Green 1979), representing the first dispersal of Austronesian-speaking horticultural peoples beyond the large "continental" islands of Western Melanesia (New Guinea and the Bismarck Archipelago). Recent advances in historical linguistics support this view: Polynesian and Fijian languages are now considered to be a subgroup of Eastern Oceanic, and are most closely related to certain languages of the southeastern Solomons and northern Vanuatu (Pawley 1972).

From the viewpoint of the Polynesianist, Western Polynesia was a gateway for the whole of the Polynesian Triangle. Furthermore, it was in the archipelagoes and scattered islands of Western Polynesia that a unique *Ancestral Polynesian Culture*, along with

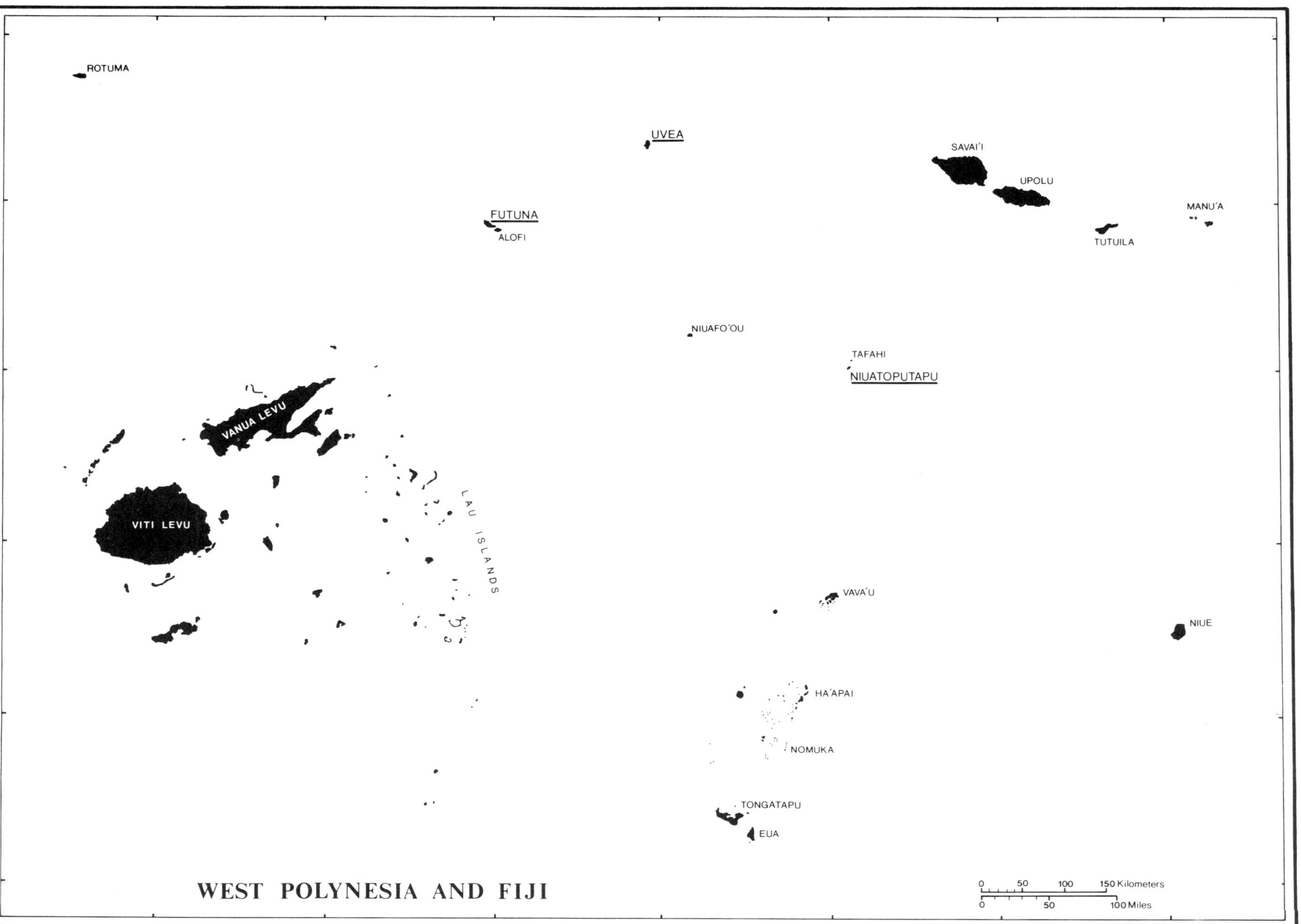

Figure 2. The Fiji-Western Polynesian region.

its associated Proto-Polynesian language, developed from an earlier Lapita ancestor (Kirch 1984a; Green 1981; Kirch and Green, 1987). It was in this *homeland region* that Polynesian ancestors first encountered the geological and biotic conditions that characterize the *oceanic* world of the eastern Pacific. Tonga lies on the structural boundary of the Pacific Basin, while Samoa, to the east, rests on the Pacific Plate. This structural boundary, which cuts right through Western Polynesia, is marked by a geological shift from complex island arc volcanics to simple oceanic basalts, and by a sharp reduction in biotic diversity, both marine and terrestrial. Thus it was that in Western Polynesia ancestral Polynesians adapted to the truly oceanic conditions which their descendants would face in the later conquest of the remote eastern Pacific.

Western Polynesia is of interest to prehistorians for yet other reasons. The relative proximity of islands and archipelagoes ensured frequent inter-island contacts, well documented in the ethnohistorical literature. Thus, at the same time that local cultural and linguistic differentiation was occurring, regional connections were exerting substantial influence on the developmental sequences of particular island communities. A major issue in Western Polynesian prehistory thus becomes the changing role and significance of inter-island contacts—especially exchange networks—in socio-cultural change. At the historic period endpoint of indigenous development, the entire Western Polynesian region was integrated into a vast exchange network controlled by the ruling chiefs of Tonga (Kirch 1984a). This Tongan polity—an object of substantial anthropological interest—ranks among the most complex chiefdoms of Oceania.

In the diversity of its ethnographically-attested subsistence and settlement systems, Western Polynesia poses still other intriguing problems. Yen (1971, 1973a) emphasized that these islands were pivotal in the development of agriculture for Oceania as a whole, and for Polynesia in particular. He notes that the border region between Eastern Melanesia and Western Polynesia exhibits remarkable diversity in agricultural systems, and is the area from which systems still farther to the east were derived. This diversity is evident, for example, in the presence of integral swidden systems, of intensive irrigation and/or drainage for taro, of greater crop diversity, of elaborate methods of food preservation (such as anaerobic pit fermentation and ensilage), and of the purposive selection of productive cultivars. Among the agronomic features of this border area, Yen (1973a:82–3) notes that (1) it is the easternmost area for sago *(Metroxylon* spp.) cultivation; (2) certain Southeast Asian genera of fruits and nuts were here developed into cultigens; and (3) "breadfruit selection did not operate against seed production." Among the area's unique developments are the use of *Alocasia macrorrhiza* as an important staple, and the regular cultivation of the bitter yam, *Dioscorea bulbifera.*

Variability in Western Polynesian settlement patterns ranged from the highly dispersed settlement of late eighteenth-century Tonga to the nucleated, fortified villages of the densely settled Fijian deltas (Parry 1977, 1981). Monumental architecture displays equally diverse distributions. Samoa and Tonga for example, are alike in the dominance of large mounds, but these mounds differ in the peculiarities of their form and function. Fortifications, a nearly ubiquitous feature of Western Polynesian settlement landscapes, likewise vary in structure and distribution.

As background to the archaeological investigation of Niuatoputapu, it is necessary to review in somewhat greater detail both the linguistic subgrouping of Western Polynesian languages and the archaeologically-attested sequences of particular islands. The linguistic picture is especially critical, since it provides a model for social and cultural differentiation.

Language Subgrouping in Western Polynesia

Grace (1959) first proposed that Fijian, Rotuman, and all of the languages of Polynesia form a distinct subgroup of the Austronesian language family, to which he later assigned the name "Central Pacific" (Grace 1967). Although the position of Rotuman within the Central Pacific group has proved refractory, in part because of complex historical influences (see Biggs 1965), the validity of the Central Pacific group as such has been widely accepted. Pawley (1972), in his seminal monograph on the Eastern Oceanic languages, located Central Pacific within a higher-order subgroup that included various languages of northern Vanuatu (New Hebrides). Central Pacific itself was seen to split rather simply into Fijic and Polynesian branches (1972, fig. 4). In culture-historical terms, the breakup of Central Pacific into Proto-Fijic and Proto-Polynesian was believed to correspond with the settlement of a Polynesian homeland (presumed to be Tonga, Groube 1971) out of Fiji.

Following upon the important work of Elbert (1953), Pawley (1966, 1967) and Green (1966) clarified the internal relationships of the Polynesian languages. Most significant was the determination of an initial split between Proto-Tongic and Proto-Nuclear Polynesian branches of Polynesian, correlating with increased isolation and cultural differentiation within Western Polynesia itself. The only modern witnesses of the Tongic subgroup are Tongan and Niuean. A further split within Nuclear Polynesian was associated with the eastern movement of colonists into the central Eastern Polynesian archipelagoes of the Marquesas and Societies (Proto-Eastern Polynesian). Within Western Polynesia, however, all non-Tongic languages could be shown to form a subgroup designated by Pawley (1967) as Samoic-Outlier (since it also incorporated the various Polynesian "outliers" on the fringes of Melanesia, cf. Kirch 1985).

This fairly simple picture of linguistic differentiation within Western Polynesia, correlating with a sequence of successive eastward population movements, has been complicated by more recent studies. Pawley and Sayaba (1971) demonstrated significant dialect chain variability within Fiji, while archaeologically, the discovery of increasingly early Lapita assemblages throughout Western Polynesia made it clear that a simple model of linguistic differentiation resulting from island colonizations was unrealistic. For example, the notion of Tonga as *the* Polynesian homeland and location of the Proto-Polynesian speech community was dealt a fatal blow by the discovery of Early Eastern Lapita ceramics in Samoa, at Mulifanua (Green and Davidson 1974). Consequently, a more complex dialect chain model has emerged.

The recent work of Geraghty (1983) on the dialect geography and history of the Fijian languages, and of Pawley (1979) on the position of Rotuman, have now amplified the historical linguistic picture for Western Polynesia. The more complicated history of linguistic differentiation indicated by these studies is outlined graphically in figure 3. Most important has been Geraghty's finding that while little evidence exists for a

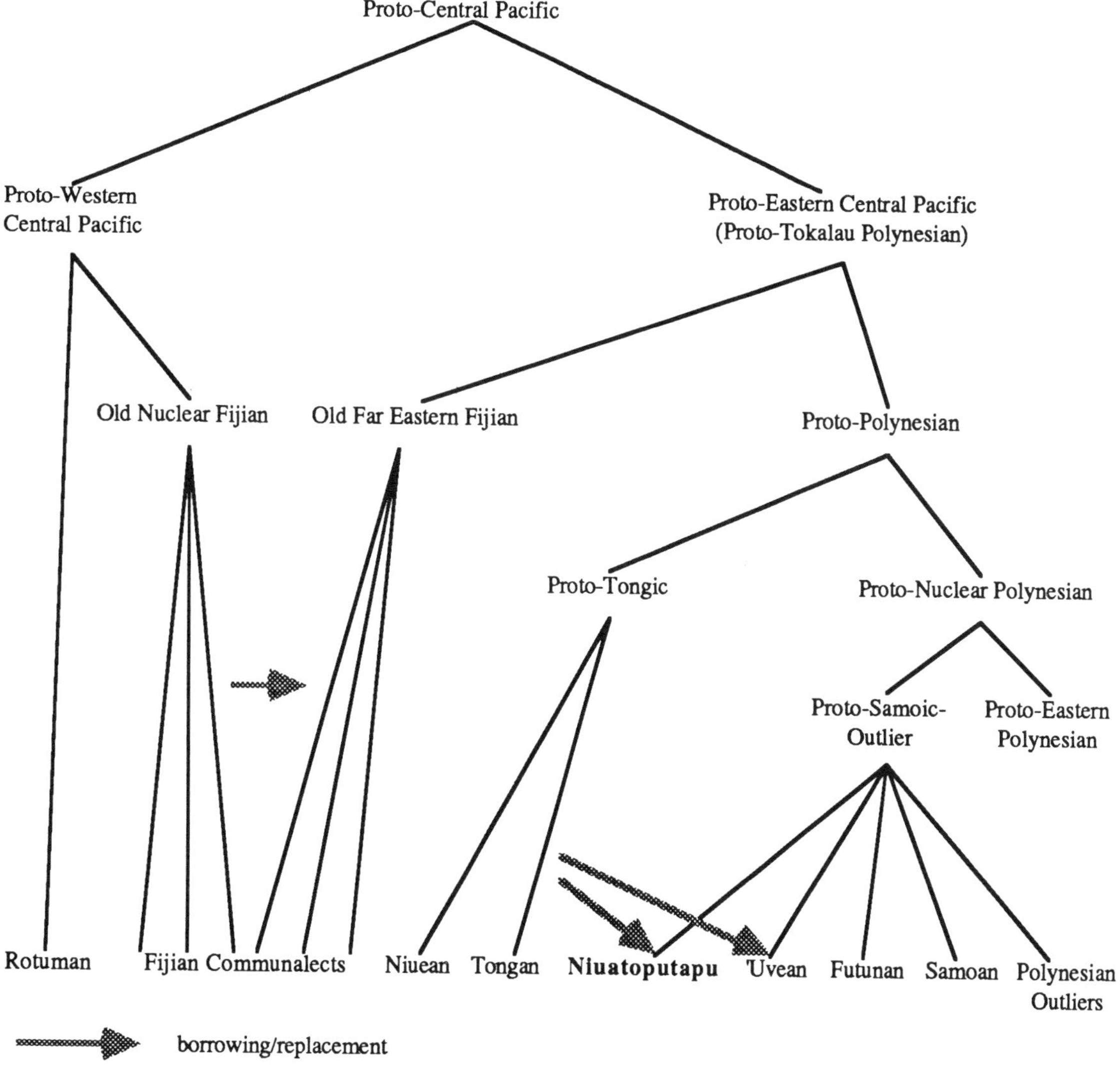

Figure 3. Subgrouping of the languages of Fiji and Western Polynesia.

"single language ancestral to all the Fijian and Polynesian languages," there is "a good deal of evidence to suggest that languages ancestral to those of Eastern Fiji, especially Lau and Eastern Vanua Levu, underwent a period of common development with the language ancestral to the Polynesian languages" (1983:348). Geraghty suggests that the dialect chain which included the languages ancestral to Tokalau Fijian and Polynesian can be called "Proto-Tokalau Polynesian." Speaking of the cultural-historical implications, Geraghty continues: "It may be assumed that the Lapita people, who came to Fiji with a homogeneous material culture, had initially also a homogeneous language, but that a dialect chain developed within Fiji before the settlement of Polynesia, and it was speakers of the dialect of Tokalau Fiji (Proto-Tokalau Polynesian) who settled Polynesia" (1983:381). Subsequently, substantial borrowing from Western Fijian in the Tokalau Fijian languages has resulted in the subgrouping of Tokalau Fijian with Western Fijian languages. Pawley (1979), incorporating the work of Geraghty, notes that Rotuman joins with the Western Fijian languages ("Old Nuclear Fijian") to form a Western Central Pacific subgroup.

Green, in a recent discussion of the Polynesian homeland problem, succinctly summarizes the revisions required by these recent linguistic investigations:

> One is that for a considerable time after much of West Polynesia was originally settled, a reasonably well unified chain of Central Pacific dialects was maintained throughout the whole Fijian and West Polynesian area.... The other revision follows from Geraghty's argument that prior to Pre-Polynesian or in its earliest stages there was a unified language community identified as Tokalau Fijian-Polynesian which also persisted for some time after Fiji and West Polynesia had both been settled. This language community straddled the current linguistic and cultural boundary generally drawn between Fiji and West Polynesia (1981:147).

In sum, the linguistic evidence indicates that the differentiation of the Central Pacific languages must be explained through the progressive breaking of a series of dialect chains extending over the entire Western Polynesian region, with the implication that no single island can be identified as *the* Polynesian homeland (Green 1981). The initial colonization of the region by Lapita people resulted in the rapid establishment of a series of Proto-Central Pacific communalects throughout the Fijian, Tongan, and Samoan archipelagoes. The dialect chain was first broken along a line extending roughly through eastern Vanua Levu and the Koro Sea, with a Proto-Tokalau Polynesian dialect chain forming in the east. Somewhat later, and presumably due to isolation and lowered frequency of inter-island contacts, a further rupture in the dialect chain led to differentiation between Old Eastern Fijian (in eastern Vanua Levu and the Lau Islands) and Proto-Polynesian. The breakup of Proto-Polynesian into Proto-Tongic and Proto-Nuclear Polynesian resulted from yet a further rupture in the dialect chain that must have extended along a north-south axis between Tonga and Samoa (but including also Niuatoputapu, and probably Futuna and 'Uvea). Finally, in relatively recent centuries, a major movement of Tongan speakers in Western Polynesia has led to massive borrowing of Tongan innovations in 'Uvean, and the replacement of an older Samoic-Outlier language in Niuatoputapu.

The Archaeological Sequences

While there are still significant geographic and temporal gaps in our knowledge of the prehistoric sequences of Western Polynesia, enough has been accomplished over three decades that we may be confident that the general outlines of regional prehistory have been well established. The sequences for Viti Levu/Taveuni, Lakeba, Tongatapu, Samoa, 'Uvea, and Futuna are graphically summarized in figure 4.

The archaeological sequence from the large, western Fijian Islands (Viti Levu and Taveuni) is the longest and most complex anywhere in Western Polynesia (Green 1963). Assemblages with Early Eastern Lapita ceramics are known from Natunuku and Yanuca on Viti Levu, and from the offshore islet of Naigani (Frost 1979; Hunt 1980; Best 1984; Kay 1984). Radiocarbon ages indicate settlement of Fiji from eastern Melanesia possibly as early as the sixteenth century B.C. Assemblages of Late Eastern Lapita are known from Yanuca and Sigatoka (Birks 1973), and Hunt has shown that the last few centuries of the first millennium B.C. are marked by the emergence of plain ware ceramics, including large quantities with parallel-ribbed paddle impressing (Hunt 1986). Thus, although the subsequent Navatu Phase (ca. 100 B.C. to A.D. 1100), with its characteristic carved-paddle impressed ceramics, has generally been interpreted as the result of a cultural "intrusion" or migration (Frost 1979), Hunt regards it as developing locally out of the earlier Lapitoid plain ware. A third major ceramic period, the Vunda Phase (ca. A.D. 1100–1600), is marked by the appearance of distinctive incised ceramics with possible relationships to the Mangaasi style of Vanuatu (Garanger 1972). In sum, the prehistoric sequence of Western Fiji is

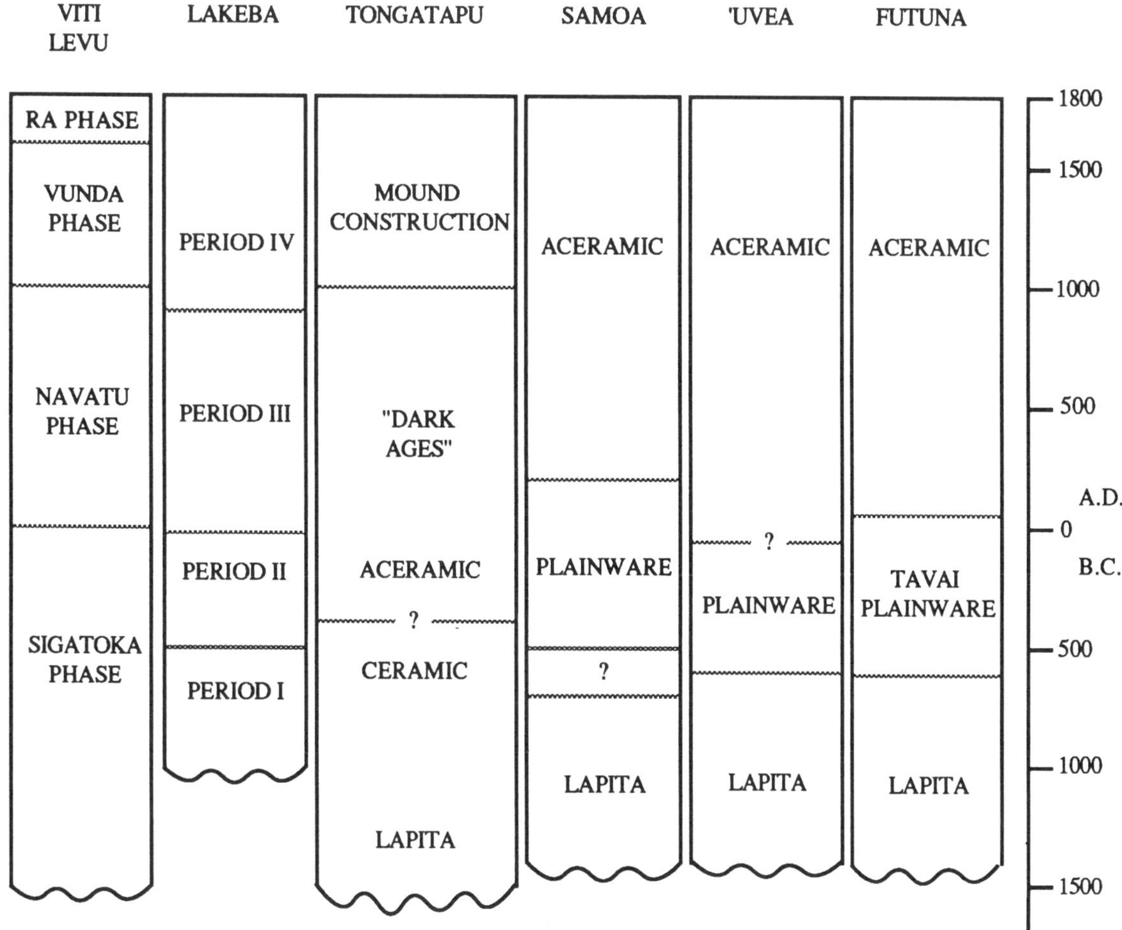

Figure 4. Archaeological sequences for Fiji and Western Polynesia.

delineated by a succession of ceramic complexes which continue into the historic period (the Ra Phase).

In the Lau archipelago of eastern Fiji, the only continuous sequence yet delineated is that from Lakeba (Best 1984), and this has also been subdivided on ceramic criteria. The Lakeba sequence begins ca. 900–1000 B.C. with characteristic, dentate-stamped Early Eastern Lapita. Period II, beginning about 500 B.C., is distinguished by Lapitoid plain ware, and continues until about the end of the first millennium B.C. Period III on Lakeba is equivalent to the Navatu Phase, with carved-paddle impressing. Period IV is subdivided into three stages, with various forms of appliqué, incised, and end-tool impressed decoration. This simple characterization of the Lakeba sequence, does not, of course, do justice to the actual complexities of ceramic change, let alone to changes in other artifact classes, in settlement pattern, and in population.

In Tongatapu, the work of Poulsen (1964, 1967, 1968, 1977, 1983), supplemented by that of Groube (1971) and Davidson (1969a), provides the outline of a prehistoric sequence, only the earlier portions of which are adequately known. The sequence commences with Early Eastern Lapita assemblages (Sites To-2 and To-5), dating as early as the thirteenth and fourteenth centuries B.C. A continuous sequence of ceramic change is indicated, with progressive loss of dentate-stamped decoration, and simplification of vessel and rim morphology (e.g., Site To-6), culminating eventually in the complete cessation of ceramic manufacture. Based on radiocarbon dates from To-6 and Vuki's Mound (Groube 1971), the abandonment of ceramic production occurred sometime after the fourth century B.C. Little is known of the aceramic portion of the sequence, leading Davidson (1979) to speak of the "Dark Ages." Sometime after about A.D. 1000, however, the construction of large earthen mounds, both faced and unfaced, became a dominant feature of the settlement landscape (McKern 1929; Kirch 1984a).

The sequence from Western Samoa has been thoroughly documented (with the exception of a slight gap in the middle of the first millennium B.C.), at a variety of excavated sites, with more than 80 radiocarbon age determinations (Green and Davidson 1969a, 1974; Jennings and Holmer 1980; Jennings et al. 1976). The sequence commences with Early Eastern Lapita from the submerged Mulifanua Ferry Berth site, dated to the tenth century B.C. Following the gap, a series of coastal and inland sites containing Polynesian plain ware ceramics range in age from the sixth century B.C. to the second century A.D. The remainder of the sequence is aceramic and is marked by changes in adz manufacture and in settlement pattern, including the construction of large earthen and stone mounds in the last 1,000 years. No periodization of the Samoan sequence has been proposed, but cultural continuity from Lapita to the Polynesian "ethnographic present" is strongly evidenced. Recent work in the Manu'a Islands of eastern Samoa (Hunt and Kirch, in press), has also yielded plain ware ceramics dated to about 2,000 years B.P. No early dentate-stamped Lapita has as yet been recovered in the Manu'a group.

Finally, in the geographically isolated islands of Futuna-Alofi and 'Uvea, recent investigations provide a few signposts in what should prove to be comparably long occupation sequences (Kirch 1975a, 1976, 1979; Frimigacci, Siorat, and Vienne 1984; C. Sand, pers. comm. 1987). Early Eastern Lapita ceramics are known from 'Uvea, and Futuna; Late Eastern Lapita and Polynesian Plain Ware are known from Futuna, Alofi, and 'Uvea. The last few centuries of the 'Uvean sequence are characterized by the construction of large earthworks of Tongan type. Futuna lacks such distinctive earthworks, although its late prehistoric settlement landscape does include fortifications and cut stone masonry tombs associated with ranking chiefs.

In summary, all known archaeological sequences in Western Polynesia commence with Early Eastern Lapita assemblages dating from the middle to the end of the second millennium B.C., suggesting a rapid colonization of the entire region by a common cultural group. The beginnings of cultural divergence are reflected materially by some differentiation in ceramics in the first millennium B.C. with the Lapitoid plain wares. Thereafter, the ceramic sequences of western Fiji and Lau depart from those of Tonga, Samoa, and Futuna-'Uvea. Whereas all of the Polynesian sequences become aceramic, those of Fiji evidence continued ceramic change, with the possibility of external influence from eastern Melanesia. A common feature of both the Samoan and the Tongan sequences is the increasing importance of large stone works and earthworks in the last 1,000 years. While skeletonized, this synopsis provides a framework into which the data from Niuatoputapu may be incorporated.

NIUATOPUTAPU AND THE TONGAN MARITIME CHIEFDOM

At the time of European entry into the Pacific, no other Polynesian society rivalled that of Tonga, either in geographic extent or in political complexity. As Guiart put it, "l'ensemble tongien pourrait être décrit comme un empire insulaire" (1963:661). A maritime chiefdom—even an 'archaic state' by certain definitions–the Tongan domain extended from the political center at Tongatapu in the south, up the 300 km length of the main Tongan archipelago to Vava'u, and yet further to incorporate the outliers of Niuatoputapu, Tafahi, Niuafo'ou, and 'Uvea (as well as Rotuma, by some accounts). But more, this political armature extended even beyond the cultural boundaries of Tonga, to penetrate Fiji to the west and Samoa to the northeast. These foreign states were linked to Tonga even over long distances by prestige–good exchange networks monopolized and organized by the Tongan elite. Thus by the seventeenth century, the Tongan maritime chiefdom dominated and integrated all of Fiji and Western Polynesia (fig. 5). (Detailed accounts of the Tongan maritime network are given in Guiart 1963; Kaeppler 1978; and Kirch 1984a:217-242). Familiarity with the structure of this Tongan maritime chiefdom is essential to understanding the prehistory of Niuatoputapu, for the island was an integral part of the larger Tongan polity in late prehistory and protohistory, though not, as we shall see, in earlier centuries.

Regarded by comparative ethnographers (e.g., Williamson 1924; Sahlins 1958; Goldman 1970) as among the most complex of all Oceanic societies, the Tongan chiefdom was strongly hierarchic (fig. 6). At the pinnacle of society were a pair of paramount chiefs, one sacred (the Tu'i Tonga), and one secular (the *hau).* Representing collateral patrilines believed to have descended from the gods, the Tu'i Tonga and *hau* were linked through regular matrilateral cross-cousin marriage (fig. 7). Giving their sisters as wives to the Tu'i Tonga, the *hau* then espoused high-ranking women from Samoa, thus securing alliances to that independent state. The highest ranked chiefesses, on the other hand—the sisters of the Tu'i Tonga—took as husbands chiefs of Fiji, giving rise to a separate line, the Ha'a Fale Fisi ("House of Fiji"). This Fijian line played an important role in the local polity of Niuatoputapu.

Functionally, the Tu'i Tonga was a ritual leader, the mediator between primal deities and humans, receiving the annual *'inasi* or tribute from throughout the chiefdom's dominions. The *hau* was the active chief, organizing agricultural activities, public works, and especially war. Below the *hau* in the reticulate hierarchy of Tongan society were the individual landed chiefs

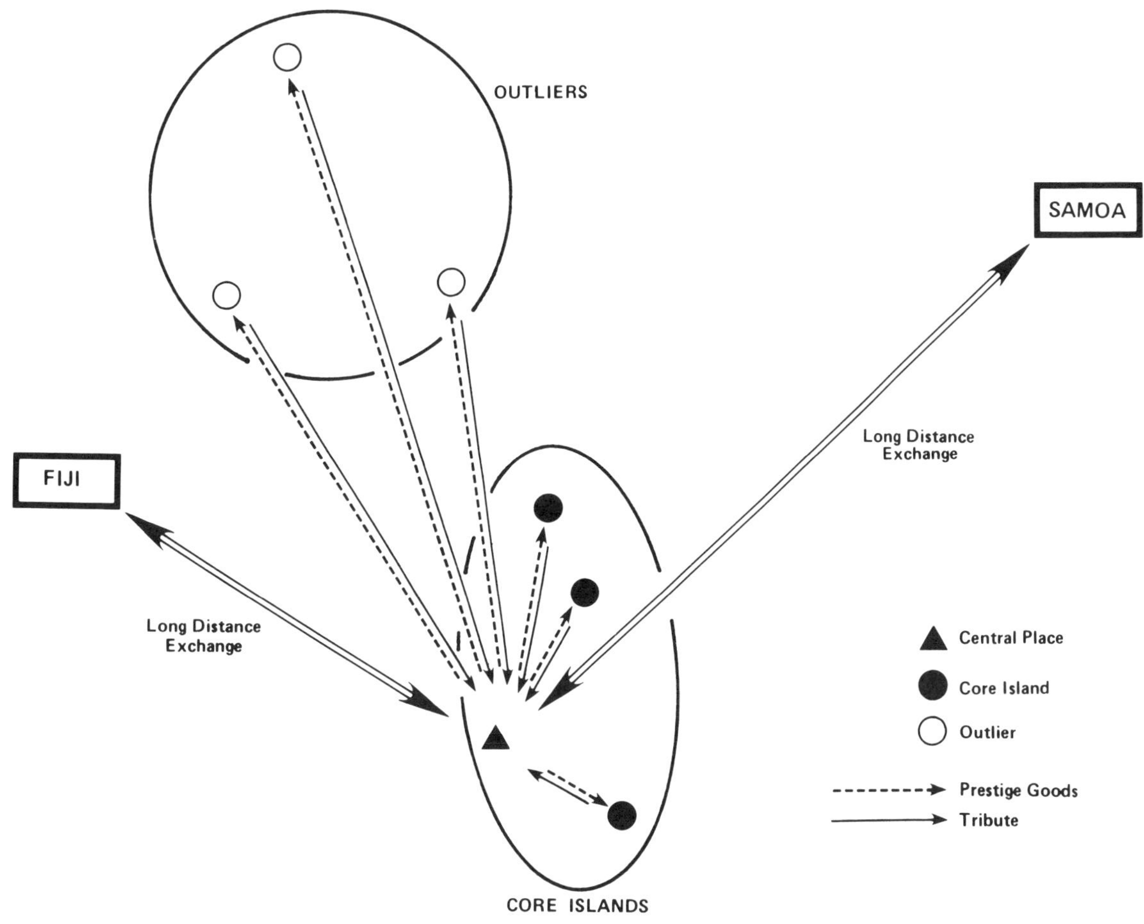

Figure 5. The topologic structure of the Tongan maritime chiefdom (after Kirch 1984a, fig. 80).

('eiki), their advisors and stewards *(matapule),* and finally the ranks of commoners (fig. 6). The distinction between chiefs and commoners was sharply drawn in protohistoric Tonga, for—unlike less stratified Polynesian societies—commoners were not affiliated with chiefs on the basis of descent but through residence on the lands of a chief. No longer the joint property of a lineage, land was allocated by the paramounts to their subordinate chiefs in exchange for tribute, labor, and support. Thus in Tonga, as in Hawai'i, we may speak of a true class disjunction between chiefs and commoners (Kirch 1984a).

The position of an outlying island such as Niuatoputapu in the larger Tongan system must be understood in terms of the local political organization and its links to the paramount lines. In the protohistoric and historic periods, Niuatoputapu was controlled by a hereditary patriline carrying the title Ma'atu. The line became defunct only in 1935 (when the last title holder passed away without legitimate issue), and traced its genealogy back eleven generations, as diagrammed in figure 8. This genealogy and numerous others of high-ranked chiefly lines throughout Tonga are well recorded and have been the subject of considerable scholarly study (Gifford 1929; Kaeppler 1971a; Bott 1982). According to these historical traditions, the Ma'atu title derives originally from a junior branch of the Fale Fisi, the offspring of unions between the Tu'i Tonga Fefine and a Fijian chief. In particular, the Tu'i Tonga Fefine named Sinaetakala-'i-Langikela married the Fijian chief Tapu'osi; Fonomanu, their male child, in turn married the Tu'i Tonga Fefine 'Ekutongapipiki, and their youngest male offspring was named Latumailangi.

A key political strategy of the Tongan paramounts was to assign junior collaterals to the outlying islands as local representatives of the ruling chiefs, a practice recorded many times in the chiefly traditions. In this manner, as Bott relates:

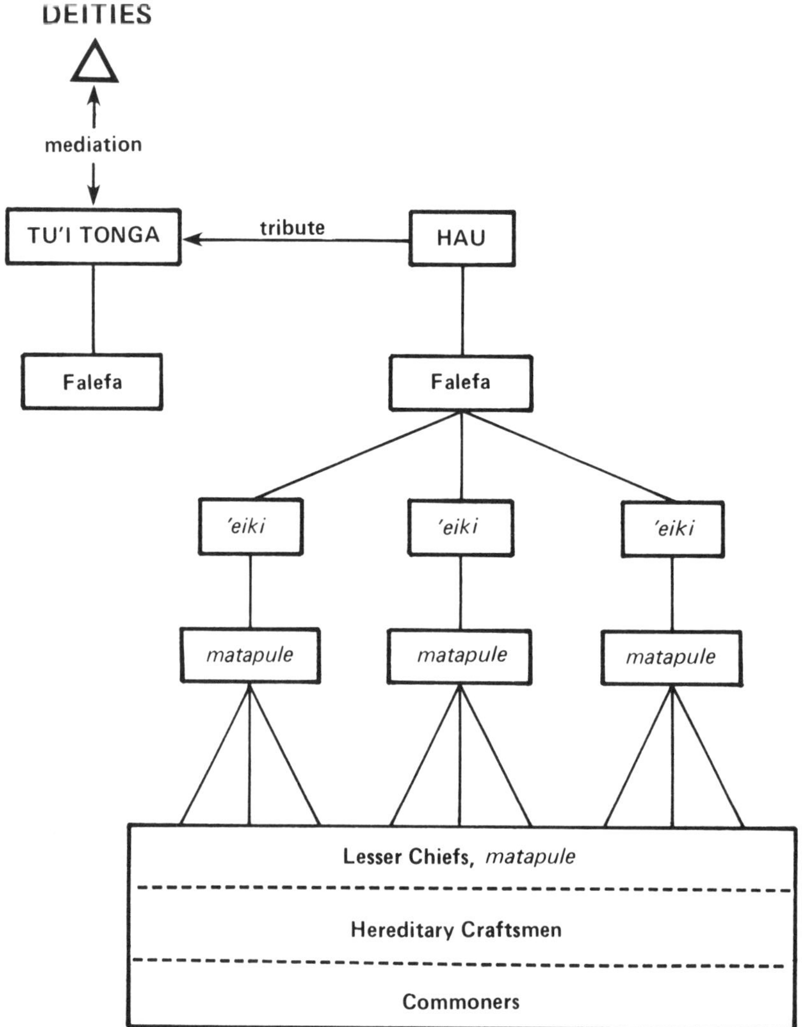

Figure 6. Hierarchical organization of the protohistoric Tongan chiefdom (after Kirch 1984a, fig. 75).

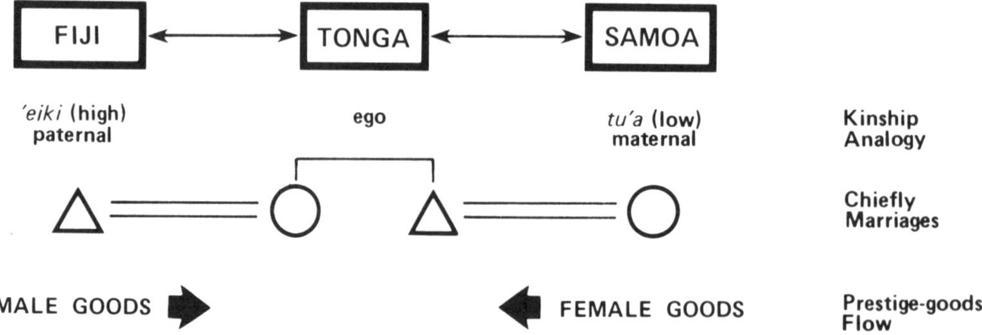

Figure 7. Structural relationships between Tonga, Fiji, and Samoa in the protohistoric era (after Kirch 1984a, fig. 79).

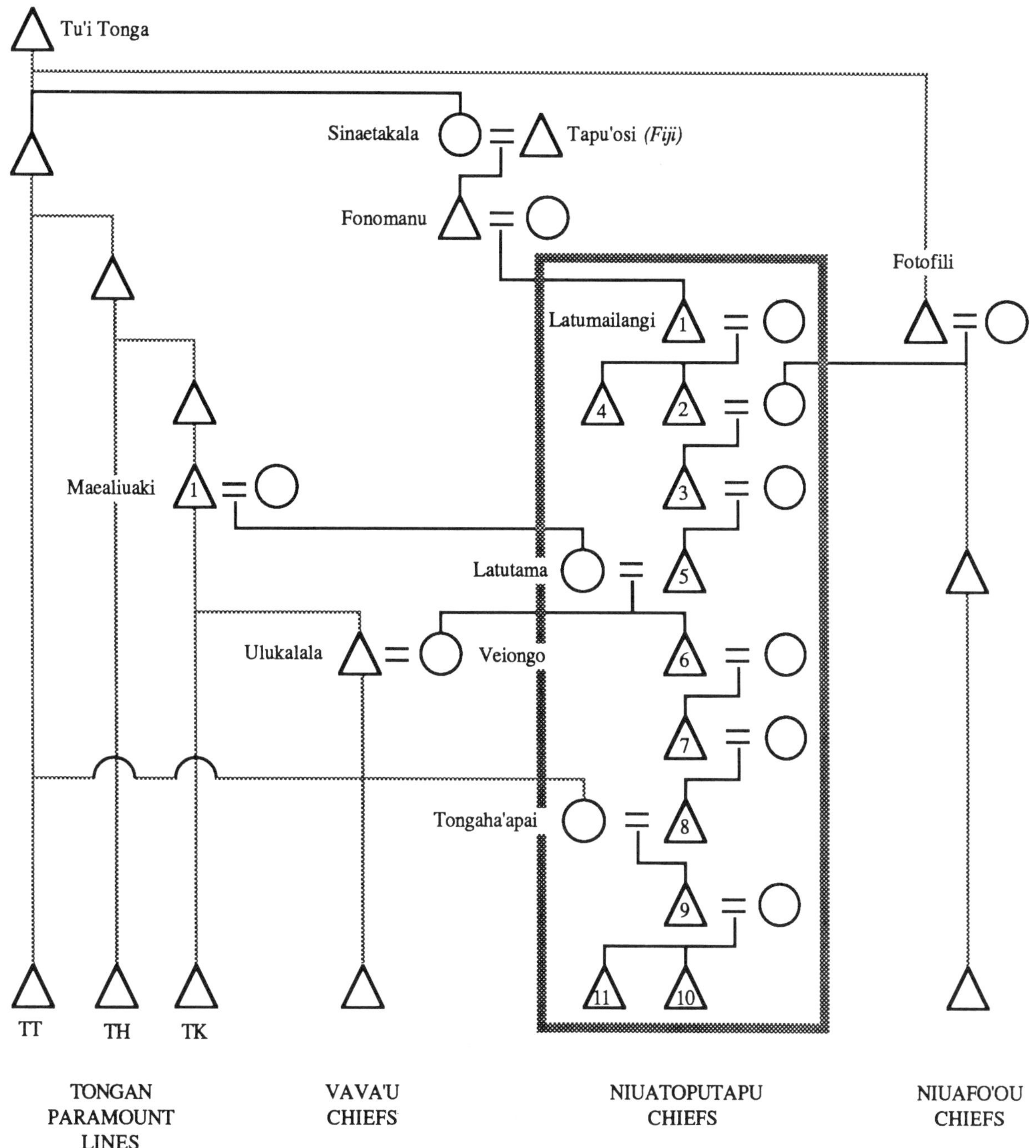

Figure 8. Genealogy of the Ma'atu line of ruling chiefs of Niuatoputapu and their relationships to the chiefly lines of Tonga, Vava'u and Nuiafo'ou (see text for discussion).

> ...the Tu'i Tonga sent Latumailangi to Niuatoputapu to see whether he could secure the loyalty of the people there. He succeeded in doing so, and became the great *'eiki* of Niuatoputapu, almost an independent king. He changed his name to Utuma'atu shortly after his arrival. There were a number of older titles already in existence there when Latumailangi arrived; all have become subordinate. It is possible that some may have been created after he arrived (Vivili, Tafea, Telai)...(1982:106).

In short, Latumailangi (who initiated the title Ma'atu) supplanted the local, indigenous polity of Niuatoputapu, henceforth linking the island to the widespread Tongan domain. This linkage was at times minimal, for, as Bott notes, Ma'atu acted as nearly independent. Thus, the Ma'atu "rarely left Niuatoputapu" (1982:107), although upon succession to the title he was obligated to send a representative to the paramount seat at Mu'a, Tongatapu, bearing the *pongipongi* or ritual offering of *kava* roots and cooked food which served to acknowledge the Tu'i Tonga as his ruler (1982:108). Likewise, Ma'atu sent to the annual ceremonies at Mu'a a tributary offering of food and valued goods as his *'inasi* (tribute).

At the time of the fifth Ma'atu titleholder, Ikamafana, the allegiance of the line shifted slightly, with Ma'atu coming under the purview of the *hau* or secular paramount, the Tu'i Ha'atakalaua. This resulted from Ikamafana's marriage to Latutama, a daughter of the Tu'i Ha'atakalaua Maealiuaki, thus forming an alliance between the two lines. Alliances also existed between Ma'atu and the local chiefly line of Niuafo'ou (Fotofili), with the marriage of the second Ma'atu (Puakailakelo) to Siulolovao, and between the ruling house of Vava'u (Ulukalala) through the marriage of Ikamafana's daughter Veiongo to Ulukalala. Yet another linkage was occasioned by the marriage of Tongaha'apai, a ranking chiefess of the Tu'i Tonga line, to the eighth Ma'atu, U. Latumailangi.

As the power of the *hau* or Tu'i Ha'atakalaua line grew in relation to that of the Tu'i Tonga, the *hau* replicated the original strategy of the Tu'i Tonga in sending junior relatives to the outlying islands as local representatives. In many cases, these new chiefs supplanted the older lines sent out by the Tu'i Tonga. "However, the Tu'i Ha'atakalaua did not send anyone to Niuatoputapu once Ma'atu was there, for Ma'atu was a very strong ruler" (Bott 1982:110). Still later, the *hau*-ship was usurped by a second collateral line of the Tongan paramount house, the Tu'i Kanokupolu (see Gifford 1929 and Kirch 1984a for details). In a repetition of this strategy of overseas rule, the Tu'i Kanokupolu sent *tehina* or junior kinsmen out as representatives. "Tangipa, a *foha* [son] of Ata, was sent to Niuatoputapu. Some say that the other Ha'a Ngata of Niuatoputapu are derived from him, others say they were sent separately. They are Motu'ahala, Lapuka, Maiava Tekimoto, and Maiava Olonuna, and perhaps also Tupo [all *hou'eiki* or chiefly lines of Niuatoputapu, to this day]." Rather than supplant the thoroughly entrenched and virtually independent chiefly line, however, these later representatives of the *hau* "all served Ma'atu, who was the lord of Niuatoputapu" (Bott 1982:131).

To the extent that these elaborate and closely interlocking traditions have historical validity, they suggest that Niuatoputapu first came under Tongan political domination late in regional prehistory, with the arrival of Latumailangi representing the Tu'i Tonga line. A rough genealogical dating would suggest that Latumailangi lived at about the end of the seventeenth or beginning of the eighteenth century. Note that in the brief account of Schouten from 1616 (see above), the "king" of Niuatoputapu was called by his people "Latou." Whether this "Latou" was *the* Latumailangi is a moot point, never to be resolved; he may have been, as Rogers suggests, "an earlier viceroy sent by the Tu'i Tonga or Tu'i Ha'atakalaua to establish his political influence on Niuatoputapu" (1975:57).

The records of the Dutch visit of 1616 do, however, provide crucial evidence on the extent of Tongan influence in Niuatoputapu at this time. As noted earlier, Le Maire collected a word list (Kern 1948), which Biggs has subjected to modern linguistic scrutiny (1971:491). As Biggs demonstrates, in 1616 the people of Niuatoputapu were *not* speaking a Tongan dialect, but rather a language which must be classified in the Samoic-Outlier subgroup of Polynesian. This is evidenced by such lexemes as *taci* 'one', *loa* 'two', *lima* 'five', and *lickasoa* 'corals', for which the Samoan equivalents are *tasi, lua, lima,* and *'asoa,* whereas the Tongan equivalents are *tahi, ua, nima,* and *kahoa.* "To clinch it the *li-* of the last Dutch item appears to be Samoan *le* 'definite article singular', an innovation of the Samoic languages" (Biggs 1971:491).

Sometime after 1616, in response to Tongan political and cultural domination, the original Samoic-Outlier language of Niuatoputapu was replaced with Tongan, so that the speech of the modern population is virtually undistinguishable from that of more southerly islands in the archipelago (in contrast to the situation with Niuafo'ou, where traces of the Samoic-Outlier language may still be detected in phonology, lexicon, and grammar; Dye 1980). Nonetheless, a few vestiges of the original Samoic-Outlier language of Niuatoputapu remain in the conservative lexical domains of fish and plant folk taxonomies. As a part of our 1976 expedition, we obtained names for 210 folk taxa of fish, of which at least 74 have reflexes in Samoan. As Dye remarks, "The twenty-two names shared exclusively by Samoa and Niuatoputapu may be Nuclear Polynesian innovations, the identifiable remnants of Niuatoputapu's once Samoic *ika* [fish] nomenclature" (1980:264).

In sum, the linguistic evidence suggests that at the time of Schouten's 1616 visit Tongan dominance in Niuatoputapu was still recent enough to have had little influence on the local language. By the close of the eighteenth century, however, there is no doubt from the records of European explorers that Niuatoputapu was thoroughly integrated into the Tongan maritime polity. Following Schouten and Le Maire, the next European ship to visit Niuatoputapu was H.M.S. *Dolphin*, under the command of Wallis, in 1767. The journal of the *Dolphin's* master, George Robertson (Carrington 1948), provides us with details of the second encounter between Europeans and Niuans:

> ...we soon Convinced them that we was no Enemys, and bargand with them for a few plantains and Bananas, which they had in their Canoes, and gave them a few smal nails, which seemd to pleas them mutch, this people hade their Ears bored, but I saw no trinkets about them, and all this men was Naked, Except their privet parts..., their Legs and thighs was painted Black [presumably, tattooed], the same as at King Georges Island [Tahiti]...—I observed two men in Each canoe, that hade lost the two first Joints of their little fingers, I suppose this is a Custom in their Country, to Cutt off this Joints on some particular Occasion, as they did not Appear to be cutt of by Accident, as no oyther part of their hands was hurt...(Carrington 1948:251)

Two aspects of this account are particularly noteworthy. The first is the custom of removing the first joints of the little finger, which is a uniquely Tongan act of mourning, especially for a ranking chief (see Kaeppler 1971b). More interesting, however, are the "smal nails" given by Robertson to the locals, for these very nails reappear in the account of an even more famous explorer, Captain James Cook, during his visit to Tongatapu in October 1773. Cook was shown one of Robertson's nails which had been carefully hafted to a bone handle and was evidently held in high esteem (Beaglehole 1969:206). The object was collected by the botanist Forster, and is illustrated by Kaeppler (1971b: plate 4b). Inquiring about this object, Cook was told that the nail:

> ...came from Onnuahtabutabu, and on asking how the people of that island came by it, he [Fattafee the King] said one of them sold a Club for five Nails to a Ship which came to the island, and these five Nails after wards came to Tongatapu and they were the first they had seen (Beaglehole 1967:162).

This incident clearly demonstrates the linkages existing between Niuatoputapu and the Tongan paramounts at Tongatapu, with so novel and highly valued an item as a nail having been despatched from the outlying island to the chiefly seat at Mu'a, where it was specially hafted and held in high esteem.

As a final commentary from the period of initial European contact, we have the account of the ill-fated French explorer La Pérouse, who called at Tafahi and Niuatoputapu in December 1787, after having visited Samoa:

> About twenty canoes immediately put off, and came towards the ships to trade.... They were laden with the finest cocoa-nuts I had ever seen, a small number of plantains, and a few yams. One of them only had a small hog, and three or four fowls. It was evident that these Indians had already seen Europeans, or heard talk of them; for they came alongside without fear, traded with tolerable honesty, and never refused, like the natives of the Navigators' Islands [Samoa], to deliver their goods before they received payment. They accepted pieces of iron and nails as eagerly as beads. They spoke the same language, however, and had the same ferocious appearance. Their dress, too, their tattooing, and the shape of their canoes, were the same: so that there can be no doubt, that they are the same people. They differed, however, in this, that every one had two joints of the little finger of the left hand cut off; and in the Navigators' Islands I never saw more than two persons, who had undergone this operation (La Pérouse 1799:163).

How much significance we should accord La Pérouse's comments on the cultural and linguistic similarities between the Niuatoputapu and Samoan populations is uncertain, although it may be that the Niuatoputapu language was still strongly Samoic-Outlier at this time. The cultural influence of Tonga, however, is very evident in the distinctive Tongan mortuary practice of finger joint removal.

DESIGN OF THE RESEARCH

The 1976 Niuatoputapu research project represents the second phase of an ethnoarchaeological program focusing on indigenous subsistence systems and settlement patterns in Western Polynesia, with the overall aim of elucidating the processes of cultural adaptation to island ecosystems (Kirch 1975a, 1976). The program began in 1974 with investigations on Futuna, Alofi, and 'Uvea islands (Kirch 1975a, 1976, 1978a,b, 1981), in which special attention was accorded the islands' agricultural systems, exemplified by both intensive irrigation and drainage cultivation of *Colocasia* taro. Initially, I planned to return to Futuna and Alofi in 1976 to build upon the results of the first season. At the last moment, political exigencies in the French-administered Territoire des îles Wallis et Futuna forced us to abandon that plan, and required that the field site be shifted to another Western Polynesian locality. The island of Niuatoputapu, which had been reconnoitered archaeologically by Rogers (1974), seemed a likely alternative. The shift in study area resulted in one significant change in the research: Niuatoputapu lacks the water-control agronomic systems that we had planned to investigate more intensively on Futuna. Consequently, less attention was devoted to the archaeological study of agricultural systems than I had originally envisioned.

Several major research topics provided orientation for the project, both during fieldwork and in the subsequent laboratory analyses which have extended over the past decade:

1. Fundamental to all other research questions, we sought to produce a culture-historical outline of the prehistoric occupation sequence of Niuatoputapu. Since the term "culture history" has become unfashionable in recent years (at least in some quarters), a further comment is appropriate. Too often, the culture-historical approach has been associated with an essentialist epistemology, in which particular sequences of continuous culture change are forced into a rigid series of temporal pigeonholes (periods or phases), succeeding each other in step-like fashion. Process is ignored, and nothing is explained. Yet it is just as certain that the study of cultural change (let alone the explanation of such changes) depends on a secure temporal framework. Thus our first and, in this sense, primary objective was to outline the temporal sequence of prehistoric human occupation on Niuatoputapu, beginning with initial human colonization and extending into the ethnographic present. While temporal labels are convenient tools for handling blocks of time ("periods"), our goal was not periodization per se. Rather, the kind of culture-historical sequence we require is one in which the material variability of archaeological phenomena is highlighted in time and space. In sum, our first objective was to delineate a cultural sequence actually composed of a large series of individual "time traces" of particular archaeological phenomena (e.g., variation in ceramic temper, vessel classes, and decoration; adz morphology; faunal class frequencies; and settlement pattern components).

2. As related earlier, Western Polynesia has been identified as the Polynesian "homeland," the region in which a distinctive Ancestral Polynesian Society developed out of an earlier and more generalized Lapita ancestor. Linguistically, a Proto-Polynesian language can be identified, with a probable age of about 1000–500 B.C.; more than 3,000 lexical items have been reconstructed for this proto-speech community (Biggs, Walsh, and Waqa 1970). The archaeological expression of the corresponding ancestral culture, however, requires further research (Kirch 1984a). This is a problem of great significance for Polynesian studies as a whole, since the accurate reconstruction of the ancestral baseline is essential for regional studies of cultural differentiation and evolution (Kirch and Green 1987). Considerable emphasis was assigned to this research topic during our study, since Niuatoputapu exhibits an extensive zone of ceramic-bearing middens dating to the first millennium B.C., the period during which Ancestral Polynesian Culture developed.

3. More recently in the culture-historical sequence, there is the problem of the expansion of the Tongan maritime chiefdom, well documented ethnohistorically but little understood from an archaeological perspective. Niuatoputapu, as an outlying island that had come under the domination of the Tongan ruling polity late in regional prehistory, offered excellent opportunities for exploring the archaeological expression of this regional political process. In particular, our studies of the island's settlement pattern—dominated by large monumental mounds of typical "Tongan" form—focused on this research issue.

4. The research strategy of both the 1974 Futuna-'Uvea Project and the 1976 Niuatoputapu project was oriented, in particular, toward the indigenous subsistence systems of Western Polynesia. One of the questions addressed was the nature of the founding or colonization economies. Whether the Lapita economy included horticulture had been a focus of some debate (e.g., Howells 1973:254-55; Shutler and Shutler 1975:82), based largely on Groube's hypothesis of the Lapita colonists as "Oceanic strandloopers" (1971:310–12). In Niuatoputapu, we sought specific archaeological evidence which might be used to test Groube's hypothesis. Also of special interest was the time frame for development of some of the unique subsistence adaptations to environmental constraints, such as the semi-anaerobic pit fermentation and storage of starchy food pastes. While documented ethnographically, the prehistory of such adaptations, unknown from archaeological data, offered a problem for investigation. In addition, we wished to pursue the issue of marine exploitation systems. In the early 1970s, there was little evidence in Western Polynesian archaeological sites for the use of sophisticated angling gear. Did the ubiquitous fishhook assemblages of Eastern Polynesian sites reflect innovations before or *after* the breakup of the Ancestral Polynesian Society? Here, too, was a matter requiring further field investigations in the Western Polynesian homeland region.

5. A final research issue which directed the 1976 Niuatoputapu project was the question of environmental dynamics and their role in the evolution of island cultures. In this we were concerned as much with the effects of three millennia of human occupation on island environments—both physical and biotic—as with the constraints and challenges posed by natural ecological conditions. As our Niuatoputapu fieldwork progressed, it became strikingly evident that the island had changed dramatically in such basic variables as land area and reef-lagoon configurations during the 3,000 years that humans had lived there. This dynamism reflects Niuatoputapu's position on the edge of one of the most active tectonic zones in the Pacific, and considerable efforts were devoted to documenting, in geomorphological as well as archaeological terms, these dramatic changes.

With these objectives providing basic orientation, the archaeological work on Niuatoputapu was carried out over a six-month period beginning in July 1976. My assistant, Thomas Dye, remained in the field through the end of January, conducting reconnaissance surveys of both Tafahi and Niuafo'ou islands. The initial reconnaissance of Niuatoputapu proceeded rapidly, with the reports of Rogers (1973, 1974) providing a useful guide. The intensive survey of surface sites was carried out in stages throughout the entire period of fieldwork, with 161 sites recorded in all. Much of our excavation effort was directed at the zone of ceramic deposits which Rogers had initially identified, and which represents at least the first half of the island's cultural sequence. Less extensive excavations were also conducted in aceramic midden deposits and in several of the larger monumental constructions.

The persistence of traditional subsistence systems in the more isolated islands of Western Polynesia provided an opportunity for simultaneous ethnoecological and archaeological research. It must be stressed that this kind of ethnoarchaeological project differs somewhat from other studies under that rubric, which have frequently aimed at producing models for the analogic interpretation of archaeological phenomena (e.g., Gould 1980), or actualistic models of site formation processes (so-called "middle range theory," e.g., Binford 1983). In Niuatoputapu, the application of ethnoecological studies was seen primarily as a means of understanding the *ethnographic endpoint* of a continuous sequence of local cultural evolution. The contemporary agricultural and marine exploitation systems of Niuatoputapu are the direct descendants of systems introduced by the first Lapita colonists. Thus an understanding of these endpoint systems provides additional *control* from which to reconstruct or retrodict cultural change in the past. Working backward in time from a known present to an unknown past provides unique opportunities for understanding evolutionary sequences. It is in this sense that Polynesia, with direct archaeological continuity from prehistory to the ethnographic present, is an ideal theater for ethnoarchaeological research.

The ethnographic and ecological components of our fieldwork were carried out more or less concurrently with the archaeological research. Both Dye and I became reasonably fluent in the Tongan language, and all of our inquiries were carried out using classic participant-observer methods. Dye assumed the primary task of studying the contemporary marine exploitation system, while I concentrated on agriculture and related aspects of terrestrial production. In the agriculture study, emphasis was placed on elucidating major patterns of cropping and agronomic practice, temporal variability, and adaptation of the agriculturalists to environmental diversity. As no scientific investigations of the Niuatoputapu terrestrial environment had been conducted, it was also necessary to concentrate on such basic descriptive factors as soil types and vegetation. A collection of 182 voucher specimens of Niuatoputapu plants was prepared, and determinations subsequently made by St. John (1977); the vouchers are deposited in the Herbarium of the Bishop Museum. In his study of marine exploitation, Dye concentrated on the material culture and techniques of fishing, the frequency and size of catch, and social aspects of fishing organization and catch distribution. Transect studies and reference collections were made of marine invertebrates and fish (all specimens are deposited in appropriate collections of the Bishop Museum).

Many of the data deriving from these ethnoecological investigations have already been published elsewhere (Dye 1983; Kirch and Dye 1979; St. John 1977), or will appear separately. Thus it was felt that a detailed account of the contemporary Niuatoputapu subsistence systems would needlessly lengthen the present monograph. In chapter 2, however, a brief synopsis of these results is presented, providing a baseline for understanding the endpoint of cultural change in Niuatoputapu subsistence systems over three millennia.

CHAPTER TWO

THE SETTING

A GEOGRAPHICAL ISOLATE WITHIN WESTERN POLYNESIA, Niuatoputapu (also known as Keppel's Island) is politically part of the Kingdom of Tonga. Most Tongans, however, regard the "two Niuas"—Niuatoputapu and Niuafo'ou—as remote outposts. Even in 1976, communications between Niuatoputapu and the rest of the Kingdom were poor; one small ship made the passage from Vava'u once a month at best. Such constraints on inter-island contact did not apply in earlier times, and from a wider geographical perspective (fig. 2), Niuatoputapu (15° 57' S, 173° 44' W) is strategically situated. To the northeast lie the Samoas (310 km to Upolu Is.), and to the south the large Tongan island of Vava'u (252 km); thus Niuatoputapu sits astride the major voyaging route between Tonga and Samoa, a crucial link in the protohistoric prestige-good exchange system monopolized by the Tongan elite. The seat of the Tongan paramounts, at Mu'a on Tongatapu, lies 515 km to the south, but once the open sea between Niuatoputapu and Vava'u had been crossed, the route lay through the virtually continuous archipelago of the Ha'apai and Nomuka groups. Directly west some 172 km is Niuafo'ou (Tin Can Is.), whose hardy population has remained undaunted by a succession of volcanic eruptions. Farther to the northwest are Futuna (386 km) and 'Uvea (261 km), the latter also a Tongan dominion in the protohistoric and early historic periods. Finally, to the southeast stretches the vast Fijian archipelago, including the main islands of Vanua Levu (675 km) and Viti Levu, and the Lau group. Source of large timber and prestige goods, the Fijis were also linked to the wider Tongan voyaging network (Kaeppler 1978; Kirch 1984a).

In 1976 the voyage to Niuatoputapu from Neiafu, Vava'u, took 28 hours on the tiny, aging steamer *Pakeina,* her rusting decks packed with passengers, bundles of mats, coconut-frond baskets full of yams and taro, and the occasional trussed pig. As dawn broke, crew and passengers alike kept a sharp watch for the 560-m high volcanic peak of Tafahi, the first sign of land to thrust above the rolling swells. This landmark allowed the captain to correct his course (for navigation is strictly by dead reckoning), and throughout the morning Tafahi rose steadily above the seas. By noon, the central volcanic ridge of Niuatoputapu (160-m above sea level) was visible, appearing like the "backbone of some mesozoic reptile" rising from the depths (Rogers 1974:311).

As *Pakeina* skirted the northeastern weather coast of Niuatoputapu, the effects of continuous exposure to the southeastern trades were obvious: the swells crash directly on the saw-toothed fringing reef, affording no possibility of a landing. An unbroken, steeply sloping white sand beach, piled up by frequent storms, rises from the reef platform. The dense scrub and forest beginning at the dune crest show no signs of permanent human occupation along this side of the island.

This untamed and forbidding windward aspect changed abruptly as *Pakeina* rounded the headland of Hikuniu, bringing into view the leeward side of the island, with its extensive system of barrier reefs and quiet lagoons. The problem now was to negotiate the single narrow, twisting passage through the reef. I still marvel at the skill of old Tolati in easing the fragile hull of *Pakeina* past razor-sharp shelves of coral into the safe waters of the sandy-bottomed lagoon. The anchor was let go a few yards from the long jetty at Falehau, where a throng awaited the arrival of returning kinfolk.

Niuatoputapu's population of about thirteen hundred resides along the leeward coast in three main villages: Falehau, Vaipoa, and Hihifo (figs. 9, 10). Hihifo, the largest village, is also the headquarters of the government representative, who maintains contact with the outside world via shortwave radio. Vaipoa village, near the center of the leeward coast, is the hereditary seat of Niuatoputapu's only noble, Tangipa, whose estate *(tofi'a)* includes the garden lands inland of the village. Formerly, the more powerful hereditary line of Ma'atu also had its seat here, but the last title-holder died without issue, and the extensive Ma'atu *tofi'a* remains under government control. Falehau village includes the residence of Fuimaono, steward of the Royal Estate, which comprises the northeastern third of the island.

Although it is a small island, only 15.2 km^2 (maximum length 6.8 km, width 1.5 to 3.8 km; Rogers [1975:14] gives the land area as 15.5 km^2), Niuatoputapu encompasses a diversity of microenvironments. This variation in landform can best be appreciated by climbing the island's central ridge, an erosional remnant of the volcanic cone which forms Niuatoputapu's structural core (fig. 11). From the inland edge of Hihifo village (situated on a series of undulating beach ridges), one traverses a series of two or three weathered escarpments of biogenic limestone, emerged reef terraces which testify to the active tectonism shaping the Niuatoputapu landscape. The track winds through a mosaic of fenced gardens of yam and aroids on a gently sloping clay terrace which represents a former stand of the sea (termed the Pleistocene Terrace in this monograph), then abruptly begins to climb the steep face of the central ridge (fig. 12). Scrambling up the active colluvial slopes through swidden clearings and second growth, one arrives at a volcanic scarp about 10 to 15 m high, where the exposed interbedded lava, breccia, and welded tuff reveal the igneous nature of the ridge itself. The scarp is scaled by climbing the entwined roots of an aged banyan tree (*Ficus* sp.), and a few steps further one emerges on the summit of Fungamuihelu, 146 m above sea level.

From Fungamuihelu and similar vantage points along the central ridge, the island reveals its mosaic of varied microenvironments. Most obvious is the contrast between windward and leeward, first noted from the sea. Windward of the central ridge (the *liku* side of the island), a broad flat plain extends out to the narrow, fringing reef, a distance of up to 2 km, or more. With the exception of the Pleistocene Terrace directly below the ridge itself, this broad plain shows few signs of cultivation; instead, it is cloaked largely in scrub or forest with light-colored open patches. These latter areas are the *toafa,* former lagoon floors now emerged through tectonic uplift, supporting only a halophytic association of sedges and occasional scrub *Pandanus* (fig. 13). Most of the windward plain itself is made up of recently emerged reef platform or accumulation ridges of reef debris, such as coral heads and other detritus, upon which a *Eugenia*-dominated rainforest has grown.

Turning to the leeward side of Niuatoputapu, we find a significant contrast. There is only a narrow coastal plain heavily marked by the signs of human occupation, between the base of the Pleistocene Terrace and the lee shoreline. From the leeward shore, a protected reef-lagoon ecosystem extends from 1 to 1.6 km offshore. In the northwest, off Hihifo and Vaipoa, this consists largely of a broad reef platform, drained at low tide, with active coral growth restricted to its outer margins. In the northeast, fronting Falehau village, a barrier reef forms an extensive lagoon, dotted with smaller patch reefs. Directly off Vaipoa village, about 1 km from shore, is Hakautu'utu'u, a small islet of reefal detritus and sand anchored to the reef platform.

Looking west, one sees a shallow passage 150 to 200 m wide, that separates Hihifo village from Hunganga Island (0.4 km^2). Heavily forested, Hunganga consists of emerged reef and is neither occupied nor cultivated. Slightly to the southeast is another complex of islets, Tafuna and Nukuseilala, barely separated from the main island by tidal passages.

Although not a main focus of our project, Tafahi Island (also known as Boscawen or Cocos Island) must be briefly described, for the populations of the two islands are closely linked, and probably have been for millennia. Displaying the classic steep-sided, conical profile of an andesitic volcano, Tafahi lies 7.25 km north of Niuatoputapu. Because it is geologically much younger, Tafahi lacks any substantial reef development, and there is no secure boat anchorage. The total land area is about 3.3 km^2; most of this consists of steep slopes rising to the 560-m summit, often cloud obscured. A single village of about 50 houses occupies a less steeply sloping ridge at the northern end of the island. Tafahi is covered in dense rain forest, and its youthful lava-and-ash derived lithosols are fertile, so that the northern and eastern slopes are dotted with shifting cultivations. In particular, Tafahi is famed throughout Tonga for its *kava (Piper methysticum)* plantations; the narcotic infusion made of roots from Tafahi Island is said to be especially potent and clean-tasting.

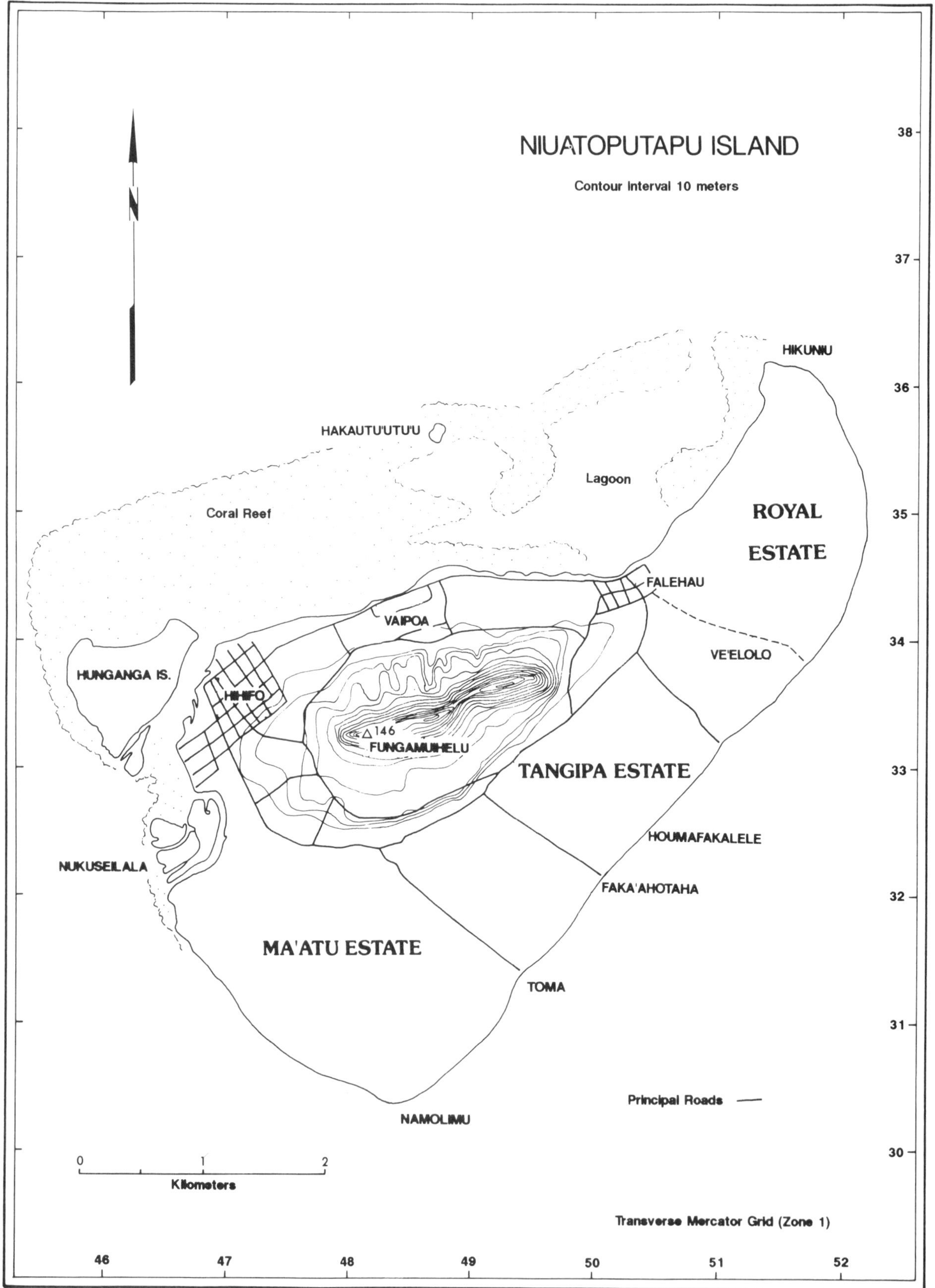

Figure 9. Map of Niuatoputapu Island (based on 1976 Directorate of Overseas Surveys, Series X872, Sheet 2, 1:25,000).

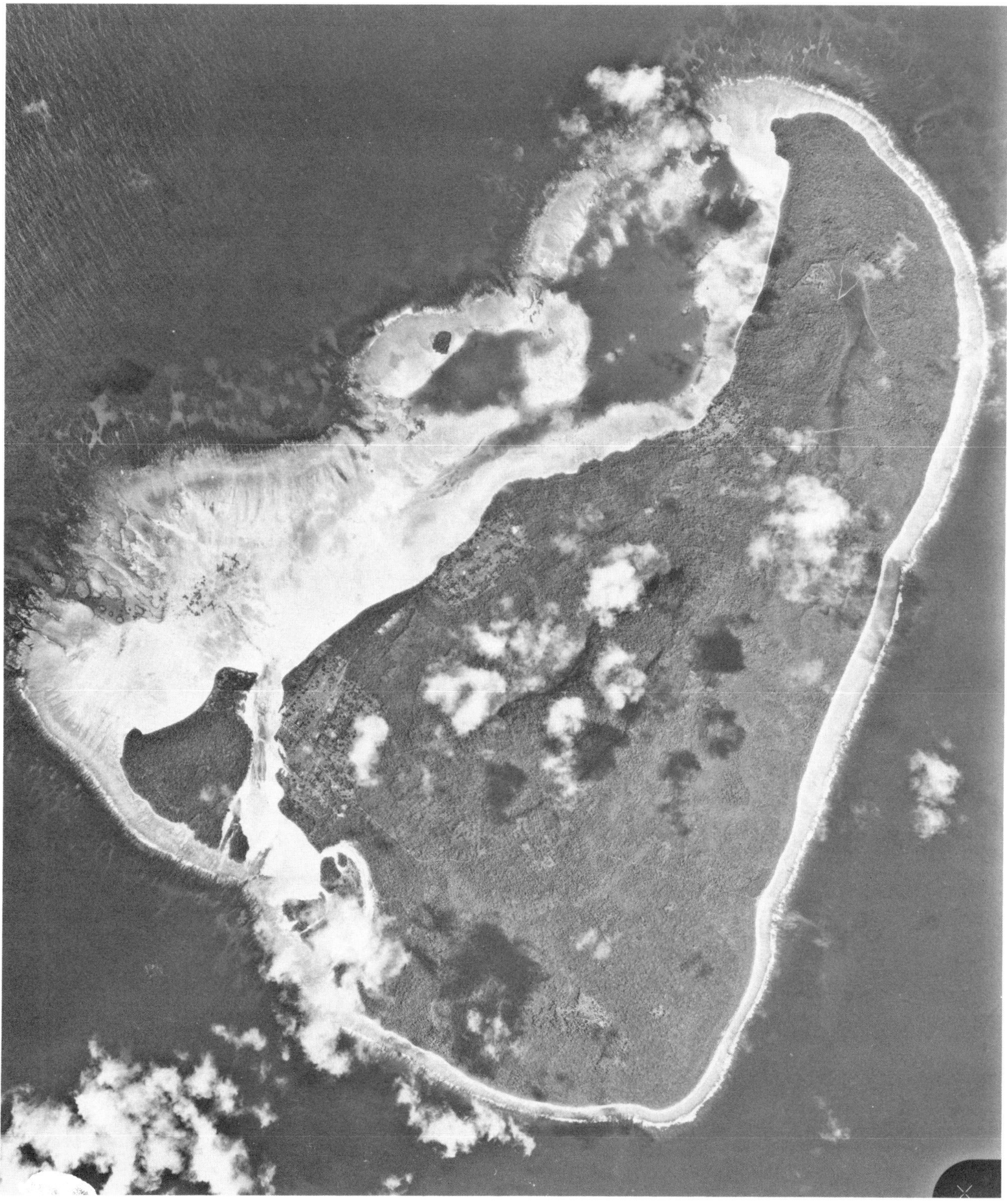

Figure 10. Aerial photograph of Niuatoputapu Island, June 14, 1971, taken from altitude of 20,000 ft. (Photo courtesy of Ministry of Lands, Survey, and Natural Resources, Kingdom of Tonga.)

GEOLOGY AND GEOMORPHOLOGY

The geological structure of Niuatoputapu, including the rapid tectonic changes that have greatly altered its landscape during the Holocene, must be understood in a regional context. The Fiji-Western Polynesian region includes islands of two major types: (1) those composed of oceanic rocks of an alkaline suite, principally olivine basalts; and (2) those composed of more complex and varied calc-alkaline suites (an andesite-rhyolite-dolerite-basalt association) with some calcareous sediments. These two types of islands are separated by the so-called "andesite line," long recognized as indicating the structural boundary of the Pacific Basin (Ladd 1934). Recent developments in plate tectonic theory have clarified the processes underlying this major structural boundary (Coleman 1973). The Tonga Trench, running north from New Zealand some 3,000 km and passing immediately to the east of Niuatoputapu and Tafahi, marks a subduction zone where the westward-moving Pacific Plate is plunging under the Australian Plate at a rate of about 8.2 cm/yr. The Tonga Ridge, the structural base of the Tongan archipelago including Niuatoputapu, is thus an active island arc system, formed by plate-melting at great depths and by consequent volcanism. Fiji and the Lau Islands were evidently similar, but now extinct, island arc systems (D. Green and Cullen 1973:131-32, 136; Gill and Gorton 1973:544). Referring to the tectonic history of the region, Gill and Gorton remark:

> Broadly contemporaneous island arc volcanism thus took place in Fiji, Tonga, and the New Hebrides during the Eocene to Lower Miocene. It thus seems likely that these areas formed a continuous volcanic ridge on the Australian side of a west-dipping subduction

Figure 11.View to the northeast along the central volcanic ridge of Niuatoputapu.

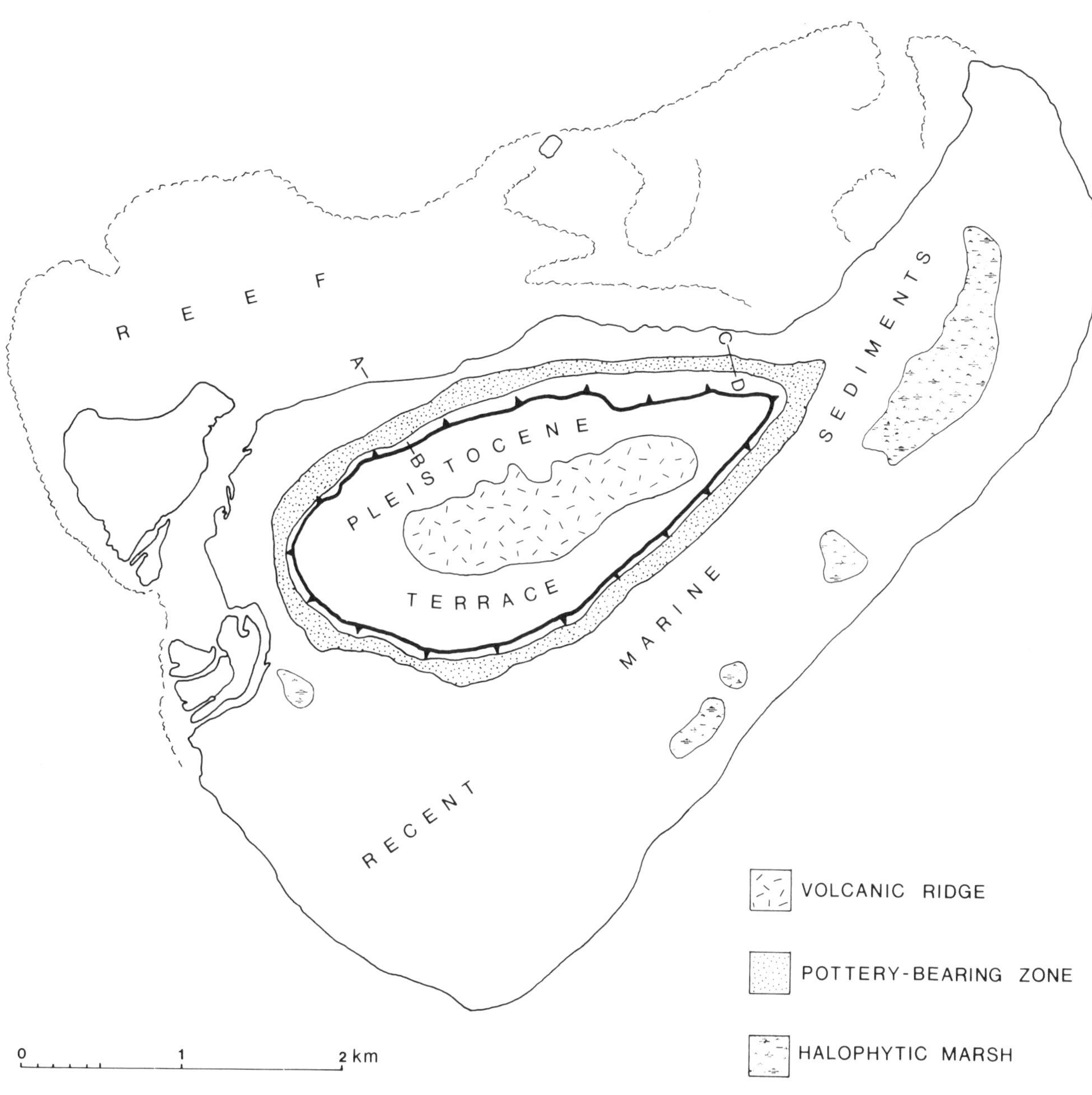

Figure 12. Geomorphologic map of Niuatoputapu Island.

zone which marked the boundary between the Pacific and Australian Plates at this time (1973:550).

Subsequent anti-clockwise rotation of the Fiji Plateau, crustal extension between the Lau and Tonga ridges, and other structural changes have resulted in the present configuration of the region (Green and Cullen 1973; Sclater et al. 1972; Chase 1971). To the east of the Tonga Trench, the Samoan archipelago reflects a relatively simple geological history of Plio-Pleistocene volcanic extrusion of oceanic basalts (Stearns 1944), probably of "hot-spot" origin. As part of the Pacific Plate, the Samoan group is slowly migrating westward toward the northern end of the Tonga subduction zone, and is undergoing gradual submergence in the process.

In this context, both Niuatoputapu and Tafahi belong to a western group of Tongan islands which are composed of young andesites associated with active island arc volcanism (Ewart and Bryan 1973).

Figure 13. View of *toafa* land, showing typical stunted *Pandanus* and *Casuarina* trees. Central volcanic ridge in the distance.

Niuatoputapu, however, is somewhat older than Tafahi, and may now have passed out of the stage of active volcanism. Niuatoputapu's volcanic core is exposed along the central ridge. Examination of exposures below Fungamuihelu reveals alternating beds of massive breccia, ash or welded tuff, and andesitic lavas, with strike ranging from 30 to 45° and dipping from 25 to 40°. Isolated volcanic outcrops, apparently northeastern erosional remnants of the central ridge, are also found at two localities inland of Falehau village.

Differences in the geological structures of various Fijian and Western Polynesian islands have significant implications for prehistoric human adaptation. As Green observed, "...on crossing the andesite line and entering the oceanic world of the geologist, the first people to settle Polynesia encountered a rather restricted suite of suitable rock types, continental equivalents of which they had largely ignored previously" (1974a:142). On Niuatoputapu and Tafahi, the available lithic resources were restricted to andesitic lavas, some suitable for adz manufacture, and a low-silica grade of obsidian or volcanic glass. The latter known especially from the younger volcanic cone of Tafahi (Ward 1974a,b), outcrops also in at least one locality on Niuatoputapu's central ridge. Indeed, the Tafahi obsidian source was probably of some importance throughout the Fiji-Western Polynesian region in the early first millennium B.C. (obsidian flakes from Lakeba Is. in the Lau group have been spectrochemically traced to the Tafahi source [Best 1984]).

The geomorphology of Niuatoputapu effectively can be described as a series of concentric zones surrounding the central volcanic ridge (fig. 12). The highest zone, between 50 to 140 m above sea level, consists of the active colluvial slopes, steep and unstable. Erosion of these slopes is encouraged by the continued clearance of vegetation and by the working of the thin lithosols for shifting cultivations. Between 30 and 50 m elevation is the gently sloping terrace that we have termed the Pleistocene Terrace, since it evidently represents a former sea level stand of Pleistocene age. The Pleistocene Terrace is most clearly defined on the southern and eastern (windward) side of the central ridge, where it can attain 400 m in width. On the northern side of the ridge, the Pleistocene Terrace is dissected by several intermittent stream valleys. The terrace appears to be formed of the igneous structural core of the island, which has perhaps been planed by wave action, and may have been capped (in places at least) by reefs. Today it is covered by several meters of volcanic sands and clays which have eroded from the central ridge. Consequently, the Pleistocene Terrace is an extremely important zone in the island's agricultural system, and is entirely covered in yam-aroid cultivations interspersed with tree crops such as coconut, breadfruit, and Tahitian chestnut *(Inocarpus fagiferus).*

The seaward edge of the Pleistocene Terrace is clearly marked on the south and east by a steep bluff of 20 to 25 m in height. On the north, the bluff is less pronounced but still discernible. Associated with this scarp, especially on the north, are outcrops of biogenic limestone, heavily pitted by solution and frequently covered with fine erosional clays. These outcrops are reef remnants, again reflecting former shorelines. Forming a concentric zone immediately below the Pleistocene Terrace bluff is a former beach terrace of unconsolidated sands, 3 to 6 m above present sea level (mean low water). This beach terrace was the setting for human occupation during the first 1,500 years of the Niuatoputapu sequence (and thus corresponds to a zone of ceramic-bearing archaeological deposits), and as a consequence has a distinctive anthropogenic soil association (the *fasifasi'ifeo* soils, see below). The geomorphological, sedimentological, and pedological characteristics of this sand terrace are the subjects of more detailed analyses in chapters 3 and 4.

Seaward of the sandy beach terrace with its ceramic zone, the remaining landscape of Niuatoputapu consists of various types of recently emerged marine sediments. In the western and northern (leeward) areas, these sediments are arrayed in a series of alternating beach ridges and intervening depressions, highly characteristic of a prograding shoreline, with the ridges representing high-energy accumulations of sand and reefal detritus. To the south, east, and northeast, the broad plains described earlier stretch for up to 2 km from the old beach terrace to the present windward coast. These plains, no more than 3 to 5 m above sea level, consist variously of exposed, solution-pitted limestone reef platforms, sandy flats representing former lagoon floors (the *toafa),* and accumulation ridges of large coral cobbles and other reefal debris.

This concentrically arrayed geomorphic structure is the direct reflection of active tectonism, resulting from the proximity of Niuatoputapu to the Tonga Trench and the major subduction zone at the edge of the Pacific Plate. The Tonga Ridge, of which Niuatoputapu is a part, lies on the leading edge of the Fiji Plate, which is sliding over the downward-plunging Pacific Plate. Consequently, islands on the Tonga Ridge are emerging at a rapid rate, sufficient even to compensate for the rapid eustatic rise of sea level in the early Holocene (from 10,000 to 6,000 years B.P.). On Tongatapu and 'Eua islands, reefs now elevated 2.2 m above sea level give radiometric ages of 5,700 to 5,900 years B.P. (Taylor and Bloom 1977). In the case of Niuatoputapu, the active shoreline at ca. 3,000 years B.P. was the seaward edge of the beach terrace bearing Lapitoid ceramic sites (see fig. 12). Thus the island has undergone approximately 3 m of uplift in the past 3,000 years, resulting in the emergence of an extensive system of former reef platforms and lagoons on the windward side of the island. The overall significance of such dynamic tectonism is indicated quantitatively: Niuatoputapu island area has increased during the past 3,000 years by about 10.9 km^2, or 312%. Furthermore, the evidence suggests that this rate of emergence is continuing. Older informants note that the passage between Niuatoputapu and Hunganga Island has become noticeably narrower and shallower within their lifetimes, a consequence of uplift accompanied by accumulation of sand and reefal detritus. Likewise, the broad reef platform seaward of Hihifo village is clearly emerging, for it no longer supports active coral growth (being tidally drained) and is heavily solution-pitted in areas. Thus it is predictable that, given the present rate of tectonic uplift, the extensive leeward reefs and lagoon of Niuatoputapu will have emerged completely within the next 1,000 to 3,000 years, and will mirror the windward expanse of uplifted marine sediments.

RESOURCES OF THE ISLAND

Niuatoputapu lies within the humid tropics, with the following key climatic parameters: annual rainfall greater than 2,000 mm, mean temperature ranging from 25 to 28° C, and relative humidity averaging about 80%. The climate, however, is distinctly seasonal. Toward the end of April the trade wind season begins, bringing somewhat cooler temperatures and lowered relative humidity. Rainfall drops to 175 mm or less per month. Throughout this "dry" season the southeastern trades blow steadily, often with considerable force, for days on end. About the end of October or early November, the "wet" season sets in. During this period the wind is irregular or absent, the weather frequently hot and sultry, and the days often punctuated by sudden torrential downpours. Monthly rainfall during this rainy season reaches 275 to 300 mm.

This seasonal climate has significant consequences for the indigenous Polynesian agricultural regime. The natural periodicity, in concert with the ecological templates of certain key crops—especially the tropophytic yams—imposes a regular scheduling of agricultural activity (see Kirch 1976 regarding the similar 'Uvean agricultural system). Even more important are two kinds of stochastically recurring climatic events: drought and cyclones. During normal years, rainfall during the dry season is sufficient to maintain the standing agricultural crop. When precipitation drops below average levels, however, as it did for four months during our stay in 1976, the aroid gardens suffer serious damage, and subsistence production is strained. Unfortunately, we have no accurate statistical data on the frequency of drought on Niuatoputapu, although informants claim it to be a recurring hazard.

Tropical cyclones can be even more disastrous, both to the agricultural system and to the villages and people themselves. Such storms, which usually move from the northeast to the southwest, are associated with the wet season; approximately 85% of all cyclones occur between December and April (Visher 1925: table 5). Although accurate figures are lacking, cyclones strike Niuatoputapu approximately every 10 to 20 years. Their destructive effects on the island's agricultural production base are greatly intensified if there is, as sometimes happens, a drought in the succeeding dry season. When we consider the balance between human population and land on Oceanic islands, such environmental hazards or perturbations are key variables, more significant as limiting factors than any average calculations of agricultural carrying capacity (Kirch 1984a:127-35).

Although a few erosional gullies dissect the leeward face of the island's central ridge, Niuatoputapu lacks permanent streams. In a few places along the coast, as at Niutoua in Hihifo village, freshwater springs issue from fissures in old, emerged reef limestones. These, along with wells *(vai tupu)* dug in the coastal plain to tap the freshwater lens (Ghyben-Herzberg aquifer), serve as the primary sources of water for drinking and bathing.

There have been no detailed pedological studies on Niuatoputapu, but the range of soils can be encompassed by a relatively simple classification. The steep colluvial slopes of the central ridge consist of relatively deep, well-drained clays and loams with substantial quantities of weathered rock fragments. The Pleistocene Terrace is mantled with finer-textured clay and silt loams, with lesser quantities of lithic fragments. These loams have been laterized in places, probably due in part to continued exposure through intensive cultivation over three millennia. Below the Pleistocene Terrace, on the old beach terrace occupied by the Lapita colonists of Niuatoputapu, the calcareous sands have been enriched through human occupation and the deposition of cultural refuse. This band of enriched sandy loams is, however, no more than 60 to 70 m wide in most places, and grades into very poorly developed sandy loams with a relatively thin A-horizon overlying sterile calcareous beach and dune sands. Much of the southern and eastern plain of recently emerged marine sediments has virtually no soil development at all.

The Niuatoputapu people utilize a folk taxonomy of soils which closely mirrors the etic categories of the Western scientist. Soils of the central ridge and Pleistocene Terrace are classed as *kelekelefatu,* in recognition of their distinctive inclusions of igneous rock *(kele* = earth, *fatu* = stone). Further distinctions are made of the *kele uli,* or darker loams of the steep slopes, and the *kele kulokula* or reddish (oxidized) soils of the Pleistocene Terrace. The concentric band of sandy loams enriched by Lapitoid occupation debris is termed the *fasifasi'ifeo,* in recognition of the numerous fragments of branch coral *(feo)* appearing there. *Tu'one* soils are the very thin, poorly developed loams on recent beach sands. Finally, the term *one'one* designates recent deposits of coral sand lacking any humus cover at all.

The flora of the Fiji-Western Polynesian region is an eastern attenuation of the Indo-Malayan Rain Forest Formation (Richards 1952; van Balgooy 1960) which, in the case of a small and anthropogenically disturbed island such as Niuatoputapu, is highly depauperate as well. Although there is considerable species-level endemicity in the region, most of the genera and higher-level taxa are found throughout insular southeast Asia and Melanesia. As a result, the early Austronesian-speaking colonists moving into this region for the first time 3,000 or more years ago would have been familiar with the main features of the vegetation. However, the Fiji-Western Polynesian region lies outside the natural distributional limits of most Oceanic cultigens and their wild ancestors. Thus it is certain that such key crops as taro, yams, bananas, and breadfruit were introduced to the region by these early colonists (Yen 1973a; Barrau 1965a).

Floristic studies of Niuatoputapu were lacking prior to our expedition; the very limited collections of H. Hurlimann (1951–52) were incorporated into Yuncker's (1959) archipelago-wide survey of the Tongan flora. In conjunction with an ethnobotanical investigation (the results of which are to be published separately elsewhere), we collected herbarium voucher specimens of as many species as possible. The 138 species represented in these collections have been determined by St. John (1977), who published a checklist of the Niuatoputapu flora, drawing also upon the earlier Hurlimann specimens. The known vascular flora of the island (which I would estimate to be approximately 90% comprehensive) includes 10 ferns and fern-allies, and 201 species of phanerogams. These latter include 1 endemic species, 113 indigenous species, 42 cultigens (including fruit-bearing trees and plants, cultivated for construction or industrial uses, introduced in both prehistoric and historic times), and 41 other introductions (including ornamentals and weeds).

The distinctive vegetation of the coastal strand includes species of virtually pan-Oceanic distribution (cf. Merrill 1945), notably coconut *(Cocos nucifera); Barringtonia asiatica,* whose large quadrilateral-sided fruit are used for fish poisoning; *Calophyllum inophyllum* and *Casuarina litorea,* the wood of which is used for carving; and other trees and shrubs *(Hernandia nymphaeifolia, Thespesia populnea, Cordia subcordata, Messerschmidia argentea, Scaevola taccada,* and others). The large *Terminalia catappa* with its reddish leaves and edible fruit dominates the shoreline in places. Lining the shores of the tidal channels between the main island and Nukuseilala are dense thickets of *Fimbristylis pycnocephala* and *Pemphis acidula.*

The vegetation of the leeward coastal plain and the central volcanic core of the island is thoroughly anthropogenic. Extensive tracts surrounding the villages constitute, in effect, managed forests in which virtually every plant is of economic value. Coconut is ubiquitous on the coastal plain, as are such fruit-bearing trees as *Artocarpus altilis, Spondias dulcis, Inocarpus fagiferus,* and the historic introductions *Mangifera indica* and *Citrus aurantium.* Also found here are the fish poison species *Derris trifoliata* and *Pittosporum arborescens;* the dye-yielding *Bischofia javanica,* used in bark cloth decoration; the medicinal *Morinda citrifolia;* various species of *Pandanus,* the leaves of which are cultivated for plaiting mats; and ornamentals such as *Gardenia taitensis.*

The lower slopes and central volcanic ridge are covered by extensive tracts of second growth, interrupted by swidden clearings. Recently abandoned cultivations are frequently dominated by *Miscanthus floridulus* canes and *Scleria polycarpa.* Feral cultigens, including *Pueraria lobata, Cordyline fruticosum,* and *Dioscorea* spp., are extensively distributed throughout the zone of second growth. Among the larger dominants are *Macaranga harveyana, Ficus scabra, Pipturus argenteus, Leucosyke corymbulosa, Hibiscus tiliaceous, Acalypha grandis, Bambusa vulgaris,* and *Melochia vitiensis.* Along the crest of the central ridge and clinging precariously to a few sheer slopes are small areas of regenerated forest which hint at the original composition of the pre-human vegetation. These include such tree or shrub species as *Eugenia clusiaefolia, Santalum yasi, Flacourtia rukam, Ficus tinctoria,* and *Decaspermum fruticosum,* with understory elements such as *Freycinetia storckii, Alyxia stellata, Piper vaupelii,* and *Peperomia* spp.

On the windward side of the island, the recently emerged marine terrain supports a young, depauperate climax forest dominated by *Eugenia clusiaefolia,* the fruit of which is the favorite food of the indigenous pigeon *(Ducula pacifica).* A unique halophytic association (the *toafa)* occupies the old, sandy floors of former lagoons, and includes stunted *Pandanus odoratissimus, Casuarina litorea, Cyperus* spp., *Fimbristylis pycnocephala,* and *Pemphis acidula.*

In terms of both floristic composition and vegetational zonation, human influences on the island's vegetation have been profound. Cultigens, ornamentals, and weeds were introduced in both prehistoric and historic times and, indeed, the process continues today. The prehistoric transfer of useful species (including endemics) from island to island in Western Polynesia is indicated by vernacular plant names. For example, the ornamental *Gardenia rotumaensis,* called *"siale lotuma,"* was transported from Rotuma Island to the west, while a single cultivated tree of *Pandanus turritus ("fala hola")* is an introduction from Samoa.

The terrestrial fauna of Niuatoputapu is rather limited, with the Polynesian-introduced domesticates of pig, dog, and jungle fowl *(Gallus gallus)* being the principal mammals. The Polynesian or Pacific rat *(Rattus exulans)* was probably transferred to the island with the original human colonists as a stowaway species. Fruit bats *(Pteropus tonganus)* are indigenous, and their meat is highly regarded.

The avifauna constitutes the richest component of the terrestrial wildlife. Seabirds commonly roosting on the island include the White-tailed Tropic Bird *(Phaeton lepturus),* the Least Man-o'-War *(Fregata ariel),* the Fairy Tern *(Gygis alba candida),* and the Common Noddy *(Anous stolidus pileatus).* All of these are taken for food. The Reef Heron *(Demigretta sacra sacra)* is frequently seen along the coast, while the Australian Gray Duck *(Anas superciliosa pelewensis)* frequents marshy areas. A common inhabitant of the undergrowth is the Banded Rail *(Rallus philippensis fosteri),* while the Purple Swamphen *(Porphyrio porphyrio vitiensis)* is a serious agricultural pest that feeds on root crops. Especially prized for its sweet meat is the Pacific Pigeon *(Ducula pacifica pacifica).* This species also figures prominently in traditional lore, and was the main object of a chiefly sport, pigeon snaring, which utilized a distinctive class of monument site (see chapter 3).

The herpetofauna is depauperate, including a few species of lizard (Gekkonidae, Scincidae), only one of which, a now extinct iguanid *(Brachylophus fasciatus)*, may have been eaten by humans. A number of the smaller lizards are synanthropic, and were probably early human introductions to the island. There are no snakes on Niuatoputapu.

Miscellaneous terrestrial food resources include several species of land crab, the most prized being the Coconut Robber Crab *(Birgus latro)*, a food usually reserved for chiefs or persons of rank. Hermit crabs *(Coenobita perlatus)* are eaten incidentally, as are several other unidentified crustaceans.

As everywhere in Oceania, the sea and its resources provide the main supply of protein in the Niuatoputapu diet. Detailed ethnographic studies of contemporary marine exploitation were a part of our 1976 field strategy, and the results of this work have been published in full elsewhere (Kirch and Dye 1979; Dye 1983). The marine environment forms an integument around Niuatoputapu that can be subdivided into three biotopes: the reef flats (7.62 km^2), the lagoon (2.63 km^2), and the reef edge (0.41 km^2).

The reef flat is broadest on the leeward side of the island, especially off Hihifo and Vaipoa villages (figs. 9, 10); its maximum width there is about 1.5 km. In contrast, along much of the windward side, the reef flat is only 60 to 85 m wide. The broad leeward flat consists of a largely dead, solution-pitted reef platform, covered in places with a veneer of shifting sand. A number of edible gastropods, such as *Trochus maculatus*, inhabit these sands, as do the edible holothurians. The leeward reef flat is a favored environment for various techniques of net fishing. The narrow windward reef platform is regularly scoured by storms. The gastropod *Turbo setosus*, which occupies small depressions in the reef, is regularly harvested from this zone, and spiny lobsters are also taken here at night.

The lagoon, with depths up to about 9 m, is limited to the area off Falehau village. It is not a major zone of fishing, but the sandy bottom is the habitat of four species of bivalve, all of which are collected for consumption. These are *Asaphis violascens*, *Laevicardium biradiata*, *Periglypta puerpera*, and *Anadara antiquata*.

The reef edge constitutes the zone of active coral growth, and supports the most diverse communities of fish and invertebrates, as well as a generally high biomass (Goldman and Talbot 1976). The windward reef edge is the scene of a rather dramatic technique of night spearfishing, *ama fakasiosio*, described by Dye (1983:255). The leeward reef edge is less often fished, due to both the fragility of its corals (making it unsafe at night) and its distance from the shore. Fishing is even more rarely undertaken in the pelagic zone, although the most prized of all fish, the *'atu (Katsuwonus pelamis)* is occasionally pursued with the traditional pearl shell trolling rig.

PRINCIPAL BIOTOPES

Based on the geologic, topographic, edaphic, floristic, and faunistic features reviewed above, the Niuatoputapu ecosystem may be subdivided into nine biotopes or microenvironmental zones. These biotopes are summarized below, and are delimited in figure 14. Whenever relevant, the biotopes will be referred to by number throughout the remainder of this monograph.

Biotope I: Central Ridge. Volcanic outcrops and lithosols, with remnants or regenerated patches of indigenous forest. Swidden gardens in places. Source locality for volcanic stone and obsidian.

Biotope II: Lower Ridge Slopes and Pleistocene Terrace. Colluvium on the higher slopes, with clay loams capping the Pleistocene Terrace. Steep on the northwest; gentler slopes on the southeast. Vegetation consists predominantly of second growth with a mosaic of yam-aroid gardens in an approximately six-year fallow cycle. Numerous tree crops, particularly breadfruit and *Inocarpus*.

Biotope III: Old Beach Terrace. Well-drained sandy loam of carbonates enriched with organic material of cultural origin. Covered by second growth and interspersed yam-aroid gardens; coconut plentiful.

Biotope IVA: Emerged Reef Platform and Beach Ridges. Below and extending out from Biotope III, terrain which has emerged within the past 3,000 years. Poorly developed sandy loams, or thin humus on sand. Typical strand vegetation on the leeward coast.

Biotope IVB: Lagoon-Flat Remnants (Toafa). Most recently emerged lagoonal areas, subject to flooding, with some drainage to the sea. Vegetation limited to halophytic association of *Pandanus*, *Casuarina*, and Cyperaceae.

Biotope V: Reef Detrital Ridges. On the south coast (and Hunganga Island), substrate of high-energy deposited coral boulders and other reefal detritus; at an earlier stage of island emergence these may have formed islets along the edge of the emerging reef (such as Hakautu'utu'u islet at present). Vegetation dominated by *Eugenia clusiaefolia*. Resources include fruit bats, pigeons, and land crabs.

Biotope VI: Reef Platform. Substrate of solution-pitted coral, covered by sand in areas; wide along leeward coast, narrow to windward.

Biotope VII: Lagoon. Shallow lagoon restricted to the area from Hakautu'utu'u Islet to Hikuniu.

Biotope VIII: Living Reef Edge. Seaward fringe of the reef platform, with highest marine species diversity and biomass.

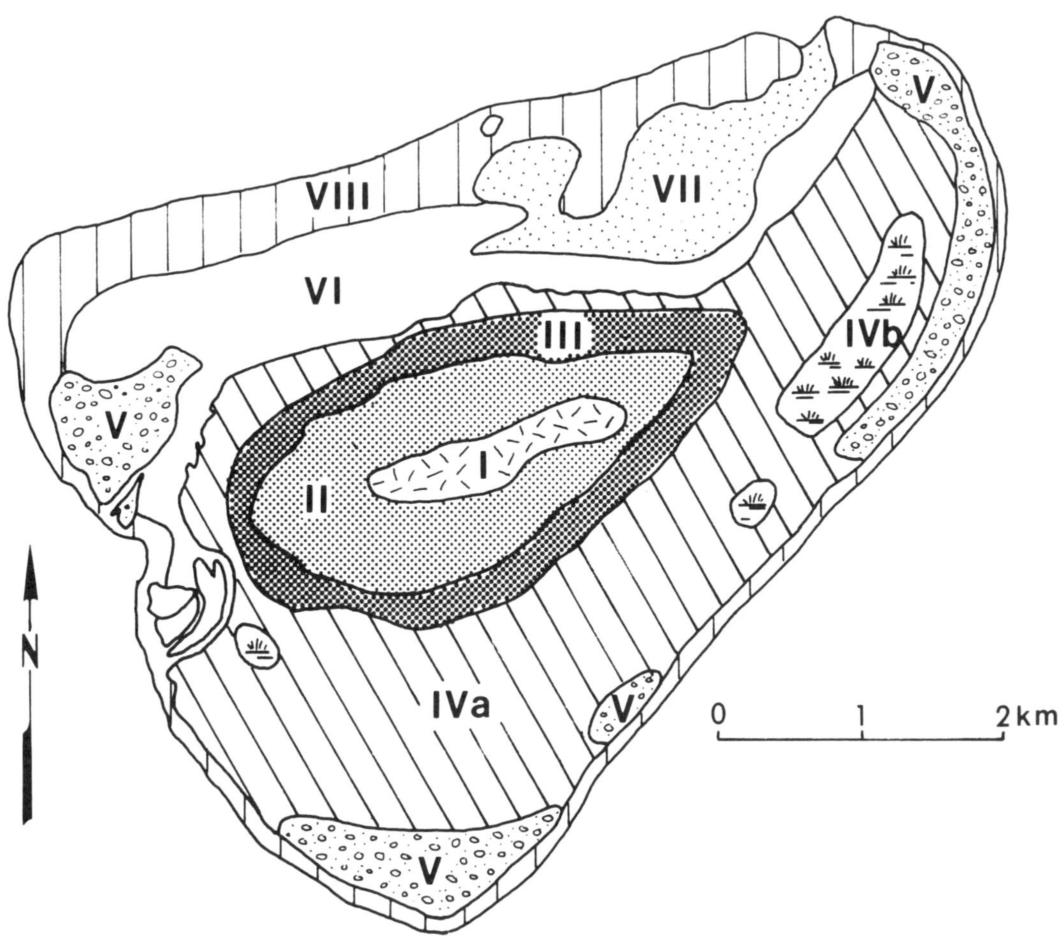

Figure 14. Distribution of principal biotopes on Niuatoputapu Island (see text for discussion).

Biotope IX: Pelagic Zone. Open pelagic zone extending beyond the reef edge, exploited occasionally by angling and trolling.

ENVIRONMENT AND SUBSISTENCE: THE ETHNOGRAPHIC BASELINE

Throughout Oceania, the continuity between prehistory and the ethnohistorically and ethnographically documented cultures of the past two centuries lends more strength to the use of ethnographic materials in prehistoric investigations than that of mere analogy. Indeed, on Niuatoputapu and elsewhere, the "ethnographic present" represents the developmental or evolutionary *endpoint* of a continuous sequence that commenced with Lapita colonization. An understanding of the indigenous culture and society in the historic period, in conjunction with archaeological analyses, provides a baseline for the retrodiction of cultural change. For this reason, and as has been detailed in chapter 1, our research design in 1976 incorporated a variety of ethnoecological studies of the contemporary Niuatoputapu subsistence system and ecological adaptation, as these were judged to have direct relevance to the understanding of the island's archaeological record.

Clearly, the island's production system was not in 1976 as it must have been in 1616, or even in 1800. Niuatoputapu is linked—albeit by a thin cable—to the world economic system, a linkage with implications for virtually every aspect of Niuatoputapu society. For that matter, it is arguable whether the island ever

TABLE 1

NIUATOPUTAPU CULTIGENS

Botanical Nomenclature[1]	English Vernacular	Tongan Vernacular[2]	Crop Type[3]	Status[4]	Age[5]
DICOTYLEDONEAE					
Moraceae					
Artocarpus altilis (Park. ex Z) Fosb.	Breadfruit	*mei*	FF	A	I
Broussonetia papyrifera (L.) Vent.	Paper mulberry	*hiapo*	I	S	I
Lauraceae					
Persea americana Mill.	Avocado	*avoka*	NF	A	H
Piperaceae					
Piper methysticum Forst. f.	Kava	*kava*	N	S	I
Leguminosae					
Inocarpus fagiferus (Park. ex Z) Fosb.	Tahitian chestnut	*ifi*	FF	A	I
Euphorbiaceae					
Manihot esculenta Crantz	Manioc	*manioke*	FT	S	H
Rutaceae					
Citrus aurentium L.	Orange	*moli*	NF	A	H
Anacardiaceae					
Mangifera indica L.	Mango	*mango*	NF	A	H
Spondias dulcis Park.	Vi apple	*vi*	NF	A	I
Sapindaceae					
Pometia pinnata J.R. & G. Forst.	—	*tava*	NF	A	I
Caricaceae					
Carica papaya L.	Papaya	*lesi*	NF	S	H
Combretaceae					
Terminalia catappa L.	—	*telie*	NF	A	I
Sapotaceae					
Burkella richii (Gray) P.H.J. Lam	—	*kau*	NF	A	I
Convolvulaceae					
Ipomoea batatas (L.) Lam.	Sweet potato	*kumala*	FT	S	H
Solanacea					
Nicotiana tabacum L.	Tobacco	*tapoka tonga*	N	S	H

Table 1, Continued

Botanical Nomenclature[1]	English Vernacular	Tongan Vernacular[2]	Crop Type[3]	Status[4]	Age[5]
MONOCOTYLEDONEAE					
Liliaceae					
Cordyline fruticosum (L.) A. Chevalier	Ti	*si*	FT	S	I
Taccaceae					
Tacca leontopetaloides (L.) Kuntze	Polynesian arrowroot	*mahoa'a*	FT	S	I
Dioscoraceae					
Dioscorea alata L.	Greater yam	*ufi*	FT	S	I
D. esculenta (Lour.) Burkill	Lesser yam	*ufi lei*	FT	S	I
D. nummularia Lam.	Yam	*palai*	FT	S	I
Bromeliaceae					
Ananas comosus (L.) Merr.	Pineapple	*faina*	NF	S	H
Gramineae					
Saccharum officinarum L.	Sugarcane	*to*	C	S	I
Palmae					
Cocos nucifera L.	Coconut	*niu*	NF	A	I
Araceae					
Alocasia macrorrhiza (L.) Schott	Elephant ear	*kape*	FT	S	I
Colocasia esculenta (L.) Schott	Taro	*talo*	FT	S	I
Cyrtosperma chamissonis (Schott) Merr.	Swamp taro	*via*	FT	SW	I
Xanthosoma sagittifolium (L.) Schott	—	*talo futuna*	FT	S	H
Pandanaceae					
Pandanus spp.	Screwpine	*fafa/kie*	I	A	I
Musaceae					
Emusa section hybrids	Banana	*hopa/pata*	FF	S	I

[1] Organized according to the family sequence of A. Engler's *Syllabus der Pflanzenfamilien* (12th Ed., Melchoir, 1964).
[2] Basic plant name; there are frequently names for specific clones as well.
[3] Abbreviations: FF, farinaceous fruit; FT, farinaceous tuber; NF, non-farinaceous fruit; I, industrial; N, narcotic; C, confection.
[4] Abbreviations: S, swidden gardens; A, arboriculture; SW, swamp planting.
[5] Abbreviations: I, indigenous (prehistoric introduction); H, historic period introduction.

constituted a closed system—the archaeological and ethnohistorical evidence certainly bespeak a varied history of external linkages (see also Kirch 1986, on closed and open systems in Oceania). From the viewpoint of subsistence production, however, Niuatoputapu is primarily a self-sustaining unit, and the fundamental strategies of agricultural production and marine exploitation pursued in 1976 were relatively little changed from those described in the historical accounts of initial European explorers to Tonga. Metal fishhooks, nylon line, and Coleman lanterns have replaced shell fishhooks, *Pipturus* cord, and coconut frond torches, while new crops have been added to the cultigen roster. Such changes, however, have not fundamentally altered the dominant strategies of yam-aroid shifting cultivation and inshore marine exploitation that have sustained human populations on Niuatoputapu for centuries.

The remainder of this chapter presents a brief synopsis of terrestrial and marine subsistence production, based on our 1976 investigations, as a baseline for the retrodiction of subsistence aspects of the prehistoric record. Again, I stress that this is a baseline or endpoint of a continuous sequence of cultural change, *not* an ethnographic "handbook" for analogic interpretation of the archaeological record. The marine exploitation strategies have been dealt with in some detail elsewhere (Kirch and Dye 1979; Dye 1983), while our ethnobotanical data have yet to be published in full.

The Agricultural System

Niuatoputapu agriculture revolves around a set of 29 adventive plant species introduced to the island in prehistory (table 1), 20 of which are indigenous to the Malayo-Oceanic humid tropics. The remaining 9 species are, with two exceptions, post-European-contact introductions of American origin. Eleven species are perennial trees, the most important being coconut *(Cocos nucifera)* and breadfruit *(Artocarpus altilis)*. The remainder are largely herbaceous, parthenocarpic species reproduced through artificial vegetative propagation of tubers and stems.

As elsewhere in Western Polynesia (Kirch 1975a, 1976, 1978a, 1979), Niuatoputapu agriculture focuses on four cultigen complexes (including 9 major species): (1) yams; (2) aroids; (3) breadfruit; and (4) bananas. The dominance in Niuatoputapu of a fifth species, the introduced manioc, provides a contrast with the more traditional Futunan and 'Uvean agricultures. These four species complexes are the primary producers of starch staple *(me 'akai)*, which forms the core of the Niuatoputapu diet. The dominant yams are *'ufi (Dioscorea alata)* and *'ufi lei (D. esculenta)*; their segregation by edaphic zone provides one of several major zonal contrasts in the spatial distribution of gardens. Another yam, *palai (D. nummularia)* is present as a minor component of gardens at the interface of Biotopes I and II. Two presently feral species, *lena (D. pentaphylla)* and *hoi (D. bulbifera)*, are widespread throughout the island's second growth and, as elsewhere in Western Polynesia, may have been a significant component of past cultivation strategies (Barrau 1965a).

Among the aroids, the dominance of *kape (Alocasia macrorrhiza)* has doubtless been favored by such selective pressures as the island's well-drained edaphic conditions, general lack of hydromorphic micro-environments, and recurring drought (to which *A. macrorrhiza* is most resistant). The central role of *kape* in Niuatoputapu is mirrored in 'Uvean agriculture (Kirch 1978a), and in Samoa. The introduced American aroid, *talo futuna (Xanthosoma sagittifolium)*, was by 1976 nearly as significant as *kape*, while *talo tonga (Colocasia esculenta)*—a hydrophytic species—plays a relatively minor role in the cultigen roster. A fourth aroid, *via (Cyrtosperma chamissonis)*, is planted in dense but restricted stands in swampy localities (the interfaces of Biotopes IVA and IVB) and serves primarily as a famine resource.

Breadfruit, used as an almost exclusive source of staple starch during the peak of fruit maturity, provides a strong arboricultural element in the Niuatoputapu agricultural system. Formerly, abundant crops of breadfruit were partially ensiled in underground pits and preserved semi-anaerobically as a resource in times of food shortage, but this practice has now ceased. (This is one impact of the island's wider economic linkages, since the availability of imported flour or rice, especially through government-sponsored relief, provides insurance against such environmental perturbations as cyclones and drought.) Bananas, particularly the *hopa* complex of *Eumusa* triploid hybrids, extend the productive phase of yam-aroid swidden gardens into the fallow period and are a significant source of staple starch during certain periods.

An American introduction of the historic period, *manioke (Manihot esculenta)* is a major contributor of staple starch. This cultigen, which may be cropped after the harvest of yams and aroids in the same swidden plot, and which is relatively hardy and resistant to drought, has the further advantage of being amenable to the filtration method *(fei hili)* of flour *(mahoa'a)* extraction. The *mahoa'a* flour, along with ensiled breadfruit paste, once provided a means of cultural buffering against the food shortages induced by cyclones and drought. In recent years, manioc has largely supplanted the traditional *mahoa'a* cultigen *(Tacca leontopetaloides)*, which, although still occasionally planted and utilized

Figure 15. Mixed yam-aroid swidden garden on clay soils of the Pleistocene Terrace. Banana and manioc in the background are a third-year planting.

as a famine resource, is plentiful only as a feral component of the island's second growth. The sweet potato or *kumala (Ipomoea batatas)*, also a historic introduction, is culturally prized (a favored food for feasts) but is a quantitatively minor source of staple starch.

In addition to these 12 staple starch producers, the remaining Niuatoputapu cultigens include 11 species of fruit- or nut-bearing trees, 2 sugar producers, 2 narcotics, and 2 species grown for "industrial" uses (table 1).

Niuatoputapu agriculture exemplifies shifting cultivation (or bush-fallow rotation) in which the dominant garden type is the mixed yam-aroid swidden (fig. 15). The tool complex (dibbles, machetes, long-handled "Tongan" spades adapted from nineteenth-century whalers' flensing spades), as well as the use of firing, are typical for Western Polynesia (Barrau 1961; Kirch 1979). Gardens in the vicinity of the villages are fenced for protection against marauding pigs. Due to the absence of suitable edaphic and hydrologic conditions, Niuatoputapu lacks the components of water control—either irrigation or drainage—that have so modified other Western Polynesian agricultural landscapes (e.g., Futuna and 'Uvea). With environmental constraint ruling out water control as an agronomic possibility, agricultural intensification in Niuatoputapu has taken the route of decreased fallow periods and, presumably, increased labor inputs (cf. Boserup 1965; Brookfield 1972; Kirch 1979). This particular form of intensified dryland cultivation is reflected as well in the more southern island of Tonga (Kirch 1984a:221–23), and in other Polynesian islands (e.g., Anuta, Yen 1973b).

The lexeme *ngoue* refers to a garden of any type, no matter what the particular crop mix. Most gardens are of the mixed yam-aroid type *(ma'ala)*, in which the yams provide the focus in terms of scheduling. This reflects their tropophytic ecologies, which require planting during the dry season. Initial swidden planting is thus concentrated on the yam crop, with some planting of *kape* and *hopa* bananas along the field borders and between individual sub-plots. Following yam harvesting (seven to nine months after planting), the field is extensively replanted in aroids and additional bananas; it is then referred to as a *tunga me'a*, or simply *ngoue*. Re-cropping in manioc, following the aroid harvest, is an option which may be chosen. Continued banana suckering generally extends the swidden's productive period into a third or fourth year, at which point ligneous and herbaceous second growth regeneration becomes dominant.

A significant zonal contrast in crop composition of yam-aroid swiddens exists between gardens of Biotopes I and II and those of Biotopes III and IVA, reflecting their differing edaphic conditions. On the central ridge and Pleistocene Terrace, *'ufi (Dioscorea alata)* is the dominant yam crop, while on the sandy loams of Biotope III and IVA *'ufi lei (D. esculenta)* assumes this role. As has already been mentioned, and will be argued further in chapter 4, the organically enriched soils of Biotope III are an artifact of human occupation; thus the possibilities of extensive yam-aroid cultivation in this zone have existed only since the abandonment of Biotope III as an occupation zone (after about A.D. 800 to 900).

Although long-term quantitative data are not available, the fallow period in Biotopes II, III, and IVA seems to average five to seven years, with a possible ten to fifteen year fallow in Biotope I. The Niuatoputapu bush-fallow regime is thus temporally more intensive than that of either Futuna or 'Uvea (Kirch 1975a, 1976, 1978a), and comparable to most of Tonga, but has not reached the state of nearly continuous cropping evidenced on the Polynesian outlier of Anuta (Yen 1973b). Second growth *(vao)* may be categorized as either *vao mui*, largely herbaceous species, or *vao taa*, fully regenerated forest. *Vao mui* is dominant and is the normal vegetative complex in which a new swidden is cut and fired. The relatively simple agricultural sequence on Niuatoputapu can thus be summarized graphically, using the indigenous land-use states: (1) *ma'ala*, first year yam-aroid swidden; (2) *tunga me'a*, second and third year swiddens; (3) *vao mui*, herbaceous second growth; and (4)*vao taa*, fully regenerated forest (fig. 16).

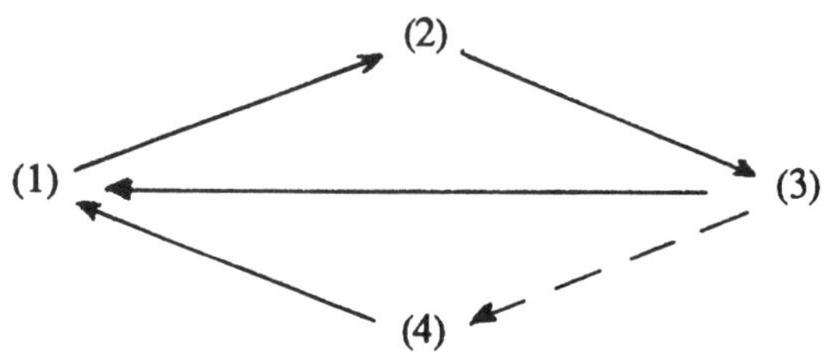

Figure 16. Directed graph showing relationship between indigenous land-use states.

The dashed line implies the infrequency with which cultivated land is allowed to regenerate forest cover. Indeed, considerable *vao taa* in Biotope IVA has recently been cut and incorporated into the zone of regular cultivations, although the terrain, due to recent tectonic emergence, supports only a thin humic layer.

The Niuatoputapu agricultural system contrasts with that of other Tongan islands in one very significant respect—the virtual absence of paper mulberry *(Broussonetia papyrifera)* cropping for the production of bark cloth. In its place, the Niuatoputapu population has specialized in the cultivation of several cultivars of *Pandanus*, used in the plaiting of mats of various types and functions (fig. 17). Niuatoputapu mats are regarded throughout Tonga as being of superior quality, and are highly sought after. Both mats and bark cloth *(ngatu)* are, however, vital objects of exchange between social groups on a number of traditional ceremonial occasions (especially marriages and funerals). Having specialized in the production of mats, the Niuatoputapu people thus obtain virtually all of their bark cloth from the more southerly islands, trading the local *Pandanus* productions for *ngatu*. We have no information on the antiquity of this economic specialization, although it may well predate the historic period.

The agricultural system includes an important animal husbandry component, focusing on pigs. Pigs are not only the most prevalent domestic animal, but are important due to the prestige value of pork in social exchange and ritual. As in other Western Polynesian islands, pigs are fed primarily on coconut, but also eat all manner of vegetable scraps, substandard tubers, etc., in addition to serving as effective scavengers in the village zone.

The constraints, both in space and in time, of a "patchy" environment are regarded as significant in the development of Western Polynesian production systems. Among the temporal, cyclically recurring constraints is drought. A four-month-long drought coincided with the 1976 fieldwork, and thus permitted the direct observation of the effects of water shortage on

Figure 17. Grove of cultivated *Pandanus* for fine mat production. Note removal of leaves from the *Pandanus* trunks.

agricultural activity. Most seriously affected of the crop plants were the two aroids, *Colocasia* and *Xanthosoma*, which suffered a heavy mortality rate, especially in the gardens of Biotopes I and II. The hill gardens took on the appearance of a wasteland, with cracked, parched soil and withered, stunted crops. *Kape* was considerably less affected than the other aroids. The *Dioscorea alata* yam crop, which had just been planted at the onset of the drought, suffered a serious delay—only about half of the crop sprouted, while the remainder lay dormant until the onset of rains in November. Those tubers that did sprout evidenced considerable stunting. The *'ufi lei* yams, favoring a xerophytic microecology, were not appreciably affected. The pig herd suffered losses, especially among the 0- to 6-month cohort, apparently from heat exhaustion and lack of mudholes for wallowing. The net effect of the drought, then, was a more or less immediate reduction in the aroid yield, and a projected reduction in the next year's yam and pig crops. The drought had become serious enough after two months to be a major topic of village conversation and a particular concern in church prayers and ceremonies. We were assured that crop shortages in the months ahead would force increased reliance on flour, rice, and other imported foods to meet subsistence demands.

The traditional importance of two indigenous food processing and preservation methods—pit fermentation and ensilage of breadfruit and other starchy tubers *(maa)*, and flour *(mahoa'a)* extraction by filtration (fig. 18)—is particularly evident in the context of such cyclic droughts. Although these methods have been largely supplanted in recent years by the importation of wheat flour and rice (the extraction technique is still practiced to a limited extent), their traditional usefulness in providing surplus food reserves is recognized by informants. The development in Western Polynesia of such preservation technologies may be viewed as an adaptation of normally non-storable tropical crops to the cyclic selective pressures of shortage due to drought and cyclonic damage (Yen 1975; Kirch 1984a).

Marine Exploitation

Although the most culturally prized flesh foods in the Niuatoputapu culinary repertoire—pig, coconut crab, and pigeon—come from the land, the sea provides the greatest variety and abundance of protein. The inshore biotopes of reef flat and reef edge are the main foci of fishing and shellfish-gathering activities, although the pelagic zone is not ignored. Prior to the decline of traditional canoe building, it is likely that pelagic trolling and benthic bottom-fishing were more important than today.

As Dye (1983:249) observes, Niuans classify fishing activities on several hierarchical levels. A fundamental distinction is recognized between *toutai*—active, male-dominated fishing strategies—and *fangota,* female-dominated gathering or collecting. Various strategies associated with particular sets of equipment and techniques in specific microenvironments are also designated, such as *uku* (diving), *kupenga* (netting), and *tau* (angling). Specific methods within a general strategy are designated lexically by modifying the general term, e.g., *tau 'otule* (fishing with hook and line for *'otule* fish).

In 1976 we observed or otherwise recorded 36 named fishing methods, including specific varieties of netting, spearing, angling, trapping, diving, and poisoning. All of these methods have been described in detail by Dye (1983). Figure 19 graphically summarizes the distribution and frequency of several major marine exploitation strategies along an idealized transect across both leeward and windward marine environments. The most evident pattern displayed in this figure is the significance of both windward and leeward reef edges and of the reef platform. The lagoon is significant only as a source of several species of large bottom-dwelling bivalves.

Twelve named netting methods contribute more fish to the Niuatoputapu diet than any other strategy. The majority of these methods utilize a long seine net on the broad leeward reef flat. Especially important is

Figure 18. Extraction of arrowroot flour *(mahoa'a)* by filtration.

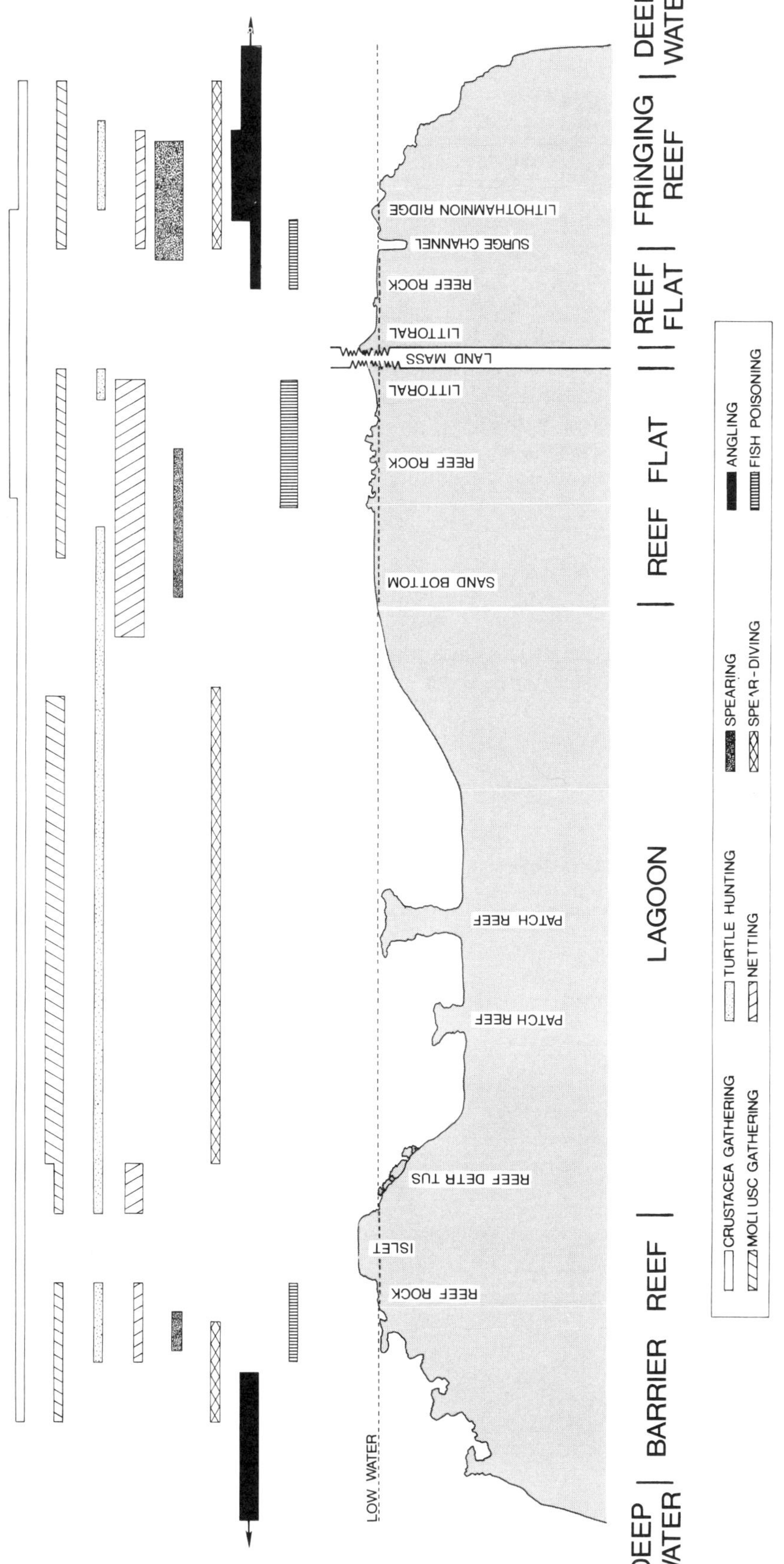

Figure 19. Schematic section through windward and leeward marine environments of Niuatoputapu Island, showing the zonal utilization of eight exploitation techniques. Bar thickness is an approximate indicator of the frequency of a given technique. The unbroken bar for crustacea gathering includes several species of land crabs that are classed with marine crabs in the local folk taxonomy.

the *kupenga fakamamaha* method, which makes use of a seine several hundred meters long to trap fish during the ebbing tide. The method requires the cooperation of several individuals, but is highly productive. Virtually all of the twelve named angling methods are practiced from boats or canoes just off the reef edge. Spearing is also heavily practiced at the reef edge, especially the nocturnal method known as *ama fakasiosio,* which is frequently used to take the large parrot fish prized for feasts. Fish poisoning is a widely practiced strategy which, unlike most other methods, frequently employs women. Rotenone, the active agent in the roots and stems of *Derris elliptica (kava 'aukava),* paralyzes the fish in shallow water (as on the reef flat at low tide), allowing them to be readily collected by hand.

Although the Niuatoputapu people recognize at least 210 mutually exclusive, lexically-marked folk taxa of fish (representing about 400 to 500 species), only about 20% of these are taken regularly enough to contribute significantly to the diet. For example, catch records for a 6-month period in 1976 (Kirch and Dye 1979, table 5) indicate that no more than 31 taxa accounted for 90% of the total catch during this period. Virtually all of these are common inshore species, such as acanthurids and scarids.

Shellfish gathering *(fangota)* is a relatively low-status activity, and while we did not obtain quantitative data, our impression was that invertebrates were a relatively minor contribution to total protein intake. Lobsters *(Panulirus* sp.) are prized for feasts, but of the variety of molluscs available, attention is regularly paid only to the gastropods *Turbo setosus* and *Trochus niloticus,* and to four species of bivalves inhabiting the lagoon. The bivalves must be taken by diving, and a few men from Falehau village specialize in this activity.

CHAPTER THREE

THE ARCHAEOLOGICAL LANDSCAPE

THE ARCHAEOLOGICAL LANDSCAPE of Niuatoputapu is dominated by two main categories of site: large, special-purpose earthworks or field monuments, particularly several kinds of mounds, and occupation deposits signalled by surface distributions of ceramics, midden, and other occupation debris. Notably absent is the array of smaller stone structures such as terrace walls and platforms—associated with household occupation units—typical of much of tropical Polynesia (especially Eastern Polynesia). In this respect, Niuatoputapu matches what is known of settlement patterns in other parts of the Tongan archipelago, especially Tongatapu, Ha'apai, and Vava'u (McKern 1929; Davidson 1971b; Anderson 1978; Kirch 1980a). However, Tonga has not yet benefited from the sort of sophisticated settlement pattern studies that have become common in other parts of Polynesia. In contrast to Samoa, for example, where several intensive surveys have documented the range of settlement components and their integration over regional landscapes, our knowledge of Tongan settlement patterns remains rudimentary at all levels. McKern's monograph (1929), based on a highly selective sampling of the largest and ethnohistorically best known field monuments (and largely focused on Tongatapu), remains the primary source. From this perspective, the archaeological survey of Niuatoputapu—begun in 1969 by Rogers and substantially extended in 1976—is significant as the only intensive sampling of any Tongan settlement landscape.

SURVEY: BACKGROUND AND METHODS

As an adjunct to his ethnographic research, Garth Rogers recorded 78 archaeological sites (111 site numbers were actually assigned, with several unexplained gaps). Most of these sites are described in Rogers (1973, 1974), and a base map on file in the Anthropology Department of the University of Auckland provides site locations. Rogers's survey was not systematic, but rather concentrated on larger and locally well known sites, such as burial mounds of the Niuatoputapu elite. Nevertheless, he recorded a number of sites unknown to the local population. In addition, Rogers correctly identified the important zone of ceramic-bearing deposits and its relationship to the island's recent geological history (1973; 1974:312). Rogers classified the surface sites he recorded by employing features from both "Niuatoputapu linguistic classification and purely morphological classification" (1973:26), with eight numbered classes (class 3 was divided into five sub-classes). Not surprisingly, such a hybrid classification proved to be of little use for meaningful settlement pattern analysis. (Indeed, because local informants often disagree in their emic classifications of particular sites, it may even be impossible to assign a given site to one of Rogers's classes.)

Using Rogers's survey results and base map as a starting point, our main objective in 1976 was to extend archaeological surface coverage of the island as intensively as possible. Of the 78 sites listed by

Rogers, 48 were re-located and examined; in many cases errors in measurement were corrected and incomplete descriptions augmented. Another 83 sites were discovered and recorded, bringing the overall total of Niuatoputapu sites to 161. Of the 131 sites checked or recorded in 1976, 35 were mapped with compass and tape, while 28 were mapped with plane table and alidade. Other sites were recorded by visual inspection with pacing or taping of primary dimensions. Sites are numbered consecutively in the order of recording, and are prefaced by the letter codes TO-NT-, for Tonga and Niuatoputapu (the TO- designation has generally been omitted in this monograph).

Although we made a concerted effort to examine virtually all geographic areas of the island—and more than doubled the known site inventory—it would be folly to claim exhaustive coverage. Large expanses of the island (especially the *Eugenia* forests of the *liku* coast) are masked with dense vegetation, in which some sites were certainly overlooked. Smaller mounds, and especially those without prominent slab facings, are easily missed even at close range. Thus it is probable that our sample remains biased toward the larger size classes. Nevertheless, the full range of settlement pattern components has probably been revealed, and the major patterns of settlement distribution shown by our survey are unlikely to be greatly affected by the discovery of additional sites.

To facilitate analysis, survey data for all sites were entered into a microcomputer database using the MINARK system; this was used for all data tabulations and statistical summaries. A complete list of sites is provided in appendix A. The site attributes recorded are: (1) local environment or biotope; (2) recorder; (3) level of recording; (4) class; (5) name, if known; (6) emic classification, if known; (7) length or diameter; (8) width or secondary diameter; (9) height; (10) basal area; (11) volume; (12) nature of facing slabs; (13) nature of paving; (14) kind of fill; (15) central depression; and (16) excavation status. Site volumes were calculated using appropriate geometric formulae, usually those for rectangular solids or frustums; these volumetric measures should be regarded as approximations only.

Rogers's site classification, which quickly proved to be unworkable, was abandoned in favor of a strictly morphological system, with local informants' emic categories recorded separately. The major site classes recognized are: (1) ceramic-bearing occupation deposits; (2) aceramic occupation deposits; (3) terraces; (4) faced platforms; (5-12) classes of faced and unfaced mounds, described in further detail below; (13) limestone quarries; (14) upright stones; (15) abandoned starch-fermentation pits (diameters generally 1 to 2 m); (16) contemporary village cemeteries; and (17) miscellaneous.

The distribution of all sites by class and biotope is given in table 2. Dominating the site inventory are the several classes of mounds, totalling 92 sites. Sites are distributed throughout the island, although the upraised lagoon flats (biotope IVA) are the favored location for most of the mound sites. Terraces are found only on the central ridge and lower slopes (biotopes I and II). The spatial distribution of sites is shown in figure 20, the archaeological base map. Particular sites may be located on figure 20 by reference to their UTM grid coordinates, provided in appendix A.

SETTLEMENT PATTERN COMPONENTS

Occupation Deposits

Two classes of occupation deposit, based upon whether the deposit included ceramics, were recognized. In the grossest terms, the Niuatoputapu prehistoric sequence can be divided into an earlier ceramic period (ca. 1200 B.C. to A.D. 900), and a later aceramic period (A.D. 900-1600), so that the classification of occupation deposits as ceramic or aceramic corresponds with earlier and later aspects of the regional sequence.

The Ceramic Zone

Ceramic-bearing deposits have a highly restricted and significant distribution (fig. 20), first recognized by Rogers (1974:312). A single, narrow zone of continuous deposits is situated at the base of the island's central volcanic ridge and terrace. The ceramic zone corresponds to an upraised beach terrace of coral sand lying immediately inland from a series of former shorelines, beach ridges, and elevated lagoons (see chapter 4 for further discussion of ceramic zone geomorphology). The ceramic zone itself constitutes a distinctive soil type, recognized by the local populace and termed *fasifasi'ifeo* (lit. "broken pieces of branch coral," *feo),* after the numerous pieces of branch coral scattered over the surface of the zone. Rogers described the zone as follows:

> [The *fasifasi'ifeo* soils] are dark loams 20-50 cm thick, containing broken igneous stones eroded down from the slopes of the central volcanic ridge and mixed with pieces of coral and shell brought up together with the underlying coarse coralline sand. This zone supports crops of sweet potato *(Ipomoea batatas),* but it is especially prized for

TABLE 2

CROSSTABULATION OF SITE CLASS WITH BIOTOPE

		BIOTOPE							
CLASS	DESCRIPTION	I	II	III	IVA	IVB	V	VI	TOTAL
1	Ceramic-bearing deposits			15					15 (9.3%)
2	Aceramic deposits				1				1 (0.6%)
3	Terraces	5	8						13 (8.1%)
4	Faced Platforms				1		2		3 (1.9%)
5	Unfaced Mound Type A			2	1				3 (1.9%)
6	Unfaced Mound Type A1	1	1	2	2				6 (3.7%)
7	Unfaced Mound Type A2		2	1	4	2	2		11 (6.8%)
8	Unfaced Mound Type A2a		1		1		2		4 (2.5%)
9	Unfaced Mound Type A2b		2		6		2		10 (6.2%)
10	Faced Mound Type B				5				5 (3.1%)
11	Faced Mound Type B1			1	12	3	14		30 (18.6%)
12	Faced Mound Type B2				18		5		23 (14.3%)
13	Quarries				2				2 (1.2%)
14	Upright Stones		1		2			1	4 (2.5%)
15	Fermentation Pits	1	4						5 (3.1%)
16	Village Cemeteries				10				10 (6.2%)
17	Miscellaneous	4	4	3	3		1	1	16 (9.9%)
TOTAL		11	23	24	68	5	28	2	161 (100%)
%		6.8	14.3	14.9	42.2	3.1	17.4	1.2	100%

producing the best crops of the shallow-rooted sweet yams *('ufi lei, Dioscorea sp.)* and bulbous yams *('ufi voli, 'ufi kaumeile,* etc., *Dioscorea spp.).* It is in and throughout this zone that abundant surface pottery sherds are found.... The explanation offered here for the presence of surface sherds throughout the *fasifasi'ifeo* soil zone is that the activities of yam-growing, involving the excavation of deep holes, has raised potsherds from their primary deposition on or just above the old beach/ lagoon sand where the Lapita-pottery people formerly lived and has scattered them, together with waterworn shells and coral from the old lagoon floor, about the surface. The pottery sherds are not waterworn (1974:312).

While the essential features of Rogers's description were borne out by our further investigations, in particular, the restriction of ceramics to the zone of *fasifasi'ifeo* soils and the role of yam cultivation in bringing sherds to the surface, some of his observations

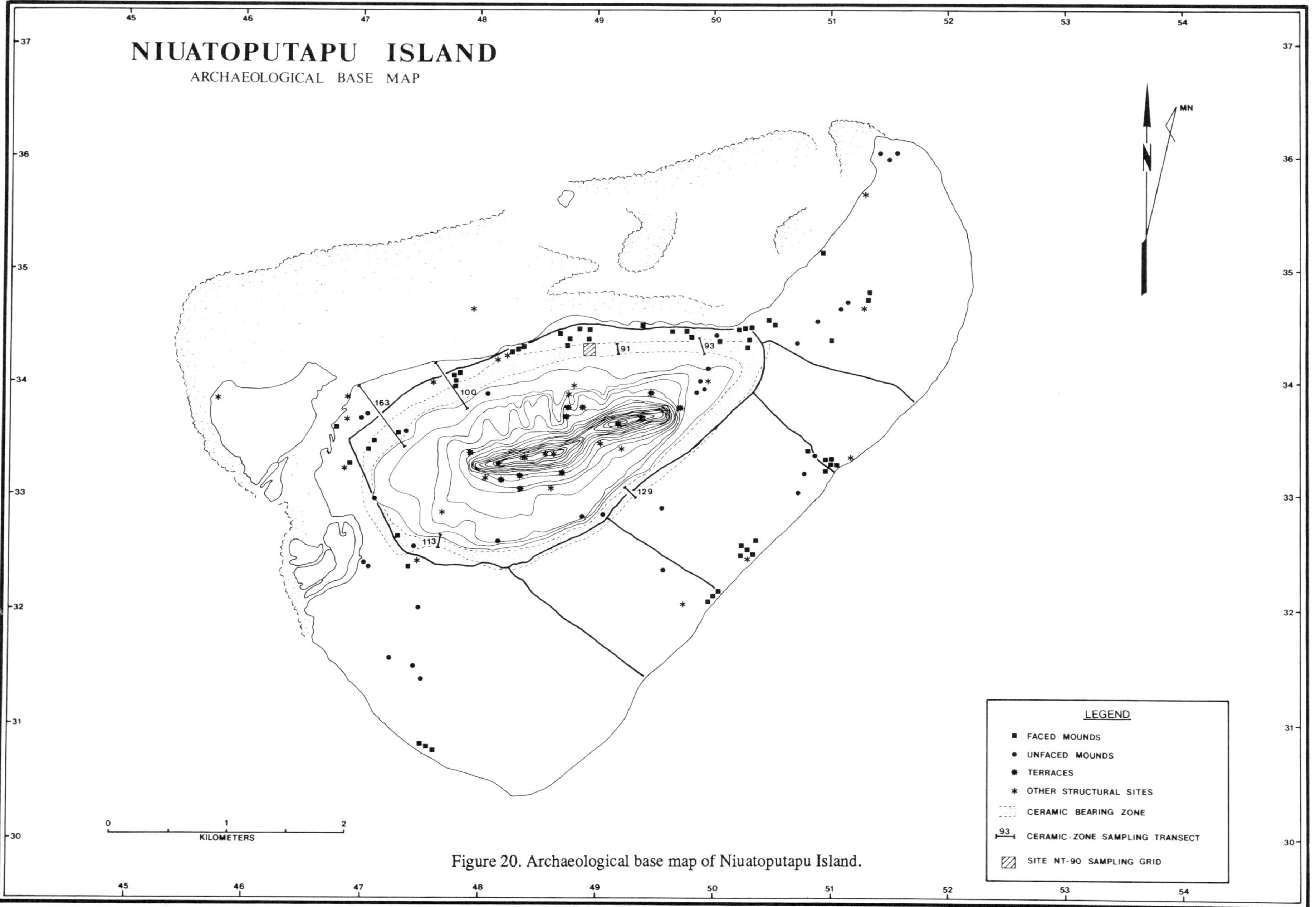

Figure 20. Archaeological base map of Niuatoputapu Island.

require further comment. First, the organic inclusions (especially finely dispersed charcoal and decomposed bone and shell) which give the zone its distinctive loamy texture are themselves the product of occupation. Thus, the *fasifasi'ifeo* loam is the result of extensive post-depositional reworking (through cultivation) of earlier occupation deposits. Second, most of the shells and coral scattered over the zone (and throughout the subsurface deposit) are not waterworn, but are culturally deposited refuse. Similarly, the igneous stones referred to by Rogers are in most cases fire-altered and shattered oven stones; although they doubtless originated on the central volcanic ridge, they were deliberately brought to the ceramic zone for use as cooking stones or for other purposes, rather than being erosionally transported to their present position.

In sum, the ceramic zone and its distinctive *fasifasi'ifeo* loam are cultural artifacts reflecting at least 1,500 years of occupation on a former beach terrace (see chapter 4 for chronological data). The various physical components of the zone, including igneous stones, large quantities of mollusc shell and branch coral, finely dispersed organic constituents, and ceramics, are all depositional products of an extended period of occupation. Because of this cultural enrichment of a well-drained coralline beach terrace with a variety of organic constituents, the *fasifasi'ifeo* zone has become a highly suitable edaphic environment for the production of certain yam cultigens, especially *Dioscorea esculenta* or *'ufi lei*. Yam cultivation over an unknown period of time following abandonment of the zone as an occupation locus has resulted in substantial mixing and reworking of the occupation deposits; the concomitant problems will be further discussed in chapter 4. The process of cultural enrichment of dune soils and the consequent creation of significant agronomic zones is not unique to Niuatoputapu, and has been noted by Kirch and Yen (1982:43, 347-49) for Tikopia. Indeed, anthropogenic creation of organic loams is a frequent occurrence on low coralline environments throughout the tropical Pacific, especially on atolls or in atoll-like situations (cf. Stone 1951).

The ceramic zone varies from 60 to 150 m in width or lateral extent, and has a total circumference of about 8.4 km. Thus its total estimated area is 0.84 km^2. The density of cultural materials within the zone varies substantially. In excavated transects across the zone, for example, sherd density ranges from 634.2 to 3.8/m^2. In general, the density of sherds and other cultural materials is highest throughout the leeward part of the zone, between Falehau and Hihifo. This density pattern suggests that the leeward coast was the preferred area of occupation throughout most of the ceramic period. Such a pattern is reasonable given the broad expanse of upraised lagoon flats to windward, which would have been tidal expanses of dead reef flat or shallow unproductive lagoon at the time of ceramic zone occupation. Excavations were conducted at several locations in the ceramic zone, and further discussion of the zone and its physical and cultural aspects are treated in conjunction with the results of these excavations in chapter 4.

Aceramic Occupation Deposits

Occupation deposits dating from the later, aceramic portion of the Tongan sequence (after ca. A.D. 800 to 900) were less evident during the surface survey, due to the absence of sherds as a visual indicator and to the general distribution of these later deposits in coastal areas not regularly cultivated. Most aceramic occupation deposits appear to underlie present or recent areas of village occupation, and are most readily identified by examining modern subsurface disturbances such as oven and trash pits for evidence of subsurface occupation strata. The seaward portion of Hihifo village overlies aceramic deposits of varying depth and complexity, as exposed, for example, in the NT-163 transect excavations (see chapter 4). A particularly noteworthy accumulation of aceramic strata in a large amorphous "mound" configuration lies adjacent to the important freshwater spring named Niutoua at the western edge of Hihifo village (Site NT-125); these deposits were sampled using a transect design (see chapter 4). In addition to these major coastal aceramic deposits, it is likely that smaller accumulations of aceramic material are scattered in inland locations, especially in association with terrace sites found on the lower slopes of the central ridge. This expectation remains to be archaeologically tested by excavation.

Architectural Sites

Aside from the subsurface occupation deposits, most Niuatoputapu sites consist of architectural features, the majority of which are large constructions of earth and stone. The basic formal classes into which such sites are categorized have already been listed; further details on the formal classification of mounds are given below, following a discussion of materials and techniques used in site construction.

Construction: Materials and Techniques

Niuatoputapu architectural sites consist basically of artificially elevated or leveled mounds, platforms, or terraces, which may or may not be faced with a veneer of stone. The fill which constitutes the mass of the site

Figure 21. Mound facing of small, natural coral cobble slabs.

may be of three main types: (1) coral sand and incorporated debris such as branch coral fragments; (2) coralline cobbles and large reef detritus obtained from high-energy beach ridge deposits; and (3) earth or clay from the central volcanic ridge and terrace. In every case, the fill used was dictated by the local environment or geological substrate. Thus, since the majority of mound sites are situated on the apron of emerged lagoon and reef flats surrounding the island's central volcanic spine, coral sand is the most common fill type represented, with 61 recorded examples (73% of cases). The use of coral cobbles was recorded in 10 cases (12%), and earth or clay in 12 cases (14%). Half of the sites with earth or clay fill are terraces situated on the lower volcanic slopes.

At the larger mound sites, fill was usually obtained by excavating one or more borrow pits in the immediate vicinity of the construction. Often these pits form a ring or "moat" around the mound, as illustrated in figures 27 to 34. Such depressions have the additional effect of heightening the outer face or slope of the mound. Generally, the borrow pits were not dug completely around the mound, but were discontinuous, leaving access causeways or ramps to the mound itself.

There is virtually no ethnographic or ethnohistoric information on techniques of mound construction (see McKern 1929:5-7), but presumably the relatively soft sand or earth fill was loosened with hardwood digging sticks and carried in baskets from the borrow pits to the mound. The test excavation of site NT-150, a large earthen-fill mound, reveals in its stratigraphic section small lens-like facies that may reflect basket-load dumping (see chapter 4). In the case of cobble fill, these needed only to be carried by hand from the adjacent terrain to the mound site.

The stone facings or veneers on some classes of mounds are usually of reef limestone or conglomerate, although some sites—particularly the inland terraces—are faced with natural cobbles or slabs of basalt. Thirty-eight sites have facings of natural slabs only; another 16 sites are faced with a combination of natural and cut-and-dressed slabs, while only 8 sites have facings entirely of artificially worked slabs. The most common facing material consists of unworked slab-like coral heads or cobbles, set on edge to form alignments ranging from 10 to 50 cm in height (fig. 21). Less common, and requiring a substantially greater energy

Figure 22. Mound facing of large, cut-and-dressed slabs of coral conglomerate.

investment, are facings made of quarried, cut-and-dressed slabs (fig. 22) of reef limestone or sandstone conglomerate ("beach rock"). The conglomerate, with its natural bedding planes, can be readily quarried as pried up slabs which are then trimmed to the desired shape. The harder and more thoroughly cemented limestone required far more effort to quarry. Some sites, such as NT-22 (the Tofi'a mound), have facing slabs significantly larger than average. Generally, the slabs utilized in a mound facing are not of uniform size, but are largest along one face (presumably the ritual "front" of the mound), and decrease along the lateral and rear facings. Often, a combination of cut-and-dressed and natural slabs is used, with the artificially worked slabs on the front face (e.g., site NT-52, see chapter 4).

No mortar was used in stone construction: the slabs were set into a foundation trench which accommodated the lower one-third to one-half of the slab and was filled in with earth or sand. After several centuries, such facings tend to be displaced by the settling of the mound fill, and the slabs gradually creep or fall outwards. Facings are also disturbed by land crabs which burrow under and around the slabs. On some of the larger burial mounds still in use as cemeteries by the local population, facings have become covered or obliterated by recent grave digging and construction. Thus, in some cases it is difficult to tell whether a particular mound was faced or not.

Most cut-and-dressed slabs were obtained from exposures of beach rock or conglomerate situated along the outer dune face or shoreline of the *liku* coast. However, two inland quarry sites were recorded. Site NT-77 at Funga'ana is a virtual cliff of reef limestone, 3 to 4 m high, which was quarried for facing slabs. Some of these doubtless were used in nearby mound sites NT-28 and NT-29. Another quarry, NT-120, lies in dense *Eugenia* forest near Faka'ahotaha inland of the *liku* coast. Here are visible a number of rectangular depressions from which facing slabs were quarried. A rectangular "moat" was dug and the slab prized up along its natural bedding plane in the emerged reef.

Some architectural sites, especially burial mounds, are covered with pebble pavings. The most commonly used material is *patapata,* waterworn pebbles 1 to 5 cm in diameter, of coral or reef debris. Thirty sites showed evidence of having been paved with this material. Two other sites were paved with a mixture of coral *patapata* pebbles and dense black waterworn volcanic pebbles, called *kilikili*. The volcanic pebbles were probably obtained from nearby Tafahi Island, as no source of *kilikili* was observed on Niuatoputapu. Both *patapata* and *kilikili* are used by modern Tongans to decorate graves, and the presence of such pavings on mound sites is regarded by informants as an indication of funereal function.

Mounds and Platforms

Formal Classification

The first attempt to deal formally with the range of structural variation in Tongan mounds and platforms was that of McKern (1929), whose approach reflected the ethnographic bias of Polynesian archaeology at that time. McKern concentrated on visually impressive and well-known sites, most of which were associated with specific oral traditions and had been categorized by his Tongan informants into one of several emic or folk categories. Thus McKern maintained that "most ancient Tongan structures of mound or platform type may be classified as belonging to one of four groups: (a) *'esi* mounds; (b) pigeon mounds; (c) house platforms; and (d) grave mounds.... In general, this classification is based both on purpose, as recorded by tradition or determined by history, and on structural form. Purpose seems to have determined basic peculiarities in form" (1929:10). In short, McKern felt that form followed function in Tongan mounds, although he did in some instances have to resort to a fifth type, "unclassified mounds," which exhibited "strong individual peculiarities."

Within these basic types, McKern recorded substantial structural variation. Thus *'esi*, or chiefly resting mounds, included "two radically different structural types, ...the rectangular and the circular" (1929:10). Pigeon mounds *(sia heu lupe)*, "places to which wild pigeons could easily be decoyed and snared" (1929:19), included two distinct types: (I) circular platforms with stone retaining walls and a large central pit lined with stone; and (II) circular mounds in which the large central pit was replaced by a smaller, shallow depression. The greatest range of structural variation was recognized in grave mounds, especially those identified by informants as *langi* or sepulchres of the Tu'i Tonga and his immediate lineage. McKern (1929:34-36, fig. 17) defined six structural types of *langi*, although he commented that there are "many variations from the type forms." Types A and B are earth mounds of conical or rectangular shape, while Type C is a rectangular earth mound with a low wall of dressed stone slabs. Types D to F are platforms or stepped pyramids with retaining walls of cut-and-dressed slabs.

McKern's classification—which relies in the first instance on informant folk taxonomy—is impossible to operationalize archaeologically. While some of the larger Niuatoputapu mounds are known to informants who retain specific oral traditions concerning them, the majority of mounds are classified by informants into one of two categories *(sia* and *fa'itoka)* based on surface attributes and a presumption of function (see Emic Classification, below). Further, it is clear even from McKern's survey data that certain structural forms cross-cut presumed functional categories. For example, his Type A *langi* is virtually identical to certain pigeon mounds (e.g., Siamoatao, McKern 1929, fig. 14), while some *'esi* are structurally identical to pigeon mounds (e.g., the Kafoa site; 1929, fig. 2). In sum, it is not feasible to use McKern's classification in Tongan archaeological settlement pattern surveys.

Davidson (1971b), who carried out a reconnaissance survey of the Vava'u group, also recognized the deficiencies in McKern's system, and outlined a new classification based solely on "descriptive" criteria of "visible features of construction." She reasonably took account of "traditionally ascribed function where this can be obtained" (1971b:30). Davidson defined four main classes: (1) large mounds with vertical coral slab facing; (2) small mounds with vertical coral slab facing; (3) mounds with coral boulder facing; and (4) unfaced mounds. Within these classes, sub-classes were defined on the basis of plan: (a) rectangular, (b) circular, or (c) pentagonal. In the case of Class 1 sites, further sub-classes were defined based on the number of courses of vertical coral slab facings.

An attempt was made to apply Davidson's classification to the Niuatoputapu site corpus, and while her system is an improvement over McKern's, it was found to be unworkable due to its arbitrary and undefined distinction between "large" and "small" mounds. While Davidson reported that "the field evidence...appears to support a clear division in the case of categories 1 and 2" (1971b:31), this is certainly not the case with the Niuatoputapu corpus (see fig. 24).

In developing a workable classification of Niuatoputapu mound sites, it was clear that distinctions had to be based on discrete qualitative attributes of structural form and construction technique, rather than on continuous variables such as height or horizontal dimension. Reviewing the structural data presented in both McKern (1929) and Davidson (1971b), along with the variation evident in our own survey corpus of 95 platform and mound sites, we selected the following attributes as encompassing the range of structural variation: (1) the presence or absence of stone facings or retaining walls; (2) the use of natural coral cobbles or of cut-and-dressed slabs as materials in facing or wall construction; (3) the presence of pebble pavings; and (4) the presence or absence of a central depression, whether stone-faced or not. Overall plan (rectangular, circular, oval, etc.) was also considered, but was found to vary widely, especially within the class of unfaced mounds; therefore, this was not selected as a primary distinguishing attribute.

Based on the above criteria, the following formal classes of platform and mound are defined:

Class	*Formal Criteria*
4	Stone-faced, rectangular platform
5	A......Unfaced mound (no further features)
6	A1....Unfaced, paved mound (no further features)
7	A2....Unfaced, unpaved mound (no further features)
8	A2a...Unfaced, unpaved mound without central depression
9	A2b.. Unfaced, unpaved mound with central depression
10	B......Faced mound (no further features)
11	B1.... Faced mound, slabs natural
12	B2.... Faced mound, slabs cut and dressed

The classification is hierarchical, as shown in figure 23, so that sites can be assigned to a particular level in the scheme based upon the quality of survey data. For example, post-constructional disturbances on some mound sites make it impossible to determine whether a site originally had a central depression; such sites are accordingly assigned to class 7.

Implicit in the classification is a primary distinction between faced and unfaced mounds, a distinction which probably has strong functional correlations. This also corresponds closely to a Tongan emic distinction between *sia* mounds (usually unfaced) and *fa'itoka* or burial mounds (usually faced).

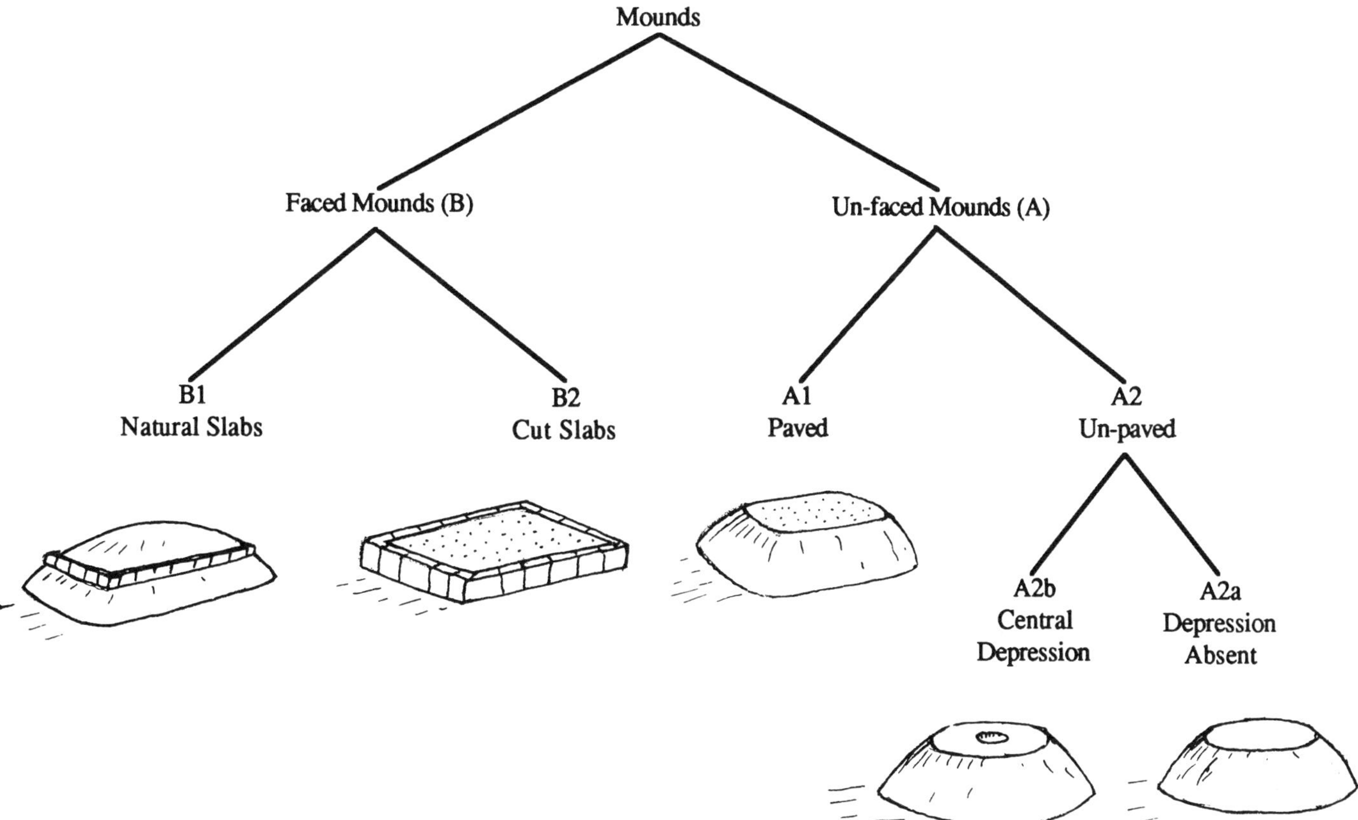

Figure 23. Diagram illustrating the hierarchical classification of Niuatoputapu mounds.

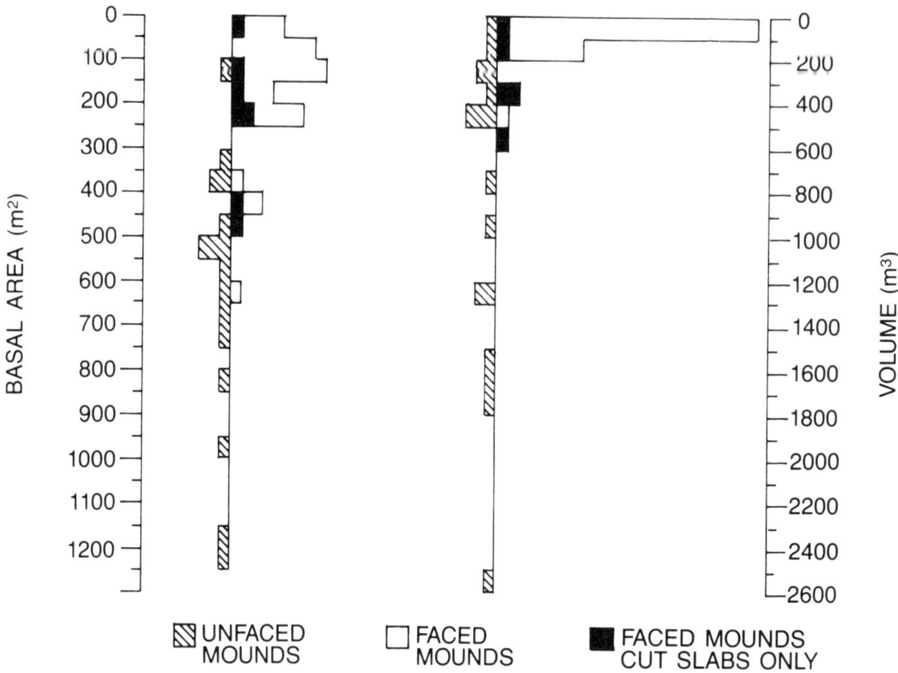

Figure 24. Basal areas and volumes of unfaced and faced mounds.

The metrical attributes of each Niuatoputapu mound class are indicated in table 3, with mean, standard deviation, and range listed for each of five variables (length or principal diameter, width or secondary diameter, maximum height, basal area, and volume). The most useful of these measures are basal area and volume, since these reflect the extent and mass of the site and are indicative of the relative energy expended on construction. Figure 24 summarizes the basal area and volume of unfaced (A) and faced (B) mounds, and also distinguishes between those mounds with facings of natural or of cut-and- dressed slabs (classes 11 and 12). In general, all of the larger mounds are unfaced, but a significant number of small mounds are also unfaced. A clear-cut distinction between "large" and "small" mounds, as maintained by Davidson (1971b), is not supported in these data.

Emic Classification and Function

While the archaeological classification of mounds must be independent of informant folk taxonomy, an understanding of Tongan mounds does require a consideration of ethnographic data. As already noted, local informants possess traditional and historical data pertaining to a significant number of structures and, indeed, the tradition of mound construction and use continues as an aspect of contemporary Tongan culture. For example, Site NT-3, the 'Esi 'o Pilolevu at Falehau, was constructed as recently as 1959 to commemorate the visit to Niuatoputapu of H.R.H. Princess Pilolevu. As Rogers rightly observes, this site "is proof of a continuing tradition of and regard for stone monuments on the island" (1973:30). In particular, the categories of *'esi* and *fa'itoka* are still very much in use by the contemporary population. On the other hand, pigeon mounds *(sia heu lupe)* have not been used at least within the last century, and are now an aspect of "memory culture."

Tongans, both on Niuatoputapu and elsewhere in the Kingdom, recognize five lexically marked categories of field monument:

1. *'esi.* These are raised platforms constructed as sitting or resting places for persons of high societal rank. In the recent past, such structures have been built for members of the royal family, as with the 'Esi 'o Pilolevu mentioned above, or in the case of a famous *'esi* on the *liku* coast of Vava'u. Frequently, these sites are situated to command sweeping views of countryside or ocean.

2. *sia.* This is not strictly a functional category, but rather is used to designate any mound, generally unfaced, for which a particular historical function is not known.

3. *sia heu lupe.* These are the "pigeon mounds" or, more properly, pigeon-snaring mounds, the loci at which the chiefly sport of pigeon-snaring *(heu lupe)* was practiced. While such mounds characteristically display a central depression, the most important criterion in their identification is historical knowledge or oral tradition to the effect that a particular mound was used for this purpose.

4. *fa'itoka.* These are burial mounds of chiefs and their lineages, often used today for commoner burial as

TABLE 3

METRICAL ATTRIBUTES OF NIUATOPUTAPU MOUND CLASSES*

MOUND CLASS	LENGTH (m)	WIDTH (m)	HEIGHT (m)	AREA (m^2)	VOLUME (m^3)
6 - Paved, Unfaced	N = 4 15.7 ± 13.0 8 - 35	N = 2 8.0 ± 2.8 6; 10	N = 5 1.1 ± 0.8 0.2 - 2.0	N = 2 79 ± 58 38; 120	N = 2 26 ± 26 8; 45
7 - Unpaved, Non-faced Mounds (not classifiable to 8 or 9)	N = 6 14.6 ± 8.1 8 - 26	N = 2 22.0 ± 1.4 21; 23	N = 6 2.0 ± 1.5 0.5 - 4.0	N = 2 491 ± 56 452; 531	N = 2 1,680 ± 126 1,591; 1,769
8 - Unpaved with Central Depression	N = 4 20.2 ± 7.2 10 - 27	N = 2 20.0 ± 1.4 19; 21	N = 3 1.1 ± 0.4 0.6 - 1.5	N = 2 476 ±136 380; 572	N = 2 384 ± 158 273; 496
9 - Unpaved without Central Depression	N = 10 28.7 ± 5.5 20.5 - 38.5	N = 10 23.2 ± 3.2 19 - 28.5	N =10 1.5 ± 0.9 0.45 - 3.0	N = 10 670 ± 254 330 - 1,164	N = 10 869 ± 745 178 - 2,518
11 - Faced with Natural Slabs	N = 21 11.3 ± 4.8 2 - 20	N = 20 9.8 ± 4.2 1.5 - 20	N = 18 0.6 ± 0.6 0.1 - 2.8	N = 17 137 ± 104 5 - 400	N = 16 62 ± 47 1 - 180
12 - Faced with Cut Slabs	N = 22 15.7 ± 8.9 1.75 - 35	N = 22 10.9 ± 4.7 1.1 - 19	N = 20 0.5 ± 0.3 0.1 - 1.3	N = 21 212 ± 161 2 - 630	N = 20 13 8 ± 157 <1 - 560

* For each measurement, sample size (N), mean, standard deviation, and range are presented.

well; they are distinct from *langi* (see below). *Fa'itoka* take a variety of structural forms, including both faced and unfaced classes. In addition to specific historical knowledge of burial use, either of two structural features will trigger a Tongan informant to assign a particular site to this emic category: (a) the presence of white coral sand, or of coral or volcanic pebble paving; or (b) the presence of facing slabs, whether natural or cut-and-dressed.

5. *langi.* The term *langi* (lit. "sky, heaven") was used figuratively for the sacred paramount chief of Tonga (the Tu'i Tonga), and referred as well to the burial mounds of these chiefs, in which members of their immediate families were also interred. Early ethnohistoric sources (e.g., Martin 1820) suggest that the burial mounds of paramounts were also called *fa'itoka,* with the term *langi* applied only during the period during and immediately following the interment of the chief. In modern Tongan, however, the sepulchre of a Tu'i Tonga is always referred to as a *langi.* In addition, the term seems to have been extended to burial mounds containing the remains of collateral branches of the Tu'i Tonga lineage, such as the Ma'atu line of Niuatoputapu. Thus six structures on Niuatoputapu (five sites in class 12) are designated by informants as *langi,* although there is specific knowledge of who is interred only in the case of NT-24 (Sioeli Kalae-Kiivalu, the Ma'atu title holder who died in 1894). The other *langi* structures are, however, regarded as associated with the Ma'atu line.

A summary correlation of emic and archaeological classifications is provided in table 4. The data in table 4 demonstrate the association of the term *sia* with unfaced and unpaved mounds of classes 6, 7, and 8. The category *sia heu lupe* consists primarily of class 9 structures (with a central depression), but also includes one example of class 8. *Fa'itoka* include all but one of the paved, unfaced mounds, as well as the majority of faced mounds. *Langi* comprise five mounds with cut-and-dressed slab facings, and one mound with natural coral slabs.

Early historic descriptions by explorers, missionaries, and other foreign residents provide additional information on the function of mounds in traditional Tongan culture. On his second voyage in 1773, James Cook had several opportunities to observe

TABLE 4

EMIC CLASSIFICATION OF NIUATOPUTAPU MOUNDS

MOUND CLASS	SIA	SIA HEU LUPE	'ESI	FA'ITOKA	LANGI	NO DATA	N
5						3	3
6	1			5			6
7	8					3	11
8	3	1					4
9		10					10
10				3		2	5
11				27	1	2	30
12				15	5	3	23
Platform			3				3
TOTALS	12	11	3	50	6	13	95

ritual behavior at mounds which his informants called "Afia-tou-ca" or *fa'itoka.* During an inland excursion on the 4th of October, Cook examined one of these mounds at first hand:

> After distributing some trifles among them we signified our desire to see the Country, this was no sooner done than the chief shewed us the way, conducting us along a lane which led us to an open green on the one side of which was a house of Worship built on a mount which had been raised by the hand of Man about 16 or 18 feet above the common level, it had an oblong figure and was supported by a Wall of Stone about three feet high, from the top of this Wall the mound rose with a gentle slope and was covered with a green turf [this would fit a class 11 site], on the top of the mount stood the house which was of the same figure as the mount about 20 feet long and 14 or 16 broad. As soon as we came before this place every one seated him self on the ground about 50 or 60 yards from the house, presently after came three elderly men and seated them selves between us and the house and began to speak what I understood to be a prayer, their discourse being wholly directed to the house, this lasted about ten minutes and then the three priests, for such we took them to be, came and sit down with us and the rest of the people when both Captain Furneaux and I made them presents of Nails, Medals &c giving them to understand that we did it to shew our respect to that house which I now desired leave to examine, the chief contrary to my expectations immidiately went with us without shewing the least backwardness and gave us full liberty to examine every part of it. In the front were two steps leading up to the top of the wall, after which the assent was easy to the house round which was a fine good Walk, the house was built in all respects like to their common dwelling houses with Posts and rafters and the Covering of Palm thatch, the eves came down to within 3 feet of the ground which space was fill'd up with strong Matting made of Palm leaves which formed a kind of Wall, the floor of the house was laid with gravel, except in the middle where it was raised with the fine blew pebbles to the height of about Six Inches and had the same form as the house that is oblong [a probable indication of a grave]. At one corner of the house stood a rude image and on one side laid a nother, each about two feet in length...(Beaglehole 1969:250-51).

After further inland exploration, Cook remarked:

> At several of the cross Roads or at the meeting of three or more roads, were generally an Afia-tou-ca, such as above described with this difference, that the Mounts were Pallisaded round in stead of a stone wall (Beaglehole 1969:252).

Summarizing his observations of Tongan culture, Cook wrote:

> We know so little of their Religion that I hardly dare mention it, the building called Afia-tou-ca before spoke of is undoubtedly set apart for this purpose. Mr. Forster and one or two of the officers think that they understood for certain that their dead was entarred in them...(Beaglehole 1969:274).

Cook, however, could not satisfy himself on this question of burial function, although he had no doubt that the prayers of the "priests or men among them who exercise the sacret function" were directed toward these *fa'itoka* mounds. (See also the observations of astronomer William Wales, in Beaglehole 1969: 812-15.)

On his third voyage in June 1777, Cook again observed ritual behavior in association with *fa'itoka,* and remarked:

> The only thing we met with worth mentioning was a larg[e] Affi-a-too-ca or burying ground belonging to the King, a Wall of stone inclosed three separate Mounts and on each of these Mounts stood a house, under which we were told, the dead are buried, but there was nothing of this sort to be seen; the floors of these houses were covered with loose fine pebbles and like wise the tops of the Mounts round the houses, there were a few rude Images of the human figure, of different ages. We were told they were there as monuments to the Memory of the dead and not the representation of any Deity (Beaglehole 1967:138-39).

Cook also noted that these *fa'itoka* were usually fronted by a grassy plaza or *mala'e,* the setting for *kava* ceremonials in both traditional and modern Tongan society. Webber, the voyage artist, drew such a *fa'itoka* mound as described by Cook (fig. 25).

Missionaries brought to Tonga by the Duff in 1797 also remarked on "fiatooka," and witnessed the burial rituals associated with the death of a high-ranking individual. Of the burial mound itself, Wilson wrote:

> This fiatooka is situated on a spot of ground about four acres. A mount rises with a gentle slope about seven feet, and is about one hundred and twenty yards in circumference at the base; upon the top stands a house neatly made, which is about thirty feet long, and half that in width. The roof is thatched, and the sides and ends left open. In the middle of this house is the grave, the sides, ends, and bottom of which are of coral stone, with a cover of the same: the floor of the house is of small stones (Wilson 1799:240-41).

Far more detailed and useful accounts of *fa'itoka* and of burial ritual are given by Mariner, a survivor of the Port au Prince massacre at Ha'apai (Martin 1820:108-111, 238-251, 390-393), who spent four years in Tonga from 1806 to 1810. Mariner was virtually "kept" by one of the highest-ranking chiefs and, in addition to learning the Tongan language, had the opportunity to observe the daily life and rituals of the Tongan elite. It is not necessary here to recount the extensive ritual details described in Mariner's account, but his brief definition of a *"fytoca"* may be cited: "a burying place, including the grave, the mount in which it is sunk, and a sort of shed over it. The grave of a chief's family is a vault, lined at the bottom with one large stone, one at each side, and one at the foot and head, and is about eight feet long, six feet broad, and eight feet deep, covered at the top with one large stone" (1820:110 fn).

These early descriptions clearly indicate that in protohistoric Tonga, the *fa'itoka* or artificial, stone-faced earthen mound surmounted with a thatched structure served both as the principal burial facility and as the site of one or more god houses at which a variety of rituals were performed (either in the house, or on the adjacent *mala'e* or plaza).

Curiously, there is virtually no ethnohistoric information on pigeon snaring (Mariner, for example, does not mention the sport). The best description is probably that of McKern, whose data were presumably obtained from chiefly informants in 1920, after the sport had ceased to be practiced:

> Briefly, the mound was used as follows: The sportsmen occupied the structure, some on the mound surface where they manipulated the heu [net] poles, and some in the pit to take the pigeons from the snare. Captive pigeons, attached to long cords, were allowed to fly among the tree tops above the mound where they served as decoys to attract their wild kin. When the wild pigeons came, lured by the calls of the decoys, the heu manipulators dropped the net over them and brought them down into the pit, where they were caught and disposed of by the men assigned to that task (1929:20).

On Niuatoputapu, where pigeons are sometimes taken today by shotgun, they remain a prized delicacy of chiefs and honored persons.

Limited information on mound function was also obtained from excavation (see chapter 4). Thus, structures of class 12 at Houmafakalele (Sites NT-52-55) were shown to be burial mounds, probably of high-ranking lineages. Testing of a class 6 mound (NT-150) revealed the presence of probable burial pits, confirming the ethnographic correlation of coral pebble paving and burial function. A class 11 mound (Site NT-126) at Niutoua, which was being mined for sand by the local residents, contained multiple interments, again validating the presumed burial function. Finally, an example of class 8 was shown to have been used neither for burial nor for habitation, thus confirming its historical designation as a *sia heu lupe*. Although limited, these tests do not contradict the functional interpretations suggested by ethnographic and ethnohistoric data. The excavations of McKern (1929) and of Davidson (1969a) in burial mounds on Tongatapu and Pangaimotu also support the funereal functions assigned to mounds of classes 6, 11, and 12.

In sum, based on ethnographic, ethnohistoric, and limited excavation data, we may suggest the following functions for the archaeological classes of mound defined for Niuatoputapu: class 4: *'esi*, or chiefly sitting platforms; class 5: data insufficient; class 6: burial in most cases; class 7: largely pigeon-snaring mounds, with *'esi* or burial functions also possible; class 8: probably pigeon-snaring mounds; class 9: pigeon-snaring mounds; class 10: burial; class 11: burial; class 12: burial, particularly of higher-ranking individuals.

Platforms (Class 4)

Three sites are included within this class; all consist of square or rectangular flat-topped platforms known to have been constructed historically as *'esi*. The most recent of these, 'Esi 'o Pilolevu, has already been mentioned. It was built under the direction of the royal estate manager Fuimaono Leonaitasi in 1959, and commands a beautiful view of the lagoon off Falehau. This monument is unique on Niuatoputapu in having two tiers (fig. 26). Site NT-1, 'Esi 'o Panuve, lies on

Figure 25. A *fa'itoka* burial mound surmounted by four thatched houses, as drawn by J. Webber, artist of Cook's third voyage, Tongatapu, in 1777.

Hunganga Island and was built to commemorate the penultimate Ma'atu titleholder, Panuve, who died in 1923. The oldest *'esi* on the island, also associated with the Ma'atu line, is NT-2, named Alo-ki-vaka-loa, situated at Atatuka on the *liku* coast. The date of construction of this monument is not known, though it is probably historic. Detailed descriptions of all three *'esi* are given by Rogers (1973:28-31).

Unfaced Mounds (Classes 5-9)

Thirty-four examples of unfaced mounds were recorded on Niuatoputapu; of these, only six had definite traces of paving (although for three mounds our data are insufficient to state whether or not the sites were paved). As indicated above, those mounds with paving were probably used for burial, while the unpaved mounds were used either as pigeon-snaring mounds or perhaps as *'esi.* Supporting the historical and traditional evidence that many of the class 8 and 9 mounds served as *sia heu lupe* is their distinct distribution pattern: largely away from the coast and from areas of dense settlement, and often situated in dense tracts of *Eugenia* forest. The *Eugenia* fruit are a major food of pigeons, which are usually hunted in these forests by modern Tongans.

The largest field monument on Niuatoputapu is Site NT-138, an unfaced circular mound (class 8) named Kamata, shown in figure 27. With a calculated volume of 2,518 m^3 of sandy fill, NT-138 represents a substantial labor outlay. The fill was obtained from five borrow pits surrounding the mound, one of which forms a virtual moat on the south and east, adding to the visual impressiveness of the monument. There is no evidence that the site was used for burial, and either an *'esi* or a *sia heu lupe* function is likely. Another example of a class 8 mound is NT-149, illustrated in figure 28. This monument has only 273 m^3 of sandy fill, which, as in the Kamata mound, was derived from five adjacent borrow pits. Aside from the fact that it lacks a central depression, it is doubtful that NT-149 was a *sia heu lupe,* because it is situated within Hihifo village in an area which has always been a locus of occupation (and thus an unlikely location in which to hunt for pigeons).

Figure 26. Two-tiered stone facing of the Esi 'o Pilolevu, near Falehau.

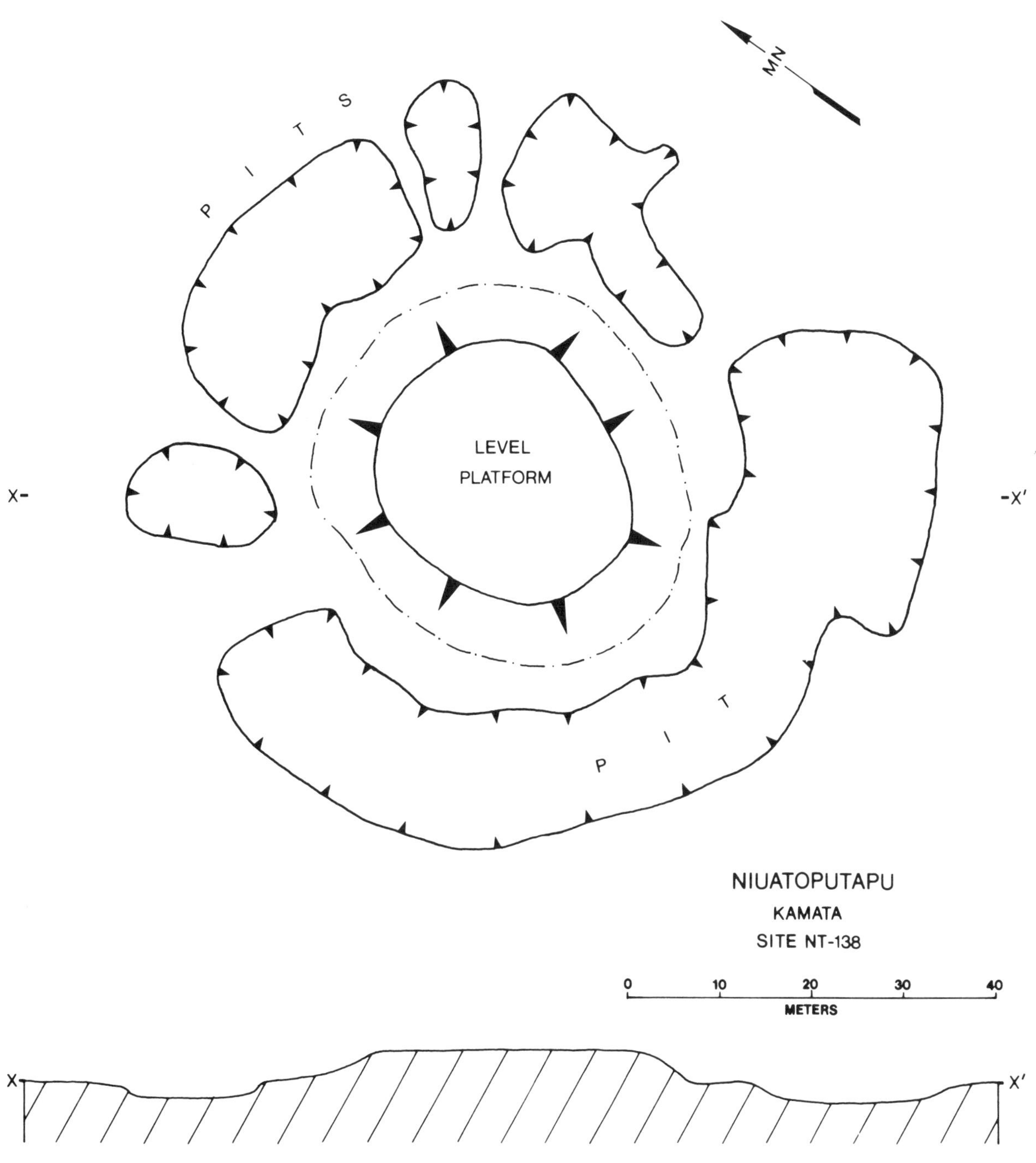

Figure 27. Plan of Site NT-138, Kamata.

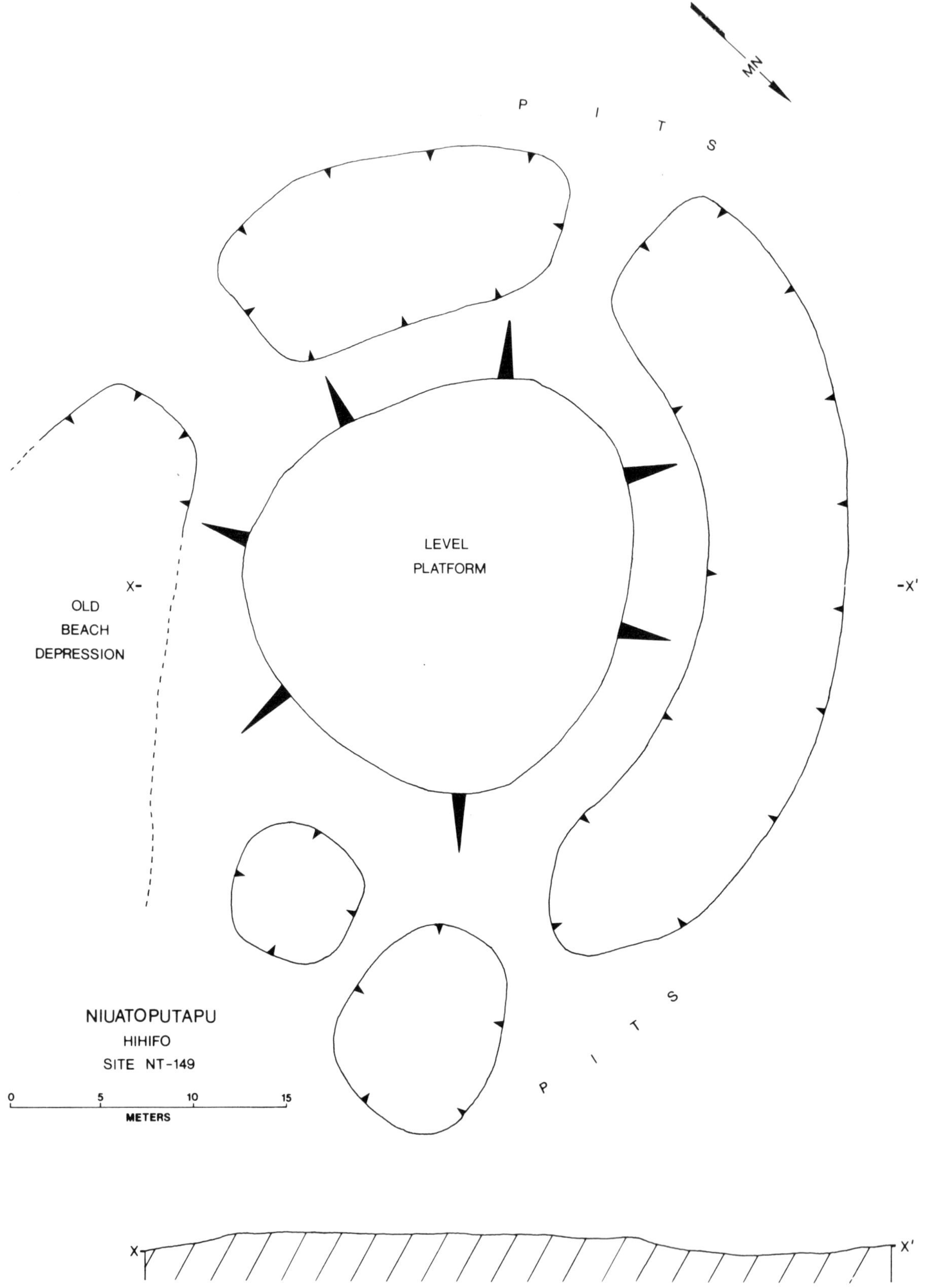

Figure 28. Plan of Site NT-149, Hihifo.

Several examples of class 9 mounds, probable *sia heu lupe*, were mapped with plane table and alidade, and are shown in figures 29 to 34. NT-146 and NT-147 (figs. 29 and 30), both located at Funga'ana, illustrate the different patterns of borrow pit excavation: nearly a continuous moat with only two access ramps in the case of NT-146, and a series of eight smaller pits in the case of NT-147. Site NT-8 (fig. 31), the Ha'afo'ou mound, is a substantial construction with 1,605 m^3 of fill, but with only a slight central depression. Site NT-7 (fig. 32), a well-known *sia heu lupe* named Fine-tenga-lelei (lit. "woman with beautiful thigh") occupies the edge of the steep bluff overlooking the broad, uplifted southeastern part of the island. This earth-filled mound has ten borrow pits flanking it on two sides. In a few class 9 mounds the central depression is stone-lined or faced. In NT-142 (fig. 33), a mound at Faka'ahotaha, the pit is lined with upright coral slabs; as with NT-7, the

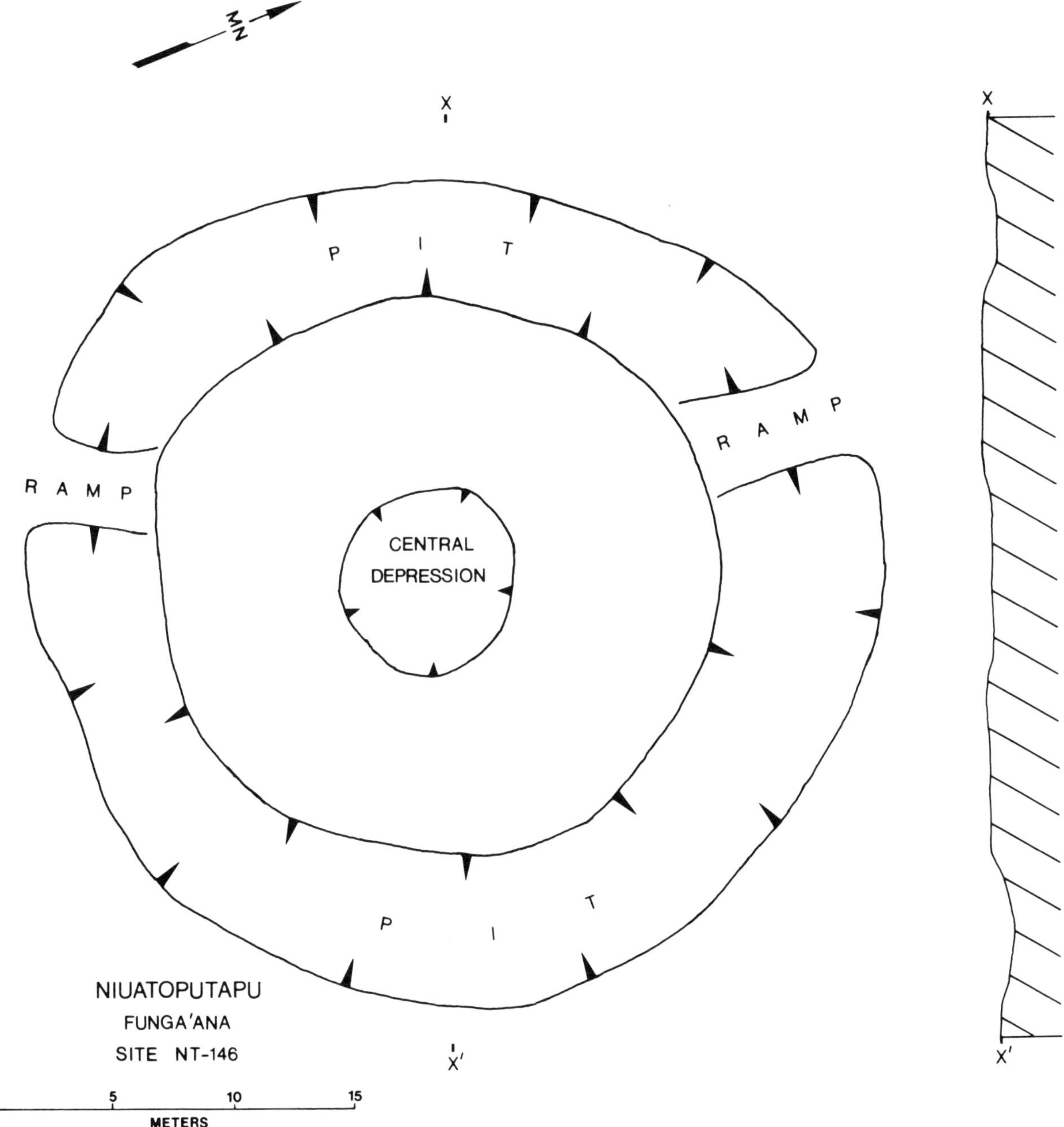

Figure 29. Plan of Site NT-146, Funga'ana.

site perches atop the steep bluff. The mound called Fakapaia or NT-178 (fig. 34) is a broad, low mound with a faced central depression and traces of stone edging along the outer rim of the circular platform.

Size variation in unfaced mounds is indicated in figure 35, with length or principal diameter plotted in relation to maximum height. Unpaved mounds are in general substantially larger than paved mounds. Indeed, the unfaced, unpaved mounds of classes 7, 8, and 9 are by far the largest field monuments on the island, with volumes ranging from 178 to 2,518 m^3. The rank-size distribution of unfaced, unpaved mounds (by volume) is shown in figure 36. The distribution departs significantly from a log-normal pattern, although the reason for this is not certain. There is no question that such mounds were constructed under the direction of powerful chiefs, and served as visual symbols of their status and dominance over the local populace. It is perhaps significant that rather than a strict hierarchical progression in the volumes of these large mounds, the

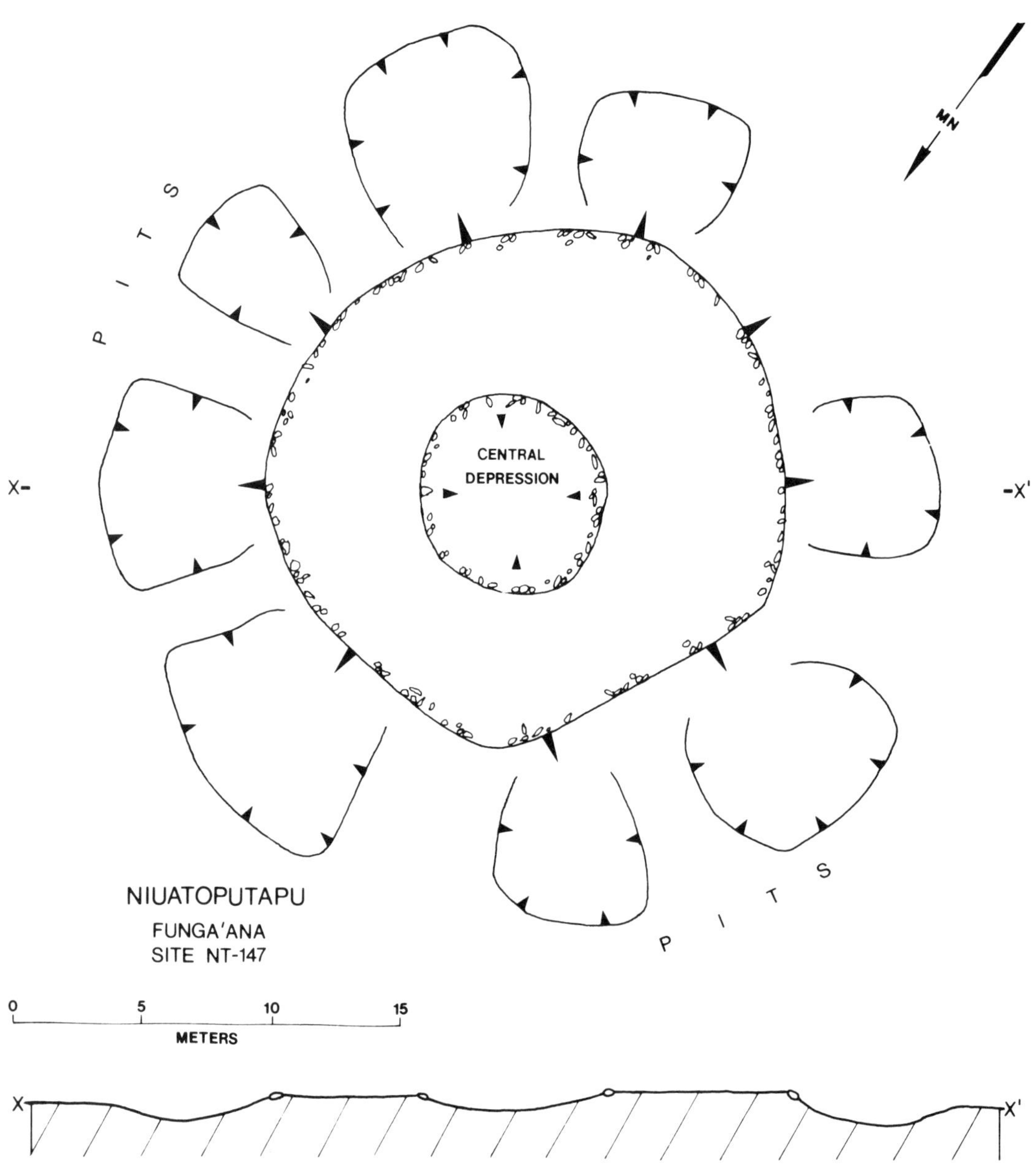

Figure 30. Plan of Site NT-147, Funga'ana.

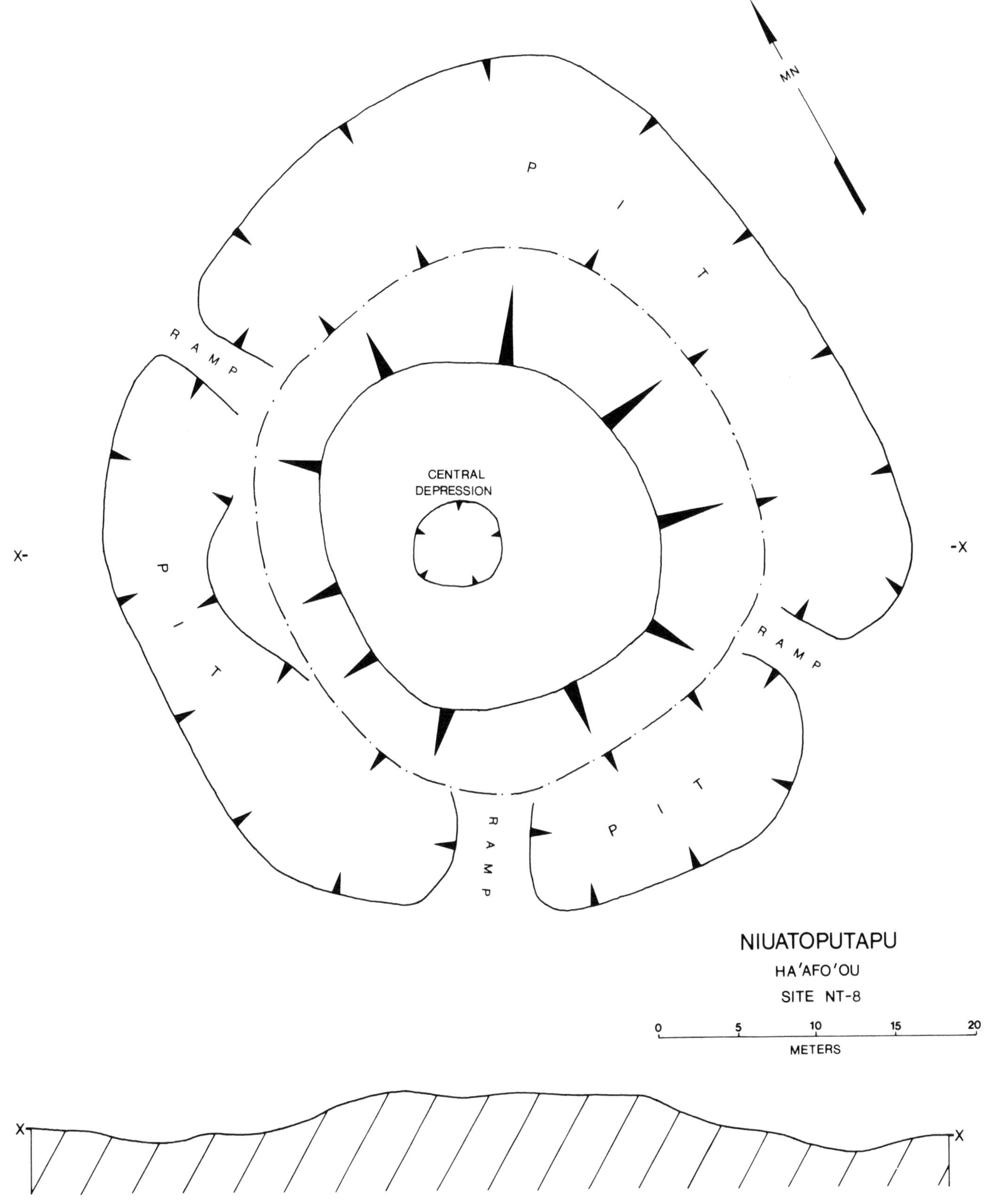

Figure 31. Plan of Site NT-8, Ha'afo'ou.

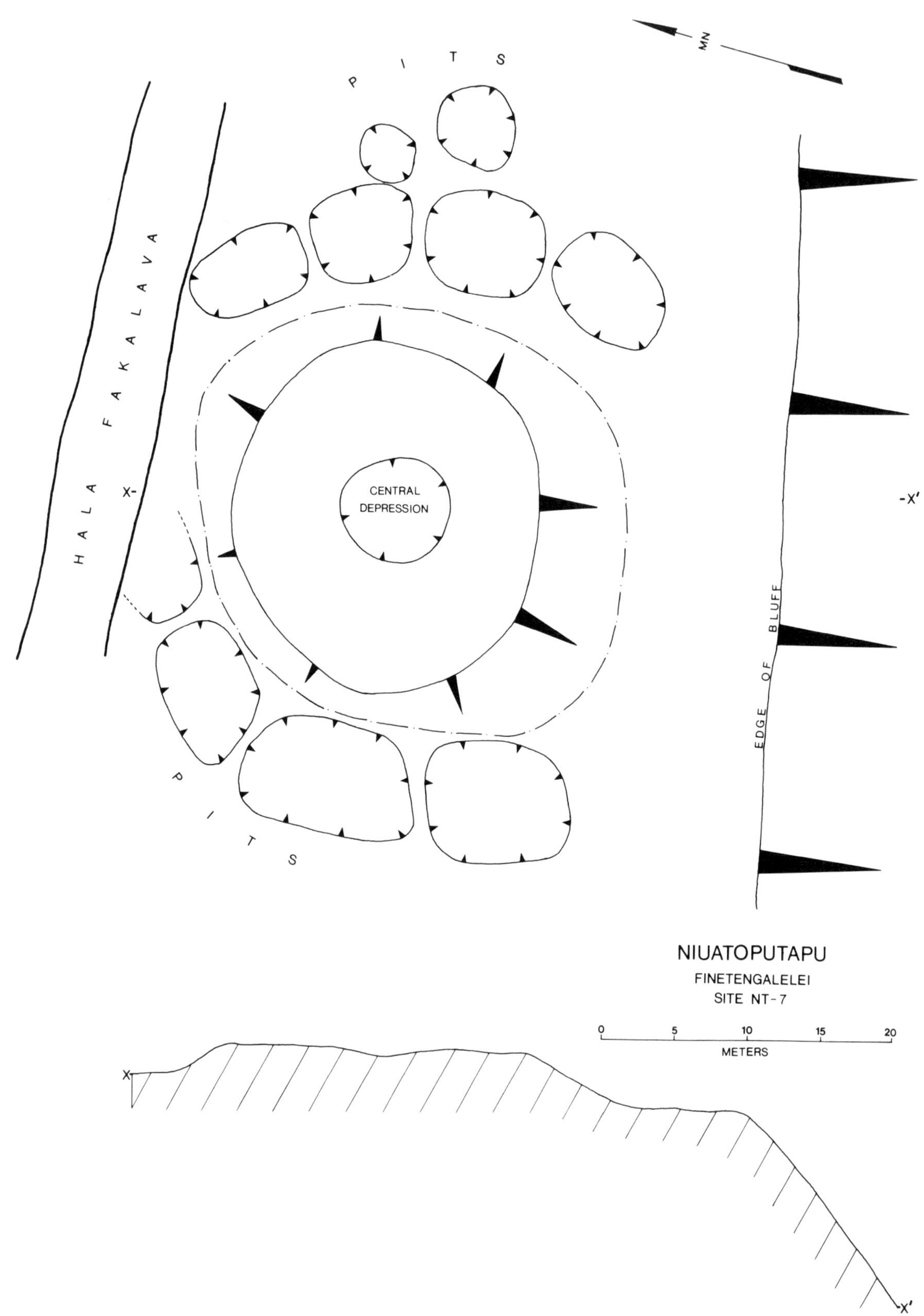

Figure 32. Plan of Site NT-7, Finetengalelei.

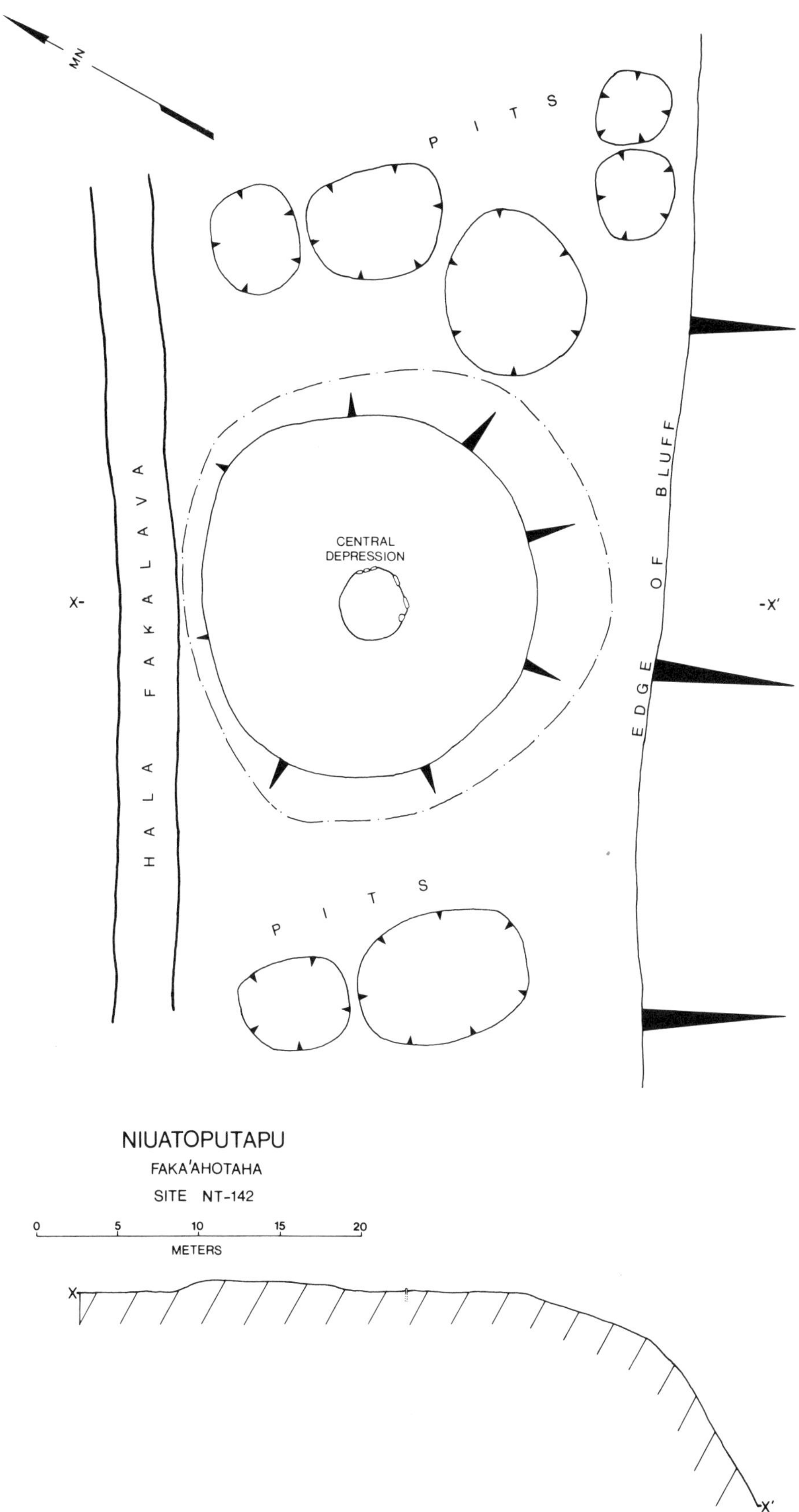

Figure 33. Plan of Site NT-142, Faka'ahotaha.

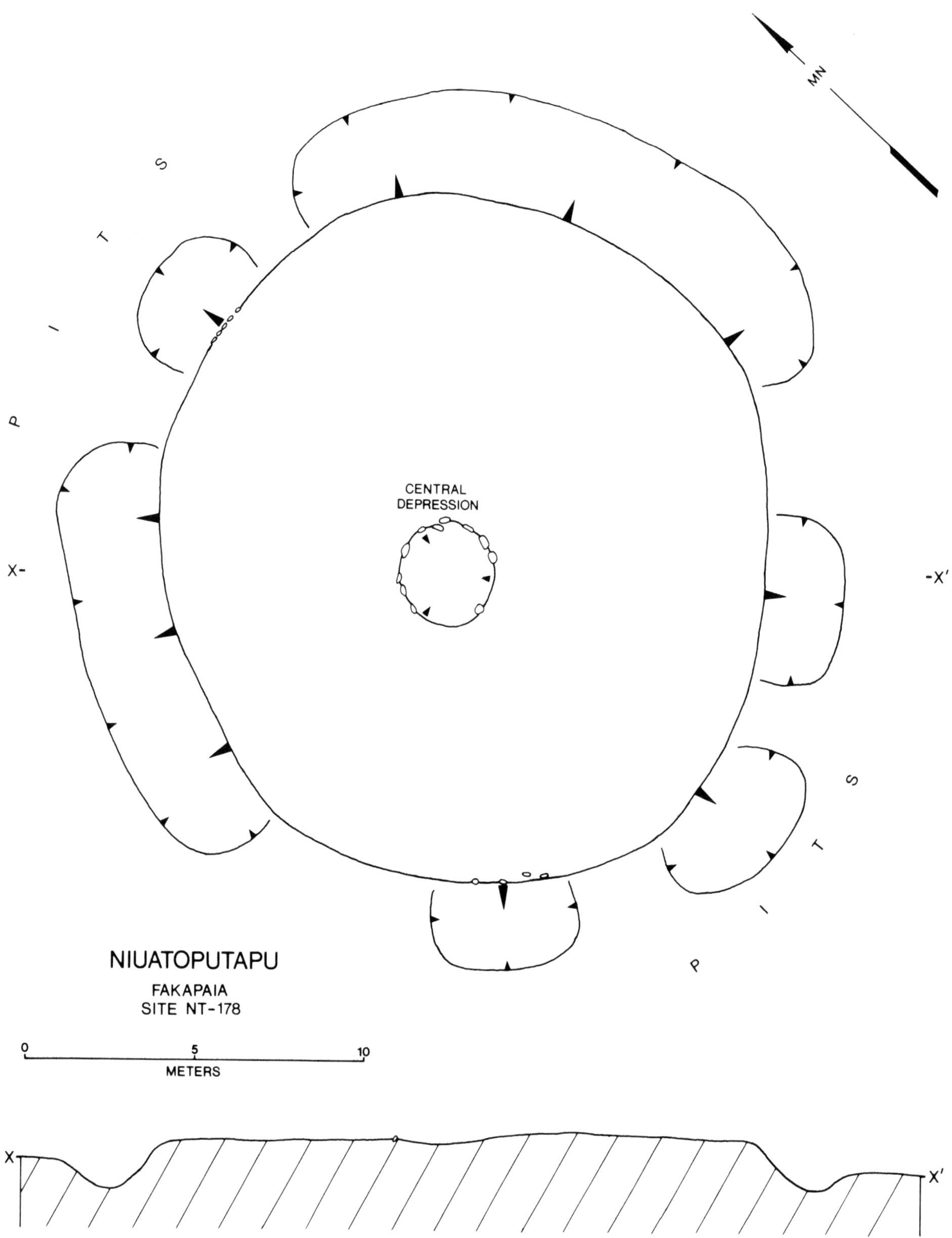

Figure 34. Plan of Site NT-178, Fakapaia.

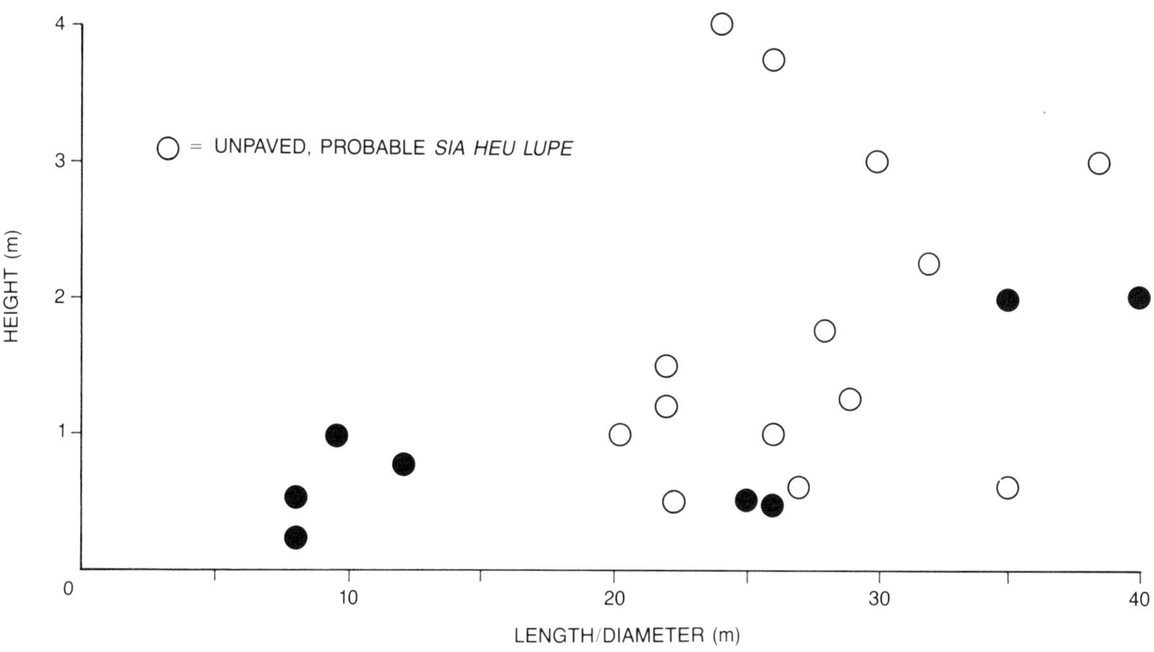

Figure 35. Size variation in unfaced mounds.

rank-size distribution is strongly convex, largely due to the sizes of the first to fourth ranked sites. In regard to convex rank-size distributions of settlement sites, Johnson has suggested that such a pattern "should then alert the researcher to the possibility that relatively autonomous settlement systems are being combined in analysis" (1977:498). It is conceivable that the comparably large volumes of the four highest-ranked mounds reflect a political system where sites of four competitive chiefly lines are represented; alternatively, the mounds may not be of the same age, in which case the largest sites might all belong to a single high-ranking lineage, in which successive paramounts each sought to validate status through construction of newer and larger mounds. Only the excavation and dating of a series of mounds can address these competing hypotheses.

Two mounds of class 7 require special discussion, because they were singled out by Rogers (1973; 1974:328-29, 339-40) as being unique in size and construction and—he maintained—particularly significant for Niuatoputapu prehistory. These are NT-4 and NT-5, named respectively Mata-ki-'Uvea (lit. "looking-towards-'Uvea") and Mata-ki-Ha'amoa (lit. "looking-towards-Samoa"). Rogers maintained that these sites were unique both in the use of stone (coral cobbles) as the main construction material and in their "huge" sizes. He gives dimensions of 27.5 m long, 23 m wide, and 4.5 m high (2,800 m^3) for NT-4, and dimensions of 21.5 m long, 15.25 m wide, and 9 m high for NT-5. Rogers continues: "...the two huge Mata mounds probably belong to a distant era and a social structure radically different from that found on the island in recent times. It is calculated that Mata-ki-'Uvea and Mata-ki-Ha'amoa each contain upwards of two million stones...it would take...100 men one year to construct each of the two Mata monuments" (1974:328-29). Caught up in this speculative fervor, Rogers suggests that the mounds "could belong to an earlier 'Samoic' period" (based on their stone construction material), or even that "they were built by the Lapita voyager-traders" (1974:340).

Because of the significance accorded these sites by Rogers, NT-4 and NT-5 were both examined and carefully mapped and measured during our survey. Site NT-4 was found to measure 25 by 21 m, and had a maximum platform height of 3.75 m above the surrounding ground surface. We calculated its basal area at 531 m^2 and its volume at 1,769 m^3. Site NT-5 measures 23 by 19 m, with a maximum height of 4.0 m, calculated basal area of 452 m^2, and volume of 1,591 m^3. Both sites have been badly disturbed by land crab hunters, who had displaced the surface stones by tunneling into the structures in search of the tasty crabs *(Birgus latro)*.

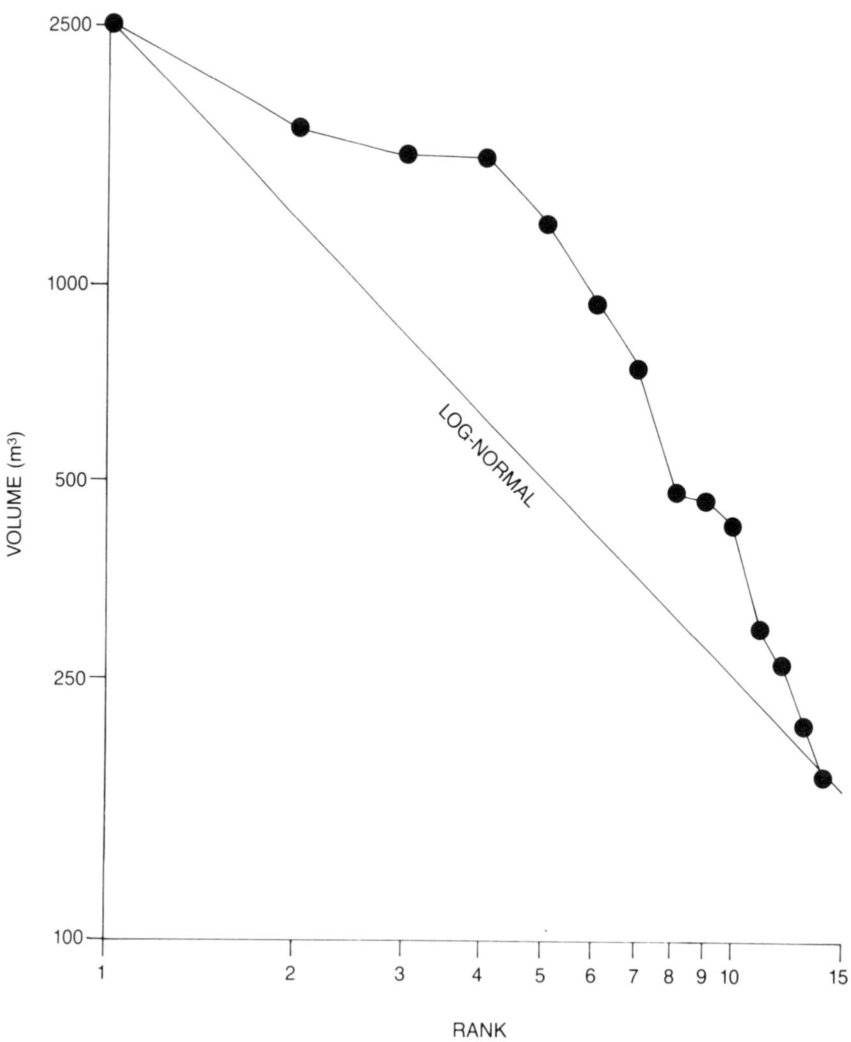

Figure 36. Rank-size distribution, by volume, of unfaced, unpaved mounds.

In addition, we located a third structure, constructed in the same style, about 60 m distant (20° E of NT-4), and clearly a part of the same site complex. This mound has a maximum diameter of 22 m; its height varies from 1.2 to 2.7 m. Although disturbed, this site bore the evidence of a faced central depression about 4 m in diameter. This feature, which may well have been present on sites NT-4 and NT-5 before disturbance, strongly suggests a *sia heu lupe* function in the protohistoric Tongan tradition. It is worth noting that these sites are all situated within a dense *Eugenia* forest.

Clearly, Rogers has exaggerated the size and significance of these sites. While NT-4 and NT-5 are large, they are not significantly more massive than other Niuatoputapu unfaced mounds. Indeed, they rank as the second- and fourth- largest mound sites in terms of volume (and eighth and ninth in basal area), putting them in a group with NT-138 and NT-7. Structurally, there is nothing to distinguish them from other mounds of classes 7, 8, or 9. The use of coral cobbles is not unprecedented on the island, and indeed is perfectly logical given that the mounds are constructed upon a former high-energy depositional ridge of coral debris. Even their indigenous names are consistent with a late prehistoric or protohistoric age, given the known voyaging contacts between Niuatoputapu, Samoa, and 'Uvea (see chapter 1). Rather than being unique signals of an earlier epoch, these sites fall unremarkably within the general range of Niuatoputapu field monuments, and in all probability functioned as pigeon-snaring mounds for the local chiefly elite in late prehistoric or protohistoric times.

Faced Mounds (Classes 10, 11, 12)

Fifty-eight faced mounds were recorded during the survey. Of these, 30 utilized only natural coral slabs in their faces or retaining walls, 23 showed partial or entire use of cut-and-dressed slabs, and 5 were not sufficiently well recorded to determine whether the facing slabs were natural or artificial. Scatterplots of length/width and area/height for faced mounds are provided in figure 37. Although many faced mounds are as large in length and width as unfaced mounds, they are generally lower, and thus significantly smaller in the critical measure of volume (see fig. 24). Furthermore, the majority of faced mounds are rather small, with volumes of less than 130 m^3. Nevertheless, when comparing faced and unfaced mounds, we cannot take volume alone into account, for significant energy was expended in the quarrying and transportation of cut-and-dressed slabs. Even the natural slabs utilized in many sites were not locally available, and had to be transported from some distance.

Three examples of class 11 structures, burial mounds faced with natural coral cobbles, are illustrated in figure 38. This particular mound group (NT-143 to NT-145) is situated near the *liku* coast at Funga'ana. The structures are rectangular, filled with sand and coral rubble. Their single-course facings of coral cobbles were derived from the immediate vicinity (an older, high-energy storm-deposited boulder ridge).

The most impressive class 12 structure on Niuatoputapu is Site NT-22, a burial mound named Tofi'a which is associated with the Ma'atu line of local paramount chiefs and classified by informants as a *langi.* Shown in figure 39, the site consists of two conjoined constructions: to the west, a massive rectangular mound with domed interior, and to the east a lower (and evidently later) addition. The carefully cut-and-dressed facing slabs of the western structure are the largest of any monument on Niuatoputapu (see fig. 22), with the longest slab measuring 3 m long and 0.4 m thick, and standing 0.6 m above the present ground surface. The main facing wall of the lower, eastern structure includes two volcanic slabs. Both structures are well paved with coral pebbles *(patapata).* The partially exposed tops of two coral slabs set at right angles, lying within the borders of the larger structure, may possibly indicate the presence of a slab-lined crypt, as described in early ethnohistoric sources (e.g., McKern 1929:32-33).

Another substantial class 12 structure is the Talitoka *fa'itoka,* Site NT-114 (fig. 40). This monument illustrates the common practice of utilizing larger cut-and-dressed slabs in the prominent "front" facing (in this case adjoining the Hala Ma'atu roadway). Other illustrated examples of class 12 monuments are NT-155 (fig. 41), NT-195 (fig. 42), and NT-31 (fig. 43).

The rank-size distribution of faced mounds by volume is shown in figure 44. As with the unfaced mounds, the distribution pattern departs from log-normal towards convex. It may be significant that four mounds again stand out as much larger than the others, replicating the pattern in unfaced mounds.

Mounds of class 12 apparently functioned as the sepulchres of the protohistoric Niuatoputapu chiefly elite, including members of the ruling Ma'atu line. As these monuments are identical in form to *langi* elsewhere in the Tongan archipelago, it is worthwhile briefly to compare the size ranges of the Niuatoputapu sites with those situated at the capital of the Tongan maritime empire—Mu'a on Tongatapu Island (McKern 1929:92-101; Kirch 1984a:227-230). The Mu'a *langi* were the burial places of the paramount chiefs of Tonga, the Tu'i Tonga line, to whom Ma'atu and other rulers of the outlying islands owed allegiance. Significantly, the largest *langi* in the Mu'a complex (McKern 1929, fig. 46), such as Tuoteau (J-1), Tauhala (J-10), or Tuofefafa (J-4), have basal areas greater than 2,500 m^2, or nearly four times larger than the largest Niuatoputapu class 12 monument. This ratio is very much in keeping with the kind of hierarchy predicted from the ethnohistoric accounts of the protohistoric Tongan polity. (Note, however, that the Mu'a complex also contains a large number of smaller class 12 monuments [such as J-5, J-6, J-11 to J-18, McKern 1929, fig. 46] with basal areas from 200-600 m^2—that is, comparable to the Niuatoputapu size range.)

Terraces

Thirteen terrace sites were recorded, all of them either on the steep central volcanic ridge (five sites) or on the lower slopes of the Pleistocene Terrace (eight sites). All are simple constructions, formed by cutting into the slope and depositing earthen fill downslope to form a level or gently sloping terrace surface. In several cases the downhill face of the terrace has a rough stone retaining wall. The terraces have maximum lengths of from 7 to 25 m, and heights of 1.5 to 2.5 m. Most, if not all, of these terraces were probably foundations for permanent or temporary habitation structures, although this interpretation has not been tested by excavation. A number of terraces are associated with abandoned starch fermentation pits.

Fermentation Pits

A widespread practice in tropical Polynesia was the semi-anaerobic ensilage and fermentation of starch pastes, especially breadfruit, in silo-like pits (Cox 1980; Yen 1975; Kirch 1984a:132-35). In Tonga, such

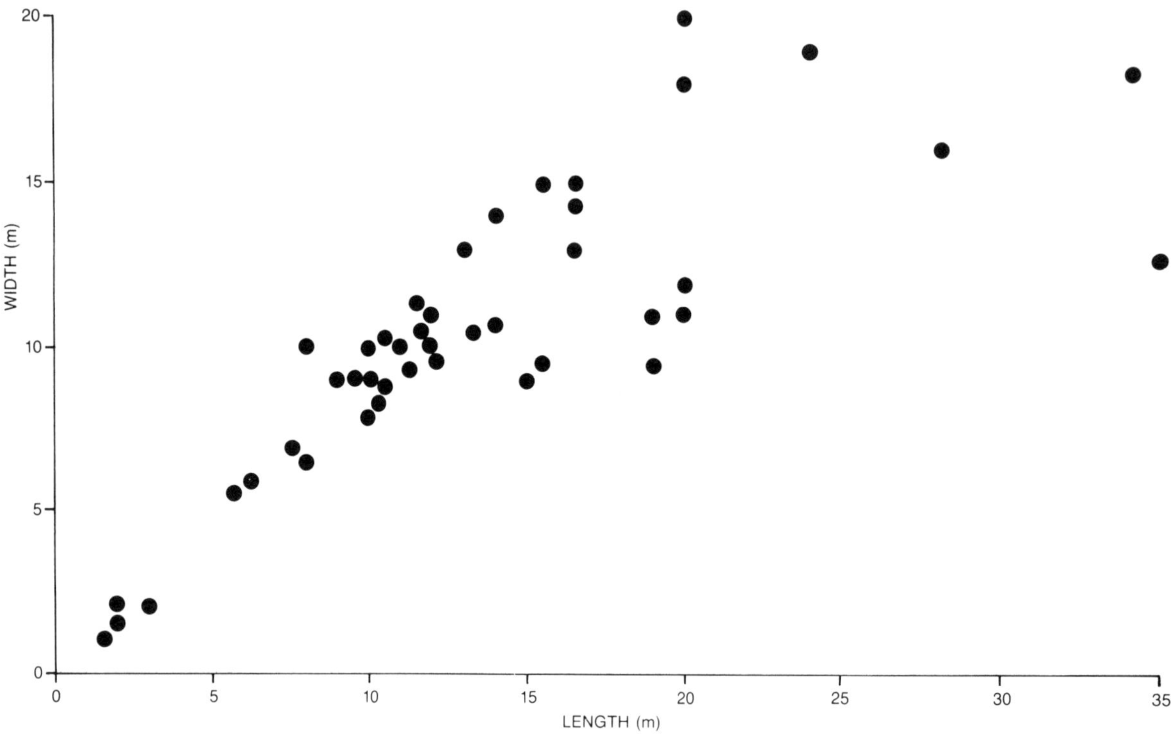

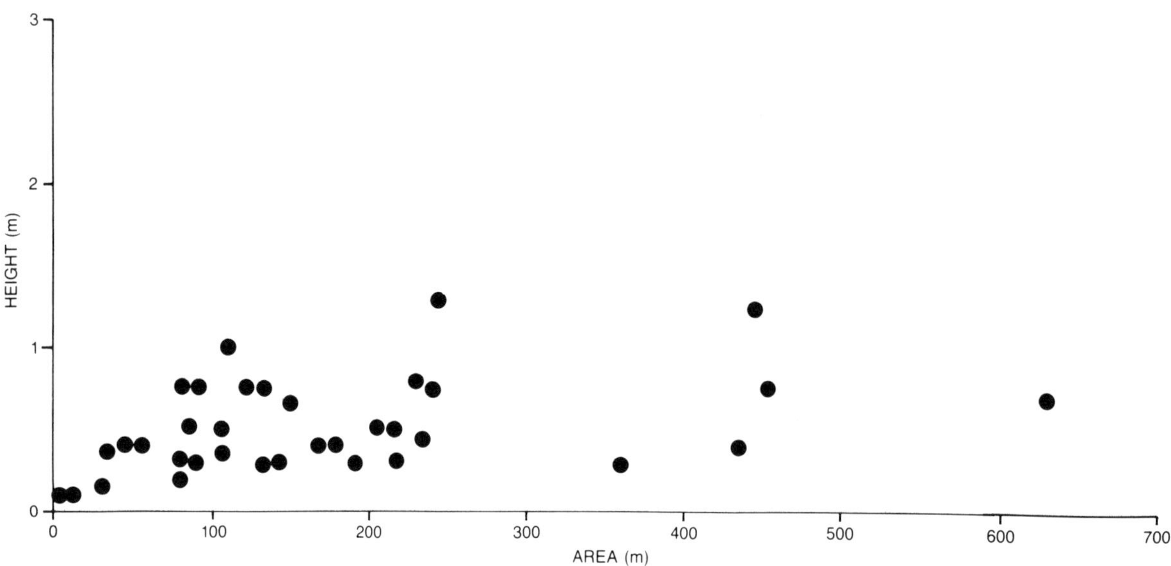

Figure 37. Size variation in faced mounds.

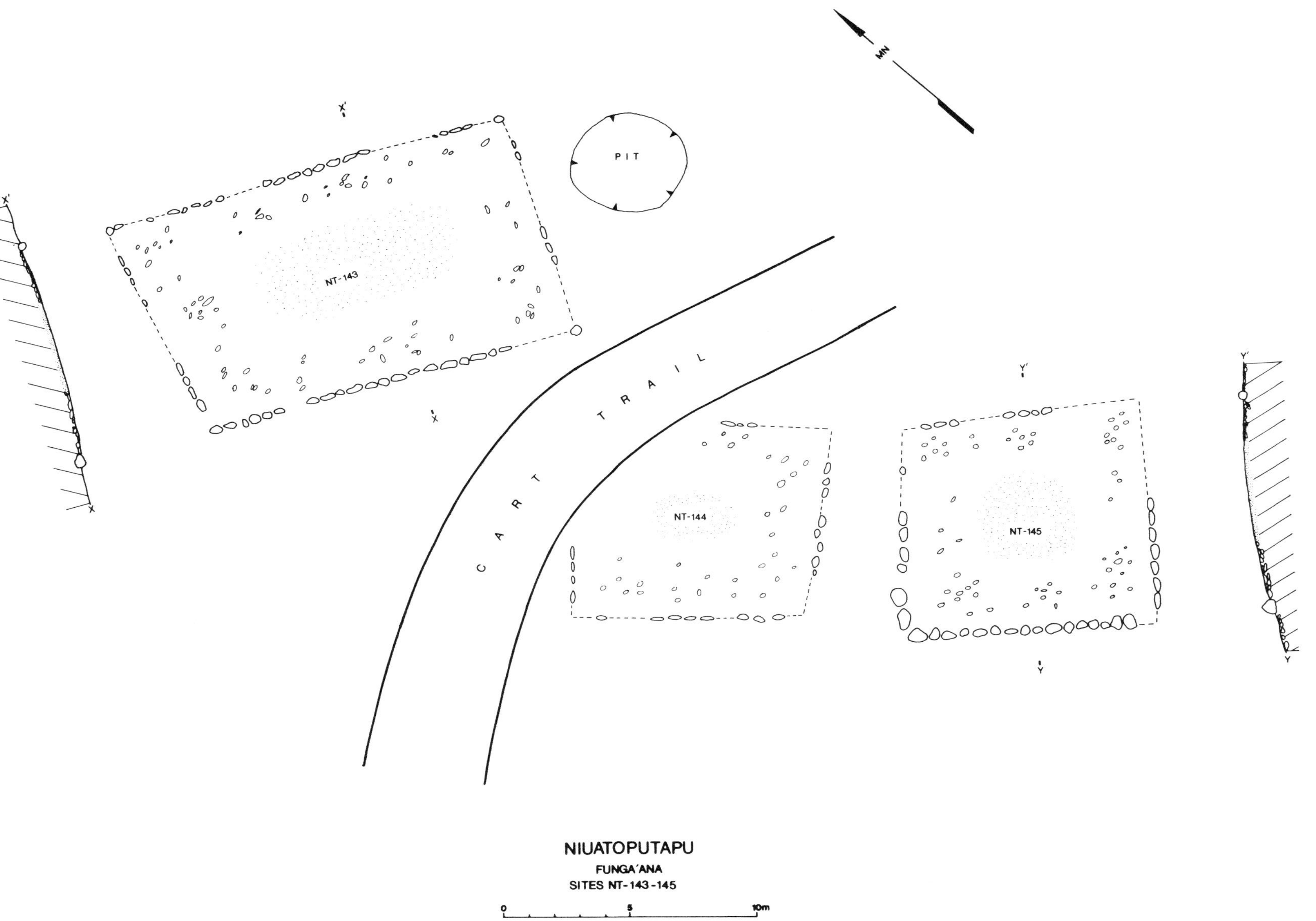

Figure 38. Plan of Sites NT-143, -144, and -145, Funga'ana.

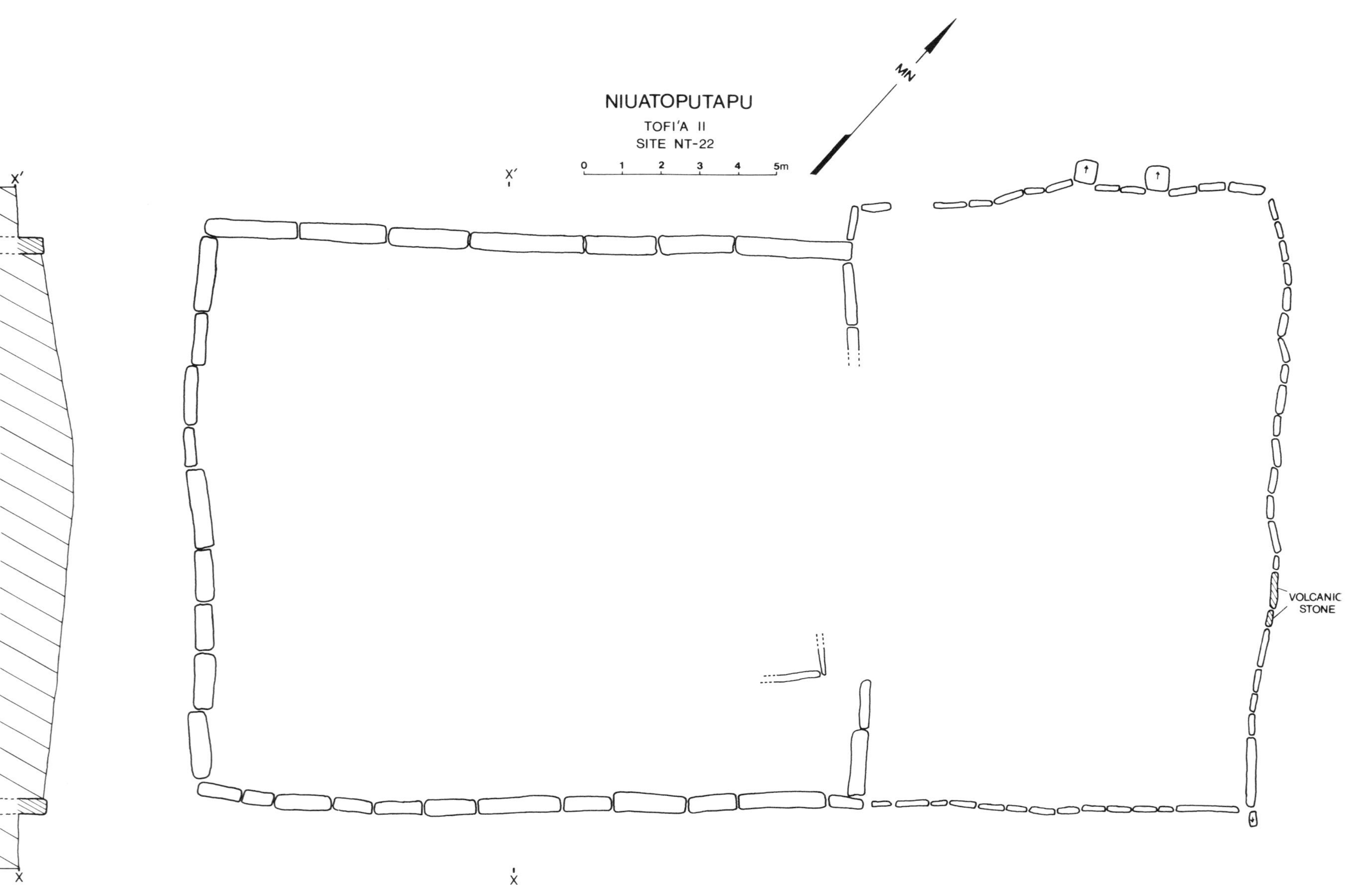

Figure 39. Plan of Site NT-22, Tofi'a.

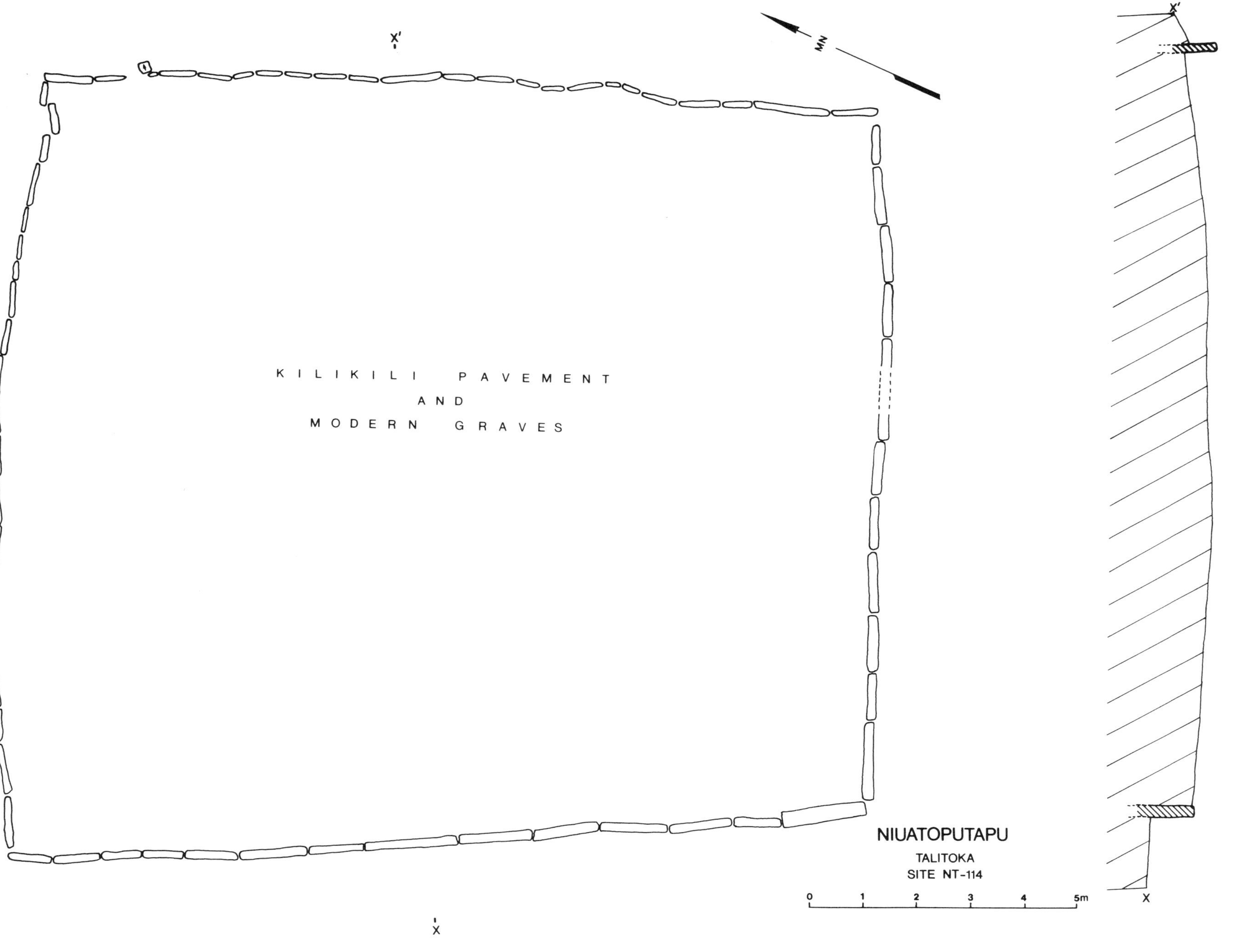

Figure 40. Plan of Site NT-114, Talitoka.

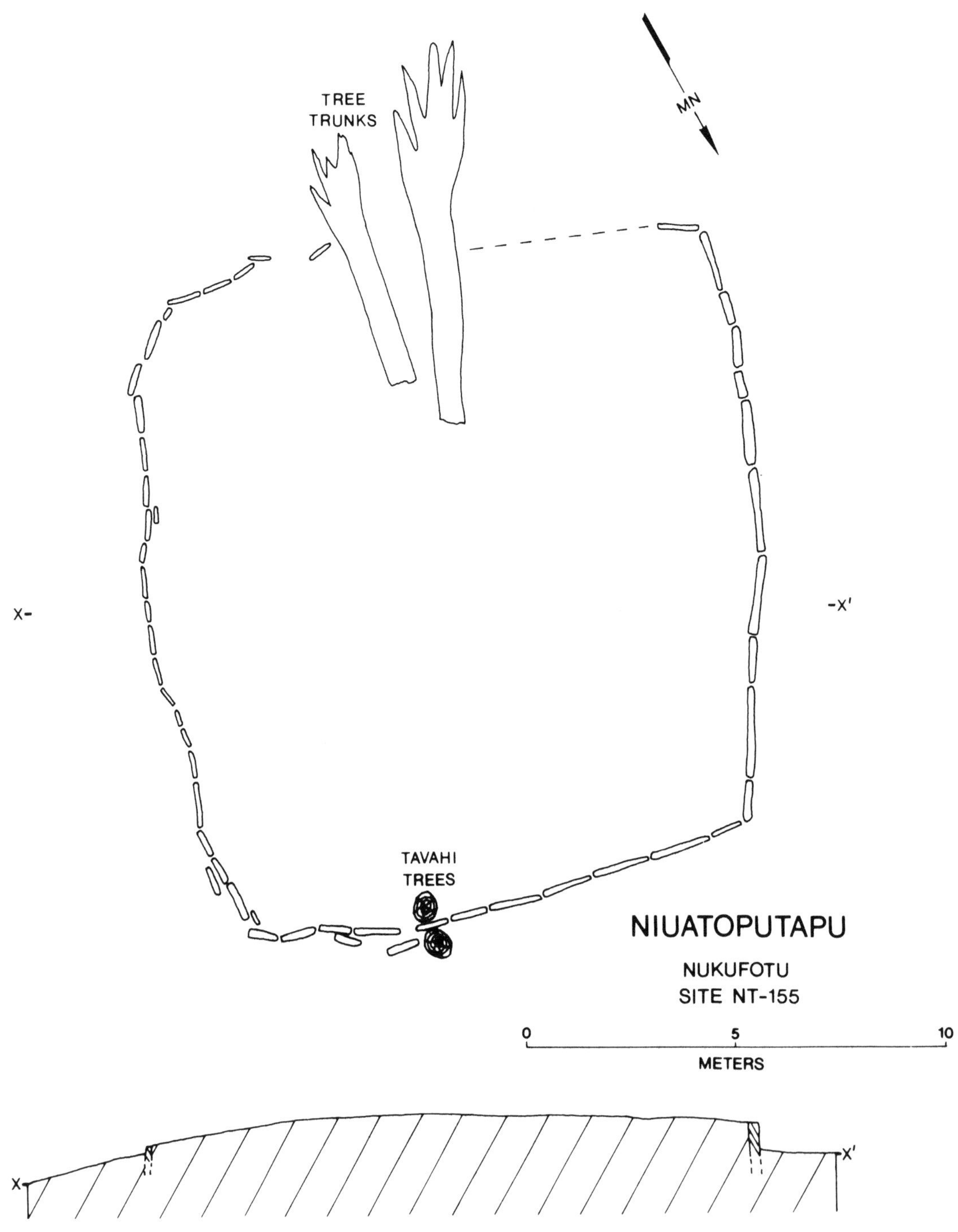

Figure 41. Plan of Site NT-155, Nukufotu.

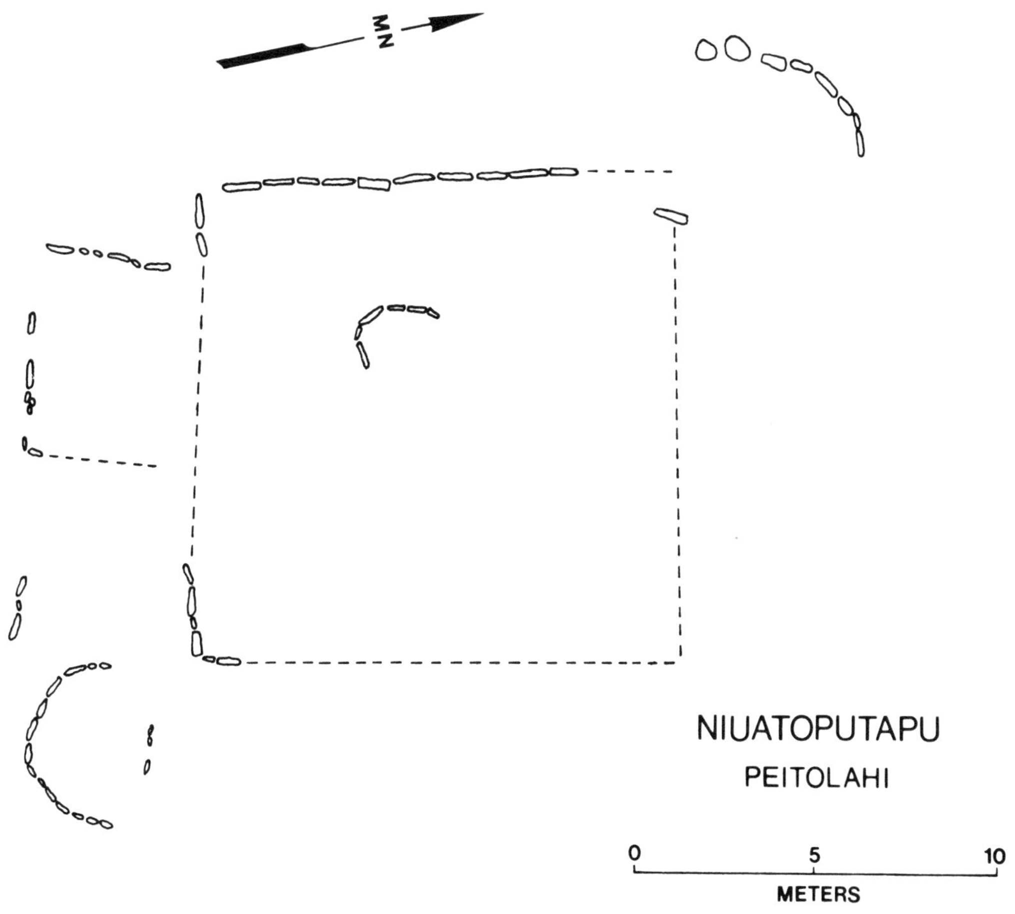

Figure 42. Plan of Site NT-195, Peitolahi.

pits were termed *luo maa—maa* being the fermented food product, *luo* designating a pit of any type. The practice of *maa* fermentation and storage has now died out on Niuatoputapu, but was remembered by several older informants from their youth. Nine fermentation pit sites were recorded, and many others probably exist on the slopes of the Pleistocene Terrace, especially near the base of the steep volcanic ridge. These pits are slightly conical, with rounded bottoms, and range from about 1 to 2 m in diameter with roughly equivalent depths.

Upright Stones

In various parts of Polynesia, artificially-set upright stones or slabs frequently had religious or ritual significance. Four sites on Niuatoputapu consist of such stones, all of which are designated with proper names. We need not repeat Rogers's (1974:335-36), descriptions here, save to note that we found no evidence of the stones at NT-70 having been dressed, or of artificial grooves or incisions in stones at NT-75 and NT-76 (the "encircling parallel lines" mentioned by Rogers are simply natural bedding lines in the rock).

SITE DISTRIBUTION AND SETTLEMENT PATTERNS

Having classified and described the individual settlement components of the Niuatoputapu archaeological landscape both formally and quantitatively, I turn now to their areal distribution, with an eye toward the socio-political implications of such distribution patterns. Given that Niuatoputapu is the only Tongan island for which there has been a systematic and relatively thorough settlement pattern survey, the significance of these data for understanding the spatial correlates of late prehistoric and protohistoric Tongan society is substantial.

One pattern that emerges from the survey data is the preference throughout the entire prehistoric sequence for the island's leeward coast as a permanent occupation or habitation area. Although the ceramic zone extends completely around the central volcanic ridge and Pleistocene Terrace, the density of occupation materials in the south and southeastern parts of the zone is significantly less than in the portion of the zone between Hihifo and Falehau. Furthermore, we found no evidence of significant aceramic occupation deposits anywhere on the *liku* or windward side of the island, in contrast to the extensive aceramic middens along the leeward coast between the ceramic zone and the present shoreline. This dominance of the leeward coast for occupation correlates with several features of the island's marine environment. First, the lee shore of Niuatoputapu is sheltered from the strong, prevailing SE trades and swells which frequently lash the *liku* coast, making canoe landings, for example, impossible. Second, even though the island's marine environment has undergone major geomorphic and biotic changes

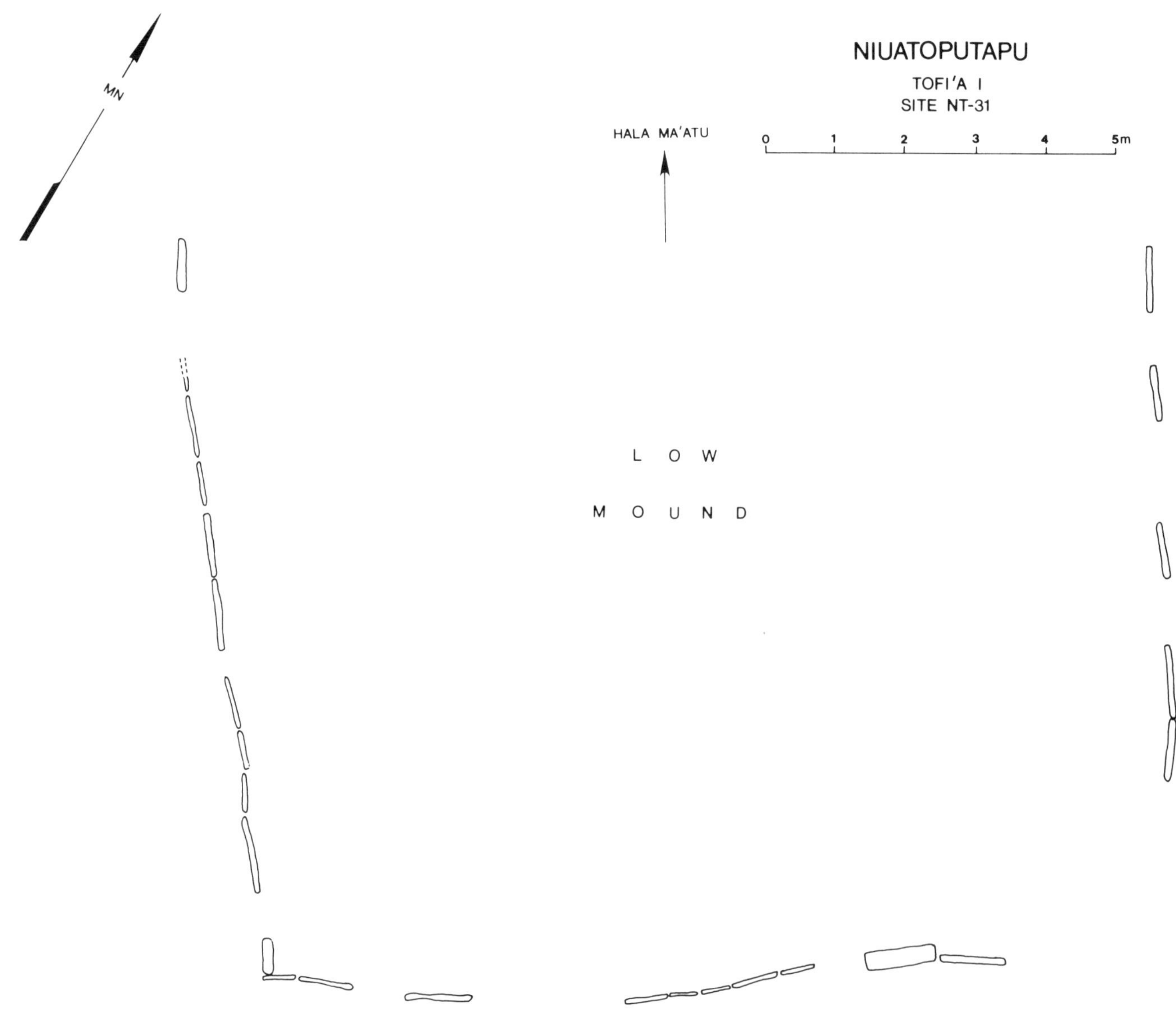

Figure 43. Plan of Site NT-31, Tofi'a.

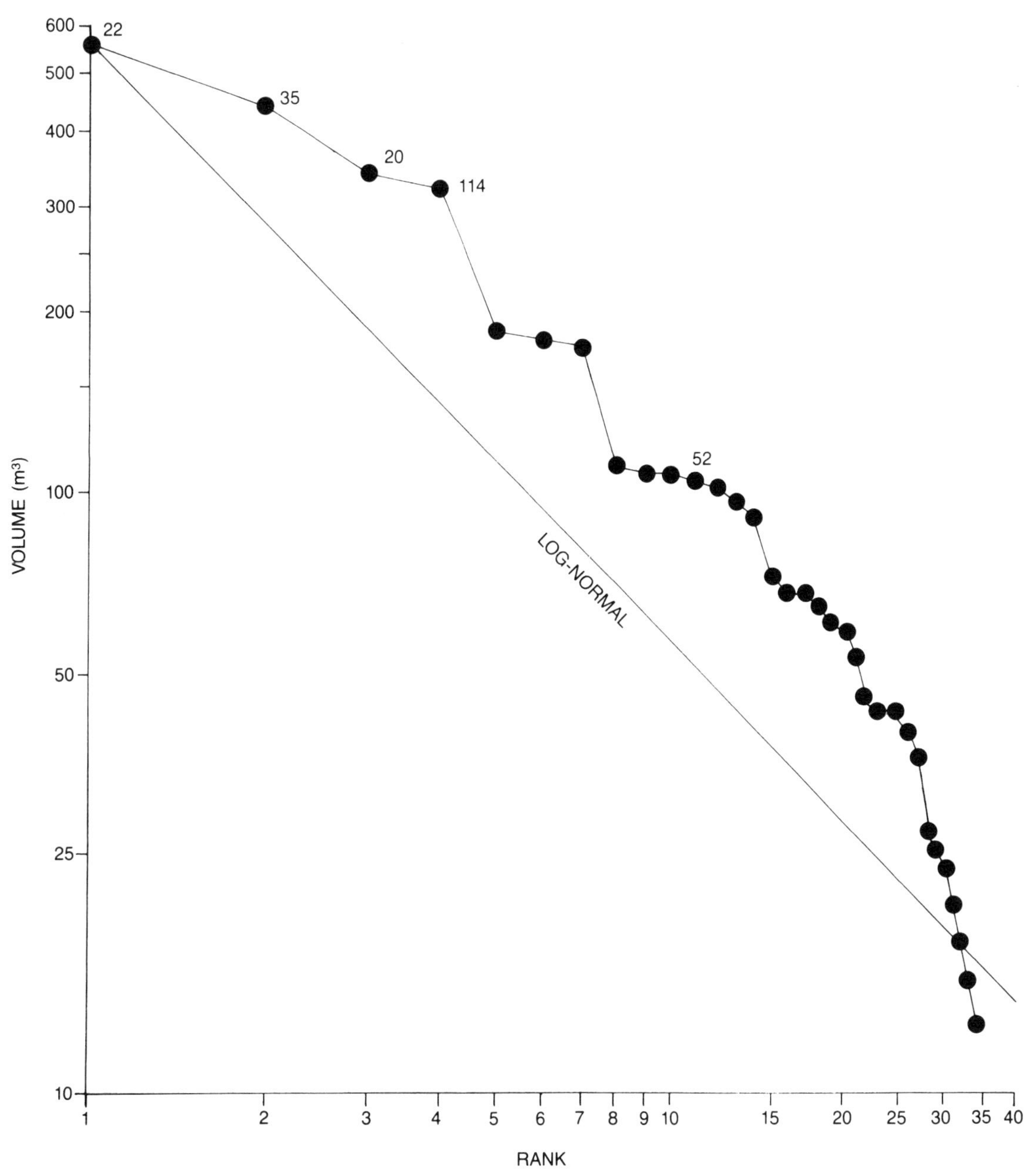

Figure 44. Rank-size distribution, by volume, of faced mounds.

over the past 3,000 years, the leeward reefs and lagoon have probably always been far more productive than those to windward. At the time of initial Lapita colonization, the broad southern and eastern plains were extensive sandy and rocky expanses of tidally exposed reef, already sufficiently uplifted to thwart active coral growth. In contrast, the sheltered leeward lagoon was, if anything, even more extensive 3,000 years ago than at present. Occupation along the leeward coastline was thus most desirable in providing immediate access to the more productive and more sheltered leeward marine ecosystem, as well as to the adjacent central volcanic biotopes which were essential for agricultural production.

Aside from the ceramic zone and leeward aceramic middens just mentioned, a number of small earthen terraces distributed over the slopes of the Pleistocene Terrace and central ridge (fig. 45) may have been used for habitation (though this hypothesis remains to be tested by excavation). The age of these terraces is not known, although the fact that they are structurally well preserved in an erosionally unstable environment suggests that they are all relatively recent. Indeed, many may be historic. It is conceivable that habitation terraces have been constructed on the central ridge and slopes since initial occupation of the island, but that older examples either are buried or have been destroyed by erosion of the colluvial slopes. Such questions cannot be further addressed without extensive excavation of terrace sites.

The larger field monuments (classes 4 to 12) are with few exceptions distributed over biotopes III (16% of sites), IVA (41%), IVB (3%), and V (18%). Biotopes IV and V are emerged marine environments which were tidal flats at the time of initial Lapita colonization of the island, and which became terra firma only within the past millennium or so. This distribution pattern thus provides a significant clue to the age of many, if indeed not all, of the large field monuments. They clearly cannot be associated with the earlier ceramic or Lapitoid period of Niuatoputapu prehistory and must belong instead to the more recent past. This pattern matches what little we know of the temporal distribution of mound sites elsewhere in Tonga. As Davidson remarks of both Tonga and Samoa, "There is little evidence until late in the first millennium A.D. of the monumental sites, particularly the earthen and stone mounds, that are now such a feature of the archaeological landscapes of both Samoa and Tonga" (1979:95). Further, it is likely that "mounds of various kinds spread relatively recently from Tongatapu to the north of the Tonga group" (1979:107; see also Kirch 1984a:232-34). Further evidence on the age of Niuatoputapu monuments will be given in chapter 4.

The distribution of unfaced, paved mounds (class 6) is shown in figure 46a. Two rather small mounds of class 6 are situated atop the central ridge. Other sites are located on the Pleistocene Terrace or below it on the uplifted terrain of biotopes III and IV. All of these larger class 6 mounds are in fairly close proximity to the main zone of occupation deposits. Unfaced mounds without pavings (classes 8 and 9) and which probably functioned either as chiefly *'esi* or pigeon-snaring mounds have a distinctive distribution pattern, shown in figure 46b. Three sites are located on the Pleistocene Terrace, two of them on the edge of the steep southern bluff. Another site lies within the confines of Hihifo village. All other class 8 and 9 monuments are found on the emerged marine sediments of biotopes IVA and IVB, generally in areas that are heavily vegetated with *Eugenia* forest and are the preferred habitat of pigeons. This is also terrain relatively remote from the main zone of habitation, or from agriculturally suitable soils. This distribution pattern offers strong supporting evidence that most of these sites were indeed *sia heu lupe*, as indicated by informants.

Faced mounds of classes 11 and 12 have highly similar distribution patterns which contrast markedly with those just discussed for classes 8 and 9. As seen in figure 47b, mounds of class 11 are with few exceptions, distributed either along the leeward coast in close association with the main occupation zone, or in discrete clusters along the windward or *liku* coast. Those mounds along the leeward coast also show signs of clustering or agglomeration. This same pattern is also indicated for class 12 mounds (fig. 47a).

In short, two major contrasts appear in comparing the distributions of unfaced (classes 8 and 9) and faced (classes 11 and 12) mounds: (1) the unfaced mounds are largely in interior locations, on recently emerged, heavily vegetated terrain, whereas the faced mounds are sited along the coasts and often in proximity to occupation zones; and (2) whereas the unfaced mounds are fairly widely spaced throughout the interior *Eugenia* forests, the faced mounds are distributed in discrete clusters. In order to test the degree of clustering or agglomeration in these various classes, the nearest neighbor statistic of Clark and Evans (1954; see also Hodder and Orton 1976:38-51) was applied to these distribution patterns. The ratio (R) between the observed mean distance to nearest neighbor (r_o) and that expected for a randomly-distributed population of points of n size (r_E) is a measure of the randomness of the spatial distribution pattern. In a random distribution, $R = 1$, while clustered or agglomerated distributions are less than 1 approaching zero in extreme cases; R values greater than 1 indicate dispersion or uniform arrangements. Table 5 provides the relevant nearest-neighbor statistics for mounds of classes 8 and 9, 11, and 12. The R value of 0.86 for classes 8 and 9 indicates substantial randomness or lack of clustering. In contrast, the values for class 11 (0.56) and especially for class 12 (0.39) indicate significant agglomeration of mounds.

These site distribution patterns, combined with what is known of the probable functions of various monument classes, are sufficient to suggest a model of late prehistoric or protohistoric socio-political grouping on Niuatoputapu (fig. 48). Throughout Polynesia, islands are typically segmented by social or political units (tribes, lineages, or chiefly alliances) into ideally radial territorial units that crosscut the environmental grain of the island (Kirch 1984a:33). As Bellwood notes, "such radial divisions, called *tapere* in the Cooks, *ahupua'a* in the Hawaiian Islands, and *nu'u* in Samoa, form the basis for any ethnohistorical interpretation of

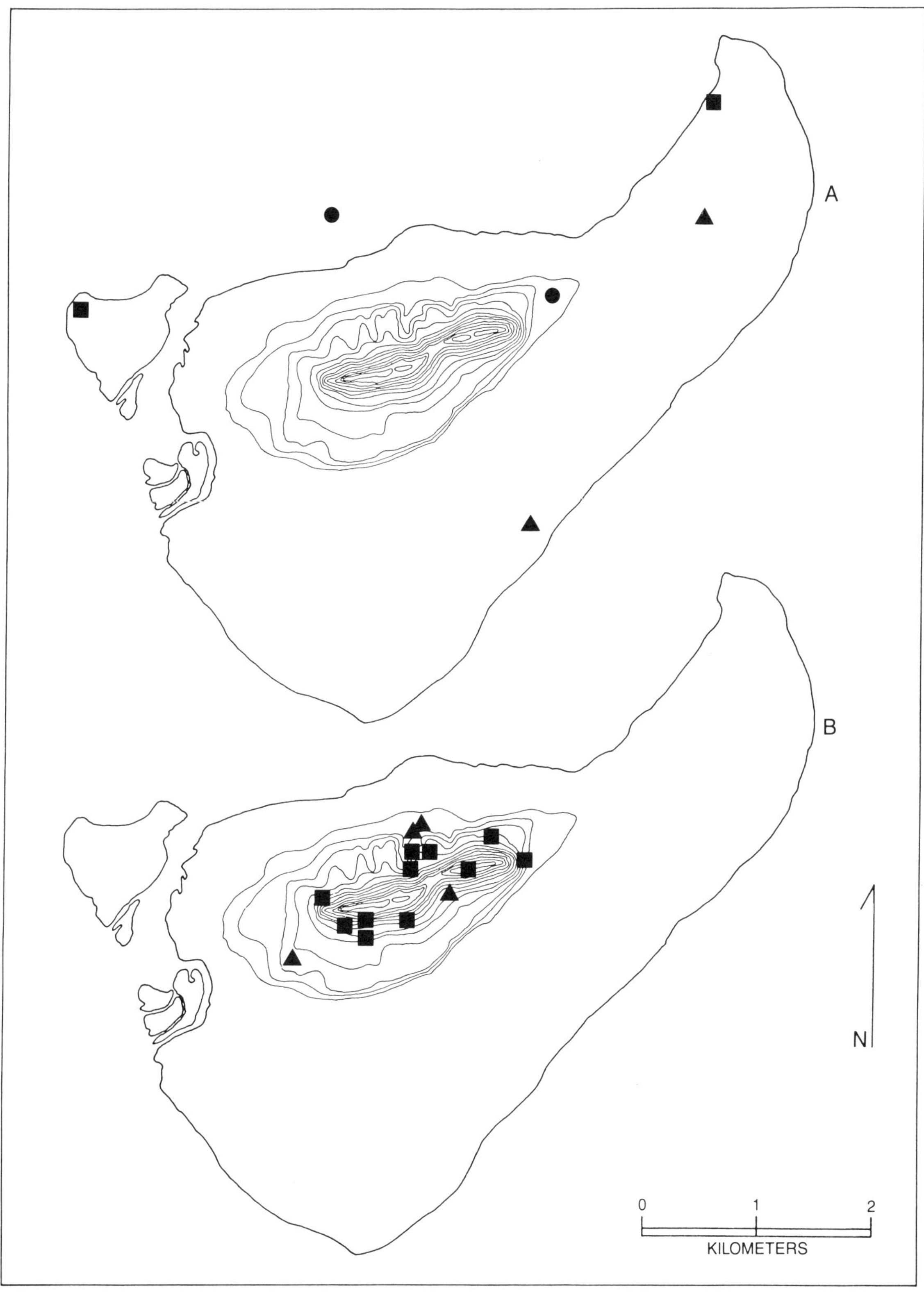

Figure 45. Distribution of archaeological site classes on Niuatoputapu Island: A, distribution of quarries (triangles), platforms, (squares), and upright stones (circles); B, distribution of terraces (squares) and fermentation pits (triangles).

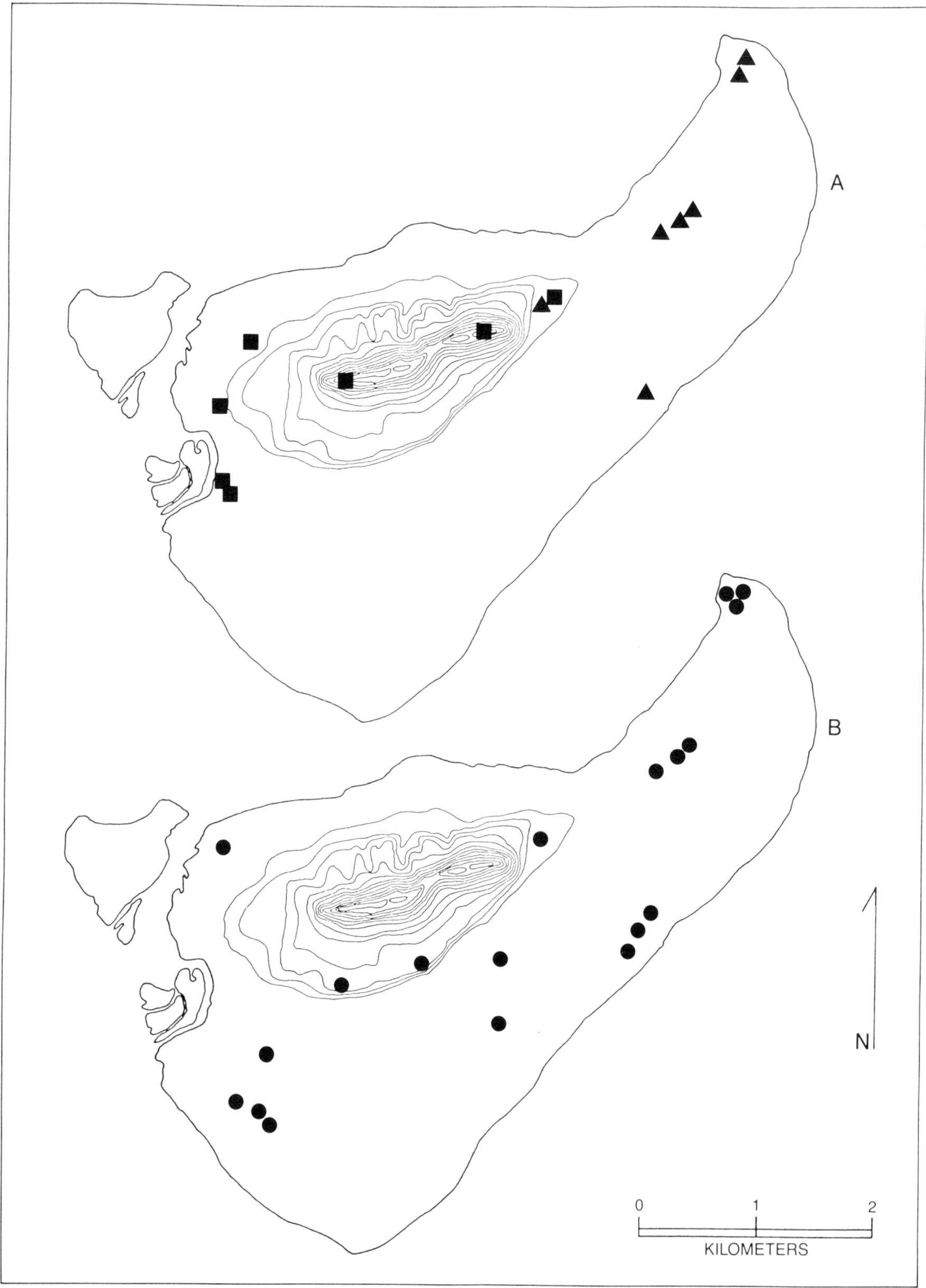

Figure 46. Distribution of archaeological site classes on Niuatoputapu Island: A, unfaced mounds of class 6 (squares), and unfaced mounds of class 7 (triangles); B, unfaced, unpaved mounds of classes 8 and 9.

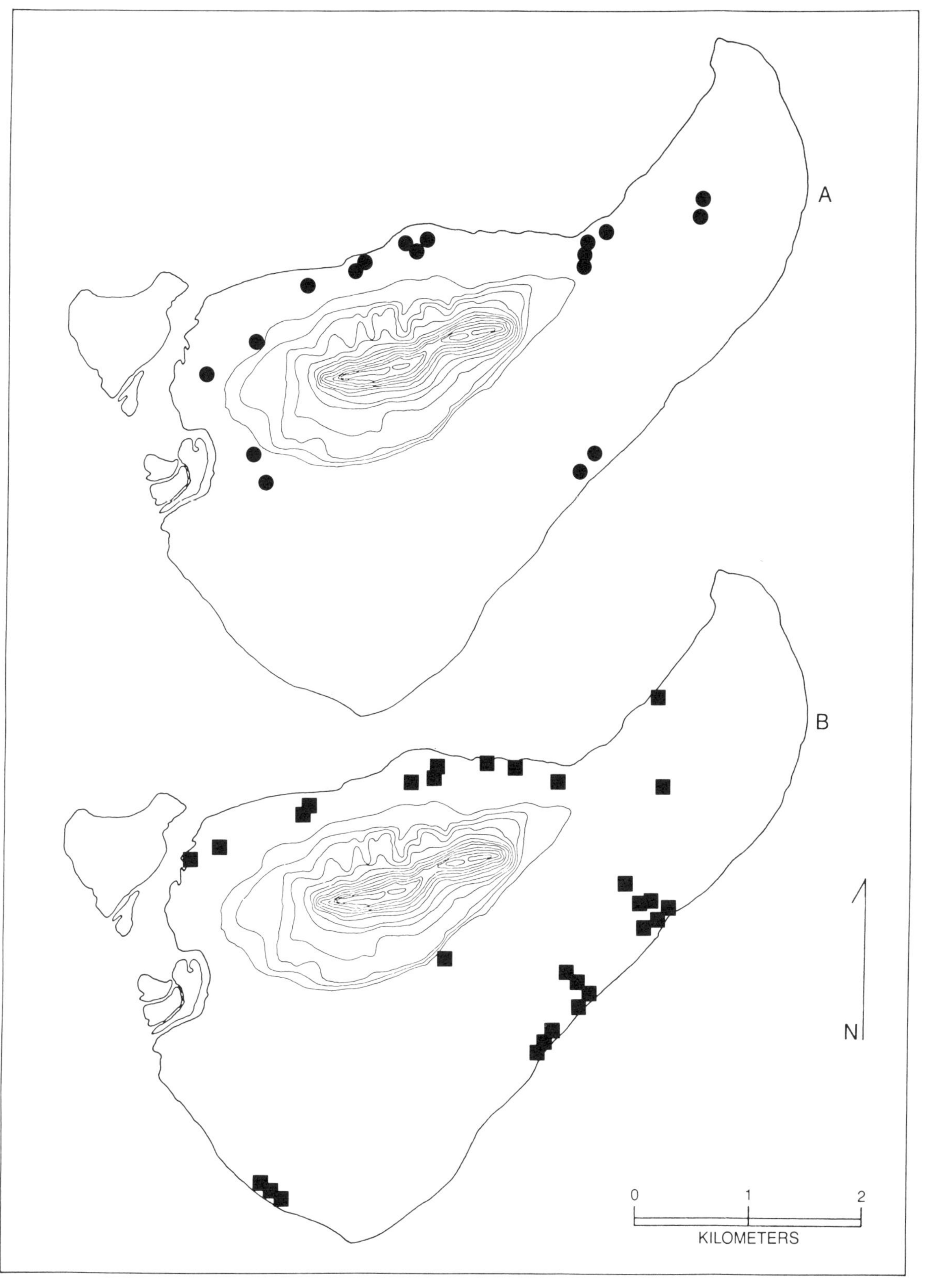

Figure 47. Distribution of archaeological site classes on Niuatoputapu Island: A, faced mounds of class 12; B, faced mounds of class 11.

TABLE 5

NEAREST-NEIGHBOR STATISTICS FOR MOUND SITES

MOUND CLASS	$\overline{r}_O$	$\overline{r}_E$	R	c
Classes 8 & 9	384.2	447.2	0.86	- 1.17
Class 11	196.7	350.1	0.56	- 4.67
Class 12	173.4	447.2	0.39	- 5.11

overall settlement patterns" (1979:309). The land within such a territorial unit was under the titular control of the chief, who might be the representative of the senior ranked line of a ramage, or, in more stratified societies (such as Hawai'i and Tonga), a member of a collateral branch of the ruling paramount who placed lesser-ranked chiefs on various land segments throughout the chiefdom.

While it would seem likely that radial land divisions were also the case in Tonga, our knowledge of contact-period Tongan social groupings in relation to land tenure is extremely scanty—indeed, worse than for virtually any other Polynesian society. The few available sources suggest that land was divided into major territorial segments (called *tofi'a* ever since the land tenure system was codified under King George Tupou I), each under the control of a ranking chief (Bott 1982; Gifford 1929). Within these major segments there were evidently smaller units, each controlled by lesser chiefs, the *hou'eiki* and their populace *(kainga).*

Since faced mounds of class 11 are evidently burial mounds associated with local descent groups, and in the case of class 12 of ranking individuals within those groups, it is to be expected that such monuments would be situated within the ancestral lands or territory of the group in question. Further, clusters of such mounds should be a clue to the territorial structure of socio-political grouping. We have already noted that on Niuatoputapu the faced mounds of classes 11 and 12 display statistically marked agglomeration. Given what we know of Polynesian social grouping in relation to land, it is thus likely that these discrete burial mound clusters (usually several class 11 mounds associated with one or two class 12 mounds) each mark the core of an associated territorial unit. If this hypothesis is correct, in late prehistory Niuatoputapu was subdivided in roughly radial fashion into approximately 12 territorial units (fig. 48). As we know from ethnohistory, of course, all of these units would have been under the higher authority of the Ma'atu line of chiefs, themselves a collateral branch of the Tu'i Tonga line (see chapter 1). Traditionally, the local seat of the Ma'atu chiefs was in the Vaipoa area, where indeed the most impressive class 12 monuments are located (designated with an asterisk on fig. 48).

According to this model, while the windward slopes of the central volcanic ridge and adjacent Pleistocene Terrace—which were economically valuable arable lands—would have been subdivided into four or five territorial units, the burial mound complexes associated with these units were actually situated some distance away on the windward coast. This reflects the apparent importance of locating burial mounds near the shoreline, for cultural reasons not clear in the ethnohistoric record, but which may have to do with widespread Polynesian notions of chiefs as foreign conquerors, "sea-people" as opposed to the indigenous occupants of the land (the so-called "stranger king" symbolic complex, cf. Sahlins 1981, 1985). Between these windward coastal burial complexes and the inland arable lands with which they were associated lay the rugged, recently-emerged terrain of *toafa* and marine sediments. This zone was of no particular significance for agriculture or other economic pursuits, and there is no reason to think it should have been territorially claimed or marked by any of the chiefly lines. However, this region did provide the principal habitat for pigeons, and it is throughout this zone that the large *sia heu lupe* or class 8-9 mounds are distributed. Chiefs of each of the territorial segments may have maintained one or more pigeon-snaring mounds in the otherwise unutilized *Eugenia* forests lying between the central volcanic ridge and the windward coast.

The model just presented is speculative in several respects, but it is consonant with Tongan ethnohistory and with certain widespread aspects of Polynesian settlement patterns. Lacking comparable archaeological surveys for other Tongan islands, it remains to be seen whether the pattern of clustered burial monuments on Niuatoputapu is reflected elsewhere in the archipelago.

EXTRA-AREAL COMPARISONS

Knowledge of Fijian and Western Polynesian settlement patterns has been advanced substantially in the past 25 years, thanks to extensive surveys in Samoa (Green and Davidson 1969a, 1974; Jennings and Holmer 1980; Jennings et al. 1976; Jennings, Holmer, and

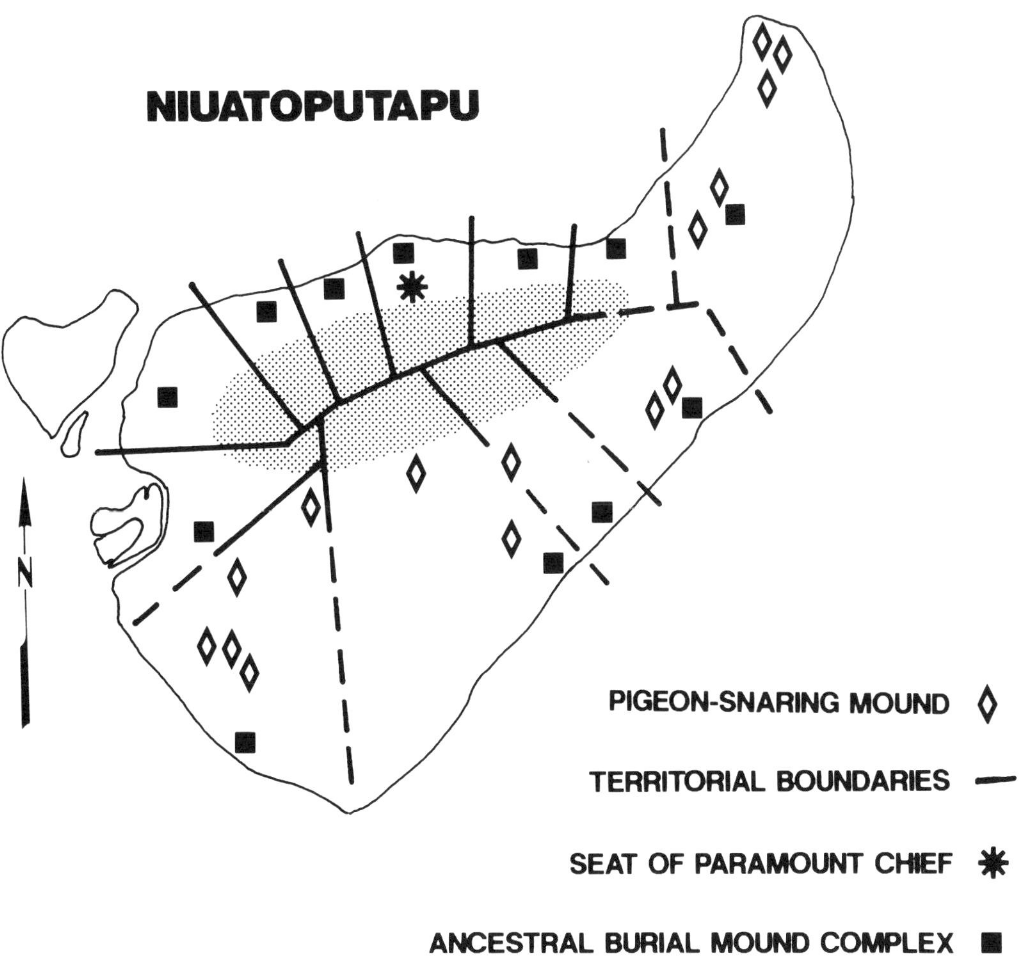

Figure 48. Diagrammatic model of late prehistoric socio-political territorial units on Niuatoputapu Island.

Jackmond 1982; Hunt and Kirch, in press), to investigations of fortification and other sites in Fiji (Frost 1979; Parry 1977, 1981; Best 1984), and to several smaller projects (e.g., Kirch 1975a; Frimigacci et al. 1984). It is thus possible to place the Niuatoputapu results in a broader regional context. Three major points bear discussion: (1) the absence on Niuatoputapu of fortifications; (2) the distinctly Tongan character of the field monuments; and (3) the absence of distinctive Samoan-type structures.

Surveys throughout Fiji, the Lau Islands, 'Uvea, Futuna, Tongatapu, Vava'u, and Samoa have shown a widespread distribution of fortifications, of which there are several major structural types (e.g., ridge-top terraced and ditched forts, ring-ditch enclosures on level or swampy ground, stone-walled constructions, etc.). In this context, the absence of any evident fortifications on Niuatoputapu is unusual. It may be that this absence reflects the small size of Niuatoputapu and the fact that it may always have been politically unified, lacking major political subdivisions which would have been competitively aligned against each other.

Perhaps the most striking feature of the Niuatoputapu settlement landscape is its distinctly Tongan character. That is, all of the classes of field monument recognized during the archaeological survey—including pigeon-snaring mounds and the various kinds of faced burial mounds—are well documented from the more southerly islands of Vava'u, Ha'apai, and Tongatapu. There is nothing in the settlement corpus of Niuatoputapu to distinguish the island from the rest of the archipelago. A corollary to the last observation is the absence in Niuatoputapu of any of the characteristic Samoan field monuments, such as star mounds, stone house platforms with curbstone edgings, or raised/sunken walkways.

The Tongan, as opposed to Samoan, character of the Niuatoputapu settlement landscape is especially noteworthy given the traditional and linguistic evidence for protohistoric Tongan domination of the Niuatoputapu polity. It is likely that most, if not all, of the major Niuatoputapu field monuments, especially the various mound classes, date to the last few centuries of the Niuatoputapu sequence, following the incorporation of the island into the Tongan "maritime empire." This conclusion is consonant with the geomorphological settings of many of the monuments on recently emerged terrain, and with the limited temporal data obtained from excavation (see chapter 4).

CHAPTER FOUR

ARCHAEOLOGICAL EXCAVATIONS

DURING THE COURSE OF OUR EXPEDITION, we excavated in 16 sites at 13 separate localities (table 6), exposing a total area of 171.25 m^2. Eight of these localities were chosen in our effort to sample the ceramic-bearing zone, while another five localities were selected to represent other site categories, including aceramic middens and architectural sites. Our efforts were biased toward the ceramic sites, in part because these localities yielded more diverse samples of both material culture and faunal remains than the later, aceramic middens and architectural sites. Nevertheless, sites of all periods were examined, providing a continuous—if in sections spotty—record of Niuatoputapu prehistory. This chapter focuses on the excavations themselves, providing details of local setting and geomorphology, excavation procedure, stratigraphy, cultural features, and chronology. The material culture recovered from the excavations is the subject of chapter 5, while the faunal remains are treated in detail in chapter 6.

EXCAVATION METHODS AND SAMPLING CONSIDERATIONS

At the time of our fieldwork, little explicit attention had been paid by Polynesian archaeologists to the sampling problems associated with excavation. Only Green (1976), in his work on Lapita sites, had raised these issues and had begun to devise strategies for assessing the adequacy of different excavation schemes. Aware of this problem, we sought in Niuatoputapu to approach the excavations with special attention to sampling considerations.

A major sampling problem was that of obtaining an accurate and representative sample of artifact and faunal variation within the extensive ceramic-bearing zone. The zone of surface sherd distribution constitutes, for all intents and purposes, a continuous site with a total surface area of about 0.5 km^2, even though sherd density varies enormously within its borders. The design of an effective sampling strategy was compounded by the observation, first made by Rogers (1973, 1974), that the pottery-bearing deposits are shallow and greatly disturbed by post-depositional agricultural activities. The relatively shallow, disturbed deposits evidently represent an occupation span presumed to be in excess of one millennium. Based on Rogers's limited test excavations, it also appeared likely that occupation components were "horizontally stratified," or spread out spatially throughout the zone, as a result of repeated shifts in settlement locality during the period of pottery production and use. Decisions on where to excavate were further compounded by the intensive cultivation of the zone by the present population, totally obliterating in situ surface manifestations of prehistoric occupation, other than scattered sherds and other cultural debris exposed by the action of digging sticks.

The sampling strategy ultimately devised consisted of two stages. First, we undertook a series of test excavations—organized as a stratified random sample (Redman 1974)—in a 2,400 m^2 sampling frame that spanned the entire ceramic-bearing zone at Lolokoka (Site NT-90; fig. 20), near Vaipoa village. This locality, initially tested by Rogers, promised to yield classic Lapita ceramics; by utilizing a stratified random

TABLE 6

SUMMARY OF NIUATOPUTAPU EXCAVATIONS, 1976

LOCALITY	SITE NO.	SITE TYPE	SAMPLING METHOD	AREA EXCAVATED (m^2)	SHERD DENSITY ($\bar{x}/m^2$)	NON-CERAMIC ARTIFACTS
Lolokoka	NT - 90	Midden, ceramic	Stratified random; areal excavation	51.25	534.2	8,985
Loto'aa	NT - 100	Midden, ceramic	Systematic transect	19.0	124.9	594
Pome'e-Nahau	NT - 93	Midden, ceramic	Systematic transect	22.0	255.8	819
Ha'afisi	NT - 91	Midden, ceramic	Systematic transect	4.0	159.5	172
Vaipoa	NT - 112	Midden, ceramic	Test pits	5.0	342.6	514
Holoiafu	NT - 113	Midden, ceramic	Systematic transect	4.0	69.2	224
Tu'afonua	NT - 129	Midden, ceramic	Systematic transect	4.0	3.8	45
Hihifo	NT - 163	Midden, ceramic and aceramic	Systematic transect	12.0	42.1	161
Niutoua	NT - 125	Midden, aceramic	Systematic transect	8.0	—	49
Matavai	NT - 110		Test trenches	4.0	288.5	237
Funga'ana	NT - 139	Midden, ceramic and historic	Trenches	9.0	—	—
Hihifo	NT - 150	Mound	Trench	6.0	6.7	—
Houmafakalele	NT - 52, -54, -55, -164, -169	Mound; ceramic midden Burial monuments	Trenches	23.0	—	—
TOTALS				171.25		11,800

sample technique we sought to obtain a controlled sample of the spatial variation within one sector of the ceramic zone. The 29 excavated units revealed lateral variation across the pottery-bearing zone. Such lateral variation in stratigraphy and artifact-faunal material concentration is evidently crucial to an understanding of the depositional history and sequence at any particular locality. The second stage of our sampling strategy focused on this problem of lateral variation through the excavation of units along systematic transects (Redman 1974) oriented laterally across the zone, at six localities chosen on the basis of variation in surface sherd density and of their environmental position along the ceramic zone. In addition, an ecological study of contemporary marine resources, carried out by T. Dye (1983, see chapter 2), was keyed to these excavation localities by extending the systematic transects out onto the reef flat and using them as the sampling frame for marine studies. Continuous elevation profiles taken with a Nikon level along the systematic transects also provided geomorphological data on the structure of former beach ridges and other shoreline features, thus aiding in the interpretation of tectonic uplift and coastal change.

This strategy was effective in sampling the temporal range represented in the ceramic-bearing zone, its internal lateral structure, and the ecological variation associated with each locality. Further, this approach to excavation procedure provided statistically comparable collections of material culture and faunal remains. Indeed, the strategy was judged sufficiently successful to be applied subsequently on Tikopia (Kirch and Yen 1982) and in a subsurface reconnaissance of Arno Atoll (Dye and Kirch 1980). Most recently, the approach has been applied in the sampling of an early Lapita assemblage in the Mussau Islands (Kirch 1987).

In other aspects, our work followed relatively standard procedures in Polynesian archaeology. Metric grid control was established at all sites, and all excavation units were 1 m^2 unless otherwise noted. For the transects, excavation units are designated by the distance from the inland origin point of the transect (e.g., Unit 210 is situated 210 meters from the zero-point of the transect). Excavation followed natural stratigraphy whenever possible, although arbitrary units were utilized in subdividing thick natural deposits. All deposits were troweled, and all excavated sediment was screened through 0.25-inch mesh. In stratigraphic descriptions, layers are designated from top to bottom with Roman numerals; occasionally an alternative system of "beds" is utilized where correlations between units is uncertain. All soil color designations are in the Munsell system. Depths of layers and features are given below surface unless otherwise indicated. Depth and thickness of stratigraphic units may be discerned from the profile sections; for sections not illustrated, depths are given with the profile descriptions.

Sediment samples were removed from each depositional unit of principal sites and returned to the Bishop Museum laboratory for physical and chemical analysis. Grain-size analysis was performed by mechanical sieving of oven-dried samples, and the gross composition of the sieved components was determined by microscopic scanning of sieve contents and of smear slides.

All vertebrate faunal material retained in the sieves was separated, washed, and returned to the Bishop Museum laboratory for identification and analysis. Molluscan remains—by far the greatest quantity of faunal material—were usually retained from one 0.25 m^2 quadrant of each excavation unit, although where density was low, samples were retained from the entire unit. Molluscs were washed in the field and sorted to taxonomic categories, with representative voucher specimens returned to Honolulu for confirmation of identifications. A complete set of molluscan voucher specimens from the Niuatoputapu excavations was deposited in the Division of Malacology, B.P. Bishop Museum.

Artifacts recovered in situ were three-dimensionally recorded; those recovered in the screens were recorded by layer or level. The majority of small, plain, non-diagnostic body sherds were washed, counted, weighed, and discarded in the field, although representative samples from all sites were returned to the laboratory along with all bases, rims, handles, decorated sherds, and other unusual or distinctive pieces. The entire artifact collection from Niuatoputapu is presently housed in the Division of Archaeology, B.P. Bishop Museum, on extended loan from the Kingdom of Tonga.

THE CERAMIC SITES

Geomorphological Considerations

Niuatoputapu geomorphology, reviewed briefly in chapter 2, reflects the active tectonic emergence resulting from the island's position on the subduction zone between the Fijian and Pacific Plates. Structurally, Niuatoputapu consists of a volcanic core with an enclosing skirt of recent marine sediments including former beach terraces, dune ridges, former lagoon floors (now halophytic marshes), and former barrier reef islets. In his reconnaissance survey, Rogers (1973, 1974:312, 338-39) correctly recognized that "pottery in Niuatoputapu encircles the mountain in a...narrow belt" and that this zone was "just above the old beach/ lagoon." He also noted prominent beach ridge depression features between Angihoa and Hihifo, but was uncertain whether these represented "the bed of a former restricted lagoon" or "a former sunken road" (1974:338). Our own archaeological survey, summarized in chapter 3, confirmed Rogers's findings regarding the restriction of ceramic-bearing deposits to what we have termed the "ceramic zone." This zone occupies a continuous raised beach terrace situated immediately below the prominent Pleistocene Terrace which is covered in volcanic clays. This ceramic distribution pattern implies that, at the time of initial Lapita settlement of Niuatoputapu, the active shoreline lay at the foot of this beach terrace. Over the course of the 3,200 to 3,300 years since colonization, tectonic uplift has precipitated substantial reef/lagoon emergence and shoreline progradation, producing the present skirt of marine sediments especially broad on the south-eastern side of the island, but present everywhere to some extent.

During our archaeological investigations at several localities in the ceramic zone, we surveyed transects running perpendicular to the axis of the zone (and thus also to the coast) from the base of the Pleistocene Terrace out onto the modern reef flat (and, where possible, to the reef edge). These transects provide geomorphological details on the sequence of coastal progradation during the past 3,200 to 3,300 years. Figure 49 shows the transect from the NT-100 locality at Loto'aa, where the location of the ceramic zone on a gently sloping beach terrace 3 to 5 m above the present reef flat is unmistakable. Immediately seaward of the ceramic zone is the depression seen by Rogers, which is clearly not an artificial feature such as a road, but a former shoreline isolated by the formation of a beach ridge immediately to the north (Martens 1939:208). Between 120 and 250 m, as measured along the transect baseline, are at least seven distinct beach ridges, each marking a formerly active berm.

A similar picture is presented by the Hihifo transect incorporting Site NT-163, although the zone of cultural deposits is somewhat wider at this point (fig. 49). Here the position of the ceramic zone on a former raised beach terrace, with an alternating series of nine beach ridges and depressions to seaward, is again clear. Evidently, the process of coastal progradation and beach ridge formation is still continuing, driven by the tectonic engine of island-wide emergence.

This geomorphological picture can be tied to a general model of Holocene sea levels and tectonic uplift (Bloom 1974; Chappell 1982; Chappell and Thom 1977; Fairbridge 1961; Stearns 1945; Taylor and Bloom 1975). It is widely accepted that the rapid rise in sea levels following the end of the last glaciation slowed and stabilized between 6,000 and 4,000 years B.P., with sea levels reaching approximately their modern stands. During the rapid post-Pleistocene rise, it is probable that the rate of eustatic rise was greater than the rate of tectonic uplift or emergence of Niuatoputapu. Thus, despite continued local tectonism, the island's coastline would have seen an effect of coastal transgression during this period. Once sea levels attained their relatively stable position by 4,000 years B.P., however, the situation would have shifted as tectonic emergence once again began to result in shoreline regression. At the time of Lapita colonization, the beach terrace upon which the colonizers settled had probably been stabilized only within the preceding 1,000 to 2,000 years, as the coastal regime shifted from one of net transgression to net regression. In the subsequent three millennia, human occupations were to be affected by continued regression, with the gradual or episodic conversion of beaches, lagoons, and reefs to dry land. The effects of such environmental change were obviously considerable, and will be further explored later in this monograph.

Lolokoka Excavations (Site NT-90)

Situated astride the ceramic zone just east of Vaipoa village, the Lolokoka Site is critical to understanding the Lapita occupation of Niuatoputapu. The Lolokoka deposits are the oldest known on the island, and the site arguably represents the original colonization settlement. In addition, Lolokoka was occupied throughout much, if not all, of the entire Lapitoid period on Niuatoputapu, spanning the ceramic transition from Early Eastern Lapita through Polynesian Plain Ware. This lengthy occupation is evidenced not only by the material culture present at the site, but by the high ceramic density of 451 sherds/m^2, greater than that at any other investigated site (table 6). Because of Lolokoka's importance, extensive excavations totalling 51.25 m^2 were carried out using both random sampling and areal excavation strategies. These yielded 31,495 ceramic sherds, 8,985 other portable artifacts, 568 specimens of vertebrate fauna, and 57 kilos of molluscan fauna.

Local Setting and Geomorphology

Site NT-90, beginning about 150 m east of Vaipoa village (as with all sites in the ceramic zone, the designation NT-90 is arbitrary) straddles the pottery-bearing zone of *fasifasi'ifeo* soil. The terrain is nearly flat, with minor undulations of about 10 cm resulting from cultivation (mounding, digging of yam pits, etc.). Seaward, a series of low beach ridges and depressions lies between the ceramic zone and the leeward lagoon shore. Inland, the Pleistocene Terrace begins about 50 m from the interior limit of surface pottery distribution.

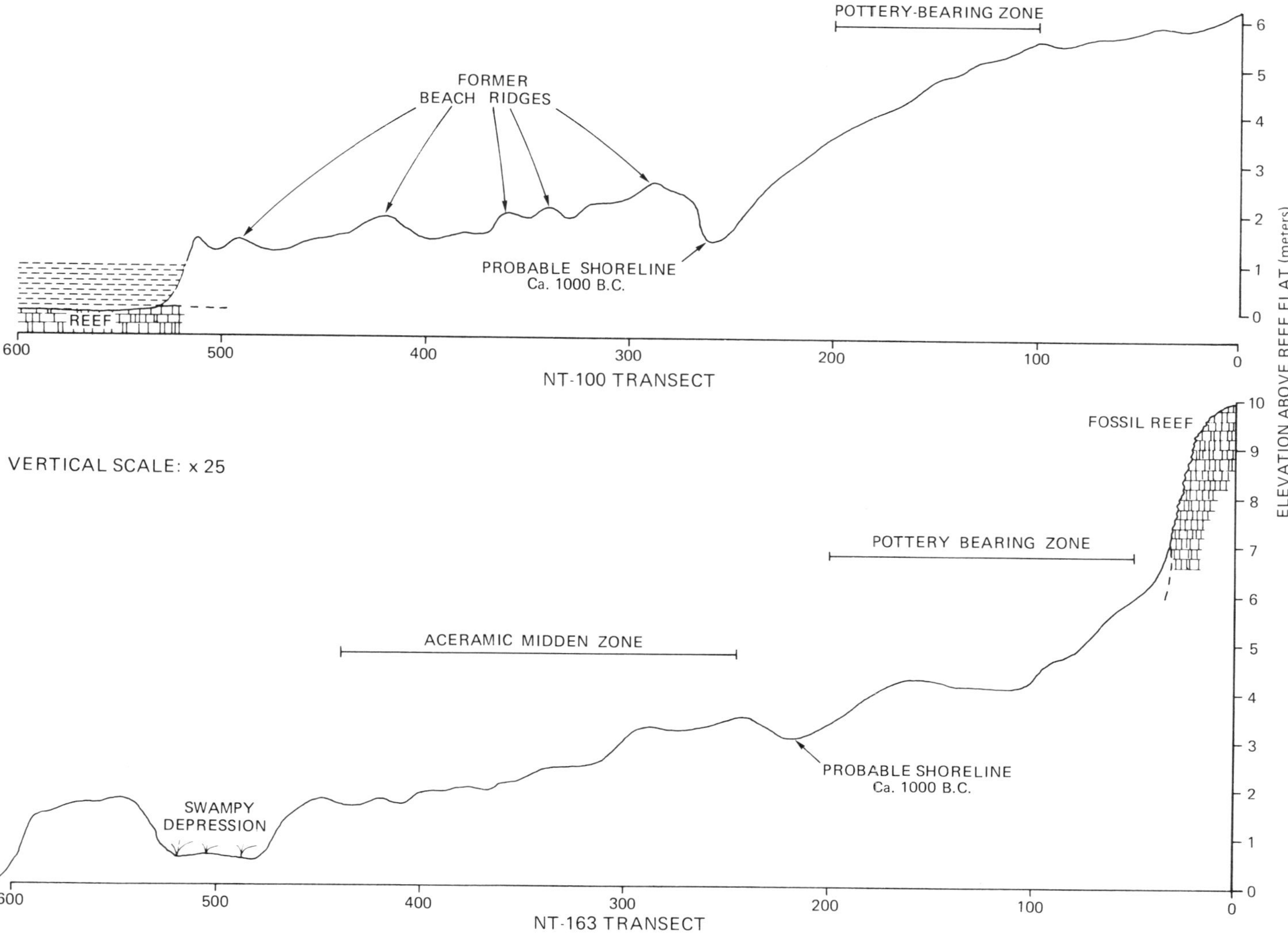

Figure 49. Transects through the pottery-bearing zone and adjacent environments at Sites NT-100 and NT-163.

In 1976, the site was planted with large aroids *(Alocasia)* and some yams *(Dioscorea esculenta);* mature coconuts dot the terrain. These food crops placed constraints on excavation strategy. In traversing the site and examining the exposed ground between gaps in the dominant weed cover *(Pueraria lobata),* we observed substantial quantities of shell midden, many fire-cracked oven stones, large fragments of heavy *Tridacna* shell (probably the detritus of shell adz manufacture), volcanic glass flakes and cores, and ceramic sherds. These materials, and the carbon-rich black organic loam in which they were found, are the dominant constituents of the indigenous soil category, *fasifasi'ifeo.* Aside from this scatter of surface cultural materials, which decreases sharply at the seaward and inland edges of the zone, there were no in situ surface indications of human occupation, such as structures or earthworks. A view of the site during test excavations is shown in figure 50.

Excavation

Previous Work. Lolokoka was discovered and designated NT-90 by Rogers in 1971 (Rogers 1973; 1974). Of the 11 locations on Niuatoputapu where Rogers discovered surface ceramics, NT-90 appeared to have the heaviest concentration of sherds, and was thus selected by him for test pitting. Rogers excavated a single test trench, 3.0 x 0.8 m, in the northwest corner of the site, and accurately described the stratigraphy: a disturbed Layer I garden soil, a relatively undisturbed cultural Layer II, and the basal sterile sand, Layer III (1973:9). The test yielded 233 sherds (1974: table 1), including two decorated with Lapita-style dentate-

Figure 50. Excavation in progress at the Lolokoka site. The central ridge is visible in the distance.

stamped motifs. Several other portable artifacts were recovered, including a complete *Tridacna* -shell adz and a fragment of a polished basalt adz. At the base of Layer II, Rogers exposed an earth oven containing fish, rat, and bird bones (1973:10).

Procedure. Initial reconnaissance of Lolokoka in 1976 indicated that the sherds, midden, and fire-cracked oven stones were distributed over a zone about 60 m wide (N–S). Lacking surface indications of specific activity areas, we decided to excavate according to a multi-stage sampling strategy. For the first stage, the zone of surface artifacts and midden was gridded out (fig. 51) over an area of 40 m E–W and 60 m N–S (2,400 m^2) and subdivided into 100 m^2 sampling strata. A test excavation unit of 0.25 m^2 was selected for each 100 m^2 stratum, using random numbers. The purpose of these 24 random sampling units (totalling 6 m^2 or a 0.25% sample of the total frame) was to obtain an assessment of sherd, artifact, and faunal distribution over the total zone at Lolokoka. The results of this first phase could then be used to select areas for more extensive excavation.

Although small, the sample provided by these random-sample units is sufficient to discover all but very rare artifact classes, and to provide a reasonable estimate of the more frequent classes such as sherds and shellfish midden. Following Nance (1981), the Negative Hypergeometric Distribution indicates the number of randomly chosen grid units necessary to discover (on average) at least one item of some class present in a given number of grid units. In our Lolokoka sampling frame, the 24 random test units were sufficient to discover at least one item of any object class present in 4.2% or more of all grid units. Thus only relatively rare object classes would not be discovered during this initial sampling procedure.

During random sampling, we observed that the density of sherds, midden, and oven stones dropped off sharply near the inland and seaward edges of the 60 m-wide sampling frame. In the second sampling stage we excavated a further 7 test units (0.25 m^2) on a transect line (the J-line shown in figure 51) extending 40 m seaward and 30 m inland of the random sampling grid. These units confirmed that our sampling grid indeed extended over the major portion of the site, since only sparse cultural materials were recovered in the additional transect pits. We could therefore be confident in the procedure of confining further work to the 60 m-wide zone defined by the inland and seaward edges of the grid.

Preliminary analysis of the random-sample tests indicated that the seaward most 20 m of the sampling frame had a substantially higher density of sherds, oven stones, volcanic glass flakes, and shellfish midden than the 40 m-wide inland portion of the zone (although, this inland area does contain "pockets" of more highly concentrated cultural material). Thus, the third stage of our sampling procedure was the excavation of five 1 x 2 m trenches within this seaward portion of the site to obtain still larger samples of cultural material and to search for intact features such as hearths, pits, and postmolds. These trenches, shown in figure 51, were placed in areas of high concentration of cultural materials as revealed by the random sampling stage. An additional 1 x 2 m trench was also dug in the east-central portion of the site grid to explore an area of unusually deep deposition (which subsequently revealed a buried well, or *vai tupu).* The 11.5 m^2 excavated by means of these trenches (two trenches incorporated initial test pits) successfully expanded our sample of decorated sherds, portable artifacts, and other cultural materials, and exposed a number of cultural features.

At this stage, the investigation of NT-90 was suspended while operations were shifted to several other localities in the ceramic-bearing zone. After completion of these latter excavations, we were able to assess adequately the significance of Lolokoka as the only site containing substantial quantities of dentate-stamped decorated Lapita sherds and other materials indicative of early settlement. We thus initiated a fourth sampling stage at NT-90 by conducting two areal excavations within the zone of highest concentration of cultural materials. Since the gridded area used for the initial sampling frame was under active cultivation (thus placing restrictions on the size of excavation units), we located these areal exposures to the west and east of the sampling frame, but within the same zone of highly concentrated artifacts and midden. Area A (fig. 52), to the east of the site grid, exposed 24 m^2, while Area B, to the west, included 8 m^2. These areal excavations revealed several intact features, and greatly expanded the sample of decorated pottery and portable artifacts.

Stratigraphy, Age, and Depositional Sequence

The stratigraphy of NT-90 is both simple and shallow, reflecting considerable post-depositional disturbance. Two major layers are recognizable: the cultural component (Layer I) with both disturbed and undisturbed facies, and the underlying parent dune sands (Layer II) which sometimes contain sparse cultural materials in the uppermost portion. Layer I has developed from Layer II parent material (calcareous marine sand with coral and shell fragments) by the addition of substantial quantities of charcoal and ash, shellfish, bone, and other organic materials, and more recently (since the pottery zone has been under second growth and shifting cultivations) by leaf litter and humus. Detailed descriptions of the layers and their

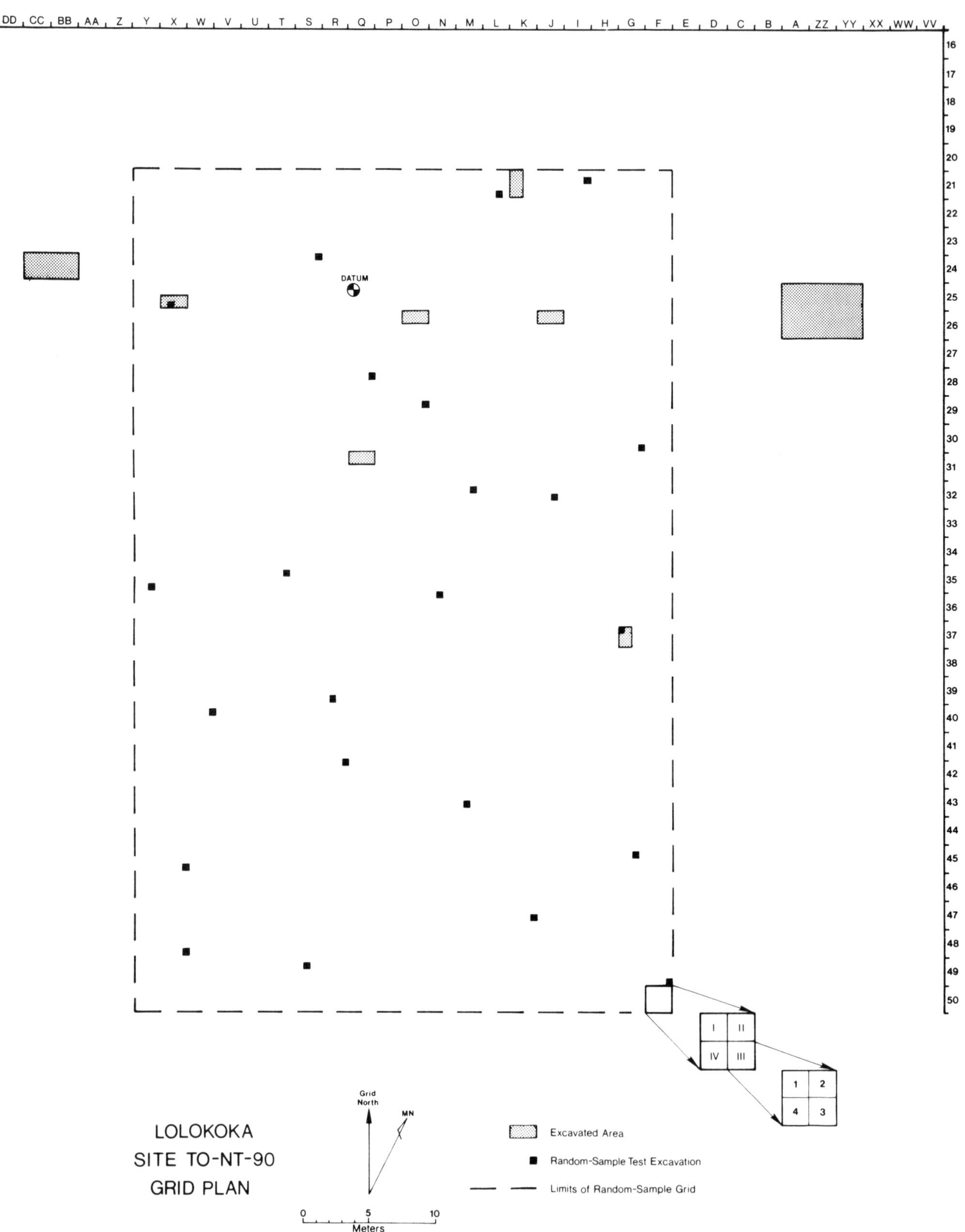

Figure 51. Random-sampling grid frame and test excavations, and locations of additional test trenches and areal excavations at NT-90, Lolokoka.

Figure 52. Completed Area A excavation at Site NT-90; view towards the north.

subdivisions follow, and typical stratigraphic profiles of the site are shown in figure 53.

Layer	*Description*
IA.	Present garden soil and extensively reworked cultural deposit. Very dark gray (5 YR 3/1) silt loam with much partially decomposed organic material. Angular to subangular blocky structure, generally very fine (5 mm). Friable consistence when moist. Sherds in this layer generally rounded, and shell midden "chalky" and weathered due to action of humic acids.
IB.	Less disturbed cultural deposit, often with intact features near base. Very dark gray (5 YR 3/1) sandy loam. Structure generally loose; very friable when moist. Sherds in this layer do not exhibit much edge wear, and shell and bone midden are well preserved.
IIA.	Unconsolidated calcareous sand, often with limited quantities of sherds or midden material in the uppermost portion. Grains sub-angular to sub-rounded, coarse (0.5-1 mm). White to very pale brown (10 YR 8/2-4). Consistence loose, non-coherent. Generally structureless but containing small dispersed concretions of sand cemented with $CaCO_3$. Concretions are weakly to strongly cemented, and range from 2 to 9 cm in diameter.
IIB.	Basal calcareous sand, strongly cemented with $CaCO_3$ (can be broken only with a crowbar), and culturally sterile. White (10 YR 8/2). Coarse sand grain size.

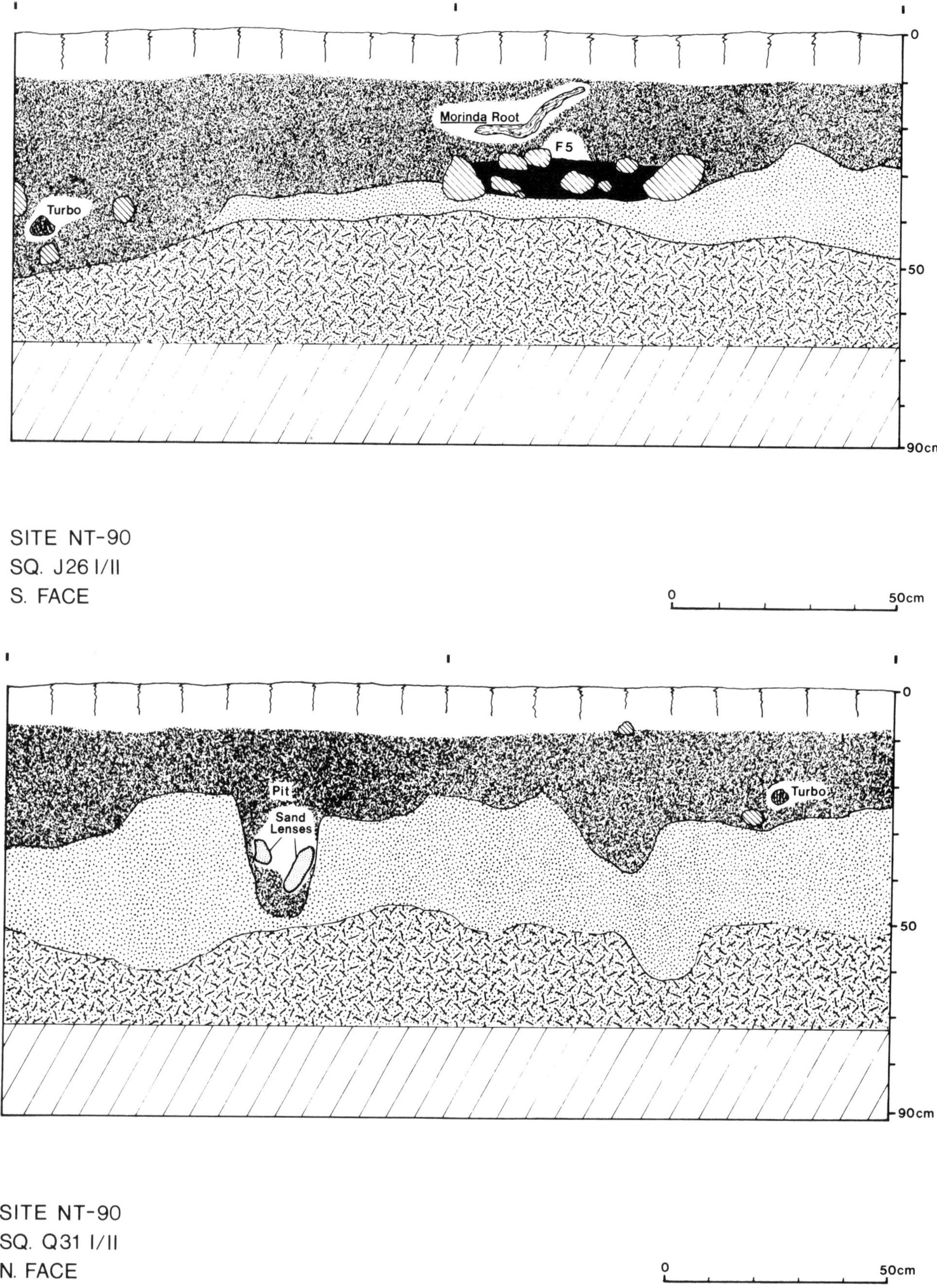

Figure 53. Stratigraphic profiles of selected excavation units, Site NT-90.

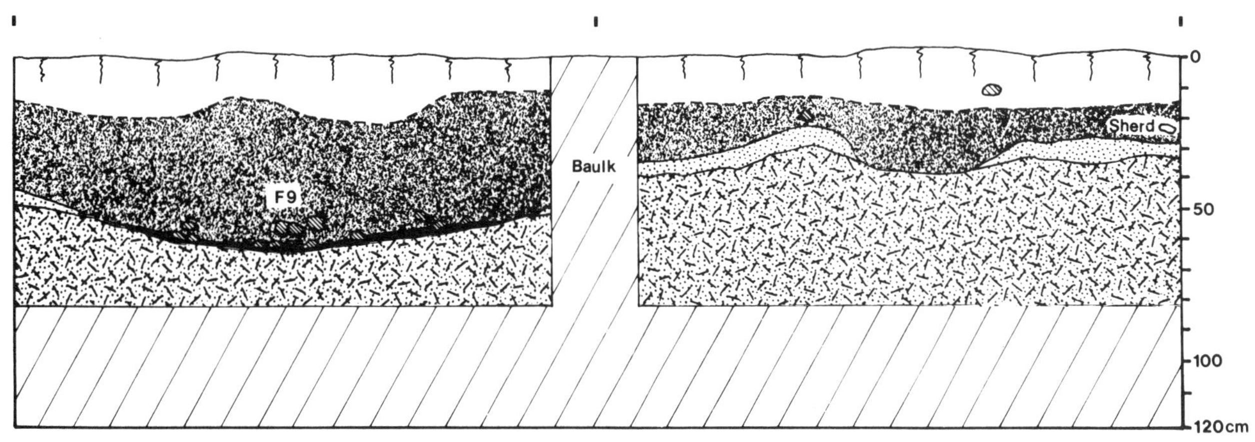

SITE NT-90
SQ. BB24, CC24
N. FACE

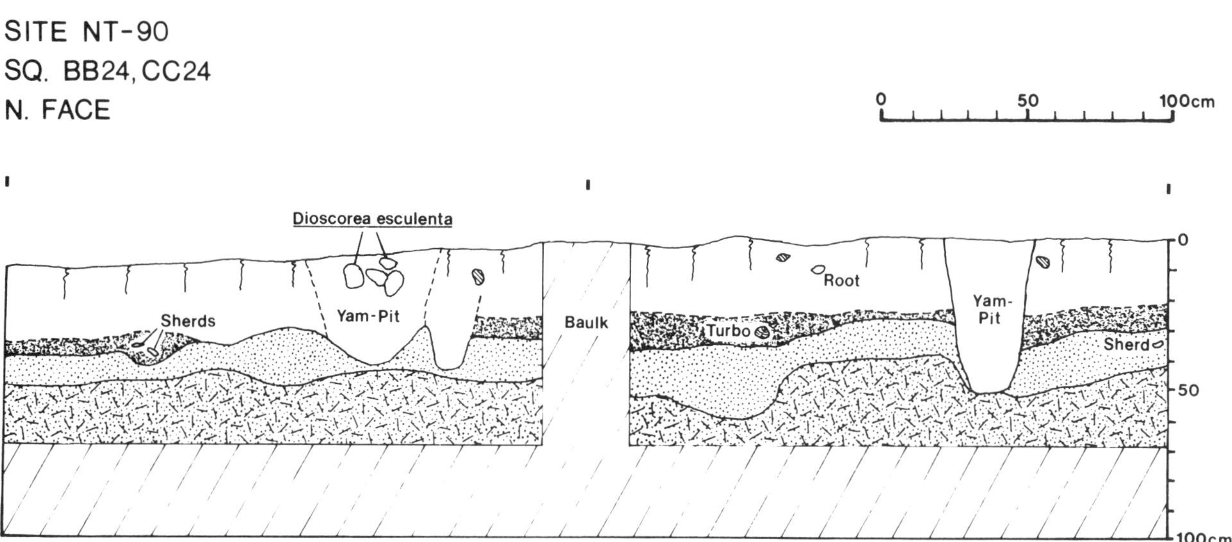

SITE NT-90
SQ. ZZ25, ZZ26
E. FACE

Key to Layers in Ceramic Bearing Sites

Ia
Ib
Ic
Id
IIa
IIb

Sediment samples from Layers IB and IIA were analyzed in the laboratory for grain size and other characteristics. The sample from IB displays a bimodal grain size distribution with a predominance of coarse sand, poorly sorted and strongly fine-skewed (see Folk 1974:46-47). Mean phi size is 0.81 ± 1.25. The Layer IIA sample shows a similar bimodal distribution (fig. 54) with a mean phi of 0.68 ± 1.22. These results clearly demonstrate the common sedimentary origin of both deposits: typical beach sand deposits (Visher 1969:1104). In both samples, 84% of grains consisted of calcareous particles, about 5% of finely-divided charcoal and other organic materials, and the remaining 10% of a mixture of small igneous rock fragments, mineral grains, and clay particles.

The shallow, disturbed stratigraphy at NT-90 and other Niuatoputapu Lapita sites creates serious problems for archaeological interpretation. Not only is a well-stratified succession of occupation horizons lacking, but the primary cultural deposit (Layer I) has suffered a great deal of mixing. Intact features and large sherds were often found at the base of Layer IB and cutting into Layer IIA, but the higher portions of Layer IB and all of Layer IA were usually thoroughly churned. Several kinds of pedoturbation are responsible for this mixing, the most important being yam and banana gardening during the period since the site was abandoned as an active habitation locus. During the planting and harvesting of yams (the principal species cultivated in the *fasifasi'ifeo* soils is *Dioscorea esculenta),* holes of about 30 to 50 cm in depth and of an equivalent diameter are dug. Since the cultural deposit rarely exceeds 50 cm in depth, the effect of this agricultural activity is obvious. Rogers first noted the pedoturbation problem with Niuatoputapu sites, and estimated that a given plot of ground might be "thoroughly disturbed every 170 years" (1973:7), assuming a 10-year fallow period, "with all successive yam holes being dug in previously undisturbed ground." If the *fasifasi'ifeo* zone has been under such a regime of yam cultivation since about the mid-first millennium A.D., it is conceivable that the zone could have been completely overturned some eight or nine times. However, the assumption that all new yam holes are dug in previously undisturbed ground is probably false, and a certain proportion of the lower cultural deposit in NT-90 and other sites has remained unchurned. This does not obviate the problem that a great deal of the cultural deposit has been reworked. This situation is not unique to Niuatoputapu, and has plagued archaeologists working on Lapita sites in Tongatapu (Groube 1971:298), the Reef Islands (Green 1976), Nendo in the Santa Cruz group (McCoy, pers. comm. 1977), and Mussau (Kirch 1987).

While mixing of the cultural deposit through cultivation destroys many intact features and breaks down or blurs the "fine-grained" structure of the site, it apparently has not affected broader or "coarse-grained" patterns of artifact and midden distribution. These patterns are amenable to analysis by trend-surface averaging of densities. A further complication with the Lolokoka site, however, is that materials deriving from a fairly lengthy period of occupation or site use (or from successive phases of occupation) cannot be temporally or stratigraphically distinguished. Radiocarbon age determinations on *Tridacna* shell from NT-90 (discussed in full below) indicate that this locality was settled as early as 1300 to 1200 B.C. However, the presence of later plain ware indicates that the site was also occupied (either continuously or intermittently) throughout the first millennium B.C. and perhaps well into the first millennium A.D. Thus, while NT-90 is the oldest known archaeological component on Niuatoputapu and probably represents a locus of initial settlement, it also contains later ceramic materials which cannot be stratigraphically separated. Fortunately, the other two major Lapitoid sites excavated (NT-93 and -100) have more limited occupation spans. Comparing the NT-90 assemblage with those from these latter sites, it is possible to argue that materials found only at NT-90 were associated with the earliest occupation phases. These include the dentate-stamped Lapita ceramics, exotic chert flakes, and certain other portable artifact classes (see chapter 5). In short, while the Niuatoputapu ceramic-zone stratigraphy is not ideal, it is not analytically intractable.

To summarize the Lolokoka depositional sequence, the site was first settled around 1300-1200 B.C., by Lapita colonists who constructed a small hamlet on a sandy flat of calcareous sand just inland of the former shoreline. Over about 1,500 years of continuous or intermittent (and certainly shifting) habitation, a concentrated deposit of carbon-rich midden accumulated to an average depth of 0.5 m over an area of several thousand square meters (the site extends both east and west beyond the 2,400 m^2 sampling frame). Following seaward aggradation of the shoreline, Lolokoka was eventually abandoned as an occupation locus and has reverted to second-growth vegetation. For an undetermined time span, beginning probably in the first millennium A.D., the site was repeatedly used for yam, banana, and aroid gardening, resulting in extensive reworking of cultural materials, especially in the upper 30 cm.

Cultural Features and Artifacts

The NT-90 excavations yielded the largest assemblage of ceramics and other cultural materials

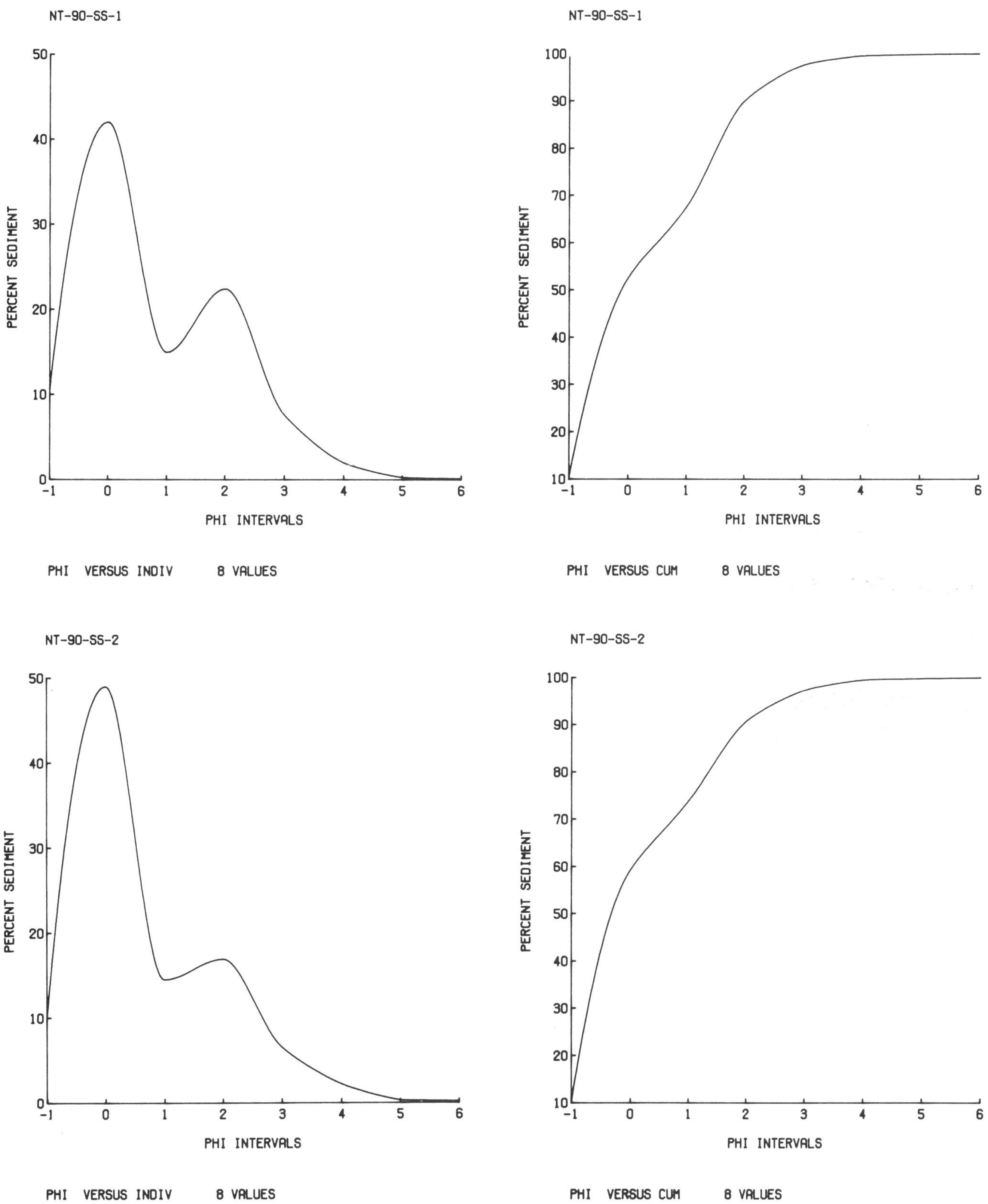

Figure 54. Frequency distributions of grain size classes (phi scale) for sediment samples from Layer IB (NT-90-SS-1) and Layer IIA (NT-90-SS-2) from Site NT-90.

from the ceramic zone. Table 7 summarizes the NT-90 cultural content, including the distribution of major categories of material from the random sampling grid units, from additional trenches within the sampling frame, and from the area excavations. Ceramic sherds dominate the assemblage, with an average density of 451 ± 270 body sherds/m^2 over the entire sampling frame. Sherd density is considerably higher in the northern or seaward portion of the zone, averaging 528 body sherds/m^2 in the Area A excavation. NT-90 was the only site investigated within the ceramic zone that yielded substantial quantities of decorated sherds, including 61 examples of "classic" dentate-stamped Lapita decoration. Carinated sherds and handles are well represented. The ceramics are fully analyzed in chapter 5.

The second most frequently encountered artifact category consists of flakes and cores of volcanic glass, with an average density of 110 ± 88/m^2 over the sampling frame. The density of volcanic glass also is higher in the northern portion of the site, and in Area A averaged 163 flakes and cores/m^2. Site NT-90 yielded 38 flakes of chert, a material exotic to Niuatoputapu Island, possibly imported from Fiji and/or Futuna (see chapter 5). Other portable artifacts represented in the NT-90 assemblage include adzes of *Tridacna* shell and of stone, sea urchin spine and coral abraders, shell scrapers, and a variety of ornaments or exchange valuables.

Fifty-seven kilograms of molluscan midden (material retained in the 0.25-inch mesh sieves) were recovered from the 24 random sample test excavation units. The average density of shellfish over the sampling frame was 9.5 ± 7.7 kg/m^2, higher than at any other locality in the ceramic zone. The density of molluscan remains at Lolokoka is only slightly less than at the early settlement site of TK-4 on Tikopia Island, which is remarkable among Oceanic sites for the concentration of shellfish remains (Kirch and Yen 1982:125, 293-97). This high density of shell midden may reflect both the site's early age (with intensive exploitation of a pristine reef ecosystem by a colonizing propagule) and its lengthy occupation.

Although the extensive pedoturbation at Lolokoka disrupted the site's fine-grained structure, the coarse-grained distribution of cultural materials appears to be intact. Using the frequency data obtained from the random-sample excavations, trend-surface distribution patterns were calculated for body sherds, volcanic glass, and shell midden (cf. Hodder and Orton 1976). These averaged trend surfaces are depicted as contour plots in figure 55, which also shows the distribution of sherds decorated with dentate-stamped motifs. There are notable correspondences in the distribution of cultural materials over the site, especially the high density of cultural materials over the northern or seaward portion of the sampling frame. The southwest quadrant is a "trough" or area of low cultural material density. An area of high sherd density along the east-central margin of the sampling frame corresponds with the former well or *vai tupu* partially exposed during excavations (see below). This locality yielded large numbers of rims and handles from globular water vessels (Vessel Form 10), and the high concentration of sherds may represent a high rate of vessel breakage around the well. The majority of cultural materials ascribable to the early phase of Lapita occupation at NT-90 were derived from the northern half of the sampling frame, evident from the distribution of dentate-stamped sherds and of exotic chert flakes (fig. 55).

Ten features or non-portable artifacts were exposed at Lolokoka, as described in table 8. All were uncovered in the lower, relatively undisturbed portions of the deposit, particularly where they penetrate the underlying Layer II. Features 1, 2, and 8 are pits, presumably dug for the disposal of trash since they contain quantities of shell and bone midden (fig. 56). Feature 1 contained the skeletal remains of a pig. Features 5, 6, and 7 are typical earth ovens, consisting of shallow basins filled with fire-cracked volcanic oven stones in a matrix of ash and charcoal. A large oven (Feature [Fe] 9), associated with a concentration of oven stones (Fe 10), was exposed in the Area B excavation. This oven is considerably larger than normal household cooking ovens known from Polynesian ethnographic sources, and may have had a special function, such as the baking of turtle, shark, or other large sea animals, or of *Cordyline* roots (cf. Firth 1939, Pl. IIIB). Two postmolds (Fe 3, 4) were also discovered in the course of excavation.

An intriguing feature, located in units G37 and G38 of the sampling frame, was a deep pit or artificial excavation that we interpret as a well. This feature, which was only partly exposed, is seen in cross section in figure 57; its sloping southern wall penetrates the cemented Layer IIB. Such wells, called *vai tupu*, are still used by the Niuatoputapu people as a vital source of potable water on an island that lacks flowing streams. Our interpretation of this subsurface depression as a well was corroborated by the high concentration of broken, handled water vessels in its vicinity.

Summary

Several lines of evidence point to Lolokoka as the earliest site excavated on Niuatoputapu, and probably the island's colonization locality. These include the high density of molluscs and other marine fauna, typical of southwest Pacific colonization sites (such as TK-4 on Tikopia and RL-2 in the Reef Islands), the presence of

TABLE 7

SITE NT–90 CULTURAL CONTENT

MATERIAL	SURFACE	RANDOM-SAMPLE TESTS			TRENCHES AND EXTRA PITS	AREA A	AREA B
		TOTAL	$\bar{X}/m^2$	s. d.			
Ceramics							
Body sherds	8	2,706	451.0	270.24	8,843	12,677	4,928
Rims	14	94	15.7	11.9	217	290	133
Bases	1	154	25.7	20.2	236	674	324
Carinated sherds	3	4	0.7	1.5	22	36	18
Handles	4	3	0.5	1.8	12	4	2
Decorated	4	15	2.5	3.1	38	50	15
Chert Lithics		4	0.7	1.5	11	19	4
Volcanic Glass Lithics		660	110.0	88.2	2,561	3,926	1,631
Other Portable Artifacts	40	10	1.7	2.3	66	46	22
Shell Midden (kg)		57.01	9.5	7.7	—	—	—
Bone Midden (g)		102	16.9	22.6	289.0	272	119

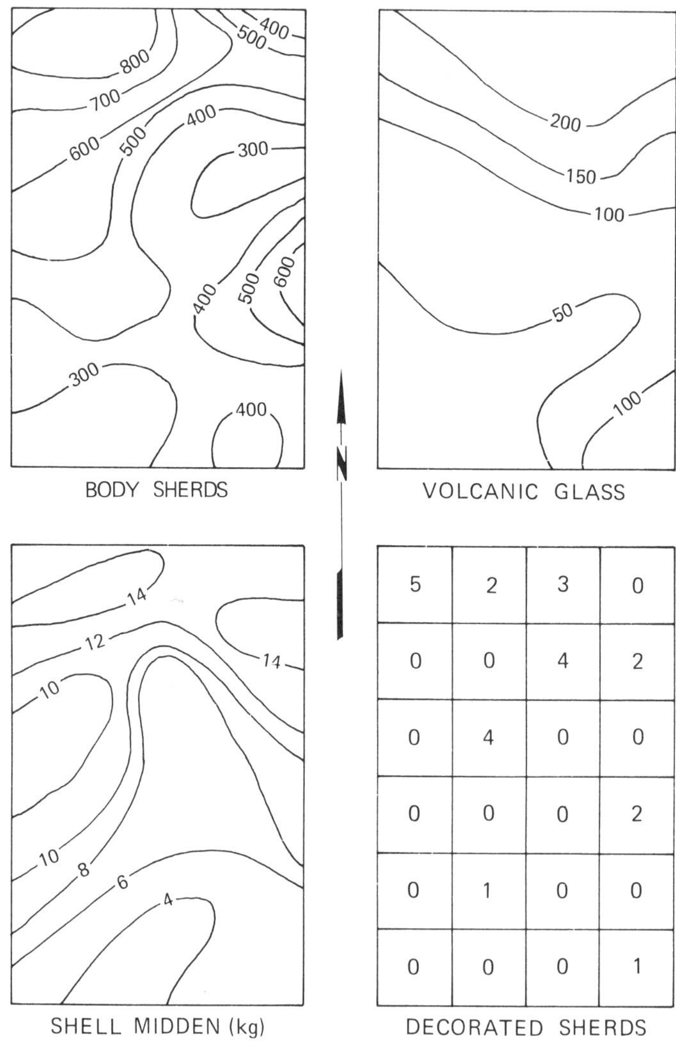

Figure 55. Trend-surface distributions of plain body sherds, volcanic glass flakes and cores, and shell midden within the NT-90 random sampling frame, and actual density of decorated sherds by 100 m^2 grid units.

Early Eastern Lapita dentate-stamped decorated sherds and exotic chert lithics, and the high density of ceramics in general. Radiocarbon age determinations indicate initial occupation late in the second millennium B.C. Occupation continued, perhaps intermittently, throughout most of the island's Lapitoid sequence.

Loto'aa Excavations (Site NT-100)

The designation NT-100 was given by Rogers (1973:13) to a portion of the ceramic zone occupied by the government agricultural farm east of Hihifo village. Rogers observed a dense scatter of sherds in "an abandoned sweet potato plot about 100 meters south of the Agricultural Officer's house," and excavated a 1 m test pit. In 1976, we included Loto'aa as one of three localities within the ceramic zone selected for intensive subsurface sampling. NT-100 lacks the Early Eastern Lapita component present at Lolokoka, but provides a good sample of Late Eastern Lapita and Polynesian Plain Ware ceramics. Loto'aa is thus later in age than the earliest NT-90 deposits, and roughly contemporaneous with those of the Pome'e-Nahau locality (NT-93).

Setting and Geomorphology

Loto'aa lies in a tract of second-growth forest and garden land between Hihifo and Vaipoa villages that is operated as an agricultural extension farm by the Tongan government. The tract is bordered on the inland

TABLE 8

CULTURAL FEATURES EXCAVATED AT SITE NT-90

FEATURE NO.	TYPE	PROVENIENCE	DIMENSIONS	DESCRIPTION AND COMMENTS
1	Pit	G30 III (3) Layer IB 20–52 cm	Appr. 1 m diam 32 cm deep	Probable trash pit with rounded bottom, only partially exposed by test excavation. Bottom of pit penetrates Layer II. Lowest 5-15 cm of pit fill consists of dark gray stained sand with pig cranial and mandible fragments, scapula. Upper 15-20 cm of pit fill consists of concentrated shellfish midden, loosely compacted, with *Cerithium* sp. dominant. Some plain sherds also in pit fill.
2	Pit	Q28 II (3) Layer IIB	unknown diam 20 cm deep	Probable trash pit, only partially exposed by test excavation. Fill of dark gray to black, carbon-rich midden with sherds, much shellfish.
3	Postmold	M32 II (4) Layer IB	20 cm diam 25 + cm deep	Circular, oval-bottom postmold cut into Layer II and first visible at Layer IB/II contact. Filled with Layer IB midden including some sherds.
4	Postmold	X48 III (3) Layer IB 38–55cm	32 cm diam 17 + cm deep	Circular, rounded bottom postmold cut into Layer II and first visible at Layer IB/II contact. Filled with Layer IB midden.
5	Oven	J 26I Layer IB	50 cm diam 10 cm deep	Shallow earth oven with concentrated fire cracked basalt oven stones (reddened) in ashy matrix. No large charcoal pieces. Base of oven lies directly on Layer IIA. Contained one small body sherd and some burned shellfish.
6	Oven	A25 I/II Layer IB 34–54 cm	125 cm diam 20 cm deep	Large, basin-shaped earth oven, filled with 214 fire-cracked, blackened volcanic oven stones. Ash and charcoal concentrated in lower 5 cm. Base of feature rests directly on cemented Layer IIB.
7	Oven	A26 I-IV Layer IB 30–50 cm	95 cm diam 20 cm deep	Shallow earth oven containing approximately 100 fire-cracked volcanic oven stones in an ashy matrix; no large charcoal pieces.
8	Pit	A26 I/IV Layer IB 36–68 cm	60 cm diam 32 cm deep	Round trash pit, filled with dense concentration of shellfish midden, *Cypraea*-shell scraper, and one decorated sherd. Cut into Layer IIB.
9	Oven	CC24 Layer IB 39–63 cm	2 x 1.3 m (partial) 24 cm deep	A large, elongated oven. Base lined with 537 fire-cracked volcanic oven stones, in a thin matrix of ash and charcoal. The feature rests directly on Layer IIB. Probably associated with Feature 10.
10	Rock Concentration	BB24 IV Layer IB 23–52 cm	70 x 94 cm (partial) 19 cm deep	Concentration of 229 volcanic rocks, some fire-cracked and blackened. Rocks range from 6 to 23 cm long. These probably represent oven stones stockpiled for use in adjacent Feature 9 oven.

side by the Hala Fakalava, and on the seaward side by the Hala Ma'atu. Running directly through Loto'aa and connecting with these two roads is a straight tractor road that has been cleared by hand. This road provided a convenient transect, perpendicularly bisecting the ceramic zone of *fasifasi'ifeo* soil. A view of the site taken along this transect is shown in figure 58.

The ceramic zone at NT-100 occupies an elevated beach terrace, with a series of old beach ridges and depressions to seaward (see fig. 49). The terrace slopes gradually seaward, ending in a depression that represents the original shoreline or active beach at the time of initial site occupation. With continued progradation of the island's leeward shoreline, a series of beach ridges have accumulated over a horizontal span of about 350 m. On the inland side, the Pleistocene Terrace rises abruptly about 100 m inland of the pottery zone.

Figure 56. Area A excavation at Site NT-90. Large circular stain in the foreground is a trash pit.

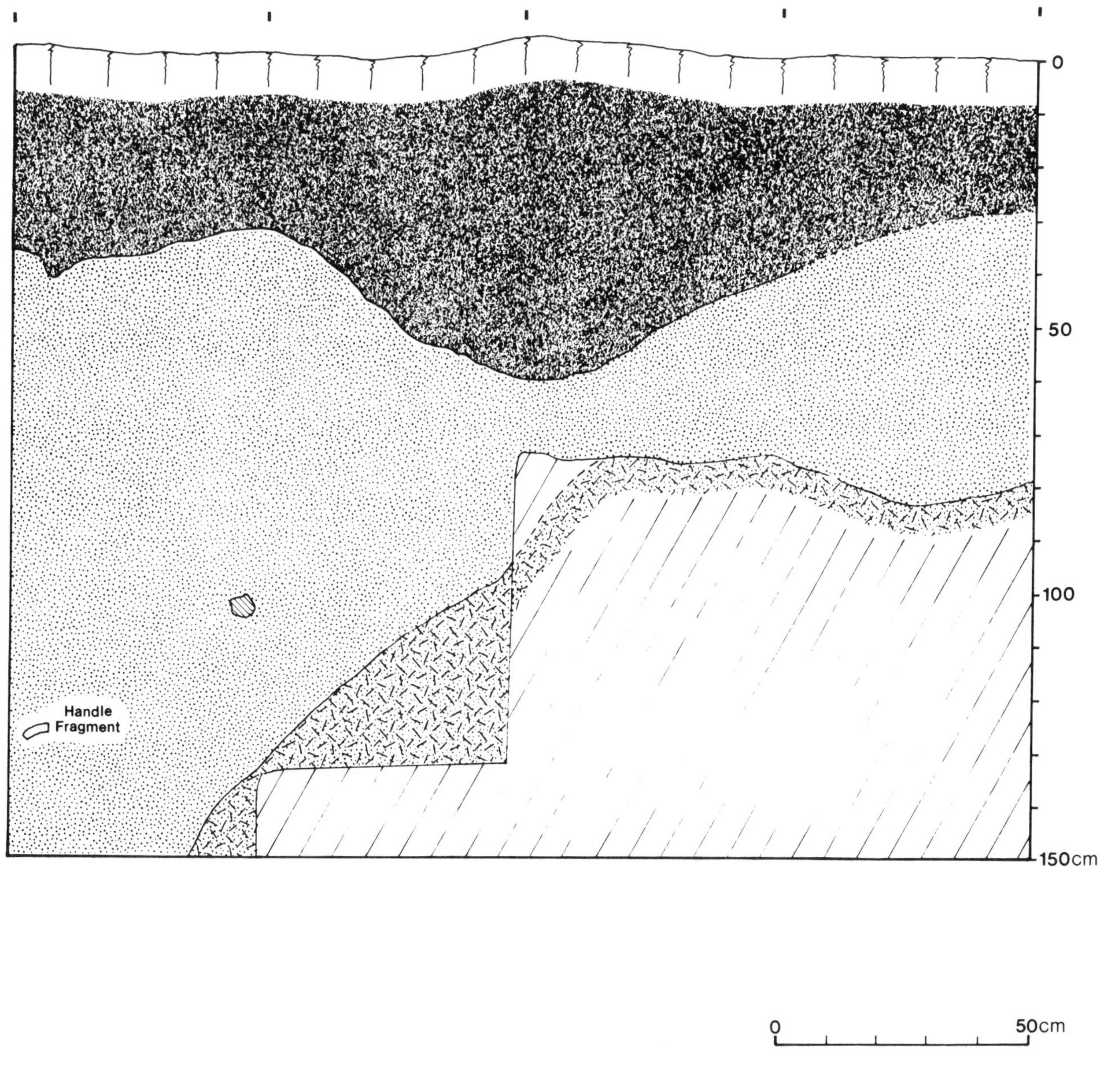

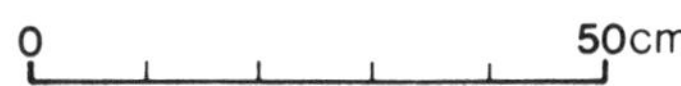

Figure 57. Stratigraphic profile of the east face of grid units G37 and G38 at Site NT-90.

Excavation and Stratigraphy

Operations at NT-100 were begun by staking out a baseline, oriented on an azimuth of 314° E, down the center of the tractor road across the Loto'aa compound. Along this baseline, elevations were taken from the base of the Pleistocene Terrace, across the old beach terrace, and over the more recent series of accumulated beach ridges, providing a picture of the geomorphological sequence of coastal progradation. The transect was later extended across the reef flat to allow for ecological sampling (the Senee transect of Dye 1983, fig. 4).

Site NT-100 was excavated along a systematic transect, with 1 m^2 units positioned at 10 m intervals across the entire width of the ceramic zone. Units were excavated along a line parallel to the baseline, but offset 5 m to the east, just off the edge of the tractor road, to avoid any disturbances caused during road clearance. Units were designated by their distance from the inland origin point of the transect baseline. This transect sampling method was chosen to: (1) determine the inland and seaward boundaries of the pottery zone; (2) determine the distribution of cultural materials laterally across the zone; and (3) relate the distribution of cultural materials to the local geomorphological setting. Once the initial transect units had been excavated and the area of highest sherd density determined, four additional 1 m^2 units were excavated to increase the sample of cultural materials from this central portion of the zone. Two of these additional units were dug adjacent to transect Unit 220, forming a 1 x 3 m trench. Two units were positioned 10 m east and west of the transect line.

Stratigraphy at NT-100 closely parallels that at NT-90. A composite stratigraphic section across the ceramic zone at NT-100 is shown in figure 59, and three representative profiles are provided in figure 60. The thickness of Layer IB (the relatively undisturbed cultural deposit) varied across the zone, disappearing completely in shallower areas where the deposit had been thoroughly reworked by gardening activity. In the central portion of the zone, however, Layer IB was quite thick (70 cm in Unit 210). In this area, a darker zone of concentrated charcoal-rich soil (dark to very dark gray in color), about 20 cm thick, could be distinguished in the middle portion of Layer IB (itself brown to yellowish brown in color).

Sediment samples from Layers IA, IB, and IIA were analyzed. All samples display bimodal distributions of coarse and medium sand typical of beach sedimentary depositional environments (Visher 1969:1104). All samples are poorly sorted; Layer IA is coarse-skewed, whereas Layers IB and IIA are fine-skewed (Folk 1974:46-47). The mean phi sizes are: IA, 1.70 ± 1.46; IB, 1.69 ± 1.37; IIA, 1.37 ± 1.51. In Layer IA, 36% of the grains are non-calcareous, including charcoal and other organic matter, igneous rock fragments, and clay particles. The percentage of non-calcareous grains decreases to 28% in IB, and to 11% in IIA.

Figure 58. View of Site NT-100 along the transect line, with excavation unit 170 in the left foreground.

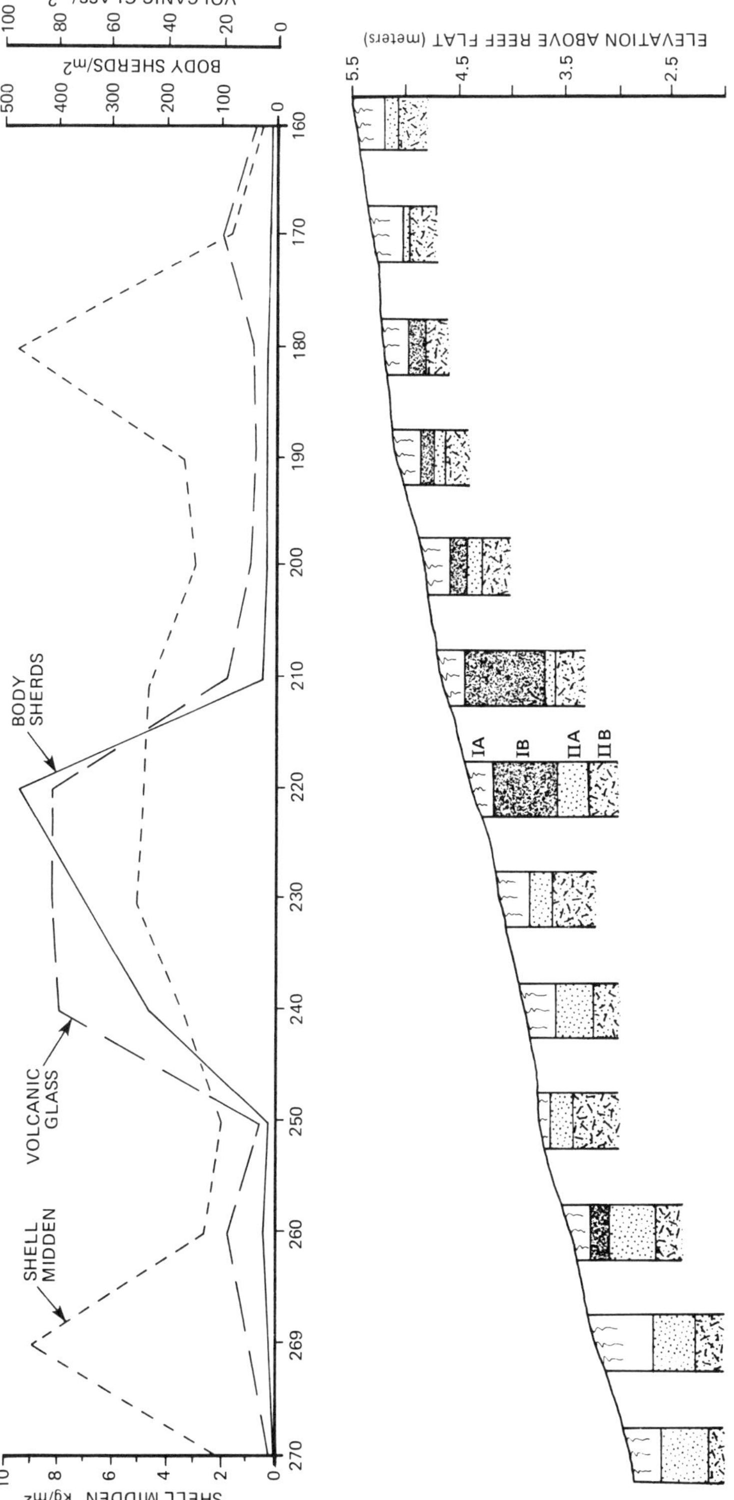

Figure 59. Excavation transect through Site NT-100, showing variation in test unit profiles, and frequency distributions of ceramic body sherds, volcanic glass flakes and cores, and shell midden.

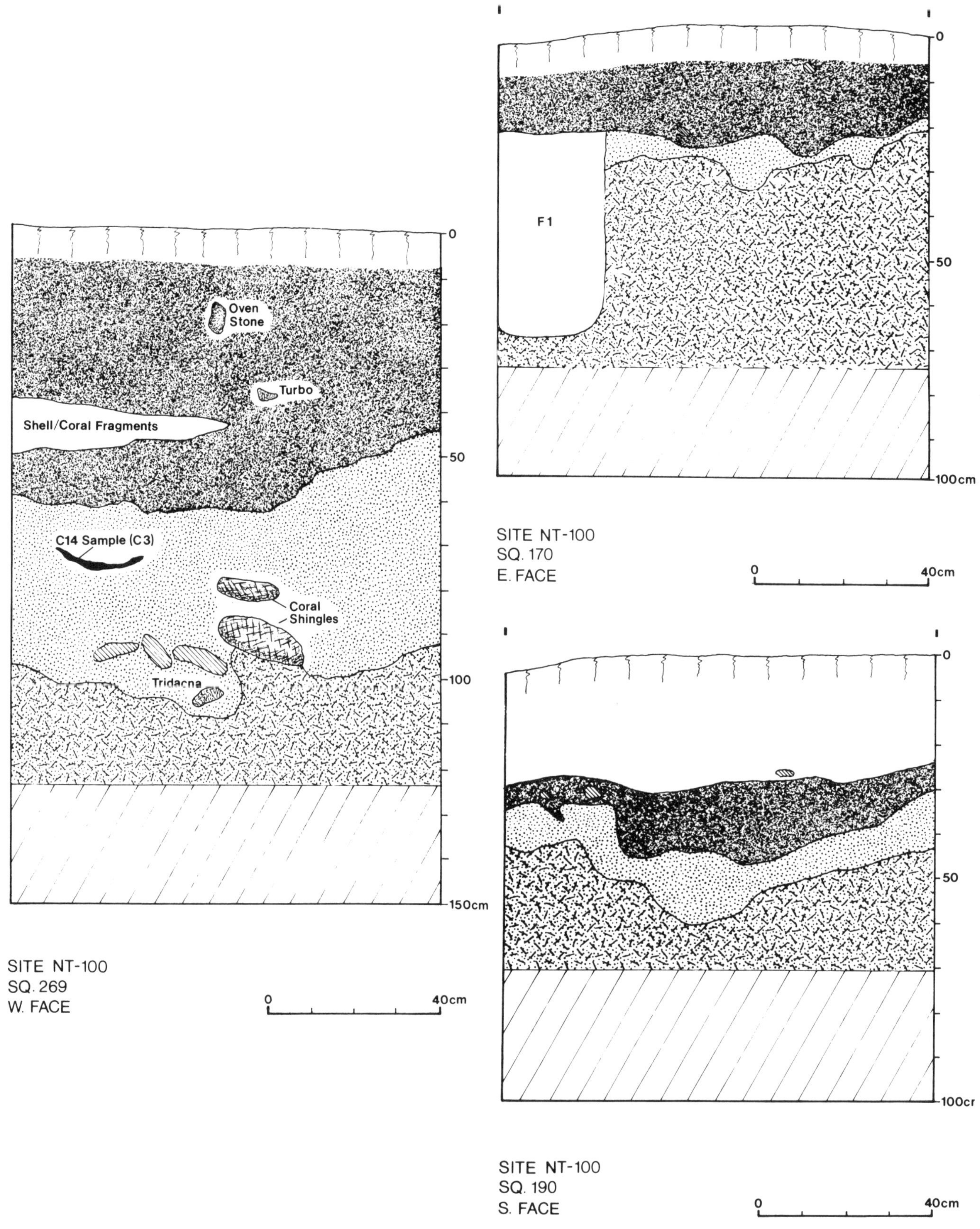

Figure 60. Stratigraphic profiles of selected excavation units, Site NT-100.

Five ^{14}C age determinations from NT-100 fall consistently in the middle to late first millennium A.D. (see Chronology, below). It is likely that the first occupation of this locality began somewhat earlier, however, based on comparison of ceramic styles with the known Lapitoid sequence in other Western Polynesian islands.

Cultural Features and Artifacts

The NT-100 excavations yielded a total of 2,385 ceramic sherds, 548 flakes and cores of volcanic glass, 1 chert flake, and 42 other portable artifacts. Analyses of bone and shellfish midden are presented in chapter 6.

Plain ware dominates the ceramic assemblage, with decorated sherds consisting of only four impressed rims and one sherd with red slip. The site also yielded one carinated body sherd and two handles. The vertical distribution of ceramics in the deep, central portion of the site is of particular interest. The following table shows the vertical distribution of sherds in the 1 x 3 m trench formed by Units 218 to 220, with the thick Layer IB subdivided into three 20 cm levels:

Layer	Level	Sherds/m^3
IA		198
IB	1	320
	2	560
	3	710
IIC		307

A steady reduction in sherd density per unit volume of cultural deposit is evidenced, from a high of more than 700/m^3 at the base of cultural layer IB, to less than 200/m^3 in the reworked Layer IA. Since the 80 cm of cultural deposit in this portion of NT-100 probably represents several centuries of Lapitoid occupation, these figures evidently reflect a gradual decline in the manufacture and use of ceramics in the latter half of the first millennium B.C. and first half of the first millennium A.D. (This conclusion assumes a relatively constant rate of deposition of the cultural deposit.)

It is instructive to compare the density of sherds in NT-100 with sherd densities in the other ceramic zone localities. The Area A excavations at NT-90 yielded an average sherd density of 1,430 sherds/m^3, more than twice that in the lowest component at NT-100. In Site NT-93, densities ranged from 284 to 470/m^3, equivalent to those of the upper portions of the Unit 218 to 220 trench at NT-100.

The horizontal distribution of cultural materials across the ceramic zone at NT-100 is shown diagrammatically in figure 59, with plots for sherd, volcanic glass, and molluscan midden density. Ceramics and volcanic glass have virtually identical distributions, with most material concentrated in a narrow band between Units 210 and 250. This pattern suggests that the main habitation zone at NT-100 was about 40 m wide. The molluscan midden, however, displays a strikingly different horizontal distribution pattern. While there is some increase in molluscan midden density between Units 210 and 250, the peaks of shellfish midden occur to either side of the area with the greatest density of artifacts. This pattern may reflect conscious disposal of food refuse away from the central habitation zone represented by the area between Units 210 and 250.

Only four features were uncovered in the NT-100 excavations (table 9). These are a typical earth oven with fire-cracked volcanic oven stones, a small single-use hearth (fig. 60), a pit of undetermined function, and a postmold.

Summary

Loto'aa was probably initially occupied in the latter half of the first millennium B.C., with the ceramics from the deepest deposits representing Late Eastern Lapita (notched rims, handled vessels, no dentate-stamping). These ceramics are similar to those from the Tavai Site (FU-11) on Futuna (Kirch 1981), dated to about 250 B.C. Loto'aa continued to be occupied until late in the first millennium A.D., as evidenced by the dominant Polynesian Plain Ware and by the radiocarbon age determinations. At the time of the site's initial use, the island's lee shore was at the foot of the beach terrace upon which NT-100 is situated. Subsequent progradation resulted in a series of dune ridges and depressions that have left the site 300 m inland of the present shoreline. Transect sampling demonstrated that a habitation zone about 40 m wide was the central focus of activity at the site, but that extensive midden dumping occurred to both landward and seaward of this zone.

Pome'e-Nahau Excavations (Site NT-93)

The ceramic zone runs immediately southwest of Falehau village, where swidden cultivations in 1976 revealed surface concentrations of fire-cracked rock, shellfish midden, and ceramics. The pottery zone here is cross cut by two named land tracts: Nahau (or Tu'akolo

TABLE 9

CULTURAL FEATURES EXCAVATED AT SITE NT–100

FEATURE NO.	TYPE	PROVENIENCE	DIMENSIONS	DESCRIPTION AND COMMENTS
1	Postmold	Unit 170 Layer IB 18 - 69 cm	35 cm diam 51 cm deep	Post mold cut from Layer IB into sterile Layer IIA sand; filled with midden.
2	Pit	Unit 269 Layer IB 40 - 60 cm	20 cm deep	Partially excavated pit (diam greater than 25 cm) with dispersed charcoal flecking.
3	Hearth	Unit 280 Layer IB 32 - 40 cm	40 cm diam 8 cm deep	Roughly circular, single-use, unlined hearth; basin-shaped. Charcoal and ash fill.
4	Oven	Unit 220/10E Layer IB 53 - 64 cm	75 cm diam 11 cm deep	Shallow earth oven filled with charcoal, ash, fire-cracked volcanic oven stones (ca. 10 cm diam).

Nahau) and Pome'e. Rogers (1973) had assigned site number NT-92 to the Nahau tract, and NT-93 to the Pome'e tract. Since the ceramic deposits constitute a continuous archaeological locality, we use the designation NT-93 to refer to the entire transect excavation conducted at Pome'e-Nahau.

Setting and Geomorphology

As shown in figure 61, the ceramic zone (defined by the limits of the excavation transect) lies approximately midway between the base of the Pleistocene Terrace and the present lagoon shore. Several late prehistoric mounds and associated borrow pits (Sites NT-9, -10, -15) are clustered on the Pleistocene Terrace. To the east of the transect are three low mounds (NT-34, -123, -124) of coral sand, one of which has been disturbed by the road running inland from Falehau and displays a remnant coral slab facing. These mounds are presumably late prehistoric *fa'itoka* or burial mounds.

Unlike that at NT-90 and -100, the terrain between the pottery zone at Pome'e-Nahau and the lagoon shoreline (a distance of 200 m) does not display prominent dune ridges and depressions. Rather, a gradual slope of sandy terrain terminates in a swampy foreshore, characterized by salt-tolerant grasses and sedges on a substrate of sandy muck and dead coral fragments. Thus the lagoon shore at Falehau has gradually prograded since initial Lapitoid settlement, but without the higher-energy events resulting in beach ridge features at sites to the southwest. The absence of beach ridge features at Falehau probably reflects the barrier reef and relatively deep lagoon lying offshore, which would have buffered high wave and surge action arising from occasional storms lashing the island's leeward side.

In 1976, the southern portion of Pome'e-Nahau was in second growth, dominated by *Hibiscus tiliaceous* and *Morinda citrifolia;* mature coconut palms dot the area. The northern portion of the Site was taken up with a large communal swidden, restricting excavation possibilities. The site surface at NT-93 was typical of the *fasifasi'ifeo* zone, with a high density of fire-cracked rock and shellfish fragments littering the dark, gray-black silt loam.

Excavation and Stratigraphy

A transect line running 330° E was cut through the tangled second growth covering the Pome'e portion of the site, and a baseline staked out. As at Loto'aa, a systematic transect was utilized, with 1 m^2 excavation

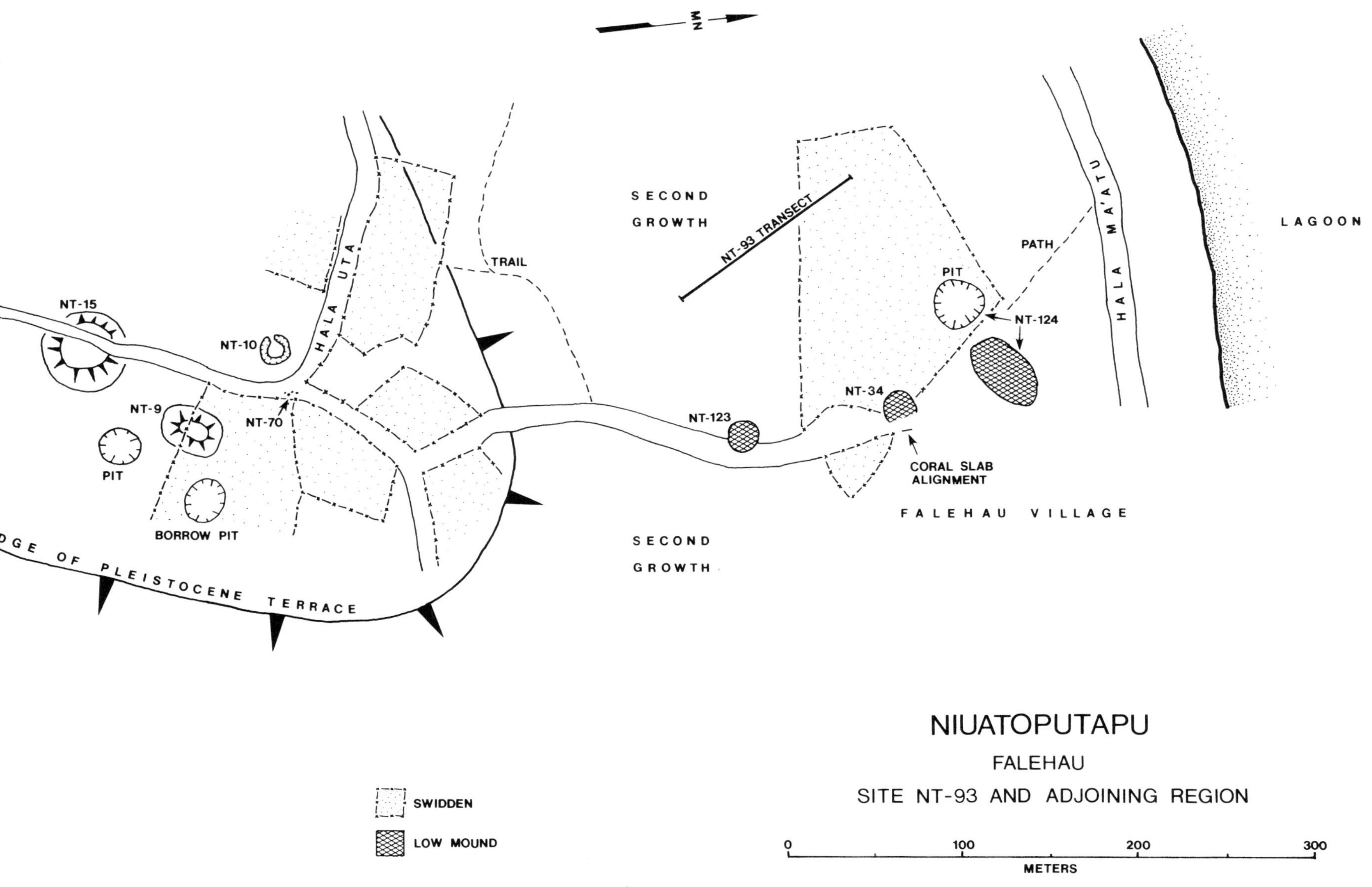

Figure 61. Map of the Site NT-93 transect and adjacent environment and archaeological features.

units placed along the transect at 10 m intervals. The 13 sampling units positioned along the transect thus provided a lateral section across the pottery zone. Additional units were opened up to expose certain features further and to obtain a larger sample of cultural materials in the central portion of the zone, in which sherd concentration was highest. Unit 90 was expanded into a 1 x 3 m trench, while four additional units of 1 m^2 were positioned 5 m to the east and west of the transect (Units 85/5E, 85/5W, 95/5E, 95/5W). Unit 150, which exposed a buried depression representing an old shoreline, was expanded into a 1 x 3 m trench, while Unit 170 was expanded an additional 1 m to the east to section fully a large earth oven. In all, 22 m^2 were excavated at NT-93.

The stratigraphy at NT-93 was more complex than at NT-90 or NT-100. A composite diagram showing the stratigraphic variation along the transect is given in figure 62, and examples of local stratigraphy are given in figure 63. The main stratigraphic units encountered at NT-93 are as follows:

Layer	*Description*
IA.	Present garden soil, consisting of a thoroughly reworked cultural deposit enriched through the addition of leaf litter and other organics. Dark brown (7.5 YR 3/2) silty loam, with granular structure, loose to friable consistence. Contains substantial quantities of fire-cracked oven stones, shellfish (molluscan remains have a chalky texture due to humic acid action), and ceramic sherds with rounded edges and eroded surfaces. Gradational contact with Layer IB.
IB.	Very dark gray (10 YR 3/1) cultural deposit; less disturbed than Layer IA, but with some signs of reworking in places. Deposit is rich in finely dispersed charcoal flecking. Sandy loam with crumb structure, or structureless; loose consistence. Discontinuous over transect, especially where gardening activities have penetrated deeply.
IC.	Cultural deposit, earlier than IB. A yellowish-brown (10 YR 5/4) to dark yellowish-brown (10 YR 4/6), medium-grained sand; structureless, with loose consistence. This deposit, containing bone and shell midden as well as ceramic sherds and artifacts, appears to represent the initial occupation at the site, and has not been much disturbed by later gardening activities. Layer IB features penetrate Layer IC in places.
IIA.	White (10 YR 8/2), medium to coarse-grained sand, representing the original ground surface upon which occupation commenced. Contains some sherds and midden in its upper portion, near the contact with IC. Otherwise culturally sterile.
IIB.	Indurated, white (10 YR 8/2), medium to coarse-grained calcareous dune sand, thoroughly cemented with calcium carbonate. Sterile.

An additional stratigraphic unit, Layer ID, was identified in Unit 150, which was subsequently expanded to a 1 x 3 m trench (fig. 64), the western profile of which is shown in figure 63. Layer ID consists of a depression with sloping sides, filled with a gray to grayish brown (10 YR 5/1-2), medium to coarse-grained sand. The base of the depression lies directly upon the Layer IIB indurated sand. Layer ID contains an unusually dense concentration of shellfish remains and ceramic sherds, as revealed in the transect diagram (fig. 62). The deposit is also completely capped by cultural Layer IC.

Layer ID represents what was originally a swampy depression just inland of a beach ridge at the time that NT-93 was initially occupied, and when the shoreline was considerably closer to the Pome'e-Nahau Site. Such swampy depressions are found today in various areas along the leeward coast, such as those between Hihifo village and the present shoreline. With the occupation of Site NT-93, this depression was used as a convenient dump for the disposal of trash, including molluscan remains and broken ceramics. (The swampy depression seaward of Hihifo village serves just such a purpose for the contemporary population.) With continued use of the depression as a trash dump, the ground surface was gradually elevated and the depression filled. Subsequently, the habitation area—which had formerly been situated inland of the depression—expanded over the filled depression (represented stratigraphically by the Layer IC cap over Layer ID).

Sediment samples were analyzed from Layers IA, IB, and IC. All samples are composed predominantly of medium sand, but IB and IC have secondary modes of coarse sand. All samples are poorly sorted. The mean phi sizes are: IA, 1.81 ± 1.23; IB, 1.76 ± 1.35; and IC, 1.66 ± 1.17.

In sum, the depositional sequence at NT-93 includes two major cultural layers, the earlier IC (representing initial settlement) and the later IB. Cultural materials in these two layers do not differ significantly, nor is there any discernible hiatus in occupation between these stratigraphic units. Layers IC

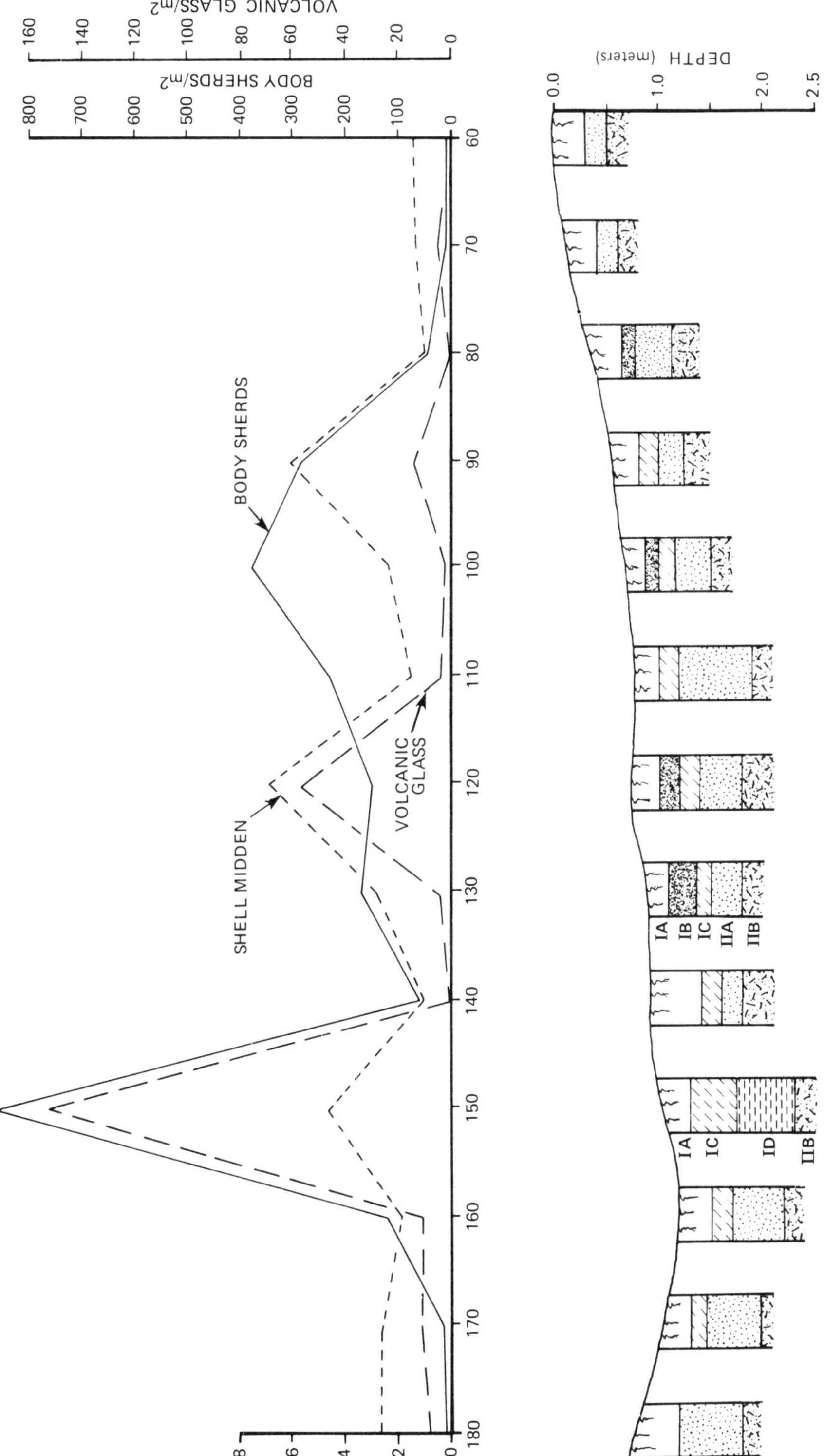

Figure 62. Excavation transect through Site NT-93, showing variation in test unit profiles, and frequency distributions of ceramic body sherds, volcanic glass flakes and cores, and shell midden.

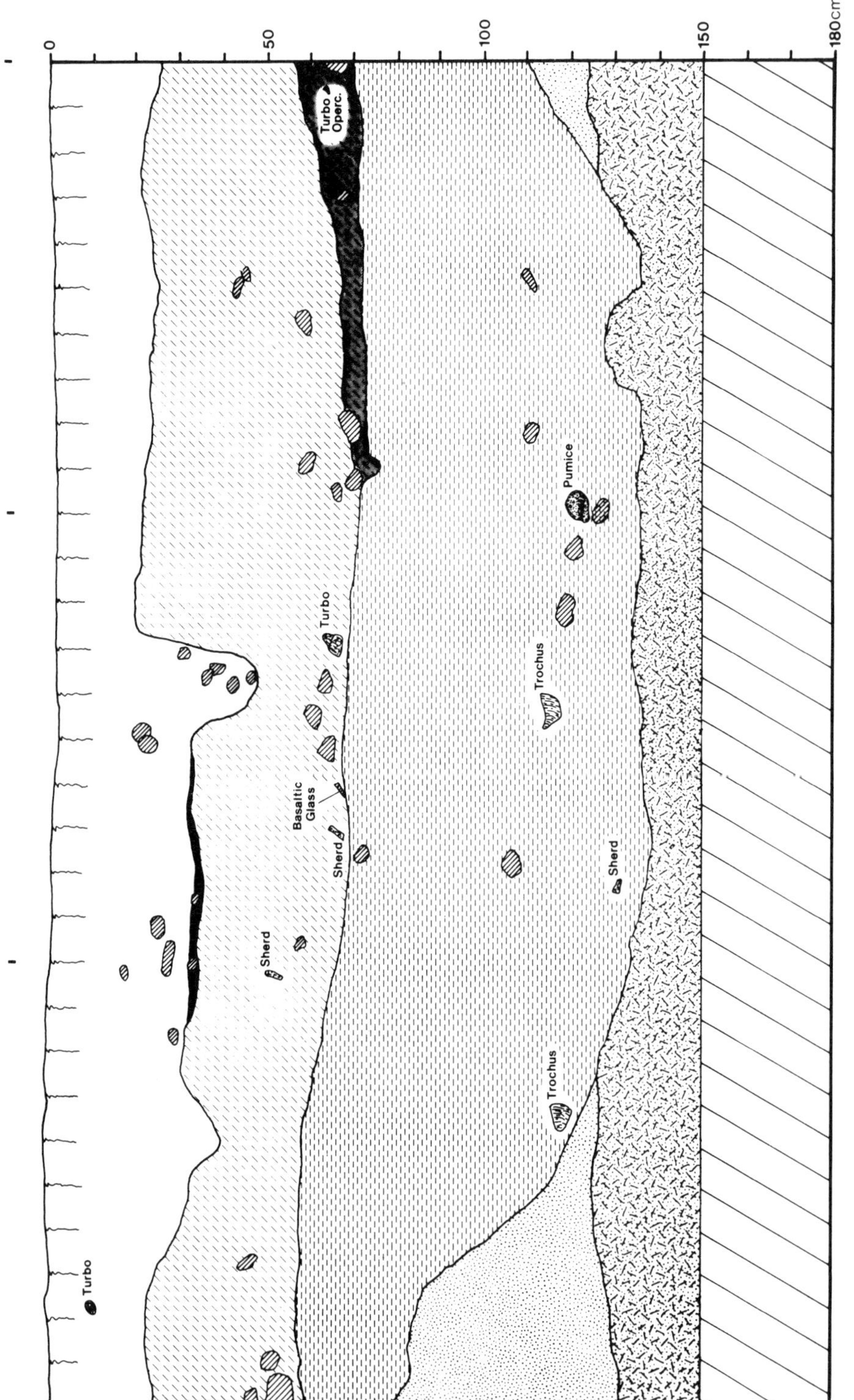
0
50
100
150
180cm
Turbo Operc.
Pumice
Turbo
Trochus
Basaltic Glass
Sherd
Sherd
Sherd
Trochus
Turbo
100cm
50
0
SITE NT-93
SQ. 149-151
W. FACE

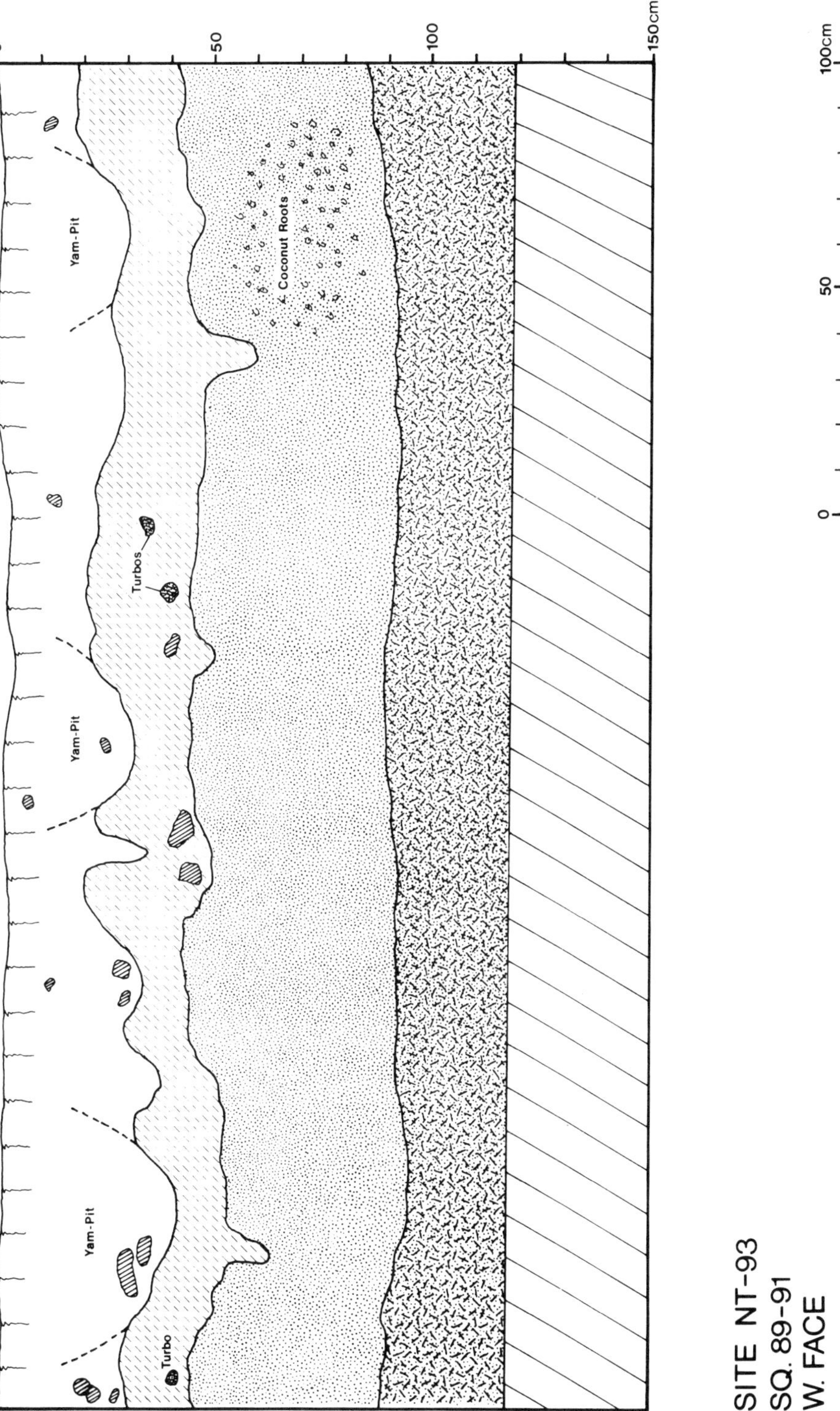

Figure 63. Stratigraphic profiles of selected excavation units, Site NT-93.

Figure 64. Units 149-151 at Site NT-93, cutting across former swampy depression.

and IB are distinguishable primarily by the greater amount of finely dispersed charcoal and clay particles contained in the latter. Over much of the site, the Layer IB occupation has been thoroughly reworked by recent gardening activities, resulting in Layer IA.

Two radiocarbon age determinations were made on samples from Site NT-93 (see Chronology, below). A sample of marine shells of several species (midden material in direct association with ceramics) from Layer IC of Unit 120 yielded a corrected age of A.D. 640 to 760, suggesting contemporaneity with the upper portions of NT-100. Charcoal from the oven (Feature 13) (see table 10) yielded a later date of A.D. 1230-1415 (corrected); however, this feature is not directly associated with the ceramics.

Cultural Features and Artifacts

The Pome'e-Nahau excavations yielded 5,635 ceramic sherds, of which 5,010 were plain body sherds.

Cores and flakes of volcanic glass total 784, but only a single flake of chert was found. Other excavated portable artifacts total 27 objects.

The ceramic assemblage from NT-93 can be characterized as Polynesian Plain Ware, since it lacks both dentate-stamped decoration and notched rims. The only decorated sherd is one example of paddle impressing. Three handles were recovered, suggesting the late persistence of the large, handled water vessel (Vessel Form 10, see chapter 5). Sherd density in the main area of the site (between excavation Units 90 and 110) ranged from 284 to 470 sherds/m^3, comparable to the upper component of Layer IB at Site NT-100.

The distribution of cultural materials along the NT-93 transect is displayed diagrammatically in figure 62. Ceramics and volcanic glass are concentrated between Units 80 and 130, suggestive of a central habitation area with an inland-seaward width of about 50 m, not unlike the situation at Loto'aa. As at NT-100, the distribution of shell midden is also bimodal, perhaps indicative of purposive dumping along the periphery of the habitation zone. A unique feature at NT-93 is the dense concentration of cultural materials in the former swampy depression centered at Unit 150.

The Pome'e-Nahau excavations exposed 13 cultural features, described in table 10. The stratigraphic relationships of these features to the main depositional units are diagrammed in figure 65. The earliest features at NT-93, all cut into Layer IIA and capped by Layer IC deposit, are two large pits (Fe 3, 4) and an earth oven (Fe 12). The pits are of particular interest, since they were most likely silos or storage pits for the semi-anaerobic fermentation of starch pastes, especially breadfruit. Pit ensilage of breadfruit and other starches was widely practiced in Polynesia; the fermented product (termed *maa* in Tongan, *masi* or *mahi* in other Polynesian languages) provided an important resource during times of food shortage induced by natural disaster (see Yen 1975; Kirch 1979:303, 1984a:132-35; Cox 1980 for discussions of food fermentation in Polynesia). Given the wide geographic distribution of this practice, and the lexical reconstruction of the term *ma/masi* to Proto-Polynesian language (Biggs, Walsh, and Waqa 1970), semi-anaerobic pit fermentation of starch must be of some antiquity in the southwestern Pacific. Direct archaeological evidence for the technique has, however, been scarce. Green (1969:121) interpreted several sealed pits beneath the Vailele Mound Site on Upolu, Samoa, as fermentation pits, while late prehistoric examples have been identified on the Polynesian Outliers of Anuta and Tikopia (Kirch and Rosendahl 1973; Kirch and Yen 1982:124, 333). Features 3 and 4 at NT-93 are thus significant in providing additional examples of a relatively early Polynesian context. An isometric projection of the stratigraphic section through Fe 4 is shown in figure 66. The pit exhibits all of the characteristic features of ethnographically documented *maa* pits, such as the nearly vertical sides, flat bottom, general dimensions, and total absence of any evidence of use for fire or trash dumping. Further validation of use for food storage was provided by several scrapers or peelers of *Cypraea* shell in and adjacent to the pit. Breadfruit must be scraped to remove the rind before ensilage, and it is probable that these scrapers were so utilized.

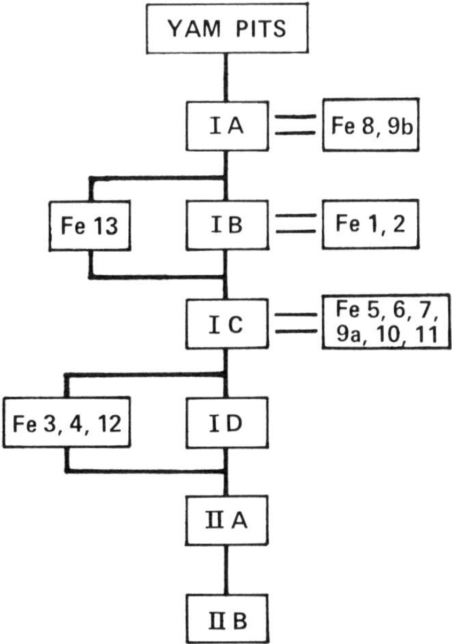

Figure 65. Stratigraphic relationships of cultural features at Site NT-93.

Two postmolds, three pits, and one hearth are associated with Layer IC. The postmolds indicate the former presence of permanent structures of some form in the area of Units 120 to 130. At least one of the pits was used as a trash dump; the function of the other pits is undetermined. Two postmolds (Fe 1, 2) are associated with the later Layer IB deposit, and indicate structures in the vicinity of Unit 100. Feature 13, a large earth oven at the seaward end of the transect (Unit 170), is capped by the disturbed Layer IA garden soil, and may postdate the Lapitoid occupation at NT-93 (note the relatively late ^{14}C age determination from this feature). A postmold (Fe 8) and a fill component of a pit (Fe 9b) are associated with the disturbed Layer IA deposit.

TABLE 10

CULTURAL FEATURES EXCAVATED AT SITE NT-93

FEATURES NO.	TYPE	PROVENIENCE	DIMENSIONS	DESCRIPTION AND COMMENTS
1	Postmold	Unit 100 Layer IB 27–75 cm	20–22 cm diam 48 cm deep	Flat-bottomed, straight-sided postmold, filled with Layer IB midden. Partially truncated by recent yam gardening disturbance.
2	Postmold	Unit 100 Layer IB 29–70 cm	18 cm diam 41 cm deep	Round-bottomed, straight-sided postmold, filled with Layer IB midden.
3	Pit	Unit 100 Layer IC/IIA 28–80 cm	78 cm diam 52 cm deep	Large, symmetrical pit with steep sides. Filled with compact, light yellow-brown sand and capped by Layer IC. Bottom of pit rests on indurated Layer IIB. Possibly a food fermentation pit.
4	Pit	Unit 110 Layer IC/IIA 30–96 cm	100 cm diam 66 cm deep	Large, symmetrical pit with nearly flat bottom and steep sides. Filled with light yellow-brown sand and capped by Layer IC deposit. Contains a few sherds and a *Cypraea* shell scraper. Interpreted as a food fermentation pit.
5	Postmold	Unit 120 Layer IC 65–90 cm	21 cm diam 25 cm deep	Steep-sided, rounded bottom postmold filled with Layer IC deposit.
6	Postmold	Unit 130 Layer IC 37–67 cm	15 cm diam 30 cm deep	Steep-sided, rounded bottom postmold filled with Layer IC deposit.
7	Pit	Unit 130 Layer IC 40–63 cm	30 cm diam 23 cm deep	Amorphous pit of undetermined function; filled with Layer IC midden deposit.

Summary

The Pome'e-Nahau excavations provide a good sample of a late Lapitoid occupation, characterized by Polynesian Plain Ware ceramics. At the time of first occupation around the beginning of the first millennium A.D., the lagoon shore was considerably closer to the site and a swampy depression separated the habitation area from the active beach ridge. This depression formed a convenient locus for midden and trash dumping, and was rapidly filled; the habitation zone subsequently expanded over the filled depression. Two occupation components, represented by Layers IC and IB, were identified, with the similarity in cultural content suggesting fairly rapid deposition (or very little cultural change). A unique find at NT-93 was two large pits, interpreted as storage silos for fermented starch pastes. As at the Loto'aa Site, the distribution of cultural materials and features across the ceramic zone suggests a main habitation area about 50 m wide, with trash or midden disposal on both landward and seaward sides of the settlement.

Table 10, Continued

FEATURES NO.	TYPE	PROVENIENCE	DIMENSIONS	DESCRIPTION AND COMMENTS
8	Postmold	Unit 80 Layer IA 34–67 cm	17 cm diam 33 cm deep	Straight-sided, conical-bottomed postmold filled with Layer IA midden.
9	Pit	Unit 90-91 Layers IA/IC 39–70 cm	35 cm diam 31 cm deep	Irregular pit filled with concentrated shellfish midden; probably trash pit (*Turbo, Cypraea* dominant). Fill includes lower component of Layer IC midden; upper fill of Layer IA midden.
10	Hearth	Unit 149–150 Layer IC 32–40 cm	32 cm diam 8 cm deep	Shallow, basin-shaped scoop hearth with charcoal and fire-cracked volcanic rocks. Probably represents single use.
11	Pit	Unit 89 Layer IC 33–89 cm	85 cm diam 56 cm deep	Possible trash pit with gently sloping sides extending into Layer IIA. Filled with Layer IC midden deposit.
12	Earth Oven	Unit 150–151 Layer C/IIA 62–90 cm	80 cm diam 28 cm deep	Broad, shallow earth oven filled with charcoal and fire-cracked volcanic oven stones. Capped by Layer IC midden.
13	Earth Oven	Unit 170 Layer IA/IC 28 - 85 cm	100 cm diam 57 cm deep	Large earth oven capped by Layer IA and cut through Layer IC. An 8 cm thick band of compact charcoal and ash lined the oven bottom.

Ha'afisi Excavations (Site NT-91)

The garden tract called Ha'afisi ("lineage of Fiji") lies roughly 200 m east of Lolokoka (the garden tract of Tutuna separates these two localities). Rogers (1973) collected a small sample of sherds at Ha'afisi from an abandoned garden, designated Site NT-91. In 1976, most of the Ha'afisi tract was covered in dense second growth, dominated by *Hibiscus tiliaceous* and *Morinda citrifolia*. The inland edge of the site bordered on a large communal *totu'u* or yam garden.

A transect line (oriented 337° E) was cut through the second growth, and four 1 m^2 excavations units were gridded out at 10 m intervals along the transect. Although sherds, shellfish, and fire-cracked oven stones were plentiful on the surface, the zone appeared to be no more than 60 m wide at this point. The stratigraphy revealed in the excavation units was identical to that described for NT-90, with the cultural deposit (Layers

IA and IB) less than 35 cm thick. Layer IIA was thin and discontinuous over the area sampled.

The NT-91 excavations yielded 638 ceramic sherds. Among the sherds was a single example of a carinated vessel decorated with dentate stamping. Also of note are two chert flakes collected on the site surface. A shell fishhook was excavated in Layer IB of Unit 40. Although the sample of cultural materials is limited, the decorated sherd, exotic chert flakes, and rim forms are sufficient to suggest that NT-91 was occupied relatively early and may be contemporaneous with the Early Eastern Lapita occupation at NT-90.

Holoiafu Excavations (Site NT-113)

Holoiafu is a garden tract just below the southwestern edge of the Pleistocene Terrace. Here the ground surface consists of a dark brown silty clay, entirely different from the *fasifasi'ifeo* characteristic of the ceramic zone at Lolokoka, Loto'aa, and Pome'e-Nahau. No shellfish, branch coral fragments, or fire-cracked rocks were exposed on the site surface at NT-113, but a scattering of ceramic sherds, including two handle fragments, some volcanic glass flakes and

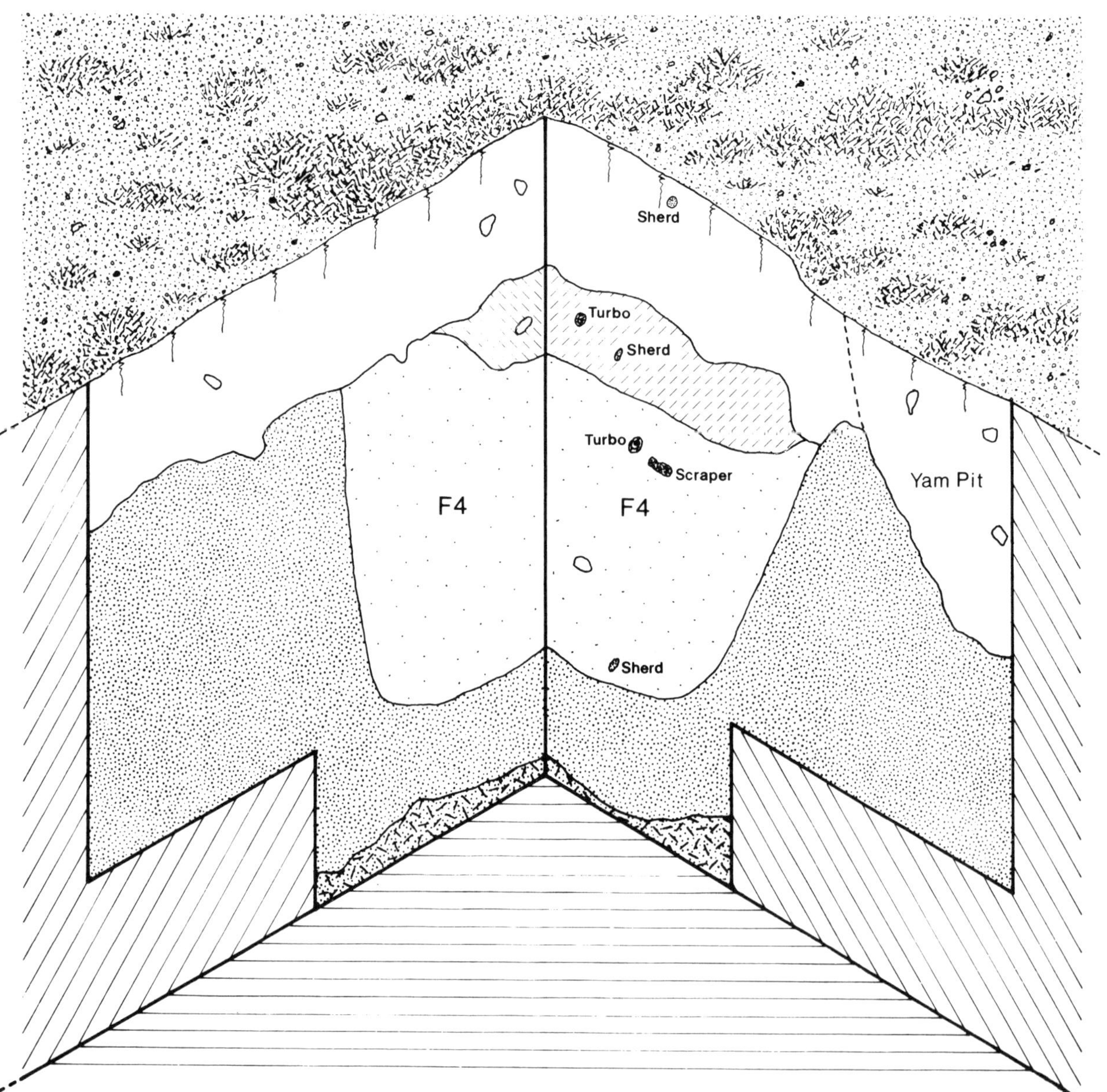

Figure 66. Isometric projection of stratigraphic profiles of the east and south faces of unit 110, Site NT-93, showing section through putative fermentation pit, Feature 4.

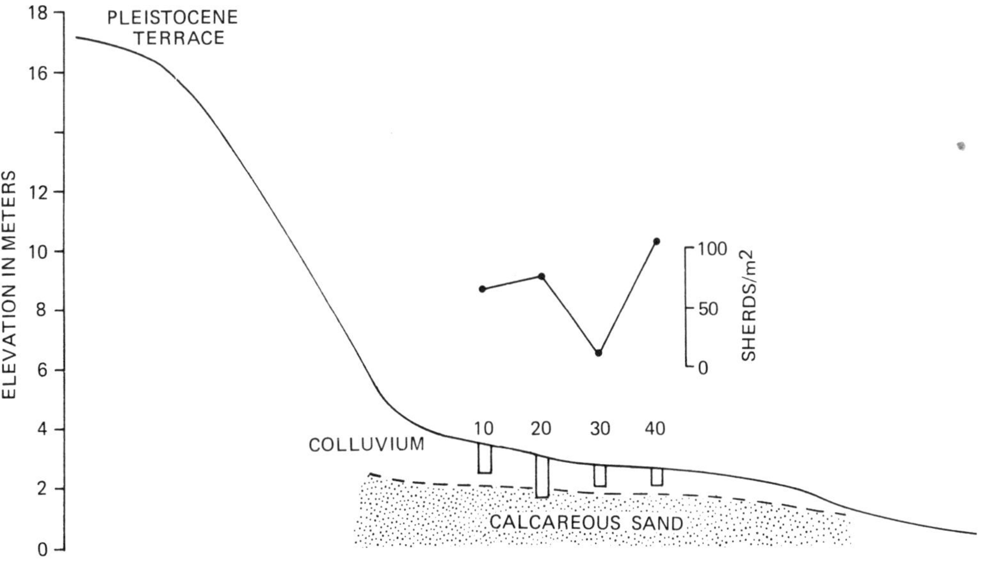

Figure 67. Excavation transect through Site NT-113, Holoiafu.

cores, and two adz fragments, indicated that the ceramic zone extends through this area just below the Pleistocene Terrace.

A systematic sampling transect oriented exactly N-S was laid out from the base of the steep Pleistocene Terrace (about 12 to 14 m high) through the Holoiafu tract toward the Hala Ma'atu. Four 1 m^2 units were excavated along the transect at 10 m intervals (fig. 67).

The stratigraphy at NT-113 differs from that in other parts of the ceramic zone, largely due to the erosion of clay soil from the Pleistocene Terrace and subsequent redeposition of clay over the Holoiafu tract and adjacent areas. The stratigraphy of Unit 20 (fig. 68) is typical of all pits in the transect:

Layer	*Description*
I.	Very dark gray to very dark grayish brown (10 YR 3/1-2) silty clay. This is a thoroughly reworked garden soil, containing eroded and worn sherds and volcanic glass. The soil has a subangular, blocky structure; it was very compact and difficult to excavate. Some charcoal flecking was evident throughout.
II.	Dark brown (7.5 YR 4/2-4) clay, largely structureless with massive character. Slightly sticky when moist. Essentially the same material as Layer I, but has not been reworked through repeated cultivation. Cultural materials were recovered only from the upper half of this stratum (to a maximum depth of 60 cm below surface).
III.	Very pale brown (10 YR 8/3) basal calcareous sand, well-sorted, structureless, culturally sterile. A zone of mixing (5-10 cm thick) lies between Layers II and III.

The basal Layer III represents a former beach terrace buried by eroded and redeposited clay from the volcanic slopes inland. In all likelihood, this erosion was itself the result of human action following Lapita colonization—specifically, forest clearance and shifting cultivation on the Pleistocene Terrace and inland volcanic slopes. Between 30 and 50 cm of clay sediment (the culturally sterile lower part of Layer II) had already been deposited at Holoiafu prior to human occupation. Following the abandonment of the site, clay continued to be deposited over the area, and the upper levels have been thoroughly reworked through cultivation. The absence of shellfish and bone midden is presumably due to the acidity of these volcanic clays.

Aside from three basalt flakes (one with polish, derived from an adz), the only cultural materials recovered from NT-113 were ceramic sherds and 221 flakes and cores of volcanic glass. A total of 277 sherds was recovered from the four excavation units, with an average density of 115 sherds/m^3. The small, eroded nature of the sherds and the absence of rims makes analysis difficult, but the Holoiafu occupation was probably late and of short duration.

Tu'afonua Excavations (Site NT-129)

Although the ceramic zone encircles the Pleistocene Terrace on Niuatoputapu, the concentration of cultural materials is substantially lower in the southeastern part of the zone. This was made apparent by examining sherd density in garden clearings on either side of the Hala Ma'atu, which runs directly over the ceramic zone for a distance of more than 2 km. Along this southeast stretch, the surface frequencies of sherds, fire-cracked rock, and molluscan remains are low, in contrast with the dense concentrations found at places such Lolokoka, Loto'aa, and Pome'e-Nahau.

To sample the southeastern portion of the zone, a systematic transect (oriented 302° E) was selected at Tu'afonua (literally, "back of the land") along the Hala Ma'atu just east of the Faka'ahotaha boundary. The selected site was a manioc garden, where a few surface sherds and volcanic glass flakes had been observed during reconnaissance. The base of the Pleistocene Terrace, which rises abruptly to a height of 20 m in this locality, lies some 50 m inland of the road.

Four 1 m^2 excavation units were positioned along the transect, two on the inland side of the Hala Ma'atu (10 m apart), and two on the seaward side of the road (again 10 m apart), with a 20 m gap spanning the road. In all units, Layer I consisted of a dark brown, granular to blocky-structured silt loam, thoroughly reworked from agricultural activities. In the inland-most unit (10), Layer I was 45 cm thick, and rested directly upon cemented calcareous beach sand (Layer II). Layer I,

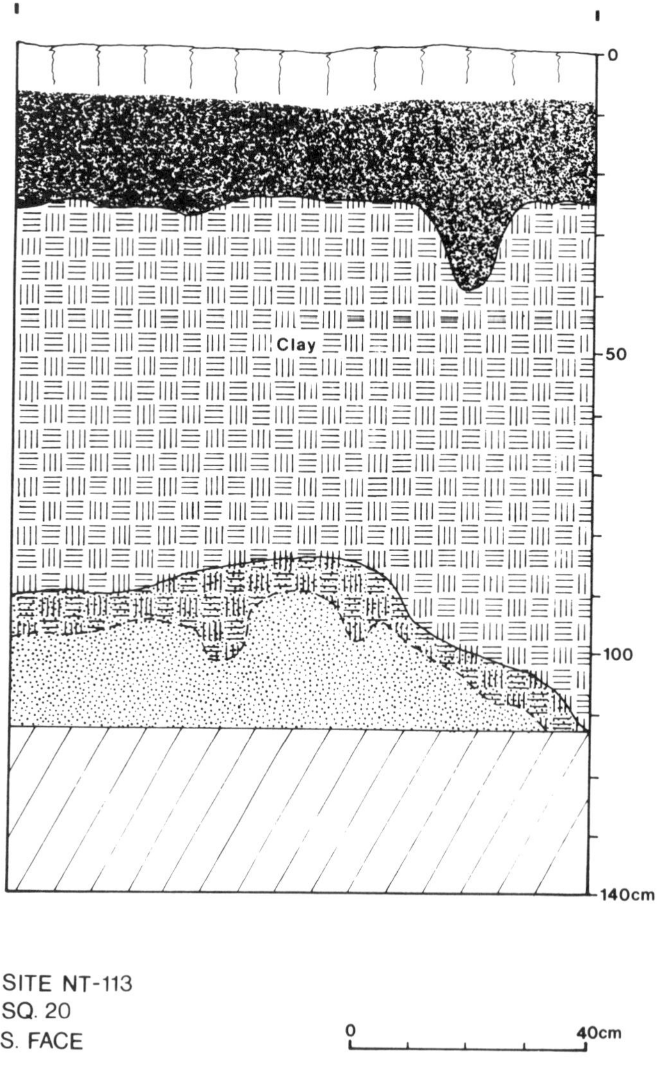

Figure 68. Stratigraphic profile of excavation Unit 20, Site NT-113.

TABLE 11

CULTURAL CONTENT OF SITE NT–129

UNIT	SHERDS	VOLCANIC GLASS
10	0	7
20	5	28
30	7	6
40	3	4
TOTAL	15	45

which consists largely of clay eroded from the Pleistocene Terrace (mixed with some sand and organic materials), gradually pinches out as one moves seaward along the transect; its depth is only 15 cm at Unit 50. Cultural materials were present in very low frequencies, as indicated in table 11. No faunal materials were present. Among the 15 sherds was a single rim.

The Tu'afonua excavations confirmed that the ceramic zone along the southeast portion of the island contains only low densities of cultural materials. Thus, while the Lapita occupation of Niuatoputapu did at one time completely encircle the island's central volcanic core, the occupation in the southeast was far less intense—and probably of shorter duration—than that along the northern part of the island. Possible ecological reasons for this difference in occupation histories are discussed elsewhere.

Hihifo Excavations (Site NT-163)

During our residence in Hihifo village, it became evident that the ceramic zone underlay the inland house lots. Although grassy yards obscure the *fasifasi'ifeo* soil, potsherds and shellfish midden were observed in bare pig runs, as well as in trash pits and other subsurface exposures. The Hihifo area provided an excellent opportunity to survey an elevation profile over a series of alternating beach ridges and depressions, testifying to continued uplift and coastal progradation of the island's leeward shoreline (fig. 49). Our final excavation transect was thus laid out along one of the main roads through Hihifo village, with sampling units positioned at 50 m intervals.

The excavations confirmed that the ceramic zone was confined to the inland portion of the village, over a 150 m-wide span from the base of an elevated reef exposure to the inland edge of a low depression representing a former shoreline. All excavation units seaward of Unit 200 failed to yield ceramics, although later, aceramic midden deposits were exposed in these seaward units.

Ceramic zone stratigraphy was not substantially different from that at NT-90 or -100, with cultural materials concentrated in Layers IA and IB. Layer IIA was present only in Units 150 and 200. Unit 50 contained unusually high quantities of molluscan and bone midden, which might indicate the former presence of a cookhouse or food preparation area in this inland part of the ceramic zone.

Site NT-163 yielded 505 sherds (table 12). Among the rim sherds are two with notched decorations; these along with the carinated body sherd, suggest that the Hihifo occupation may extend back to the Early Eastern Lapita phase, although the majority of the ceramics are assignable to later Polynesian Plain Ware.

Excavations at Other Ceramic Zone Sites (Sites NT-110, -112, -150)

Vaipoa Faleako Site (NT-112)

Shortly after arriving on Niuatoputapu, we observed ceramic sherds in a recent borrow pit adjacent to the Catholic school in Vaipoa village. The school is constructed on top of a former beach terrace about 60 m inland of the present shoreline, and the borrow pit was dug to obtain fill material for a playing field. Two trenches with a total area of 5 m^2 were excavated, by the researchers, from the edge of the borrow pit into the highest portions of the beach terrace. In both cases, ceramic-bearing strata virtually identical to those at NT-90 were exposed, but here these strata were heavily disturbed by post-Lapitoid phase and recent activities, such as trash pits and postmolds. A sample of 1,714 sherds was recovered from the two trenches, along with 497 volcanic glass flakes and cores and a few other portable artifacts. Because the ceramic zone in this locality was so highly disturbed, excavations at NT-112 were terminated with the completion of the two test trenches.

Matavai Village Site (NT-110)

Site NT-110 is an early historic village at which two test trenches were excavated (see below). In one trench, a portion of the circum-island ceramic zone was uncovered beneath a historic-period midden deposit. In

TABLE 12

CULTURAL CONTENT OF SITE NT–163

MATERIAL	UNIT 50	UNIT 100	UNIT 150	UNIT 200
Ceramics				
Body sherds	80	216	128	3
Rims	3	7	2	—
Bases	13	24	25	1
Carinated	—	1	—	—
Handles	—	1	—	1
Volcanic Glass Lithics	58	82	18	1
Other Artifacts	6	—	—	1
Bone midden (g)	254	16	78	—
Shellfish midden (kg)	20.9	2.0	4.1	2.1

the second trench, to seaward, the pottery zone was absent as a distinct stratigraphic unit, but a few sherds were incorporated into the historic-period midden deposit. In all, 482 sherds and 220 flakes and cores of volcanic glass were recovered from the NT-110 excavations.

NT-150 Mound Site

NT-150 is a large earthen mound of late prehistoric age, partially sectioned by the Hala Ma'atu road. A cut made into the mound from the road side to determine the internal stratigraphy and construction sequence (see below) revealed that the mound had been constructed on top of the ceramic zone (exposed at the base of the excavated trench). The few sherds from the ceramic deposit were small and worn, and were not retained for further analysis.

Surface Sherds on the Pleistocene Terrace

Potsherds were found outside the ceramic zone in two localities on the Pleistocene Terrace. A single, heavily worn sherd was collected from the surface of a new yam swidden on the Terrace southwest of Falehau village (near Site NT-15). A second locality, designated Site NT-183 and situated near the bluff about midway along the southern face of the Pleistocene Terrace, yielded a few small, worn sherds and volcanic glass flakes scattered over about 2,500 m^2. There was no indication of intact subsurface cultural deposits at either locality.

ACERAMIC OCCUPATION SITES

Niutoua Excavations (Site NT-125)

One objective of the excavation program was the testing of occupation deposits spanning the so-called Tongan "dark ages" (Davidson 1979), between the cessation of ceramic production and use and the historic period. A promising locality, observed early during our field program, was the Niutoua area at the western edge of Hihifo village.

Setting and Geomorphology

Niutoua is properly the name of a small freshwater spring which issues from a fissure in an exposed scarp of upraised reef platform (figs. 69 and 70), and drains into a swampy depression behind an old beach ridge.

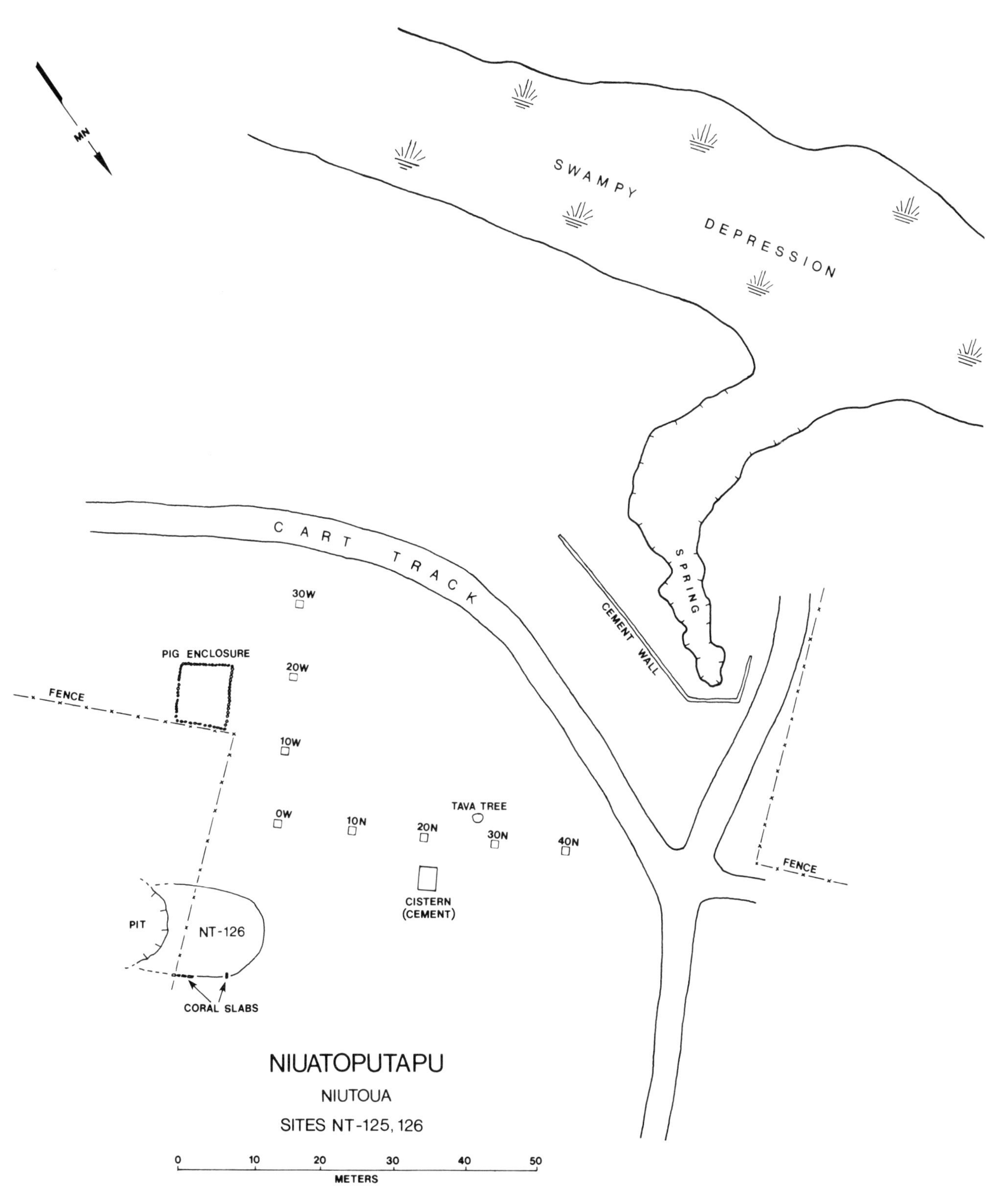

Figure 69. Map of Niutoua and vicinity, showing the location of transect excavation units.

Prior to the installation of a piped water system in Hihifo, Niutoua was the primary source of fresh water for the western portion of the village, and remains an important bathing spot, especially for younger men and women who gather there in the early evening from social as much as hygienic considerations.

As shown in the plan (fig. 69), Site NT-125 is a gently sloping mound rising on the inland side of the spring, from which it is currently separated by a cart track. A dwelling was formerly located atop the mound, and the ruins of a cement cistern remained in 1976. On the eastern side of the mound is a small *fa'itoka* burial mound with traces of coral facing slabs (Site NT-126). (At the time of our excavation, a group of Hihifo men were systematically mining the *fa'itoka* for sand for concrete mix, oblivious to the burials that were disturbed in the process. The burial mound was not claimed by any extant lineage group, nor had it been used in recent memory, and thus it was not protected by any sanctions.)

Geomorphologically, NT-125 lies about 100 m seaward of the ceramic-bearing zone, on a slightly lower terrace of which the reef platform escarpment mentioned above forms the seaward edge. This locality was presumably an active reef platform or beach at the time of initial Lapita occupation, and would have become suitably elevated for permanent occupation only some time later, following the progression of tectonic uplift already described. Subsequent exposure of the freshwater spring (which may originally have been sub-tidal) would have been an inducement to adjacent occupation.

Figure 70. View of the freshwater spring at Niutoua.

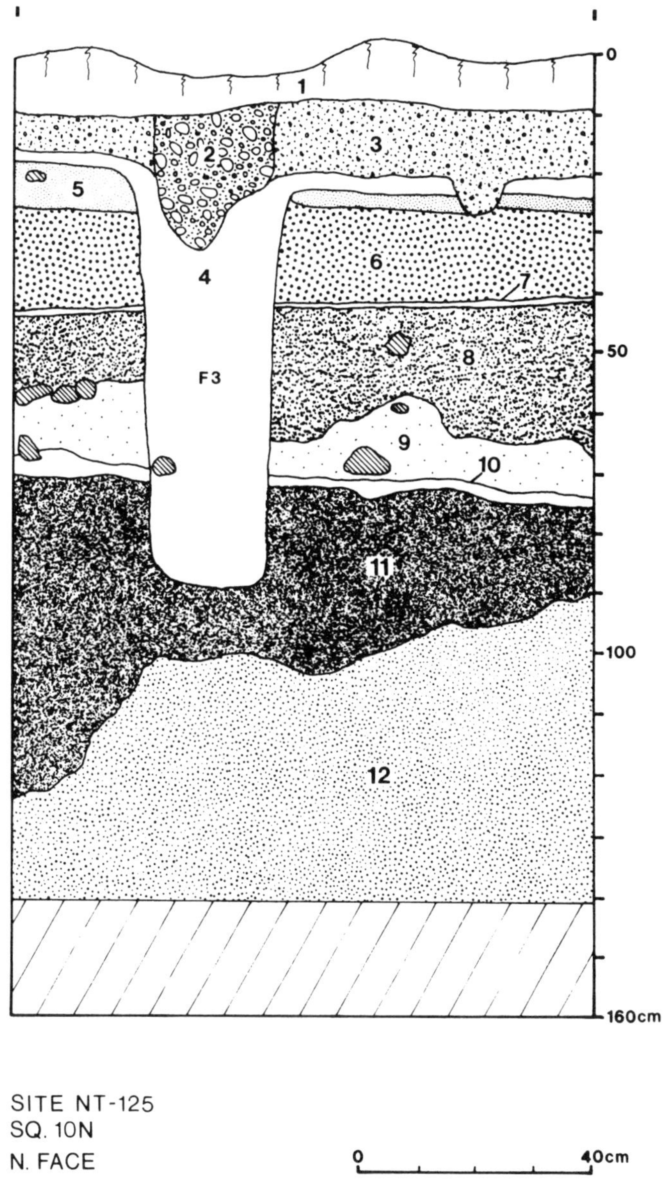

Figure 71. Stratigraphic profile of Unit 10N, Site NT-125.

Excavation and Stratigraphy

To sample this large, amorphous mound with no evident surface features, we positioned a series of 1 m^2 test pits at 10 m intervals along two systematic transects oriented perpendicular to each other. One transect (designated N) ran across the highest portion of the mound, where the strata could be expected to be deepest and most complex. The second transect (W) followed the gentle slope of the mound seaward toward the cart track (fig. 69). A total of 8 m^2 was excavated in both transects.

The excavations revealed a succession of historic and prehistoric occupation deposits, with the greatest depth of occupation debris along the N transect between 0W and 30N. The deepest and most complex stratigraphic profile was that exposed in Unit 10N, shown in figure 71, summarized as follows:

Bed	*Description*
1	Recent historic midden and sandy humus (10 YR 5/1).
2	Fill of waterworn coral pebbles *(patapata).*
3	Sand mixed with coral pebbles (10 YR 8/3).
4	Sandy loam with shellfish midden, also constituting the fill of postmold Fe 3 (10 YR 6/1).

5 Thin lens of medium-grain sized sand, probably laid down as house floor (10 YR 7/1).
6 Sandy midden (10 YR 6/1).
7 Thin lens of white sand, probably laid down as house floor (10 YR 8/2).
8 Sandy midden with considerable charcoal flecking throughout (10 YR 5/1).
9 Lightly stained sand lacking shellfish midden (10 YR 6/1).
10 Thin lens of white sand, probably laid down as house floor (10 YR 8/2).
11 Sandy midden with some charcoal flecking (10 YR 4-5/1).
12 Sterile coral sand, weakly cemented in places (10 YR 8/1-2).

Historic period artifacts were contained only in the uppermost midden deposits (Beds 1 and 3), with Beds 6, 8, and 11 representing prehistoric occupations. The thin sand lenses of Beds 10, 7, and 5 appear to represent house floors. A large postmold, Fe 3, was dug following the deposition of Bed 5, and both the floor and post presumably derived from a structure constructed in late prehistoric or early historic times.

Twenty meters to the northwest along the N transect, in Unit 30N, the stratigraphy was less complex (fig. 72). Here a recent historic-period midden deposit capped a shallow oven pit containing glass, iron, and other historic-period objects. The oven pit truncated two vertical postmolds (Beds 3 and 4), probably derived from a historic-period structure. The

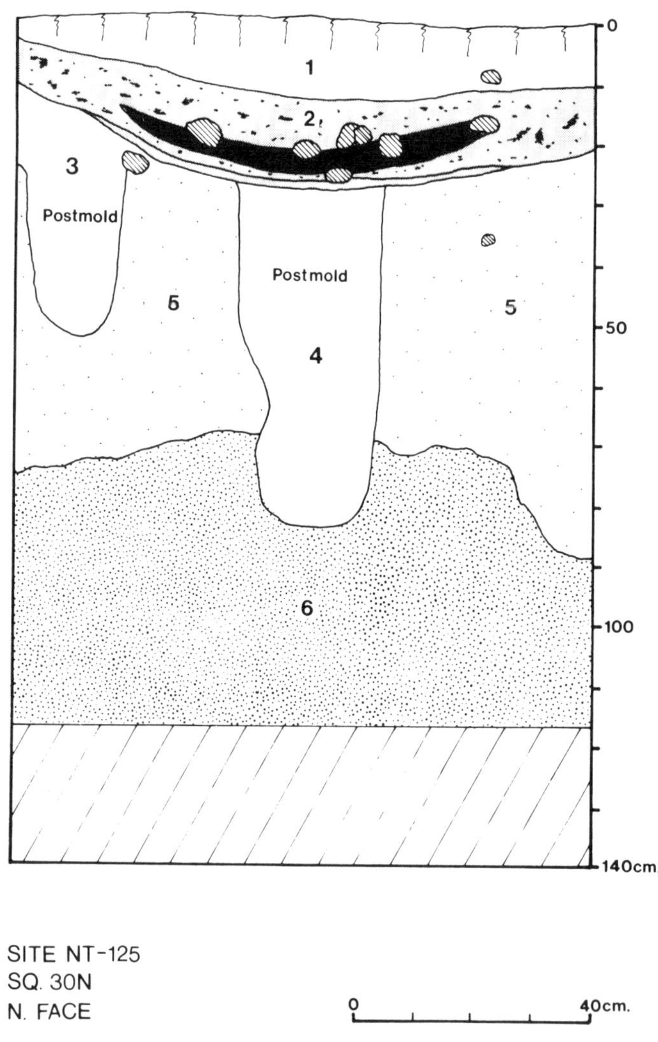

Figure 72. Stratigraphic profile of Unit 30N, Site NT-125.

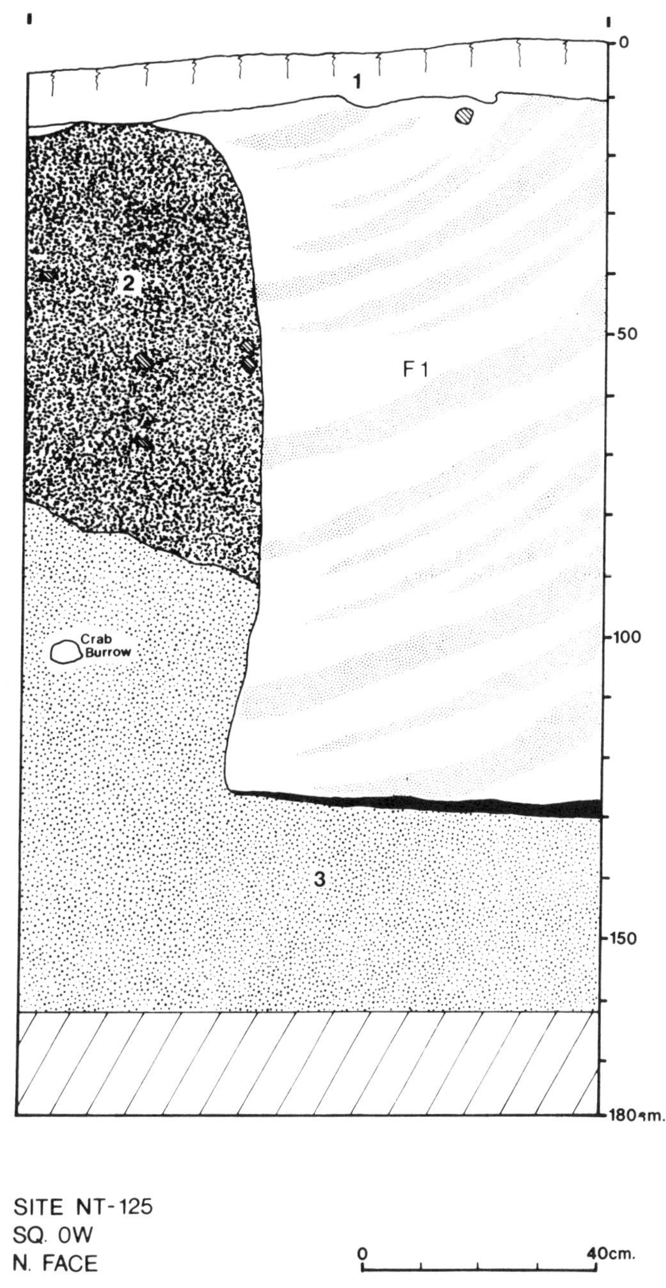

Figure 73. Stratigraphic profile of Unit OW, Site NT-125.

postmolds themselves penetrate a relatively thick (ca. 40 to 50 cm) deposit of sandy midden with some charcoal flecking, lacking in historic period artifacts, and correlating with Beds 6 through 11 in Unit 10N.

In Unit OW, at the intersection of the two transects, the simple stratigraphic situation was disturbed by a large, vertical-sided pit (Fe 1), shown in figure 73. This pit, probably of historic age, penetrated a prehistoric deposit of sandy midden (Bed 2), and both were capped by Bed 1, a thin deposit of historic-period midden.

The prehistoric midden deposit represented by Bed 2 in OW gradually diminishes in thickness as one moves seaward along the W transect, and disappears between Units 20W and 30W. This latter unit, adjacent to the modern cart track, displays only the recent, thin historic midden deposit of Bed 1.

The age of the prehistoric deposits at NT-125 is indicated by two ^{14}C samples (see Radiocarbon Dating). One sample, TORC-14, was obtained from Unit 20N, at the base of the major prehistoric deposit (Bed 4), and produced a result of 1140 ± 75 B.P. The second sample was obtained at a depth of 50 to 60 cm within the prehistoric midden deposit in Unit 10W, and yielded an uncorrected age of 650 ± 85 years B.P. These ages would appear to be stratigraphically consistent, since both the greatest depth of deposit and probably the oldest part of the site are situated in the vicinity of Units 10N to 20N. These radiocarbon age assessments suggest that Niutoua was occupied more or less continuously from around the close of the first millennium A.D. into the historic period.

Cultural Features and Artifacts

The Niutoua deposits were disappointing in cultural content. The prehistoric occupations produced only an echinoid-spine abrader and a shell ring ornament, along with a few basalt and volcanic-glass flakes. In addition, 22 potsherds were recovered, but we do not believe that these are in primary context. All sherds were worn and rounded, and were probably derived from the pottery-bearing zone situated a few meters inland of Niutoua. Green (1974b:245-47) has cogently described the problem of pottery in secondary contexts in Polynesian sites, and the interpretive issues which have resulted.

Several cultural features, including pits, postmolds, and an oven, were exposed during the excavations. A large firepit containing burnt coral cobbles, exposed in Unit 20W, is illustrated in perspective view in figure 74. The pit was fully sealed by the prehistoric midden deposit. It is much too large to have been an ordinary household oven, but would match closely with ethnographic descriptions of large ovens used for cooking *Cordyline* root in Western Polynesia and the Polynesian Outliers (see, for example, Firth 1939, Pl. IIIB).

Summary

The Niutoua excavations document continued occupation from the latter part of the first millennium A.D. through the historic period, a time during which ceramics were no longer in production or use. Unfortunately, the impoverished cultural content of the site yielded little evidence of material culture or technological adaptation. The faunal evidence for subsistence patterns during this period is discussed in chapter 6.

Hihifo Transect Excavations (Site NT-163)

The Hihifo transect has already been described in connection with the ceramic zone, and the transect profile is diagrammed in figure 49. No ceramics were recovered from any of the eight 1 m^2 units excavated seaward of Unit 200. These seaward units, located from 250 to 650 m along the transect, revealed shallow midden deposits on the gently undulating former beach ridges that descend to the modern coastline. These aceramic middens are concentrated in the area between Units 200 and 500, thus spanning a zone about 300 m wide. Today this area is covered by the modern houses of Hihifo village.

The stratigraphy of Unit 300 is typical for the aceramic portion of the Hihifo transect:

Layer	*Description*
I.	Non-concentrated midden, sandy loam, ranging from dark grayish brown to brown (10 YR 4/2-5/3). Shellfish remains present but relatively sparse. Contact with Layer II uneven and gradational. Depth varies from 30 to 35 cm.
II.	Very pale brown (10 YR 7/4) sterile sand, fine- to medium-grained. To 63 cm below surface.
III.	Very pale brown sterile sand, weakly concreted to indurated.

As at NT-125, the artifact content of the aceramic deposits in the Hihifo transect was limited. One pearl shell fishhook fragment was recovered from Unit 400. All other cultural material was faunal, either bone or shellfish; no cultural features were exposed. The primary result of the NT-163 transect excavations was to confirm the continued occupation of the island's leeward coastline, with a gradual seaward shift in settlement location as tectonic uplift continued to result in a westward migration of the active beach.

Matavai Village Excavations (Site NT-110)

The historic-period village of Matavai lies along the Hala Ma'atu southeast of Hihifo. The *hou'eiki* (chief) Telai told us that his grandfather had resided here, and that the *hou'eiki* Vivili and a few others had continued to live in Matavai as recently as 1948. A large, oval mound with entryway pavings in three locations, situated on the inland side of the Hala Ma'atu, is said to be the foundation of the former Wesleyan church.

Our interest in Matavai (Site NT-110) lay in the possibility that occupation had extended back into the late prehistoric period. Accordingly, test excavations were carried out in two localities to determine whether the historic period features had overlaid prehistoric deposits. The first trench (1 x 2 m) was positioned on

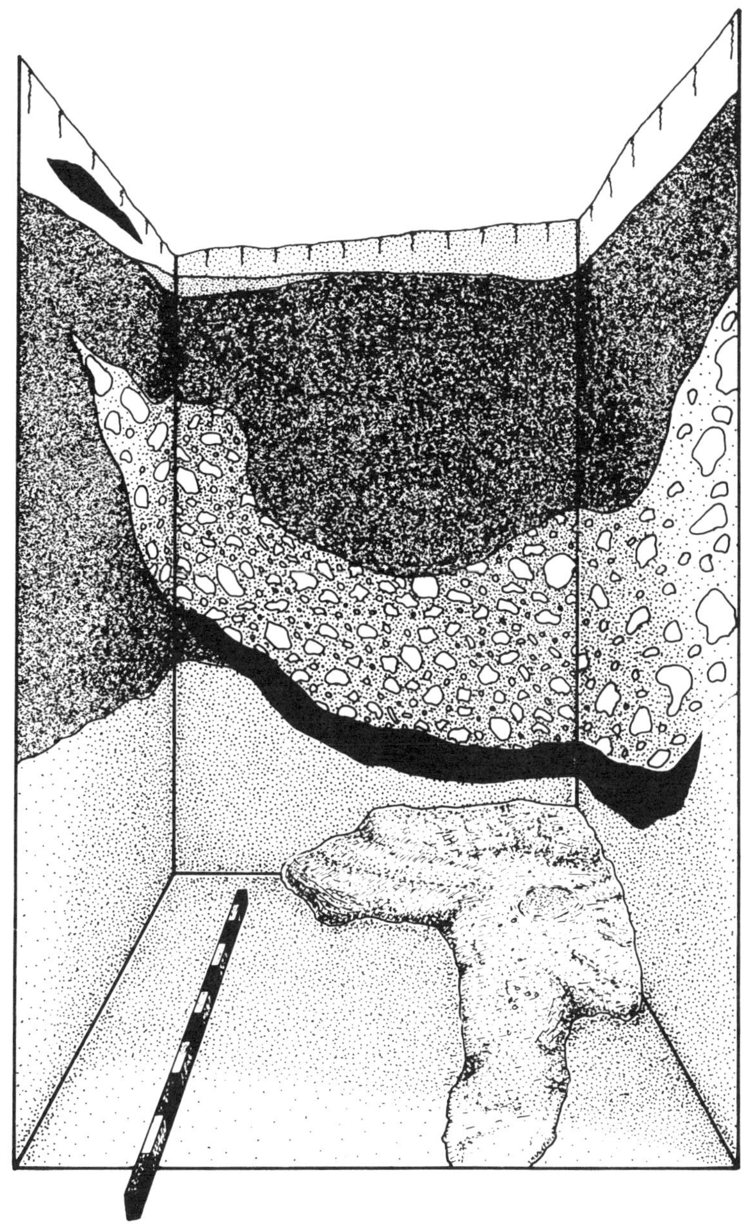

Figure 74. Perspective view of large earth oven exposed in Unit 20W, Site NT-125.

the seaward side of the Hala Ma'atu, about 7 m from the road, on the highest portion of a low mound through which a road cut revealed shellfish midden and coral *patapata* paving gravel. An upright coral slab, probably part of a house edge, was noted a few meters seaward of the test trench. The second test trench (1 x 2 m) was placed 35 m further seaward on another low, amorphous mound or gentle rise in the terrain. Lying about halfway between the two test trenches were an abandoned well *(vai tupu)* and two circular, flat-topped volcanic stones, which may have served as seats or door steps (fig. 75).

Situated further seaward of the second test trench was a large depression filled with stagnant water and supporting a dense growth of the aroid *Cyrtosperma chammissonis (via),* a famine resource. Telai said that the depression was named Tolungohue, and that it was a spring, like Niutoua, with an exit channel to the sea. It had served as the main bathing place for the occupants of Matavai village. A final feature in the vicinity of the test excavations was a large *fa'itoka* burial mound located about 40 m southeast of the seaward test trench.

Figure 75. Flat-topped volcanic stones at historic Matavai Village, Site NT-110.

The seaward test trench revealed a thin (ca. 15-20 cm) deposit of sandy midden, containing sparse shellfish remains and historic period artifacts directly overlying sterile sand. In the trench near the Hala Ma'atu, the stratigraphy was slightly more complex (fig. 76). Here a thin historic-period midden (8-10 cm thick), Bed 1, overlay a deposit of beach sand (Bed 2) representing the floor of a historic period dwelling. Bed 3, about 40 cm thick, was a ceramic-bearing deposit containing potsherds and volcanic glass flakes, indicating that Matavai village was constructed over part of the circum-island ceramic zone. The interface between Beds 2 and 3, however, represents a gap of at least 1,000 and probably 1,500 years during which the locality was unoccupied. No evidence was uncovered at Matavai of an aceramic, late prehistoric occupation phase.

ARCHITECTURAL SITES

Although most of our excavations were directed at occupation sites, particularly within the ceramic zone, three architectural sites were investigated to obtain details of internal structure and construction technique and, in the case of the Houmafakalele burial complex, to attempt to assess the age of this type of monumental architecture.

Funga'ana Mound (Site NT-139)

Site NT-139 is a typical *sia* mound located in uncultivated scrub on recently uplifted terrain in the southeast portion of the island, in the tract called

Funga'ana. The mound has a maximum diameter of about 40 m, and a height above the surrounding terrain of 75 to 100 cm. The *sia* is surrounded by the borrow pit from which its fill was derived. This pit or ditch is bridged in two places by causeways (fig. 77). The typical central depression is not stone lined. There are no *paepae* or retaining walls, and the site appears to be constructed entirely of sand and coral rubble.

Two trenches were excavated in the mound, with the following objectives: (1) to determine the construction sequence, whether a single event or one involving multiple stages or uses; (2) to locate datable materials; and (3) to determine whether the mound was ever used for habitation. A 1 x 6 m trench was excavated into the east side of the mound to expose the internal stratigraphy. A second trench, 1 x 3 m, was then cut through part of the central depression in a further search for any occupation debris or datable material.

The extremely simple stratigraphy of Trench 1 is shown in figure 78. A layer of brown humus ("A" horizon, 7.5 YR 4-5/2) less than 10 cm thick, which caps the entire mound, developed on the site after abandonment as a result of decomposing vegetation. Layer II is the mound fill, consisting of white (10 YR 8/2) coarse beach sand and coral rubble; there is no internal structure or features. Separating the Layer II fill from the underlying basal sterile sand (Layer IV) is a thin, ancient "A" horizon of grayish brown to light grayish brown (10 YR 5-6/2) color, representing the ground surface at the time of mound construction. This paleosol is very poorly developed and, given the recently uplifted nature of the local terrain, may have existed for only a few centuries prior to its burial by the mound fill.

In sum, the NT-139 excavations revealed that the mound was constructed as a single event, by excavation and the heaping up of sand and coral rubble from the adjacent borrow pits. The lack of any midden, artifactual materials, or structural features argues against the use of this mound for occupation. Unfortunately, datable material was not recovered, but the location of the site on recent marine sediments restricts its age to the late prehistoric period.

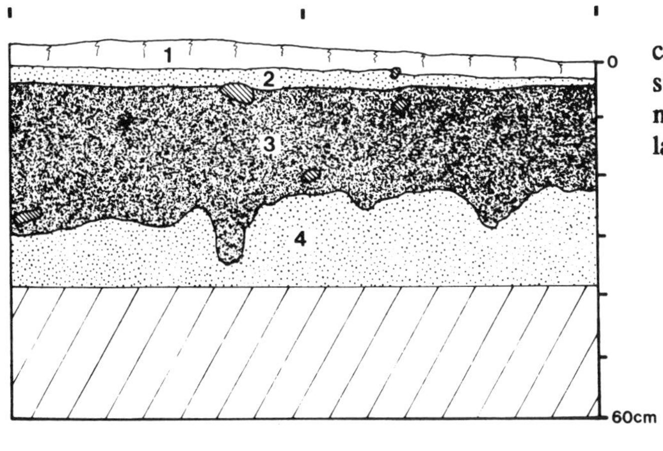

Figure 76. Stratigraphic profile at Site NT-110.

Hihifo Burial Mound (Site NT-150)

A large earthen mound at the southeastern edge of Hihifo village had been partially sectioned by the Hala Ma'atu road, providing an opportunity to obtain a cross-section through one of these large architectural sites. The mound is roughly oval, with a maximum diameter of about 35 m (the site was badly disturbed by the road cut), and maximum elevation above the surrounding terrain of no more than 2 m. The borrow pit from which the mound fill was derived lies immediately inland of the site. That the mound had functioned as a *fa'itoka* rather than a *sia* was suggested by the presence of scattered *patapata* pebbles and a few displaced coral slabs (the latter presumably set as upright edging stones). Local residents had no name for the site, nor could they supply any functional details.

Working back from the face of the Hala Ma'atu road cut, we excavated a 3 x 2 m trench, exposing a stratigraphic section through the central portion of the mound (fig. 79). The section consisted of the following layers:

Layer	*Description*
I.	Brownish yellow to yellow (10 YR 6-8/8), highly mottled clay mound fill, containing many subangular saprolitic pebbles. Silt-clay texture, highly compact. Capped at the surface by a thin A horizon (ca. 5 cm) (7.5 YR 4/4).
II.	Very dark gray (10 YR 3/1) horizon containing potsherds and volcanic glass. Silt-loam texture, granular structure. Contact with Layer I very sharp and regular. Contact with Layer III irregular and somewhat gradational.
III.	Dark brown to brown (7.5 YR 4/4), sterile clay subsoil. Extremely compact.
IV.	White (10 YR 8/1) concreted reef rock.

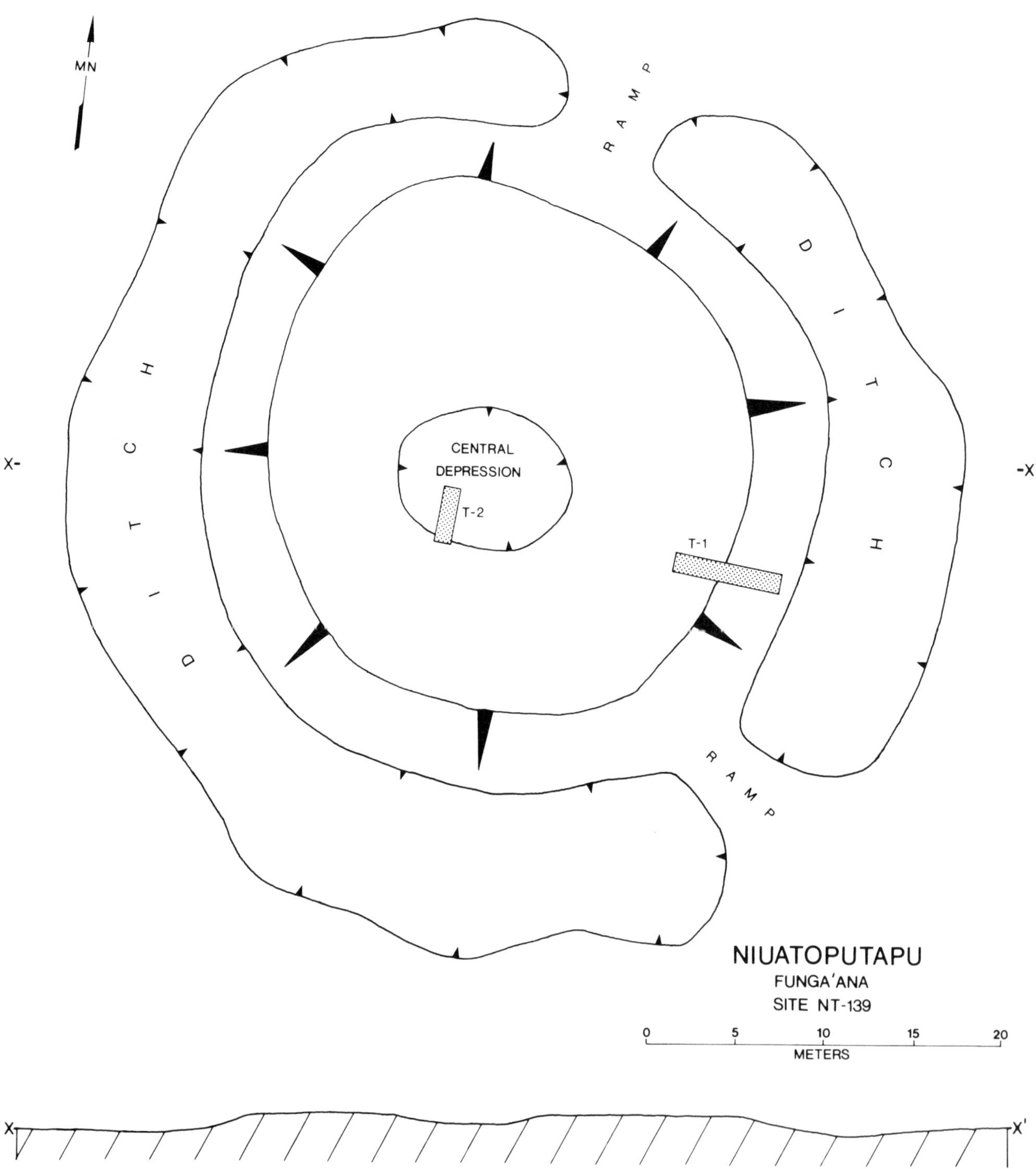

Figure 77. Plan of Site NT-139.

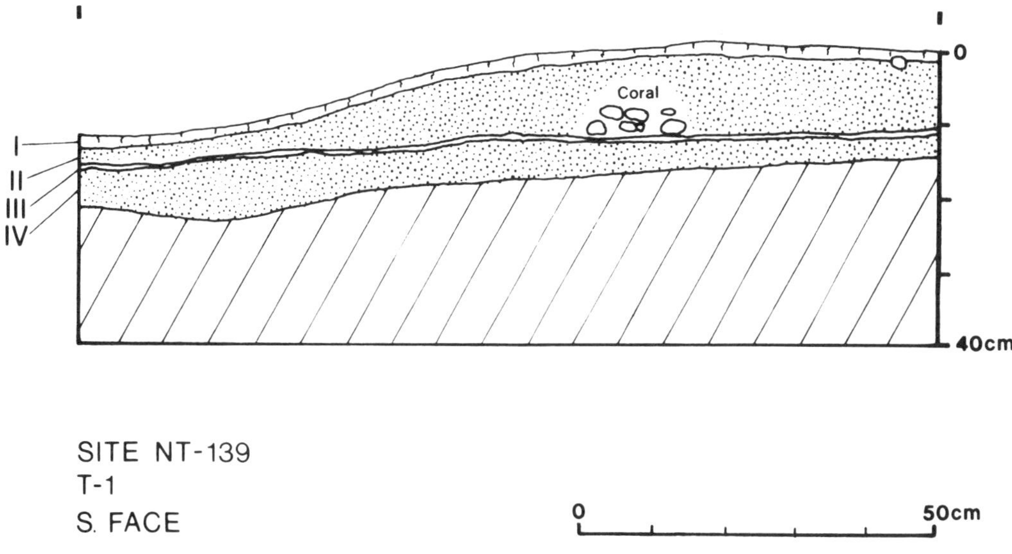

Figure 78. Stratigraphic profile through Site NT-139.

Layer II is a portion of the circum-island ceramic zone which had been completely sealed by mound construction. This stratum contains no features, and has been thoroughly reworked, probably from gardening prior to mound construction. The potsherds recovered from Layer II were extremely rounded and fragmentary. The mound itself, represented by the Layer I fill, was built in a single phase, as no internal components were recognizable. A few discrete lenses of clay, seen in the section (fig. 79), probably represent individual basket-loads dumped during the construction process.

Three pit features were revealed in the section, all of them cut from the mound surface. Fe 1 is a round-bottomed pit, filled with brown clay (10 YR 4/3) and numerous waterworn coral pebbles of the type called *patapata* and associated with burials. Fe 2 is a large, straight-sided pit, also with brown clay fill but lacking pebbles. Fe 3 is a shallow pit, again with brown clay fill. Although no skeletal material was noted, it is likely that all three pits are burial features. In all respects, these pits closely match burial pits in two Tongan *fa'itoka* excavated by Davidson (1969a).

No datable material was obtained, but the age of the mound relative to the Lapitoid occupation of the island is indicated by the superposition of the mound over the ceramic-bearing zone. The reworked nature of Layer II suggests that the mound was constructed a considerable time after the abandonment of the ceramic zone as an occupation locus. It can thus be confidently assigned to the final third of the island's sequence, sometime after A.D. 1000.

Houmafakalele Complex (Sites NT-52, -54, -55, -164 through -169)

The distribution of most large mound sites on the geologically recent, uplifted marine terrain indicates that they postdate the ceramic occupations. It was nonetheless desirable to confirm this rough sequence with datable material from at least one major mound complex. Furthermore, although informants had no doubts as to the burial function of many of the large, stone-faced mounds, we wished to confirm this through excavation, and to obtain specific information on interment style and details of mound construction. Most of the large burial mounds are the sepulchres of highly ranked individuals recorded in genealogies and oral traditions, many of whom are ancestors of present-day Tongans. Excavation of such sites is a sensitive matter. Indeed, we initially assumed that the excavation of any burial mounds would be impossible for these cultural reasons. Toward the end of our stay on Niuatoputapu, however, after becoming familiar with the local socio-political scene and following discussions with the island's secular and religious leaders, we were informed that it might be feasible to excavate a burial mound for which there was no extant traditional information on lineage affiliation or interred individuals. A large mound complex on the *liku* coast, named Houmafakalele, seemed a likely choice, and after formal discussions with the *hou'eiki* and *fakafofonga puleanga* (government agent), permission was granted to undertake work at this complex. Recognizing that such work would be sensi-

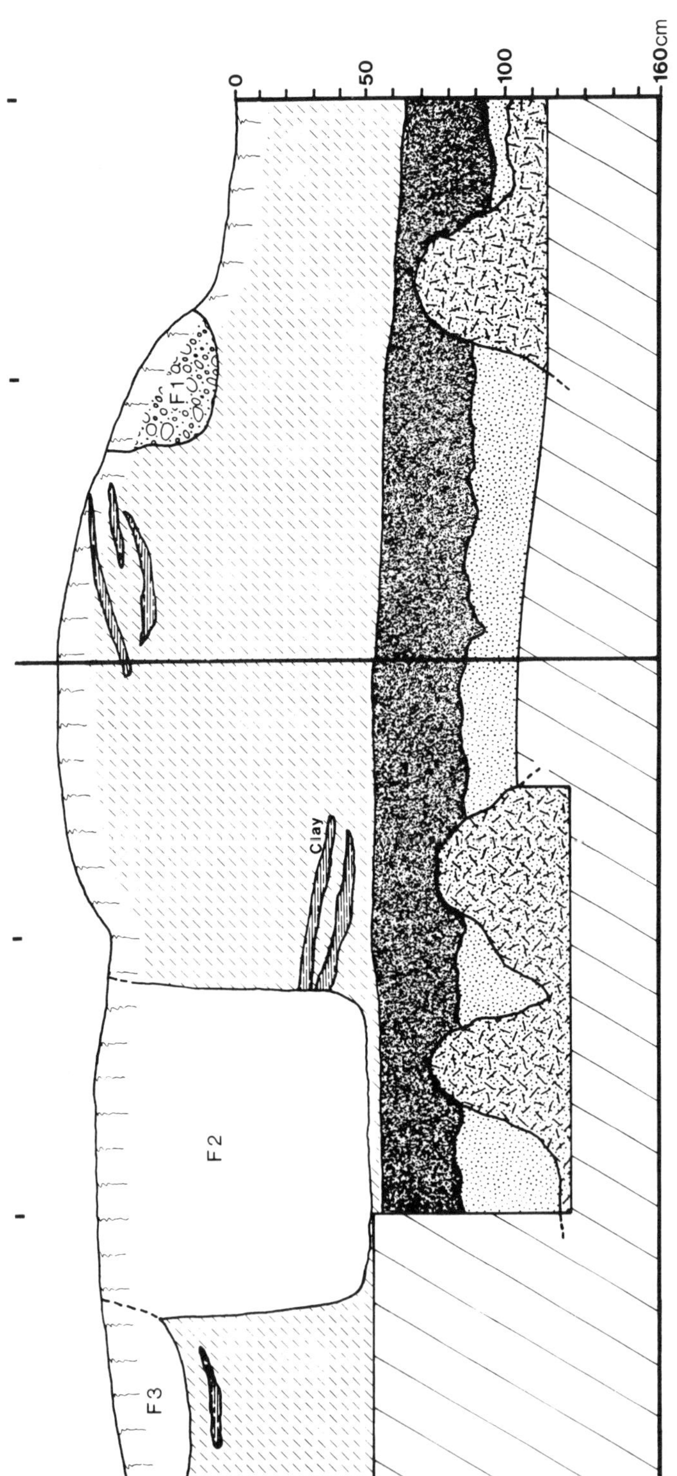

Figure 79. Stratigraphic profile through Site NT-150, Hihifo burial mound.

tive, we asked a leading minister of the Siasi Tonga Tauataina to perform a blessing ceremony at both the commencement and the conclusion of the excavations.

The Houmafakalele Mound Complex

The Houmafakalele complex lies midway along the windward or *liku* coastline, in dense scrub and open-canopy *Eugenia* forest about 100 m inland of the beach. Rogers (1973, 1974) recorded the site, assigning site numbers 50 to 57 to as many separate structures. After clearing, we were able to match his descriptions for Sites NT-52 (Houmafakalele III), -54 (H IV) and -55 (H V) with individual archaeological features. It was impossible, however, to determine which features corresponded to his minimal descriptions for other sites. Therefore, we assigned new site numbers NT-164 to -169 to the six additional features cleared and mapped. The complex was plane-table mapped at 1:75 (figs. 80 and 81).

The complex has a symmetrical layout, with the largest and most impressive mound, NT-52 or Houmafakalele III, to the south. The front of Houmafakalele III, with the largest cut-and-dressed slabs, faces three smaller stone-faced mounds, NT-54, -55, and -164. Of these, the best constructed is the central NT-54 mound, the highest side of which faces south towards Houmafakalele III. Three small structures, NT-167, -168, and -169, lie seaward of the main group, and may have been added later. The four largest structures, however, appear to have been laid out according to some overall plan, perhaps reflecting the relative rank or status of the interred individuals (see Kirch 1980a for further discussion of the social aspects of Tongan burial monuments).

Sites NT-52, -54, and -164 are examples of Class 12 mounds (utilizing cut-and-dressed slabs in their facings) described in chapter 3. Formally, NT-169 also falls within this class, although it is the smallest example on the island. The other mounds in the Houmafakalele complex belong to Class 11, since they utilize only natural (unworked) coral slabs in their facings.

Houmafakalele III (Site NT-52). This impressive monument (figs. 80, 82, 83) is rectangular, with dimensions of 16.5 by 14.3 m. With an average elevation of 0.45 m, the mound has an estimated cubic volume of 106 m^3; the sandy fill was derived from an oval borrow pit adjacent to the mound on its west, or inland, side. The northern mound face was intended to be its "front" and is constructed of carefully cut and dressed rectangular slabs of coral reef rock, ranging from 0.6 to 1.95 m long. Most of these front-facing slabs stand about 0.3 to 0.5 m above the ground surface, but one especially large slab rises 0.9 m (fig. 83). Some cut-and-dressed slabs are incorporated into the east and west mound facings, but parts of these, as well as the entire south or rear facing of the mound, are constructed of natural coral heads or cobbles. The rear facing stands only 0.1 to 0.2 m above the ground surface. The interior surface of the mound is sandy, with no traces of *patapata*.

Houmafakalele IV (Site NT-54). Facing south toward Houmafakalele III is Site NT-54, a nearly square mound with a front facing of cut-and-dressed slabs (fig. 81). The mound measures 10.0 by 9.5 m and, with an average height above the adjacent terrain of ca. 35 cm, has an estimated volume of 33.25 m^3. In the prominent south face, the largest slab is situated in the southwest corner, and stands 55 cm high. The two longest slabs in the south face are 1.25 and 1.14 m long; the face averages 0.3 to 0.4 m high. The other three faces are constructed of natural, unmodified coral heads and cobbles about 0.3 to 0.6 m long and 0.1 to 0.2 m above the ground surface. The interior fill is sand, with a few *patapata* pebbles scattered over the central part of the mound.

Houmafakalele V (Site NT-55). This monument, northeast of Houmafakalele IV, is nearly square in plan, with dimensions of 8.5 by 9.0 m. Its facings are entirely of unmodified coral cobbles, and rise only 0.1 to 0.2 m above the ground surface. The mound thus has an estimated volume of only 11.5 m^3. A faint depression was noted in the central part of the mound.

Site NT-164. Lying about 10 m northwest of Houmafakalele IV, this monument has a distinctive, polygonal plan rather than the usual rectangular shape. With maximum dimensions of 12.5 by 11.5 m (approximate average radius 6 m) and an average elevation of 0.40 m, the monument has an estimated volume of 46 m^3. Eleven well-trimmed and dressed coral slabs are aligned along the western edge of the mound. The largest of these is 1.3 m long, with a maximum thickness of 0.21 m. The remaining faces are constructed of natural coral cobbles, decreasing in average size toward the rear, or eastern, face. Most of these natural slabs range in length from 0.2 to 0.4 m, and stand only 0.1 to 0.25 m above the surrounding terrain. Some *patapata* pebbles are scattered over the western part of the structure.

A 1 x 2 m test trench was excavated into the western portion of this mound, in the area of greatest *patapata* concentration. No human skeletal remains were recovered, although we did find the mandible of a fruit bat *(Pteropus* sp.). The original ground surface, marked by an old A horizon, was reached at 49 cm.

Site NT-165. This structure is an outlier situated some distance from the main complex. It is nearly square, with faces ranging from 9.0 to 9.8 m in length,

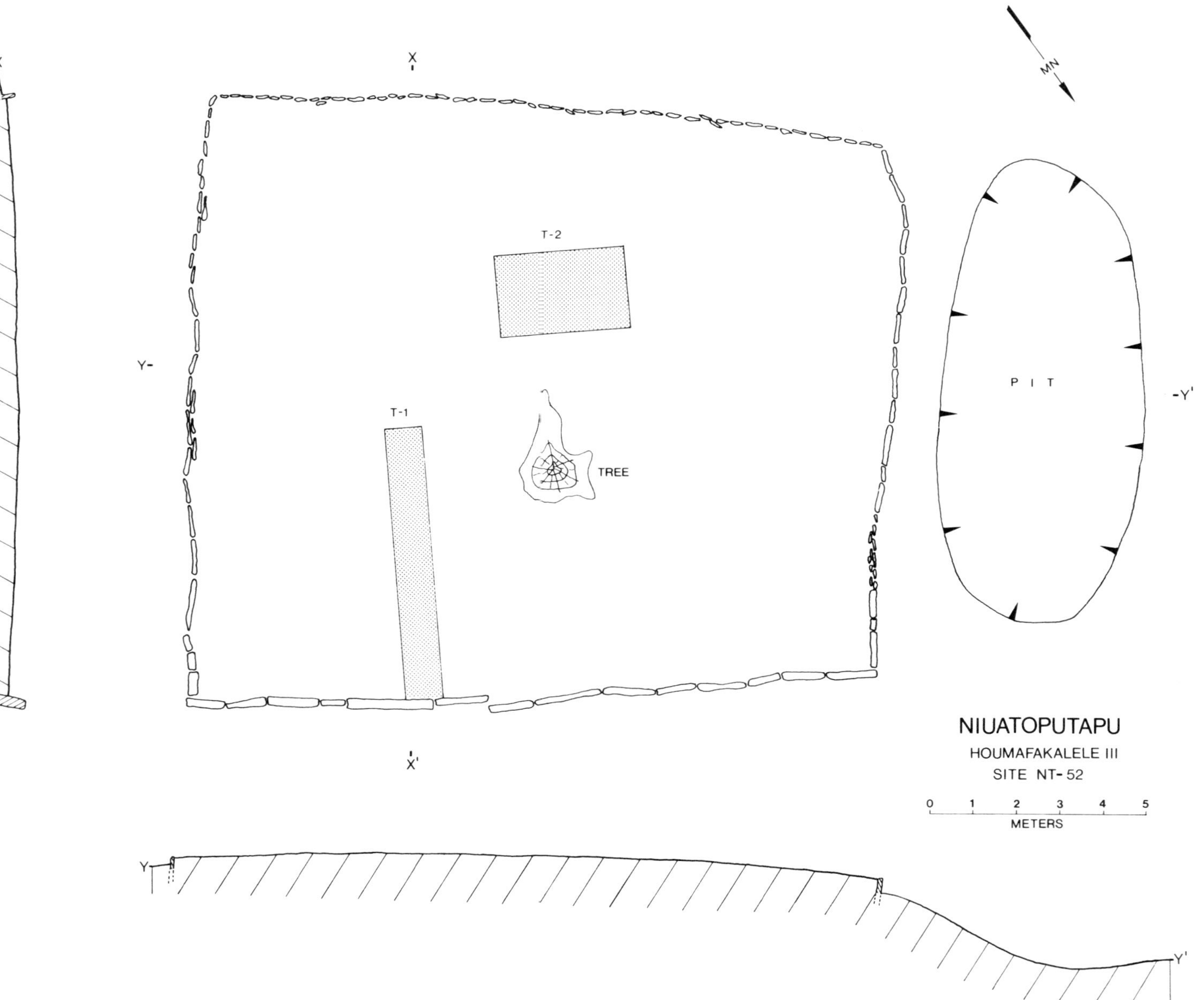

Figure 80. Plan of Site NT-52, the Houmafakalele III burial mound, showing locations of excavation trenches 1 and 2.

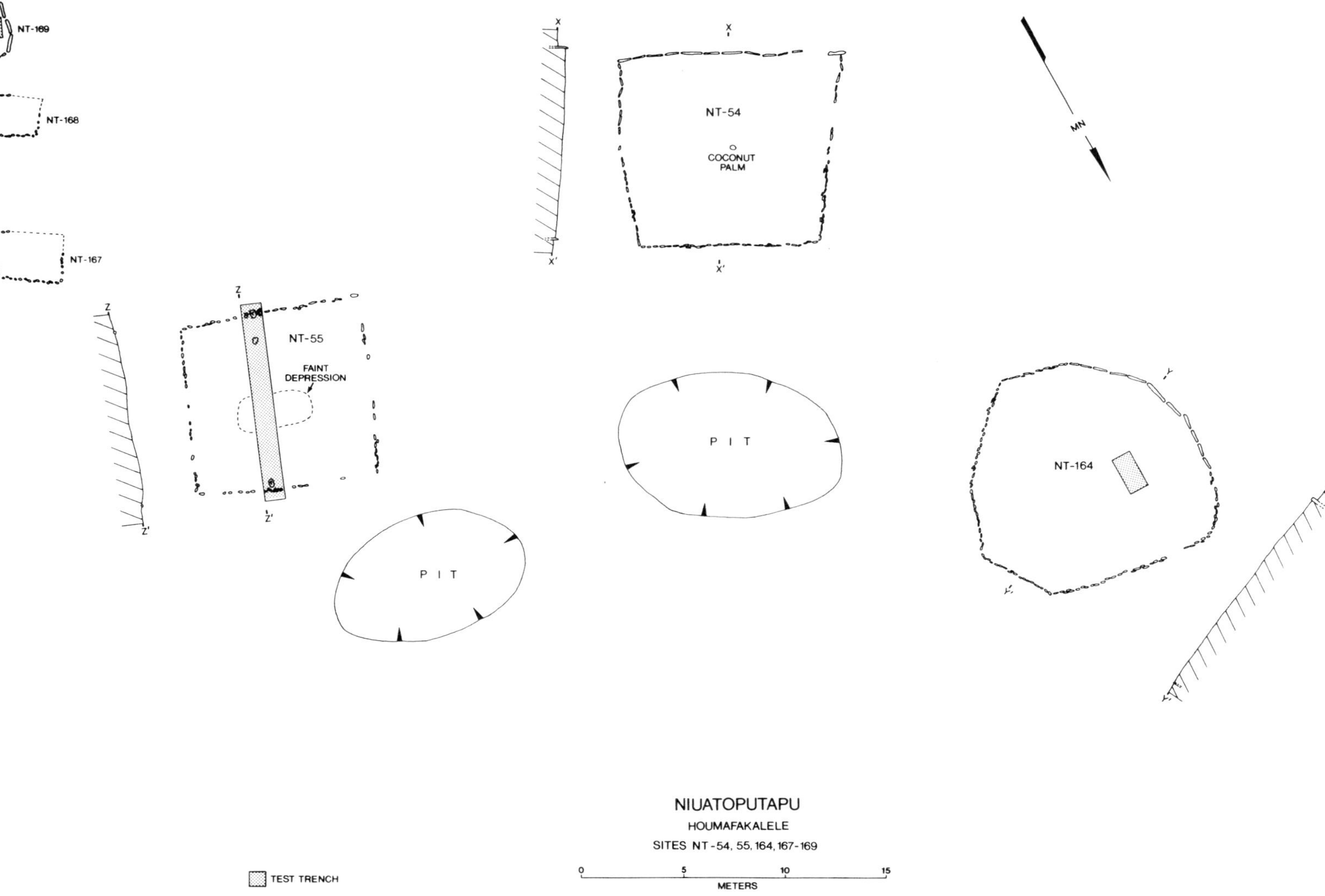

Figure 81. Plan of Sites NT-54, -55, -164, -167, -168, and -169, showing location of excavated trench through mound NT-55.

Figure 82. Cut-and-dressed coral facing of Site NT-52, Houmafakalele III.

and with an elevation of about 0.5 m above the surrounding terrain (volume 44.1 m^3). The facings are constructed entirely of unmodified coral heads and cobbles, and range from 0.2 to 0.4 m in height. There is a distinct central depression, suggesting either that the tomb was robbed at some point or that a collapsed crypt is present. Some *patapata* pebbles are scattered over the platform surface.

Site NT-166. Another outlier situated 66 m from NT-55, this is a small crypt formed of crudely dressed slabs of conglomerate or reef rock, measuring 1.75 by 1.1 m. The highest slabs stand 0.35 m high, and are 0.15 to 0.2 m thick.

Site NT-167. This is one of three small structures located in a cluster seaward of the main Houmafakalele group (fig. 81). It is rectangular, outlined with upright natural coral slabs, each about 0.3 m long and standing only 0.05 to 0.1 m high. The interior is paved with *patapata* pebbles.

Site NT-168. This rectangular structure is identical in form to NT-167 except that it is in better condition and the facing slabs are slightly larger (ca. 0.4 m long).

Site NT-169. This small rectangular structure (fig. 84) has a western face (oriented toward the main group) of three cut slabs of reef rock, each about 0.25 m thick and 0.15 m high. The other three faces are composed of unmodified coral slabs, as with NT-167 and -168. The surface is paved with coral cobbles and *patapata.* A test trench excavated across the interior of this structure (fig. 81) produced no evidence of an interment, but revealed 30 cm of humus and coral pebble fill overlying an original A horizon, with sterile sand below (tested to 1.1 m). This suggests that the group of three small rectangular structures may not be tombs at all, but foundations for small houses of a ritual nature, or for some similar purpose.

Figure 83. Large, central facing slab in Site NT-52, Houmafakalele III.

Excavations in Houmafakalele III (NT-52)

Trench 1. The first excavation in this large mound was a trench 1 m wide and 7 m long (fig. 85), beginning at the interior edge of the largest facing slab and running toward the highest part of the mound. No in situ interments were discovered, but screening of the sand fill produced three human bones: 1 phalange, 1 carpal, and 1 broken fragment of a long bone shaft. The stratigraphic section follows:

Layer	*Description*
I.	0-15/25 cm. Sandy humus, heavily penetrated by rootlets and large roots of *pukovai* tree (7.5 YR 4-5/2).
II.	15/25-55/65 cm. Fill of clean white beach sand, derived from borrow pits (7.5 YR 8/1).
III.	55-65/60-70 cm. Thin buried A horizon of old humus; original soil surface. The very slight development of this layer, less than the present Layer I horizon, is notable, as it suggests the relative recency of emergence of this part of the island (7.5 YR 5-6/2).
IV.	60-70+ cm. White coral sand; sterile.

Trench 2. The second excavation began as a 1 x 3 m trench perpendicular to trench T-1 in the south-central portion of the monument. After the discovery of two interments, the trench was expanded to 2 x 3 m (fig. 80). Three complete, articulated burials were uncovered, as shown in figures 86 and 87. The burials were in an excellent state of preservation, owing to their sandy $CaCO_3$ matrix. That they were interred simultaneously is suggested by their parallel orientations, the fact that they lie at the same level, and the absence of any

disturbance of one interment by the others. The burials are described individually below; all observations had to be conducted with the skeletons in situ, as we had agreed that they would not be removed for study. No metric observations were taken, other than femur and tibia lengths for Burial 2 (these bones were removed, with permission, for ^{14}C age assessment).

Burial 1. A fully articulated skeleton in supine position, extended, with the head turned to the right. The knees and feet were touching, suggesting that the legs had been bound at the time of interment. Hands were at the sides of the pelvis. The symphysis pubis is lipped, granular, and pitted, and cranial sutures are fairly well fused, all suggesting a mature adult (probably 35 to 50 yr of age). The pelvis shape, gracile bone structure, cranial bossing, and lack of prominent brow ridges indicate a female. Osteoarthritis of the lumbar vertebrae (lipping) is strongly pronounced, and the loss of several molars during life suggests periodontal disease (rolled alveolar margin). The skeleton is oriented 115° E.

Burial 2. A fully articulated skeleton in supine, extended position with the head oriented forward; right hand over the abdomen, left hand clasped over the right wrist; knees wide apart, with heels nearly touching and toes pointed outwards. The cranial sutures are well fused and a mature adult is indicated. The skeleton is very robust, with numerous muscle markings; pelvic form and the absence of bossing indicate a male. No osteoarthritis is apparent, but the left femur has a healed fracture, and the left calcaneus appears also to have been fractured at one time. There are numerous caries, and considerable wear on the occlusal surfaces of the molars. All teeth are present but there is some rolling of the alveolar margin, suggesting slight periodontal disease. The third molar is present. The skeleton is oriented 110° E.

The femora and tibia of Burial 2 were removed for ^{14}C dating. This also presented the opportunity to measure these bones and to attempt a reconstruction of stature. The femora had lengths of 46.2 and 46.0 cm, while the tibia had lengths of 39.4 and 39.1 cm. Using the formula provided by Trotter and Gleser (1958), the stature of this individual would have been approximately 174.95 ± 3.74 cm (about 5 feet 10 inches).

Figure 84. Site NT-169.

Figure 85. Trench 1 in Site NT-52, Houmafakele III.

Burial 3. This skeleton is articulated but rather disturbed by root action; one large root had fractured the left radius and ulna and pushed across the thoracic cage. The innominate bones were also crushed and deformed by root action. The burial is supine, extended, with the head lying to the right. Both hands lie over the right side of the pelvis. Knees and feet are close together, suggesting binding as with Burial 1. General robustness, muscle markings, brow ridges, and lack of bossing all suggest a male. The individual was clearly a mature adult. No osteoarthritis or evidence of trauma were observed. The teeth are in good condition, with little wear on the occlusal surfaces. The third molar is present. The burial is oriented 105° E.

Other Burials. Portions of two other interments were exposed. A complete, articulated foot was exposed

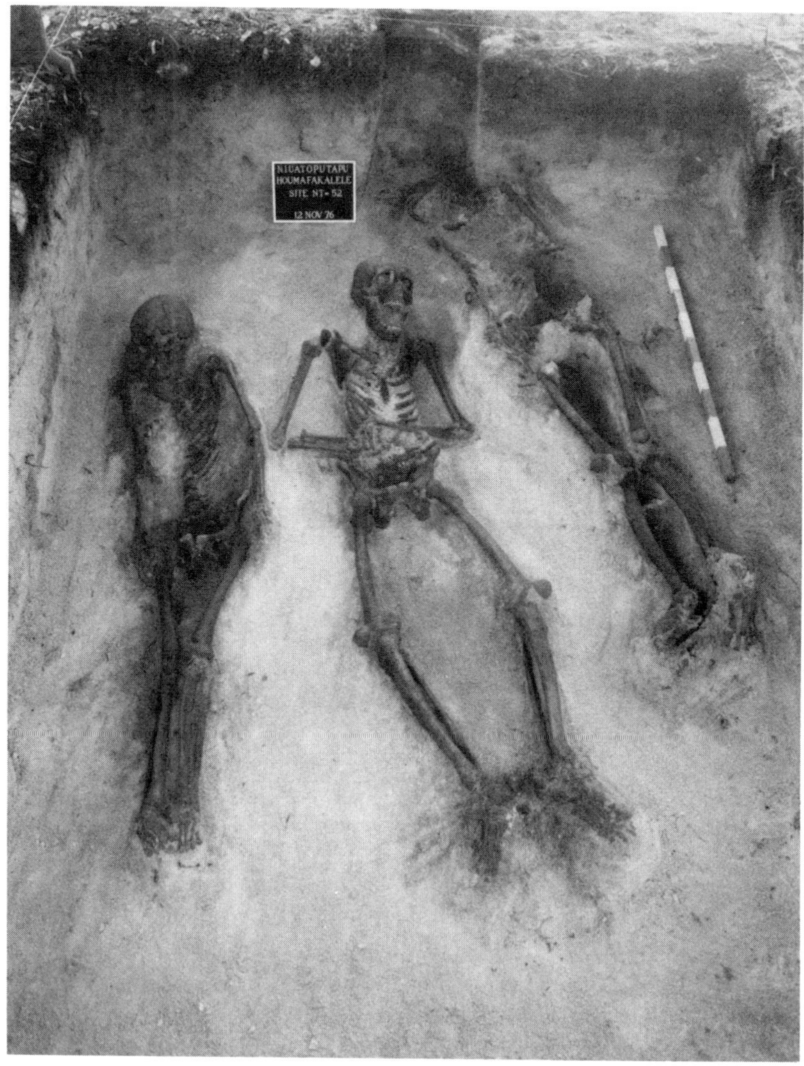

Figure 86. Burials in Trench 2 of Site NT-52, Houmafakalele III.

along the south side of the trench, suggesting another individual in that direction. A single calcaneus was discovered in the northern corner of the trench.

All three burials had a dark gray or blackish stain on the sandy matrix surrounding them. This may have resulted simply from the decomposition of the bodies following interment, or may represent black pigment on burial shrouds or mats.

One objective of the Houmafakalele excavations was to obtain datable material for ^{14}C age assessment. The femora and tibia of Burial 2 in NT-52 fortunately provided material for this purpose. The ^{14}C age of 270 ± 75 years (sample number TORC-16) confirmed our original expectation that this monument, and probably others of its class, date to the late prehistoric or early protohistoric periods.

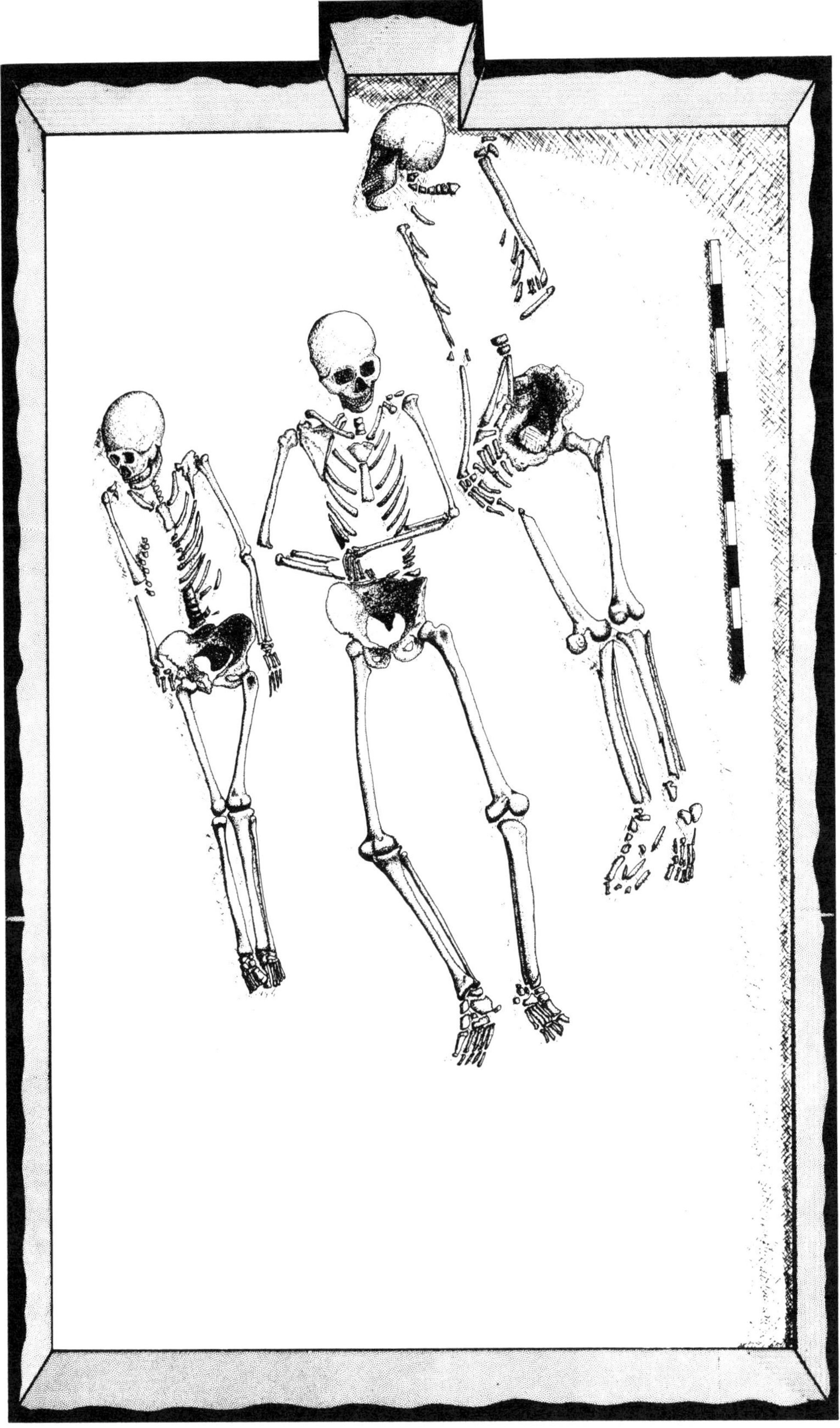

Figure 87. Plan of burials in Trench 2, Site NT-52, Houmafakalele III burial mound.

Excavations in Houmafakalele V (NT-55)

A 1 m wide trench was excavated completely across this monument, bisecting the slight central depression noted earlier. The trench revealed a simple stratigraphic profile similar to that described for NT-52. No articulated skeletal remains were encountered, but the highly disturbed remnants of a burial were discovered under the central depression. These included an articulated right hand, a left ulna and radius, scattered ribs, the proximal end of a humerus, a second metatarsal, fourth metatarsal, and a phalange, as well as two isolated molars. All of these were found within an area of 0.7 by 1 m. It appears that the monument originally contained at least one articulated burial which, excepting the few bones discovered in the trench, was later exhumed. When this exhumation took place, or for what purpose, could not be discerned.

Extra-Areal Comparisons

Ethnohistoric data on protohistoric Tongan burial practices, recorded in the southern islands of Vava'u and Tongatapu, are relevant to the interpretation of the Houmafakalele monuments, as are the results of archaeological excavations in Tongatapu and 'Uvea. Mariner, one of the few Europeans to observe Tongan chiefly burial rites at close hand prior to missionization, remarks that "the body is always placed in a house in front of the fytoca during the time the grave is digging. If there be no house near, a small one is immediately brought for the purpose, which, from the construction of their houses, is readily done by the aid of 50 or 60 men" (Martin 1820:242). This structure is later referred to as a "temporary house" (1820:245). Gifford (1929:199) was told by informants that a temporary house specially constructed for a dying chief was termed *faletolia*. The missionary Baker (quoted in Gifford 1929:200) also refers to a "house built near the god's house [i.e., the burial mound] for the reception of the sick," which he says was termed *falefeao*. These descriptions suggest a probable function for the three small rectangular faced pavements situated seaward of the main monument cluster (structures NT-167, -168, -169). As noted above, the absence of any skeletal remains in NT-169 indicates that these structures are not interments. They could have served as foundations for small, temporary houses or sheds erected to shelter the corpse of the deceased prior to burial.

Excavations in burial monuments in Tongatapu were carried out by McKern (1929) and Davidson (1969). In a circular burial mound (unfaced) on Pangaimotu Islet, McKern (1929:104, fig. 47) excavated multiple interments, all in extended, supine position. No grave goods were present. Davidson investigated two mounds, locally termed *fa'itoka*, at 'Atele on Tongatapu, and found them to contain multiple burials, apparently of local lineage or descent groups; one mound had been enlarged in a second construction phase. The majority of interments were also extended and supine. These results, combined with the Houmafakalele excavations, confirm the widespread dominance of the extended, supine burial position, as well as the general absence of grave goods, throughout the Tongan archipelago in the late prehistoric or protohistoric periods. It should be noted, however, that none of the sites investigated by McKern or Davidson were rectangular, faced-stone monuments like Houmafakalele III.

On 'Uvea Island, also known to have been under Tongan influence and political domination after ca. A.D. 1600 (Kirch 1984a), Frimigacci et al. (1984) excavated a high-status tomb at Atuvalu (Site WF U MU 020A) with features remarkably similar to those of Houmafakalele III. The burial monument is a rectangular platform (6 by 8 m), delimited by a facing of upright basalt slabs (Frimigacci et al. 1984:119, fig. 50), which surmounts a large, oval, earthen mound (20 by 37 m). Excavation within the rectangular platform revealed two interments, one of a large adult male in supine, extended position, with knees apart, ankles touching, and hands on the pelvic region, much like Burial 2 in NT-52. To this individual's left was a female who is interpreted as having been buried alive with the deceased male (Frimigacci et al. 1984, photo no. II). No dates were obtained, although this burial is presumably of late prehistoric or protohistoric age.

CHRONOLOGY OF THE SITES

Assessment of the chronological age of excavated deposits was attempted using radiocarbon dating and the experimental technique of measurement of hydration rinds on volcanic glass flakes. A suite of 14 radiocarbon samples provides a reasonably firm chronology for the principal ceramic sites, the aceramic middens, and the Houmafakalele burial complex. The 30 hydration-rind measurements are "dates" in relative terms only, and are useful primarily in verifying the temporal relationships of the primary ceramic sites.

Radiocarbon Dating

Fourteen radiocarbon age determinations were made on Niuatoputapu samples, eleven by the laboratory of Teledyne Isotopes, Inc., and three by the laboratory of Beta Analytic. The results of these determinations are summarized in table 13; some comment, however, is necessary on the method of data presentation. The column in table 13 labeled "^{14}C Age Years B.P." is the conventional radiocarbon age of Stuiver and Polach (1977:356-57), calculated on the basis of the Libby half-life of 5568 years, and given in years before 1950. For dates made on charcoal, a value of –25 per mil ^{13}C was utilized by both laboratories in calculating the conventional radiocarbon age. When the three samples were submitted to Beta Analytic, we also requested that $^{13}C/^{12}C$ ratios be determined; the two shell samples yielded ^{13}C values of –3.44 and –2.05 per mil. A review of the earlier Teledyne Isotopes determinations suggested that the values reported for shell samples were inaccurate, and an inquiry was made regarding the method used in calculating the conventional radiocarbon age. According to James Buckley, laboratory manager, the three Teledyne Isotopes shell determinations had originally been cited based on a –25 per mil ^{13}C basis, rather than the 0 per mil typical of marine shell (Stuiver and Polach 1977, fig. 1). Buckley then provided normalized ages for these three shell samples based on a 0 per mil calculation for ^{13}C (Buckley, letter to Kirch dated 29 March 1985). In table 13, the bracketed values in the ^{14}C Age column thus provide the conventional radiocarbon age values for shell samples, with ^{13}C normalized to 0 per mil in the case of the Teledyne Isotopes samples, and adjusted to the precisely determined ^{13}C values for the Beta Analytic samples. These bracketed values, along with those for the charcoal samples, thus adhere to Stuiver and Polach's recommendations for presentation of conventional radiocarbon ages as ^{13}C corrected only.

The conversion of these ^{14}C ages into calendrically meaningful ranges required further manipulation of the data, and different procedures were used for the charcoal and marine shell samples. For charcoal samples, the ranges given in the "Corrected Age" column of table 13 are based on the calibration of the radiocarbon time scale using dendrochronologically dated bristlecone pine and sequoia wood, following the procedures and calibration tables in Klein et al. (1982). The ranges given are at the 95% confidence level.

For the marine shell samples, it is necessary to take into account the reservoir effect, which results in deficient ^{14}C levels reflecting "oceanic surface water in ^{14}C equilibrium with the atmosphere, and the rate of exchange with deeper (and older) waters" (Stuiver 1984:8). Stuiver (pers. comm., 1985) notes that the reservoir effect varies considerably in different parts of the world, depending on several factors. For coastal waters of the United Kingdom, a reservoir value of 405 ± 40 years has been determined (Stuiver 1984:8), while in New Zealand, Law (1984) suggests that an age of 336 years is empirically validated. Based on Australian samples, Gillespie and Swadling (1979) have used a value of 450 ± 35 years.

For the Niuatoputapu samples, a tentative local reservoir correction value can be suggested on the basis of the compared charcoal and shell samples from Site NT-100. (I am grateful for the assistance of M. Stuiver in deriving this correction value.) The three charcoal samples from NT-100 have remarkably close conventional ^{14}C ages, with a pooled mean of 1173 years B.P. The two shell samples also overlap well within one standard deviation, with a pooled mean (^{13}C normalized values) of 1,680 years B.P. If we assume that all of these samples are dating phenomena of approximately the same real age (a reasonable working assumption), then the difference between the two pooled means, 507 years, is an approximate estimate of the reservoir value for this area. Alternatively, if we confine ourselves to the two Beta Analytic samples for which actual ^{13}C values were determined in the laboratory (Beta-8682, -8684), the difference between the normalized ages is 480 years. For the purpose of providing a working correction for the reservoir effect on the marine shell samples from Niuatoputapu, the value of 500 years has been used here. Researchers wishing to apply another reservoir correction value which they feel more appropriate can readily do so based on the data provided in table 13. For shell samples, therefore, the "Corrected Age" column in table 13 gives age ranges at one standard deviation based on a reservoir correction factor of 500 years.

Age of the Lapitoid Sites

Before discussing the Niuatoputapu age determinations from sites with Lapitoid ceramics, the presently accepted chronology for Lapita and Polynesian Plain Ware in Fiji and Western Polynesia must be briefly summarized. The earliest dates for Early Eastern Lapita range from 3240 ± 100 at Natunuku and 2980 ± 90 at Yanuca in Fiji to 3090 ± 95 at To-2 in Tongatapu and 2890 ± 80 at the submerged Mulifanua Site on Upolu, Samoa (Green 1979, table 2.1). These ages thus suggest initial colonization of the region between about 1500 and 1200 B.C. Green (1979) further suggests a date of approximately 1000 B.C. for the division between Early and Late Eastern Lapita. Based on ^{14}C determinations from sites such as Sigatoka (Fiji), Mangaia Mound (Tongatapu), and Tavai (Futuna), a date of approximately 500 B.C. has been suggested for the division between Late Eastern Lapita and Polynesian Plain Ware. In Fiji, Late Eastern Lapita gives way to the impressed Navatu Phase ceramics by about 100 B.C. (Frost 1979). In Samoa, the cessation of ceramic production and use has been placed by Green and

TABLE 13

NIUATOPUTAPU RADIOCARBON AGE-DETERMINATIONS

FIELD NO.	LAB. NO.	SITE	PROVENIENCE	MATERIAL	^{14}C AGE YEARS B.P.[a]	^{13}C	CORRECTED AGE[b]
TORC-1	I-10,481	NT-90	Q28II(3), IB, 32-36 cm	Charcoal	1110 ± 75	—	A.D. 650-1135
TORC-3	I-9934	NT-90	A25,IB,34-54 cm	Charcoal	1815 ± 130	—	155 B.C.-A.D.460
TORC-17	I-10,633	NT-90	I21III(3), IB	*Tridacna*	3210 ± 85 [3620 ± 85]	—	1255-1085 B.C.
TORC-18	I-10,632	NT-90	S24 II (2), IB	*Tridacna*	3350 ± 90 [3770 ± 90]	—	1410-1230 B.C.
TORC-7	I-9936	NT-100	220, IB, 57-66cm	Charcoal	1120 ± 165	—	A.D. 615-1210
TORC-9	I-9937	NT-100	269, IIA, 67-75 cm	Charcoal	1220 ± 95	—	A.D. 605-1010
TORC-19	I-10,634	NT-100	269, IIA	*Tridacna*	1305 ± 80 [1720 ± 80]	—	A.D. 650-810

TABLE 13, Continued

FIELD NO.	LAB. NO.	SITE	PROVENIENCE	MATERIAL	^{14}C AGE YEARS B.P.[a]	^{13}C	CORRECTED AGE[b]
—	Beta-8682	NT-100	210, 40-60 cm	*Tridacna*	1290 ± 100	-3.44‰	A.D. 710-910
—	Beta-8684	NT-100	269, IIA, 67-75 cm	Charcoal	1180 ± 60 [1160 ± 60]	-25.82‰	A.D. 655-1010
TORC-5	I-9935	NT-93	Fe13, 65-85 cm	Charcoal	645 ± 95	—	A.D. 1230-1415
—	Beta-8683	NT-93	120, 40-60 cm	Marine Shell	1380 ± 60 [1750 ± 60]	-2.05‰	A.D. 640-760
TORC-13	I-9938	NT-125	10W, 50-60 cm	Charcoal	650 ± 85	—	A.D. 1230-1415
TORC-14	I-10,482	NT-125	20N, Bed 4	Charcoal	1140 ± 75	—	A.D. 635-1045
TORC-16	I-9943	NT-52	Burial 2	Human Bone	270 ± 85		A.D. 1420-1815

[a]Bracketed values for ^{13}C corrections, either based on the $^{13}C/^{12}C$ ratio in the case of the Beta samples, or on an assumed 0/00 ^{13}C in the case of the shell samples processed by Isotopes.
[b]For charcoal dates, corrected for secular variation based on Klein et al. (1982), at 95% confidence intervals. For shell dates, correction for reservoir effect only (see text for discussion).

Davidson (1974:224) at about the end of the third century A.D., on the basis of a large suite of radiocarbon age determinations from several Polynesian Plain Ware assemblages. For Tonga, Groube (1971) argued that pottery production did not extend beyond about 200 B.C., based on a reconsideration of Poulsen's dates and on additional ^{14}C determinations from Vuki's Mound.

For reasons discussed above, and based also on a detailed stylistic analysis of the ceramics (see chapter 6), Site NT-90 is clearly the earliest site excavated on Niuatoputapu. Furthermore, given our intensive survey of the ceramic zone, we believe that it represents the island's initial colonization site. However, the site contains not only the characteristic Early Eastern Lapita style of dentate-stamped decoration but large quantities of Plain Ware as well, suggesting that it was occupied over a lengthy period. The four ^{14}C age determinations from NT-90 confirm this interpretation. The two dates obtained on *Tridacna* shell can be taken as reasonable estimates of the time of initial human colonization of the island, sometime in the last three or four centuries of the second millennium B.C. (The *Tridacna* shells used for dating were culturally modified, probably for shell adz production, and X-ray analyses showed them to be nearly pure aragonite, indicating no significant recrystallization or calcite formation. We believe that the molluscs were probably taken alive from the Niuatoputapu lagoon.) Furthermore, these two determinations closely match those cited above for the Natunuku and To-2 sites, reinforcing the established chronology of Lapita settlement in the Fiji-Tonga-Samoa region.

The two charcoal dates from NT-90, on the other hand, suggest that occupation continued at this locality for more than 1,500 and perhaps as long as 2,000 years. Indeed, the TORC-1 assessment, of A.D. 650 to 1135 when corrected, at first appears unacceptably late in comparison with Polynesian Plain Ware sites in Tongatapu and Samoa. This initial reaction, however, is belied by the consistent dating results from the two principal Plain Ware sites, NT-100 and -93.

Seven samples were processed from Sites NT-100 and -93. The results are highly consistent, which is remarkable considering that both charcoal and marine shell samples are included, and that determinations were made by two independent laboratories. The only sample that does not overlap at one standard deviation is TORC-5, from Fe 13 at NT-93. This oven pit is sealed by the disturbed Layer IA garden soil, and may well be a later feature. The other six samples are in unquestioned association with the Plain Ware ceramics that were abundant at both sites.

These consistent results from NT-100 and -93 can only be interpreted as evidence for the persistence of ceramic production on Niuatoputapu well into the first millennium A.D. Indeed, they present a strong case for the continuance of ceramics as late as A.D. 800 to 900. Although this chronology is at variance with the accepted scenario from both Samoa to the north and Tongatapu to the south, the Niuatoputapu ^{14}C data are too consistent to be discounted.

Age of the Aceramic Sites

Two charcoal samples from NT-125 provide some indication of the age of these aceramic deposits (a third sample, from the aceramic portion of the NT-163 transect, was submitted to Teledyne Isotopes but proved too small to be measurable). These samples, with corrected age ranges of A.D. 635 to 1045 and A.D. 1230 to 1415, are consistent with the Plain Ware site determinations reviewed above and suggest a tentative age of about A.D. 900 for the cessation of ceramic production and use on Niuatoputapu.

Finally, the dated sample of human bone from Burial 2 in the Houmafakalele III mound (NT-52) provides one chronological marker for this class of large chiefly mortuary structures. The corrected age range, A.D. 1420 to 1815, is consistent with the age predicted from an analysis of chiefly genealogies and oral traditions (Kirch 1984a), as well as from the geomorphological location of most of these sites on the recently uplifted apron of marine sediments surrounding the island.

Hydration-Rind Dating of Volcanic Glass Flakes

At the time that the Niuatoputapu excavations were undertaken, some effort was being made to develop the method of hydration-rind age assessment of volcanic glass in the Hawaiian Islands (Barrera and Kirch 1973; Morgenstein and Riley 1974; Morgenstein and Rosendahl 1976). Since the volcanic glass recovered from the Niuatoputapu sites appeared to be similar in chemical composition to that from Hawaiian sources, it was decided to experiment with the measurement of hydration rinds on flakes from the principal excavated sites. This work was undertaken by M. Morgenstein, then with Hawaii Marine Research of Honolulu. No attempts at artificial inducement of hydration were made, nor was a rate of hydration or alteration established. Furthermore, subsequent work with the Hawaiian volcanic glass by Olson (1983) raised a number of questions as to the physical and chemical

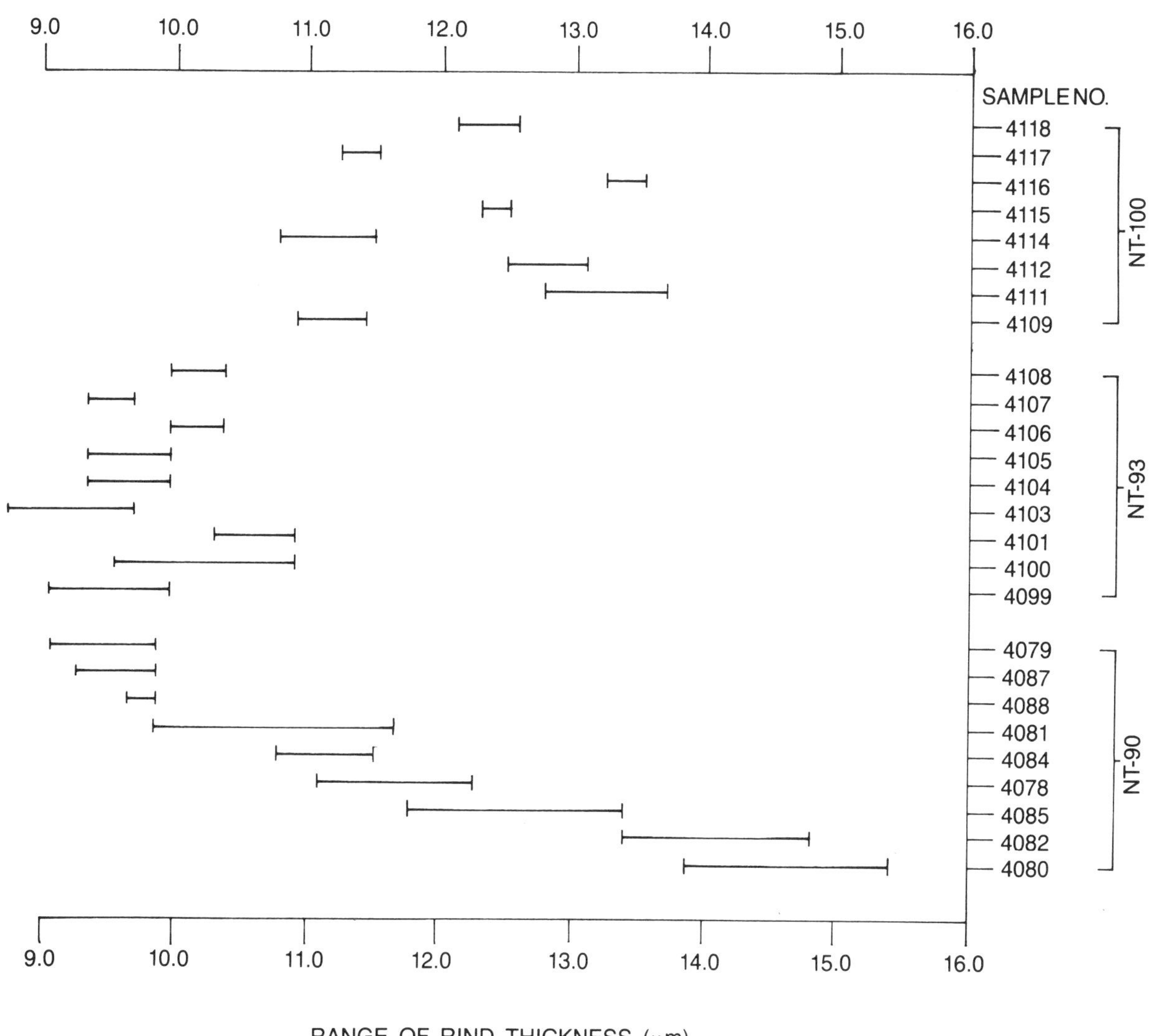

Figure 88. Graph of hydration rind thicknesses for volcanic glass flakes from Sites NT-90, -93, and -100.

properties involved in the hydration-alteration of these low-silica forms of glass. Thus, the hydration-rind measurements taken on the Niuatoputapu flakes cannot be considered as chronometric in any but a very approximate, relative sense.

Thirty flakes—10 each from Sites NT-90, -93, and -100—were thin-sectioned for rind measurement. Morgenstein (pers. comm.) reported that "the rinds are inconsistent with abrupt and gradational lateral terminations, are sometimes masked by abundant ferruginous dust in flow orientations, and in general the petrographic identification of the cortex is almost impossible except for the very thick hydration bands. We have observed no evidence of perlite or perlitic texture, rather the rinds are enriched with ferruginous oxyhydroxides giving them an apparent similarity to palagonite. We are uncertain if the rinds are an iron rich perlite, an iron poor palagonite, or a phase we are unaccustomed to intermediate between the both."

The rind thickness measurements are graphically summarized in figure 88, showing the range of rind thicknesses determined for each of 26 flakes for which a rind could be isolated. If we assume that rind thicknesses are proportional to age, the primary significance of these data is, first, to confirm the long occupation span for Site NT-90 relative to the other two sites and, second, to confirm the later ages of NT-93 and NT-100. The placement of NT-100 between NT-90 and -93, however, is inconsistent with the radiocarbon dates, which suggest that these two sites are more or less contemporary.

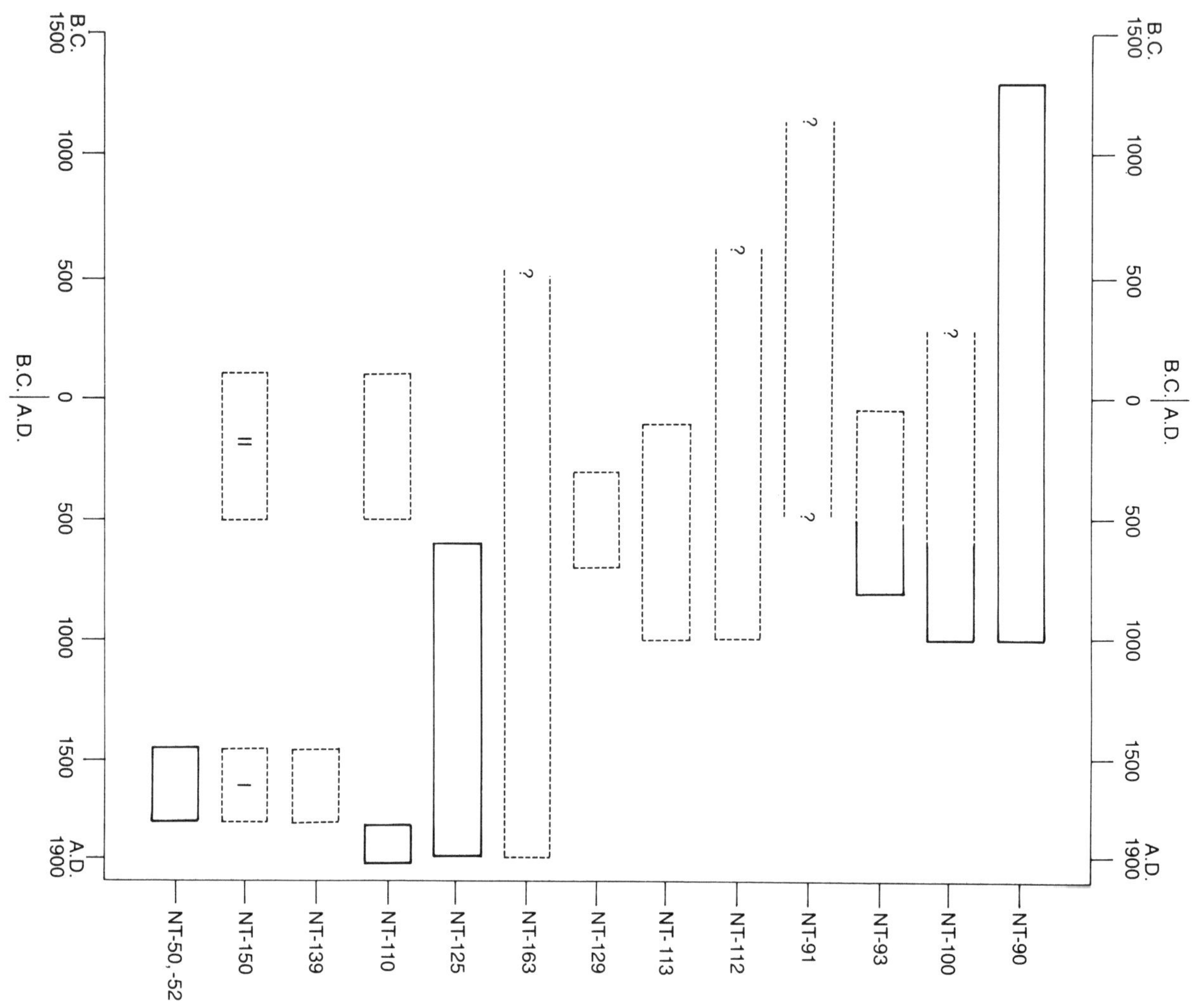

Figure 89. Suggested temporal correlation of Niuatoputapu excavated sites.

It is possible that with further study, especially the artificial inducement of hydration-alteration rinds and determination of the particular chemical processes involved, the Niuatoputapu volcanic glass flakes will provide a useful medium for chronometric analysis. The very preliminary results summarized above do not seriously conflict with the chronology derived from radiocarbon dating, but neither do they add any precision to the prehistoric time scale for the Niuatoputapu sites.

SITE CORRELATIONS

The suite of radiocarbon dates obtained from five key sites provides a chronological framework into which the other excavated sites may be placed on the basis of stylistic, architectural, geomorphological, and other indicators. The suggested correlation of sites is shown graphically in figure 89, in which the solid bars represent sites that have been dated, while dashed bars denote those that have been correlated by means of comparative data.

CHAPTER FIVE

MATERIAL CULTURE AND TECHNOLOGICAL CHANGE

Our archaeological investigations on Niuatoputapu yielded a collection of 54,900 artifacts, with an additional 56 specimens recovered during the reconnaissance of Tafahi Island. As indicated in table 14, which shows the distribution of major artifact classes by site, the collection is dominated by ceramic sherds (78%) and flaked stone (21%), with less than one percent (222 objects) representing all other categories. The most significant assemblages are those from Sites NT-90 (73% of the entire collection), NT-93, and NT-100. There is also a temporal imbalance in the collection, since only a handful of adzes and other non-ceramic objects were obtained from sites outside the ceramic zone. Thus, while technological changes that occurred over the first 1,500 to 2,000 years of the Niuatoputapu sequence are reasonably well evidenced, changes that may have occurred after about A.D. 700 to 800 are largely undocumented. This problem is not unique to Niuatoputapu, and affects the whole of Tongan prehistory, as reflected in Davidson's use of the term "the dark ages" to characterize the later prehistoric period (1979).

In this chapter, the excavated and surface-collected artifacts are analyzed according to the major classes indicated in table 14, categories in wide use in Oceanic archaeology. For each general class, analytical procedures and descriptions of the specimens are followed by extra-areal comparisons with similar artifacts from other Western Polynesian and southwest Pacific sites.

CERAMICS

The Ceramic Sample

The excavations and surface collections in the Niuatoputapu ceramic zone and on Tafahi Island yielded 43,131 ceramic sherds, the site-by-site distribution of which is shown in table 15. Of these, the majority (92.4%) were plain body sherds. Another 5% of the collection consists of heavy base sherds. Only 2.6% of the collection (1,106 sherds) is classified as diagnostic—i.e., rims, carinations, handles, or sherds carrying decoration.

Seventy-three percent of the entire sample derives from Site NT-90, where the density of sherds per square meter was nearly twice that at any other site. Reasonably large collections were obtained from NT-93 and -100; together, these three assemblages provide the focus for the ceramic analysis. As noted in chapter 4, Site NT-90 is believed to have been the initial colonization site on Niuatoputapu, although the occupation there spanned a long period. Sites NT-93 and -100, on the other hand, represent later phases of the Lapitoid ceramic series in Western Polynesia. Consonant with its status as an Early Eastern Lapita locality, Site NT-90 yielded 93% of all decorated sherds recovered on the island. Nonetheless, these account for less than 1% of the total ceramic assemblage at the site.

TABLE 14

DISTRIBUTION OF GENERAL ARTIFACT CLASSES FROM NIUATOPUTAPU AND TAFAHI

CLASS	SURFACE FINDS	NT-90	NT-91	NT-93	NT-100	NT-110	NT-112	NT-113	NT-125	NT-129	NT-163	TAFAHI ISLAND	TOTALS
Ceramics		31,405	638	5,635	2,385	482	1,714	277	22	15	505	53	43,131
Adzes	29	25	2	5	12	4	7	3				3	90
Fishing Gear		12	1	6	3		2						24
Ornaments		20		2	1	1	2		1		1		28
Food Preparation Gear		7		4	1		1				1		14
Tools		12		4	3	2	1		1				23
Miscellaneous		2											2
Worked Bone		2		2									4
Worked Shell		11		3	3		1						18
Lithics		8,891	161	793	571	220	497	221	45	45	159		11,603
Historic Period Artifacts	1	3				10	3		2				19
TOTAL	30	40,390	802	6,454	2,979	719	2,228	501	71	60	666	56	54,956

TABLE 15

THE CERAMIC SAMPLE

SITE	TOTAL SHERDS	DENSITY No./m2	DIAGNOSTIC SHERDS	BODY SHERDS	BASE SHERDS	DECORATED	
						NO.	%
NT - 90	31,405	612.8	854	29,162	1,389	122	0.39
NT - 91	638	159.5	11	593	34	1	0.16
NT - 93	5,635	256.1	124	5,010	501	1	0.02
NT - 100	2,385	125.5	58	2,242	85	4	0.17
NT - 110	482	241.0	11	420	51	1	0.21
NT - 112	1,714	342.8	30	1,644	40	—	—
NT - 113	277	69.2	1	259	17	—	—
NT - 125	22	—	1	21	—	—	—
NT - 129	15	3.7	1	14	—	—	—
NT - 163	505	126.2	15	427	63	2	0.40
TF - 5	26	—	0	26	—	—	—
TF - 12	27	—	0	27	—	—	—
TOTAL	43,131		1,106 (2.6%)	39,845 (92.4%)	2,180 (5.0%)	131	—

Analytical Procedures

During excavation, sherds were regularly processed by washing and drying, weighing, and sorting into major categories (plain body sherds, bases, rims, and other diagnostics). Plain body sherds, most of which were small (less than 5 cm^2) and rounded, were generally discarded after counting and weighing. However, representative samples from various grid units and stratigraphic levels at each site were retained for detailed laboratory analysis. All diagnostic sherds were retained.

Laboratory analysis proceeded separately for the samples of plain body sherds and of diagnostic sherds; all data were recorded in two separate SPSS computer files (Nie et al. 1975). In the case of the plain body sherds, the analytical focus was on attributes of material and manufacture, and only samples from the three principal sites noted above were considered. The SPSS data file for the plain body sherds included the following variables:

1. Provenience (site, grid unit, layer, level);
2. Sherd thickness (mm);
3. Exterior color (hue, value, chroma in Munsell system);
4. Carbonized core (+ / -);
5. Temper type (calcareous, volcaniclastic, mixed);
6. Temper texture, following the ranges defined by Bennett (1974:88);
7. Temper density, following Bennett (1974:105);
8. Nature of surface treatment (slipped, impressed, wiped, burnished, or eroded);
9. Anvil impressions (+ / -).

A total of 379 plain body sherds from Sites NT-90, -93, and -100 was examined and coded for the variables listed above.

All diagnostic sherds (1,106) were coded in a separate SPSS file, with a focus on formal and stylistic attributes. The variable list for this file follows:

1. Provenience (site, grid unit, layer, level);
2. Sherd form (rim with lip, rim without lip, lip only, carination, handle, decorated body sherd);
3. Vessel type (pot/jar, non-carinated jar, carinated jar, open bowl, carinated bowl, restricted neck vessels, plates);
4. Decoration position (absent, exterior, interior, both sides, lip only, both sides plus lip, exterior plus lip);
5. Temper type (calcareous, volcaniclastic, mixed);
6. Basic rim form (vertical, inverted, everted, upturned inverted, upturned everted, aberrant);
7. Rim thickening (interior, exterior, divergent, parallel, reduced);
8. Rim thickening position (high, low);
9. Lip form (pointed, rounded, flat, flat-rounded, outwardly beveled, inwardly beveled, aberrant);
10. Reconstructed rim diameter (cm);
11. Lip thickness (mm);
12. Maximum rim thickness (mm);
13. Carination angle (°); and
14. Surface treatment (slipped, impressed, wiped, burnished, eroded).

The analyses described above were applied not only to the ceramic samples from Niuatoputapu and Tafahi, but to collections obtained by the author from Futuna, 'Uvea, and Vava'u islands, to facilitate detailed inter-site and inter-island comparisons of Western Polynesian Lapitoid ceramics. (For the Futunan results, see Kirch 1981.) All ceramic data from these sites are on file in punched-card format in the Anthropology Department, B.P. Bishop Museum.

Body Sherd Analysis

Paste

Although paste was not included as a variable within the original analytical framework, subsequent work with the ceramic collection indicated that the Niuatoputapu and Tafahi sherds could readily be sorted into three paste groups. Each of 399 sherds from NT-90, -93, and -100 and from Tafahi was examined by grinding a fresh cross-section on a hand-held whetstone and examining the exposed surface under a binocular microscope at 10X. A selection of 16 sherds, typifying each of the paste groups, was photographed using a scanning electron microscope at the University of Washington. These SEM photos (fig. 90) clearly illustrate the major structural differences in paste composition. The three paste groups are described below:

Paste A. Dominating the Niuatoputapu samples (ranging from 40 to 96% of any sample), this paste has medium porosity, with numerous small interstices in the range of 0.05-0.1 mm. Sherds of Paste A tend to have crumbly surfaces, and individual grains are readily detached by rubbing the sherd between the fingers. Individual clay particles agglomerate into "peds" about 0.1 to 0.5 mm in diameter, giving the paste a grainy texture. Temper is volcaniclastic, including both light and dark minerals, lithic fragments, and pumice. Temper particles range in size from 0.1 to 1.9 mm, with most in the range of 0.2 to 0.5 mm. Temper density ranges from 15% to 25%. Color of the paste in cross-section is frequently red (10 R 4-5/6-8).

Paste B. Paste B is less frequent in the Niuatoputapu samples, but dominates the Tafahi collections. It is very compact and dense, much less porous than Paste A. There are few interstices in cross-section. Individual clay particles are very fine and do not agglomerate into "peds" as in Paste A. Rubbing the sherd between the fingers generally does not result in the detachment of fine particles. The temper is invariably volcaniclastic with both light and dark minerals, lithic fragments, and pumice. Temper particles range in size from 0.15 to 2.9 mm, with most in the range from 0.2 to 0.5 mm. Temper density ranges from 20% to 30%. Usual color in cross-section is weak red to red (10 R 4-5/3-6). A variant of Paste B noted in TF-5 and certain Niuatoputapu samples has better-sorted and smaller-grained temper, with temper density of 25% to 30%.

Paste C. This paste is common only at Site NT-90, with few examples from other sites. Paste C is the least compact and most porous of the three paste groups. Frequent, linear, parallel interstices ranging from 0.1 to 0.4 mm in width give the sherds a platy texture in section. Sherds are crumbly, and particles are readily detached by rubbing the sherd between the fingers. The silty clay agglomerates into "peds" ranging from 0.1 to 0.7 mm in diameter, as in Paste A. Temper always includes calcareous sand grains as well as volcaniclastic grains, and individual samples range from calcareous dominant to volcaniclastic dominant. Volcaniclastic temper grains are in the same size range as for Paste A; calcareous grains range from 0.1 to 1.1 mm. The density of calcareous grains ranges from 5% to 40%, while overall temper density (calc + volcani-

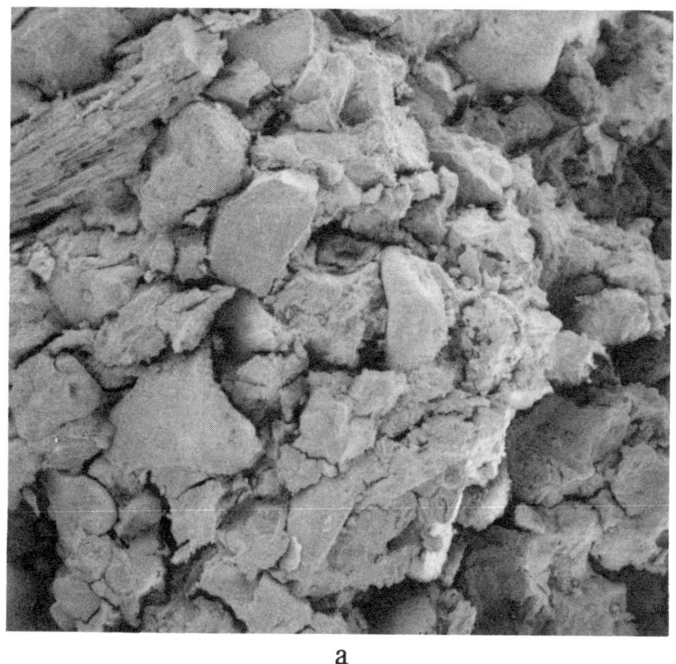

a

b

Figure 90. Scanning electron microscope photos of Niuatoputapu ceramic paste (40X): a, Paste A; b, Paste B.

clastic) ranges from 20% to 40%. Usual color in cross-section is weak red to red (10 R 4/4-8).

These paste groups are significantly distributed with regard to site, as shown in table 16. Paste C with calcareous temper is dominant only at early Site NT-90, where it accounts for between 12.5% and 60% of any given sample (average for the entire site is 35%). Site NT-100 yielded only one example of Paste C, as did Tafahi Site TF-12. Two sherds from Site NT-93 were provisionally classed as Paste C variants, although the frequency of calcareous grains in these examples was very low. Paste C is thus clearly early, and comprises approximately two-thirds of sherds from NT-90 bearing Lapita style dentate-stamped decoration. Elsewhere, I have observed that calcareous sand tempering is characteristic of Early Eastern Lapita ceramic technology (Kirch 1981:137, 142), a point further emphasized below.

The spatial distribution of Pastes A and B is also significant. As indicated in table 16, Paste A dominates all Niuatoputapu assemblages: 55% of sherds at NT-90, 82% at NT-93, and 82% at NT-100. The pattern is reversed in the two Tafahi assemblages, in which Paste B accounts for 88% and 78% of the sherds respectively. This suggests that Paste A derives from a local Niuatoputapu clay source, while Paste B is from a Tafahi Island source. The presence of about 20% of sherds of the non-dominant type on either island can accordingly be explained by some transport of ceramics across the 5 km-wide channel between islands. This suggests some regular contact or exchange between populations on the two islands, as indeed occurs at the present time.

There is also evidence that Paste B increased in frequency in the Niuatoputapu sites over time. In Unit S24II at NT-90, Paste B is absent in the lowest level and gradually increases from 7% to 27.5% as one moves up the stratigraphic column. A similar pattern is evidenced in Unit 219 at Site NT-93. The NT-100 pattern is not so clear, but does not contradict the evidence from the first two sites. If confirmed by future work, an increased frequency of Paste B sherds in Niuatoputapu sites over time might be indicative of the increased importation of Tafahi ceramics.

Temper

Dickinson (1974) thin-sectioned and petrographically analyzed nine sherds collected by Rogers on Niuatoputapu, and classified these into three distinctive temper types: (1) calcareous sand; (2) ferromagnesian sand; and (3) pumiceous sand. Subsequently, 18 sherds collected during our 1976 excavations (from NT-90, -93, and -100) were sent to Dickinson for petrographic study; his report on these specimens is included here as appendix B. Non-plastic inclusions identified within the clay matrix of these sherds include calcareous sand (reef detritus), pyroxenes, plagioclase feldspar, volcanic rock fragments including pumiceous types with distinctively stretched vesicles, opaque iron oxides, olivine, and occasional quartz. Sorting and rounding of non-plastic inclusions varies

TABLE 16

DISTRIBUTION OF CERAMIC PASTE TYPES BY SITE

SITE/LEVEL	PASTE A		PASTE B		PASTE C	
	N	%	N	%	N	%
NT–90	38	55	7	10	24	35
NT–93 Unit 151	144	82	29	17	2	1
NT–100 Unit 219	78	82	16	17	1	1
TF–5	4	12	29	88	—	0
TF–12	5	19	21	78	1	4

TABLE 17

DISTRIBUTION OF CERAMIC TEMPER BY SITE

TEMPER TYPE	NT–90	NT–93	NT–100	TF–5–6	TF–12–3
Calcareous	30	—	—	2	1
Ferromagnesian	45	109	96	11	26
Pumiceous	—	16	3	7	—
Feldspathic	—	1	—	—	—
Unclassified	—	6	5	6	—
TOTAL	75	132	104	26	27

from sherd to sherd, indicating that temper sands were obtained from a variety of depositional environments, including beaches, ravines, and pyroclastic accumulations. Based on the mineralogy of the non-plastic inclusions, Dickinson concluded that all of the necessary depositional environments could be found locally on either Niuatoputapu or Tafahi, although in his opinion available data were not sufficient to rule out sources on other Tongan island-arc volcanoes. No examples of the distinctive Fijian or Samoan temper types were found among the Niuatoputapu sherds.

Based on the relative proportions of the various non-plastic inclusions within the observed sample of sherds, Dickinson described three temper types and three variant temper types from Niuatoputapu. The three main types, the same at those enumerated above, are numerically superior to all other grain types combined. The Calc-FM variant is of a ferromagnesian temper with a significant calcareous component (ca. 10%). The crystal lithic variant is intermediate in composition between ferromagnesian and pumiceous temper types. The placer variant is similar to the crystal-lithic variant, but with the addition of a significant opaque iron oxide component (ca. 20%).

As a facet of his research into the production and distribution of Tongan pottery, T. Dye in 1983 further examined temper in 311 sherds from Niuatoputapu and Tafahi. All sherds were examined in hand sample at magnifications of 10 to 30X. Most sherds contain ferromagnesian crystals, lithic fragments, and pumice in varying proportions, while a few (largely from NT-90) contain significant proportions of calcareous beach sand. The non-plastic inclusions in the 311 sherds were grouped into three major categories, corresponding approximately to Dickinson's three temper types, while the variants were grouped according to which non-plastic constituent was dominant. One sherd contains a majority of feldspars, while 17 others defy assignment to a group on the basis of hand-sample examination. As indicated in table 17, sherds with dominant ferromagnesian non-plastic inclusions are most common in both Niuatoputapu and Tafahi sites, making up 79% of the entire collection. Calcareous temper is frequent only in Site NT-90, although this type is represented also in both Tafahi sites.

Fifty of the sherds studied by Dye were also thin-sectioned and examined under the petrographic microscope because they appeared to deviate from the usual non-plastic inclusion blend of ferromagnesian crystals, lithic fragments, and pumice. The 50 thin sections were compared and contrasted with the 19 sections submitted to Dickinson by Kirch. Under petrographic examination, all of these sherds were seen to fall within the range of types and variants described earlier.

In sum, the petrography of the Niuatoputapu and Tafahi sherds examined to date strongly supports the conclusion of local manufacture. Although the mineralogical similarity of Tongan island-arc volcanics precludes a definitive statement, no evidence for importation of ceramics from Fiji or Samoa was obtained (the exception being two decorated sherds of almost certain Fijian origin, not petrographically examined, but described below under "Decoration"). The only significant inter-site temper difference is the common occurrence of calcareous reef-detritus sand grains at Site NT-90, an attribute of Paste C.

Temper density was also analyzed for the plain body sherd samples; cumulative density curves for the principal Niuatoputapu assemblage and two Tafahi assemblages are shown in figure 91. The curves are similar, although the TF-12 assemblage is slightly less dense than average, and TF-5 has a small component

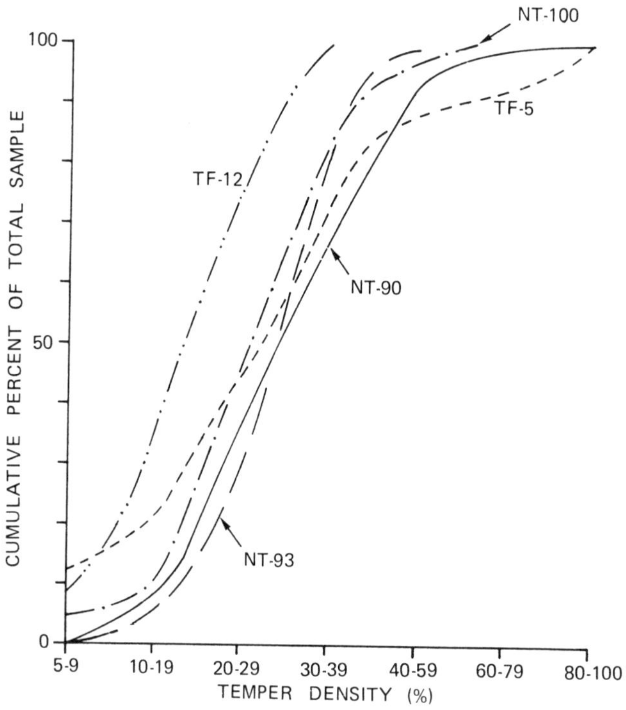

Figure 91. Cumulative frequency plots of temper density for ceramics from Niuatoputapu and Tafahi sites.

with higher than usual density. Most sherds contain temper or non-plastic inclusions in the density range of 20% to 35%.

Exterior Color

Sherd color reflects a complex set of conditions and processes, including the nature of the original paste, firing attributes, subsequent use (i.e., fire blackening), and post-depositional processes. Despite this potential for variation, the color range in Niuatoputapu sherds is not great. The majority fall within the range from weak red and reddish brown to red, dusky red, and dark red in the Munsell system (5 YR - 10 R, 3-6/2-6). Of the three sites, NT-90 exhibits the least color variation, NT-100 the greatest.

Sherd Thickness

In Samoa, considerable significance has been accorded to sherd thickness as an index of ceramic change, with "thick" and "thin" classes proposed for Polynesian Plain Ware (Green and Davidson 1969a, 1974). Accordingly, we attempted to determine whether the Niuatoputapu assemblages display comparable changes in sherd thickness. A total of 1,932 sherds from the principal Niuatoputapu and Tafahi assemblages were measured for thickness, and the results plotted as histograms (fig. 92). The curves were not only invariably unimodal—indicating a continuum in vessel wall thickness rather than two discrete groups—but showed no significant inter-site or stratigraphic differences. As summarized in table 18, the Tafahi samples have mean sherd thicknesses of about 1 mm greater than the Niuatoputapu samples, but these do not appear to be statistically significant. Most importantly, the later prehistoric NT-93 and -100 assemblages do not reveal any significant difference in sherd thickness from the earlier NT-90 assemblage. These results are a

TABLE 18

THICKNESS OF PLAIN SHERDS (mm)

SITE	MEAN, S.D.	RANGE
NT–90	6.61 ± 1.39	4–11
NT–93	6.98 ± 1.43	4–11
NT–100	6.61 ± 1.62	4–13
TF–5	7.85 ± 1.91	5–12
TF–12	7.96 ± 2.08	4–12

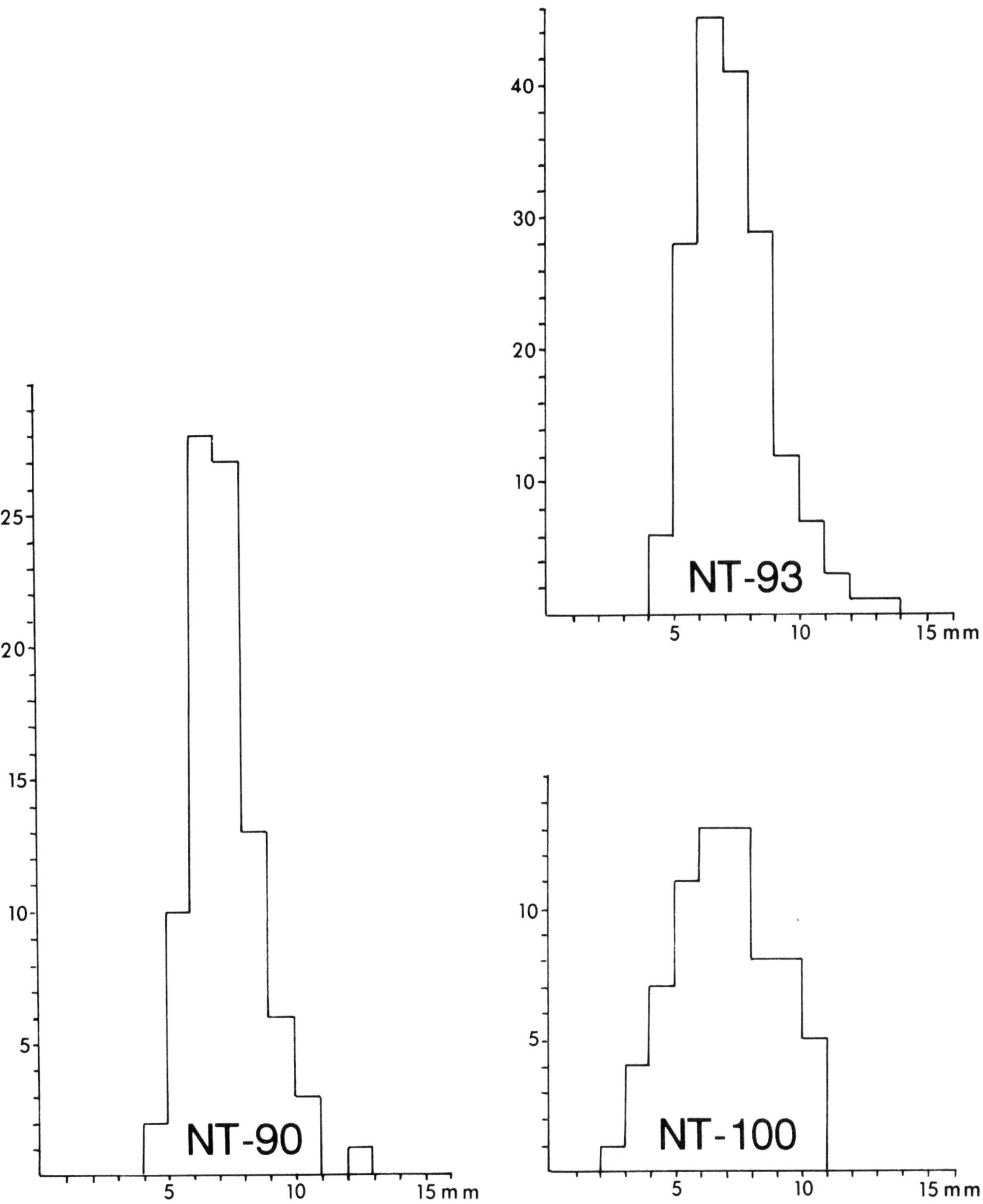

Figure 92. Histograms of body sherd thickness for representative samples from Sites NT-90, -93, and -100.

significant contrast with the Samoan case, and underscore the point that ceramic change did not proceed in a uniform fashion throughout Western Polynesia (cf. Kirch 1981).

Manufacture

Some techniques used in vessel forming, finishing, and firing may be inferred from the ceramics themselves. Yet, as Birks (1973:19) aptly notes, many of the most interesting aspects of pottery production—such as the procurement of raw materials, organization of labor, and inter- or intra-community specialization—cannot be determined from present evidence. Based on the analysis of non-plastic inclusions, the raw materials are presumed to be from local Niuatoputapu and Tafahi Island sources. Purposive, manual addition of temper is evident in the calcareous-tempered vessels (Paste C). It

TABLE 19

PLAIN SHERD ANALYSIS

ATTRIBUTE	TF - 5 (N = 26)	TF - 12 (N = 27)	NT - 90 (N = 151)	NT - 93 (N = 118)	NT - 100 (N = 110)
Carbon Core					
Present	3.8 %	0.0 %	3.3 %	1.7 %	3.6 %
Absent	96.2	100.0	96.7	98.3	96.4
Temper Type					
Calcareous*	0	3.7	33.8	0.0	0.9
Volcanic	100.0	96.3	66.2	100.0	99.1
Surface Treatment					
Slip	8.0	0.0	0 ++	3.6	6.7
Wiped	8.0	18.5	38.5	81.8	79.8
Burnished	4.0	18.5	0.9	5.5	3.8
Eroded	80.0	63.0	60.6	9.1	9.6
Anvil Impression					
Present	15.4	11.1	0.7	22.9	30.9
Absent	30.8	29.6	9.3	39.8	20.0
Indeterminate	53.8	59.3	90.1	37.3	49.1

* Includes mixed calcareous and volcanic temper.
++ 2% of diagnostic sherds slipped.

Figure 93. Earthenware pots immediately after firing with coconut shells and fronds, at Sigatoka, Fiji, 1982.

is not certain, however, whether some or all of the volcaniclastic inclusions in Pastes A and B were manually added to the clay body as temper or grog. Such non-plastic inclusions may, in fact, have been naturally present in local clay deposits. If so, the cessation of calcareous tempering would imply the cessation of purposive tempering altogether (cf. Kirch 1981 on the Futunan ceramics). This issue will not be resolved until a range of local clay samples has been collected, fired, and petrographically examined for comparison with the prehistoric ceramics.

Incomplete slab-welds in numerous sherds suggest that slab-building was a common technique used in vessel forming. Bases were thickened and strengthened by the addition of a second slab to the vessel bottom. Evidence for the use of a paddle and anvil to thin the vessel walls consists of anvil impressions on interior wall surfaces and, less frequently, of parallel-ribbed paddle impressions on exterior surfaces. Table 19 provides data on the frequency of anvil impressions on the plain body sherd samples.

Exterior surfaces were most commonly finished by wiping, leaving fine, roughly parallel striations visible under a low-power lens. Burnishing, perhaps with a waterworn cobble, resulted in smooth, hard finishes on some vessels (table 19). A few vessels were also finished with a reddish-brown or red slip. Although none of the plain body sherds in the NT-90 sample exhibit such a slip, 2% of the diagnostic sherds are slipped. All sites have sherds with highly eroded, patinated, or encrusted surfaces for which determination of surface treatment is not possible (table 19).

No evidence of kilns was excavated at any of the Niuatoputapu sites, nor have such structures been reported in other Oceanic archaeological contexts. Ethnographic descriptions of Oceanic pottery production usually refer to open firing in which a small number of vessels are surrounded with kindling or dry coconut fronds. In August 1982, I observed such a firing technique in the lower Sigatoka Valley on Viti Levu, Fiji (fig. 93). Such open firing was probably used in the production of the Niuatoputapu vessels, in which

TABLE 20

STANDARDIZED CANONICAL DISCRIMINANT FUNCTION COEFFICIENTS FOR PLAIN WARE ATTRIBUTES

ATTRIBUTE	CANONICAL FUNCTION 1	CANONICAL FUNCTION 2
Thickness	–0.072	–0.321
Hue	–0.526	–0.732
Value	–0.326	0.685
Chroma	0.551	–0.822
Carbon Core	0.057	–0.253
Temper Type	0.250	–0.098
Temper Texture	–0.420	–0.165
Temper Density	0.160	–0.109

low firing temperatures are indicated by the presence of inoxidized carbon cores (table 19). The interior portions of vessel bases are also frequently inoxidized, which may indicate that firing took place in an inverted position, thus creating a reducing atmosphere in the vessel interior.

Discriminant Analysis of Plain Body Sherds

Differences and similarities in the samples of plain body sherds have been discussed above in terms of individual attributes. Proceeding with such a discrete, attribute-by-attribute analysis, it is difficult to measure or form an impression of the overall similarity between whole assemblages. For this purpose, the multivariate statistical technique of discriminant analysis is useful (Sneath and Sokal 1973:400-408). Discriminant analysis creates linear combinations ("discriminant functions") of a set of variables so as to best separate a set of groups or assemblages. In this case, the groups to be discriminated among are the plain body sherd assemblages from the three principal Niuatoputapu sites. The variables used were hue, value, and chroma of exterior surface, wall thickness, carbon core, temper type, temper texture, and temper density. Discriminant functions were computed using SPSS (Nie et al. 1975:434-67) with the direct method in which all independent variables are entered into the analysis concurrently. A total of 291 cases was used in the analysis. Table 20 reports the canonical discriminant function coefficients for each variable, while figure 94 is a scattergram of cases for the first two discriminant functions.

One hundred percent of sample variance was accounted for by only two discriminant functions. Function 1, which accounts for 76.2% of variance, has high positive loadings for chroma, and to a lesser degree for temper type. High negative loadings on Function 1 are for hue, value, and temper texture. Function 2, accounting for 23.8% of total variance, has high positive loadings for value and high negative loadings for hue, chroma, and, to a lesser extent, thickness and carbon core.

The NT-90 assemblage is most distinct from those of NT-93 and -100 on Function 1 (fig. 94), in part reflecting the high frequency of Paste C in the former site. The NT-93 and -100 assemblages are virtually indistinguishable on Function 1. These latter groups sort out slightly better on Function 2, with considerable overlap with NT-90. In general, however, the results of this analysis suggest that the differences between the NT-93 and -100 assemblages are slight. This is demonstrated further by the classification results of individual cases. Whereas 73% of the NT-90 sherds were correctly assigned to their predicted group membership, the figures for NT-93 and -100 were substantially lower (47 and 52%). In sum, discriminant analysis supports the interpretation of the NT-90 assemblage as the most distinct, whereas the two later assemblages are only minimally distinguishable.

Diagnostic Sherd Analysis

A total of 1,106 diagnostic sherds was recovered from 10 Niuatoputapu sites (the Tafahi collections contain only plain body sherds). The distribution of these diagnostic sherds by site and sherd type is provided in table 21, from which it can be seen that the majority of diagnostics derives from NT-90. About one-half of all diagnostic sherds are lip fragments, generally too small to determine overall rim form. Most useful for analysis are the 209 complete rims with lips intact, although many of the 194 rims with missing lip edges are also classifiable to vessel form. Other categories of diagnostic sherd include carinations, handles, and miscellaneous (e.g., body sherds with decoration).

Vessel Form

Ten vessel forms are reconstructable from the Niuatoputapu assemblages, with most of these restricted in distribution to NT-90. Two or more variants (designated by letters) are recognized for four of these vessel forms. The assemblages yielded a total of 18 forms and variants, as indicated in table 22. Vessel forms are illustrated in figures 95 and 96.

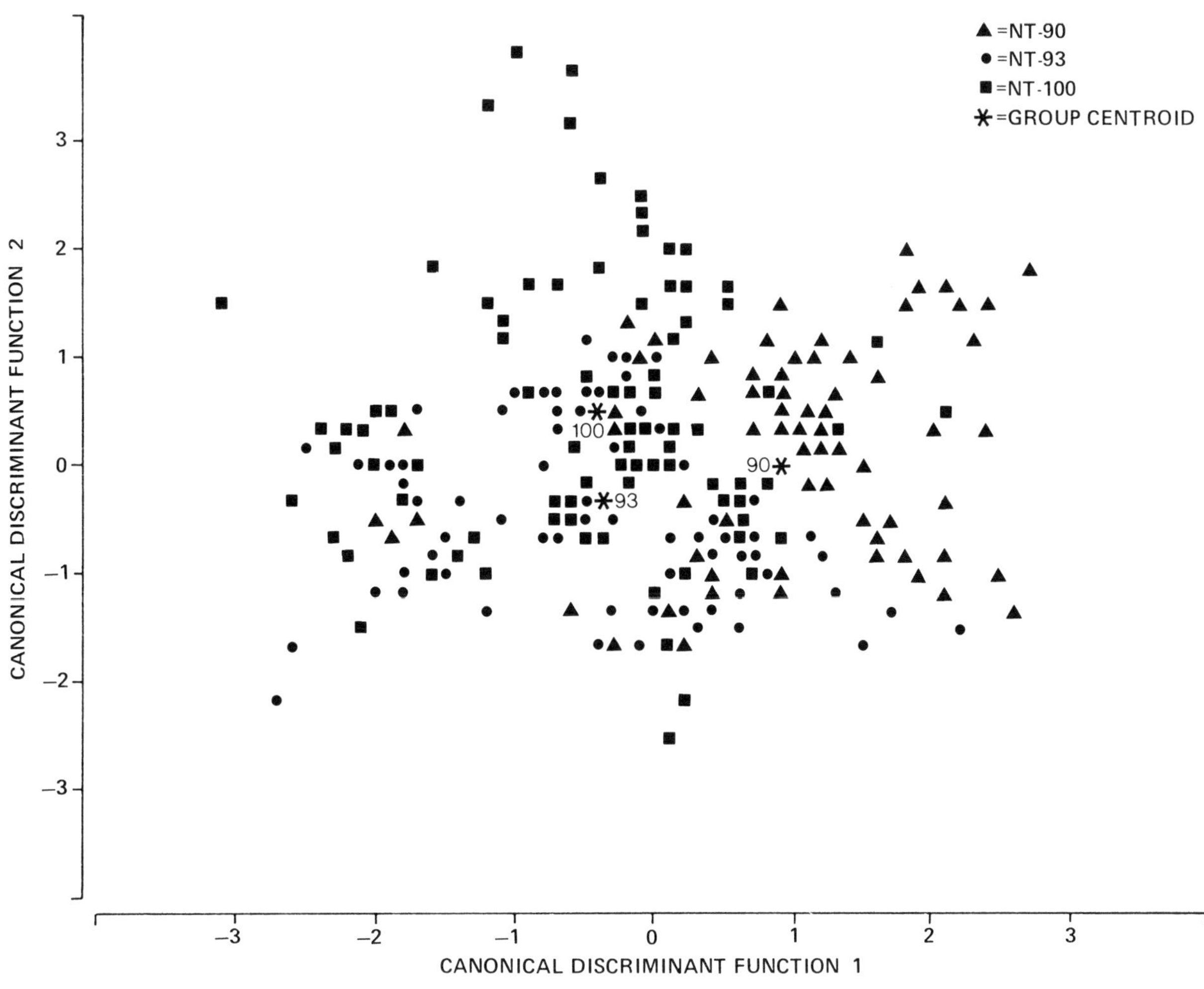

Figure 94. Discriminant analysis scatterplot of plain body sherds from Sites NT-90, -93, and -100.

Vessel Form 1: Small Bowls/Cups. Form 1 consists of small bowls or cups with rim diameters ranging from 10 to 16 cm. Three variants are recognized.

Vessel Form 1A: Plain Ware. Two examples of plain ware bowls or cups from Site NT-90 are shown in figure 97. These vessels were evidently shallow-bottomed, and the smaller ones closely resemble coconut-shell drinking cups known ethnographically throughout Western Polynesia. Such cups are still in use today in Tonga for *kava* drinking. The rims are simple and not thickened, and the lip is rounded or flat-rounded. Form 1A lacks decoration, although in several examples from Site NT-90 these bowls/cups have a fine red-orange slip. The smallest of these vessels probably served as drinking cups, although some of the larger ones might have been used as serving vessels.

Vessel Form 1B: Decorated Cup. Form 1B, represented by a few sherds from NT-90, consists of a small cup with a rim diameter of about 10 cm. The lip is flat-rounded, and the cup is decorated on both exterior and interior surfaces and on the lip, as shown in figure 98, g-h. The decoration includes dentate-stamped lines, incised lines, and notching on the rim. The vessel was probably used as a drinking cup, perhaps for serving *kava*. It is conceivable that the decoration distinguished these cups from Form 1A, marking them as reserved for persons of particular status or rank.

Vessel Form 1C: Decorated Cup. These cups were evidently about the same size as 1B, but they differ in two respects. The vessel walls are quite thin (ca. 2 to 5 mm), and expanded at the interior of the lip. The flat-rounded lip edge is decorated with a dentate-stamped zig zag motif (fig. 98, c-f). At least three different examples

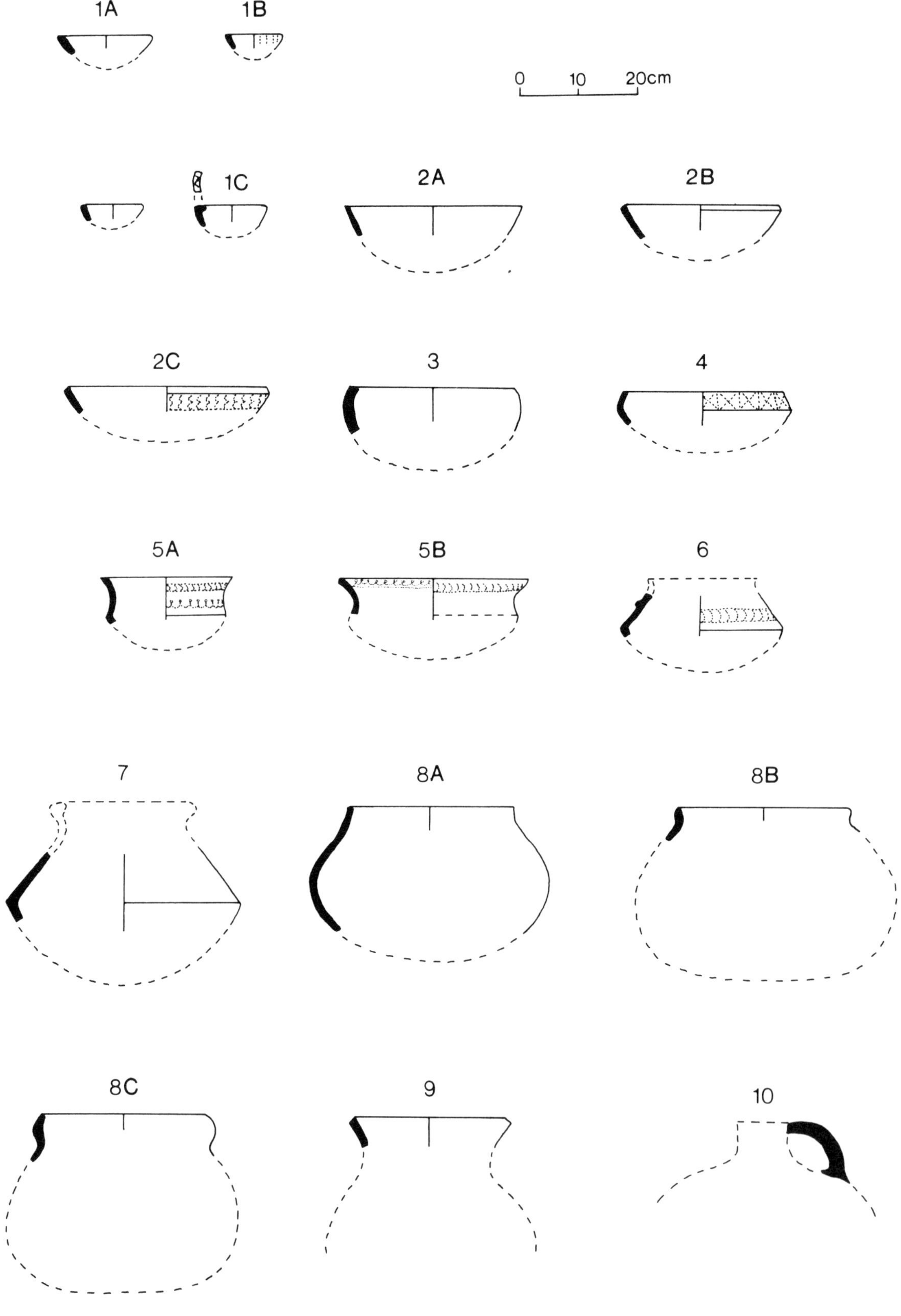

Figure 95. Niuatoputapu ceramic vessel forms (see text for description).

TABLE 22

CLASSIFICATION OF VESSEL FORMS

	FORM
I. Unrestricted Vessels	
A. Simple Vessel Contours	
1. Rim diameter < 20 cm	1
a. Undecorated	1A
b. Decorated	
(1) Simple, direct rim	1B
(2) Interiorally thickened rim	1C
2. Rim diameter > 20 cm	2
a. Undecorated	
(1) Flat rim	2A
(2) Beveled rim	2B
b. Decorated	2C
B. Composite Vessel Contours	5
1. Rim diameter = carination diameter	5A
2. Rim diameter > carination diameter	5B
II. Restricted Vessels	
A. Simple Vessel Contours	3
B. Composite Vessel Contours (carinated)	
1. Inverted rim	4
2. Everted rim	
a. Decorated	6
b. Undecorated	7
C. Inflected Vessel Contours	
1. Upturned inverted rim	8
a. Rim parallel, direct	8A
b. Rim thickened, "rolled"	8B
c. Rim thickened exteriorally	8C
2. Everted rim	9
3. Constricted neck, handled	10

TABLE 21

DIAGNOSTIC SHERD SAMPLE

SITE	RIM WITH LIP	RIM WITHOUT LIP	LIP ONLY	CARINATION	HANDLE	OTHER	TOTAL
NT–90	149	178	412	79	24	12	854
NT–91		4	4	1	2		11
NT–93	30	9	82		3		124
NT–100	19	1	34	1	2	1	58
NT–110	2	1	7		1		11
NT–112	4		25	1			30
NT–113					1		1
NT–125			1				1
NT–129		1					1
NT–163	5		7	1	2		15
TOTAL	209	194	572	83	35	13	1,106

of this vessel type are known from NT-90. Form 1C may also have functioned as a *kava*-serving cup.

Vessel Form 2: Large Bowls, Thin Ware. Form 2 vessels consist of several varieties of thin ware bowls, both plain and decorated.

Vessel Form 2A: Large Bowl, Plain. This Form 2 variant has a rim diameter of about 30 cm and vessel wall thickness of about 7 mm (fig. 99, b). The rim is simple and parallel, with a flat lip. The probable function of Form 2A was as a serving vessel of some sort.

Vessel Form 2B: Large Bowl, Plain. This Form 2 variant is distinguished from 2A by its outwardly slanting lip and straighter sides. The rim diameter of the single reconstructed example is 27 cm (fig. 99, a). This form probably also functioned as a serving vessel.

Vessel Form 2C: Large Bowl, Decorated. An example of a Form 2C bowl from NT-90 (fig. 100, a) has a rim diameter of 34 cm, and an outwardly slanting lip as in 2B. The bowl carries simple dentate-stamped decoration on both the lip edge and the exterior surface. A food serving function is again suggested.

Vessel Form 2D: Large Bowl with Incurved Rim, Plain. A few rim sherds from relatively large bowls with slightly incurved rims were excavated at NT-90 (fig. 98, a-b), although none was sufficiently large to facilitate accurate reconstruction of the rim diameter. These rims have flat or flat-rounded lips, and are plain.

Vessel Form 3: Large Bowl, Thick Ware. This vessel form (fig. 99, c) consists of a large, massive bowl with rim diameter of about 29 cm and wall thickness of 12 to 13 mm. The rim curves slightly inward and the lip is flat-rounded. The vessel is entirely plain.

Vessel Form 4: Carinated Bowl, Decorated. This vessel form, of which a good example was reconstructed from NT-90 (fig. 100, b) has a rim diameter of 27 cm and a distinct carination about 30 to 33 mm below the rim. The lip is flat-rounded. Simple dentate-stamped decoration (Motif M30.1) is carried on the vessel exterior in the zone defined by the rim and carination.

Figure 96. The ceramic assemblage of Site NT-90.

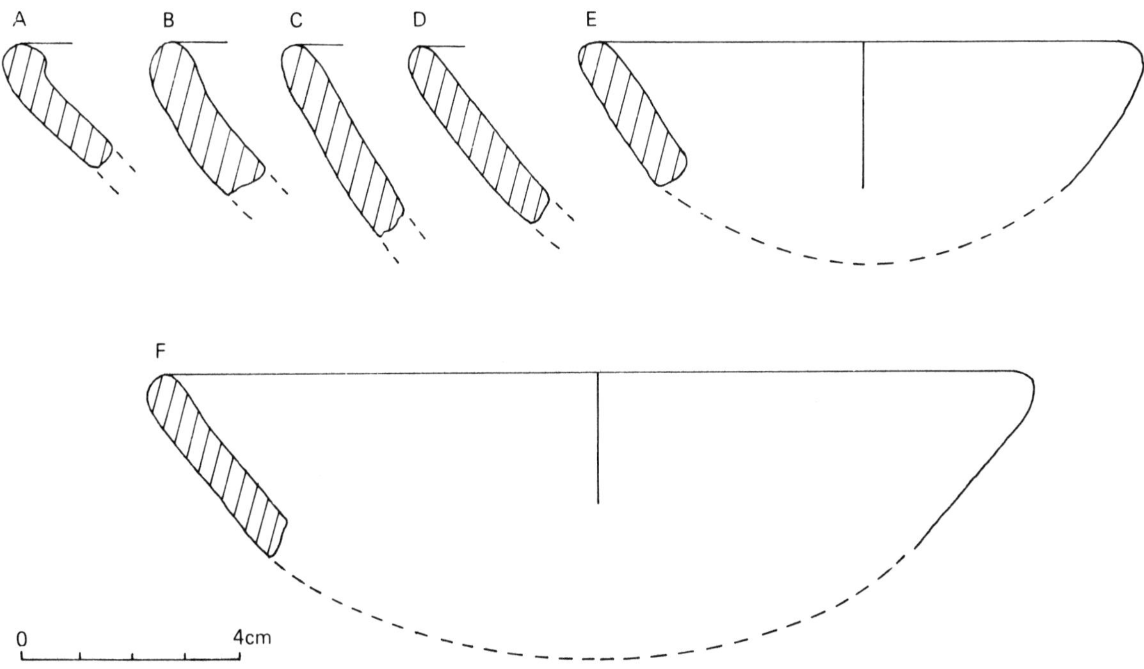

Figure 97. Rims and reconstructed vessels of Form 1A.

Vessel Form 5: Collared Bowls, Decorated. This vessel form, of which two variants are recognized, consists of distinctly carinated vessels with flaring, outturned rims, resulting in a collared effect. All known examples carry dentate-stamped decoration.

Vessel Form 5A. This variant is represented by a reconstructed example from NT-90 with a rim diameter of 23 cm and a distinct carination about 6 cm below the rim (fig. 100, c). The lip is missing. A dentate-stamped zone marker (GZ2) runs along the carination and defines a zone, between the marker and the rim, which is filled in with several dentate-stamped motifs. This was presumably a serving vessel of some kind.

Vessel Form 5B. The reconstructed 5B example (fig. 100, d) differs from 5A in its larger rim diameter (32 cm) and in its more pronounced flaring of the rim. The lip tapers slightly and is rounded. Dentate-stamped motifs are present both on the rim exterior and on the interior surface, where the flaring angle of the rim makes the design prominent to the viewer. It is possible that both Form 5 variants were *kava* bowls, as their form would be reasonably well suited to this purpose. (Note that a lexeme for '*kava* bowl', **taanoa*, is reconstructable to Proto-Polynesian.)

Vessel Form 6: Carinated Jar, Decorated. This vessel form, known from at least nine examples from NT-90 (fig. 104, f-n), consists of a sharply carinated jar with a somewhat restricted orifice. Unfortunately, there are no examples with a complete rim, or for which rim diameter can be reconstructed. These jars carry dentate-stamped and incised decoration on the outer surface above the carination. There may also have been plain ware variants of this vessel form.

Vessel Form 7: Large Carinated Jar. This vessel form, known only from several examples from NT-90 (fig. 101, d, e), consists of a large, sharply carinated jar, the upper part of which slopes sharply inward. Two reconstructed examples have maximum diameters at the body carination of 30 and 44 cm. The vessel walls are thick and massive, generally between 12 to 15 mm, up to 20 mm thick at the carination point. The rim form is unknown. These vessels are evidently entirely plain. They could have functioned for either serving or storage.

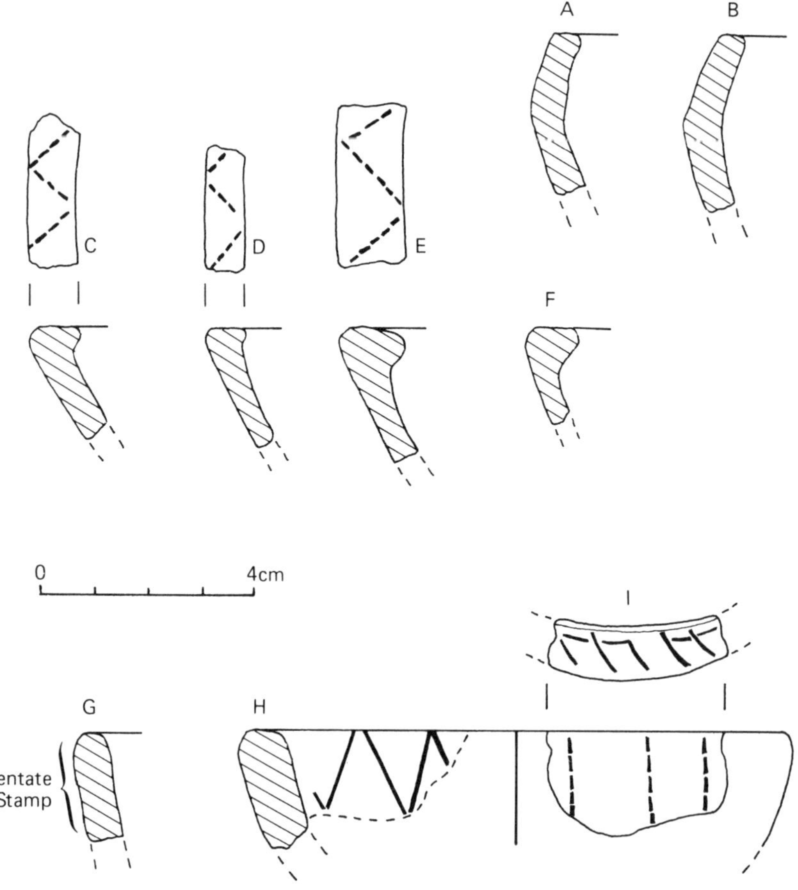

Figure 98. Decorated bowls of vessel Forms 1B, 1C, and 2D.

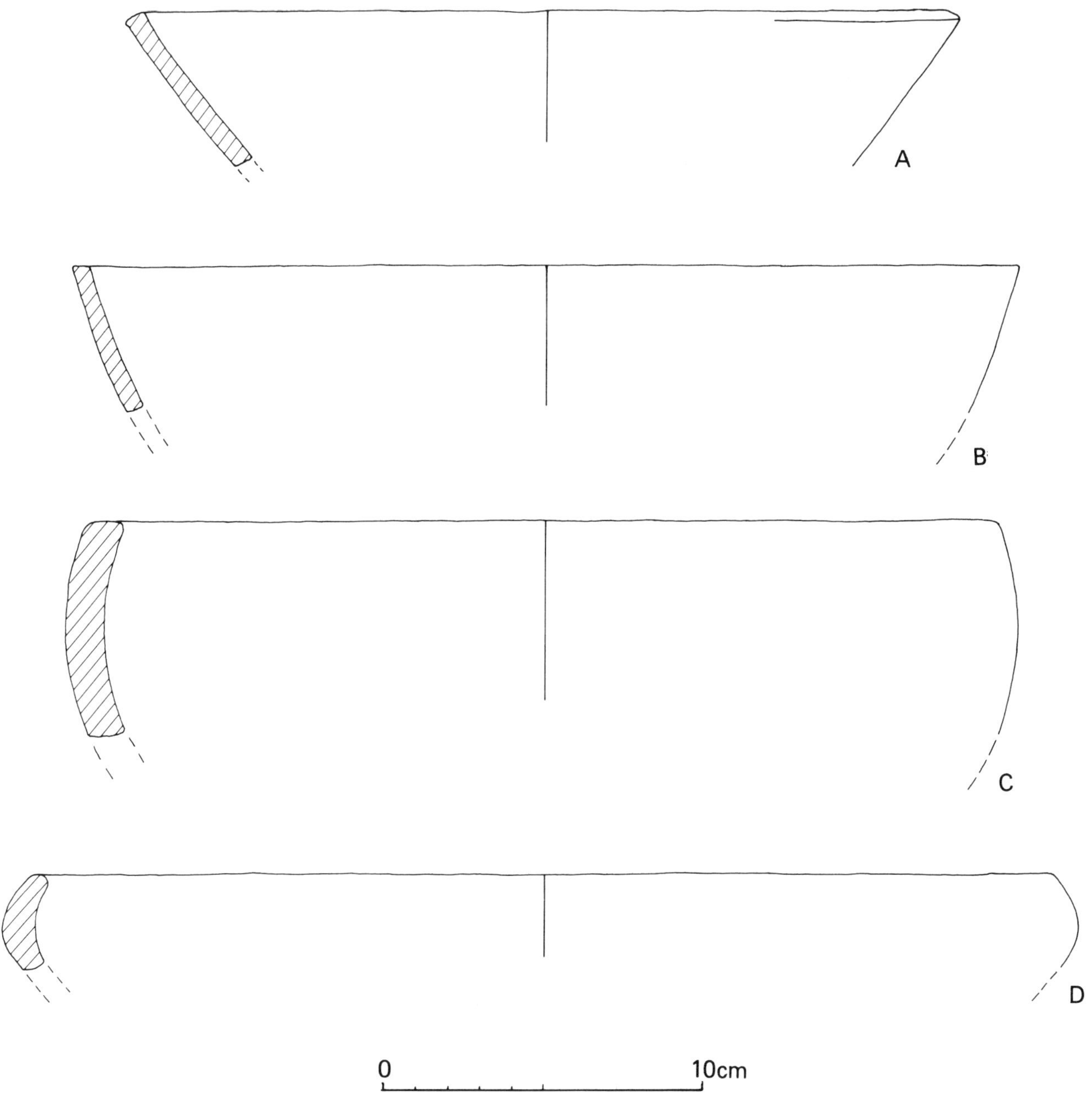

Figure 99. Reconstructed large bowls of vessel Forms 2A, 2B, and 3.

Vessel Form 8: Large Jars, Plain Ware. Three variants of large Form 8 jars have been distinguished, largely on differences in rim form. All are plain and appear to have had a utilitarian function, presumably as either storage or cooking vessels.

Vessel Form 8A. Two reconstructed examples of this form have rim diameters of 24 and 28 cm (fig. 102, b, c); the large example, the largest single sherd recovered from the NT-90 excavations, includes the rim and most of one side wall (fig. 102, c). The vessels have simple parallel rims, with flat lips. These are large, globular jars with slightly restricted orifices. The lip itself is generally rounded.

Vessel Form 8B. Also large, globular jars with restricted orifices, these vessels are distinguished by having slightly everted, "rolled" rims, sometimes with a slight exterior thickening at the lip (fig. 101, c).

Vessel Form 8C. This vessel form, quite common in the NT-90 assemblage, is distinguished from other Type 8 variants by its unique, thickened rim (fig. 101, a, b), which has a number of minor variations. The rims are slightly inverted, with exterior thickening just above a constriction in the neck; the rim then tapers to a rounded lip.

Vessel Form 9: Large Jar with Constricted Neck. This vessel form consists of a large, globular jar with a constricted neck which flares strongly outward to the rim (fig. 102, a). A reconstructed example from NT-90 has a rim diameter of 26 cm. On this example, the lip is outwardly beveled. The vessel is undecorated, although the outer surface bears traces of parallel-ribbed

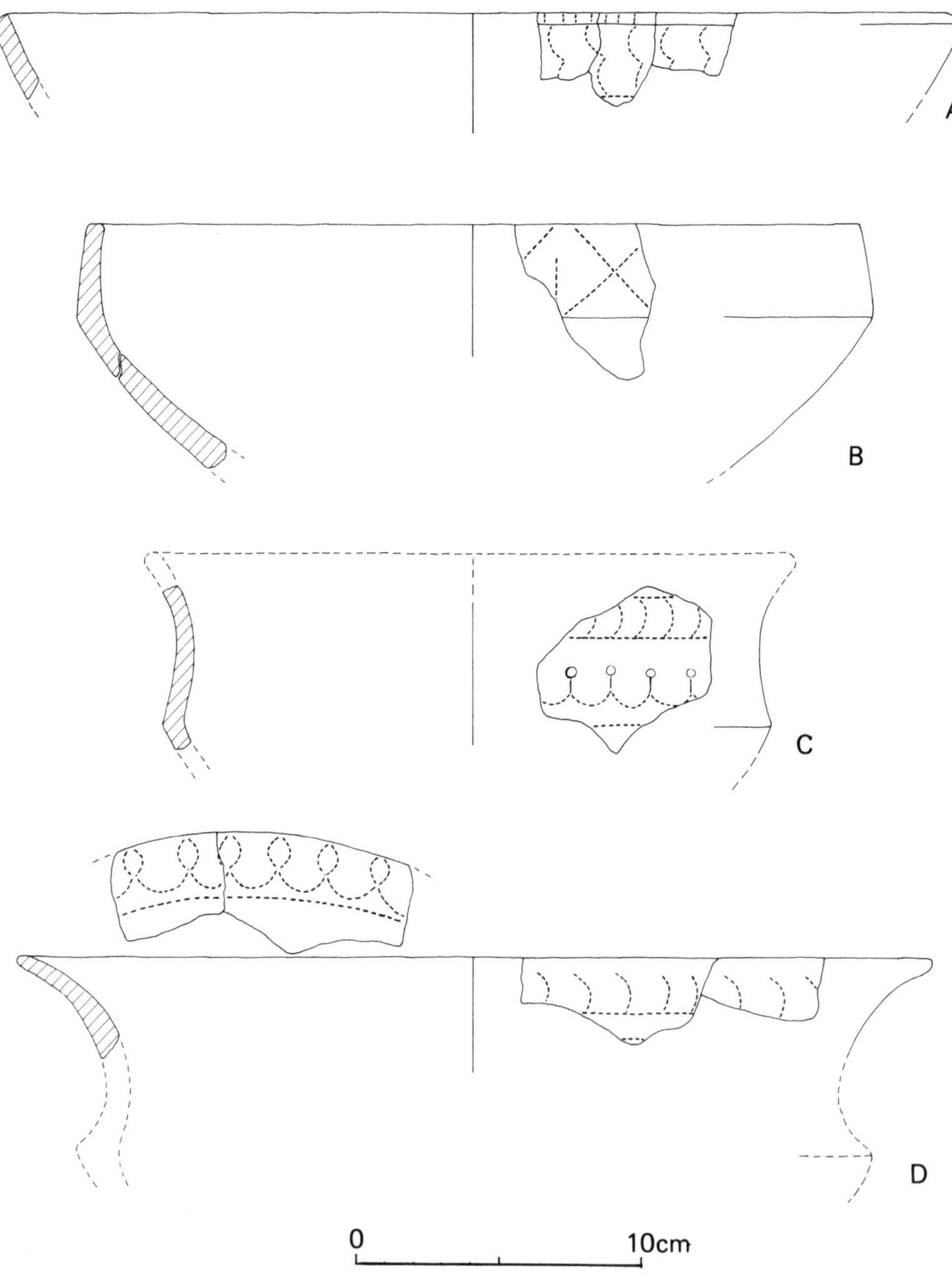

Figure 100. Reconstructed decorated vessel Forms 2C, 4, 5A, and 5B.

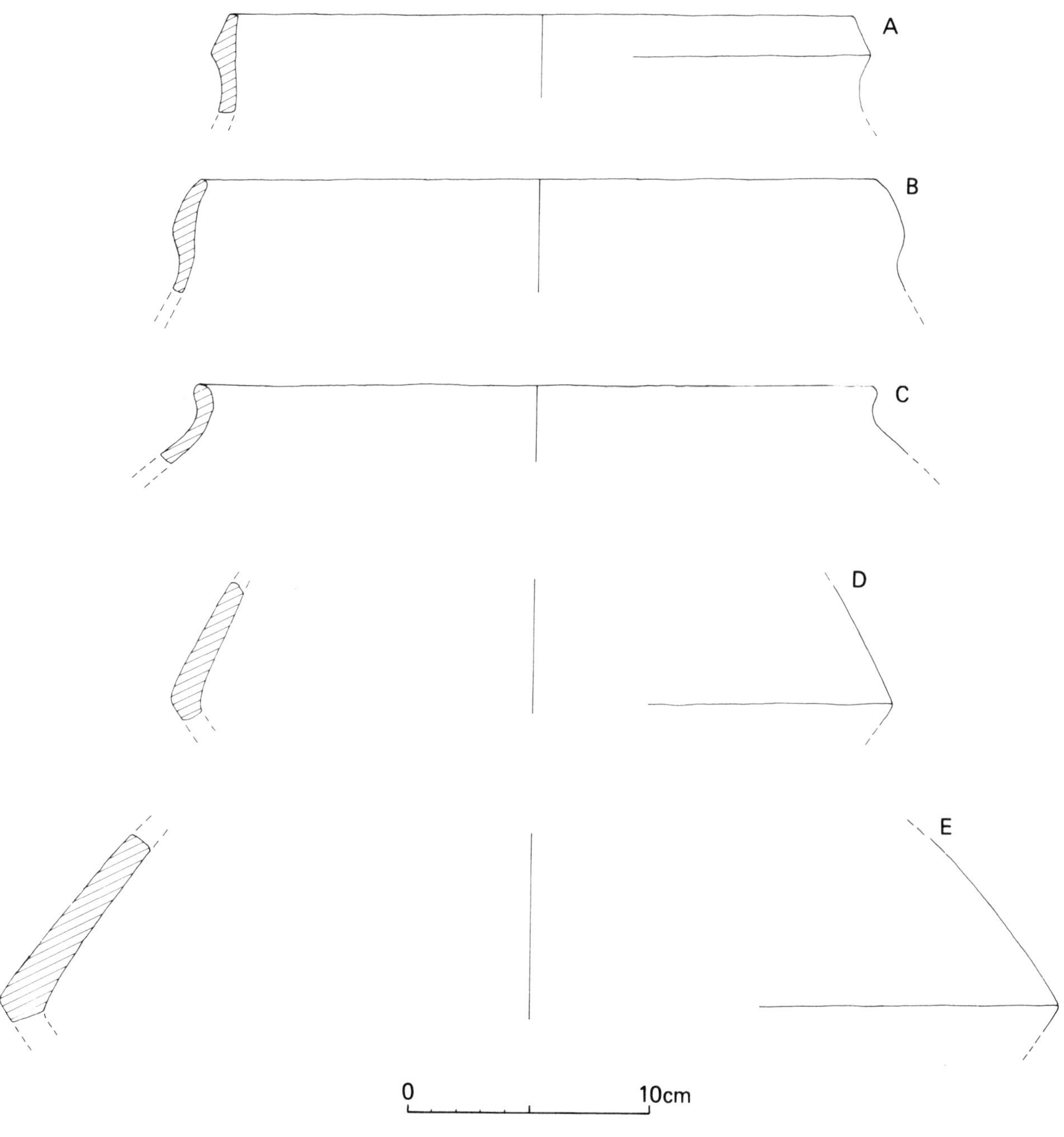

Figure 101. Reconstructed plain ware vessel Forms 7, 8B, and 8C.

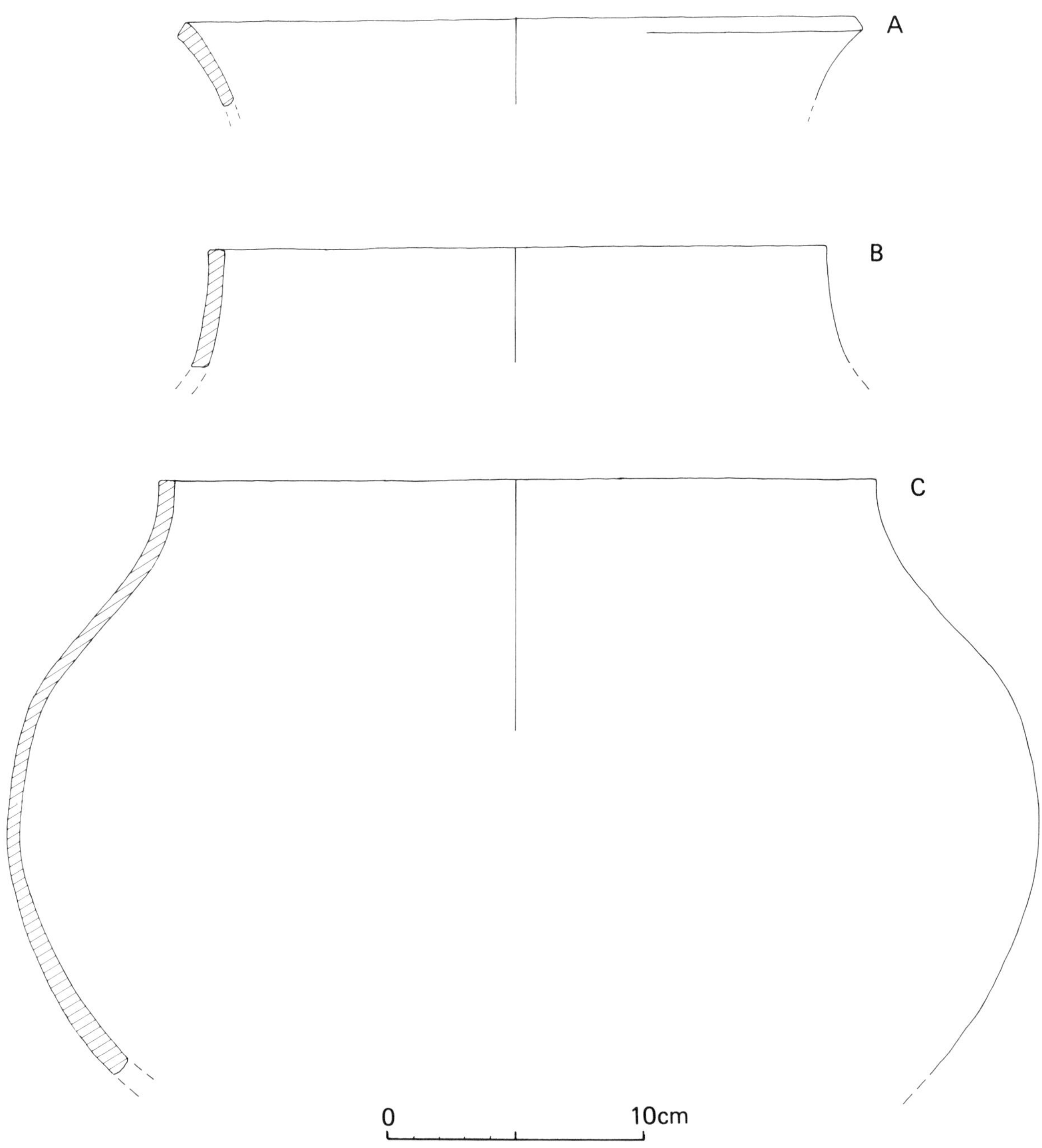

Figure 102. Reconstructed plain ware vessel Forms 8A and 9.

paddle impressing. This vessel form would have been suited either to storage or to cooking.

Vessel Form 10: Large Water Jar. No reconstructable examples of this vessel form were recovered, but the presence of the type is indicated by numerous handles (fig. 103). This vessel form was presumably of the general shape known from other Lapitoid assemblages such as Sigatoka and FU-11 on Futuna (Birks 1973; Kirch 1981). With a restricted orifice and large, globular body, such vessels were presumably used to carry and store water, and possibly other liquids.

Vessel Form and Temper

For 44 individual vessels we were able to distinguish calcareous versus volcaniclastic tempers. For most vessel forms, the distribution between temper types was more or less equal. However, Vessel Forms 1 and 5 show a somewhat greater proportion of calcareous temper. This is particularly clear for Form 5 vessels, where 10 examples are of calcareous temper and only 3 of volcaniclastic temper. Since the use of calcareous temper is regarded as an early trait, this strongly suggests that Form 5 vessels are a component of the earliest Lapita vessel array.

Inter-Site Distribution of Vessel Forms

The distribution of vessel forms by site is presented in table 23. The early NT-90 site yielded all forms and variants, most commonly simple bowls/cups (Form 1A), medium-sized carinated jars with decoration (Form 6), large plain ware jars of Form 8 (all variants), and large, handled water jars (Form 10). The two later sites with reasonably large samples, NT-93 and -100, display less variation in vessel form. These assemblages are dominated by small bowls/cups (Form 1A) and by two variants of large jars (Forms 8A, B). The large water jars (Form 10), and possibly also the large plain ware jars with flaring rims (Form 9), are still present. Site NT-90 also yielded a single rim sherd from a Form 8C jar. The four other assemblages listed in table 23 have rather small samples, but generally reflect the same pattern as at NT-93 and -100. The presence at NT-163 of small fragments of a Form 1C decorated cup and a large Form 7 carinated jar might be taken to indicate some temporal overlap between the NT-90 and -163 assemblages, but this hypothesis would need to be confirmed by further excavations and radiocarbon age assessment.

Rim Form

The 975 rims and lip fragments from 10 Niuatoputapu sites are analyzed in table 24, following terminology outlined in Kirch and Rosendahl (1973). As with vessel form, the NT-90 assemblage displays the greatest variability in all attributes of rim and lip form. Everted rims predominate in the NT-90 assemblage, and continue to dominate the later NT-93 and -100 assemblages (figs. 104-108). While the NT-90 assemblage has a large percentage of exteriorally thickened rim courses, later assemblages are dominated by divergent and parallel rim courses. The large number of rims which have a low thickening position, reflecting the numerous Form 8C vessels in Site NT-90, are largely absent from later assemblages. Lip form follows a similar pattern: the diversity in early NT-90 is absent in the later assemblages, which are characterized mainly by flat-rounded lip forms. In short, a consistent pattern of reduction in variation of rim and lip form is indicated by the Niuatoputapu data.

Analysis of Decoration

Only a small component of the ceramic collection from Niuatoputapu exhibits decoration, and nearly all of these sherds are from the early NT-90 site. In general terms, the decorated sherds can be divided into those displaying features of the "Lapita style" (Mead et al. 1973), and those which evidence some other style or non-Lapita technique.

Decorative Techniques

By decorative technique, I refer to the method of applying a decorative pattern to the pot surface, rather than a particular style or design motif. The Lapita style, for example, makes use of five distinct techniques, often in combination. As indicated in table 25, six decorative techniques are evidenced in the Niuatoputapu ceramic collection. All of these are represented in the NT-90 assemblage, but only incising and notching are found in the small samples from NT-100 and NT-163.

Dentate Stamping. This is the classic technique associated with the Lapita style. It consists of the application of one or more forms of carved, "toothed" (dentate) stamp into the damp clay. As no stamps have ever been archaeologically recovered, it is assumed that they were of a perishable material such as wood or bamboo. R.C. Green (pers. comm., 1982), in experimenting with the replication of stamps, has had excellent success with stamps carved of hardwood. The individual stamps include circles and straight and curved lines of various lengths and weights. The individual design elements and motifs formed with these stamps are treated in detail below.

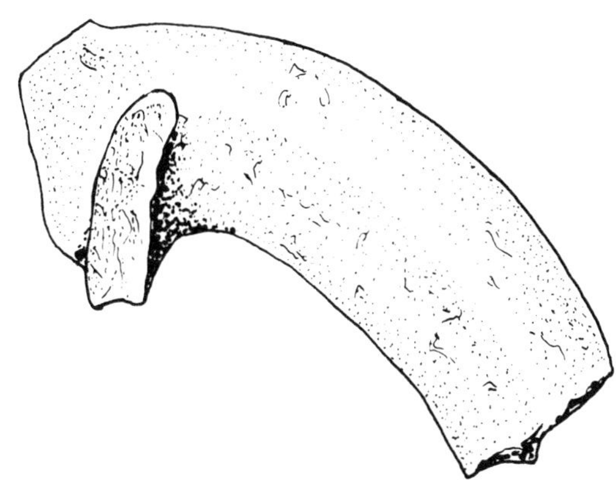

Figure 103. Handle from vessel Form 10.

TABLE 23

DISTRIBUTION OF VESSEL FORMS BY SITE

VESSEL CATEGORY	VESSEL FORM	SITE						
		NT–90	NT–93	NT–100	NT–112	NT–110	NT–91	NT–163
Small bowls/cups	1A	++	++	++	+	+	+	+
	1B	+	0	0	0	0	0	0
	1C	+	0	0	0	0	0	?
Large bowls	2A	+	0	0	0	0	0	0
	2B	+	0	0	0	0	0	0
	2C	+	0	0	0	0	0	0
	2D	+	0	0	0	0	0	0
	3	+	0	0	0	0	0	0
Carinated bowls	4	+	0	0	0	0	0	0
	5A	+	0	0	0	0	0	0
	5B	+	0	0	0	0	0	0
Carinated jars	6	+	0	0	0	0	0	0
	7	+	0	0	0	0	0	?
Large jars	8A	++	++	++	+	?	?	+
	8B	++	++	++	0	+	?	0
	8C	++	(+)	0	0	+	+	0
	9	+	?	?	?	0	0	0
Water jar	10	++	+	+	0	+	+	0
Forms/variants present		10/18	4(5)	4(5)	2(3)	4(5)	3(5)	2(4)

++ = common, + = present, 0 = absent, ? = uncertain
(+) = single example only

TABLE 24

ANALYSIS OF RIM FORMS

ATTRIBUTE	SITE									
	NT–90	NT–91	NT–93	NT–100	NT–110	NT-112	NT-113	NT-125	NT-129	NT-163
Basic Rim Form										
Vertical	24			2						
Inverted	52			1						2
Everted	123	1	25	12	3	8		1		6
Upturned-Everted	32									
Upturned-Inverted	49		2							
Aberrant	2			1						
Indeterminate	574	10	97	42	8	22	1		1	7
Rim Course										
Exteriorally-Thickened	100	3	7	3	2	3				
Interiorally-Thickened	17		2	1						
Divergent	119	2	63	16	3	12				3
Parallel	350	2	41	30	5	12		1		9
Reduced	11									
Thickening Position										
High	156	3	71	20	4	15				3
Low	79	3	1		1					
Lip Form										
Pointed	3		1							
Rounded	170	1	7	4		2		1		1
Flat	29			2		2				
Flat-Rounded	294	3	101	46	9	20				9
Outward-Beveled	33		3			2				2
Inward-Beveled	1									
Aberrant	1					2				

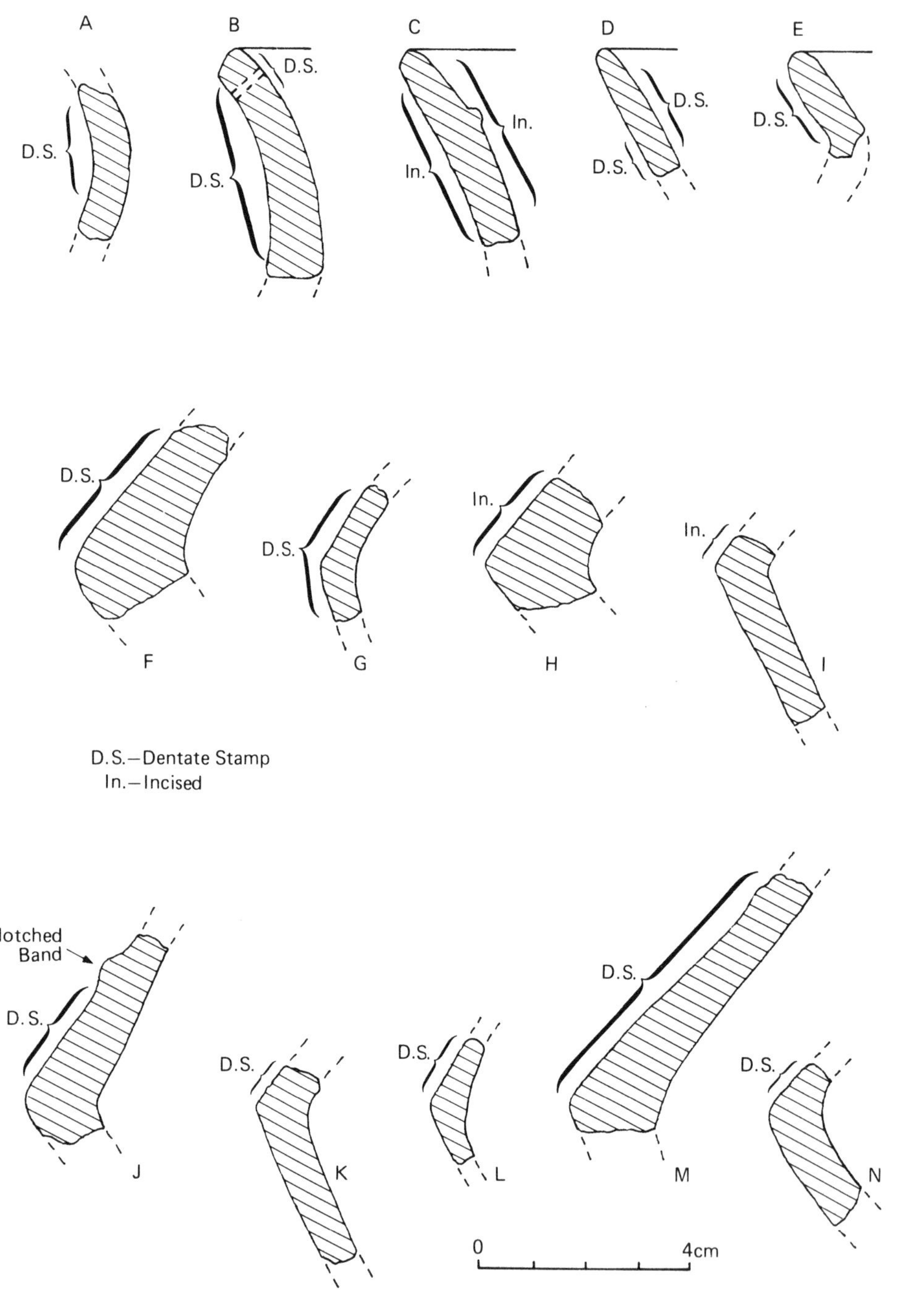

Figure 104. Profiles of rim sherds and carinated sherds bearing dentate-stamped or incised decoration (D.S. = dentate-stamping; In. = incising).

Incising. Incision of the clay surface with a pointed or blunt implement is a technique characteristic of the Lapita style (where it sometimes occurs in combination with dentate stamping), but it is also found in non-Lapita contexts—for example, at the plain ware sites NT-100 and NT-163. On sherds from these sites, incising has been applied to the rims of small bowls or other (indeterminate) vessels, to form simple patterns of cross-hatched or parallel oblique lines (fig. 108, b-c; 109, a). Incised design elements of the Lapita style are discussed further below. A distinctive incised sherd, probably of Fijian origin, is also discussed below.

Appliqué/Modeling. A third decorative technique, limited to the Lapita style, involves the raising of a three-dimensional band above the pot surface either by the application of a narrow "wire" of clay or by modeling of the pot surface.

Punctation. A single sherd from NT-90 displays this decorative technique. This is a fairly thick, unelaborated rim, probably from a simple bowl or cup,

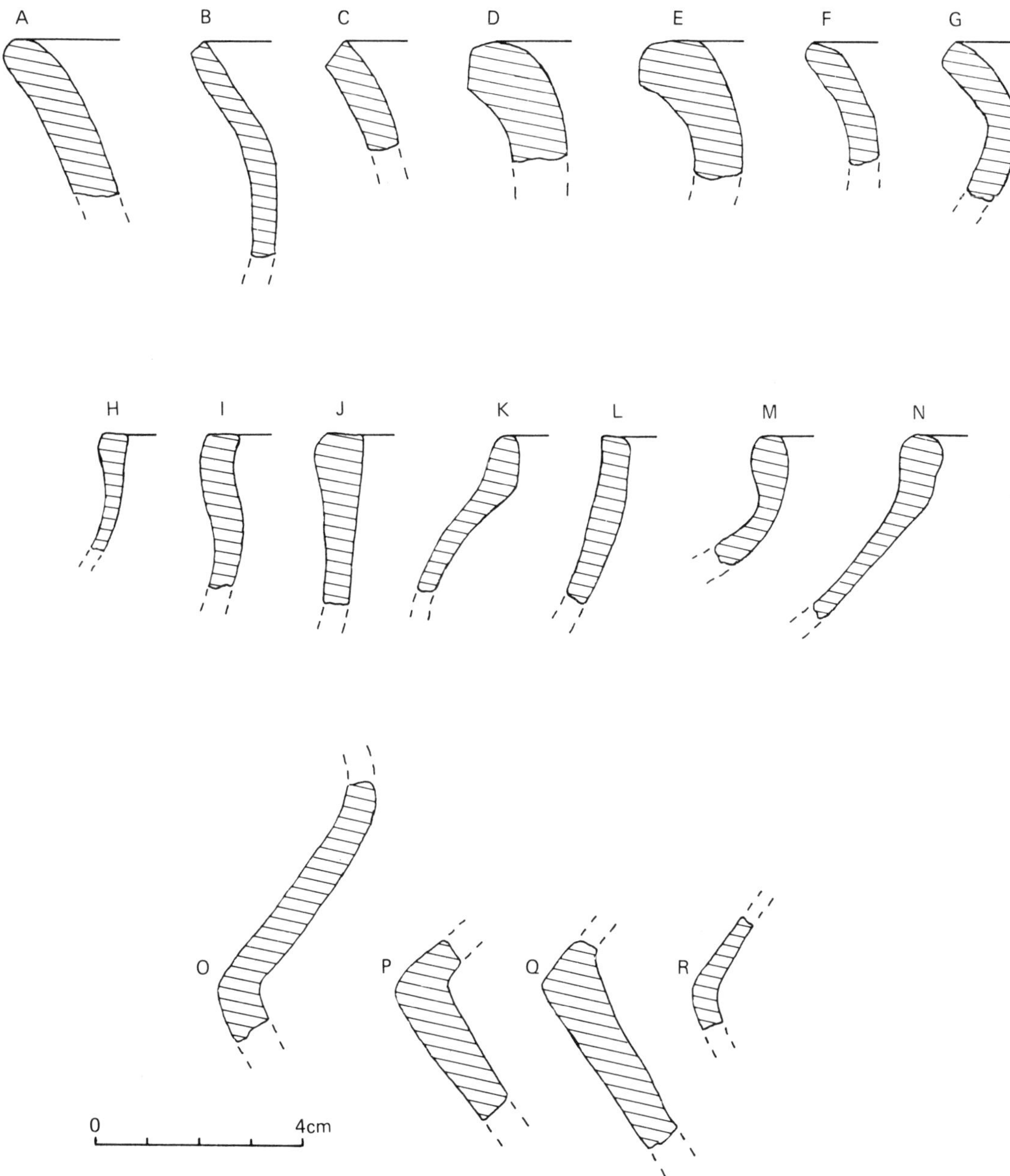

Figure 105. Rim profiles: top row, vessel Form 9; second row, vessel Form 8; bottom row, carinated plain ware jars.

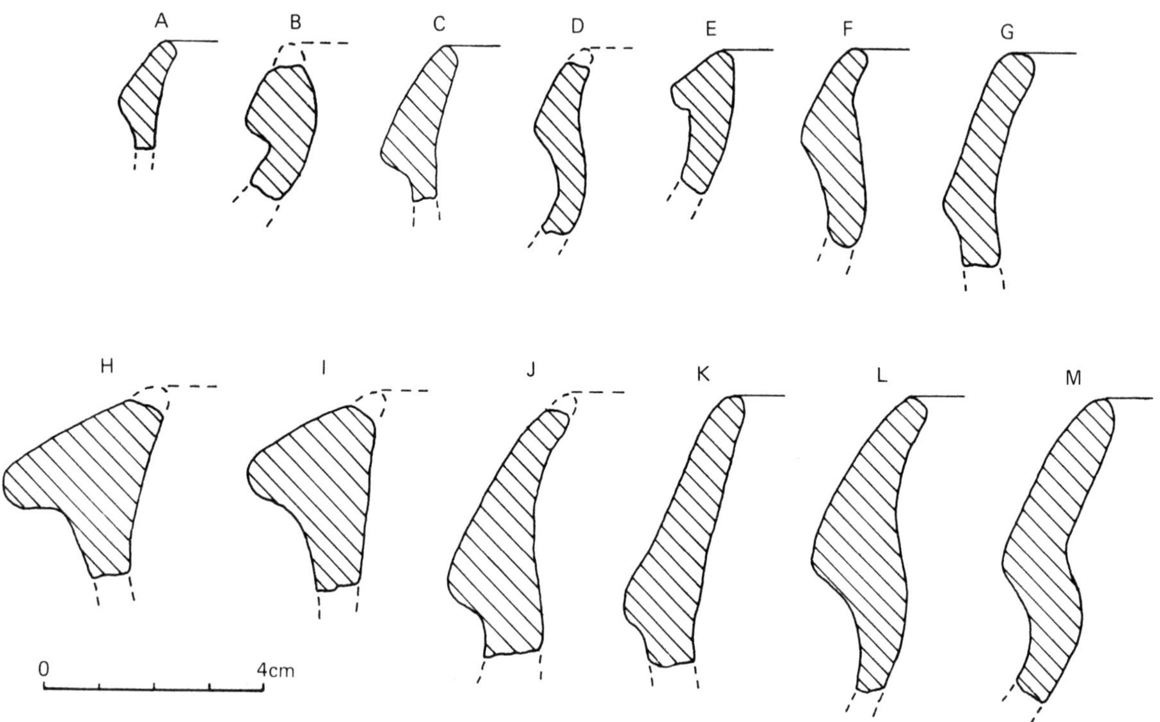

Figure 106. Rim profiles of vessel Form 8C.

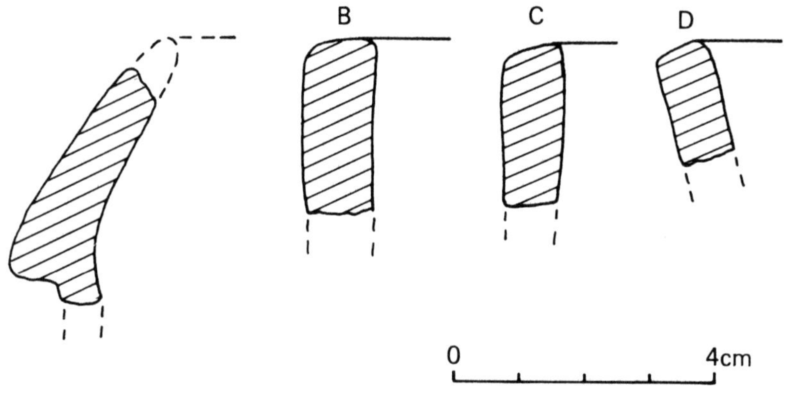

Figure 107. Rim profiles of Tafahi Island sherds.

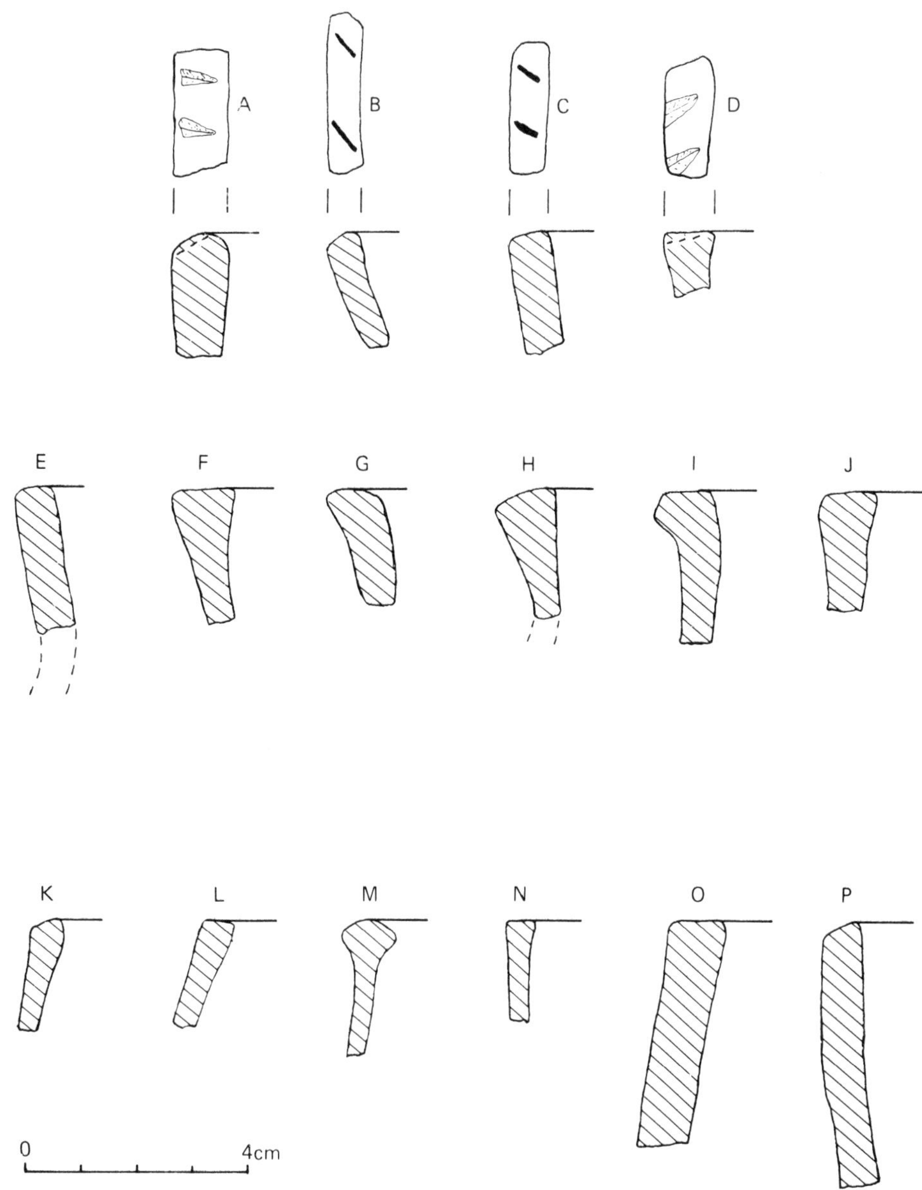

Figure 108. Rim profiles of sherds from Site NT-100.

with the flat surface of its lip dotted with punctate depressions in two roughly parallel but irregular rows. As discussed below, this sherd is probably of Fijian origin.

Paddle Impressing. This technique is evidenced by 34 sherds, from Site NT-90, whose surfaces are marked by distinctive parallel impressions. These impressions occur in groups which are oriented in slightly different directions, thus suggesting a tapping action with a narrow paddle back and forth over the pot surface. The parallel lines are not deep enough to indicate a carved paddle surface, but suggest that the paddle might have been wrapped with some kind of fabric. It is questionable whether this form of surface treatment should really be classified as "decoration." Identical paddle impressions have been noted on sherds from other Western Polynesian and Fijian sites, including the Vailele site in Samoa (Green and Davidson 1969a, pl. 17), the Yanuca site in Fiji (Hunt 1980:133, pl. 4.4), and the FU-11 site on Futuna (Kirch 1981:136-7, fig. 10, c, d). Hunt (1980:133) also mentions the occurrence of such paddle impressions on sherds from Tongatapu. Thus, this technique was a fairly widespread component of Lapitoid or Polynesian Plain Ware ceramic technology in the region.

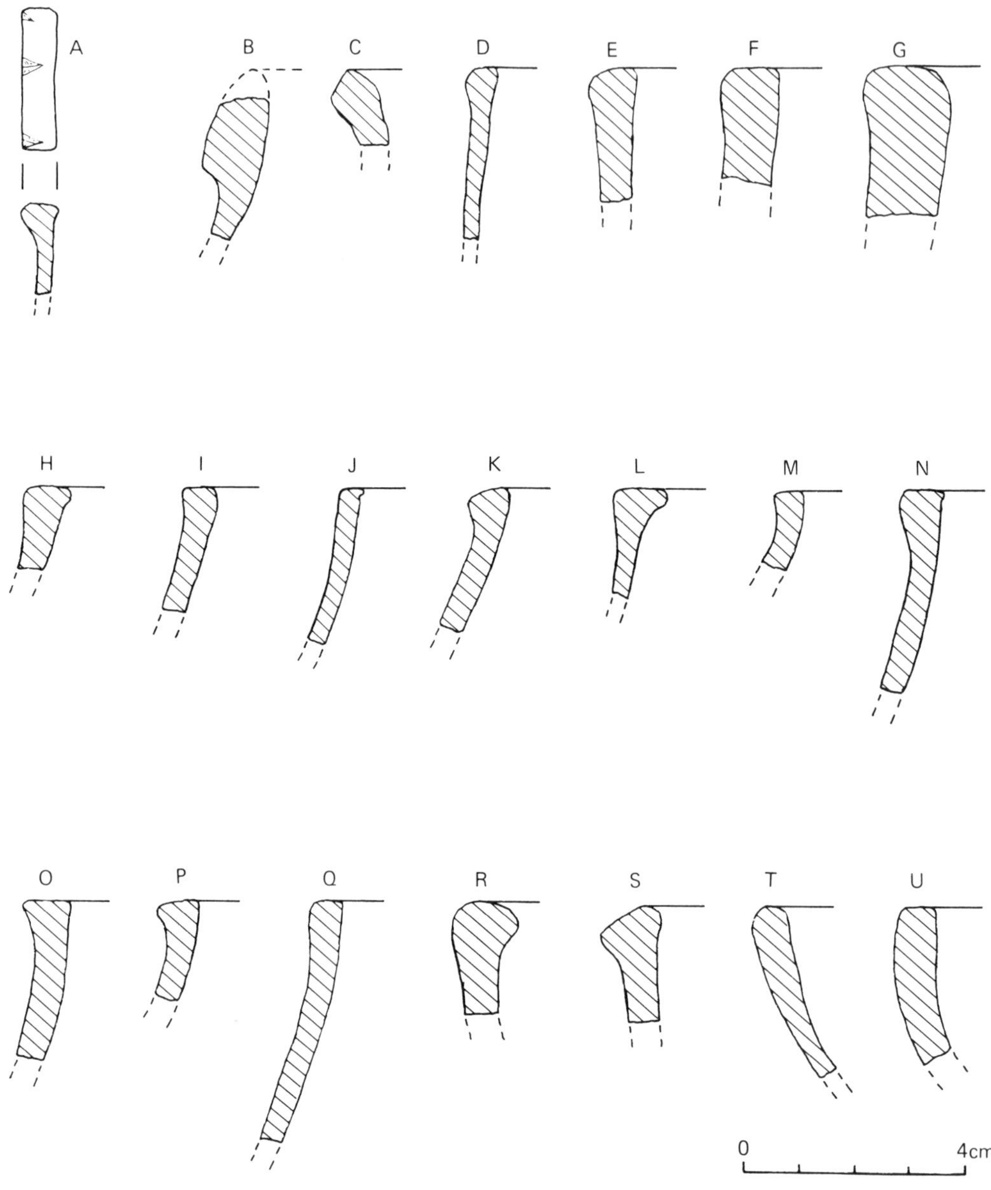

Figure 109. Rim profiles of sherds from Site NT-93.

Notching. Notching is represented by a few examples, primarily from Sites NT-100 and NT-163, and by a stray surface find. It is applied solely to the rim, and consists of a series of parallel, V-shaped notches cut perpendicular to the rim's curvature (fig. 108, a, d). A different kind of notching is evidenced by a single sherd from NT-90, where a thickened band about 2 cm below the lip on the vessel exterior has been notched with a series of parallel vertical grooves. This particular form of decoration was extremely common at the Late Eastern Lapita site of Sigatoka in Fiji, where it appears on vessels of Type 1 (see, for example, Birks 1973, fig. 21, no. 57, for an example nearly identical to the NT-90 specimen).

Slipping. A form of surface treatment that may be classed as decoration is the addition of a thin slip of orange or reddish color. As indicated in Table 19, a small percentage of sherds from each of the principal sites carries traces of slipping.

Table 25 also indicates the distribution of decoration relative to its position on vessels. In Site NT-90, most decoration is carried on the upper exterior of the vessel, usually just below the rim and above the carination if one is present. A smaller number of sherds

TABLE 25

CERAMIC DECORATIVE TECHNIQUES AND POSITION DISTRIBUTION BY SITE

ATTRIBUTE	NT-90	NT-100	NT-163
Decorative Technique			
Dentate-Stamping	61		
Incising	17	2	1
Appliqué/Modeling	16		
Punctate	1		
Paddle-Impressing	34		
Notching	1	2	1
Decoration Position			
Lip	10	4	2
Exterior	111		
Interior	11		

have some interior decoration, again contiguous to the lip on the exposed or visible inner portion of the rim. Most sherds with interior decoration also have exterior designs. Ten sherds have decoration along the lip itself, sometimes in combination with interior and exterior designs. At Sites NT-100 and NT-163, decoration is limited to vessel lips, and consists of simple incised or notched patterns as described above.

In order to determine whether decoration was more commonly carried out on vessels of a particular temper type, all decorated sherds were characterized as of either calcareous or volcaniclastic temper (table 26). Calcareous temper is an early trait, evidenced primarily at Site NT-90. Whereas the incidence of paddle impressions and incised designs appears with more or less equal frequency on sherds of either calcareous or volcaniclastic temper, it is significant that dentate stamping and appliqué/modeling appear more frequently on calcareous-tempered sherds. This correlation may not mean that calcareous-tempered pots were preferred for decoration. Rather, it is probably reflective of the fact that the use of calcareous temper and of decoration in the Lapita style are both early techniques which disappeared rather quickly from the ceramic repertoire.

The Lapita Decorative System

I turn now to the analysis of the sherds from Site NT-90 that display features of the classic Lapita style. The pioneering work of Mead, Birks, Birks, and Shaw (1973) on the Lapita decorative system of Fiji, supplemented by later work of Donovan (1973) on the decorative system of the Reef Islands, provides a rigorous framework for analysis. The reader unfamiliar with the terminology and procedures used here is referred to the above works for a detailed exposition.

The Design Field

NT-90 vessels were commonly decorated on the exterior or outside walls, sometimes on the lip edge, and sometimes on the visible interior portion of an everted rim. As Mead et al. have noted, however, Lapita potters apparently never regarded the entire outer surface of a pot as, "one large design field." Instead, it was conceived as a space which could receive so many transverse bands of decoration. Associated with the idea of arranging the patterns in bands was the notion that a pattern ought to be confined within a clearly demarcated zone and not left hanging in space (1973:21).

Design zones are defined by "zone markers" which generally run transversely around the pot, subdividing its surface into areas which then receive one or more motifs. Five discrete types of zone marker, all of them well known from other Lapita assemblages in Fiji, Tonga, and the Reef Islands, are present in the NT-90 assemblage. These consist of three types of general zone (GZ) markers, and two types of transverse bands (TB), the latter produced by modeling or appliqué.

Zone Marker GZ1. This marker consists of a double line of dentate stamping, and is represented by a single example.

Zone Marker GZ2. Consisting of a single line of dentate stamping (e.g., fig. 110, f), this type of zone marker, represented by numerous examples, dominates the NT-90 assemblage.

Zone Marker GZ3. This marker consists of a single line of incising (e.g., fig. 111, f), and is represented by a few examples.

Zone Marker TB3.2. This is a transverse band with a rounded cross-section, formed either by adding a narrow clay wire to the pot surface or by raising the band through modeling. TB3.2 is represented by 13 examples. In several cases, the makers have elaborated the band by notching across it at regular intervals (fig. 111, e), or by stamping GZ2 lines immediately adjacent to it (fig. 111, j).

TABLE 26

DISTRIBUTION OF CERAMIC DECORATIVE TECHNIQUE BY TEMPER TYPE

DECORATIVE TECHNIQUE	CALCAREOUS TEMPER	VOLCANICLASTIC TEMPER	TOTALS
Site NT–90			
Dentate-stamping	40	21	61
Paddle-impressing	19	15	34
Incising	8	9	17
Appliqué/modeling	12	4	16
Notching	1	0	1
Punctate	0	1	1
Site NT–100			
Incising	0	1	1
Notching	0	3	3
Site NT–163			
Incising	0	1	1
Notching	0	1	1
TOTALS	80	56	136

Zone Marker TB3.3. Represented by three examples, this zone marker consists of a transverse band with distinctly triangular cross-section (fig. 112, c).

The zone markers described above were applied to individual vessels in a variety of configurations to produce several types of discrete design zones (Mead et al. 1973:24, fig. 2.16). Many of the NT-90 sherds are too small and fragmentary to allow for determination of the type of design zone represented. For those sherds large enough to provide diagnostic information, however, the following frequencies were determined:

Zone Type	Frequency
A	9
B	2
C	1
E	1
F	8
G	9
H	14

Following Mead et al. (1973), these zones may be briefly characterized as follows: Zone Type A, a continuous band with upper and lower boundaries clearly defined by zone markers; Zone Type B, a single border divided into rectangular or square areas by the use of vertical zone markers; Zone Type C, a series of Type B borders, one below the other, forming a design grid; Zone Type E, borders in which one of the boundaries is defined by the lower structural limits of the vessel, e.g., by a carination; Zone Type F, narrow borders on the inside of the rim in which the lower boundary is formed by a zone marker or a transverse bar, or both; Zone Type G, the flat edge of the lip in which both boundaries are structurally defined; and Zone Type H, a border in which the upper boundary is defined by the rim and the lower boundary consists of a zone marker.

Design Elements

In addition to the zone markers and the zone types they define, the Lapita style is composed of a small number of discrete design elements which are then combined according to a specifiable set of rules and processes to form motifs. Of the eight design elements defined by Mead et al. (1973:29, fig. 2.17-2.24) for Fijian Lapita, all but one (DE7) are represented in the NT-90 assemblage. These elements may be formed either by dentate stamping or by incising, although stamping is more frequent. Since these elements have been thoroughly described and illustrated by Mead et al. (1973), their definitions will not be repeated here.

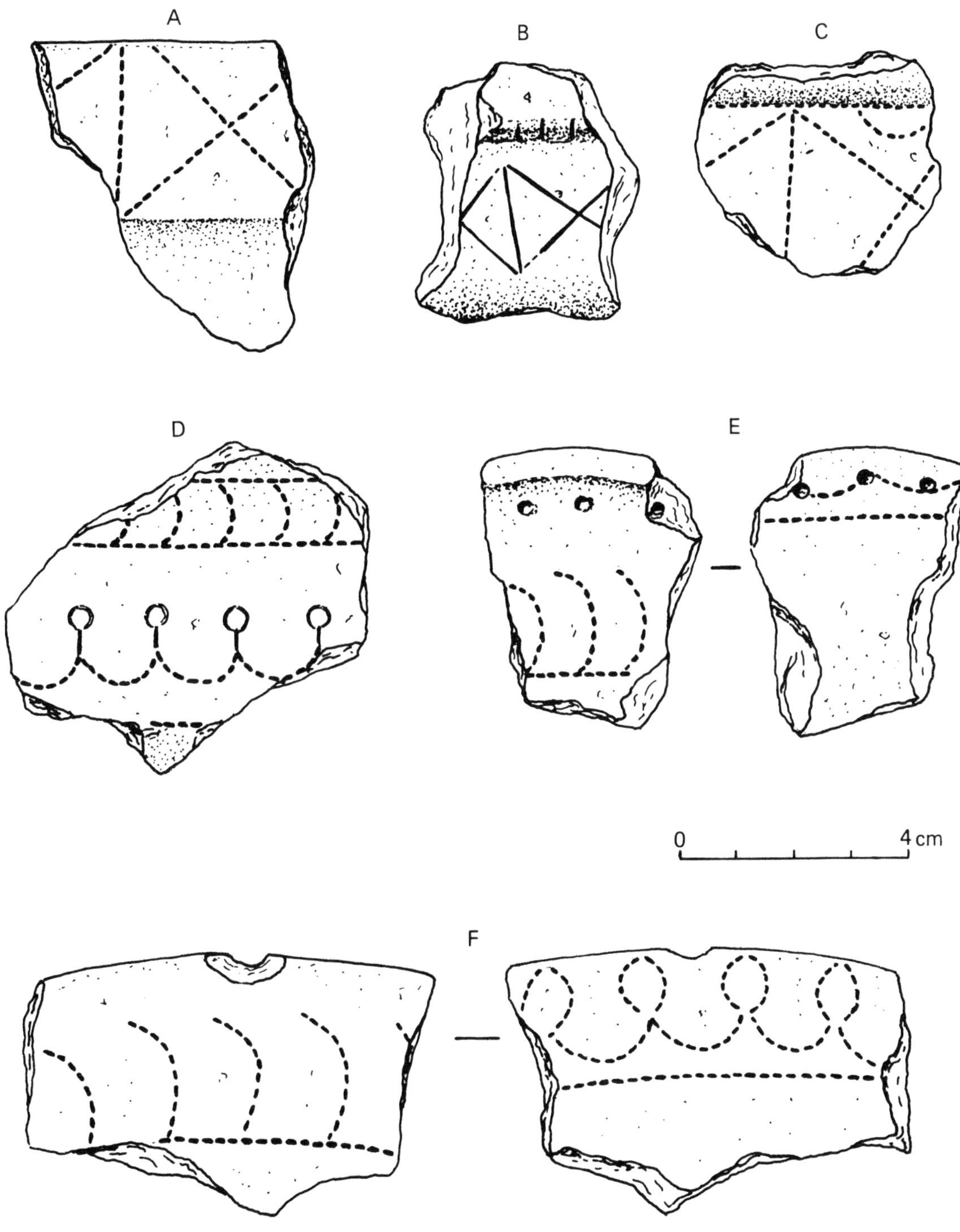

Figure 110. Lapita style decorated sherds from Site NT-90.

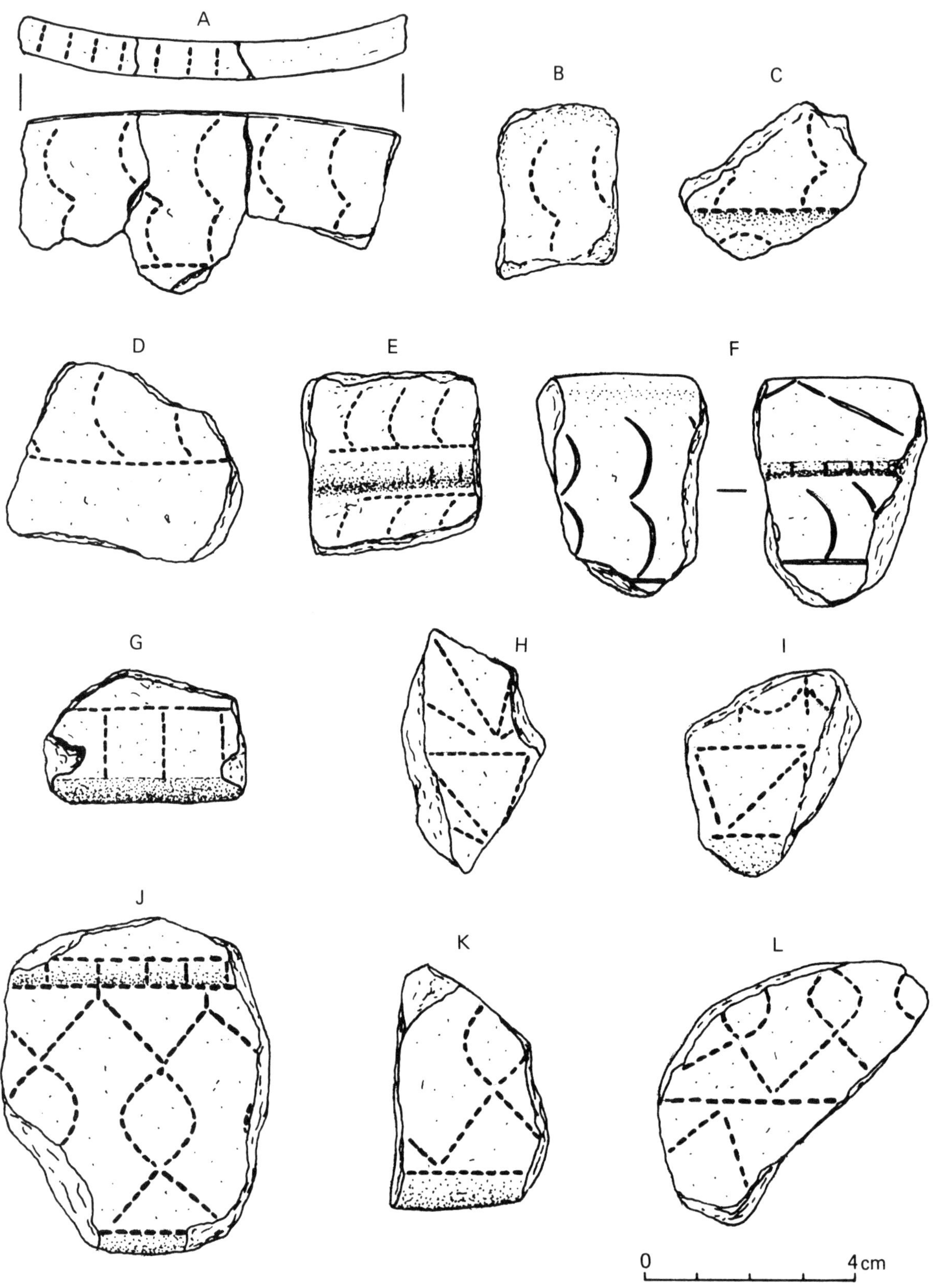

Figure 111. Lapita style decorated sherds from Site NT-90.

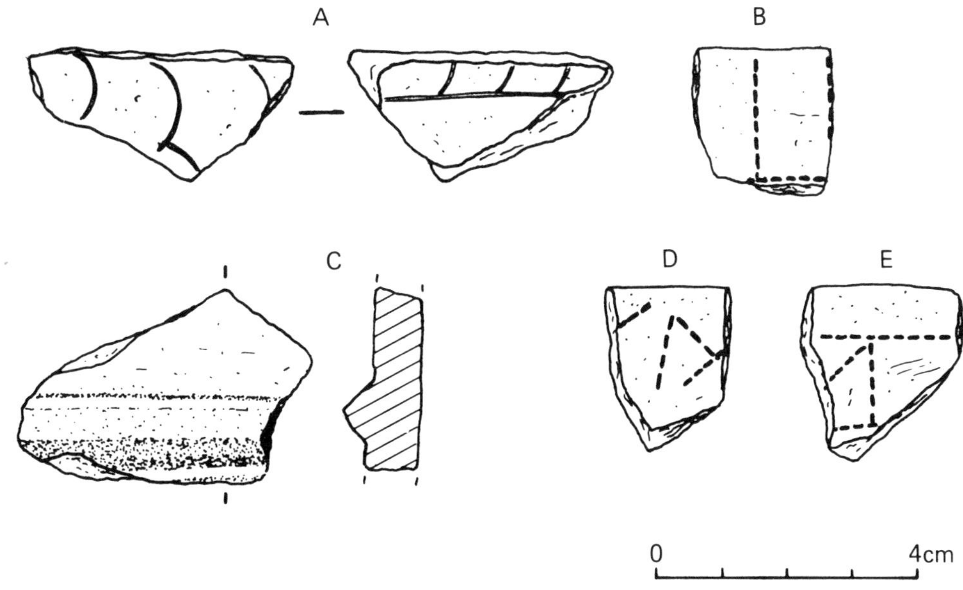

Figure 112. Lapita style decorated sherds from Site NT-90.

The Motifs

Eleven discrete motifs, two of them with distinctive alloforms, are represented in the NT-90 assemblage. In addition, there are regular occurrences of two design elements in patterns which are not defined as motifs by Mead et al. (1973), but which do in effect form motifs and are therefore described below. Many sherds in the sample are very small and do not exhibit complete motifs, so that the catalog presented below probably is not exhaustive for the design system used by the early Niuatoputapu potters. The motifs are discussed individually, using the numbering system of Mead et al. (1973) and Donovan (1973), with data on frequency, variation in technique, and statement of the decorative rule applied. Table 27 presents a summary of the correlations between vessel type, design zones, design elements, and motifs.

DE2.1 Pattern. Although not formally recognized as a motif by Mead et al. (1973), design element DE2.1 is in fact the second most common design in the NT-90 assemblage, with seven examples. Consisting of two DE1.1 crescents placed one above the other, the design is repeated according to the rule P = DE2.1 —> DisR/E-W. In four cases the design is stamped (fig. 111, a-c), while in three it is incised (fig. 111, f; 112, a). It occurs in design zones bordered by GZ2, GZ3, TB3.2, and TB3.3 zone markers. This pattern occurs on vessels of Forms 2C, 5, and 6.

Motif M1. This motif consists of a stamped DE1.1 crescent placed horizontally, and repeated contiguously according to the rule P = M1 —> ConR/E-W. It appears only on a single rim sherd of a Form 5A vessel, in a Type F design zone with the lower border defined by a GZ2 zone marker. This sherd is also unique in having, through its rim, perforations that are aligned with the M1 pattern (fig. 110, e). The outer surface of the same rim carries an M99.1 motif.

Motif M12. A clear example of M12 occurs on a rim of a Form 5B vessel in a Type H zone, where it was produced by dentate stamping (fig. 110, f). This particular example appears to represent the alloform M12.2 of Mead et al. which follows the familiar rule P = M12.2 —> DisR/E-W. The interior surface of the same rim carries an M99.1 motif.

Motif M13/M14. A large sherd of vessel Form 6 carries an example of an alloform of either M13 or M14 in a Type A zone bounded above by a TB3.2 band with GZ2 elaboration, and below by a structural carination also defined by a GZ2 line (fig. 111, j). Motif 13, as originally defined by Mead et al. (1973, fig. 2.40), involves a double-line technique. This example could alternatively be classified as a modification of M14.2, in which the units are placed contiguously according to the rule P = M14.2 —> ConR/E-W/CLS.

Motif M12/13/14 Alloforms. There are four examples of motifs which represent one or more alloforms of the above three closely related motifs;

TABLE 27

CORRELATION BETWEEN VESSEL FORM AND DESIGN ZONES, ELEMENTS, AND MOTIFS

VESSEL FORM	DESIGN ZONES	ELEMENTS	MOTIFS
1	H	TB 3.3 DE 5	M15
1B	F,G,H	DE 5, DE 8	M16, M15
1C	G		M16 variant
2C	G,H	GZ 2 DE 1.1 DE 2.1 DE 5	DE 2.1—> Dis R/E–W
4	H		M30.1
5	F,H	GZ 2 DE 1.1 TB 3.3 DE 2.1	M99.1, M18(?), M1, M16 DE 2.1—>Dis R/E–W
5A	A,F,H	TB 3.3 GZ 2 DE 1.1 DE 3	M1, M16, M99.1, (M53)
5B	F,G,H	GZ 2 DE 1.1 DE 4	M12, M46, M99.1
6	A,B,E	DE 2.1 DE 4 DE 5 DE 6 TB 3.2 GZ 2	M13, M15, M16 (?), M19 (?), M30.1, M30.2 DE 2.1—>Dis R/E–W M12/13/14 variants M53

exact determination is difficult because the motifs are fragmentary. All of these are stamped (figs. 111, k, l), and all appear to be from Form 6 vessels in a Type A zone pattern. One is executed rather crudely in comparison to the others.

Motif M15. This motif consists of vertical lines or bars according to the rule P = M15.1 —> DisR/E-W. In two cases it is stamped, and appears on the exterior of small bowls or cups of Forms 1 and 1B, in a Type H zone with the lower boundary formed by a GZ2 line. In the third example, the pattern is incised and borders an incised GZ3 line on the exterior of a carinated pot, probably of Form 6.

Motif M16.4. This motif was recognized by Mead et al. (1973:91) from Natunuku, Fiji, and follows the rule P = M16.4 —> ConR/E-W/CLS. It is represented by a single example on the interior rim of what is probably a Form 5 vessel.

Motif M16 Alloforms. There are three examples of what appear to be additional variations on the M16 motif. The first of these (fig. 98, h) is incised on the interior rim of a small Form 1B vessel. A second example occurs as a stamped design along the lip (Type G zone) of a Form 1C cup in which the rim is expanded and flattened, probably to receive the decoration (Fig. 98, c-e). In the third case, the motif is incised in a Type F zone along the inner rim of a Form 5 vessel, with the lower boundary formed by a TB3.3 band. Lying below the band is an M99.1 motif; the exterior of the same vessel carries the DE2.1 pattern (fig. 111, f).

Motif M18. One small example of what may be M18 in dentate stamping, from a Form 5 vessel, is represented.

Motif M19. Motif M19 is known from a single, somewhat problematic example (fig. 111, h) where it is stamped on the exterior wall of what may be a Form 6 vessel. Part of this fragmentary motif may actually be another instance of motif M16.4 (see above).

Motif M30.1. This alloform of M30 consists of a Type A zone defined above and below by GZ2 lines, which is then subdivided into rectangular spaces by vertical bars; each rectangular unit is further partitioned with an "X." This motif is represented in Site NT-90 by three specimens. The first of these occurs on a Form 4 vessel in which the design zone is actually defined by the structural limits—i.e., by the lip edge above and a carination below (fig. 110, a); this design is dentate-stamped. In the second example, which is incised, M30.1 appears in a Type A zone on a Form 6 vessel (fig. 110, b). Here the design zone is bounded below both by the vessel carination and by an incised GZ3 line, and above by a notched TB3.2 band. The third instance of this motif is on the narrow, flattened lip of a small vessel, possibly a bowl or cup. This design has been finely incised in a Type G zone.

Motif M30.2. This is a slightly more complex alloform of M30, with the addition of DE1.1 elements (see Mead et al. 1973, fig. 2.57). It is represented by a single example, stamped on a Form 6 vessel, apparently in a Type A zone (fig. 110, c).

Motif M46. This motif was designated M46 by Mead et al. (1973) based on Poulsen's Type K1 from Tongatapu (Poulsen 1967); Donovan (1973) terms it motif M62 in her study of the Reef Islands. It is quite close to M12 in structure. Basically, the pattern consists of an M1 motif elaborated by the addition of stamped circles above the junction of the DE1.1 elements (fig. 110, f). It is known here from two matching sherds from a Form 5B vessel, where it occurs on the inner rim (Type F zone) with the lower boundary defined by a GZ2 line. The outer surface of the same vessel carries motif M99.1.

Motif M53. This motif was originally recognized from Poulsen's Tongatapu material (Poulsen's Type K16) and given the designation M53 by Mead et al. (1973); Donovan (1973), who discovered it in the Reef Islands material, terms it M110. At NT-90, it is represented by a single large sherd (fig. 110, d) with fine execution in dentate-stamping technique. The motif consists essentially of an M1 pattern which has been elaborated by the addition of short vertical bars extending upward from the juncture of the DE1.1 elements, and by stamped circles (DE3.1) at the top of these bars. The entire motif follows the rule P = M53 —> ConR/E-W. It occurs on a large Form 6 vessel in a Type A zone bounded below by a carination and above by a GZ3 line. Directly above the zone of M53 motifs is a zone of M99.1.

Motif M99.1. This motif, recognized by Donovan (1973), is the most common in the NT-90 assemblage, with ten examples. It is very simple, consisting of single vertical DE1.1 crescents repeated according to the rule P = M99.1 —> DisR/E-W. It appears on both interior and exterior surfaces, is executed by either stamping or incising, and is found on vessels of Forms 5A and 5B. Various examples are illustrated in figures 110, e, f and 111, d, e.

Probable Fijian Sherds

Two decorated sherds from Niuatoputapu are probably of Fijian origin. One is a small body sherd found on the sandy flat seaward of Site NT-90. The sherd is dark gray to black, well burnished on the exterior, and is decorated with two zig zag incised lines, each about 3 mm wide. This incised motif is common in later prehistoric Fijian ceramics of the Vunda and Ra phases, after about A.D. 1100 and on into the historic period (Green 1963; Frost 1979). The second sherd, which was excavated from the upper 20 cm of Site NT-90, is a thick (13 mm), crude rim, decorated with a double row of tool punctations. This motif is not associated with the Lapita style, but is known from the later Fijian ceramics. Indeed, a virtually identical rim was excavated by Gifford (1951, pl. 21, w) from Location B of his Site 17 of Vunda Phase. The presence of such Fijian sherds in Niuatoputapu is not surprising, given the ethnohistoric evidence for Tongan voyages to Fiji in the protohistoric period (Kirch 1984a). James Cook, on his second voyage in 1773, observed two pots in Tongatapu which he believed to be "the Manufactory of some other isle" (Beaglehole 1969:265). Mariner reported that the

Tongans "perform the process of boiling in earthen pots, of the manufacture of the Fiji islands" (Martin 1820:421).

Extra-Areal Comparisons

Although McKern (1929) excavated Lapita pottery on Tongatapu and 'Eua in 1921, the significance of these ceramics for the origin and development of Ancestral Polynesian Society was not recognized until Golson's renewed excavations in Tonga and his discovery of plainware pottery in Samoa (1957), along with Suggs's recovery of a few plainware sherds in early levels of the Marquesas (1961). With the recognition by Gifford and Shutler (1956) that the decorated ware from their Site 13 (named "Lapita") in New Caledonia closely matched McKern's ceramics from Tongatapu, as well as pottery from Fiji (Gifford 1951) and Watom (Meyer 1909), interest in these early ceramic assemblages heightened. In a synopsis of the "Lapita" phenomenon (as it had by then been labeled) at the 1969 Sigatoka conference, Golson (1971) proposed that the early wide distribution of these ceramics throughout the southwestern Pacific represented a "community of culture" ancestral to both eastern Melanesia and Polynesia. "The Lapita settlement of Tonga, and...of Samoa...develops in substantial isolation the pattern of culture we call Polynesian" (1971:76). This viewpoint has been upheld by additional excavations and analyses of Lapita assemblages, not only in the Fiji-Western Polynesian region but in New Caledonia, Vanuatu, the Reef-Santa Cruz Islands, and the Bismarck Archipelago. Green (1978, 1979), especially, has furthered the concept of the Lapita Cultural Complex as the founding cultural group throughout what he has termed "remote Oceania." Moreover, Green has demonstrated that Lapita ceramics can be readily subdivided into two major groups: (1) a Western Lapita group, which includes assemblages from the Bismarcks, the Reefs-Santa Cruz, Vanuatu, and New Caledonia; and (2) an Eastern Lapita group, including all known assemblages in the Fiji-Tonga-Samoa region. While both groups share many attributes including ceramic manufacture technique, vessel form, and certain widespread decorative motifs (as well as the basic structural rules of the Lapita decorative style), they are clearly distinguishable by other attributes, especially decorative motifs. As Green (1979) argues, the colonization of the Fiji-Western Polynesian region late in the second millennium B.C. led to the isolation of a splinter group of Lapita people, who subsequently developed the ceramic innovations that characterize Eastern Lapita.

Subsequent change in the Eastern Lapita ceramic complex has been dealt with by Green (1974b, 1978, 1979), based on local sequences of ceramic change in Tonga (Poulsen 1964, 1968, 1976), Fiji (Birks 1973; Mead et al. 1973; Hunt 1980), and Samoa (Green and Davidson 1969a, 1974; Jennings et al. 1976; Jennings and Holmer 1980). Green subdivided the Eastern Lapita sequence into three phases: (1) Early Eastern Lapita, characterized by well-decorated ceramics with a broad range of vessel types, dating from ca. 1300 to 1000 B.C.; (2) Late Eastern Lapita, with minimal dentate decoration and a more restricted range of vessel types, dating from ca. 1000 to 500 B.C.; and (3) Polynesian Plain Ware, lacking significant decoration, with vessel types restricted essentially to simple bowls and cups, dating from ca. 500 B.C. to A.D. 300. The change in vessel types represented in this ceramic sequence is illustrated in figure 113.

In his characterization of this sequence, Green (1974b:250-51) takes issue with Golson's (1971:75) proposal of a "Lapitoid ceramic series," emphasizing instead the change from the Late Eastern Lapita ceramic style to Polynesian Plain Ware. He does, however, stress the demonstrable continuity between Late Eastern Lapita and Polynesian Plain Ware. As I have argued elsewhere (Kirch 1981:127; 1984a), there are compelling reasons for retaining Golson's proposal, which makes use of the ceramic series concept as defined by Rouse and Cruxent (1963:23-26). Without belaboring the argument, I will simply note that the term "Lapitoid" is retained here in Golson's sense, as the series that encompasses not only Eastern Lapita and Polynesian Plain Ware, but Western Lapita and its derived plain ware assemblages as well.

I have also pointed out, in conjunction with an analysis of Lapitoid ceramics from Futuna (Kirch 1981:138, 142), that the tripartite division of the Lapitoid sequence in the Fiji-Wesern Polynesian region must not be taken as more than a generalized schema. As with the Futunan FU-11 ceramic assemblage, it is often pointless to force such variable and plastic artifacts as ceramics into a pigeonhole like "Late Eastern Lapita." In a region as extensive as Fiji-Tonga-Samoa, and when dealing with ceramic change over perhaps two thousand years, we must anticipate, and be equipped to deal with, substantial variation. Green's tripartite sequence of Early Eastern Lapita —> Late Eastern Lapita —> Polynesian Plain Ware is accepted here as a generalized, heuristic framework for speaking of regional ceramic change, not as a model that accounts for the full range of regional variation.

It is within this general framework of the Lapitoid ceramic series that the Niuatoputapu assemblages must be compared and their significance assessed. The specific excavated assemblages of Lapitoid pottery from the Fiji-Western Polynesia region that are of interest may be

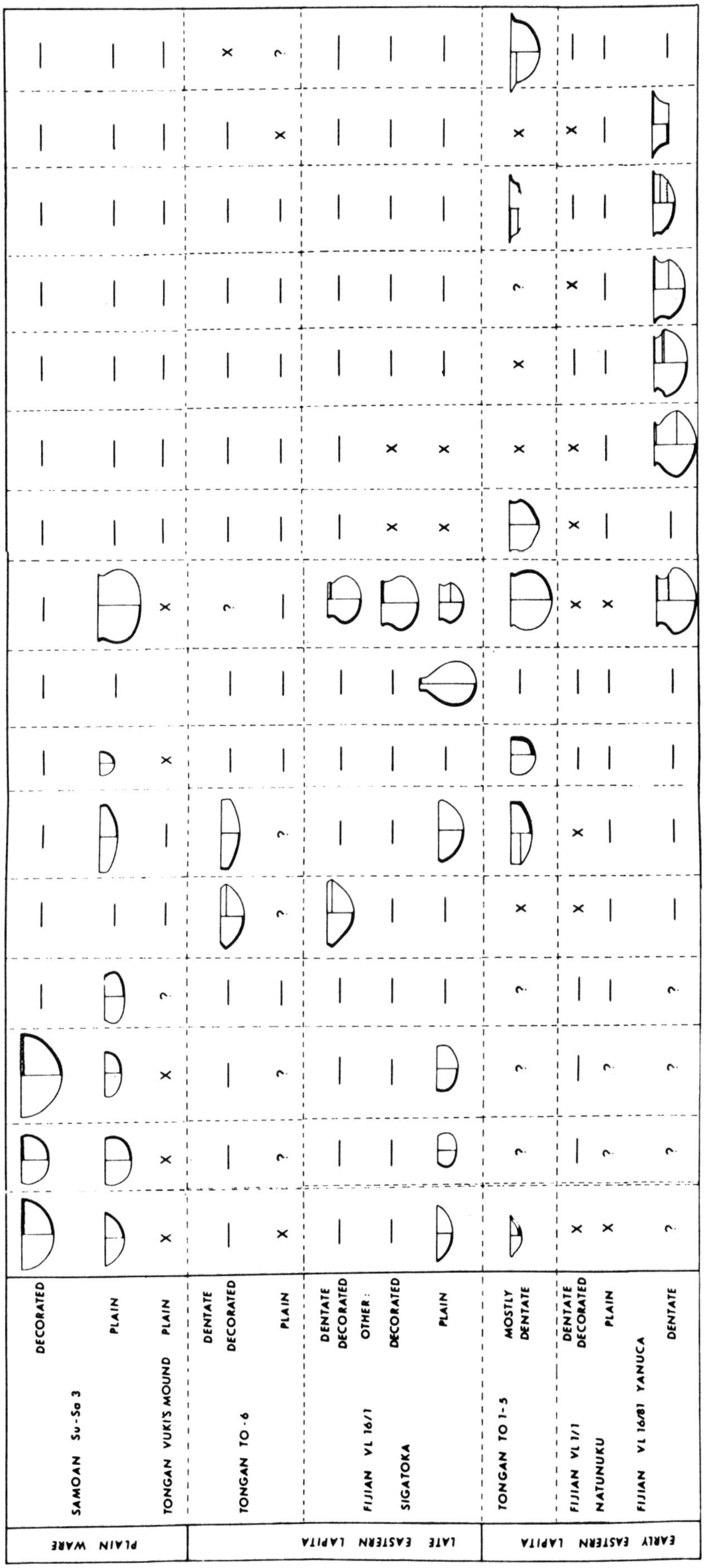

PLAIN WARE
SAMOAN Su-Sa 3 — DECORATED
PLAIN
TONGAN VUKI'S MOUND — PLAIN

LATE EASTERN LAPITA
TONGAN TO-6 — DENTATE DECORATED
PLAIN
FIJIAN VL 16/1 — DENTATE DECORATED
OTHER:
SIGATOKA — DECORATED
PLAIN

EARLY EASTERN LAPITA
TONGAN TO 1-5 — MOSTLY DENTATE
FIJIAN VL 1/1 — DENTATE DECORATED
NATUNUKU — PLAIN
FIJIAN VL 16/81 YANUCA — DENTATE

Figure 113. The sequence of ceramic change from Early Eastern Lapita, to Late Eastern Lapita, and Polynesian Plain Ware, as reflected in vessel forms (courtesy R. C. Green).

briefly reviewed. In Samoa, the submerged Ferry Berth or Mulifanua site has yielded a small collection of dentate-stamped ceramics of Early Eastern Lapita attribution, the earliest known assemblage from that archipelago, with an associated ^{14}C date on shell of 2890 ± 80 B.P. (Green and Davidson 1974). The Polynesian Plain Ware component of the Samoan sequence is extremely well documented through a number of sites on Upolu (Green and Davidson 1969a, 1974; Jennings et al. 1976; Jennings and Holmer 1980), and some temporal change within the late plain ware (e.g. from thin, fine to thick, coarse wares) has been demonstrated. On 'Uvea (Wallis) Island, Kirch (1975a, 1976:50-51) discovered six pottery-bearing sites; recent excavations by Frimigacci, Siorat, and Vienne (1984) at Utulei have now revealed the presence of typical dentate-stamped Lapita style ceramics. Four Lapitoid sites are known for Futuna and Alofi Islands (Kirch 1975a, 1976, 1981), although only one of these (FU-11) has been excavated, yielding a ^{14}C age of 2120 ± 80 B.P. One small assemblage from a disturbed site (FU-13) is arguably of Early Eastern Lapita age (even though no dentate-stamped decorations are present in the restricted sample), while the FU-11 assemblage is transitional between Late Eastern Lapita and Polynesian Plain Ware.

In the Tongan archipelago, Poulsen (1964, 1968, 1976, 1977) excavated at six sites distributed along the innerlagoon shore of Tongatapu. Although Poulsen's chronology for the Tongatapu ceramic sequence has been rejected as too protracted (Groube 1971; Green 1972a), his assemblages reflect the general tripartite sequence of ceramic change summarized above. The critical assemblages are those from Site To.2, with Early Eastern Lapita-style decoration and a wide range of vessel types, and the upper levels of To.6, with Polynesian Plain Ware. Site To.2 has an associated ^{14}C age of 3090 ± 95 B.P., while To.6 has two reliable dates of 2380 ± 51 and 2350 ± 200 B.P. Limited surface collections of pottery in the Ha'apai group and Vava'u (Groube 1971; Kaeppler 1973; Davidson 1971b) have indicated the presence of ceramic sites throughout the northerly islands of the archipelago, and T. Dye (pers. comm., 1984) has recently excavated well-stratified deposits containing both Early Eastern Lapita and Plain Ware from several sites in the Ha'apai group.

In Fiji, dentate-stamped Lapita was first recovered by Gifford (1951) from "Sites 20 and 21" at Sigatoka on Viti Levu; subsequent excavations there by the Birks (1973) yielded a collection of nearly whole vessels, some with minimal dentate stamping, dated to 2460 ± 90 B.P. The nearby Yanuca rockshelter, also excavated by the Birks, produced a larger array of decorated sherds in association with other artifacts, dated to 2980 ± 90 B.P. Hunt (1980, 1986), who carried out further excavations at this site, has dealt with the local ceramic sequence in admirable detail. Another Viti Levu site with Early Eastern Lapita ceramics is Natunuku, on the northwest coast, excavated by Shaw (in Mead et al. 1973), and yielding an associated ^{14}C age of 3240 ± 100 B.P. While Shaw has analyzed the Lapita design system at Natunuku, no complete site report exists. Most recently, a site containing elaborately decorated Lapita was discovered on the small offshore islet of Naigani, for which reports by Best (1981) and Kay (1984) are available. The Naigani site may be the oldest Lapita occupation yet known in the Fiji-Western Polynesian region. Finally, on Lakeba in the Lau group, Best (1984) excavated a series of Lapita and plain ware sites encompassing a lengthy sequence of ceramic change.

The NT-90 Assemblage

As has been demonstrated, the NT-90 assemblage differs significantly from those of NT-93 and -100 (as well as the smaller assemblages), is chronologically the oldest site on Niuatoputapu, and probably represents the island's initial colonization. It is the only site containing dentate-stamped Lapita decoration, although it also contains substantial quantities of plain ware. Based on the ^{14}C indications of second millennium B.C. age, the presence of a number of dentate-stamped Lapita motifs, and the range of vessel types present, the NT-90 assemblage (or a component of it) would clearly be assigned to Early Eastern Lapita as defined by Green (1974b). Specific comparisons, however, may help to precisely define the spatial and temporal position of this assemblage in the framework of Western Polynesian prehistory.

In terms of material and manufacture, the NT-90 assemblage falls squarely within the Lapitoid series: slab-constructed, paddle-and-anvil finished, relatively low fired earthenware. Of particular note is the high frequency of calcareous temper (about one-third of the sherds from NT-90), represented by Paste C. This paste group is virtually absent from later Niuatoputapu sites. Indeed, the use of calcareous sand temper in Fiji-Western Polynesian Lapitoid ceramics seems to be a distinctly early trait (Kirch 1981:137). In Samoa, for example, only the Mulifanua ceramics and the relatively early "Faleasi'u Fine" ware contain calcareous temper (Holmer 1980). In Futuna, only the enigmatic and putatively early FU-13 site contains sherds with calcareous temper. Unfortunately, we lack data on the frequency of calcareous temper in other assemblages from Tonga or Fiji, but the generality of this trend may be determined by future work.

As Green (1974b, 1979) demonstrated, and as is graphically summarized in figure 113, the transition from Early Eastern to Late Eastern Lapita involves a loss not only of decorative complexity but of several vessel forms. The NT-90 assemblage displays 10 vessel forms with 17 individual variants (fig. 95), and in this respect clearly falls within the Early Eastern Lapita group. Table 28 summarizes the distribution of NT-90 vessel forms in other important Lapitoid assemblages. The closest assemblages in terms of range of vessel forms are Tongatapu (To.2, which also exhibits a number of forms not present in NT-90), Yanuca, and Sigatoka. Most of the Sigatoka vessels, however, lack dentate-stamped decoration. The small collections from 'Uvea contain a number of the NT-90 vessel forms, and it is likely that others will be found once extensive excavations are undertaken. The evidence from Mulifanua is least satisfactory, since most of the sherds are small and reveal little of the range of vessel shapes. Although only the presence of Forms 6 and 8C vessels can be confirmed, it is probable that other forms were present. (The submerged geomorphic position of this site unfortunately renders the acquisition of further samples unlikely.) The NT-90 assemblage is most dissimilar to the FU-11 assemblage (which is transitional between Late Eastern Lapita and Polynesian

TABLE 28

DISTRIBUTION OF VESSEL FORMS IN EASTERN LAPITA SITES

NT-90 VESSEL FORMS	MULIFANUA	'UVEA	FUTUNA (FU-11)	YANUCA	SIGATOKA	TONGATAPU (To. 2)	TIKOPIA (TK-4)
1A						X	X
1B							
1C							
2A		?	?	X	X		
2B		?		X	X		
2C							
3		?	?	X	X	X	
4	X			X	X	X	
5A	X	X		X	X	X	X
5B	X	X		?	X	X	?
6	X	X		X		X	
7					X	X	
8A		?	X	X			
8B		?		X	X	X	X
8C	X	?		X	X		X
9			X				X
10		X	X		X		

X = definitely present; ? = possibly present

TABLE 29

DISTRIBUTION OF DECORATIVE DESIGN ELEMENTS AND MOTIFS IN SELECTED LAPITA SITES

NT–90 DESIGN ELEMENTS, MOTIFS	MULIFANUA	'UVEA	TONGATAPU	YANUCA	SIGATOKA	NATUNUKU	MALO	RL–2	TIKOPIA
GZ 1	X	X	X	X	X		X	X	X
GZ 2	X	X	X	X		X	X	X	X
GZ 3	X		X	X			X	X	
TB 3.2	X	X	X	X			X	X	
DE 1.1	X	X	X	X	X	X	X	X	X
DE 2.1	X	X	X	X			X	X	
DE 3.1	X	X	X	X		X	X	X	
DE 4	X	X		X		X	X	X	
DE 5	X	X	X	X	X	X	X	X	
DE 6	X	X	X	X		X	X	X	
DE 8		?	X	X		X	X	X	
M 1	X	X	X	X	X	X	X	X	
M 12/13/14	X	X	X	X				X	
M 15	X	X	X	X	X	X		X	X
M 16	X		X	X		X	X	X	
M 18	X	X	X	X		X	X	X	
M 19			X	X		X	X	X	
M 30.1	X		X	X		X	X	X	
M 30.2	X		X	X	X	X	X	X	
M 46			X					X	
M 53			X					X	
M 99.1	X	X	?				?	X	X
Motifs not in Niuatoputapu	3/4	2 (?)	40	24	1	26	34	74	1
Simple Matching Coefficient	0.91	0.93	0.66	0.78	0.85	0.72	0.61	0.40	0.85

Plain Ware) as well as the plain ware assemblages from Upolu.

Associated with the wide range of vessel forms in Early Eastern Lapita is a comparable variability in rim form. Of the Niuatoputapu assemblages, only that from NT-90 displays substantial rim variability, with high frequencies of expanded or thickened rims (table 24). The NT-90 ceramics strongly resemble those from To.2 in Tongatapu (Poulsen 1967, 1976), and to some extent the limited sherd sample from 'Uvea (Frimigacci et al. 1984). Unfortunately, the Mulifanua sample contains few rims, and the range of variation in that assemblage thus remains enigmatic.

The most efficacious strategy in analyzing the relative position of NT-90 is the comparison of Lapita design systems. Using the formal analytical procedure provided by Mead et al. (1973), Green (1976, 1978, 1979) has constructed quantitative distance models of differentiation among various Lapita assemblages. Following these models, table 29 shows the design elements and motifs in the NT-90 assemblage in relation to their counterparts in other critical sites of the region. Data from Western Lapita sites in Malo (Hedrick n.d.) and the Reef Islands (Site RL-2, Green 1976 and Donovan 1973) are provided for a broader regional perspective. (The relevance of the Tikopia data, also included, will be discussed shortly.)

Some initial indication of the similarity (or, alternatively, distance) between these assemblages is provided by the number of motifs not present at NT-90. Within the Fiji-Western Polynesia area, the Tongatapu, Natunuku, and Yanuca assemblages all contain a much wider array of design elements and motifs, indicating more elaborate decorative styles. Given the regional trend of decline over time in the complexity of decoration in the Lapitoid series—a trend leading ultimately to the total loss of decoration—one might conclude that the NT-90 assemblage is younger than the other three assemblages just named. (It is also evident that NT-90 differs substantially from the Western Lapita assemblages—particularly RL-2, which contains at least 74 motifs not present in NT-90.) On the other hand, the NT-90 assemblage shares many elements and motifs with both the 'Uvea and Mulifanua assemblages, neither of which exhibits many motifs or elements not present in Niuatoputapu. This observation supports the hypothesis that these latter three assemblages are more closely linked, either temporally, spatially, or both. Finally, the Sigatoka and Tikopia assemblages, while not exhibiting substantial numbers of elements or motifs absent from NT-90, display a reduced number of correspondences. In other words, they appear as even more simplified derivatives of the NT-90/'Uvea/Mulifanua complex.

These observations can be formalized through quantification. Table 30 provides Simple Matching Coefficient (SM) values for each of the above sites in relation to the NT-90 assemblage. The SM Coefficient, suited for presence/absence data such as those available here, is calculated according to the formula MC = (a + d)/(a + b + c + d), where a is the number of attributes present in both samples under consideration, b is the number presented only by sample i, c the number only in sample j, and d the number of attributes that occur elsewhere in the matrix but not in either sample under consideration. Table 30 presents these and other SM values in a matrix format for the Fiji-Western Polynesian sites under comparison. The close relationship between the NT-90, Mulifanua, and 'Uvea assemblages is indicated by high SM values, while the divergence of these three units from the early Yanuca and Tongatapu assemblages is revealed by low SM values. Sigatoka also corresponds closely to the first group.

TABLE 30

SIMPLE MATCHING COEFFICIENTS FOR LAPITA CERAMIC DESIGN ASSEMBLAGES

	'UVEA	NIUATOPUTAPU	MULIFANUA	SIGATOKA	YANUCA	TONGATAPU
'UVEA (U)	1.0	0.93	0.89	0.90	0.76	0.60
NIUATOPUTAPU (N)		1.0	0.91	0.85	0.78	0.66
MULIFANUA (M)			1.0	0.85	0.77	0.65
SIGATOKA (S)				1.0	0.69	0.54
YANUCA (Y)					1.0	0.59
TONGATAPU (T)						1.0

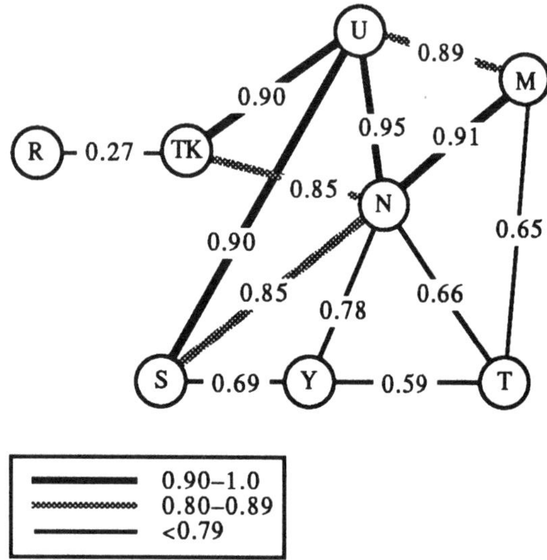

Figure 114. Diagram showing relationship between Lapita ceramic assemblages, based on shared design motifs.

Based on these comparative data, we can propose the existence of a "northern group" of Early Eastern Lapita sites which—while characterized by a broad range of vessel types with typical dentate-stamped and incised Lapita-style decorations—share a simplified set of design elements and motifs. I would further suggest that these sites are slightly younger (perhaps 200 to 400 years) than Natunuku, basal Yanuca, To.2, or Naigani. Given that these northern assemblages possess a common set of decorative elements and motifs, we may advance the hypothesis that their makers were either in relatively continuous contact or were settled from a common source community. This latter hypothesis needs to be tested by additional excavations in both 'Uvea and Samoa, but is reasonable given the geographic propinquity of these locations. Keeping in mind that both time and space are involved in the ceramic assemblage relationships described above, we can attempt to portray the situation in a two-dimensional diagram (fig. 114).

A Digression: Tikopia Reconsidered

The colonization of Tikopia, a Polynesian Outlier some 2000 km west of Niuatoputapu, was achieved about 900 B.C. by a population that manufactured Lapitoid ceramics termed Kiki Ware (Kirch and Yen 1982). This pottery is largely plain, with only five sherds bearing dentate-stamped designs, although a number of rims are crenated or notched. Calcareous temper dominates the assemblage (79% of sherds), and vessel forms include five or possibly six types known from the NT-90 site (table 28). In comparing Kiki Ware with other Lapitoid assemblages, both in Fiji-Western Polynesia and in Melanesia, Kirch and Yen (1982:205) remarked on the similarities with Niuatoputapu sites NT-90 and -100, FU-11 on Futuna, and Sigatoka. Although the presence in the early Tikopian settlement of several exotic items of material culture with *westerly* derivations (e.g., metavolcanic adzes, Talasea obsidian, and chert) would tend to imply connections with the Western Lapita exchange network, Kirch and Yen hesitated to conclude that Tikopia was actually settled from the west. An early likely alternative was that Tikopia had been peopled from Western Polynesia, as an early "outlier" phenomenon. Rather, the issue was left unresolved, with three alternative hypotheses proposed for the immediate source of the Tikopia colonists (Kirch and Yen 1982:337-38).

The detailed analysis of the NT-90 design system, and the regional comparison given above, strengthen Kirch and Yen's third hypothesis for the origin of the Kiki Ware makers: "...initial settlement was from the east, in an early Outlier pattern of westerly voyaging or drift from the Fiji and West Polynesian area" (1982: 337). The argument can be advanced that the Tikopia colonizing population originated in one of the "northern group" islands identified above. The evidence in support of this hypothesis is the close similarity between Kiki Ware and the northern group ceramic assemblages in (1) technique of manufacture, such as the use of calcareous temper; (2) vessel form; and most importantly, (3) decoration. The few dentate-stamped elements and motifs present in Kiki Ware are all present in the northern group represented by Mulifanua, NT-90, and 'Uvea. Indeed, Kiki Ware can readily be characterized as a further simplification of the northern group ceramic complex. Moreover, the dating of Tikopia colonization at ca. 900 B.C. fits well with the NT-90 age assessments.

Equally significant for this hypothesis is the fact that Kiki Ware does not compare at all closely with contemporary Lapitoid assemblages in the geographically proximate Reef Islands or Santa Cruz (Green 1976; Donovan 1973), which were marked by rather elaborate decoration, as late as 900 B.C. An SM coefficient calculated between Kiki Ware and RL-2 ceramics yields a value of only 0.27. It is not parsimonious to derive Kiki Ware from Reefs-Santa Cruz Lapita, whereas this early Tikopia pottery can readily be seen as a derivative of the northern group of Early Eastern Lapita.

If this hypothesis is accepted, we still must account for the presence of exotic items of westerly derivation in the Kiki site. A likely explanation would be that the early Tikopia colonists established some intermittent contact with Lapita peoples in the Reef-Santa Cruz islands, which are only 250 to 300 km distant, and received from them the few items under consideration. All of these exotic materials are, indeed, known to have been elements of the wide-spread Western Lapita exchange system (Green 1979).

A further comment will conclude this digression. The diminutive outlier of Anuta, only 137 km from Tikopia, was also colonized about 900 B.C. Its settlement site contains Lapitoid pottery very similar to Kiki Ware (although no dentate-stamped sherds were recovered; Kirch and Rosendahl 1973, 1976; Kirch 1982b). A chert nodule of exotic origin recovered in association with this pottery has been shown by XRF characterization to be of probable Futunan origin (Kirch and Yen 1982:344; Kirch 1981:139). This find is suggestive of a Western Polynesian origin for the initial Anuta population. Chert flakes of probable Futunan origin also occur in Site NT-90 (see Flaked Stone, below). Although no chert specimens from the early TK-4 site on Tikopia have been sourced, two specimens from later contexts compare closely with the Futuna and Niuatoputapu materials.

In sum, we now have excellent grounds to entertain the hypothesis that Tikopia, and probably Anuta as well, were initially colonized by voyagers (either purposeful or adrift) from one or more of the northern islands of Western Polynesia. Specific tests (such as the characterization of the chert from Tikopia site TK-4) can and should be designed and implemented in an effort to reject or confirm this hypothesis.

The Plain Ware Assemblages (NT-93, -100)

The assemblages of Sites NT-93 and -100, as well as the other excavated collections, represent later phases in the local sequence of ceramic change. Since neither is well stratified, and both probably span several hundred years, they unfortunately do not give us a finely partitioned sequence of change. They do, however, exhibit attributes characteristic of both transitional Late Eastern Lapita (as in the FU-11 and Sigatoka assemblages) and Polynesian Plain Ware (as in the Samoan assemblages). The absence of calcareous temper is a feature of note. These assemblages also display a substantial reduction in the variability of rim morphology. Numerous vessel forms were dropped from the ceramic inventory, leaving only the Form 1A cups/bowls, large jars of Forms 8A and 8B (and possibly 8C), probable Form 9 vessels, and the large, handled water jars of Form 10. With the exception of the Form 1A cups/bowls, this suite of vessels closely matches the FU-11 assemblage from Futuna (Kirch 1981). It differs, however, from the Samoan Polynesian Plain Ware assemblages, which are restricted almost entirely to small and medium-sized open bowls (Green 1974b). A further point of differentiation between the assemblages from Niuatoputapu and Samoa is in vessel wall thickness. Whereas the late Samoan ceramics underwent a significant increase in wall thickness, the Niutoputapu assemblages clearly do not show such a pattern (table 18).

Along with a change in tempering and reduction in rim variation and vessel forms, there was a near-total loss of decoration in the later assemblages. Decoration was limited to a few examples of rim notching or incising (figs. 108, 109), a feature also seen in the late Samoan ceramics.

ADZES

Of all Polynesian artifact classes, adzes—particularly those of stone—have been most utilized for culture-historical purposes (Cleghorn 1984). Although variations among adz collections from Polynesian islands have long been recognized (e.g., Duff 1959; Figueroa and Sanchez 1965), it was not until the recovery of substantial assemblages from stratigraphically documented contexts in the 1960s that the significance of such variability for the temporal development of the early Polynesian adz kit was determined (Emory 1968; Green 1971, 1974b). Focusing on excavated adz assemblages from Tonga, Samoa, and the Marquesas Islands, Green delineated both the development of an early Polynesian stone adz kit from earlier Lapita adzes in both stone and *Tridacna* shell and the elaboration of this kit in Eastern Polynesia with its several innovations, including the tang. Adzes of shell have, until recently, been largely ignored as objects of classificatory study. The recent recovery of large excavated samples of shell adzes from early Lapitoid contexts in the southwestern Pacific has, however, prompted reconsideration of this artifact class (Davidson 1971a; Garanger 1972; Kirch and Rosendahl 1973; Craib 1977; Kirch and Yen 1982). In particular, the detailed analyses of Kirch and Yen (1982) on the Tikopia shell adz assemblage provide a baseline for employing these protean artifacts in culture-historical frameworks.

The Niuatoputapu investigations yielded 87 stone and shell adzes or adz fragments (table 14); a large number of these consist of small fragments or flakes lacking diagnostic features. However, 25 stone and 11 shell adzes or adz fragments have sufficient attributes to render them useful for classificatory and comparative studies. Three additional stone adzes were recovered on Tafahi Island. A constraint in the use of these artifacts for tracing temporal change in adz variation is that many of them were surface finds, lacking stratigraphic association. Despite these limitations, the Niuatoputapu adz collection adds significantly to our knowledge of the

TABLE 31

BASALT ADZES: DESCRIPTIVE DATA

CATALOG NO.	TYPE[1]	CROSS-SECTION	BEVEL[2]	LENGTH (cm)	CUTTING-EDGE WIDTH (cm)	MID-POINT WIDTH (cm)	POLL WIDTH (cm)	THICKNESS (cm)	WEIGHT (g)	REMARKS
NT–GEN–3	III	Trap.	C	9.36	4.18	4.0	2.96	1.74	111.3	well polished
NT–GEN–4	X	Trap.	S	15.96	4.6	5.1	4.4	3.4	507.8	well polished
NT–GEN–5	IX	Trap.	C	12.67	4.4	4.8	3.4	3.8	380.2	partly polished
NT–GEN–6	X	Trap.	—	14.6	4.1	4.6	3.3	2.8	363.4	well polished, bevel damaged
NT–GEN–7	IX	Trap.	—	8.3	3.2	3.3	2.1	2.3	113.8	partly polished, bevel damaged
NT–GEN–8	III	Rect. Quad.	S	7.5	3.8	3.6	3.0	1.1	56.4	well polished
NT–GEN–9	I (?)	Quad.	C	9.2	7.0	6.8	6.2	1.9	213.8	partly polished
NT–GEN–10	IX	Trap.	C	12.9	3.6	4.5	4.2	2.9	301.3	partly polished
NT–GEN–13	—	Trap.	S	20.1	1.6	2.9	2.8	1.5	249.2	well polished chisel/ aberrant type
NT–93–85/SE(2)–1	VI	Triang.	—	—	—	3.7	3.0	3.6	—	bevel missing, preform
TF–GEN–2	IX	Trap.	S	8.8	3.5	3.2	2.8	2.7	115.5	partly polished

[1] After Green and Davidson (1969b).
[2] C, curved; S, straight.

TABLE 32

BASALT ADZ FRAGMENTS: DESCRIPTIVE DATA

CATALOG NO.	TYPE[1]	CROSS-SECTION	BEVEL[2]	CUTTING-EDGE WIDTH (cm)	MID-POINT WIDTH (cm)	THICKNESS (cm)	REMARKS
NT–GEN–1	—	Quad.	—	—	—	2.7	partly polished, midsection
NT–GEN–2	IX?	Trap.	—	—	4.8	2.0	midsection
NT–GEN–28	X	Trap.	—	—	2.5	1.4	well polished, butt section
NT–GEN–36	III	Trap.	—	—	2.9	1.2	well polished, midsection
NT–90–SA–7	Va	Plano-convex	—	—	3.9	2.0	well polished, bevel, midsection
NT–90–SA–16	IX/X	Trap.	—	—	4.4	4.5	partly polished, midsection
NT–90–SA–34	III?	Trap.	—	—	3.2	1.5	partly polished, midsection
NT–90–SA–40	III	Trap.	—	—	3.5	0.9	well polished, midsection
NT–90–SA-46	IX	Trap.	S	5.0	5.7	3.6	partly polished, bevel section
NT–90–A26I(4)–1	—	—	S	—	—	—	corner of bevel, well polished
NT–100–SA–2	IX/X	Trap.	—	—	3.0	2.4	partly polished, butt section
NT–100–219–1	—	Circ.	S	0.9	1.3	1.1	well polished, chisel, bevel section
NT–110–SA–1	—	Trap.	—	—	3.5	2.4	partly polished, butt section
NT–110–SA–2	—	Trap.	—	—	3.8	1.4	partly polished, midsection
NT–112–SA–1	IX/X?	Trap.	S	—	—	2.2	bevel corner, well-ground
TO–TF–2–1	VI?	Triang.	—	—	4.1	4.0	partly polished, midsection
TO–TF–GEN–1	IX	Trap.	—	—	4.1	3.7	partly polished, midsection

[1] After Green and Davidson (1969b).
[2] C, curved; S, straight.

variability and distribution of this important artifact class in Western Polynesia, and confirms certain interpretations of the temporal development of the Ancestral Polynesian adz kit.

Stone Adzes

Eleven complete adzes and 17 fragments with diagnostic attributes from Niuatoputapu and Tafahi provide the material for analysis. Descriptive data on these specimens are provided in tables 31 and 32. The 59 smaller fragments and flakes lacking diagnostic attributes are not further considered here.

All stone adzes are of fine-grained grayish or blue-black volcanics, either basalt or andesite. Some variation in petrology is evident in hand specimens, and these artifacts probably derive from several sources, some of them non-local. T. Dye (pers. comm., 1984) reports discovering, during investigations on Niuatoputapu in 1983, a source of local fine-grained stone suitable for adz manufacture.

Building upon the earlier work of Buck (1930), Green and Davidson (1969b) produced a classification of Samoan stone adzes that has proven applicable to adzes from other Western Polynesian and Polynesian Outlier contexts (e.g., Futuna and Uvea, Kirch 1976, Frimigacci et al. 1984; Tikopia, Kirch and Yen 1982). The Green and Davidson classification, with minor revisions suggested by Green (1974b:254), is used here, and the appropriate type designations are indicated in tables 31 and 32. Not all of the Samoan types are represented in the Niuatoputapu collection. Indeed, the majority of the specimens fall into types III, IX, and X, with minor representation of I, Va, and VI. The distinctions between these types can be concisely displayed using the following taxonomy, modified from Green and Davidson (1969b:21; see also Kirch 1976:52):

Type

A. Quadrangular Section
- 1. Back > Front
  - a. Partially Ground
    - 1. Thin .... I, II
    - 2. Thick IX
  - b. Fully Ground
    - 1. Thin III
    - 2. Thick X
- 2. Front > Back IV

B. Plano-Convex Section
- 1. Thin .... Va
- 2. Thick .... Vb

C. Triangular Section
- 1. Apex Up .... VI, VII
- 2. Apex Down VIII

A small number of specimens cannot be accommodated within this taxonomy, and appear to represent either the reworking of established types or idiosyncratic or individualistic crafting.

Type I Adz. Only one Niuatoputapu specimen (fig. 115, d) has been classified, somewhat tentatively, in Type I. This is a fairly large adz with rectangular outline, trapezoidal section, and minimal grinding. It does not, however, display the typical longitudinal reduction of Samoan Type I adzes, and probably has been reworked from an originally larger adz. The absence of any other specimens of Type I is significant, since this class dominates Samoan adz collections (Green 1974b, table 28).

Type III Adzes. Two whole and three fragmentary Type III adzes are represented (fig. 116). As indicated in the taxonomy, these are characterized by thin, trapezoidal sections and by extensive grinding and polishing. Three of these adzes are surface finds from locations outside the pottery-bearing zone, but two fragments were surface-collected at Site NT-90.

Type Va Adz. Type V adzes, distinguished by their plano-convex sections, are closely associated with Lapitoid contexts in Western Polynesia and carry over into early Eastern Polynesian assemblages as well, making them an important component of the Ancestral Polynesian adz kit (Green 1971, 1974b; Kirch 1976, 1981). Only one fragment of this type, a surface find from Site NT-90, was recovered (fig. 115, a). The specimen had been displaced from its archaeological context by recent gardening, and presumably is associated with the NT-90 ceramic assemblage.

Type VI Adzes. One nearly complete example of a triangular-sectioned adz was excavated from Site NT-93, in association with plain ware ceramics. This adz (fig. 115, c) lacks only the bevel, and the absence of grinding suggests that it was in the preform stage of manufacture when the bevel section broke away, perhaps as a result of end shock. The other example of a triangular-sectioned adz, a midsection, comes from Tafahi Island.

Type IX and X Adzes. These types are essentially variants of the same general form, distinguished primarily by the degree of grinding and polish. Fragmentary specimens, in which it is often difficult to discriminate between types, can be unambiguously assigned to the general category IX/X. Most of these adzes are large. Two smaller examples, one each of types IX and X, are illustrated in figure 117. Large examples of Type IX and of Type X are shown in figures 118 and 119. In all, 13 IX/X adzes are represented in the Niuatoputapu and Tafahi collection, establishing them as the dominant type. All specimens were surface finds: two from the surface of Site NT-90,

Figure 115. Basalt adzes from Niuatoputapu.

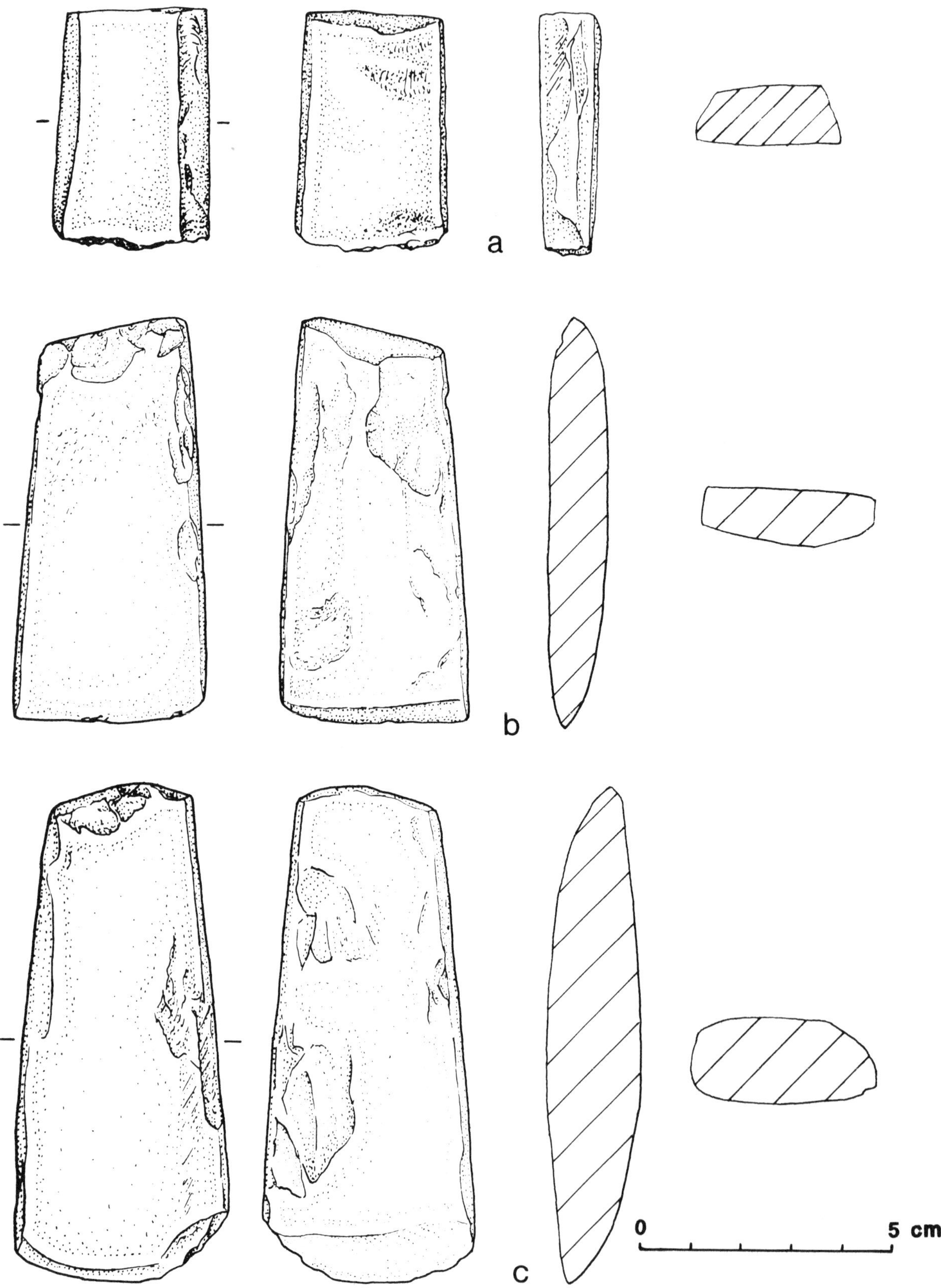

Figure 116. Type III basalt adzes from Niuatoputapu.

Figure 117. Type X and Type IX adzes from Niuatoputapu.

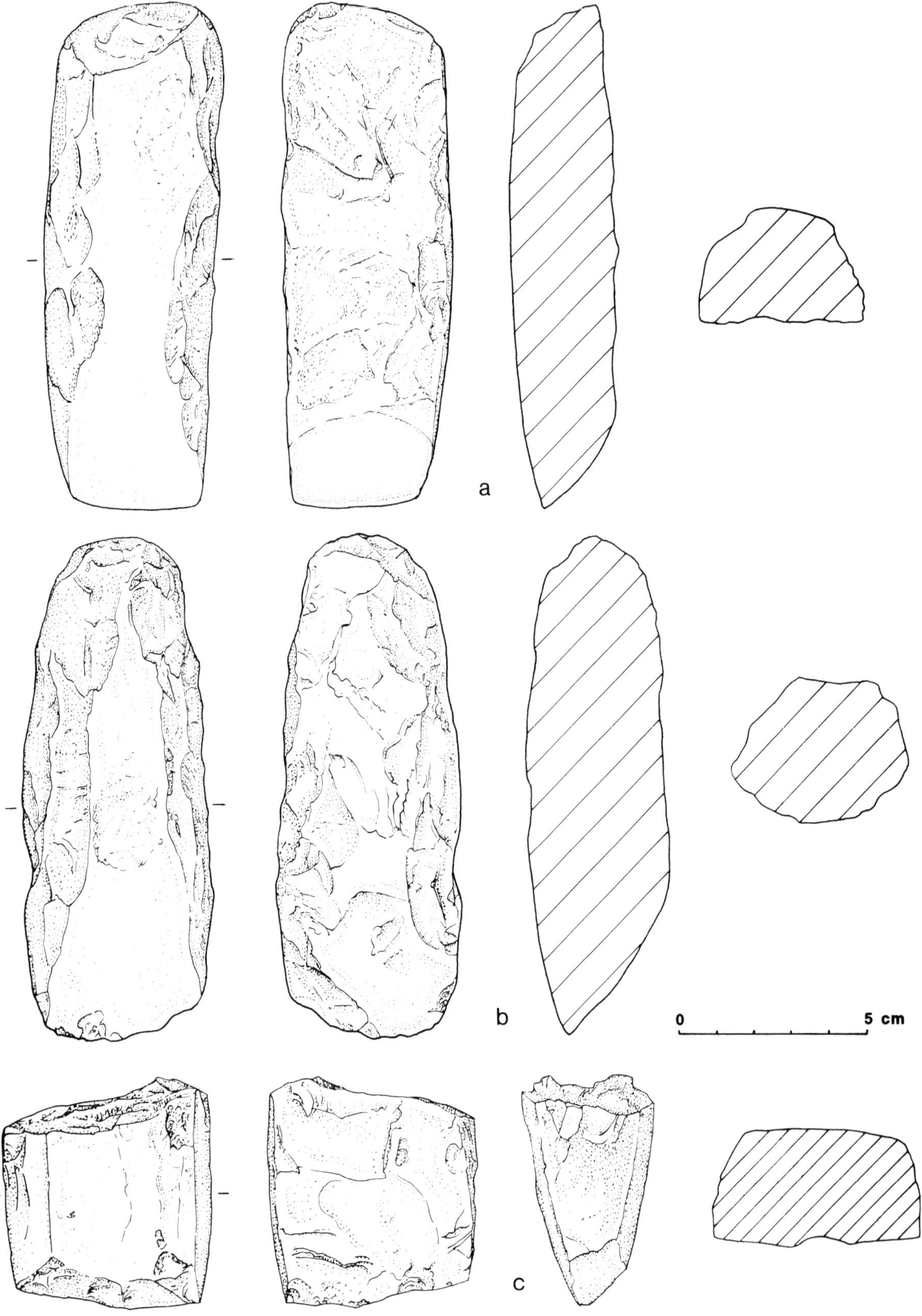

Figure 118. Type IX adzes from Niuatoputapu.

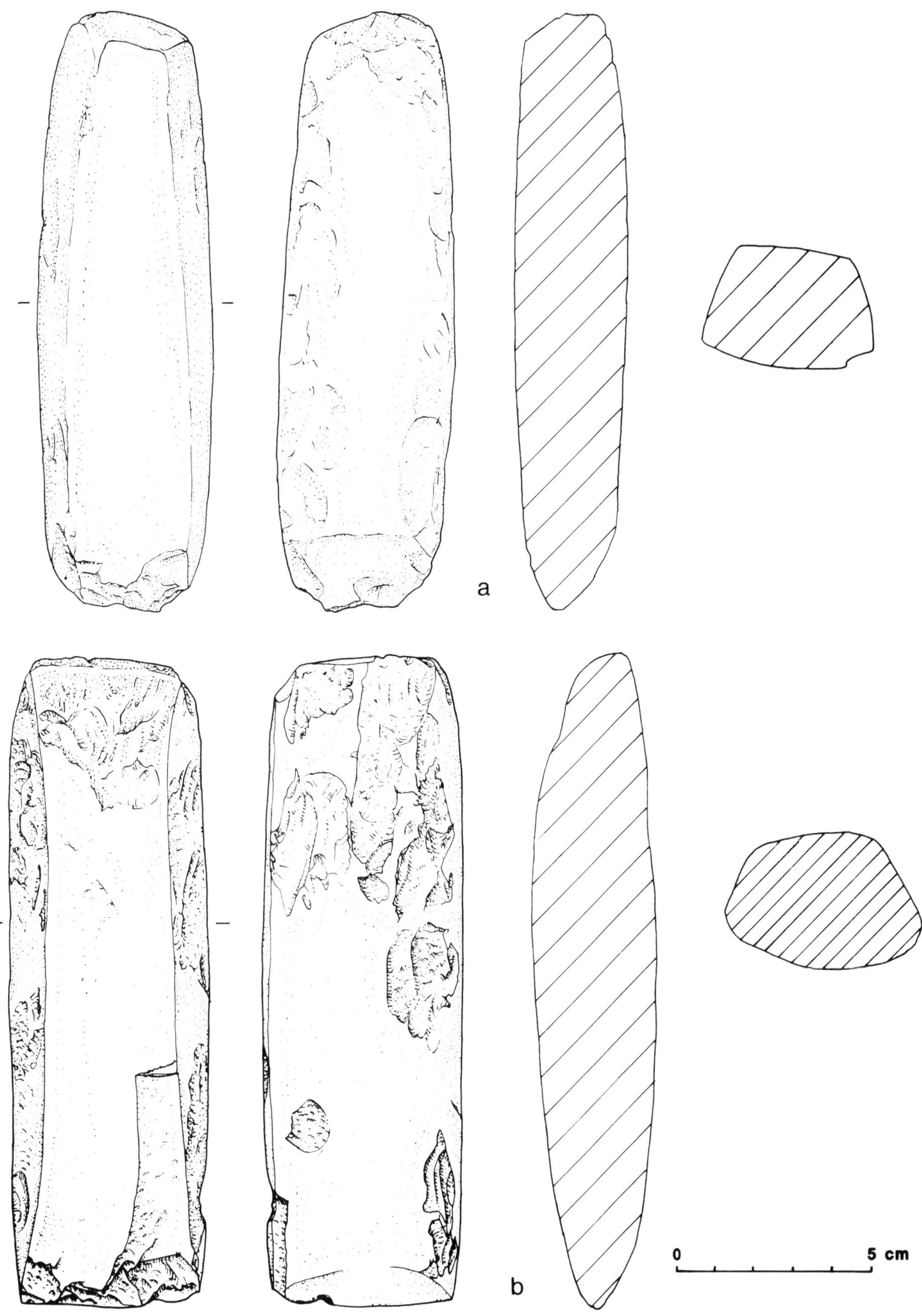

Figure 119. Type X adzes from Niuatoputapu.

one from NT-100, and one from NT-112. While none can be unambiguously associated with ceramics, this possibility is not precluded. However, the distribution of Type IX/X adzes over other parts of the island, particularly in association with monument sites on the more recently uplifted terrain, does suggest that types IX/X dominated the later prehistoric adz kit.

Aberrant Types. Two specimens cannot be accommodated within the above classification. One of these (fig. 115, b), excavated from Site NT-100 in association with plain ware ceramics, is the bevel end of a small chisel, nearly circular in cross-section, well polished on all surfaces. The other specimen (fig. 120) is unique, and appears to have no counterpart in other Tongan or Western Polynesian collections. This is a long narrow adz (or possibly a chisel), well ground on all surfaces, with a plano-convex section. The specimen was given to us by Loketi of Hihifo village, who discovered it while excavating an outhouse pit on his *api.* The precise stratigraphic context of this artifact is not known, although the outhouse lay within the ceramic zone.

Shell Adzes

The Niuatoputapu collection includes 11 adzes of shell, all associated with the island's ceramic zone occupations either through excavation (four specimens) or as surface finds within the zone. Eight adzes are of *Tridacna* shell and one each of *Cassis, Terebra,* and *Conus.* Descriptive data for shell adzes is provided in table 33.

Tridacna-shell Adzes. Extensive grinding on all adzes makes the determination of species difficult, but the massive size of several specimens precludes the smaller species *Tridacna maxima* and indicates the large *T. gigas.* Some of the smaller adzes may be of *T. maxima.*

Kirch and Yen (1982:206-232) developed a taxonomy of shell adzes based upon an exhaustive analysis of 234 specimens from Tikopia; their types are applicable to the Niuatoputapu artifacts. All but one of the eight Niuatoputapu *Tridacna* adzes were manufactured from the massive hinge region of the valve and thus fall into either Type 7 or Type 8, depending upon whether the transverse section is ovoid or quadrangular. Type 7 adzes are illustrated in figure 121, b, and 122, c; Type 8 adzes are shown in figure 121, a, c, and 122, b. Although the Niuatoputapu specimens can be identified with the two Tikopia types, they encompass considerable variation. For example, two of the adzes are quite massive (figure 121, b, c), while two have narrow, chisel-like bevels (figure 121, a; 122, c). The massive Type 7 adz from Site NT-93 is noteworthy for its "hollow-ground" bevel (concave transverse bevel section), a feature also found in some *Tridacna* adzes from early Lapitoid contexts on Tikopia and Anuta. One *Tridacna-* shell adz (fig. 122, a), from Site NT-91, is made from the dorsal region of the valve and would be classified in the Tikopia system as Type 3.

Cassis-shell Adz/Chisel. The bevel of a small adz, or perhaps a chisel, of *Cassis*-shell lip was found within the ceramic zone near Matavai village (fig. 123, b). It has a curved bevel, and is very similar to *Cassis*-shell chisels known from Anuta (Kirch and Rosendahl 1976), Tikopia (Kirch and Yen 1982), and the Marquesas (Suggs 1961:115-117, fig. 35).

Terebra-shell Chisel. A surface find at Site NT-100 was a chisel or gouge of *Terebra* shell, with the shell apex ground down to a narrow cutting edge (fig. 123, c). Such chisels are also known from early Eastern Polynesian contexts (e.g., Sinoto and McCoy 1975).

Conus-shell Adz. The bevel of a small adz of *Conus* shell was excavated at Site NT-100. The adz is made from the body whorl of a large cone shell, and has a curved cutting edge (fig. 123, a).

Extra-Areal Comparisons

The range of variability and the temporal development of adzes are better known for Samoa than for any other Polynesian group, due to the work of Buck (1930), Green and Davidson (1969b, 1974), and Jennings and Holmer (1980), which provides a basis of nearly 800 individual artifacts, many from well-dated stratigraphic contexts. Green (1974b) provides a thorough analysis of temporal change in Samoan adzes, of which a few critical points must be mentioned. First, no shell adzes have ever been excavated in Samoa (although Buck [1930:353-54] records two Bishop Museum specimens). Green (in Green and Davidson 1974:141-44, 264-65) argues convincingly that many of the early innovations in the Samoan adz kit were due to the limited numbers of rock types on these geologically "oceanic" islands, and to the absence of large *Tridacna* shells. "When people crossed the andesite line to settle Samoa and the rest of Polynesia, they found it necessary to manufacture their entire adz kit from a restricted range of fine-grained basalts whose flaking properties and strengths differed from those of the materials previously used" (1974:144). Among the stone adz types developed during the first millennium in Samoan prehistory were Type I, Type III, Type IV, and Type V with its plano-convex section. Of these, Types I, III, and IV continue throughout later periods of Samoan prehistory, while Type V was not manufactured after the cessation of pottery production. Other innovations led to the development of additional adz types early in the first

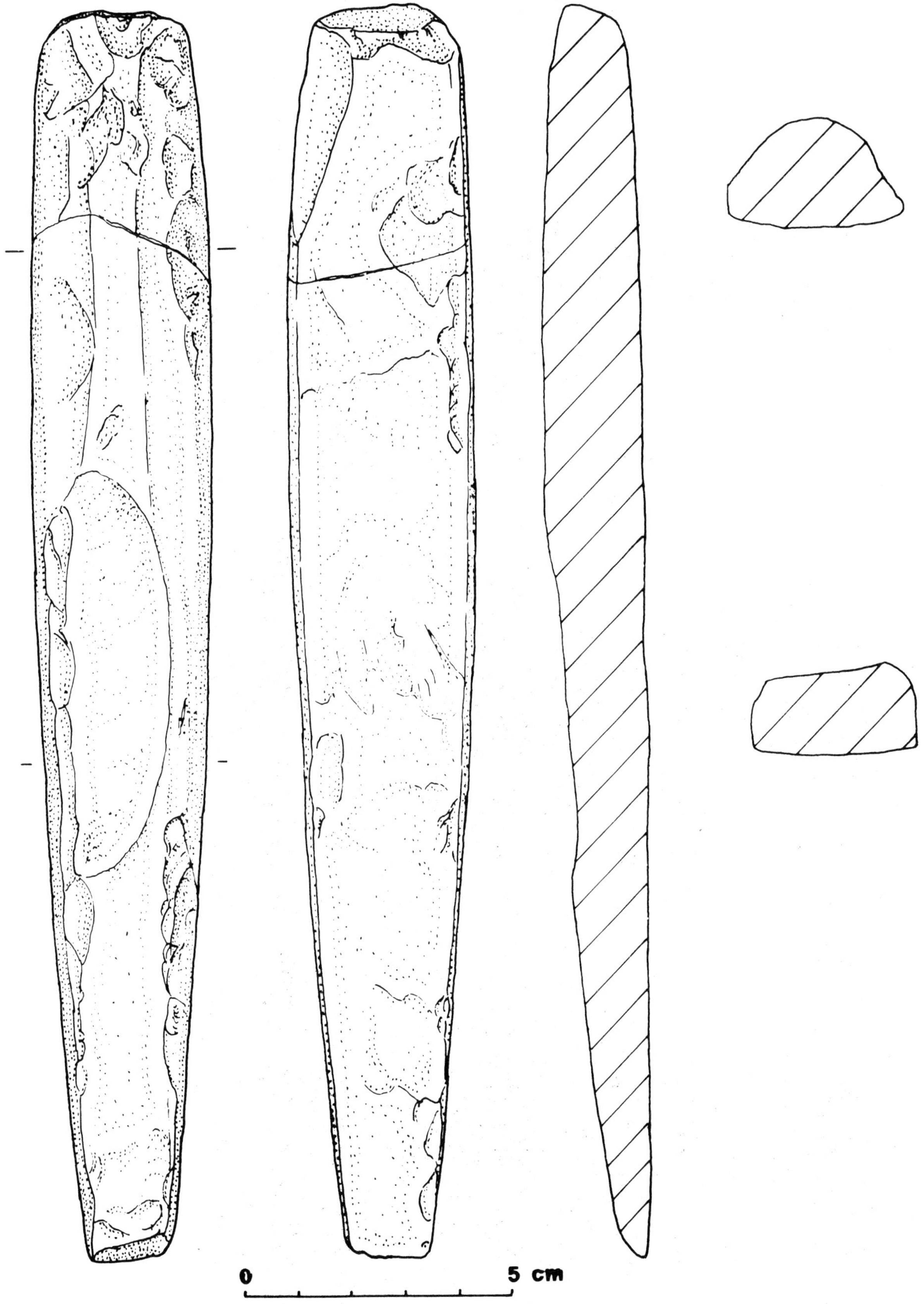

Figure 120. Unique adz or chisel from Hihifo Village area.

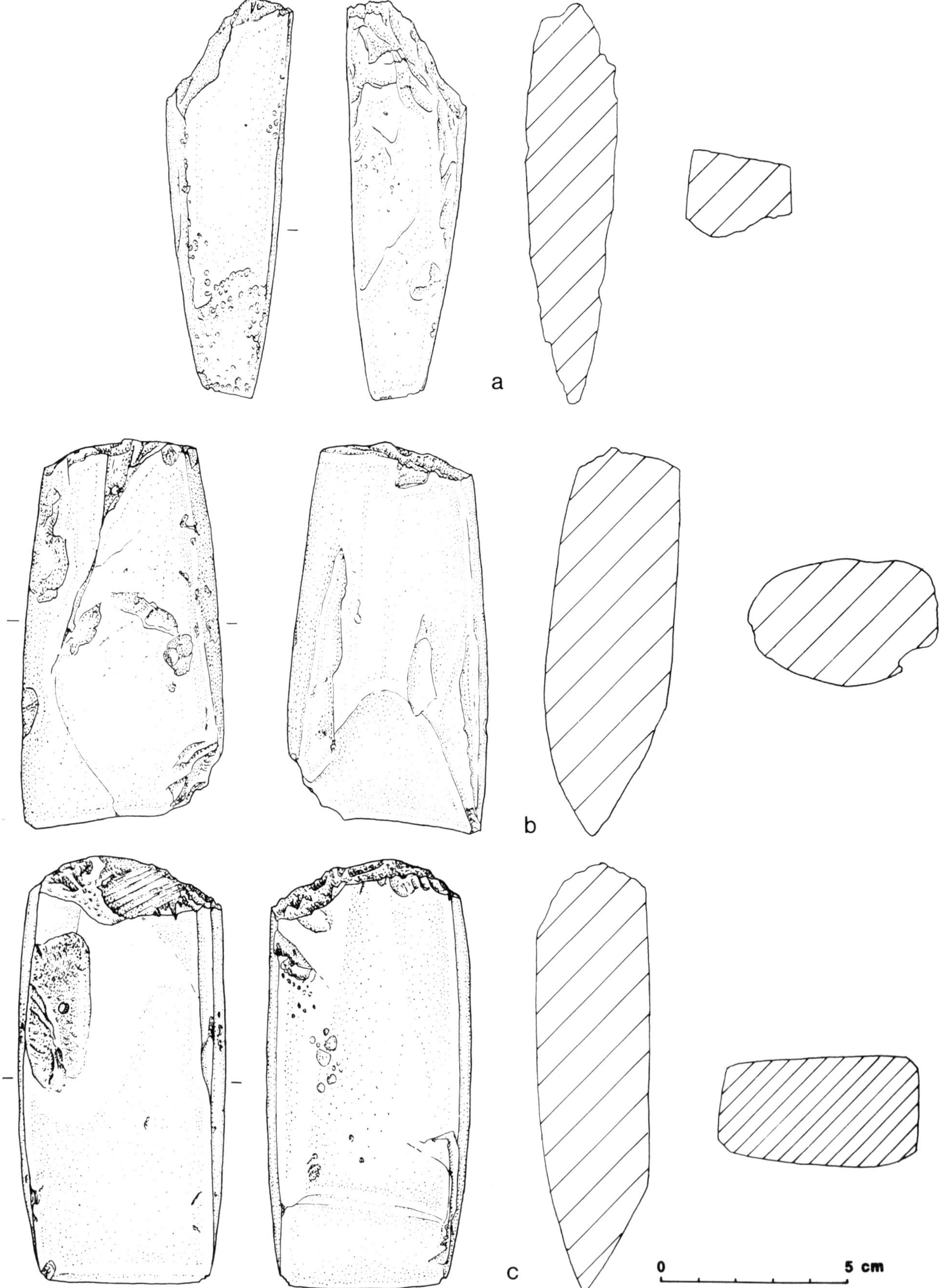

Figure 121. *Tridacna*-shell adzes from Niuatoputapu.

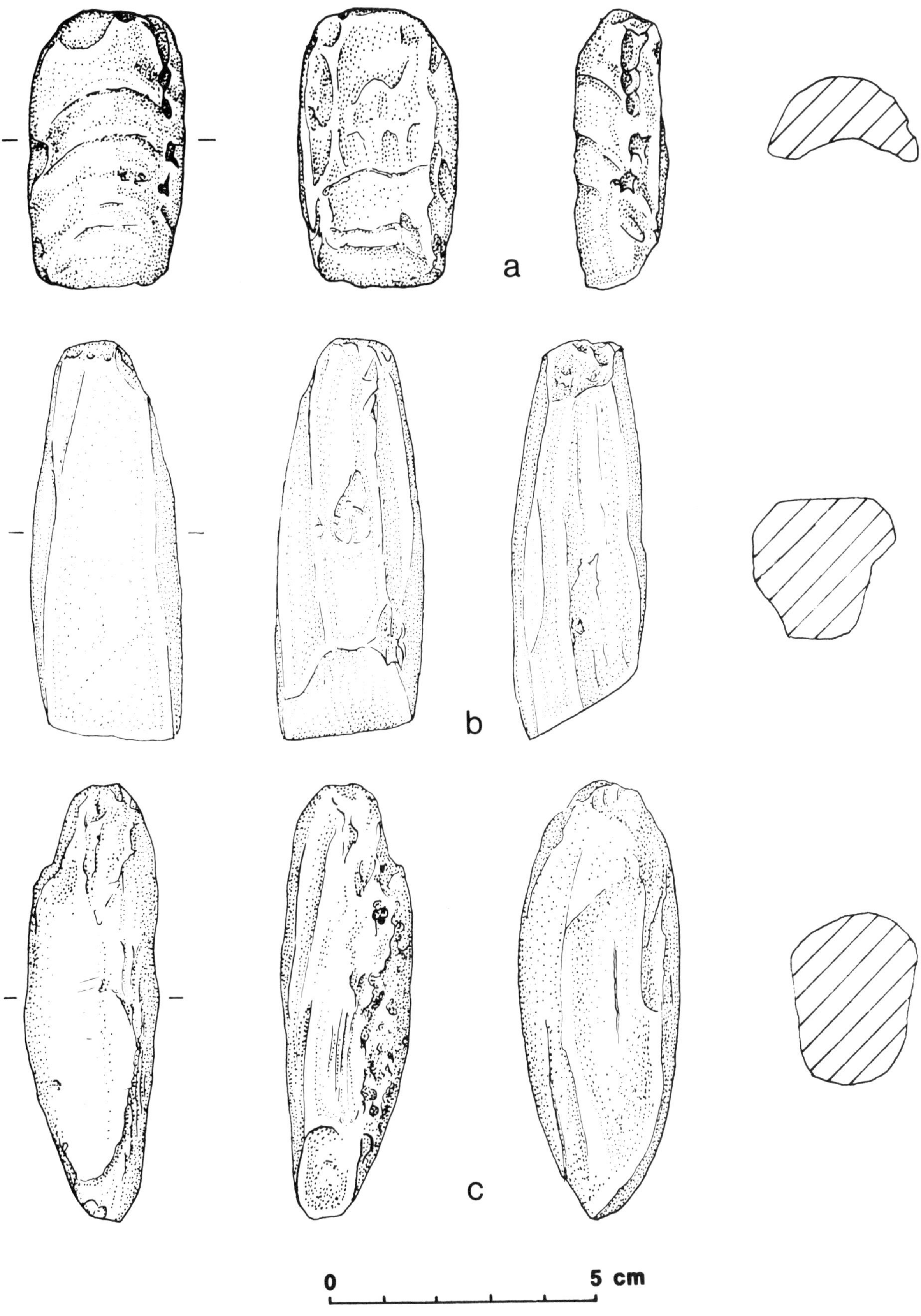

Figure 122. *Tridacna*-shell adzes from Niuatoputapu.

TABLE 33

SHELL ADZES: DESCRIPTIVE DATA

CATALOG NO.	MATERIAL	TYPE[1]	SHELL MORPHOLOGY	CROSS-SECTION	BEVEL EDGE[2]	DEGREE OF GRINDING[1]	LENGTH (cm)	CE WIDTH (cm)	MID-POINT WIDTH (cm)	POLL WIDTH (cm)	THICKNESS (cm)	WEIGHT (g)	REMARKS
NT-93-SA(5?)	*Tridacna*	7	hinge	oval	S	4	10.0	4.3	5.5	4.6	3.4	302.3	
NT-GEN-12	*Tridacna*	8	hinge	quad	S	4	10.9	4.9	5.2	5.2	2.9	354.7	
NT-90-X25III-1	*Tridacna*	8	hinge	quad	S	4	10.2	1.8	2.8	2.1	2.1	113.9	chisel-like
NT-91-SA-2	*Tridacna*	3	dorsal region	oval	C	3	5.7	2.2	2.9	2.3	1.3	34.3	
NT-93-91-1	*Tridacna*	8	hinge	quad	S	4	7.0	2.2	2.7	1.5	2.6	81.0	
NT-93-SA-5	*Tridacna*	7	hinge	oval	—	4	—	—	2.8	—	1.8	—	mid-section
NT-93-SA-4	*Tridacna*	7	hinge	oval	C	4	7.9	1.2	2.4	1.3	3.1	91.2	chisel-like
NT-100-180(1)-1	*Conus*	11	whorl	oval	C	3	—	2.9	2.8	—	0.4	9.7	
NT-100-SA-1	*Terebra*	—	whole shell	—	—	1	7.7	0.5	2.3	3.2	3.2	47.2	chisel/gouge
NT-100-218-1	*Tridacna*	7?	hinge	oval	—	4	—	—	—	1.9	1.9	—	butt fragment
NT-GEN-15	*Cassis*	9	lip	oval	C	4	—	0.9	2.0	1.4	1.4	—	chisel

[1] After Kirch & Yen 1982.
[2] C, curved; S, straight.

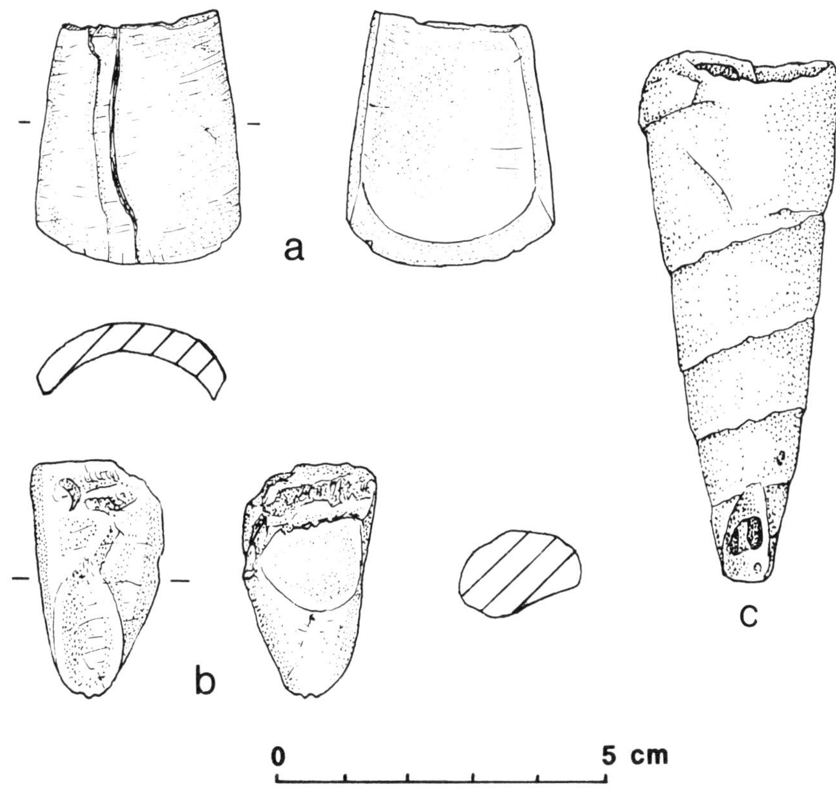

Figure 123. Shell chisels: a, *Conus* shell; b, *Cassis* shell; c, *Terebra* shell.

millennium A.D. Among these are the triangular-sectioned adzes (Types VI and VII) and quadrangular forms IX and X. The latter two types became particularly common during later phases of Samoan prehistory. Adzes from the small Western Polynesian islands of Futuna and 'Uvea are known from the work of Burrows (1936, 1937), Kirch (1976, 1981), and Frimigacci (1984); few of these are from excavated contexts. Of the 44 stone adzes studied by Kirch (1976), most can be accommodated within the Samoan typology of Green and Davidson (1969b). Types I, III, IV, V, VI, IX, and X are all represented. Significantly, three Type V adzes from Futuna were excavated in association with ceramics of Late Eastern Lapita style. In my 1981 study I found that the association of these plano-convex sectioned adzes with Lapitoid ceramics at Site FU-11 reinforces Green's interpretation of Type V as a significant marker of Lapita and early Polynesian assemblages throughout the Fiji-Western Polynesian region (Kirch 1981:139).

Tongan material culture has never been systematically treated, and although several museums hold extensive surface collections of adzes, the range of adz variability and the relationship of Tongan adzes to the Samoan classification remains unknown. In his excavations of Lapitoid sites on Tongatapu, Poulsen (1967, 1968) recovered 37 adzes of both stone and shell that provide some indication of the early Tongan adz kit. The relationship of these adzes to the Samoan sequence has been discussed by Green (1974b:262-64). The early Tongan assemblages are characterized by several varieties of oval- or lenticular-sectioned stone adzes, by both quadrangular- and oval-sectioned *Tridacna*-shell adzes, and by stone adzes of Samoan types V, I, III, and V. The first category of stone adzes, with oval or lenticular sections, resemble adzes in Lapita contexts in Melanesia, and are absent from Samoa. As Green argues, the early Tongan materials thus form a link between the Western Lapita adz kit, ancestral to that of Polynesia, and the later early Polynesian adz kit represented by the Samoan Plain Ware assemblages.

Finally, the well-dated shell adz assemblages of Anuta and Tikopia, found in stratigraphic association with Lapitoid ceramics of the first millennium B.C., are relevant to understanding the Niuatoputapu materials (Kirch and Rosendahl 1973, 1976; Kirch and Yen

1982). While these assemblages include adzes of both hinge and dorsal regions, it is only in the early contexts that hinge-region adzes dominate. As Kirch and Yen (1982:231) observe: "...hinge-region Types 6 through 8 were closely associated with Lapitoid ceramic series assemblages in the southeastern Solomons, New Hebrides, and Western Polynesia. Such hinge-region adzes may, in fact, be of considerable antiquity in the western Pacific."

The Niuatoputapu adzes may now be discussed in their spatial and temporal contexts. During the period that ceramics were in use on Niuatoputapu, adzes made of the massive hinge region of *Tridacna* shell were common, perhaps dominant. The Niuatoputapu materials thus correspond closely with the evidence from Poulsen's Tongatapu excavations. They also reinforce Kirch and Yen's interpretation of hinge-region *Tridacna* adzes as a significant marker of Lapitoid assemblages in the southwestern Pacific. Although the Niuatoputapu collection is small and its stratigraphic associations often ambiguous, there are indications that several stone adz types may also have been developed before the end of the ceramic-use period. Foremost among these is Type V with its plano-convex section, represented at Site NT-90 and well-documented in association with Late Eastern Lapita and Plain Ware sites in Futuna and Samoa. Also present at ceramic-bearing sites on Niuatoputapu, albeit as surface finds, are Types III, VI, and IX/X. The presence of any of these types in association with plain ceramics is consistent with the Samoan sequence (Green 1974b). Finally, the frequent surface finds of Types III and IX/X adzes in various parts of the island suggest that these became the dominant adz forms during the last 1,000 to 1,500 years of Niuatoputapu prehistory. It is significant that Types I and II, so common in late prehistoric Samoa, were never common in Niuatoputapu.

FISHING GEAR

In marked contrast with Eastern Polynesian sites, where fishing gear and the detritus of its manufacture often dominate artifact assemblages, Western Polynesian excavations generally yield few objects associated with marine exploitation. This difference may be explained in part by the extensive barrier reef-lagoon marine ecosystems of most Western Polynesian islands, which favor the use of nets, poisoning, traps, and other fishing techniques that do not leave substantial material traces (Kirch and Dye 1979). The Niuatoputapu excavations were no exception, and only 24 objects can be assigned to the general category of fishing gear. Fully half of these are from Site NT-90, with the remainder distributed among Sites NT-91, -93, -100, and -112.

One-Piece Fishhooks

Four one-piece hooks, none complete, were excavated. The largest specimen, from Unit 40 of Site NT-91, is of massive *Turbo* shell, probably from the species *T. marmoratus* (fig. 124, b). Since the point is missing, it cannot be determined whether the hook was of rotating or jabbing form. The shank is intact and has a line-lashing device consisting of five notches (the lower two very shallow) filed into the outer shank edge. The shank is 4.0 cm high and 0.8 cm thick; hook width exceeded 3.3 cm.

The second hook, from a depth of 40 to 43 cm in Unit 90 at Site NT-93, is also of *Turbo* shell, but is less massive than that described above (fig. 124, a). The point is missing, and the bend has a U-shape. In this case the line-lashing device consists of three outer shank notches. This specimen has a shank height of 3.3 cm, a shank thickness of 0.55 cm, and originally had a total width of more than 2.9 cm. A third specimen, from Unit 151 of NT-93, consists of a point fragment of a fairly massive *Turbo* shell hook.

The fourth hook, excavated from Unit 200 of Site NT-100, consists of an angular pearl-shell fragment, presumably the point (fig. 124, c). The point height is 2.6 cm and the point thickness 0.36 cm. The hook appears to be unfinished, and may have broken during manufacture.

Fishhook Tabs

Seven ovoid or subrectangular pieces of *Turbo* shell from Site NT-90, as well as another specimen from NT-100, have been classified as fishhook tabs or "blanks" based on comparison with similar materials from Anuta and Tikopia (Kirch and Rosendahl 1973; Kirch and Yen 1982). The tabs are all made from the body whorl of a large species of *Turbo* and display filing marks along their edges.

Net Weights

Net fishing techniques dominate the contemporary Niuatoputapu marine exploitation strategy (Kirch and Dye 1979), and the prehistoric use of nets is indicated by 12 net weights or sinkers. Most common, represented by 8 specimens from Sites NT-90, -93, -100, and -112, are small to medium-sized *Cypraea* shells with two perforations in the dorsum or, in one instance, with the entire dorsum removed. These shells range from 2.5 to 5.4 cm in length, and from 3.2 to 36.4 g in weight. Such cowrie shells are known from ethnographic collections from several Western Polynesian islands where they were attached as weights

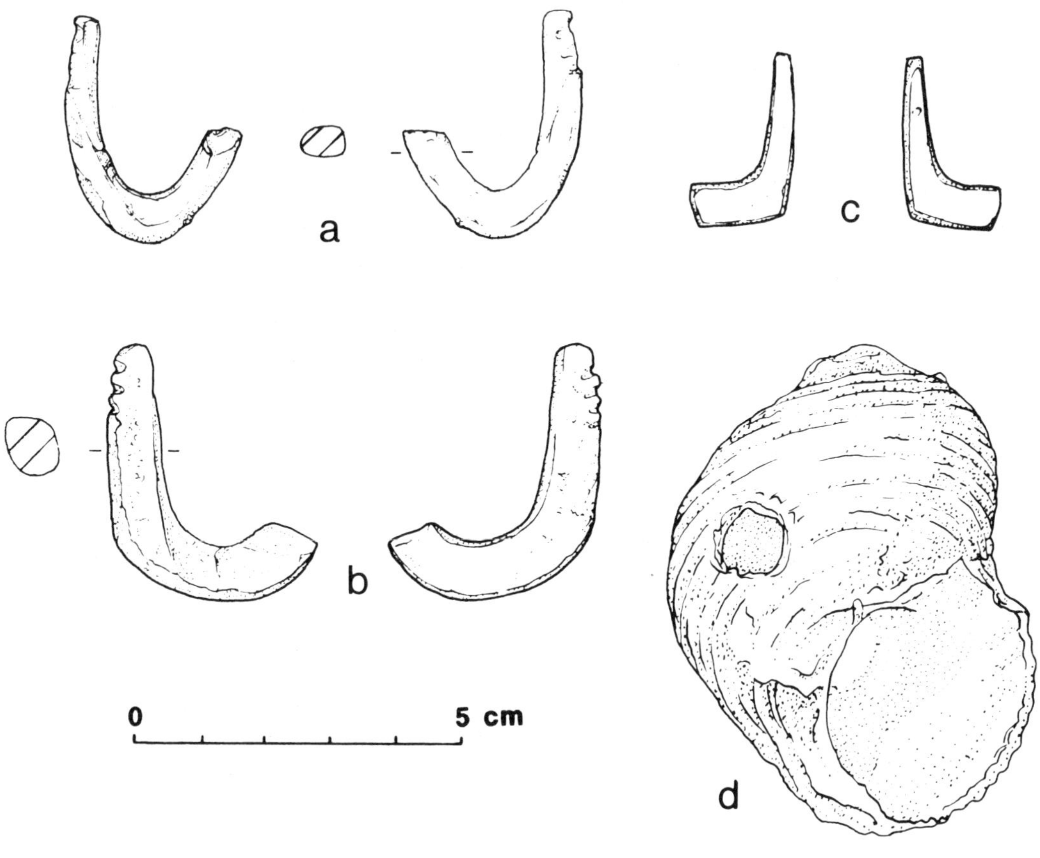

Figure 124. Fishing gear: a, b, *Turbo*-shell one-piece fishhooks; c, pearl-shell one-piece fishhook; d, *Turbo*-shell net weight.

to the bottom edges of scoop or dip nets; I have observed them used in this manner on Futuna Island and on the Polynesian outlier of Tikopia (see Extra-Areal Comparisons, below).

Three large *Turbo* shells with perforations through the body whorl probably functioned as weights for larger nets such as seines. One of these is illustrated in figure 124, d. These objects weigh 36, 92, and 110 g. Finally, a perforated bivalve shell from Site NT-90 has also been classified as a net weight.

Extra-Areal Comparisons

Prior to the Niuatoputapu excavations, only two one-piece fishhooks had been recovered from Western Polynesian sites. Poulsen (1968:87, fig. 2:18) excavated a small jabbing hook of *Turbo* shell at Tongatapu (along with a second, problematic specimen), while Davidson (1969b:244, fig. 103, a, pl. 23) recovered a small *Turbo* shell hook fragment (probably unfinished) from the Lotofaga coastal midden site on Upolu, Samoa. Neither of these hooks displays any sophisticated features, such as line-lashing devices. From excavations in Western Samoa conducted at the same time as our Niuatoputapu work, Jennings and Holmer (1980:123-25, fig. 43) obtained five small one-piece hooks or hook fragments, one of which "has two slight but unmistakable grooves on the outer side of the shank, causing a slight knobbing at the head."

The two Niuatoputapu one-piece hooks with intact shanks, illustrated in figure 124, find their closest parallels in assemblages from the Polynesian outliers of Anuta and Tikopia, where excavations (Kirch and Rosendahl 1973, 1976; Kirch and Yen 1982) yielded almost 300 specimens of fishing gear, including numerous hooks of *Turbo* shell. Several types of line-lashing device are present on the Anuta and Tikopia hooks, including the outer-shank notched technique found on the Niuatoputapu hooks (termed type HT1 in Kirch and Rosendahl 1973:63). The Anuta and Tikopia assemblages date to the first millennium B.C., making them roughly contemporaneous with the hooks from NT-91 and -93, as well as with Poulsen's Tongatapu specimen.

Although pearl shell occasionally appears in Western Polynesian and Polynesian Outlier hook assemblages, *Turbo* was clearly the preferred material. The fishhook tabs of *Turbo* shell identified from NT-90 and -100 are also paralleled by large numbers of such specimens, in various stages of manufacture, from Anuta (Kirch and Rosendahl 1973, figs. 16, 17) and Tikopia (Kirch and Yen 1982, fig. 94).

The finds from Western Polynesia, along with the Polynesian Outlier materials, leave no doubt that one-piece *Turbo*-shell fishhooks were a component of the Ancestral Polynesian fishing kit. The low frequency in which such hooks have appeared in Western Polynesian sites probably reflects an emphasis on fishing strategies other than angling.

Shell net weights have not often been identified from Western Polynesian sites, although I suspect that this reflects a lack of recognition by archaeologists unfamiliar with ethnographically documented material culture, or a failure to discriminate such artifacts from shell midden. Poulsen (1968:87) observed that net sinkers of *Arca* shell were common in his Tongatapu sites. No weights or sinkers of shell were identified in any of the Western Samoan sites excavated by Green and Davidson or their colleagues (1969a, 1974); Jennings and Holmer (1980), however, illustrate six *Cypraea* shells with double perforations in the dorsum, identical to the net weights identified from Niuatoputapu. Jennings and Holmer classify these objects as scrapers, an unlikely attribution since the perforations are punched and not ground (as in *Cypraea* scrapers or peelers known from the Marquesas or Tikopia) and since the columellar lip has not been removed to prevent scrapings from clogging the implement.

Cypraea shells are known as net weights on Futuna Island (Burrows 1936, pl. 4a) and on Tikopia, where they were also common in archaeological excavations (Kirch and Yen 1982:244-45). Buck (1930:480, fig. 279, pl. XLVI, a) illustrates and describes the use of cowrie shells, with dorsa removed, as weights along the edge of a shrimp net in Samoa. I have little doubt that the *Cypraea* shells from the Niuatoputapu sites, along with those excavated by Jennings and Holmer in Samoa, were utilized as net weights rather than as scrapers.

ORNAMENTS

Twenty-eight objects have been assigned to this category; 20 of these are from Site NT-90, which had representatives of all but one specific ornament class. The term "ornament" must not be narrowly interpreted in terms of personal or bodily adornment, for we are uncertain how these items were worn or displayed. While some were probably worn on the body as items of decoration, others probably functioned as component pieces of exchange valuables, composite artifacts linked with perishable line or cord. This interpretation is further explored in chapter 7.

Tridacna-shell Rings

Two fragments of *Tridacna* ring or circlet were excavated at NT-90; the larger of these is illustrated in figure 125, d. (The term "ring" is used here and below only in the sense of a circular object, without any qualifications as to size.) The illustrated example has an oval cross-section with a diameter ranging from 1.15-1.35 cm. The reconstructed diameter of the whole ring is approximately 16 cm. The second ring has a nearly circular cross-section with a diameter of 1.05 cm; the fragment is too small to allow accurate reconstruction of the diameter, although this must have been close to 15 cm.

Conus-shell Rings

This is the most prevalent ornament class, represented by nine examples from NT-90, two from NT-93, and one each from NT-125 and -163. These rings are manufactured from the outer portion of the cone shell spire, where it joins the body whorl. Most have been well ground on all facets. Several specimens are illustrated in figure 125, c, e-g. The nine rings from Site NT-90 indicate the range of metrical variation: overall diameter, $\bar{x}$ = 4.64 cm, s.d. = 1.38, range 2.2-6.5 cm; width, $\bar{x}$ = 0.39 cm, s.d. = 0.09; thickness, $\bar{x}$ = 0.66 cm, s.d. = 0.22. Most of these would have been too small to wear as bracelets or armbands, and too large to wear on the finger. It is likely that they functioned as parts of composite artifacts joined by lashing.

Trochus-shell Rings

Three rings of *Trochus niloticus* are represented by fragments from Site NT-90 (2) and NT-112. With reconstructed diameters of 6 to 7 cm, these might have been worn as armbands, particularly since *Trochus*-shell armbands are ethnographically documented from various southwest Pacific societies.

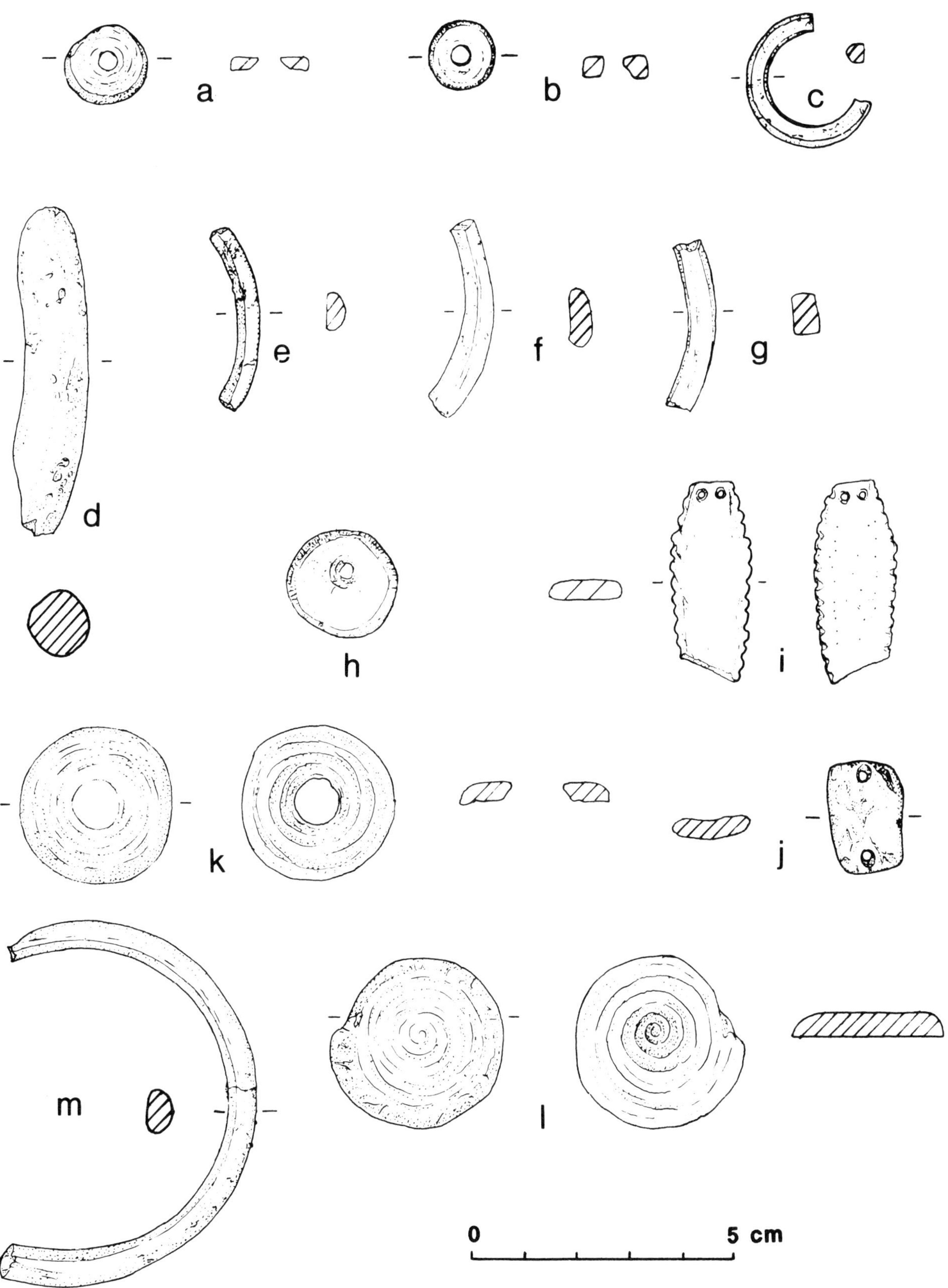

Figure 125. Ornaments from Niuatoputapu sites.

Spondylus-shell Bead

A single example of a bead (or possibly a bracelet segment) of *Spondylus* shell was excavated at NT-90 and is shown in figure 125, j. The artifact is rectangular in plan view, with two perforations drilled in each face. It measures 2.0 cm long, 1.45 cm wide, and 0.35 cm thick.

Bi-perforate Shell Bead

A small bead of shell (possibly *Tridacna* or *Spondylus)* that had been perforated by drilling from both ends was recovered at Site NT-90. In plan view the bead is rectangular, while in cross-section it is plano-convex. It measures 1.2 cm long, 1.0 cm wide, and 0.55 cm thick.

Shell Disk/Bead

Another unique specimen from Site NT-90 is a disk-like bead, probably of *Spondylus* shell, with a double-drilled central perforation, shown in figure 125, h. The bead has a diameter ranging from 1.9 to 2.0 cm and a thickness of 1.15 cm.

Conus-shell Disks

Site NT-90 yielded two disks made by grinding down and flattening the spires of medium-sized cone shells (fig. 125, k, l). One of these has a central perforation. The disks have diameters of 3.1 and 2.8 cm and thicknesses of 0.4 and 0.5 cm.

Conus-shell Beads

These items are similar to the disks described above, except that they are made from much smaller cone shells, and both have central perforations (fig. 125, a, b). One each was recovered from Sites NT-90 and -110. They have diameters of 1.9 and 1.3 cm, thicknesses of 0.3 and 0.4 cm.

Perforated Cone Shell

Site NT-90 yielded an example of a small *Conus* shell with a drilled perforation through the central wall of the body whorl, enabling the attachment of a string for lashing. The cone shell is 2.7 cm long.

Bone Pendant

The most striking ornament in the collection is a fragment of a carved bone pendant recovered from the early historic village site of NT-110. Shown in figure 125, i, the pendant is elongate, with two carefully drilled perforations at the upper end, and has notched sides. It is 3.6 cm long, 1.6 cm wide, and 0.3 cm thick.

Extra-Areal Comparisons

The distribution of ornaments from other Western Polynesian and Polynesian Outlier contexts is discussed further in chapter 7, where the possible role of these objects as exchange valuables is considered. In brief, the most common and widely distributed items are the various beads, rings, and disks of *Conus* shell. Larger rings or armbands of *Tridacna* shell are also reported from Samoa and Tongatapu, as well as Tikopia. Of particular interest are the various types of "bracelet segment," which appear to be characteristic of Lapitoid pottery assemblages in Tongatapu, Ha'apai, Samoa, Tikopia, and possibly Fiji. Whether these actually were strung as bracelets is open to question. The possible significance of these ornament classes as items of exchange or as indicators of social rank differentiation is further explored in chapter 7.

FOOD PREPARATION EQUIPMENT

Cowrie-shell Peeler

Site NT-90 yielded one example of a peeler. Made from the dorsum of a large species of *Cypraea*, this peeler has smoothed edges along three sides; the fourth edge has been highly fractured (along the lamellar structure lines of the shell) by use in peeling and/or scraping. In plan view, the implement measures 5.8 by 5.4 cm.

Bivalve-shell Scrapers

Large bivalve shells with fracturing and use wear along their dorsal margins (fig. 126, c) were recovered from Site NT-90 (2 specimens), NT-100, and NT-112. Although these have been identified as scrapers for food preparation (such as removing the skins of tubers or breadfruit), it is possible that they were utilized for other scraping tasks as well.

Cowrie-shell Scrapers

These implements constitute the most problematic class of food preparation equipment. They consist of the bases or ventral portions of *Cypraea* from which the dorsa have been removed by hammering. On several specimens, the curved, fractured edge displays evidence of use in some sort of scraping operation. The shells

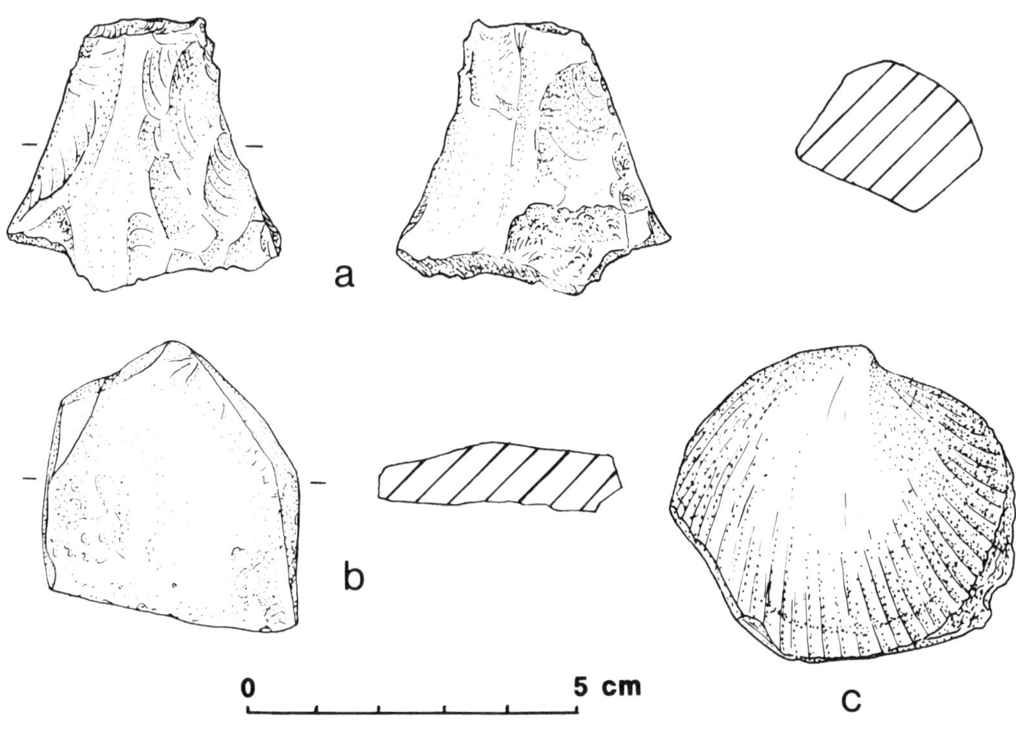

Figure 126. Miscellaneous artifacts: a, basalt drill fragment; b, abraded hematite; c, bivalve scraper.

range in length from 7.8 to 8.6 cm. There are four specimens each from Sites NT-90 and -93. Although they have been identified as scrapers, it must be noted that such modified cowries could also have served as weights for large nets, in the manner described ethnographically by Buck (1930:480, fig. 279) for Samoa.

Nut-cracking Hammer

From Unit 200 of Site NT-163 we excavated a small hammer, made from a subrectangular volcanic cobble, with pecked finger grips on both sides as illustrated in figure 127, a. The hammer shows evidence of use on one end only. Based on comparison with similar artifacts from other Western Polynesian sites and on ethnographic analogy, it is classified as a hammer for cracking hard-shelled nuts such as *Canarium* or *Terminalia*. This interpretation is somewhat speculative; it is possible that this implement could have functioned in other ways.

Extra-Areal Comparisons

The *Cypraea*- shell peeler from Site NT-90 has exact equivalents in several specimens excavated in association with Lapitoid ceramics on the Outliers of Tikopia and Anuta (Kirch and Yen 1982:252, fig. 102; Kirch and Rosendahl 1973:88-89, fig. 29). Buck (1930:109) notes the use of various mollusc shells as scrapers or peelers for food preparation in Samoa into the historic period. Large cowrie bases like those described above as problematic scrapers were also recovered in Samoa by Jennings and Holmer (1980:125, fig. 44, h), who also classify these objects as scrapers.

The nut-cracking hammer has close parallels from a number of Western Polynesian contexts, including Samoa (Green and Davidson 1969a:134; Jennings and Holmer 1980, fig. 48), Tongatapu (Birks and Birks 1972), Fiji (Birks and Birks 1972), and Futuna (Kirch 1981:141, fig. 13). All of these specimens share such features as the pecked finger grips and the light traces of

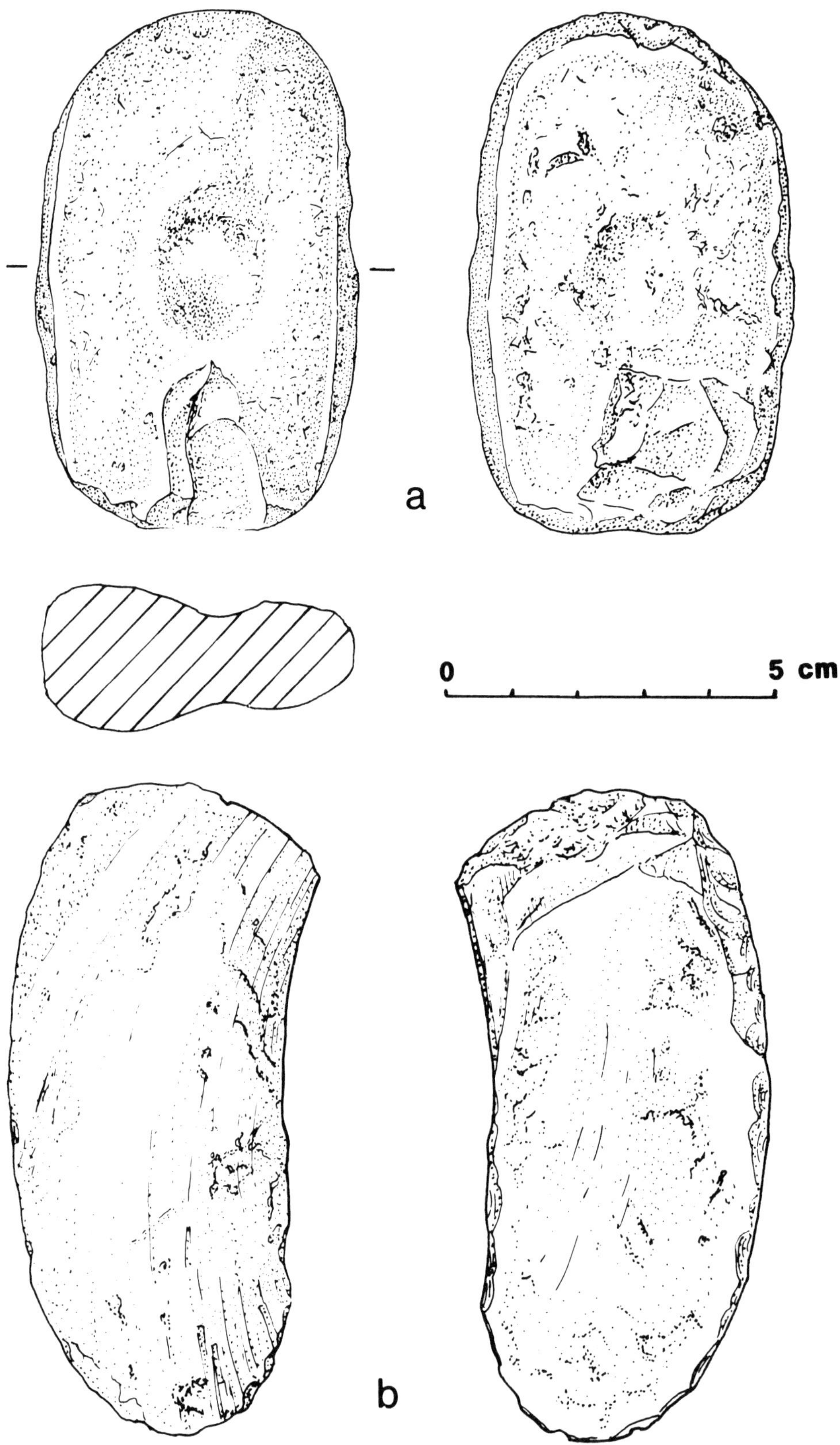

Figure 127. Miscellaneous artifacts: a, nut-cracking hammerstone; b, large *Tridacna* flake tool.

battering which suggest hammering a relatively soft object, rather than stone. I have discussed elsewhere the possible ethnobotanical significance of these hammers (Kirch 1981:142).

MANUFACTURING TOOLS

This general category of implements includes six specific classes, each of which was presumably used in the manufacture of other implements and objects. Twenty-three artifacts are included in this category, slightly more than half of them from Site NT-90.

Echinoid-spine Abraders

The naturally abrasive spines of the slate pencil sea urchin *(Heterocentrotus mammillatus)* were widely utilized throughout Oceania as files or abraders in the manufacture of shell and bone artifacts. Nine of these were excavated on Niuatoputapu, seven from Site NT-90, one from NT-93, and one from NT-110. A selection of these abraders is illustrated in figure 128, a-e. All abraders were worked only on the distal end or tip, except for one specimen from Site NT-90 which is worn flat along one side for the entire length of the spine.

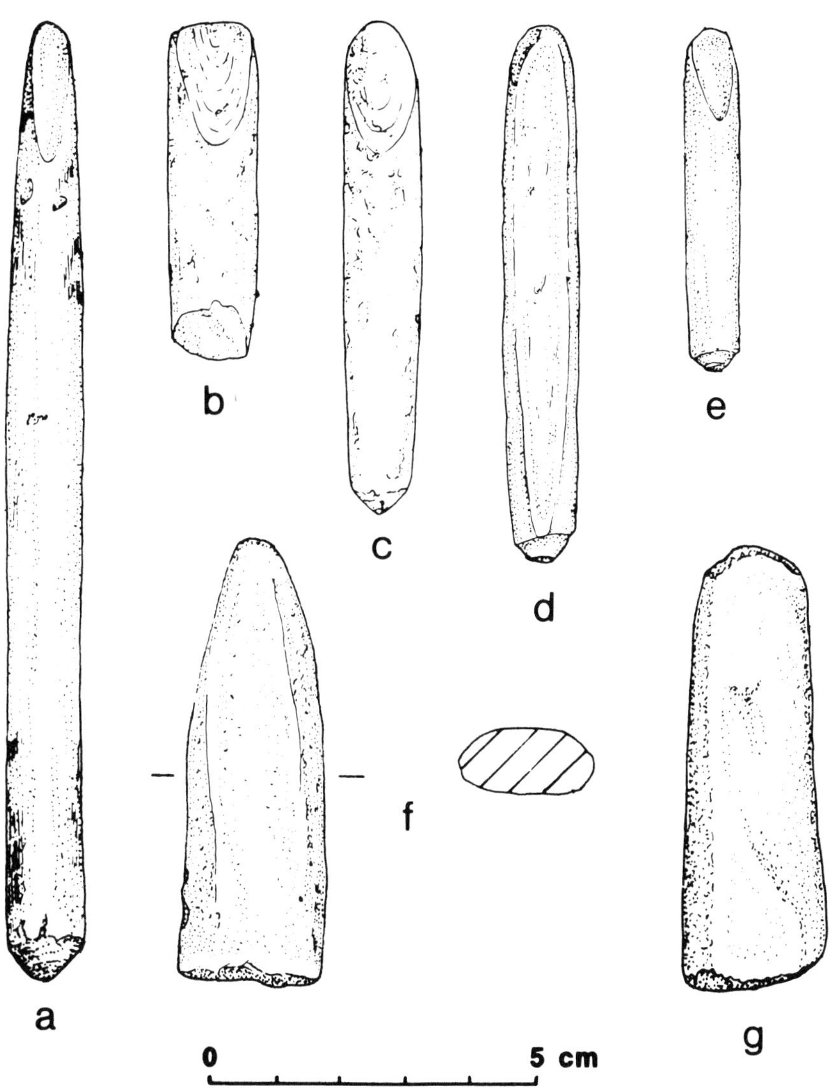

Figure 128. Abraders: a-e, echinoid spine; f-g, stone.

The abraded tips of the other spines show variable wear patterns; on most the abraded surface is slightly convex, suggesting a rocking motion during use. On one specimen the abraded facet is perfectly flat, suggesting a back-and-forth movement against a flat surface.

Acropora Coral Abraders

The collection includes two abraders or files of *Acropora* branch coral, in which the rough natural protuberances of the coral provide an abrasive or rasp-like surface. Both specimens came from Site NT-93. One has a diameter of 1.5 cm and length of 7.9 cm, the other a diameter of 2.6 cm and length of 4.4 cm.

Block Coral Abrader

A single abrader of an undetermined species of block coral (possibly a species of *Porites)* was excavated in Unit 10W of Site NT-125. The longest edge (4.8 cm) has been used for abrading or filing.

Stone Abraders

From the surface of Site NT-90 we collected a rectangular abrader (6.6 cm long) of dark gray, somewhat vesicular stone, possibly of local origin (fig. 128, g). The stone has been worn smooth from use on all its longitudinal facets. At Site NT-110 we excavated (in TP2) a lanceolate abrader of fairly compact pumice (fig. 128, f), 6.6 cm long, with an ovoid section.

Hammerstones

Six volcanic stones with battering or crushing around their perimeters, indicative of hammering or pounding, are included in the collection. From Site NT-90 come two ovoid and one spherical stone of vesicular basalt or andesite, with weights of 723, 230, and 156 g. Site NT-93 yielded a small spherical stone weighing 192 g. The two specimens from Site NT-100 are both elongate with a single battered end (one, however, is broken). The complete hammerstone, with several flakes removed from the battered end, weighs 1,065 g and is 15 cm long.

Coral Hammers

Three spherical pieces of block coral appear to have been utilized as hammers. The first, found at NT-90, is disk-shaped, 7.26 cm in diameter and 4.3 cm thick, weighing 350 g and showing signs of battering around its perimeter. Another specimen, from NT-100, is a rather small spheroid, 3.3 cm in diameter and weighing only 27 g. A spherical coral stone found at the surface of NT-112 has a pecked depression on one surface, perhaps for a grip; it is 6.3 cm in diameter and weighs 114 g.

Extra-Areal Comparisons

The classes of manufacturing tool described above have parallels from other Western Polynesian sites. In Samoa, echinoid-spine abraders have been excavated at coastal dune sites (Green and Davidson 1969a:245; Jennings and Holmer 1980:129, fig. 43; Jennings et al. 1976:73, fig. 17). In all cases, only the distal end was faceted from use. Abraders of branch coral and block coral are also noted by these authors. For Tongatapu, Poulsen (1968:87, fig. 2) briefly notes and illustrates branch coral and echinoid-spine abraders. Hunt (1980:169) describes a single echinoid-spine abrader from the Yanuca site in Fiji, along with branch coral files. Branch coral abraders and stone "files" are mentioned by Best (1981:14, pl. 12) from the early Lapita site of Naigani. Birks (1973:49) reports abraded pumice from the Sigatoka site on Viti Levu. On the Polynesian outliers of Anuta and Tikopia, echinoid-spine and branch coral abraders occurred frequently with the Lapitoid ceramics (Kirch and Rosendahl 1973:82; Kirch and Yen 1982:253-55), and on Tikopia block coral and pumice abraders were excavated as well.

All of the echinoid-spine abraders from Western Polynesian and Polynesian outlier sites are faceted only on the distal end or tip (except in the case of the longitudinally ground specimen from Niuatoputapu). This contrasts strikingly with abraders of the same type from certain Eastern Polynesian sites, especially Hawai'i and the Marquesas, where proximal as well as distal ends are worked.

FLAKED STONE

The second largest class of excavated artifacts from the Niuatoputapu sites is flaked stone, with 11,603 specimens. Nearly 99% of these are of volcanic glass, with small quantities of chert and basalt/andesite. The distribution of flaked stone by material and site is provided in table 34. Following initial segregation of the collection by material type (volcanic glass, chert, basalt/andesite), we selected representative samples from each major site for more detailed study. In all, 535 pieces were analyzed, with a standard set of morphological and metrical attributes recorded and entered into an SPSS data file. Data on these specimens are on file in the form of punched cards at the Anthropology Department, B.P. Bishop Museum, Honolulu.

Chert

Forty chert flakes were recovered, 38 from Site NT-90 and one each from NT-91 and -100. In NT-90, chert is present at an average density of about 0.66 flake/m^2, whereas at NT-91 and -100 the respective densities are 0.05 and 0.06/m^2. Chert is clearly a component of the earliest occupation phase on Niuatoputapu, and one which dropped relatively quickly from the technological repertoire.

Chert varies somewhat in both color and texture, but basically can be classified as a siliceous micro-crystalline rock, usually with some impurities or inclusions, including vugs with quartz crystals in some specimens. (Similar material excavated on Tikopia was termed "chalcedony" by Kirch and Yen 1982:260.) Clear, white, red, pink, purple, and yellow variations are present; specimens vary from somewhat translucent to opaque. The material is moderately isotropic.

Chert does not occur locally on either Niuatoputapu or Tafahi, and thus was imported to the island. These siliceous rocks are probably of marine origin. One known source is Futuna, a geological "fragment" of the old Fijian Plate with uplifted marine limestones. Chert cores and flakes were present at the FU-11 site (Kirch 1981), and source material, in the form of water-rolled nodules, was observed in nearby streams at Tavai. Chert sources may also be present on one or more of the larger Fiji islands, especially Viti Levu (Ladd 1934). Birks (1973:49) reports a "knife or scraper of chalcedony" from Level 1 of the Sigatoka site, while Hunt (1980:144) reports the presence of flaked chert at the Yanuca site. At the early Lapita site of Naigani, near Viti Levu, Best (1981:13, pl. 11; Kay 1984:134) excavated a large number of cores and flakes of siliceous stone which he terms "chert"; in his illustration, they appear very similar in both material and lithic technology to the NT-90 assemblage. One further source

TABLE 34

FLAKED STONE FROM NIUATOPUTAPU SITES

SITE	VOLCANIC GLASS	CHERT	BASALT/ ANDESITE	TOTALS
NT–90	8,778	38	75	8,891
NT–91	160	1	0	161
NT–93	784	0	9	793
NT–100	548	1	22	571
NT–110	220	0	0	220
NT–112	497	0	0	497
NT–113	221	0	0	221
NT–125	45	0	0	45
NT–129	45	0	0	45
NT–163	159	0	0	159
TOTALS	11,457	40	106	11,603

location may be the island of 'Eua in the southern Tonga archipelago, with an ancient geology that includes uplifted marine limestones (Hoffmeister 1932).

Ward and Smith (1974) are the only investigators who have attempted to source chert materials in the southwest Pacific, and four flakes from Niuatoputapu (three from NT-90, one from NT-91), along with four archaeological and two geological samples from Futuna (Kirch 1981:139), were submitted to them for characterization by X-ray flourescence. Analyses were run for four elements: vanadium, chromium, manganese, and barium. In reporting these data, Ward (pers. comm. 1980) stressed their preliminary and tentative nature. Two of the NT-90 samples and that from NT-91 are virtually identical with regard to the four elements considered, while the third NT-90 specimen clearly differs. Interestingly enough, the first group matches quite closely with two of the Futunan samples. While it is conceivable that Futuna was the source of these materials, more extensive characterization of samples with the use of a larger array of elements must be made from a wide variety of Fijian and Western Polynesian localities. At present, we can state that the Niuatoputapu cherts are exotic to the island, and that Futuna remains a likely source area.

The chert assemblage from NT-90 consists generally of small flakes that lack any evidence of secondary retouch or formal tool types. Flakes were probably produced by hard hammer percussion, using a "bi-polar" technique with an anvil. A sample of 25 chert

TABLE 35

VOLCANIC GLASS FLAKES: MORPHOLOGICAL ATTRIBUTES

ATTRIBUTE	NT–90 (N = 62)	NT–93 (N = 203)	NT–100 (N = 47)
Cortex			
present	3 %	1 %	0 %
absent	97	99	100
Dorsal Ridges			
0	18	8	10
1	39	35	58
2	24	32	16
3	8	18	10
4+	10	6	7
Bulb of Percussion			
absent	30	22	52
positive diffuse	61	61	48
positive salient	9	18	0
Termination			
feather	38	49	43
hinge	28	21	29
step	34	29	29

TABLE 36

VOLCANIC GLASS FLAKES: METRICAL ATTRIBUTES

ATTRIBUTE	NT-90		NT-93		NT-100	
	FLAKES	CORES	FLAKES	CORES	FLAKES	CORES
Length (mm)	18.7 ± 4.6	26.0	23.0 ± 7.1	25.6 ± 3.9	19.8 ± 6.1	24.3 ± 11.7
Width (mm)	15.7 ± 3.8	20.0	18.1 ± 5.6	20.6 ± 5.2	17.09 ± 5.5	21.3 ± 12.1
Thickness (mm)	5.6 ± 1.7	15.0	6.4 ± 2.9	14.4 ± 5.6	4.8 ± 2.0	13.0 ± 4.4
Weight (g)	1.6 ± 0.9	7.0	2.4 ± 2.2	6.1 ± 3.9	1.8 ± 1.6	5.7 ± 5.0
Striking Platform Thickness (mm)	3.2 ± 1.4	—	4.2 ± 2.4	—	3.4 ± 1.7	—
Striking Platform Width (mm)	8.2 ± 3.6	—	10.0 ± 4.3	—	10.1 ± 5.8	—
N	51	1	184	7	42	3

flakes recovered from the NT-90 Area A excavation yields the following metrical attributes:

Length (mm)	22.1 ± 6.4
Width (mm)	16.6 ± 4.4
Thickness (mm)	7.2 ± 2.0
Weight (g)	2.5 ± 1.3
Striking platform thickness (mm)	2.8 ± 1.9
Striking platform width (mm)	8.8 ± 5.0

Volcanic Glass

Flakes and cores of volcanic glass were recovered from every excavated locality within the ceramic zone. The highest density averaging 159.2 specimens/m^2 was recorded from Site NT-90 while Sites NT-93 and NT-100 had densities of 35.6/m^2 and 32.2/m^2 respectively. These substantially lower densities at the later sites may reflect a diminution in the use of volcanic glass over time, although the lengthy occupation span of NT-90 should also be taken into consideration. Nonetheless, volcanic glass is infrequent outside the ceramic zone, and does not appear to have been in use during the proto-historic period.

Unlike chert, volcanic glass occurs locally on both Niuatoputapu and Tafahi. Rogers (1974) collected source material on Tafahi, which he submitted along with archaeological flakes to Ward for XRF analysis (Ward 1974a, b). The specimens from both localities matched closely, and Ward concluded that it is "highly likely that the natural volcanic glass from the Lapita sites at Niuatoputapu derives from the Tafahi source" (1974a:345). In 1976, an outcropping of volcanic glass was discovered on the central volcanic ridge of Niuatoputapu. This material has not been characterized by XRF analysis, but it may well fall within the elemental ranges already determined. Although Ward uses the term "obsidian" for this glass, I prefer the more general term "volcanic glass" because the Niuatoputapu and Tafahi rocks are not translucent, and are apparently lower in SiO_2 than true obsidian. This glass would probably be best characterized as an andesitic or basaltic phase of volcanic glass.

The volcanic glass assemblages show no evidence of attempts at formal tool production, although there are occasional flakes with secondary retouch, probably to produce a fresh cutting edge. No studies of use wear or edge damage were carried out, but it is probable that these flakes were utilized in a variety of cutting and scraping tasks. Morphological attributes of samples from the three main assemblages are provided in table 35, metrical attributes in table 36. Flakes are fairly small, generally lacking cortex, usually with one or two dorsal ridges, with percussion bulbs either lacking or

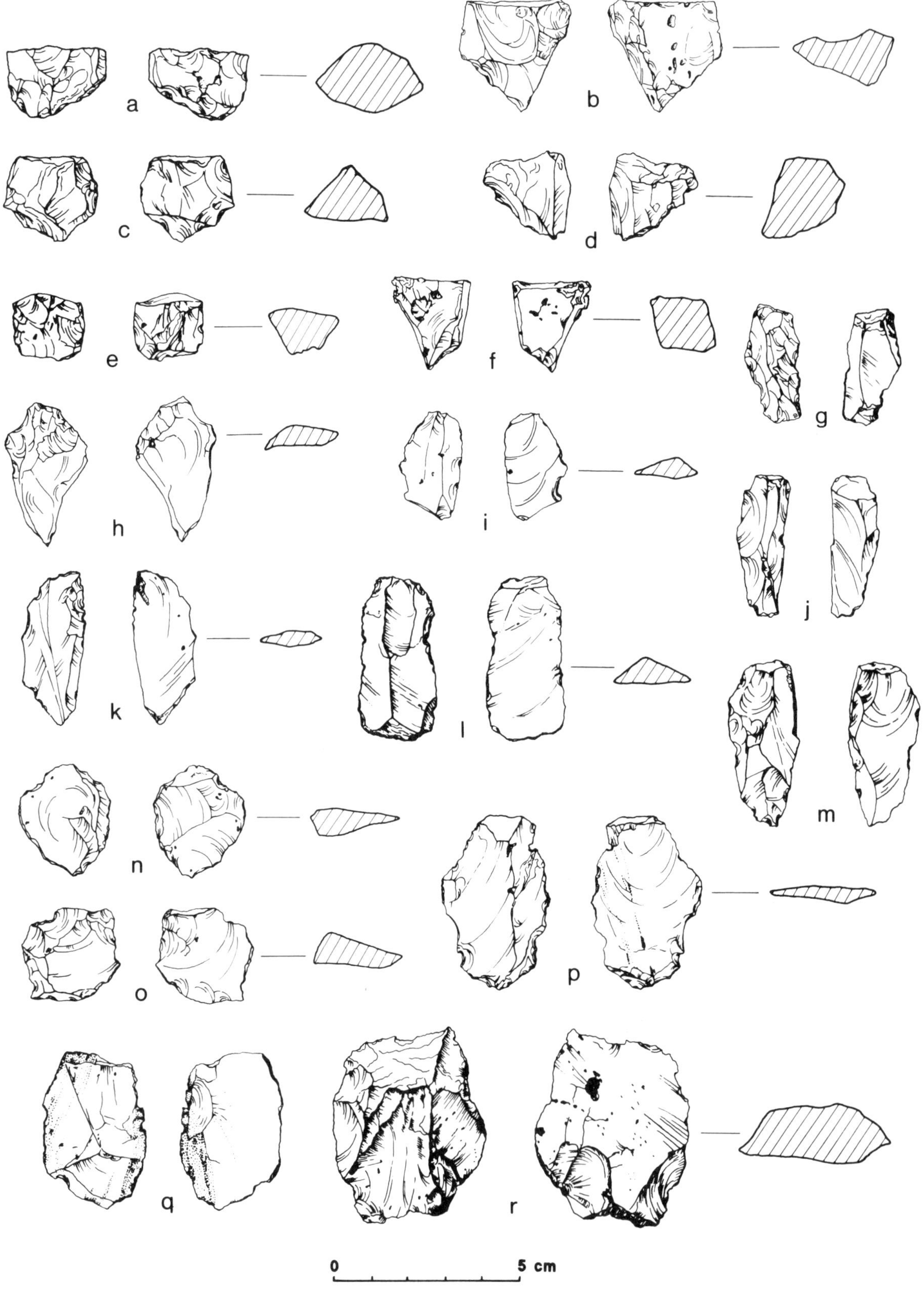

Figure 129. Selected flakes and cores of volcanic glass from Niuatoputapu ceramic-zone sites.

diffuse, and with termination edges varying from feather to hinge to step. Flakes were produced using a hard hammer technique, probably in association with an anvil (i.e., "bi-polar" percussion). A selection of these artifacts is illustrated in figure 129.

Basalt/Andesite Flakes

One hundred six flakes of basalt and/or andesite were recovered during excavations at the three main sites. Most of these are probably fragments of stone adzes, although they lack any signs of grinding or polish and therefore cannot with certainty be identified as adz fragments. A few may have been used as scraping tools. As indicated in table 37, they are slightly larger than the flakes of chert or volcanic glass.

TABLE 37

BASALT FLAKES: METRICAL ATTRIBUTES

ATTRIBUTE	NT-90	NT-100
Length (mm)	27.0 ± 11.3	30.9 ± 16.7
Width (mm)	21.0 ± 7.9	23.0 ± 10.3
Thickness (mm)	6.8 ± 3.6	7.2 ± 3.3
Weight (g)	4.7 ± 5.8	7.7 ± 12.1
Striking Platform Thickness (mm)	5.4 ± 5.0	4.4 ± 2.2
Striking Platform Width (mm)	13.7 ± 8.1	12.3 ± 8.8
N	66	21

Extra-Areal Comparisons

Aside from the flaked basalt assemblages of Samoan sites analyzed by Green and Davidson (1969a, 1974) and their colleagues, relatively little attention has been paid to flaked stone in Western Polynesia or Fiji, making detailed comparisons difficult. A small number of "obsidian" and chert flakes were excavated in association with ceramics at several Samoan sites (Green 1974b:268-69). The source for the obsidian, which was more prevalent, is not known, although Ward (in Green and Davidson 1974) does not rule out a local source (possibly the Fagaloa Volcanics). The chert, of which only two flaked pieces were excavated, certainly seems to be an import. Green (1974b:269) notes that chert is a component of Lapita assemblages in Melanesia as well as Tonga, and regards its presence in Samoan pottery-bearing sites as a terminal manifestation of the use of an exotic material.

Chert occurs locally on Futuna Island, and a number of cores and flakes were excavated at the FU-11 and FU-19 sites (Kirch 1981:139-40). Analysis of these assemblages suggested production of small flakes by direct percussion of stream-worn nodules. Site FU-19 also yielded 59 cores and flakes of volcanic glass, of unknown but probably local derivation. These again were produced by a bi-polar direct percussion technique.

Little has been written concerning flaked stone assemblages in Fiji. Hunt (1980: 143-67, pl. 5.3) briefly describes a range of flaked plutonics, argillites, sandstones, and cherts from the Yanuca site, while Birks (1973:49, pl. 49) mentions worked basalt, dolerite, diorite, chalcedony, and other stones. The most extensive assemblage to date is that associated with the early Lapita site on Naigani (Best 1981; Kay 1984), in which small flakes of a whitish siliceous stone were fairly common; this assemblage has yet to be reported in full.

The most extensive analysis of comparable flaked stone materials is of the Polynesian Outlier of Tikopia in a technological study by McCoy (in Kirch and Yen 1982:255-69). The 869 pieces of flaked stone from Tikopia include both obsidian and volcanic glass (from probable Talasea and Banks Island sources), as well as several varieties of siliceous rocks or cherts (again, from multiple sources). McCoy (1982:262) notes an "emphasis on the manufacture and use of small, generally amorphous flake tools of varied lithologies." He believes that manufacture involved "variable use of freehand and bipolar percussion techniques on predominantly subangular to well-rounded nodules" (1982:265).

In sum, while the data on flaked stone assemblages in Western Polynesia, Fiji, and the Polynesian Outliers is scanty, a consistent association of both obsidian or volcanic glass and chert with Lapitoid assemblages seems clear, and in this the Niuatoputapu materials are comparable. In Fiji, the only site containing substantial quantities of chert is early Naigani, which parallels the situation in Niuatoputapu where only the early NT-90 site yielded a significant density of chert flakes. The Niuatoputapu and other Fiji-Western Polynesian materials just summarized also provide evidence for what McCoy (1982:262) tentatively defines as a "not yet fully described pan-Oceanic small-tool tradition with a time-depth of 3,500 years or more in eastern Melanesia."

MISCELLANEOUS ARTIFACTS

Flaked Stone Awl

A fragment of a carefully flaked core tool, possibly an awl or drill, was found on the surface of Site NT-90. As shown in figure 126, a, the object has been bifacially worked, and tapers toward a point which is broken off. The fragment is clearly not an adz preform, and the tapering end is suggestive of an awl or drill. The material is basalt or andesite, probably local. It measures 4.0 cm long.

Abraded Hematite

A pentagonal slab of hematite or similar iron oxide with evidence of abrasion on several facets (fig. 126, b) was excavated at Site NT-90. Similar abraded pieces of hematite or iron oxide ores have been noted from other Western Pacific sites (e.g., Tikopia, Kirch and Yen 1982:271; Vanikoro, Kirch 1983a:107), where they may have been ground to produce a reddish pigment.

Worked Bone

Four small pieces of turtle bone, two each from Sites NT-90 and -93, show evidence of working. In all cases, one edge of the plate-like bone has been beveled, suggesting that these objects may have been scrapers such as are known, for example, from the early Eastern Polynesian site of Vaito'otia in the Society group (Sinoto and McCoy 1975). Similar fragments of beveled turtle bone were excavated on Tikopia (Kirch and Yen 1982:252).

Worked Shell

Eighteen miscellaneous pieces of worked shell were excavated; unambiguous identifications are not possible. Twelve of these are of *Tridacna* shell, and include two shaft-like fragments, nine small chips or flakes (probably detritus from shell adz manufacture), and one large flake (fig. 127, b) with edge damage suggestive of use as a scraper. This latter specimen, 9.5 cm long and 4.3 cm wide, could readily have been mounted on the end of a wooden stool for use as a coconut grater. This type of artifact is known ethnographically throughout Micronesia and Polynesia.

The remainder of the worked shell consists of two fragments of pearl shell, three of *Trochus*, and one of *Cypraea*.

HISTORIC PERIOD ARTIFACTS

A small assemblage of 19 historic-period artifacts was obtained during the excavations, largely from Site NT-110. Included are a bowl and a stem fragment of clay pipes, the bowl bearing a molded design (crossed leaves and crown); one small glass vial and five glass sherds; two ceramic sherds; two small pieces of metal; and seven fragments of slate (probably from school slate boards).

CHAPTER SIX

FAUNAL ANALYSIS AND SUBSISTENCE PATTERNS

THE NIUATOPUTAPU EXCAVATIONS produced a faunal sample comprising 1,555 vertebrate remains, and more than 300 kg of molluscs. Included are the following taxa: 5 mammals, at least 5 birds, 2 reptiles, 14 fish, and 32 molluscs. While this assemblage is not as large or diverse as, for example, that from Tikopia (Kirch and Yen 1982), it is one of the most extensive faunal collections yet recovered from a Western Polynesian locality, providing significant archaeological data on the origins and development of regional subsistence patterns. Most of the vertebrate faunal materials come from four main sites: NT–90, NT–100, NT–125, and NT–163, with an additional modest assemblage from NT–93. Smaller quantities of material were obtained from NT–91, –110, –112, and –113. All sites yielded large quantities of molluscan remains.

The faunal materials were recovered by sieving (0.25 inch mesh) in virtually all excavation units. As noted earlier, molluscs were sorted to taxon and weighed in the field. Voucher specimens of molluscs, as well as representative quantitative samples, are deposited in the Bishop Museum. Vertebrate remains were returned to the Museum laboratory, where identification of non-fish bone was undertaken by Dr. Alan C. Ziegler (formerly Vertebrate Zoologist, Bishop Museum), based on reference collections available to him. Bird bones were further examined and identified by Dr. David Steadman (New York State Museum). Fish bone was identified by the author based on a comparative skeletal collection, which was established in the Archaeology Laboratory of the Bishop Museum and which included a number of species collected during our expedition on Niuatoputapu. Molluscan vouchers were identified with the assistance of Prof. E. Alison Kay of the University of Hawaii and of Dr. Carl C. Christensen of the Bishop Museum.

I have purposely avoided complex statistical manipulation of the quantitative data, since I believe that these faunal samples are too limited in size and diversity to warrant such an approach. As Grayson (1984) has demonstrated, quantitative measures such as those of faunal diversity and richness are highly responsive to sample size variations. Thus, the preferred approach to the present data set is more qualitative, with an attempt to identify major components of prehistoric subsistence strategy and how these may have changed over time.

THE VERTEBRATE SAMPLE

Vertebrate remains from all sites, totalling 1,555 bones or bone fragments, are tabulated in table 38. Slightly more than half (51%) of this assemblage consists of fish bone, while another large component (27%) is made up of medium vertebrates which cannot be identified to lower-order taxa. Mammals constitute 7% of the collection, birds 9%, and reptiles 6%.

Some comments on the categories listed in table 38 are necessary. The category "large mammal" refers to fragments of larger bones of either old adult *Homo* or *Sus;* no cetaceans are included. The more frequent "medium mammals" are in the size range of *Homo,*

TABLE 38

VERTEBRATE REMAINS FROM NIUATOPUTAPU SITES (NISP)

TAXON	NT–90	NT–91	NT–93	NT–100	NT–110	NT–112	NT–113	NT–125	NT–163	TOTAL	
MAMMALS											(114) 7%
Sus scrofa	2		3	5		3		19	1	33	
Canis familiaris	4				7			3		14	
Rattus exulans	1			16						17	
Pteropus sp.	1									1	
Homo sapiens	8			20				4		32	
Large Mammal	2									2	
Medium Mammal	3			3		1		8		15	
BIRDS											(139) 9%
Gallus gallus	12		6	7	1	37		3	26	92	
Sula sula	5									5	
Puffinus sp.									1	1	
Sterninae sp.	1									1	
Gygis alba	6									6	
Anous stolidus	3									3	
Large Bird	3									3	
Medium Bird	13		1	3	1	7		4	4	28	
REPTILES											(94) 6%
Marine Turtle	71		6	10		2		3	1	93	
Lizard				1						1	
FISH	296	4	48	153	32	9	1	49	197	789	(789) 51%
UNIDENTIFIABLE											(419) 27%
Medium Vertebrate	141	2	48	76	12	16		92	31	418	
Large Vertebrate	1									1	
TOTAL	568	6	112	294	53	75	1	185	261	1,555	

Canis, and *Sus*, although most are probably not *Canis*. The "large birds" are in the size range of boobies (Sulidae), and some of this material may well belong to one or more species in this family. The category "medium bird" is in the general size range of smaller individuals of *Gallus gallus;* most material is probably of this species. Finally, the general category "medium vertebrate" consists of material other than bird, not identifiable to class. Ziegler (pers. comm.) suggests that 99% of this is probably referable to *Sus*, marine turtle, and *Homo*, with very little fish. While the material could not be positively identified, Ziegler had the impression that it included a fair amount of adult *Homo* cranial and limb bone fragments.

Mammals

Aside from fragmentary bones of *Homo sapiens*, the mammal bones consist principally of the two main Polynesian domestic species, *Sus scrofa* and *Canis familiaris*, along with the widespread Malay or Pacific Rat, *Rattus exulans*. Pig appears to have been more numerous than dog, and its presence in all of the principal sites with Lapitoid ceramics (including NT–90) is significant, reinforcing the argument that pig husbandry was an aspect of Lapita and Ancestral Polynesian subsistence (Kirch 1979). Four dog bones were excavated at NT–90, which suggests that this animal has also been present on Niuatoputapu since initial colonization. Dog bones are absent from the NT-93 and -100 assemblages; they are, however, present in the later NT–125 and –110 sites. One suspects from this evidence that dogs were never plentiful on the island.

Interestingly, the bones of *Rattus exulans* are not present in any sites except NT–90 (1 bone) and NT–100 where there are 16 specimens. This is in marked contrast to, for example, the Tikopia situation, where *Rattus* bones were extremely plentiful in all deposits (Kirch and Yen 1982:table 39). *R. exulans* is extremely widespread in the Pacific, clearly having been distributed by human agency, as Tate recognized (1951:97). The only fruit bat represented among the mammal bones is a humerus of *Pteropus*, probably *P. tonganus*, from Site NT–90.

Birds

Most of the identifiable bird material (including that in the category "medium bird") consists of the domestic jungle fowl, *Gallus gallus* (Ball 1933), one of the three domestic species widely distributed throughout Oceania. The presence of this species in ceramic zone sites, especially at NT–90, is again significant for the argument that Lapita colonists in Western Polynesia brought with them a horticultural economy incorporating animal husbandry.

Bird taxa other than *Gallus* are few, and are largely restricted to the NT–90 assemblage. These include five bones from NT–90 referred to *Sula sula* (Mayr 1945:18–19). Site NT-163 yielded a single humerus of a species of *Puffinus;* the humerus is definitely not referable to *P. pacificus* or any of the smaller species, but could represent any of several other petrels or shearwaters. Among the NT–90 assemblage, three species of larids (gulls and terns) are represented. One is an undetermined species of Sterninae (tern). Six wing elements are of *Gygis alba*, the Fairy Tern, while three other wing elements are of *Anous stolidus*, the Common Noddy.

Reptiles

With the exception of one bone, all of the reptile material consists of marine turtle, which probably includes both the Green Sea Turtle (*Chelonia mydas*) and the Hawksbill Turtle (*Eretmochelys imbricata*). Most of this material consists of osseous carapace and plastron fragments, limbs, and cranial fragments, none of which are identifiable to genus. Both species of turtle occur in Tonga, where they are collectively termed *fonu*, and prized as food for chiefs; the Hawksbill is further termed *fonu koloa* because its keratinous plates provide the material for making valued ornaments known as *koloa*, "valued goods."

The distribution of turtle bone in the Niuatoputapu sites is quantitatively significant, the majority of specimens from Site NT–90. Turtle bone at NT–90 has a density of approximately 1.39 bones/m^2, which drops to 0.53/m^2 at NT-100, and 0.27/m^2 at NT–93. Prior to the human colonization of Niuatoputapu, the lagoon and beaches presumably supported a sizable nesting colony of marine turtles, offering a ready food source to the first Lapita settlers. The reduction in turtle frequency from the early NT–90 site to that in the later sites probably reflects this initial situation of high resource abundance. Such a pattern has been delineated in the Tikopia case discussed by Kirch and Yen (1982:285).

The single lizard jaw fragment from NT-100 may be of the iguanid genus *Brachylophus*, known from Fiji.

Fish

About 51% of the total vertebrate sample, or 789 individual bones, consists of fish, including rays and sharks as well as teleosts. Of these, 230 (29%) could be identified to taxon, using a reference collection in the

TABLE 39

FISH REMAINS FROM NIUATOPUTAPU SITES (NISP)

TAXON	NT-90	NT-91	NT-93	NT-100	NT-110	NT-112	NT-113	NT-125	NT-163
SUBCLASS ACTINOPTERYGII									
Acanthuridae									
Acanthurus	4			2					2
Other	5		1	1	3				
Balistidae	1			2		1			
Carangidae				1				2	
Diodontidae									
Diodon hystrix (jaw plates)	18		4	1			1	1	2
Diodon hystrix (spines)	19		2						4
Labridae	2		1	1		1			
Lethrinidae	2			1					3
Lutjanidae									
Lutjanus	1								1
Scaridae									
Calotomus	1			2					
Other (beaks)	25		2	15	5	1		1	9
Other (lower pharyngeal grinding plates)	13		2	1	1			2	6
Other (upper pharyngeal dental plates)	3	1		4	2				1
Scombridae									2
Serranidae									
Cephalopholus				1		1			
Sparidae									
Monotaxis grandoculis	6		2	6					3
SUBCLASS ELASMOBRANCHII	7		1	8				6	1
TOTALS	107	1	15	46	11	4	1	12	34

Bishop Museum and published references (Fowler 1955; Schultz 1958; Barnett 1978). Most of the identified bones are mouth parts, particularly dentaries and premaxillaries, and pharyngeal grinding plates for scarids and labrids. Other identifiable bones include the spines of *Diodon hystrix* and the vertebrae of elasmobranchs. The distribution of identified bones by site is provided in table 39. Kirch and Dye (1979: table 8) provided conversions to MNI for the bone counts from the three principal ceramic sites (these conversions primarily affect the number of scarids). The eleven families and one subclass of fishes represented in this collection are briefly discussed below with regard to habitat, food value, and possible implications for prehistoric fishing strategies. In this discussion I draw on the detailed ethnographic and ecological studies of contemporary fishing on Niuatoputapu conducted as a part of our 1976 investigation, and published in detail elsewhere (Kirch and Dye 1979; Dye 1983). Information on fish taxonomy and ecology are drawn from a variety of sources, including Fowler (1959), Jordan and Seale (1906), Munro (1967), Bagnis, Mazellier, Bennett, and Christian (1972), and Tinker (1978).

Acanthuridae. The surgeon fishes, including the diverse genus *Acanthurus*, are herbivorous and live upon shallow water algae. They are an inshore reef group, various species of which frequent such habitats as surge channels, the outer reef edge, or the shallower waters of the reef platform. Most range from 20 to 35 cm in length. Several species of *Acanthurus,* including *A. guttatus, A. triostegus,* and *A. lineatus* were among the most commonly taken fishes recorded over a six-month period on Niuatoputapu (Kirch and Dye 1979: table 5). *Acanthurus guttatus* and *A. triostegus* were the second and third highest-ranked of 31 commonly caught fish taxa, with a total of 465 individual fish of these species. *Acanthurus guttatus* was taken more frequently by night spearing on the outer, windward reef edge (the *ama fakasiosio* method). This species, in fact, accounts for 28% of all fish recorded during *ama fakasiosio* sorties (Kirch and Dye 1979: table 4). A particular netting method used for *A. guttatus,* called *kupenga ha'oha'o,* involves the use of a 20 m seine (Dye 1983:253). The species *A. triostegus,* on the other hand, is more frequently taken by netting. Both species, however, may be caught by either technique, as well as by the use of poisons. We have no records, however, of their being taken on hooks.

Balistidae. The triggerfish family includes several genera and many species of carnivorous or partly herbivorous fishes, the flesh of which can at times be toxic to humans (Munro 1967:557). Tinker (1978:470) observes that the triggerfishes also are the source of ciguatera toxin, which in turn affects humans who eat the fish. Despite this danger, they are regularly eaten. Balistids are solitary, coral reef dwellers which frequent the reef bottom, where they graze on crabs, echinoderms, corals, and other reef animals. In Niuatoputapu, a number of species (known under the generic term *humu)* were taken by informants, primarily by poisoning, although more occasionally by netting, angling, or spear-diving.

Carangidae. This is a very large family with several genera and more than 200 species, much prized for food. As Tinker (1978:254) notes, they are "active, fast swimming, carnivorous predators which feed upon a wide variety of fish and crustacea." In length they may range from about 15 cm to as much as 75 cm. They are a generally schooling fish, and frequent the inshore areas or outer reef edge. Younger fish tend to live closer to the reef, while the larger and older individuals move toward the deeper waters. In Niuatoputapu, some species, such as *lupo (Caranx ignobilis),* are highly prized. The most frequently captured species recorded during our stay was *Trachurops crumenopthalmus* or *'otule,* represented in three separate catches. This species is the object of a named angling strategy *(tau 'otule),* practiced at night from a boat or canoe off the reef edge (Dye 1983:250). *Caranx ignobilis* is also taken by this method, as well as by netting and spear-diving.

Diodontidae. The spiny puffers or porcupine fish are represented in the Niuatoputapu faunal assemblage by spines and bony jaw plates of the genus *Diodon,* especially the large species *D. hystrix.* These fish frequent quiet reef waters, where they prey upon various invertebrates; their massive, bony jaws, which are so well preserved in archaeological contexts, are adapted to crushing crabs, molluscs, and other prey. Although Bagnis et al. (1972:227) report that the Tahitians are very fond of the species *D. holacanthus,* in general these fish are toxic and shunned as food. On Tikopia, for instance, *D. hystrix* is regarded as *tapu,* associated with malevolent deities, even though its skeletal parts are abundant in early archaeological deposits on the island (Kirch and Yen 1982:292). *Diodon* not only concentrates the ciguatera toxin, but carries its own crinotoxin (Cameron 1976). Nevertheless, it was taken prehistorically on Niuatoputapu and is represented in other Polynesian archaeological contexts, including Tikopia and the Reef Islands Lapita sites (Green 1986). The spiny puffers are said to be taken by spearing, diving, and netting, though they did not occur with high frequency in our catch records.

Labridae. The wrasses are a highly varied and colorful group of reef fishes, including about 600 species worldwide, many of these widely distributed in the Indo-Pacific region. They are primarily carnivorous and non-schooling, feeding on molluscs which they crush between their powerful jaws (Fowler 1959:390). Fowler records 19 genera in Fiji, and it is probable that they are one of the most diverse groups in the Niuatoputapu fish fauna. They range in size from ca. 15 cm to larger than 60 cm, and are prized as food. Labrids are taken by the modern Niuatoputapuns primarily by spearing and netting. The species *Thallasoma purpureum* is taken by the *ama fakasiosio* method on the windward reef edge (Kirch and Dye 1979: table 4). Dye (1983:253) also describes the capture of wrasses with the *kupenga taliava* method, in which a net is used to close a channel at the island's western end; fish trapped in the channel with the dropping tide are then speared. We have no records of wrasses being taken by angling.

Lethrinidae. This family of valued food fishes has one genus *(Lethrinus)* and several species in this area. These emperor fish, as they are commonly termed, frequent "shallow coastal waters around rocky outcrops and coral reefs" (Munro 1967:324), and are noted for readily taking baited hooks. Barnett indicates that they are found in a variety of reef habitats, including the outer reef edge, in passes, and inside lagoons (1978:14). Although they are as noted above, easy to catch by angling, Bagnis et al. (1972:132) report that the Tahitians frequently net or trap schools of young emperors in lagoon shallows, while Akimichi (1978:315) records the seine netting of emperors among the Lau of Malaita. On Niuatoputapu, one species of *Lethrinus*, called *tanutanu*, occurred in four of our recorded catches. The methods used were netting, especially the use of a large seine in the *kupenga fakamamaha* technique (Dye 1983:252), and poisoning, or *'aukava* (1983:256). Despite indications in the literature of emperors taking baited hooks, we have no records of their capture by angling on Niuatoputapu.

Lutjanidae. Fowler (1959:227) describes the snappers as "active, voracious, and carnivorous." Three genera occur in Fiji-Western Polynesia, the most important of which is *Lutjanus*. Like the emperors, they frequent a variety of reef habitats, including deeper lagoon waters, passes, or off the outer reef edge. Green (ms.) notes that large individuals are sometimes toxic (presumably due to ciguatera poisoning), so that smaller individuals from lagoons are preferred. Several species of *Lutjanus* are well represented in our Niuatoputapu catch records. *Lutjanus fulvus* was taken in 13 catches by five different techniques for a total of 52 fish, placing it well up on the list of 31 most frequently caught species (Kirch and Dye 1979: table 5). *Lutjanus monostigma* was taken four times with three techniques, while an unidentified species was taken three times by two techniques. Of particular techniques, Dye (1983) mentions *lafolafo* or casting for *L. fulvus* on the windward reef flat, the *tau 'otule* and *tau tu'u* angling techniques, as well as the *kupenga fakamamaha* and *kupenga hokohoka* netting strategies, as well as spearing and poisoning. *Lutjanus fulvus* and *L. monostigma* were both taken during noctural *ama fakasiosio* spearing sorties on the windward reef flat (Kirch and Dye 1979: table 4).

Scaridae. The parrotfish are noted as one of the most dominant of coral reef groups in terms of total biomass (Goldman and Talbot 1976), which probably accounts for their high frequency not only in the Niuatoputapu faunal assemblage, but also in faunal suites from other Pacific island sites (e.g., Green 1986; Kirch and Yen 1982; Kirch and Rosendahl 1973; Kirch 1973, 1979; Leach and Ward 1981). Although the identification of the distinctive mouth parts, including dentaries, premaxillaries, and upper and lower pharyngeal clusters, is a straightforward matter at the family level, the systematics of the group are "enigmatic and bewildering" (Bagnis et al. 1972:145; see also Schultz 1958). Scarids reach fairly large sizes (ranging from ca. 25 cm to 120 cm), and are everywhere prized as good eating. On Niuatoputapu these fish, termed *menenga*, are regularly sought for presentation at important feasts. They occur in a variety of coral reef habitats, but on Niuatoputapu especially frequent the outer reef edges and surge channels, where they feed upon marine algae. They are the principal quarry of the *ama fakasiosio* night spearing sortie and, as Kirch and Dye remark, "no *ama fakasiosio* expedition is judged successful unless the catch includes a *menenga*" (1979:64). Parrotfish were, in fact, captured on 56% of the spearing sorties recorded, although in terms of the total numbers of fish obtained they fell well below *Abudefduf* and *Acanthurus*. Parrotfish are also taken in several netting strategies, such as *kupenga ha'oha'o* and *kupenga taliava*. Dye (1983:253) describes a dramatic net technique termed *kupenga menengakalia*, which is used to take an especially large and prized species of parrotfish named after the large, inter-island sailing canoe *(kalia)*. We have no records of parrotfish being taken with hook and line.

Scombridae. Only two mouth parts of a mackerel or tuna were archaeologically recovered; these came from Site NT-163. These are probably from one or two of the larger pelagic, carnivorous species such as the bonito or albacore *(Katsuwonus, Thunnus*, and other genera). These specimens are, notably, the only representatives of open-ocean pelagic fish in the Niuatoputapu faunal assemblage. For want of large canoes or boats, such species are not often taken on Niuatoputapu today, although the technique of bonito trolling *(hi 'atu)* is occasionally practiced. The single *hi 'atu* sortie carried out during our stay on the island yielded 67 fish in just two hours. The status attached to these fish, and to the fishermen who obtain them, is indicated by the performance of a *kava* ceremony in which the first cup is offered to the *'atu* fish (Dye 1983:251-52).

Serranidae. The two specimens of serranids recovered archaeologically are both referable to the genus *Cephalopholus*, a member of the sea bass or grouper family. According to Fowler (1959:586), the principal species in our area is *C. argus*, with lengths up to 37 cm. This species is taken by spearing, netting, and poisoning, and is represented in eight different catches recorded during our stay (Kirch and Dye 1979: table 5). Other serranids, however (there are a large number in several genera), are often taken by angling, especially bottom fishing or handlining off the reef edge and in the lagoon.

Sparidae. All of the sparids or porgies in our archaeological material are unquestionably of the species *Monotaxis grandoculis*, called *muu* by the Tongans. They reach lengths of 50 cm and frequent the reef edge and reef flats. During our stay on Niuatoputapu they were infrequently taken by spearing and angling. Out of all *ama fakasiosio* sorties recorded, *muu* was captured just once (Kirch and Dye 1979: table 4).

The archaeologically recovered fish species from our Niuatoputapu sites consist almost wholly of inshore fishes, with minimal representation of pelagic and benthic species. This dominance of inshore fish resources is highly consistent not only with the ethnographic data on contemporary Niuatoputapu fishing, but with the faunal pattern from most southwest Pacific archaeological sites, especially those of Lapita affinity (Green 1986). (Additional comparisons with other Western Polynesian and Fijian sites are provided at the end of this chapter.)

Our ethnographic data on the fishing strategies used to take the various taxa represented archaeologically also provide some indication of the range of strategies which may have been pursued prehistorically. In terms of material culture (chapter 5), net weights and one-piece fishhooks of *Turbo* shell are archaeologically attested. It is certain, however, that the majority of fish taxa represented in the faunal suites were not taken with hook and line. Rather, both netting and spearing strategies must have been important to the prehistoric Niuan fisherman, and probably accounted for the major portion of fish captured. These points have been argued in full in Kirch and Dye (1979).

Finally, there are a few intriguing differences between the suite of fish taxa represented archaeologically and the quantitative patterns of fish catches recorded ethnographically. We must be cautious in such comparisons, of course, since the incomplete status of our reference collection precluded identification of a significant component of the archaeological fish bone sample. We can, however, remark on those taxa which are dominant or common in the archaeological record, yet do not figure prominently in the contemporary Niuatoputapu diet. Most striking is the high frequency of *Diodon hystrix* in the excavated sites. Today this species hardly figures in the fish catches of the modern Niuan fishermen, yet it is the second most frequent species in the archaeological record. Kirch and Dye (1979) suggest that differential preservation may account for some over-representation in the archaeological record (this species having massive jaw plates and substantial spines), but this explanation is not entirely satisfactory (cf. Green, ms.). Interestingly, a similar situation occurs on Tikopia (Kirch and Yen 1982), where *Diodon* was extremely common in archaeological deposits, but is never eaten by the contemporary population. Kirch and Yen (1982:292, 357) suggest that repeated experiences with ciguatera poisoning may have led to an aversion to the consumption of this species, and the same might have been true on Niuatoputapu. Also noteworthy are the high frequencies of pelagic tunas and of *Lutjanus* in the contemporary fish catches, in relation to their lower archaeological representation. At the present time, it is impossible to say whether this skewing represents sampling factors, differential preservation, or real differences in fishing strategies over time.

MOLLUSCS

Molluscan remains dominate the faunal assemblages of all excavated sites. Here we present the data on only four key sites (NT-90, -93, -100, and -163 aceramic component), although detailed statistics for all excavation units, with recorded weight by taxon, are on file with the excavation records. Molluscs were sorted into 37 categories, most of which represent single species, but some of which are multiple species combinations within a genus or family. Voucher specimens for each of these categories have been deposited in the Malacology Division of the B.P. Bishop Museum. Table 40 presents basic data on these categories, including their English vernacular names (when known), and their habitat ranges. The most important species are illustrated in figures 130 and 131.

Quantitative data on molluscan composition of the four main sites under consideration are provided in tables 41 to 44. The first column of each table indicates the actual excavated weight per taxon (all values are in kilograms). The second and third columns display the mean weight and standard deviation per 1 m^2 excavation unit. Since the depth of deposit varies somewhat both within and between sites, the fourth column presents a standardized concentration index (CI) of weight per cubic meter, which can be utilized for between site comparisons. Finally, the fifth column shows the relative importance of each taxon, calculated as a percentage of total shell.

In all sites, gastropods were more frequent than bivalves, ranging from 62 to 70% of all molluscs by weight; there is also a greater number of gastropod taxa represented. It is intriguing that the aceramic component of NT-163 displays substantially less taxonomic richness than any of the ceramic zone sites. This is more in keeping with the contemporary exploitation of molluscs, in which relatively few species are regularly harvested for food (table 40).

Inter-site differences in dominant taxa can be seen in figure 132, which shows the percentage composition of molluscan assemblages with six gastropod and five bivalve taxa. All assemblages display relatively high values for *Turbo* and *Strombus* in the gastropods and for *Gafrarium* in the bivalves. Site NT-93 is distinctive for its low quantities of *Rhinoclavis*, which is otherwise prominent. Similarly, Site NT-100 has unusually high quantities of *Gafrarium*. Also notable are the low values for *Trochus* and *Cypraea* in the NT-90 assemblage.

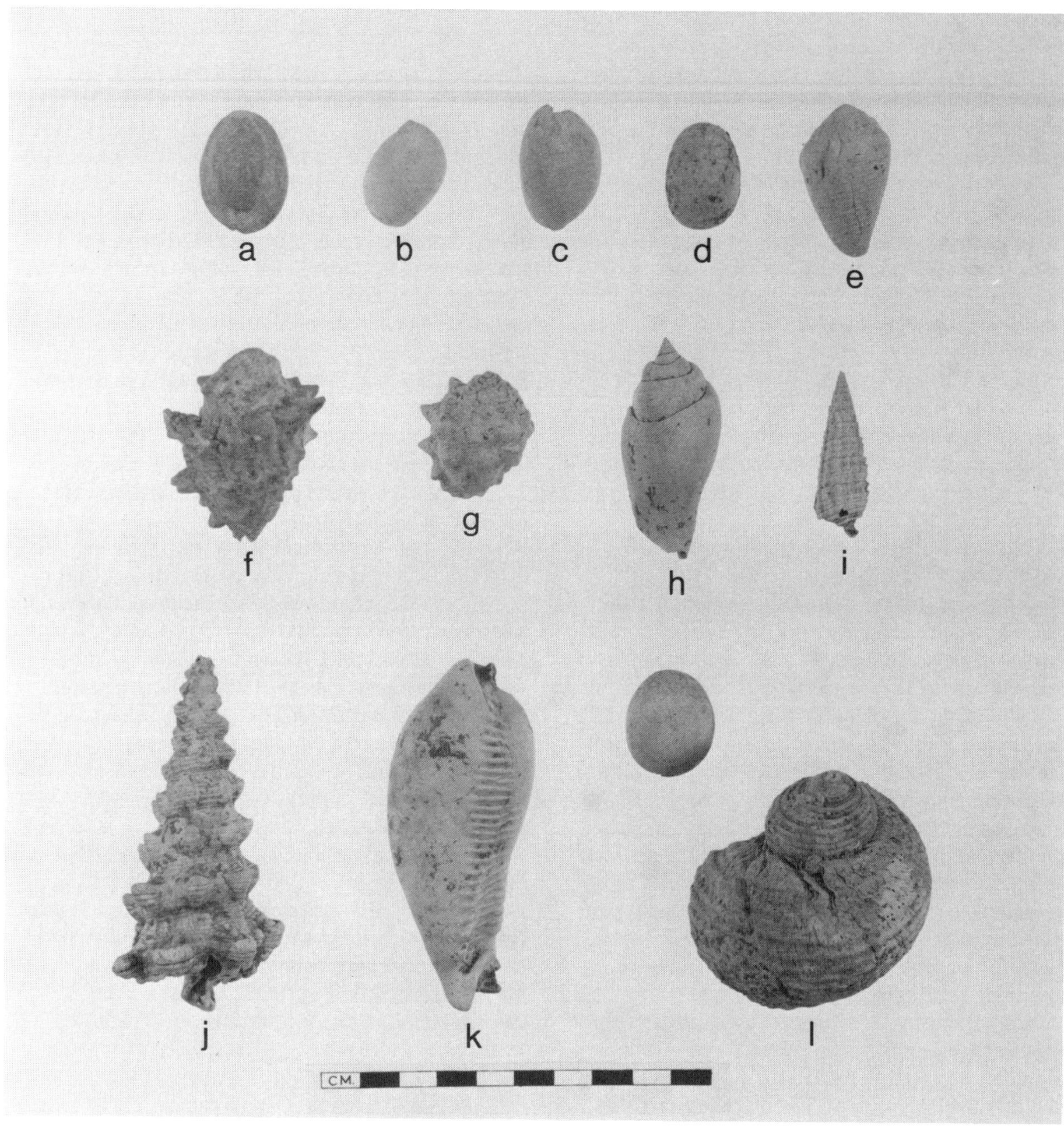

Figure 130. Dominant gastropods from Niuatoputapu sites: a, *Cypraea caputserpentis;* b, *Polinices simiae;* c, *Bulla* sp.; d, *Nerita* sp.; e, *Conus* sp.; f, *Thais armigera;* g, *Drupa ricina;* h, *Strombus mutabilis;* i, *Rhinoclavis asper;* j, *Cerithium nodulosum;* k, *Cypraea* sp. (fragment); l, *Turbo setosus* (shell and operculum).

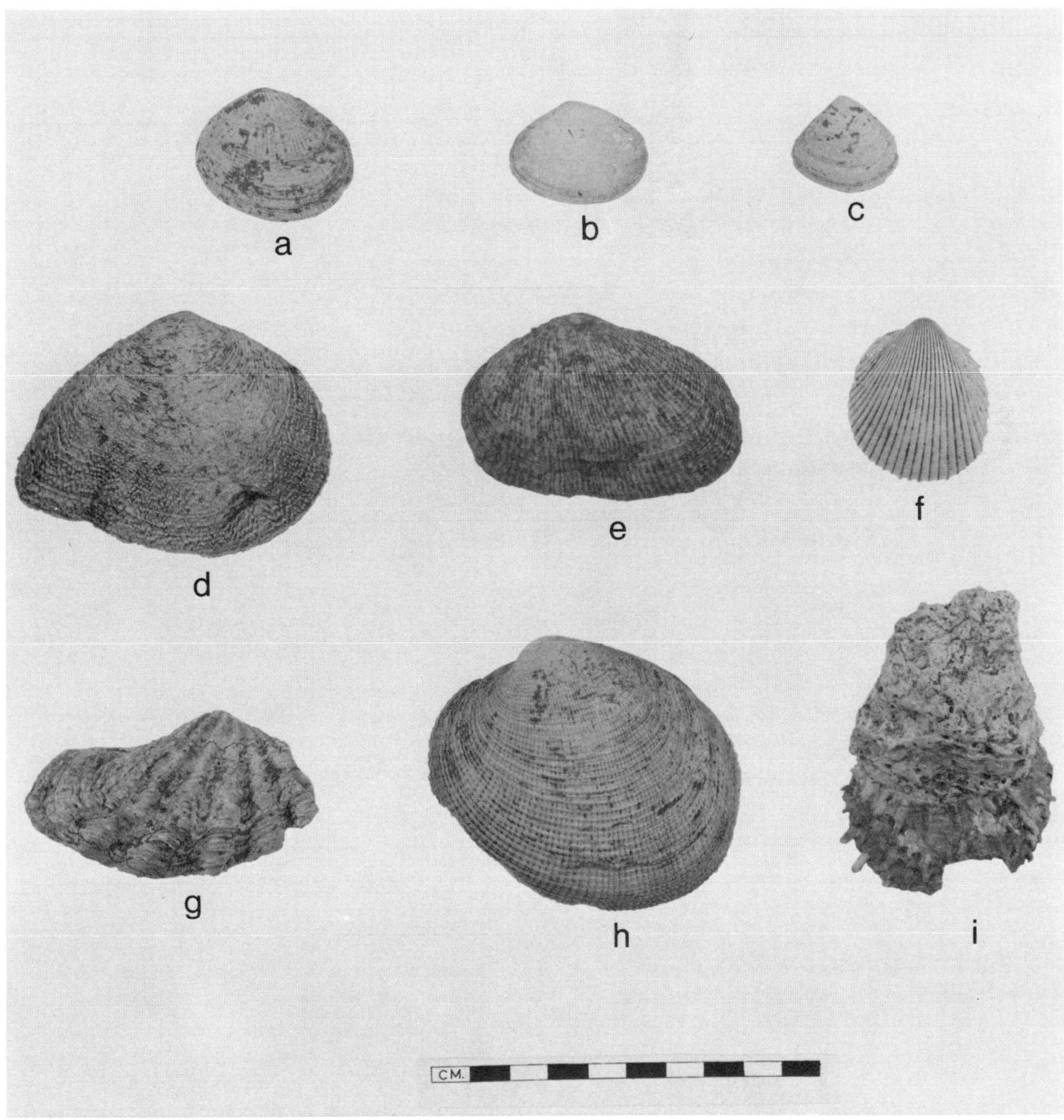

Figure 131. Dominant bivalves from Niuatoputapu sites: a, *Gafrarium puerpera;* b, *Tellina* sp.; c, *Arcopagia* sp.; d, *Quidnipagus palatam;* e, *Asaphis violascens;* f, *Fragum fragum;* g, *Tridacna maxima;* h, *Periglypta pectinatum;* i, *Spondylus* sp.

TABLE 40

EXCAVATED MOLLUSCS: BASIC DATA

FAMILY	SPECIES	ENGLISH VERNACULAR	HABITAT*
GASTROPODA			
Trochidae	*Trochus niloticus* L.	Pearly Top Shell	1
	Trochus maculatus L.	Maculated Top-Shell	
Turbinidae	*Turbo setosus* Gmelin	Setose Turban	1
Neritidae	*Nerita polita* L.	Polished Nerite	2
	Nerita plicata L.	Plicate Nerite	2
Planaxidae	*Planaxis sulcatus*	Ribbed Clusterwink	
Cerithiidae	*Rhinoclavis asper* L.	Rogh Creeper	
	Cerithium nodulosum Brugiere	Giant Knobbed Cerith	3
Strombidae	*Strombus mutabilis* Swainson	Mutable Conch	3
Cypraeidae	*Cypraea tigris* L.	Tiger Cowrie	2
	C. caputserpentis L.	Serpent's Head Cowrie	2
	C. annulus L.	Ring Cowrie	2
	C. moneta L.	Money Cowrie	2
Naticidae	*Natica* sp.	Moon Shell	
	Polinices simiae	Moon Shell	3
Cymatiidae	*Cymatium* spp.	Triton	2
Thaididae	*Thais armigera* Link	—	1
	Drupa morum Röding	Mulberry Drupe	4
Mitridae	*Mitra* spp.	Mitres	

* Habitat classes: 1, algal crest, reef edge; 2, inter-tidal reef platform; 3, sand- or mud-dwelling; 4, rocky surge zone.

Given the massive quantity of molluscan remains excavated from these sites, we are certain that these differences are significant, and do not represent sampling error. However, we cannot offer ready explanations for these patterns. Site NT-93, for example, is adjacent to the most extensive lagoon and might be expected to yield higher percentages of the lagoon-floor dwelling bivalves such as *Asaphis*, *Periglypta*, and genera of Cardiidae. Yet this is not the case; environmental factors do not explain these faunal differences.

One of the most significant trends in these data is the reduction in total molluscan content over time, indicated by the CI values from the four main sites (table 45). Site NT-90, the oldest known occupation component and probable colonization site, has a total molluscan concentration index of 19.74 kg/m^3. Site NT-100, which spans the Late Eastern Lapita to Polynesian Plain Ware sequence, has a CI of 8.32, while the overlapping and generally Polynesian Plain Ware deposits of NT-93 have a CI of only 4.76. Lowest of all is the aceramic NT-163 site, with a CI value of 2.50. This trend probably represents a combination of two factors: (1) the heavy exploitation of a pristine reef ecosystem with high standing-crop biomass by the island's first human occupants, and (2) the steady reduction in area of exploitable reef caused by the gradual tectonic uplift of Niuatoputapu during the period in which humans have occupied the island. This pattern is extremely similar to that on Tikopia, where the CI values for the early Kiki Phase deposits far exceed those

Table 40, Continued

FAMILY	SPECIES	ENGLISH VERNACULAR	HABITAT*
Conidae	*Conus ebraeus* L.	Hebrew Cone	2
	Conus coranatus Gmelin	Crowned Cone	2
	Conus spp.	Various Cones	2
Terebridae	*Terebra* spp.	Augurs	3
Bullidae	*Bulla* sp.	Bubble Shells	
BIVALVIA			
Arcidae	*Anadara antiquata*	Ark Shell	3
Pteriidae	*Pinctada* sp.	Pearl Oyster	2
Isognomonida	*Isognomon perna* (L.)	—	2
Spondylliidae	*Spondylus* sp.	Thorny Oyster	2
Chamidae	*Chama iostoma* Conrad	Rock Oyster	4
Cardiidae	*Fragum fragum* L.	White Strawberry Cockle	3
	Laevicardium sp.	Common Egg Cockly	3
Tridacnidae	*Tridacna maxima* (Röding)	Elongate Clam	2
Tellinidae	*Tellina* sp.	Tellin	3
Psammobiidae	*Asaphis violascens* (Forskal)	—	3
Veneridae	*Gafrarium pectinatum* (L.)	—	
	Periglypta puerpera L.	Purple Venus	3
	Veneridae spp.	Venus Clams	3

* Habitat classes: 1, algal crest, reef edge; 2, inter-tidal reef platform; 3, sand- or mud-dwelling; 4, rocky surge zone.

of subsequent occupation horizons (Kirch and Yen 1982:293, table 47). Indeed, the concentration indices for the Zone C1 and C2 deposits at the base of the Sinapupu dune sequence on Tikopia are virtually identical to that from NT-90.

Our data on molluscan concentrations in the ceramic zone deposits also permit a rough calculation of the total shellfish content represented by the leeward portion of this extensive pottery-bearing occupation zone (i.e., that portion of the zone between Hihifo and Falehau). This portion of the zone, which was the most heavily occupied (see chapter 5), covers an area of about 0.32 km^2. Using an average value of shell density per square meter, derived from the three main sites, of 5.4 ± 3.6 kg, we obtain an estimate for the total molluscan content of the zone of 1,728 ± 1,148 metric tons. The actual edible flesh weight represented by this quantity of shellfish can be crudely estimated using a ratio of flesh/shell weight of 0.4 (derived from data presented in Meehan 1982): 691 ± 459 metric tons. While this is undeniably a large quantity of shellfish, its probable significance in the total prehistoric Niuan diet must be assessed in terms of the approximately 2,000-year duration of ceramic zone occupation. The 691 metric tons of shellfish meat estimated above would amount to a mere 345 kg/yr on the average. While the error factors inherent in calculations of this sort deter me from further numerical exercises, the implication seems indisputable: molluscs (despite their overwhelming dominance in the archaeological deposits) were never

TABLE 41

MOLLUSCAN AND ECHINODERM FAUNA FROM SITE NT–90

TAXON	TOTAL WEIGHT (kg)	WT/m^2 (kg)		CI/m^3	% (of total shell)
		$\bar{x}$	s.d.		
GASTROPODA					
Trochus maculatus	1.94	0.08	0.10	0.17	0.85
Turbo setosus	47.98	1.99	1.52	4.15	21.04
T. setosus operculae	20.65	0.90	0.39	1.79	9.06
Nerita polita	4.66	0.19	0.17	0.40	2.04
Nerita plicata	0.12	0.005	0.007	0.01	0.05
Planaxis sulcatus	3.56	0.15	0.28	0.31	1.56
Rhinoclavis asper	41.47	1.73	5.95	3.59	18.18
Cerithium nodulosum	0.96	0.04	0.08	0.08	0.42
Strombus mutabilis	29.42	1.22	0.78	2.55	12.90
Cypraea tigris	0.97	0.04	0.06	0.08	0.43
Cypraea spp.	1.93	0.08	0.05	0.17	0.85
Natica spp.	1.50	0.06	0.06	0.13	0.66
Polinices simiae	0.10	0.004	0.009	0.009	0.04
Cymatium spp.	0.44	0.02	0.05	0.04	0.19
Thais armigera	1.09	0.05	0.07	0.09	0.48
Drupa morum	0.04	0.002	0.006	0.004	0.02
Mitra spp.	—	—	—	—	—
Conus spp.	3.80	0.16	0.17	0.33	1.67
Terebra spp.	—	—	—	—	—
Bulla sp.	0.12	0.005	0.014	0.011	0.05
TOTAL GASTROPODA	160.75	6.74	6.75	13.92	(70.49)
BIVALVIA					
Pinctada sp.	0.02	0.0008	0.0004	0.002	0.01
Isognomon perna	0.04	0.001	0.0003	0.003	0.02
Spondylus sp.	0.45	0.019	0.05	0.04	0.20
Chama iostoma	1.96	0.08	0.11	0.17	0.86
Tridacna maxima	11.68	0.49	0.50	1.01	5.12
Tellina spp.	12.42	0.52	0.43	1.08	5.45
Fragum/Laevicardium	1.86	0.08	0.08	0.16	0.82
Asaphis violascens	8.57	0.36	0.35	0.74	3.76
Gafrarium pectinatum	19.12	0.80	0.49	1.65	8.38
Periglypta puerpera	2.75	0.11	0.17	0.24	1.21
Veneridae spp.	3.26	0.14	0.11	0.28	1.43
TOTAL BIVALVIA	62.13	2.59	1.78	5.38	(27.24)
Miscellaneous Taxa	5.17	0.21	0.25	0.45	2.27
TOTAL MOLLUSCA	228.05	9.50	7.75	19.74	100.00
ECHINODERMS	0.40	0.02	0.04	0.03	—

TABLE 42

MOLLUSCAN FAUNA FROM SITE NT–100

TAXON	TOTAL WEIGHT (kg)	WT/m² (kg)		CI/m³	% (of total shell)
		$\bar{x}$	s.d.		
GASTROPODA					
Trochus niloticus	0.26	0.02	0.04	0.05	0.57
Trochus maculatus	0.38	0.03	0.05	0.07	0.83
Turbo setosus	5.67	0.47	0.36	1.03	12.40
T. setosus operculae	1.83	0.15	0.11	0.33	4.00
Nerita polita	0.20	0.02	0.02	0.04	0.44
Nerita plicata	0.32	0.03	0.04	0.06	0.70
Planaxis sulcatus	0.09	0.007	0.01	0.02	0.20
Rhinoclavis asper	9.26	0.77	0.93	1.68	20.24
Cerithium nodulosum	0.08	0.007	0.02	0.01	0.17
Strombus mutabilis	7.76	0.65	0.69	1.41	16.97
Cypraea tigris	0.56	0.05	0.12	0.10	1.22
Cypraea spp.	1.25	0.10	0.08	0.23	2.73
Natica sp.	0.65	0.05	0.07	0.12	1.42
Cymatium spp.	0.47	0.04	0.04	0.08	1.03
Thais armigera	0.20	0.02	0.03	0.04	0.44
Mitra spp.	0.13	0.01	0.04	0.02	0.28
Terebra spp.	0.008	0.0007	0.002	0.001	0.02
TOTAL GASTROPODA	29.12	2.43	1.64	5.29	(63.66)
BIVALVIA					
Isognomon perna	0.004	0.0003	0.001	0.007	0.01
Spondylus sp.	0.13	0.01	0.01	0.02	0.28
Cardiidae spp.	1.72	0.14	0.13	0.31	3.76
Tridacna maxima	0.38	0.03	0.06	0.07	0.83
Tellina spp.	1.53	0.13	0.08	0.28	3.34
Asaphis violascens	1.19	0.10	0.10	0.22	2.60
Gafrarium pectinatum	9.68	0.81	1.32	1.76	21.16
Periglypta puerpera	0.30	0.02	0.02	0.05	0.66
Veneridae spp.	1.00	0.08	0.07	0.18	2.19
TOTAL BIVALVIA	15.93	1.36	1.39	2.90	(34.83)
Miscellaneous Taxa	0.69	0.06	0.06	0.13	1.51
TOTAL MOLLUSCA	47.75	3.85	2.82	8.32	100.00

TABLE 43

MOLLUSCAN FAUNA FROM SITE NT-93

TAXON	TOTAL WEIGHT (kg)	WT/m² (kg)		CI/m³	% (of total shell)
		$\bar{x}$	s.d.		
GASTROPODA					
Trochus niloticus	—	—	—	—	—
Trochus maculatus	1.45	0.14	0.26	0.24	5.07
Turbo setosus	8.91	0.89	0.86	1.48	31.18
T. setosus operculae	—	—	—	—	—
Nerita polita	0.21	0.02	0.02	0.03	0.73
Nerita plicata	—	—	—	—	—
Planaxis sulcatus	0.22	0.02	0.03	0.04	0.77
Rhinoclavis asper	0.46	0.05	0.05	0.08	1.61
Cerithium nodulosum	0.67	0.07	0.13	0.11	2.34
Strombus mutabilis	5.64	0.56	0.62	0.94	19.73
Cypraea tigris	0.75	0.07	0.09	0.12	2.62
Cypraea spp.	0.73	0.07	0.07	0.12	2.55
Natica sp.	0.16	0.02	0.01	0.03	0.56
Polinices simiae	0.11	0.01	0.01	0.02	0.38
Cymatium spp.	—	—	—	—	—
Thais armigera	0.30	0.03	0.07	0.05	1.05
Drupa morum	—	—	—	—	—
Mitra spp.	—	—	—	—	—
Conus spp.	0.46	0.05	0.05	0.08	1.61
Terebra spp.	—	—	—	—	—
Bulla sp.	—	—	—	—	—
TOTAL GASTROPODA	20.07	2.00	1.71	3.35	(70.22)
BIVALVIA					
Pinctada sp.	—	—	—	—	—
Isognomon perna	0.02	0.002	0.004	0.003	0.07
Spondylus sp.	0.03	0.003	0.01	0.005	0.10
Chama iostoma	0.01	0.001	0.003	0.002	0.03
Fragum/Laevicardium	0.39	0.04	0.04	0.06	1.36
Tridacna maxima	0.54	0.05	0.13	0.09	1.89
Tellina spp.	0.43	0.04	0.04	0.07	1.50
Asaphis violascens	0.18	0.02	0.02	0.03	0.63
Gafrarium pectinatum	1.68	0.27	0.08	0.28	5.88
Periglypta puerpera	0.28	0.03	0.07	0.05	0.98
Veneridae spp.	1.05	0.10	0.09	0.17	3.67
TOTAL BIVALVIA	4.31	0.46	0.24	0.77	(16.13)
Miscellaneous Taxa	3.90	0.39	0.41	0.65	13.65
TOTAL MOLLUSCA	28.58	2.85	2.18	4.76	100.00

TABLE 44

MOLLUSCAN FAUNA FROM ACERAMIC UNITS, SITE NT-163

TAXON	TOTAL WEIGHT	WT/m² (kg)		CI/m³	% (of total shell)
		$\bar{x}$	s.d.		
GASTROPODA					
Trochus maculatus	0.08	0.02	0.04	0.08	3.20
Turbo setosus	0.39	0.08	0.13	0.39	15.60
T. setosus operculae	0.04	0.008	0.02	0.04	1.60
Nerita polita	0.02	0.004	0.009	0.02	0.80
Planaxis sulcatus	0.02	0.004	0.009	0.02	0.80
Rhinoclavis asper	0.50	0.10	0.06	0.50	20.00
Strombus mutabilis	0.28	0.06	0.06	0.28	11.20
Cypraea tigris	0.18	0.04	0.08	0.18	7.20
Cypraea spp.	0.004	0.0008	0.002	0.004	0.16
Cymatium spp.	0.04	0.007	0.02	0.04	1.60
Drupa morum	0.01	0.002	0.003	0.01	0.40
TOTAL GASTROPODS	1.56	0.31	0.26	1.56	(62.40)
BIVALVIA					
Tridacna maxima	0.06	0.01	0.03	0.06	2.40
Tellina spp.	0.12	0.02	0.03	0.12	4.80
Cardiidae	0.10	0.02	0.02	0.10	4.00
Asaphis violascens	0.12	0.02	0.03	0.12	4.80
Gafrarium pectinatum	0.32	0.06	0.04	0.32	12.80
Veneridae	0.22	0.04	0.08	0.22	8.80
TOTAL BIVALVIA	0.94	0.19	0.16	0.94	(37.60)
TOTAL SHELL	2.50	0.50	0.31	2.50	100.00

more than a supplementary source of protein and did not constitute a dominant component of the overall diet. This conclusion is consistent with that of Meehan (1982:171-72) on the "supportive role" of shellfish in coastal economies. As Meehan (1982:161) observed for the Anbarra of Australia, and as we did for the contemporary Niuans, shellfish are often valued more for the variety they bring to a diet than for their actual caloric contribution, especially in Polynesia where the bulk of the daily caloric intake is provided by relatively bland starch staples.

TERRESTRIAL GASTROPODS

Aside from the larger marine molluscs deposited in the Niuatoputapu sites as food remains, the ceramic zone sites also contain the diminutive shells of various taxa of non-marine gastropods, or land snails. Such terrestrial gastropods from Pacific archaeological sites have begun to attract some notice from prehistorians, both as indicators of former environmental conditions, and because some synanthropic taxa were evidently transported from island to island by early Oceanic peoples (adherring to plants or buried in soil) (Christensen and Kirch 1981, 1986; Kirch and Christensen, in press; Hunt 1980; Kirch and Yen 1982:308-309). Samples of cultural deposit from sites NT-90 and -93, when processed in the laboratory for grain-size analysis, also yielded small numbers of sub-fossil terrestrial gastropods, of the following taxa: *Pleuropoma* sp. (Helicinidae; Site NT-93 only); *Assiminea* sp. and *Omphalotropis* sp. (Assimineidae); *Lamellidea* cf.

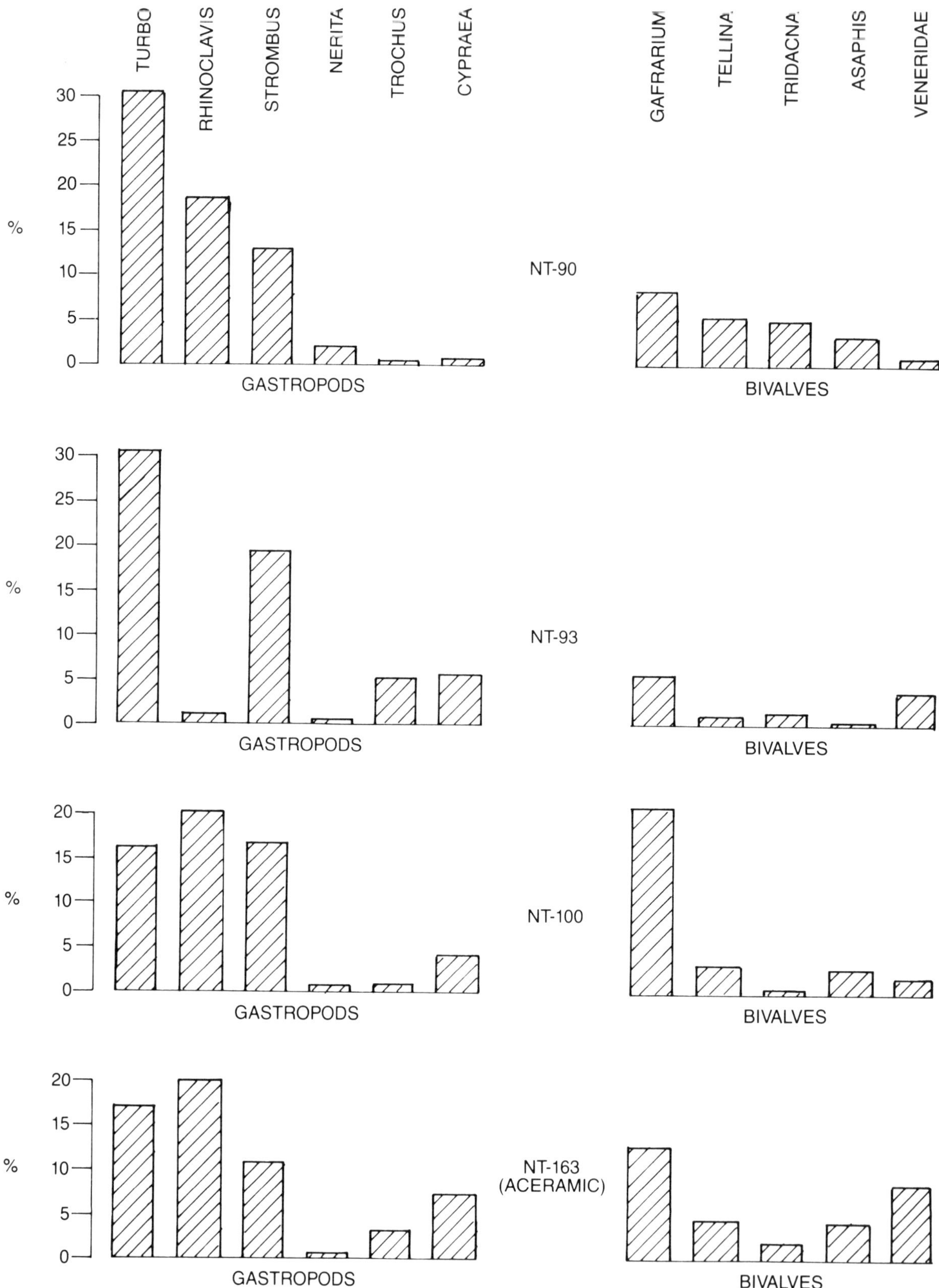

Figure 132. Relative frequencies of dominant gastropod and bivalve molluscs at Niuatoputapu Sites NT-90, -93, -100, and -163.

TABLE 45

MOLLUSCAN CONCENTRATION INDICES FOR PRINCIPAL SITES (kg/m^3)

SITE	GASTROPODS	BIVALVES	TOTAL SHELL
NT–90	13.91	5.38	19.74
NT–93	3.35	0.77	4.76
NT–100	5.29	2.90	8.32
NT–163*	1.56	0.94	2.50

* Aceramic excavation units only

pusilla (Achatinellidae); *Gastrocopta pediculus* (Pupillidae); *Discocharopa aperta*, and *Sinployea* sp. (Charopidae): and *Lamellaxis gracilis* (Subulinidae).

Of particular significance is the presence of *Lamellidea pusilla, Gastrocopta pediculus,* and *Lamellaxis gracilis,* as these three species have now been confirmed as occuring in early archaeological contexts throughout the southwestern Pacific, and in the case of *Lamellaxis gracilis,* extending even into Eastern Polynesia (Society Islands and Hawaii). *Discocharopa aperta* is also widespread, although it has not been identified as a specifically human-transported species. The presence of these synanthropic snails in ceramic period sites in Niuatoputapu further strengthens the arguments made elsewhere by Christensen and Kirch (1981, 1986; Kirch and Christensen, in press) and by Hunt (1980), that these species reflect the inter-island transfer of plants and adhering soil, both during and after the human colonization of islands.

CHANGING SUBSISTENCE PATTERNS

The faunal assemblages from Niuatoputapu provide a broad picture of the "protein component" of the prehistoric diet, and of its changes over time. Missing from this portrait, of course, is the contribution of horticulture, which—as today—is presumed to have been the mainstay of subsistence. Based on evidence presented above, the main sources of protein in the islanders' diet have always been fish, shellfish, marine turtle, the domestic trio of pig, dog, and fowl, and the occasional wild bird and fruit bat. The contribution made by each of these categories has not, however, remained constant. This has been demonstrated for the molluscs, with reductions in the quantity of shellfish deposited from early to later sites in the prehistoric sequence. Changing patterns among the vertebrate fauna are also indicated (table 46). The concentration indices for particular taxa in several key sites used as a basis for comparison suggest several major trends. First, there is a reduction in the quantities of fish bone deposited from early to later sites, which presumably reflects a concomitant reduction in the role of fish in subsistence. The NT-90 deposits show higher CI values for fish than those of any other locality, followed by the slightly later NT-100 deposits. As with shellfish, this reduction is an indication of both the changing marine environment of the island (the reduction in local marine habitat occasioned by tectonic uplift) and the effects of continued human predation. The same general pattern is reflected in the concentration indices of marine turtle, as remarked upon earlier, with the NT-90 deposits exhibiting the highest densities. Turtle populations are particularly sensitive to the effects of predation, and the rapid reduction in their exploitation probably resulted from the initial decimation of the local breeding population. An identical pattern has been demonstrated in the Tikopian faunal record (Kirch and Yen 1982).

Other long-term trends are suggested for the wild birds and for the domestic animals. The only site with any significant quantities of wild birds is NT-90, where modest quantities of *Sula* and larid bones were recovered. These taxa probably had breeding populations on Niuatoputapu prior to human colonization, providing easy-to-exploit resources for the first human propagule. Initial predation quickly led to a decimation and perhaps even extirpation of the species, a pattern witnessed on other Pacific Islands (Kirch and Yen 1982; Olson and James 1984; Cassels 1984). The figures for the domestic animals, however, display a rather different trajectory. Most interesting is the pig which, while never represented in large numbers, does significantly increase over time. In the ceramic zone deposits, pig is never present in a CI of more than 0.56 bone/m^3, while in the two aceramic sites it has CI values of 1.0 and 2.38. The capacity of the local production system to support pig herds likely increased over time as the island's agricultural support base was developed and expanded. On the other hand, the dog and fowl do not display any obvious trends, and appear always to have been relatively minor or supplementary components in subsistence.

In this discussion, I have concentrated upon temporal trends for individual faunal groups, without any assessment of the *relative* contribution of particular groups or taxa to one another. Given the problems and

TABLE 46

CONCENTRATION INDICES (NISP/m^3) OF VERTEBRATE FAUNA FOR PRINCIPAL SITES

CATEGORY	NT–90 RANDOM SAMPLE	NT–90 GENERAL SAMPLE	NT–100	NT–93	NT–125	NT–163 ACERAMIC COMPONENT
Pig	0.33	0.08	0.56	0.23	2.38	1.00
Dog	0.00	0.16	0.00	0.00	0.38	0.00
Fowl[a]	1.67	0.88	1.11	0.54	0.88	0.00
Sula	0.00	0.16	0.00	0.00	0.00	0.00
Larids[b]	1.00	0.36	0.00	0.00	0.00	0.00
Turtle	2.00	2.84	1.11	0.46	0.38	0.00
Fish	26.33	11.84	17.00	3.69	6.13	9.00

[a] Includes "medium bird" category
[b] Includes "small bird" category

potential error sources associated with quantitative zooarchaeology (Grayson 1984), one hestitates to venture further. Yet it may be instructive (as an exercise for which the lack of precision is admitted) to estimate the relative contribution of each of the main faunal categories to the prehistoric Niuan diet. This exercise is here restricted solely to the faunal assemblage from the random sample units at Site NT-90. In order to assess the relative importance of taxa, minimum numbers of individuals must be calculated—not an easy task given the highly fragmentary nature of much of this material. The best available estimates are shown in table 47. If these estimates are multipled by an assumed "average" flesh weight per individual, a crude approximation of the total edible meat weight per taxon is derived. Given the potential for error in such estimates, their only value is in the implication that fish were the most significant items in the subsistence base, followed by pigs and turtle in an intermediate range, and finally by the relatively small contribution of domestic fowl and wild birds. For the later sites, of course, these ratios would be somewhat different, with the total contribution of fish and turtles declining, and that of pigs rising.

NIUATOPUTAPU SUBSISTENCE IN REGIONAL PERSPECTIVE

The evidence from Western Polynesia, Fiji, and the Polynesian Outliers for reconstructing prehistoric subsistence patterns is rather poor and uneven; many of the excavated sites did not contain significant quantities of faunal materials (often due to poor preservation in acidic inland soils), or else analyses were incomplete or superficial. Since the Western Polynesian-Fijian region is that in which Ancestral Polynesian adaptive strategies developed (Kirch 1984a), more attention needs to be paid to acquiring detailed subsistence data in future archaeological studies.

Samoa. Despite the extensive archaeological work of the Auckland expedition in Western Samoa (Green and Davidson 1969a, 1974), only one site yielded significant quantities of faunal material. This was the Lotofaga coastal midden, excavated and analyzed by Davidson (1969b), with a basal ^{14}C age of 735 ± 85 B.P., making the site roughly contemporaneous with NT-125 and the aceramic portions of NT-163 on Niuatoputapu. Unfortunately, while substantial effort was expended in determining the "content" of the midden in terms of basic categories such as stone, coral, shell, bone, and charcoal, the identifications of bone and molluscs were incomplete and largely nonquantitative. Davidson notes the presence of pig (said to predominate among the bone material), dog, rat, and bird. Small numbers of fish bone were present, but were not identified to specific taxa. The only shell analyzed was that from Level 4b of Excavation Unit C (volume not specified), which totalled 1.99 kg in weight. This sample was dominated by *Turbo* spp., *Trochus*, and *Tridacna;* also present among the bivalves were *Periglypta, Asaphis,* and *Tellina.*

More detailed faunal analyses in Samoa were conducted by Janetski (1976, 1980) on materials from three sites excavated by Jennings et al. (1976) and Jennings and Holmer (1980): Jane's Camp on Upolu, and Potusa and Falemoa on Manono Islet. All of these sites are associated with Polynesian Plain Ware, and in the case of Jane's Camp date as early as 2550 ± 50 B.P. They are roughly comparable in age to NT-100 and -93 on Niuatoputapu. Jane's Camp yielded bone of porcupine fish (Diodontidae), parrotfish (Scaridae), and other unidentified fish taxa, *Gallus gallus,* and turtle. Molluscs dominated the faunal assemblage, with the common gastropods being *Cypraea, Trochus, Turbo,* and *Cerithium;* common bivalves included *Gafrarium* and *Quidnipagus (Tellina).* Little was noted concerning the Potusa site, except that it yielded fish and 37 fragments of pig bone. For Falemoa, however, Janetski provided useful quantitative data on both the bone and the shellfish. In the earliest stratum, molluscs were present in a density (CI) of 21.71 kg/m^3, but declined in higher stratigraphic layers to 11.28 and 2.99 CI values. The bone showed a similar pattern, with an initial CI value of 209.7 g/m^3, declining to 76.04 and 19.38. For this site, Janetski noted the presence of parrotfish, crab, turtle, fruit bat *(Pteropus* sp.), and bird. Dominating the molluscs were *Cypraea, Trochus, Nerita,* and *Strombus.*

The decline in concentrations of both molluscs and bone at Falemoa is significant in its parallels with Niuatoputapu. Janetski (1980:118-22) interprets this change in terms of "...a general decrease in dependency on reef collecting through time," which he feels might be "...equated with the increased reliance on horticulture." He cautions, however, that "depletion of supply through the pressure of continuous exploitation is equally likely to account for the decrease noted."

Tongatapu. Poulsen (1968:89) briefly summarizes the faunal content of his Tongatapu excavations. He characterizes all sites as "heavily concentrated shell middens," with restricted quantities of bone. Among the latter were chicken, wild birds, pig, dog, rat, and turtle. Poulsen remarks that "both early and late levels hold bones of domesticated animals, so the early settlers seem to have been well equipped in this respect."

Although he presented little substantive data, Groube (1971:310-12) hypothesized that toward the close of the first millennium B.C., Tongan economy underwent a radical change, from a "restricted maritime/lagoonal economy," of "Oceanic 'strandloopers'" to a horticultural economy following the introduction of crop plants and of the domestic pig. The hypothesis engendered some debate and inspired further analyses of Lapita faunal remains and settlement patterns (e.g., Kirch 1978b, 1979; Green 1978; Best 1984). In my view, the numerous finds of pig bone in early Lapita contexts, as well as artifacts such as food peelers (including those from Niuatoputapu), permit the

TABLE 47

ORDER-OF-MAGNITUDE ESTIMATES OF RELATIVE SIGNIFICANCE OF VERTEBRATE FAUNA FOR SITE NT-90 (RANDOM-SAMPLE UNITS)

CATEGORY	ESTIMATED MNI	FLESH WEIGHT PER INDIVIDUAL (kg)	ESTIMATE OF TOTAL EDIBLE WEIGHT (kg)
Fish	40+	4	160+
Turtle	2	30	60
Pig	1	60	60
Fowl	4	0.75	3.0
Larids	2	0.5	1.0

falsification of Groube's "strandlooper" hypothesis. It remains to be clarified whether the pattern of shell midden dumping along the inner Tongatapu lagoon shore also radically changed at the end of the first millennium B.C., as Groube claimed.

Fiji. Despite the size and importance of the Fijian archipelago, few sites have been excavated, and fewer still have had adequate faunal analyses. Best (1981) and Kay (1984) report on the study of the early Lapita site on Naigani Island, which yielded small quantities of fish bone, turtle, bird, fruit bat *(Pteropus)*, rat, and dog. Sixty percent of the fishbone is of Lethrinidae, while the bird includes an extinct species of megapode. Among the shellfish, *Trochus niloticus* is dominant, and *Gafrarium* and *Asaphis* are included among the bivalves.

Hunt (1980) includes a study of the faunal remains in his report on the Yanuca Rockshelter on Viti Levu, although the bulk of the shell midden excavated by the Birks could not be located for analysis. The vertebrate remains associated with Lapita pottery (1980, table 6.6) included fish *(Diodon,* scarids, and serranids), turtle, wild birds, *Pteropus,* dog, rat, pig, and fowl *(Gallus gallus).* A large range of gastropods and bivalves are listed by species but not quantified, and include virtually all of those present in the Niuatoputapu sites. Hunt remarks on the "exploitation of the diverse maritime and estuarine microenvironments adjacent to the rockshelter" (1980:183). Elsewhere, Hunt (1981) comments further on the significance of the pig, dog, and fowl, along with terrestrial molluscs of synanthropic association (cf. Christensen and Kirch 1981), as evidence for a horticultural subsistence base in the Lapita period of Fiji.

The most complete faunal analyses from Fiji are those of Gifford (1951) for materials excavated at his Sites 17 and 26 on Viti Levu. As Green (1963) suggests, these sites span the post-Lapita, Navatu and Vunda Phases of the Fijian sequence. Bone was plentiful in both sites (3.1 kg fish bone, 4.95 kg other bone), and the fish bone was studied in detail by Fowler (1955). More than 23 genera were identified, primarily inshore reef taxa. Of particular note in regard to Niuatoputapu are the genera *Balistes, Coris, Diodon, Lethrinus, Lutjanus, Monotaxis, Mugil, Scarus,* and *Serranus.* Turtle bones were frequent in both sites. Also represented were pig, dog, fowl, the Pacific rat *(Rattus exulans),* and fruit bat. The molluscan remains were not quantified, although Gifford notes that they were plentiful, and he provides an exhaustive list of taxa which includes virtually all of those in the Niuatoputapu middens.

Summary. This brief regional comparison highlights several points. First, the association of domestic animals with Lapita ceramics is undisputed—pig, dog, and fowl were a part of the Lapita subsistence base. A further implication is that Lapita economy was also horticultural, which can be argued on the basis of other evidence as well (Kirch 1984a; 1987). At the same time, the Lapita colonists took full advantage of the rich marine resources in their new-found island homes. As the first exploiters of "pristine" ecosystems, these colonists harvested high biomass levels of molluscs, fish, turtle, and other marine animals on reefs and in lagoons. Such resources were not restricted to the marine environment; local populations of seabirds, megapodes, pigeons, and other avifauna were also exploited, leading to rapid decimation or extirpation. The initial abundance of these wild food resources presumably assisted in the maintenance of small, founding human populations prior to the establishment of stable agricultural systems.

Another pattern, perhaps of widespread distribution but most notable at present in the data from Niuatoputapu and the Falemoa site in Samoa, is the gradual decrease over time in the contribution of marine resources to the subsistence base. While in part this reflects the expansion of local agricultural systems, it probably also resulted from continuous predation pressure on reefs and lagoons, and perhaps from environmental change including degradation of reef ecosystems through runoff and siltation. Such a pattern has also been demonstrated for Tikopia over a three-thousand-year sequence (Kirch and Yen 1982).

To date, only the fish bones from Niuatoputapu and Gifford's sites have been adequately identified. In these cases the dominance of inshore fishing, a pattern which persists from initial Lapita settlement through to the ethnographic period, is unmistakable. This is not to deny the practice of offshore trolling for larger and culturally prized game fish such as tuna, but it was the more abundant inshore reef fish which were the main contributors of protein to local diets.

The lack of quantitative data on molluscs from Western Polynesian and Fijian sites thwarts attempts at comparison. The available qualitative data suggest that a similar range of taxa was being exploited in most cases, with a few dominant taxa (such as *Turbo, Trochus, Strombus, Asaphis,* and *Gafrarium)* recurring in the faunal lists.

As further archaeological investigations are undertaken in the region, more attention needs to be paid to detailed, quantified faunal evidence which may advance our understanding of prehistoric subsistence patterns. The full identification of vertebrate materials, especially fish and birds, and the quantification of molluscs (including data on concentration indices) are especially important.

CHAPTER SEVEN

SYNTHESIS

THE NIUATOPUTAPU RESEARCH was oriented around five main objectives: (1) to provide an outline of the island's prehistoric cultural sequence; (2) to add to our understanding of Ancestral Polynesian technology, economy, and social organization, as reflected on Niuatoputapu[1]; (3) to obtain archaeological information on the ethnohistorically-attested late Tongan expansion throughout Western Polynesia; (4) to trace the local sequence of subsistence strategies and economic change on the island; and (5) to assess the role of environmental dynamics in the Niuatoputapu cultural sequence. Preceding chapters have outlined in detail the ethnographic, geomorphological, and archaeological evidence gathered in the course of our expedition and subsequent analyses. The task of synthesizing this evidence in the broader regional context of Western Polynesian prehistory begins with the construction of a local phase sequence for Niuatoputapu, which is then compared and contrasted with what is currently known of prehistoric sequences in Fiji, Tongatapu, Samoa, and Futuna-'Uvea. From this foundation, I then consider the internal evidence for environmental dynamics and for the local evolution of the Niuatoputapu production system over three millennia. The role of Niuatoputapu in the changing configurations of regional exchange systems over three millennia is also reviewed. The synthesis concludes with a discussion of the protohistoric Tongan expansion in Western Polynesia and its dramatic effect on the socio-political system of Niuatoputapu.

THE NIUATOPUTAPU SEQUENCE

A casualty of the paradigm shift between the late 1960s and the late 1970s from "culture history" to "processual archaeology" (Dunnell 1986) was the periodization or phase sequence model of culture change which had formerly dominated the discipline. Critics of such periodization frameworks (e.g., Groube 1967; Plog 1973) quite rightly pointed to the problems of reducing continuous change and variation to a series of normalized or essentialist "time capsules," and to an overemphasis on homologous aspects of culture change (i.e., the invocation of migration, diffusion, and cultural replacement to explain changes in the archaeological record). Nonetheless, the "new archaeology" has in turn failed to produce a compelling alternative which can effectively replace the phase sequence as a framework for summarizing long spans of prehistoric cultural change (several of the most recent syntheses of regional North American prehistory still rely solidly on the phase sequence model, e.g., Cordell 1984; Moratto 1984). My own view is that phase sequences are essential tools in understanding local and regional prehistory, especially in Oceania where the cultural sequences for individual islands must be carefully constructed on internal

1. The contribution of the Niuatoputapu project to objective 2 was dealt with extensively in Kirch (1984a) and hence is not further considered here.

archaeological evidence before regional synthesis is possible (cf. Kirch 1985; Davidson 1984). At the same time, the inherent limitations of periodization schemes (the need for arbitrary temporal divisions; the unavoidable tendency toward 'normalization' of variability) must be fully recognized, and construction of such schemes can constitute only one step toward the ultimate goal of understanding prehistoric change. Phase sequences provide a convenient framework for summarizing a lengthy span of time, and for making inter-island comparisons. They cannot in themselves provide a satisfactory model of the *dynamics* of cultural change.

With the above caveats in mind, a local prehistoric sequence for Niuatoputapu can be constructed, from the data presented in this monograph, as a heuristic device for comparing prehistoric change on Niuatoputapu with the sequences for other Western Polynesian islands. In constructing this sequence, the evidence of portable artifacts, settlement patterns, and faunal remains has all been taken into consideration. The portable artifacts, which are especially critical in deciding where to "cut" the sequence into its component phases, are diagrammatically summarized in figure 133. The periods indicated along the top of the chart (Early Eastern Lapita, Late Eastern Lapita, Polynesian Plain Ware, Aceramic) are those of Green's ceramic chronology for Western Polynesia (1974b). Solid bars indicate the known temporal distribution of particular artifact classes, while dashed lines represent probable but less certain temporal distributions. Ideally, we should

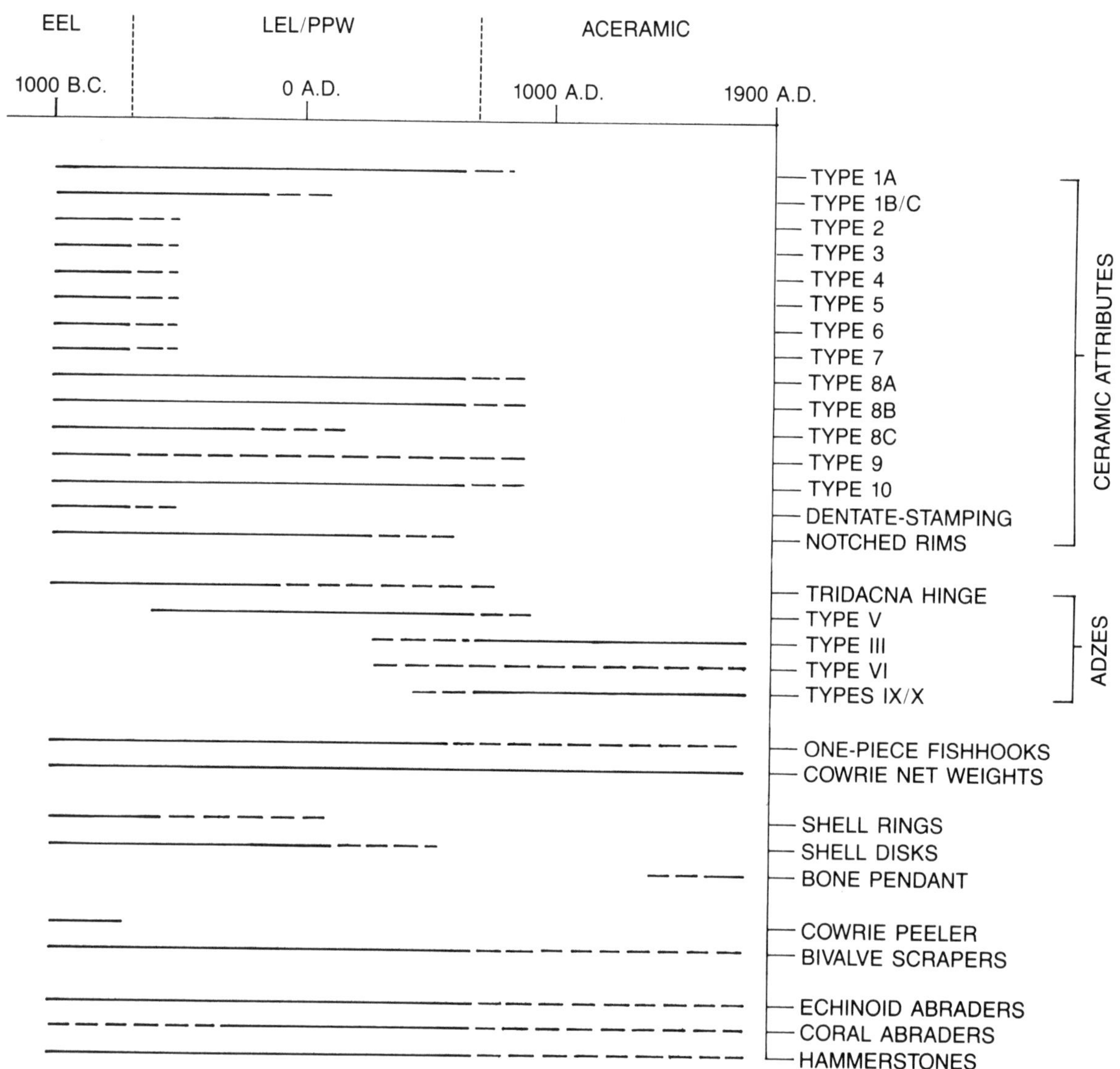

Figure 133. Temporal distribution of key artifact classes throughout the Niuatoputapu cultural sequence.

represent the temporal distribution of each artifact class not in nominal terms as in figure 133, but as continuous frequency distributions. Unfortunately, the nature of the Niuatoputapu sites themselves, lacking deep stratification, as well as the small sample sizes, preclude such an analysis.

In constructing this local phase sequence for Niuatoputapu, I follow my own precedent of using the names of key site localities to designate each phase (cf. the Halawa Valley and Tikopia sequences, Kirch 1975b, Kirch and Yen 1982). This practice not only underscores the *local* nature of the sequence, but avoids the charged theoretical connotations of such phase labels as "developmental," "expansion," or "classic." The latter, in my view, are appropriate only at a higher level of regional synthesis (e.g., the Hawaiian archipelago, Kirch 1985).

The Lolokoka Phase (1400/1200—500 B.C.)

Named after the key site locality that provides the evidence for initial human occupation of Niuatoputapu, the Lolokoka Phase spans at least five centuries. *Precise* beginning and end dates for this phase cannot, however, be fixed given the nature of the ^{14}C corpus. While Niuatoputapu was certainly settled by the close of the second millennium B.C., the two shell dates from NT-90 suggest initial colonization as early as 1400-1200 B.C. Only additional excavation and radiometric dating may tighten this chronology, and even then the absence of deep stratification may thwart further attempts at chronological refinement.

At the close of the second millennium B.C., the physiography of Niuatoputapu differed radically from its modern configuration. The island had a land area of only 4.9 km^2 (as opposed to its modern area of 15.2 km^2), defined by the seaward edge of a narrow beach terrace lying immediately below the Pleistocene Terrace and central volcanic ridge. South, east, and north of this much smaller island were extensive reefs and tidally-exposed sand flats that provided a range of microenvironments suitable for exploitation by a variety of fishing and shellfishing techniques (especially netting and spearing). We may make two further assumptions about the local environment at the time of initial colonization: first, the island itself was forested in a typical southwest Pacific rainforest association; and second, populations of marine invertebrates, fishes, turtles, and nesting seabirds were at maximal equilibrium levels, not having been subject to any form of intensive predation. Thus, the terrestrial environment was rich in exploitable timber and other forest resources, but correspondingly poor in edible plants (though providing fertile terrain for shifting cultivation), while the marine environment offered extremely high biomass levels of edible invertebrates and vertebrates.

It was into this small pristine high-island ecosystem that a propagule of Lapita colonists intruded, at the close of the second millennium, to establish a permanent human population. Based on our sampling of the ceramic zone, permanent habitation during the Lolokoka Phase was limited to the leeward (western) beach terrace, and was especially concentrated in the area of Lolokoka. Small numbers of calcareous-sand tempered sherds from NT-163, NT-91 and NT-100 do suggest low-density occupation extending south and north of Lolokoka. This focus on what is presently called the Vaipoa area of Niuatoputapu is not surprising, since occupants of this area would have been centrally situated with regard to all primary microenvironmental zones (leeward and windward reef habitats and arable slopes). The early Lapita settlement structure is not well understood, though it likely consisted of individual dwellings (perhaps with separate cookhouses) dispersed in a linear fashion, parallel to the shoreline. The only structural features exposed at Lolokoka are postmolds, trash pits, and earth ovens, and while these are consistent with what is known of other early Lapita sites (Green 1979), the sample is not large enough to provide further details of architecture or community patterning.

The first colonists on Niuatoputapu came from a community which manufactured Lapita-style ceramics, and the tradition of pottery production was continued on Niuatoputapu, using local clays and calcareous beach sand as temper. At least ten major vessel forms were in use, with only several of these carrying elaborate dentate-stamped decoration. Other vessel forms, especially bowls and large jars, were plain; these forms numerically dominated the ceramic assemblage.

In other aspects of material culture, the Lolokoka Phase resembles other early Lapita assemblages from Tonga and Fiji. Adzes were predominantly made from the hinge portion of large *Tridacna* clams, although plano-convex sectioned stone adzes may also have been present. Fishing gear is represented by one-piece angling hooks of *Turbo* shell and by cowrie-shell net weights. Manufacturing tools include echinoid-spine abraders, coral abraders, and hammerstones. Food processing activities are reflected in a *Cypraea*- shell vegetable peeler (a type known from other Lapita sites) and in scrapers of bivalve shell. Of particular note is the variety of shell objects that would ordinarily be classed as "ornaments:" *Tridacna* shell rings, *Conus* shell rings and disks, various beads, and pendants. For reasons elaborated below, these probably functioned as exchange valuables in a long-distance exchange network linking several Lapita communities in the Fiji-Western Polynesian region.

The economic system of the early Lolokoka Phase colonists relied on a broad-spectrum subsistence strategy typical of early Austronesians throughout the southwest Pacific. This included intensive exploitation of rich marine resources (fish, turtle, molluscs, and other invertebrates) through gathering, angling, spearing, netting, poisoning, and other techniques, as well as hunting of the more limited terrestrial resources such as birds and fruit bats. Equally important was the cultivation of a range of root and tree crops and the husbandry of pigs, dogs, and fowl. While domestic animals are evidenced by faunal remains, the evidence for cultivation is admittedly more slender, consisting primarily of starchy-food preparation equipment such as peelers and scrapers and of anthropophilic terrestrial gastropods known to be readily transported with planting stocks. Were this evidence unique to Niuatoputapu, the case for agricultural production might be more tenuous. Given, however, that the Lolokoka data are consistent with similar archaeological evidence from a wide range of Lapita sites, as well as with linguistic data indicative of a well developed Proto-Oceanic horticultural complex (French-Wright 1983), the inference of root and tree crop horticulture for the Lolokoka Phase seems entirely reasonable.

The Lolokoka Phase population of Niuatoputapu continued to maintain external contacts with other Lapita communities, as evidenced by the presence of exotic chert flakes at NT-90 and -91 and by the presence of Niua-Tafahi obsidian at other Lapita sites. The probable nature of these external relations is explored in greater detail below.

Recalling the caveats mentioned earlier, we must avoid the facile notion that the Lolokoka Phase represents a "static" period during which there was no significant cultural change. Unfortunately, in the absence of well-stratified deposits, such change as must have occurred is not archaeologically visible— certainly not in fine-grained detail. Yet it is probable that many aspects of early Niuatoputapu culture changed significantly during the half-millennium represented by the Lolokoka Phase: the ceramic complex was undergoing the first stages of simplification in vessel form and design system complexity; experimentation probably occurred with local isotropic stone suitable for adz production; and the role of shell valuables in the sociopolitical system may have decreased significantly. Then too, it is only reasonable to suppose that there was some measure of population increase and settlement expansion, that the island's original forest vegetation was modified through clearing and cultivation to a mosaic incorporating human introductions, and that the marine biota suffered significant population reductions due to regular exploitation by humans. Unfortunately, many of these changes are only dimly, if at all, reflected in the archaeological record.

The Pome'e Phase (500 B.C.— A.D. 800)

The Pome'e Phase, named for one of several localities containing plainware ceramics, spans thirteen centuries, and corresponds to the Late Eastern Lapita and Polynesian Plain Ware ceramic periods of Green (1974b,c). Several changes occurred during the course of this lengthy phase, but the nature of the Niuatoputapu sites does not permit finer temporal divisions.

The Pome'e Phase settlement pattern was a continuation of that established in the Lolokoka Phase, with a narrow zone of habitations (about 50 m wide) situated on the beach terrace. Dumping of shellfish and other midden was concentrated on both seaward and landward edges of this habitation zone. The settlement zone gradually expanded during the course of the Pome'e Phase such that it eventually encircled the island, forming the continuous ceramic zone lying on the old beach flat seaward of the Pleistocene Terrace. This expansion of settlement also signaled an increasing human population. Based on the density of occupation materials in the ceramic zone, however, this population remained most concentrated along the leeward side of the island. This leeward orientation may reflect the increased impoverishment of the windward reef flats and lagoons as tectonic uplift gradually exposed the eastern and southern reefs, greatly reducing their productivity.

The ceramic complex of the early Pome'e Phase was a much simplified reflection of Lolokoka Phase ceramics. All of the elaborately decorated dentate-stamped vessel forms had been dropped from the ceramic inventory, and decoration was confined to simple notching of rims. Even rim notching was eliminated by the later Pome'e Phase, leaving a simple ceramic complex of plainware bowls and large jars. Calcareous sand was no longer used as temper.

Other major changes occurred in the adz kit, reflecting innovations in stone adz technology throughout the Western Polynesian region (Green 1974a,b). The use of *Tridacna* clam shell for adzes was discontinued early in the Pome'e Phase, and was replaced by the Oceanic basalt/andesite suite of volcanic rocks. Throughout most of the Pome'e Phase, the dominant form of stone adz was Type V of Green and Davidson (1969b), with a distinctive plano-convex cross-section. Toward the end of the Pome'e Phase, Type V declined and was replaced by several new forms of quadrangular and triangular sectioned adzes (Types III, VI, and IX/X).

Other aspects of material culture exhibit continuity from the Lolokoka Phase. One-piece fishhooks of *Turbo* shell and net weights of cowrie-shell suggest stability in fishing gear. Bivalve scrapers, echinoid-spine abraders, coral abraders, and hammerstones are also represented in the Pome'e Phase without significant changes in form.

An important change from the Lolokoka to the Pome'e Phase is the disappearance of exotic chert flakes from the flaked stone inventory. Along with the early discontinuation of shell rings, disks, and other probable exchange valuables, this suggests a major decline in long-distance exchange links with other Western Polynesian communities. The significance of this change will be explored further below.

The Pome'e Phase subsistence economy continued the mix of terrestrial production (horticulture and animal husbandry) and marine exploitation established by the island's first colonists. In this phase we have the first clear evidence for the widespread Polynesian practice of pit ensilage and fermentation of starch pastes. A quantitative shift is also clear in the reduced contribution of marine resources. Fish, turtle, and molluscs, while well represented in Pome'e Phase middens, are at density levels substantially below those of the Lolokoka Phase. Rather than any change in fishing or shellfishing strategies, this trend most likely reflects declining reef/lagoon biomass as a result of: (1) continual human predation pressure on marine species populations; and (2) reductions in the area of exploitable marine biotopes due to tectonic uplift.

The Niutoua Phase (A.D. 800—1550)

Davidson (1979) has referred to the post-ceramic portion of the Tongan and Samoan sequences as the "dark ages" because the archaeological record for this period is so thinly represented. Unfortunately, the situation in Niuatoputapu does not offer much of an improvement. The only stratified site which produced material dating to this phase is Niutoua (NT-125), for which the phase has been named. (The NT-163 transect probably also includes deposits of Niutoua Phase age, although this has not been checked with radiocarbon dating.) Unfortunately, NT-125 produced few cultural materials.

By the close of the first millennium A.D., the Niuatoputapu landscape had changed substantially from its configuration at the time of initial human settlement. Tectonic uplift had resulted in progradation of the leeward shoreline, and in the emergence of the broad reef/lagoon flats in the eastern and southern portions of the island. Consequently, leeward settlement shifted seaward off the old beach terrace which had been the main locus of habitation during the preceding two phases, onto the newer beach ridges closer to the shoreline. It is also likely, although we lack direct evidence for this, that the settlement pattern began to change from one of concentrated coastal habitations to a more dispersed pattern with nucleated hamlets scattered throughout the interior portions of the island. Such a shift would explain the apparent absence of extensive coastal midden deposits dating to the Niutoua Phase. Unfortunately, with ceramics no longer a part of the material culture assemblage, the detection of such putative inland hamlet sites becomes a difficult task. Certainly, the presence of scattered stone flakes and adzes over the inland parts of the island (frequently turned up in the process of clearing new shifting cultivations) suggests the former presence of inland occupation. As indicated in Chapter 3, there are also various terraces and stone wall constructions, revealed during surface survey, which probably indicate interior occupation; however, none of these were excavated or dated, and the archaeological demonstration of a shift to dispersed, inland settlement in the Niutoua Phase remains a task for future research.

Relatively little can be said of Niutoua Phase material culture. Ceramic production had ceased entirely by the beginning of this phase, and it is probable that the pottery bowls and dishes that had been dropped from the inventory of material cultured were functionally replaced by wooden equivalents (as known from contact-period ethnography). Based largely on surface finds from the interior portions of the island, basalt/andesite adzes of Types III and IX/X, and possibly Type VI, dominated the adz kit. The earlier Type V had certainly been dropped from the cultural inventory, as had adzes of *Tridacna* shell. Fishing nets are indicated by the presence of *Cypraea*-shell weights, but one-piece hooks can only be inferred from their presence earlier in the sequence and later at European contact. Similarly, it is likely that such tools as echinoid abraders, coral abraders, and hammerstones were also present, but the impoverished nature of the Niutoua Phase deposits precluded direct archaeological representation.

The Niutoua Phase subsistence economy continued the general mix of agricultural production, animal husbandry, and marine exploitation established in earlier phases. The relative contribution of marine resources including fish, turtle, and molluscs, however, had declined substantially from previous levels. This declining emphasis on marine resources reflected both the reduction in area of exploitable reef/lagoon biotopes resulting from tectonic uplift, and the continued effects of human predation pressure on marine species populations. At the same time, there is the suggestion that agricultural production had been extended and intensified. Certainly the faunal record from NT-125 and -163 indicates higher levels of pig production, and—given the close integration of pigs in Oceanic agricultural systems—this can probably be taken as a signal of agricultural intensification.

There is essentially no evidence from the Niutoua Phase of external contacts or exchange linkages with other islands. Some of the stone adzes may be of exotic origin (particularly Samoa and/or 'Uvea), and petrographic sourcing would be essential in confirming this.

The Houmafakalele Phase (A.D. 1550-1830)

The Houmafakalele Phase spans a somewhat hazy boundary between prehistory and history. Niuatoputapu received its first European visitors, Schouten and LeMaire, in A.D. 1616, but visits of foreign vessels were extremely rare events until early in the nineteenth century; even then, the island remained a backwater of western cultural contact. Nonetheless, the reports of early visitors, such as Schouten (1619), La Pérouse (1799), Wallis (Carrington 1948), and others, in conjunction with knowledge of indigenous Tongan traditions (Bott 1982; Gifford 1924; Kirch 1984a), augment the scanty archaeological evidence pertaining to this final phase of the Niuatoputapu sequence.

Fixing dates for the Houmafakalele Phase is a troublesome matter. The main distinguishing criterion for this phase is Tongan political domination, reflected archaeologically in the late prehistoric field monuments described in Chapter 3. The only monument which was directly dated, Houmafakalele III (NT-52), yielded an age determination in the seventeenth century. Schouten's account, however, along with Tongan political traditions, suggests that Tongan dominance over the indigenous Niuatoputapu chiefly lines had been achieved by at least the beginning of the seventeenth century. Thus, for the present, the beginning of the Houmafakalele Phase is set slightly earlier at A.D. 1550. Clearly, however, more extensive excavation in the large "Tongan-style" field monuments, accompanied by radiocarbon dating, will be essential for accurately determining the commencement date for Tongan political hegemony in Niuatoputapu. Deciding upon a closing date for the Houmafakalele Phase is a more arbitrary matter. I have chosen 1830 because this is the approximate date of the establishment of Wesleyan missionaries on the island (Collocott 1972:104).

In almost all respects, the cultural patterns described for the Niutoua Phase continued unchanged into the Houmafakalele Phase. Archaeologically, the Houmafakalele Phase is distinguished primarily by the apparently sudden proliferation of field monuments, including burial mounds with stone facings and large earth or sand mounds lacking stone facings. All of these structures represent distinctly Tongan styles of monument construction, and reflect the incorporation of Niuatoputapu into the expanding late prehistoric Tongan "maritime empire" (Guiart 1963; Kirch 1984a). The implications of this Tongan political hegemony are discussed in detail below.

NIUATOPUTAPU AND WESTERN POLYNESIAN PREHISTORY

The Niuatoputapu sequence may now be compared to sequences for other islands in Western Polynesia (including Fiji), with an eye to essential similarities or differences that inform as to the broad pattern of cultural change in this region. The sequences of Tongatapu, Samoa, Futuna-'Uvea, Viti Levu, and Lakeba are reviewed in chapter 1 (see fig. 4).

Of particular interest is the date of initial settlement of Niuatoputapu, and the implications for the rate of colonization of the entire Western Polynesian region. Initial archaeological results in Tonga and Samoa suggested a substantial lag in the settlement of the latter archipelago, fitting closely with linguistic data (Green 1966). This led Groube (1971) to argue that Tonga had been *the* Polynesian "homeland." Subsequently, the discovery of the Early Eastern Lapita site at Mulifanua in Samoa, and Geraghty's work on regional linguistic history (see chapter 1), indicated that the gap between the settlement of Tonga and Samoa was very slight, if indeed there was a gap at all. Rather, the hypothesis has been advanced that there was a rapid settlement of the entire Western Polynesian-Fijian region, and that linguistic and cultural differentiation occurred through the gradual breakup of dialect chains and inter-community contacts, rather than as a result of island colonization per se (Green 1981).

Table 48 lists the earliest available ^{14}C age determinations for sites containing Early Eastern Lapita ceramics in Fiji-Western Polynesia. Almost all of these ages cluster between about the twelfth and ninth centuries B.C. Clearly, there is no cline or lag evident in the initial settlement dates for the entire region. Rather, on present evidence, it appears that Fiji-Western Polynesia was settled very rapidly indeed, and that Niuatoputapu was colonized as a part of this process.

To date, much of Western Polynesian archaeological research has focused on the complex sequence of changes in the ceramic inventory, which begins with a sophisticated and elaborate set of both decorated and plain wares early in the sequence, and ends with the complete loss of pottery in the first millennium A.D. (or, in the case of Fiji, its replacement with strikingly different ceramic wares). The Niuatoputapu data reinforce this general regional picture of ceramic change.

There are some striking similarities in the Niuatoputapu and regional sequences of ceramic change.

TABLE 48

INITIAL SETTLEMENT AGES FOR FIJI-WESTERN POLYNESIA

LOCALITY/SITE	SOURCE	CONVENTIONAL ^{14}C AGE		CALIBRATED AGE RANGE (95%)
FIJI				
Natunuku	Green 1979	GAK–1218	3240 ± 100 (charcoal)	1755–1355 B.C.
Yanuca	Green 1979	GAK–1226	2980 ± 90 (charcoal)	1435–895 B.C.
Lakeba Site 197	Best 1984	NZ 4594	2960 ± 70 (charcoal)	1380–910 B.C.
		NZ 4906	2960 ± 160 (bone)	1550–825 B.C.
Naigani	Kay 1984	NZ 5615	2850 ± 50 (shell)	870–570 B.C.
		NZ 5616	2860 ± 50 (shell)	880–580 B.C.
TONGA				
Site To. 2	Green 1979	ANU 541	3090 ± 95 (shell)	1045–745 B.C.
SAMOA				
Mulifanua	Jennings & Holmer 1980	NZ 1958	2980 ± 80 (shell)	1035–555 B.C.

Especially notable is the early reduction in the range of vessel forms, accompanied by the loss of complex dentate-stamped and incised decoration. This reduction in the range of formal variation from Early Eastern Lapita to Late Eastern Lapita occurs throughout the Fiji-Western Polynesian region, evidently within two or three centuries following colonization, and must signal some fundamental changes in the functional role that ceramics played in these early societies. Rather than viewing this ceramic change as simply a reduction in ceramic variability, we should perhaps think of it as the wholesale elimination of the decorated ceramic component, leaving only a restricted group of plainware vessel forms. The possible social implications of this reduction are considerable, for the decorated vessels likely served a symbolic role as visual markers. The difficulty comes in knowing the particular semiotic value of these decorated vessels: were they markers of hierarchical or rank differences, of differential sex roles, of lineage or household differences, or of some other contrasts within early Western Polynesian societies? However, it would be premature to assume that the loss of material symbols which must have been correlated with some form of social differentiation implies a corresponding loss of the social distinction itself. Rather, it may be that the ceramic change is an indirect reflection of a shift in the visual form of marking status distinctions in early Polynesian societies. Yen (n.d., p. 6) has commented with considerable insight on this possibility:

> The adduction of Lapita pottery sequences to social terms may be the proletarianization of its use, as the societies move to more highly organised forms...Indeed, what we could be viewing... are the transformations of symbols of rank that were to be eventually replaced in large part by other symbols that may have had material expression, but whose ultimate manifestation, with the rise of heredity in social ranking, could have been the importance of genealogy in Polynesia.

The concept of the proletarianization of ceramics is an intriguing one that deserves to be pursued further as we attempt to explain the so-called "devolution" of Western Polynesian ceramics. As Green (1974b) and others have already made clear, the decline and ultimate loss of pottery in Polynesia cannot be explained on any of the obvious environmental or technological models (e.g., absence of suitable clays or tempering materials). It is clearly within the social realm that we shall have to seek our explanations.

Following the relatively rapid elimination of the decorated vessel forms from the Niuatoputapu ceramic complex, the remaining plain wares continued in use for a lengthy period, perhaps as long as 1600 to 1800 years. During this time, further change in the ceramic inventory was minimal, aside from a gradual quantitative reduction in frequency of pottery production and deposition (this, at least, as based on the evidence from sites NT-90, -100, and -93, with depositional frequencies declining from ca. 1,430 sherds/m^3 to 300 sherds/m^3). Here, again, the Niuatoputapu evidence seems to match closely the sequences from Tongatapu and Samoa.

Another apparently regional pattern of ceramic change highlighted by the Niuatoputapu data is the shift from calcareous sand temper to strictly volcaniclastic tempers later in the sequence. Unfortunately, not all ceramic analyses have paid close attention to changes in tempering, but the pattern seems to hold not only for Niuatoputapu, but for Samoa, Futuna, and probably Tongatapu as well. Whether this change in the use of tempering materials implies some broad-scale innovations in ceramic manufacture itself remains to be determined.

While the Niuatoputapu evidence supports the general sequence of a ceramic transition from Early Eastern Lapita, through Late Eastern Lapita, and Polynesian Plain Ware, to the loss of ceramics entirely (Green 1974b, 1979), there are several important local differences between the Niuatoputapu ceramic sequence and those of neighboring islands. This underscores a point I made earlier with regard to the Futunan ceramics (Kirch 1981), that we must not permit *generalized* models of regional change to mask significant variability at the local level. It is precisely such minor, local variation which may provide vital clues to the processes of cultural differentiation in the early stages of divergence among Western Polynesian societies.

With regard to local differentiation, analysis of the design components of the Early Eastern Lapita assemblage from Site NT-90 (chapter 5) demonstrated distinctions between a northern group of assemblages (including Mulifanua, 'Uvea, and Sigatoka, as well as Niuatoputapu) and those of Tongatapu and other parts of Fiji (e.g., Natunuku). Such a possible northern Lapita network is, furthermore, suggested by the restricted geographical distribution of one vessel form, the large, handled "water jar." Thus far, this vessel form is known from Sigatoka (Fiji), 'Uvea, Futuna, Niuatoputapu, and Vava'u (Kirch, surface collections, 1976), but is wholly absent in the extensive collections from Tongatapu, or from the Yanuca and Natunuku sites in Fiji. The possible implications of such geographic differences in ceramic variation for early Lapita inter-island contacts or for differentiation between island communities remain unexplored. Such evidence, however, will prove vital as we move beyond gross regional patterns of cultural change to an understanding of divergence at the local level.

Another contrast in local sequences of ceramic change may be drawn between Niuatoputapu and Samoa. In Samoa, the work of Green and Davidson (1969a, 1974), and of Jennings (Jennings et al. 1976; Jennings and Holmer 1980) has demonstrated that in the final stages of Polynesian Plain Ware production there was an increasing thickening of vessel walls over time, so that one may distinguish "thin ware" from "thick ware." In Niuatoputapu, however, there is no evidence of such a trend. Thus, while both Samoan and Niuatoputapu assemblages of Polynesian Plain Ware are very similar, the local sequences of ceramic change are not in fact identical.

Finally, the chronology of ceramic change in Niuatoputapu raises questions about the timing of the disappearance of pottery in Western Polynesia. In Samoa, an extensive array of ^{14}C age determinations analyzed by Green and Davidson (1974) led them to conclude that pottery production had ceased in that archipelago by about A.D. 300. In Tongatapu, Poulsen (1967, 1968) originally interpreted his radiocarbon and stratigraphic data to suggest that ceramics had remained a part of Tongan material culture throughout most of the Christian era. Subsequently, however, Groube (1971) and Green (1972a), with the Samoan ceramic sequence as a model, argued that Poulsen had been misled by sherds in secondary depositional contexts, and that in Tongatapu ceramics did not persist later than the end of the first millennium B.C. The Niuatoputapu data, however, indicate that pottery production on that island persisted as late as the ninth century A.D. The question thus arises whether Niuatoputapu was unique in the late persistence of ceramics, continuing to produce pottery after it had been abandoned in Samoa to the north and Tonga to the south, or whether the chronological data for Samoa and Tonga should be further scrutinized. Green and Davidson (1974:213 passim) at least hint that other interpretations of the Samoan radiocarbon corpus are possible, and in my view the issue of the date(s) for final loss of ceramics in Western Polynesia remains an open one.

In other aspects of material culture, the Niuatoputapu data reinforce several other regional trends. Although the corpus of adzes from Niuatoputapu sites is not extensive, it is sufficient to indicate that the temporal progression in adz forms from Early Eastern Lapita through the later aceramic periods closely parallels that known from other Western Polynesian localities. Thus, adzes manufactured from the thick hinge portion of the *Tridacna* clam are associated with the earliest colonization phase in Western Polynesia; by the late first millennium B.C. these had been replaced by adzes of locally available basalt or andesite. Dominant among these volcanic adzes associated typically with Polynesian Plain Ware was the plano-convex sectioned form, Type V in the Green and Davidson (1969b) system. These plano-convex forms were themselves to be replaced, however, with a greater variety of trapezoidal-, quadrangular-, and triangular-sectioned adzes, which persisted throughout the final 1,500 years of Western Polynesian prehistory. The consistency of these temporal trends throughout Western Polynesia renders adze assemblages an important tool for relative chronological ordering of sites, especially in cases where ceramics and radiometrically datable materials are scarce or absent.

Another pattern of apparent regional significance is evident in the simple assemblages of flaked stone, especially cherts and obsidian (or volcanic glass). The use of chert for flake tools appears to be a consistently early phenomenon, associated with Early Eastern Lapita; chert rapidly drops from site inventories later in the first millennium B.C. The use of obsidian, on the other hand, was carried on considerably longer, although evidently not into the aceramic periods of Western Polynesian sequences. Acceptable explanations for these losses or eliminations from the material culture inventory have not been forthcoming, although the disappearance of chert may be related to a breakdown in an early intensive long-distance exchange network (see further discussion on this point, below).

Turning from portable artifact arrays to settlement components and patterns, we see that the Niuatoputapu archaeological landscape falls squarely within the pattern previously documented for Tonga, with several characteristic forms of large field monument (especially earthen mounds, both faced and unfaced), but lacking smaller structures associated with normal household activities. In this, the Tongan and Niuatoputapu patterns contrast markedly with those of Samoa and 'Uvea, where the landscapes are literally blanketed in complex arrangements of stone walls, platforms, and associated features, which constitute a reticulate mosaic of "household units" (Jennings et al. 1982). The Samoan landscape is also dotted with larger monumental constructions that reflect the supra-household polities, but the particular forms constructed in Samoa (such as the "star-mound") differ considerably from those in Tonga and Niuatoputapu. In 'Uvea, on the other hand, the larger monumental constructions are, as in Niuatoputapu, of distinctly Tongan form. These contrasts and similarities suggest that, while 'Uvea and Niuatoputapu developed their patterns of domestic household grouping and organization distinctively over millennia of relative isolation, their late prehistoric settlement landscapes both reflect the political process of Tongan conquest and hegemony in the final centuries prior to European contact. This episode of Tongan expansion and its reflection in the archaeological record are further discussed in the conclusion to this chapter.

One final parallel among the prehistoric sequences of Western Polynesia, including Niuatoputapu, must be mentioned. This is the lamentable thinness of the archaeological record between about the mid-first millennium A.D. and the protohistoric period, what Davidson (1979) has aptly termed the "dark ages." In part because several highly visible classes of material culture (especially ceramics) disappear from Western Polynesian assemblages at this time, sites from this period are either difficult to find or, when excavated, yield relatively little for the archaeologist to work with. This is clearly a problem that must be redressed in future investigations in Western Polynesia, for while we have now achieved substantial understanding of the development of Ancestral Polynesian Society out of its Lapita ancestor, the subsequent emergence of distinctive Samoan and Tongan cultures in the last fifteen centuries is as yet but dimly understood.

THE DYNAMIC ENVIRONMENT

A major objective of our research was to understand the Niuatoputapu landscape in terms of the varied processes—both natural and cultural—which had shaped the local ecosystem during three millennia of human occupation. The island's contemporary landscape is a complex mosaic of artificial or anthropogenic micro-environments, and the keen observer discovers in time that the composition of the flora, zonation patterns in the vegetation, distribution of the terrestrial fauna, even the existence of certain soil zones, are artifacts of human actions over 3,000 years. Indeed, there is little that could be said to represent a "natural" environment.

Some of the most dramatic changes in the Niuatoputapu environment during the time span of human occupation, however, resulted not from human actions, but from the engine of global plate tectonics. Poised on the edge of the abyssal Tonga Trench, Niuatoputapu is being rapidly upthrust as the vast

Pacific Plate slides under the margin of the Fiji Plate. Indeed, the very existence of Niuatoputapu can be traced to plate melting and andesitic-arc volcanism typical of the western Pacific Rim.

The changes that tectonic uplift has wrought in the basic physiography of the island have been nothing short of astounding. Fig. 134 is a reconstruction of the probable configuration of Niuatoputapu about 1000 B.C., based on geomorphological survey data. Rather than a relatively high ratio of land to reef/lagoon, three millennia ago the situation was precisely reversed: reef and lagoon microenvironments covered an estimated 21.5 km^2, with a land area of about 4.9 km^2. Thus, in the simplest terms, the net effect of tectonic uplift during the period of human occupancy has been an increase of 312% in the amount of land, and a concomitant decrease of 50% in reef/lagoon microenvironments. To date, we know of no other island in the Pacific where there has been such a dramatic shift in basic island physiography over so short a time span.

What of the implications of these massive changes for the human population? We must avoid facile assumptions: for example, that as island size increased by a factor of three, so the human carrying capacity would correspondingly rise. Not so. Virtually all of the terrain that was converted from reef/lagoon to land has remained wholly unsuited to agriculture. The uplifted terrain consists of unconsolidated calcareous sands, or larger bioclastic ridges of coral shingles and debris, and the time period since uplift and exposure to colonizing vegetation has been insufficient to develop soil other than the thinnest organic A horizon. Thus, most of the uplifted terrain is cloaked in an extremely low-diversity vegetation of hardy, shallow-rooted trees or shrubs of little economic value, especially *Eugenia clusiaefolia*. Where attempts have been made, as in recent years, to clear this scrub forest for shifting cultivations, the results are disastrous. Not only do the tuberous crops find the sandy, infertile substrate an unsuitable edaphic matrix, but even the scrub *Eugenia* fails to recolonize the site once the thin organic surface horizon has been disturbed. These ill-advised attempts at expansion of the island's agricultural system have left only bare patches recolonized by, at best, a few sedges *(Cyperus)* and stunted *Pandanus*. The old, uplifted lagoon floors (the *toafa;* see chapter 2) are even more inhospitable environments—open expanses dotted with salt-tolerant *Pandanus, Casuarina, Cyperus, Fimbristylis,* and *Pemphis.*

In short, the massive increase in land area has had little impact on *terrestrial* carrying capacity, other than in relatively minor ways, such as the addition of areas of scrub forest exploitable for firewood, edible land crabs, or pigeons and fruit bats. Rather, it is in the area of *marine resources* that uplift and physiographic change has had the greatest impact upon the human occupants of Niuatoputapu. The fundamental effect of tectonic uplift was to eliminate extensive areas of reef and lagoon which must formerly have supported significant populations of inshore fishes, as well as invertebrates. Indeed, since much of the uplifted area consisted of sandy substrates, the impact may have been greatest on the populations of bottom-dwelling molluscs, such as *Anadara, Asaphis, Codakia,* and other bivalves, and gastropods such as *Strombus* and *Conus*. Rather than having a net positive effect on the human carrying capacity of Niuatoputapu, the tectonic conversion of reef flats and lagoons into scrub forest-covered terrain and halophytic intermittent marshes has resulted in a net reduction of exploitable marine food resources, without any significant increase in land area suitable for agricultural expansion.

Against this background of tectonically-induced changes in island physiography, we may examine the impacts of human actions themselves. Some of these are directly evidenced in the archaeological record (e.g., certain faunal introductions, soil enrichment, erosion), while others are inferable from ecological analysis of the contemporary environment. One such anthropogenic process is that of continual forest clearance, firing, and shifting cultivation on the island's central volcanic ridge and Pleistocene Terrace. The few clumps of rainforest species that cling precariously to the most inaccessible sections of the central ridge provide only the slimmest reflection of a former climax vegetation that cloaked the island prior to human colonization. That this forest has been virtually eliminated, and replaced with a mosaic of aggressive and hardy second-growth species, is reflected as well in the remarkable absence of any floral endemics (save a single species of *Pandanus,* assigned to endemic, specific-level status by a taxonomist noted as an extreme "splitter," St. John 1977).

The cycle of clearance, firing, gardening, and secondary regrowth, which has gone on, presumably, since initial Lapita colonization, has affected not only the floristic composition and vegetative zonation of the island's volcanic core, but the land surface as well. The central volcanic ridge is actively eroding as a result of continued exposure and gardening manipulation of the upper soil zone. Largely through surface water transport (and secondarily through mass wasting), finer sediments are continually transported off the central ridge to the Pleistocene Terrace, where the gentler terrain encourages deposition. This process can be documented even off the Pleistocene Terrace, as at Holoiafu (Site NT-113), where a thick layer of fine clay has been deposited over the original calcareous beach terrace. The effect of such erosion and deposition has doubtless been beneficial,

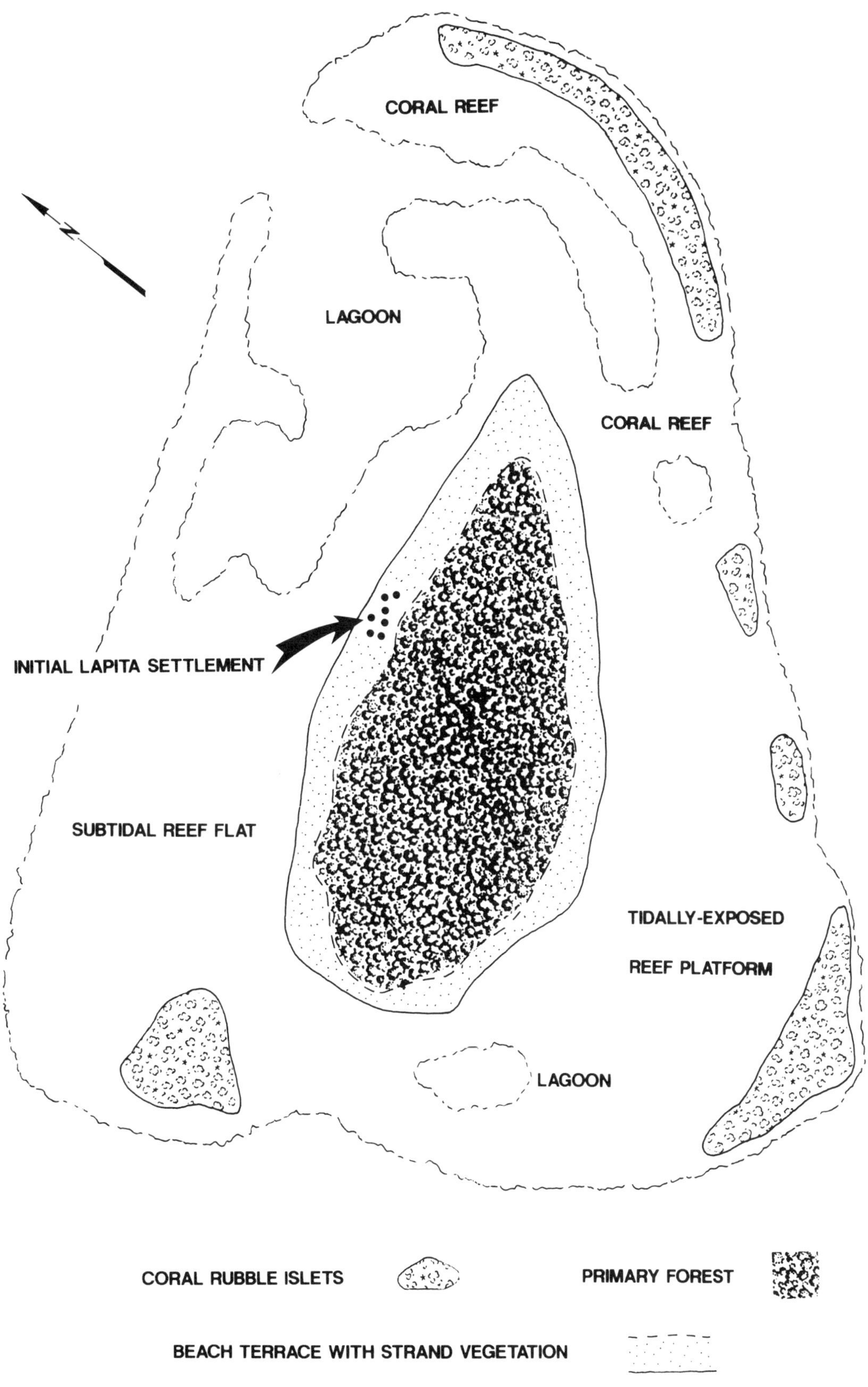

Figure 134. Paleogeographic reconstruction of Niuatoputapu Island about 1000 B.C.

continually enriching the soils of the Pleistocene Terrace upon which the island is heavily dependent for intensive agricultural production.

Human habitation was—quite literally—responsible for another form of edaphic transformation of major importance to the island's agricultural system. This was the gradual enrichment, over at least 1,500 years of continued occupation, of the old beach terrace that became the "ceramic zone." Through the deposition of organic debris of all kinds, including shell, bone, and charcoal (especially oven rakeouts), this zone of calcareous beach sand developed a thick cap of extremely fertile organic sediment, so distinctive in its physical properties as to be recognized by its own term in the local folk taxonomy of soil types: *fasifasi'ifeo*. Once the island's settlement pattern shifted in the period after about A.D. 800/900, this former occupation zone, covering an area of about 0.84 km^2, was opened up for cultivation. In the present agricultural system, the *fasifasi'ifeo* is the dominant zone for cultivating the yam *'ufi lei* or *Dioscorea esculenta*, in a mixed-gardening system that also incorporates the large aroid *Alocasia macrorrhiza*. While the anthropogenic creation of this intensive garden zone through organic enrichment of the calcareous soil can hardly be said to have been a purposive effort on the part of the human population, its long-term impact on Niuatoputapu agricultural production cannot be underestimated.

Three millennia of human occupation have had other impacts on the island biota as well. Elsewhere, I have used Edgar Anderson's concept of *transported landscapes* to refer to the introduction by Oceanic peoples of a wide array of synanthropic species to formerly remote and ecologically vulnerable island ecosystems (Kirch 1983b, 1984a; Kirch and Yen 1982). Niuatoputapu is certainly no exception. The introduction—both purposeful and inadvertent—of exotic species began with initial Lapita colonization, and included domestic animals (pigs, dogs, and fowl), anthropophilic terrestrial gastropods, a range of crop plants, and various other plant and animal species such as weeds, geckos and skinks, and insects, which are not yet directly represented in the archaeological record. These were not mere additions to the island's biotic diversity, for most of these species are either subject to direct human manipulation or are natural competitors themselves. Thus over time they tend to outcompete and replace other species in the "natural" biotic community (Fosberg 1963).

Finally, there have certainly been reductions in the population levels of many indigenous species as a result of centuries of direct human exploitation. This trend is evidenced in the archaeological faunal record for birds, turtles, fish, and shellfish. The greatest impacts of this type probably occurred relatively early in the island's settlement sequence, at least to judge from the archaeological record of faunal reductions.

The varied means by which humans have transformed the Niuatoputapu environment into a thoroughly cultural, manipulated landscape are certainly not unique in the southwestern Pacific. Rather, the Niuatoputapu evidence adds a parallel case to sequences of human-induced ecological and landscape change already documented for such islands as Aneityum, Tikopia, Futuna, and Lakeba (Spriggs 1981, 1986; Kirch and Yen 1982; Kirch 1975a, 1981; Hughes et al. 1979). Instead of viewing the Pacific archaeological record of technological and settlement changes as occurring in a relatively stable and static environmental milieu—as was for many years the unquestioned assumption—we now recognize that entire island ecosystems must be understood as the consequences of human actions.

DEVELOPMENT OF THE PRODUCTION SYSTEM

In its most general features—shifting cultivation, arboriculture, husbandry of pigs and chickens, diversified fishing and marine gathering, and limited hunting of wild birds—the ethnographically documented subsistence system of Niuatoputapu is rather unremarkable, and indeed could stand as a model for virtually any tropical Oceanic system. On closer scrutiny some distinctive features emerge, among them the specialization and intensification of *Pandanus* production and mat making, and the zonal arrangement of *Dioscorea* yam cultivation. The zonality of yam cultivation offers a perspective on the developmental *history* of the Niuatoputapu production system since, as we have just seen, the particular edaphic zones in which yams are grown—the *fasifasi'ifeo* and the fine clays of the Pleistocene Terrace—are to a large extent anthropogenic creations. Thus this aspect of local production must clearly be a development of the later part of the local sequence, after the environmental transformations of erosion and organic enrichment of the old beach terrace had been effected. To attempt to fill in the broader canvas of production system evolution in Niuatoputapu is no facile task, and must depend more than one might wish on indirect inference. Figure 135 is a schematic portrayal of what this developmental sequence may have looked like in terms of major components of production. The transformations of the production system have been plotted adjacent to the major environmental changes already discussed, and the two categories are intimately linked, as both causes and effects of one another. Also graphed is the cultural phase sequence determined from traditional archaeological (primarily material culture) criteria.

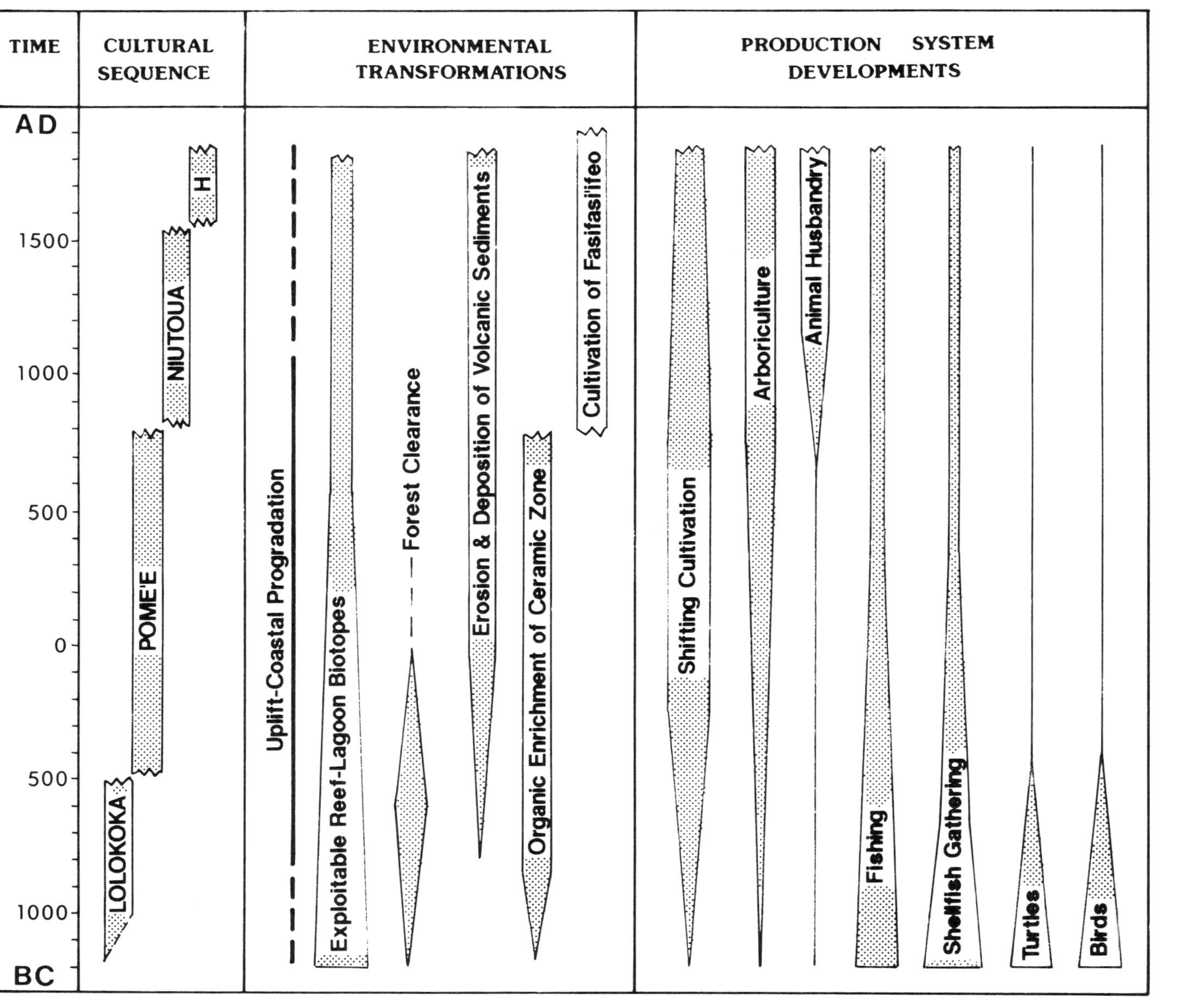

Figure 135. The development of the Niuatoputapu production system, in relation to the cultural phase sequence and major environmental transformations.

Based on several lines of evidence documented in this monograph, the hypothesis of Groube (1971) that the Lapita settlers of Fiji-Western Polynesia were Oceanic "strandloopers" with a "restricted maritime/ lagoonal economy" who "expanded ahead of colonization by agriculturalists" (1971:312) can be rejected, despite recent efforts by Best (1984) to resuscitate the argument. Not only does the *direct* archaeological evidence of vegetable scrapers/peelers, pig and fowl faunal remains, anthropophilic garden snails, nut-cracking hammers, and so forth from Fijian-Western Polynesian Lapita sites (Kirch 1984a) testify to the agricultural capabilities of these colonists, but new work in more westerly Lapita sites, immediately ancestral to those of Fiji-Western Polynesia (Kirch, in press), has confirmed Lapita agricultural production on the direct evidence of cultivated plant remains. Thus, any effort to retain the strandlooper hypothesis now requires the invocation of a highly implausible sequence, in which agricultural Lapita colonists from western Melanesia suddenly abandon cultivation in their eastward expansion to Fiji-Western Polynesia, only to readopt tillage a few centuries later. Both ethnobotanical and linguistic evidence (Barrau 1963, Yen 1971, 1973a; Shutler and Marck 1975; French-Wright 1983) have long informed us that the initial expansion of Austronesian speakers into the southwest Pacific was achieved, at least in part, due to a highly successful colonization strategy that included a tropical tuber-, fruit-, and nut-crop complex. Groube's contrary hypothesis provided a very important stimulus for archaeologists to seek the often elusive evidence of agricultural production which, in my view, has now become incontrovertible for the Lapita complex as a whole.

To argue that Lapita colonists were cultivators who transported an array of crop plants with them is not, however, to deny the significance of marine exploitation, especially in the initial founding period of a new settlement. As the first large omnivorous predators to enter the remote island ecosystems of the southwestern Pacific, Lapita people had the significant advantage of being able to exploit pristine habitats with large "standing crops" (high biomass levels) not only of shellfish, turtles, and fish, but of land birds and nesting seabirds. The recent and often remarkable finds of extinct or extirpated avifauna in early archaeological levels in Hawaii, Henderson, the Marquesas, the Cook Islands, Tikopia, and Anuta provide eloquent testimony to the former biotic diversity and faunal population levels that greeted Lapita voyagers (Olson and James 1984; Steadman and Olson 1985; Steadman 1985; Steadman and Zarriello, in press; Steadman and Kirch, in prep). During the initial and surely tenuous stages of transfer and establishment of a cultivation complex on newly settled islands, such abundance in the natural marine and terrestrial fauna offered a significant "buffer" for Lapita subsistence. Not surprisingly, such exploitation of wild fauna by early Lapita populations is strongly reflected in the archaeological deposits, with the danger that such faunal suites can readily be mistaken for the signature of a "strandlooper" subsistence economy.

It is in this context that the early phase of subsistence production on Niuatoputapu must be understood. The archaeological evidence from Site NT-90 can most plausibly be interpreted as signalling this kind of colonization-agricultural transfer stage, with the significant exploitation of local fauna, especially fish, shellfish, turtles, and birds. Regrettably, the lack of fine stratification within NT-90, or for that matter, within any of the ceramic-zone localities, denies us the opportunity to track the putative increase in agricultural system production and decrease in wild faunal exploitation in other than the most general terms. Nonetheless, the contrasts in the faunal assemblages of NT-90 and the successive NT-100 and -93 localities support the contention that initial exploitation of marine and avifaunal resources was at levels never again matched in later phases of the Niuatoputapu sequence. Both fishing and shellfishing, however, continued throughout the entire prehistoric sequence, and their ethnographically-attested roles in subsistence have been documented in this monograph (chapter 2) and elsewhere (Dye 1983; Rogers 1975). Although the quantitative contribution of fish and shellfish to Niuatoputapu subsistence certainly must have declined from initial levels, the *cultural* importance of such foods at all periods cannot be overlooked. Throughout Polynesia, starch staples provide the caloric bulk of subsistence intake, but supplementary flesh foods such as fish, molluscs, lobster, and crabs assume great cultural importance, especially in the regular exchange of food between social groups as implemented in the feasting cycle (Kirch 1979, 1984a).

The inference of a gradual expansion of shifting cultivation must be largely on the basis of the settlement evidence for a gradually expanding population during the Lolokoka to Pome'e phases, corroborated by the geomorphological indications of erosion and deposition of volcanic sediments at localities such as Holoiafu (NT-113). The intensive yam-aroid cropping of the *fasifasi'ifeo* soil zone, however, was a somewhat later development that had to await the abandonment of the ceramic zone as a habitation locus and the shift of settlement to newly-emerged beach terraces and to dispersed inland localities, thus making the organically-enriched former village sites available as garden sites.

The relative significance of arboriculture is virtually impossible to track in direct archaeological terms. At the ethnographic endpoint, both breadfruit

(Artocarpus altilis) and Tahitian chestnut *(Inocarpus fagiferus)* play substantial roles, and, until very recently, the pit ensilage of breadfruit *(maa)* was an important strategy for buffering the stochastic effects of hurricanes and drought on the production system. The evidence of fermentation pits at Site NT-93 is thus significant, indicating that both breadfruit cultivation and pit ensilage were components of local subsistence by about the close of the first millennium B.C. Green (1969) has noted archaeological evidence of breadfruit storage pits in Samoa at similar dates, and—given the ethnobotanical evidence for the distribution of the ensilage technique in Oceania (Yen 1973a, 1975; Cox 1980)— the Fiji-Western Polynesian region is a likely candidate for the area in which this technology was first developed.

Animal husbandry, especially of pigs but also of chickens, was unquestionably a component of Lapita subsistence, and was presumably introduced to Niuatoputapu upon initial colonization. Certainly the bones of both pigs and fowl in the NT-90 site support this contention. However, pigs do not appear to have played a major role in subsistence production until much later in the island's cultural sequence—that is, until at least the Niutoua and Houmafakalele phases. Thus, the cultural significance of pork as a virtual necessity in presentation feasts *(katoanga)* may be a somewhat recent innovation, perhaps correlating with the rise of sociopolitical hierarchy throughout Western Polynesia.

As noted earlier, the steady expansion of terrestrial production on Niuatoputapu, including the swidden, arboricultural, and animal husbandry components, must be roughly correlated with gradual increases in the island's human population, even though we have no archaeological index to the latter other than that of the expansion of settlement area from the Lolokoka to Pome'e phases. Without going so far as to engage in futile exercises in the calculation of potential carrying capacity, we must nonetheless address the issue of human population-resource balance. Niuatoputapu is a relatively small island, which, lacking the hydrologic requirements for intensive irrigation, can support only a limited population even on an intensified shifting cultivation-arboricultural regime. Further, the dietary contribution of wild terrestrial and marine fauna had declined from initial levels, not only through steady exploitation, but due also to the decreased areas of productive reef/lagoon resulting from tectonic uplift. Given these constraints on demographic increase, we might have anticipated the cultural development of various controls on population growth, as are so well documented on, for example, the similarly small Polynesian island of Tikopia (Firth 1936, 1939; Borrie, Firth, and Spillius 1957; Kirch and Yen 1982). Such controls might be expected to include not only the regulation of human fertility, but inter-group conflict and territorial conquest. The striking absence of such cultural developments—at least if the silence of Niuatoputapu oral traditions in this regard has any significance—may well highlight the importance of nearby Tafahi Island as a kind of "safety valve" for population-resource imbalances on Niuatoputapu. Though very steep and lacking any reef/lagoon resources, Tafahi is extremely fertile (consisting almost exclusively of geologically young volcanic sediments) and has the potential to substantially increase the agricultural subsistence base for Niuatoputapu. Today, owing to outmigration and lessened agricultural pressures on Niuatoputapu, there is little call on Tafahi to contribute subsistence products to the larger island, although Tafahi does serve as a major exporter of *kava* root on a cash-crop basis (not only to the Kingdom at large, but even to Samoa). In the past, however, Tafahi's link to Niuatoputapu may well have been that of a politically subservient territory, able—by virtue of its extremely fertile geography—to produce a surplus essential to the maintenance of high population levels on politically dominant Niuatoputapu.

The general sequence of production system development for Niuatoputapu that has just been sketched is matched in many of its essential features by those sequences that have been archaeologically revealed in other tropical Polynesian islands. As one example, we may cite the evolution of the Tikopia production system (Kirch and Yen 1982), which displays a broadly similar (though by no means wholly identical) expansion and intensification of agricultural production, an initial heavy emphasis on wild faunal exploitation, later prehistoric intensification of pig husbandry, and steady contribution of fishing and shellfish gathering. The Marquesan sequence as well reveals many of the same general trends (Kirch 1984a:156-59), although it too has unique features, not the least of which is the addition, in late prehistory, of human flesh to the dietary repertoire (Kirch 1973). The intersection points between the developmental sequences of subsistence production in Niuatoputapu, Tikopia, the Marquesas and other Polynesian islands, however, do begin to inform us as to those trends that may have been common to most, if not all, islands. Once such common trends are understood, the task of sorting out the unique adaptations of particular times and places will be more readily accomplished.

CHANGING CONFIGURATIONS OF LONG-DISTANCE EXCHANGE

Even in the late twentieth century, Niuatoputapu remains connected to other islands in Western Polynesia through a network of long-distance exchanges. These include tributary obligations of the Niuatoputapu noble (Tangipa) and chiefs *(hou'eiki)* to the royal family in Tongatapu and to other high-ranking elite elsewhere in the Kingdom, exchange among church groups, and reciprocal exchanges between various household groups. The latter are materially evident whenever an inter-island ship sails from Niuatoputapu, carrying basket-loads of yams, pigs (live or cooked), dried *kava* roots, and especially the fine mats for which Niuatoputapu is famous. Returning household members or visiting relatives on ships arriving at Niuatoputapu are likewise burdened with food, *ngatu* or barkcloth, and items of foreign manufacture not available on the island. The more occasional visit of a prominent church leader, government official, or member of the royal family calls for yet more elaborate exchanges of barkcloth and fine mats, and presentations of yams, pig, and *kava*.

To judge from ethnohistoric sources the present flow of goods to and from the island is certainly reduced from what it appears to have been in protohistory and in the early decades after European contact. Regular voyaging to Samoa and 'Uvea (now restricted due to modern political boundaries), as well as to Tongan islands to the south, assured a diversity of traffic through Niuatoputapu. The missionary John Williams, at Niuatoputapu in 1832, saw a large canoe carrying perhaps 130 persons bound for Samoa from Ha'apai. Williams noted the frequency of contact between Niuatoputapu and other islands (in Gunson 1977:258, fn 4).

Archaeologically, we face the problem of assessing the extent to which Niuatoputapu was, in prehistoric times, linked with other islands in the Fiji-Western Polynesian region as part of various long-distance exchange networks. Our evidence, naturally, is restricted to those material items that can be analytically "sourced" to exotic localities (or, if not definitively sourced, at least shown to be of non-local origin). Given the material paucity of the Niuatoputapu archaeological record after about A.D. 800, this means that we shall be restricted in our discussion of prehistoric long-distance contacts to the Lolokoka and Pome'e phases.

The clearest material evidence for long-distance exchange in the Lolokoka phase is the exotic chert or chalcedony found almost exclusively in the NT-90 site, and associated with the earliest dentate-stamped ceramics. Preliminary analysis (see chapter 5) indicates that Futuna Island was the probable source for some, but not necessarily all, of these flakes. A source of chert nodules known on the western end of Futuna (Kirch 1981) was being locally exploited by at least 200 B.C., and probably earlier. The recent igneous geological structures of Samoa and 'Uvea eliminate these islands as probable sources, but many of the islands in the Lau group, as well as the main Fiji group, contain older limestones that may yield biogenic cherts. Biogenic cherts, chalcedonies, or jaspers may also occur on Tongatapu or 'Eua. For the present, however, we can be certain only that during the Lolokoka Phase the Niuatoputapu population was importing chert for flake tools, some of it from Futuna but some possibly from one or more other sources.

Other material imports have not been clearly identified, although adzes are a very likely category, given the evidence for their localized production and wide geographic distribution throughout the Fiji-Western Polynesian area (Best 1984). Despite evidence for its inter-island movement elsewhere among Lapita communities, we can rule out the importation of pottery to Niuatoputapu (though it could, of course, have been an exported item). All of the sherds petrographically examined were locally manufactured.

Niuatoputapu provided at least one important export to the early Fijian-Western Polynesian Lapita exchange network, of which it controlled the only source: obsidian. Tafahi Island obsidian flakes were excavated by Best (1984:431) at his Lapita sites 196 and 197 on Lakeba Island in the Lau group. Poulsen (1967) reports obsidian flakes from Tongatapu that, while they have not been spectrochemically analyzed, most probably derive from Tafahi-Niuatoputapu. Other Lapita sites have been reported to contain flaked stone, including obsidian which has not, unfortunately, been sufficiently described or analyzed to identify possible sources. It is likely, however, that with further attention to the flaked stone components of early Lapita assemblages, Tafahi obsidian will prove to have been fairly widely distributed throughout the region.

All ethnographically known Oceanic long-distance exchange systems are characterized by the flow not only of utilitarian goods and raw materials but of various forms of *exchange valuables,* most often manufactured of shell. The classic examples of such exchange valuables are the *mwali* armrings and *soulava* necklaces of the famous Kula-ring (Malinowski 1922; Campbell 1983), but many other forms of shell exchange valuables (often colloquially referred to as "shell money") are found ethnographically throughout Melanesia and central-eastern Micronesia. In light of this ethnographic corpus, the variety of shell "ornaments" associated with early Lapita assemblages, including long units, broad or rectangular units, disks, beads, rings, and pendants, may be interpreted as having been an integral component of Lapita long-distance exchange. A detailed consideration of the probable role of these artifacts in Lapita exchange has been presented elsewhere (Kirch, in press), and need not be repeated in full here.

The early NT-90 site yielded a range of shell objects that have been interpreted as exchange valuables, including *Spondylus* long units, *Conus* rings, *Tridacna* rings, *Conus* discs, and *Spondylus* beads. All of these objects appear in the NT-90 site as whole or broken *finished* artifacts; there are no examples of unfinished ornaments, nor is there an assemblage of cut or worked shell manufacture detritus. As I have argued elsewhere (Kirch, in press), such evidence strongly suggests that Niuatoputapu was an *importing* node for shell valuables. Within the Fiji-Western Polynesian region, only two Lapita sites have thus far yielded evidence for specialized production of shell valuables: Naigani and Lakeba. Naigani shows evidence for the manufacture of *Conus* rings, beads, and possibly discs (Kay 1984). Lakeba sites display the evidence for production of *Tridacna* long units; *Conus* rectangular units, rings, and beads; *Trochus* rings; and possibly *Tridacna* rings (Best 1984). It is, of course, impossible to state which of these localities (if either) was the source(s) of the valuables found at NT-90. Nonetheless, given the absence of any evidence for shell manufacturing at Niuatoputapu, the status of these objects as high-value imports seems a plausible hypothesis.

Although scanty, the evidence outlined above does allow us to sketch a model, however tentative, of Niuatoputapu's position within an early Eastern Lapita exchange network (see also Kirch, in press). The Niuatoputapu community was importing chert and possibly other exotic stone materials (adzes, for example), as well as high-value shell objects; it is likely that a range of other, perishable materials was also imported but has not left any archaeological witness. Niuatoputapu was exporting obsidian, for which it was the only source in the region. It may have been exporting ceramics, all of which were locally produced. A direct link with Futuna Island is indicated by the chert, and direct or indirect linkages with the Lau Group and southern Tonga are suggested by the obsidian.

Some further insights into the possible role of Niuatoputapu in such an early Lapita exchange network are offered by a graph theoretic analysis of known Lapita communities in this region. Graph theory has been applied by a number of investigators in Oceania as a heuristic device to explore topologic or relational dimensions of spatial distributions that may not be intuitively obvious (Hage 1977; Hage and Harary 1983, and in press; Irwin 1983, 1985; Terrell 1986). In figure 136, the known Lapita sites of Fiji-Western Polynesia are portrayed as a network in which sites have been connected by the first through third *proximal points* for each node. (In this figure, nodes 5 through 8 are based on reported southern Lau Lapita sites mentioned in Best 1984:556. A further assumption is made that Vava'u, which has several reported ceramic sites but has not been subjected to detailed survey, will prove to have been occupied since the Early Eastern Lapita phase.) The possible importance of Niuatoputapu in such a network is indicated by examining the *centrality* of particular nodes. Table 49 is a short-path connectivity array derived from the graph in figure 136, in which each cell indicates the shortest path or geodesic linking of each pair of nodes. Summing the rows or columns of the matrix gives an index of relative centrality for any node, which may then be rank-ordered. Two sites within this network are equally ranked with the greatest centrality: Lakeba and Futuna. The second rank is held by Niuatoputapu. All other sites in this network are substantially less centralized than these three. It may be particularly significant that both Futuna and Niuatoputapu, each of which is a known source for lithic materials (chert and obsidian), occupy nodes critical to movement between the Fiji and Tonga-Samoa sections of the network. The central position occupied by Lakeba is also interesting in light of the archaeological evidence for this node as a major center of shell valuable manufacture.

Of course, we must be cautious not to take graph theoretic models such as that presented above too literally, since they represent no more than a *possible* set of connections based on the locations of presently known archaeological sites and on certain basic assumptions of interaction between nodes (in this case, limitation of interaction to the first through third proximal points). The discovery of new Lapita sites (for example, on Vanua Levu) would to some degree alter the centrality of nodes. Nonetheless, much of the structure inherent in figure 136 is fixed by the basic geography of the region, and it is likely that the actual Lapita exchange network that we seek to understand was indeed constrained by this very structure. Certainly the use of graph theoretic models such as that in figure 136 provides a valid means for generating hypotheses about Lapita exchange, which may in turn help in the design of new archaeological research in the region.

The lack of fine-grained stratigraphy in the Niuatoputapu sites makes it impossible to determine the duration of the long-distance exchange network that initially linked the island to other early Lapita communities. However, the absence of both exotic cherts and shell exchange valuables from the NT-100 and NT-93 sites indicates that by the Pome'e Phase the original network had either collapsed entirely or, at least, changed significantly in terms of the materials being imported. Unfortunately, for the Pome'e and Niutoua Phases the archaeological record regarding foreign contacts is virtually mute, in part due to its paucity. It is thus difficult to determine whether Niuatoputapu

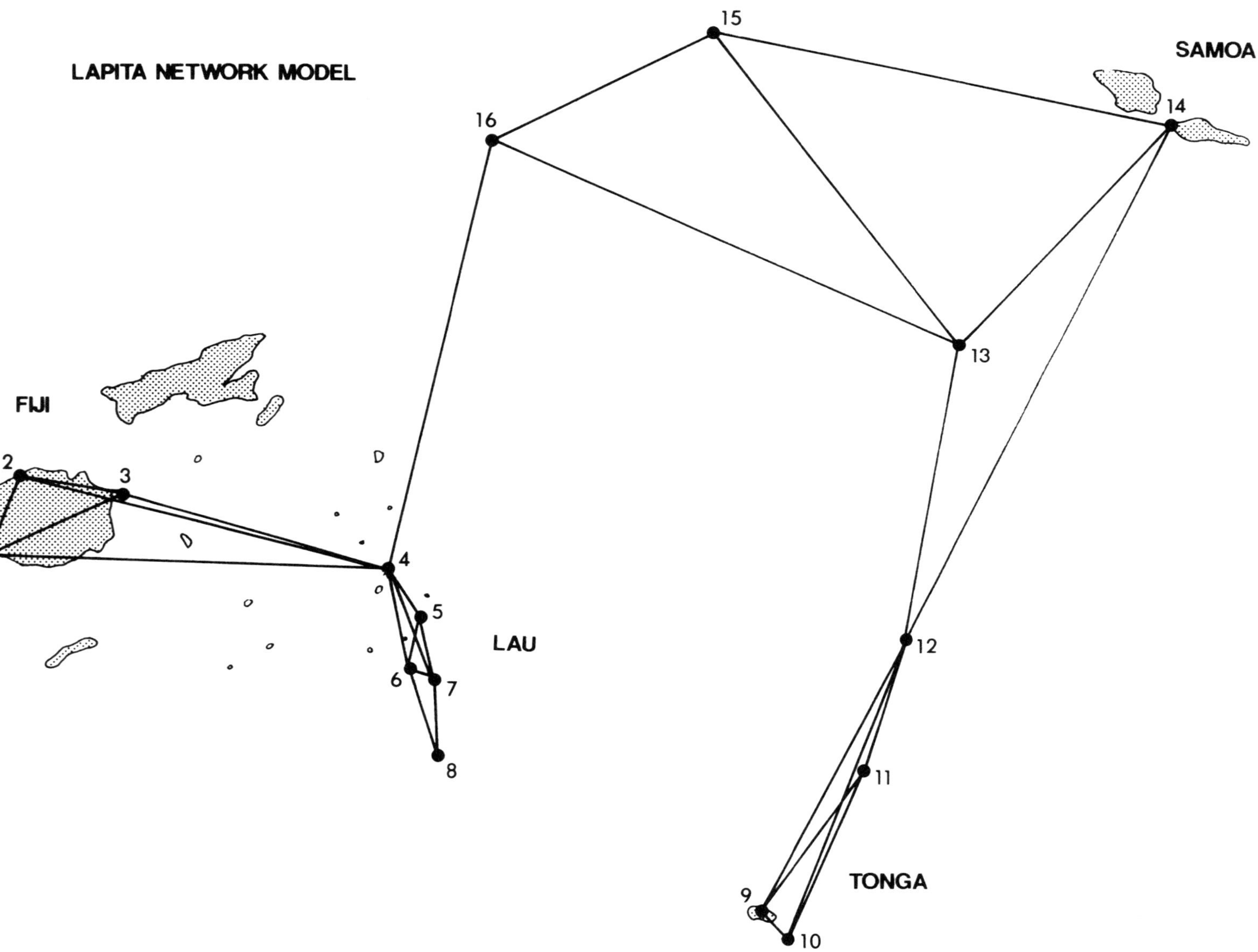

Figure 136. Graph network of Lapita sites (1st to 3rd proximal points), based on short-path connectivity matrix of table 49.

TABLE 49

LAPITA SITE NETWORK: SHORT-PATH CONNECTIVITY MATRIX

	1	2	3	4	5	6	7	8	9	10	11	12	13	14	15	16	
1	0	1	1	1	2	2	2	3	5	5	5	4	3	4	3	2	Yanuca/Sigatoka
2	1	0	1	1	2	2	2	3	5	5	5	4	3	4	3	2	Natunuku
3	1	1	0	1	2	2	2	3	5	5	5	4	3	4	3	2	Naigani
4	1	1	1	0	1	1	1	2	4	4	4	3	2	3	2	1	Lakeba
5	2	2	2	1	0	1	1	1	5	5	5	4	3	4	3	2	Oneata
6	2	2	2	1	1	0	1	1	5	5	5	4	3	4	3	2	Fulanga
7	2	2	2	1	1	1	0	1	5	5	5	4	3	4	3	2	Mothe
8	3	3	3	2	1	1	1	0	6	6	6	5	4	5	4	3	Ono-i-lau
9	5	5	5	4	5	5	5	6	0	1	1	1	2	2	3	3	Tongatapu
10	5	5	5	4	5	5	5	6	1	0	1	1	2	2	3	3	'Eua
11	5	5	5	4	5	5	5	6	1	1	0	1	2	2	3	3	Ha'apai
12	4	4	4	3	4	4	3	5	1	1	1	0	1	1	2	2	Vava'u
13	3	3	3	2	3	3	1	4	2	2	2	1	0	1	1	1	Niuatoputapu
14	4	4	4	3	4	4	5	5	2	2	2	1	1	0	1	2	Mulifanua
15	3	3	3	2	3	3	1	4	3	3	3	2	1	1	0	1	'Uvea
16	2	2	2	1	2	2	2	2	3	3	3	2	1	2	1	0	Futuna
	43	43	43	31	41	41	37	52	53	53	53	41	34	43	38	31	Σ
	6	6	6	1	5	5	3	6	7	7	7	5	2	6	4	1	= Rank

actually entered a period of substantial isolation, or whether long-distance exchange continued in configurations not archaeologically visible. Two sherds of almost certain Fijian origin (see chapter 5) can be stylistically assigned to the Vunda Phase of the Fiji sequence, dating to sometime after A.D. 1100 (Frost 1979). We should not assume that these necessarily indicate *direct* contact with Fiji, however, as they may well have been derived indirectly via either Futuna or a southern Tongan source. Many of the basalt adzes dating to the post-ceramic part of the Niuatoputapu sequence are probably also imports, quite likely from either 'Uvea or Samoa (or both); determination of actual sources must await detailed petrographic or chemical study of these artifacts.

In the protohistoric Houmafakalele Phase, Niuatoputapu became integrally connected with the rapidly expanding Tongan "maritime empire" (Guiart 1963; Kaeppler 1978; Kirch 1984a; Mahina 1986), a system based substantially on long-distance prestige-good exchange between chiefly elites in Tonga, eastern Fiji, and Samoa. This system, which is known to some degree from ethnohistoric sources, was centrally controlled by the dual paramountship located at Mu'a, in Tongatapu, and was operationalized primarily by Tongan navigators and sailors. The flow of goods through this system, and its topologic structure, have been analyzed elsewhere (Kirch 1984a:217-42). Here it is important only to specify the geographic role of Niuatoputapu, which is again illuminated through graph theory. Figure 137 portrays the primary links between nodes in the protohistoric Tongan long-distance exchange network, as based on ethnohistoric sources. Converting the graph to a short-path connectivity matrix (table 50), it is clear that Niuatoputapu and Vava'u occupied equally central positions in this network (though it must be understood that in this case "centrality" has a highly specific, topologic definition and does not refer to political or economic dominance in the system as a whole). Indeed, given that sailing in this region is best effected along a north-south axis, Niuatoputapu occupies a critical "way-station" between politically dominant Tongatapu in the south and its subjugated outliers of Niuafo'ou and 'Uvea, along with Samoa, in the north. It is not surprising, perhaps, that Niuatoputapu became the object of Tongan hegemony during the late protohistoric expansion of the Tongan chiefship.

NIUATOPUTAPU AND THE TONGAN MARITIME CHIEFDOM

The structure of the protohistoric Tongan maritime chiefdom, and what can be inferred of its historical development, have been discussed in detail elsewhere (Kirch 1984a:217-42) and are briefly reviewed in chapter 1 of this monograph. Because much of our knowledge of this chiefdom—with its complex hierarchy, long-distance prestige-good exchange, and system of tribute—is based on ethnohistoric sources, an important contribution of the Niuatoputapu research has been the archaeological confirmation of the putative history of Tongan hegemonic expansion in about the sixteenth and seventeenth centuries A.D. Based on oral traditions and ethnohistoric accounts, the Tongan polity expanded northward beyond Ha'apai and Vava'u to conquer the formerly independent chiefly states of Niuatoputapu, Niuafo'ou, 'Uvea, and Rotuma during the reign of the 24th Tu'i Tonga, Kauulufonuafekai. Following the subjugation of these islands, junior kinsmen of the Tu'i

TABLE 50

ETHNOGRAPHIC NETWORK MODEL: SHORT-PATH CONNECTIVITY MATRIX

	1	2	3	4	5	6	7	8	9	10	
1	0	1	2	3	4	5	6	5	5	2	'Eua
2	1	0	1	2	3	4	5	4	4	1	Tongatapu
3	2	1	0	1	2	3	4	3	3	1	Ha'apai
4	3	2	1	0	1	2	3	2	2	2	Vava'u
5	4	3	2	1	0	1	2	1	1	3	Niuatoputapu
6	5	4	3	2	1	0	1	2	2	4	Samoa
7	6	5	4	3	2	1	0	3	3	5	Manu'a
8	5	4	3	2	1	2	3	0	1	4	Niuafo'ou
9	5	4	3	2	1	2	3	1	0	4	'Uvea
10	2	1	1	2	3	4	5	4	4	0	Lakeba
Σ	33	25	20	18	18	24	32	25	25	26	Σ
	7	4	2	1	1	3	6	4	4	5	= Rank

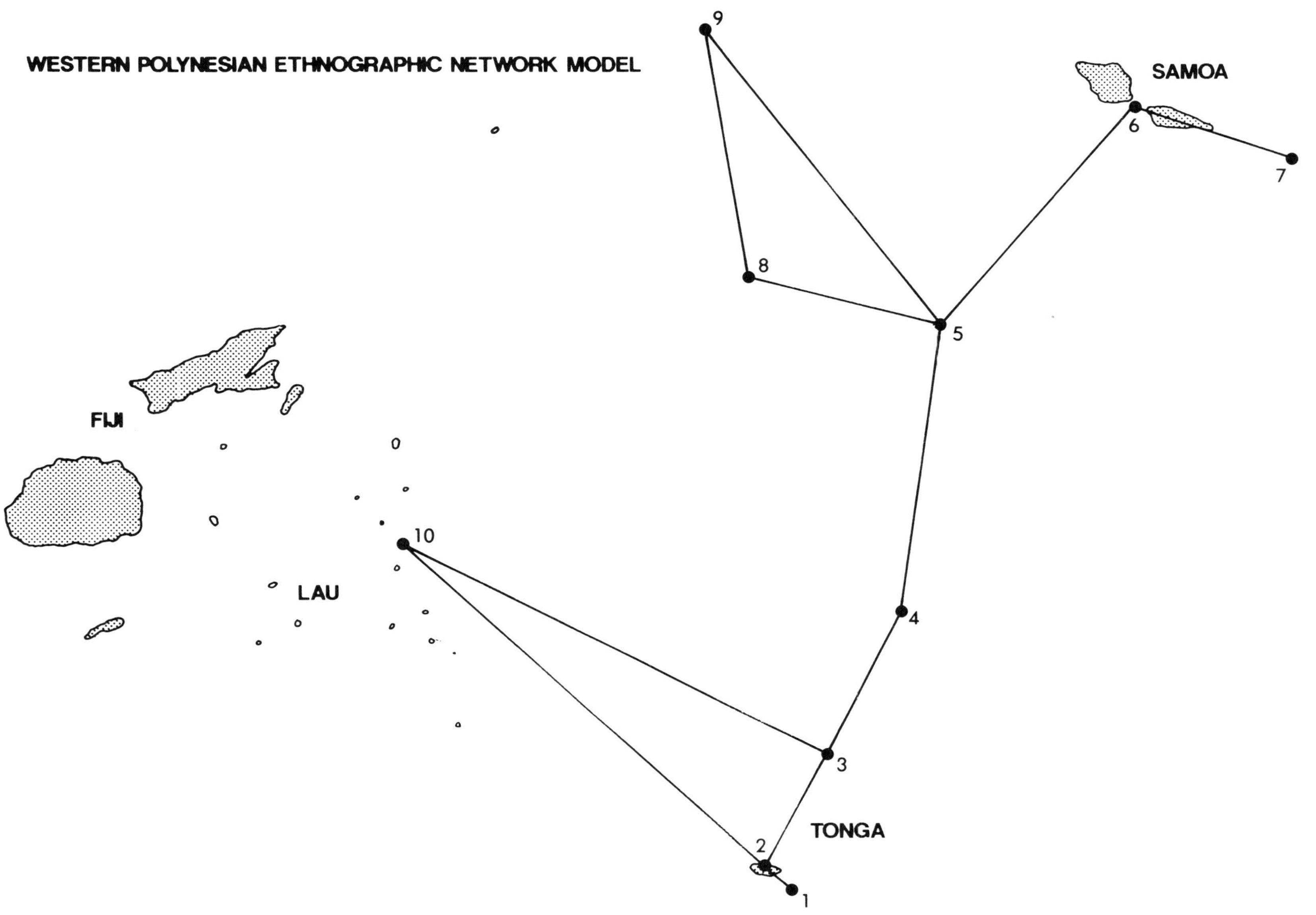

Figure 137. Graph network of protohistoric long-distance exchange within the Tongan "maritime empire," based on short-path connectivity matrix of table 50.

Ha'atakalaua were sent to rule over the new possessions; in Niuatoputapu, this was the origin of the Ma'atu line (see figure 8).

The Niuatoputapu archaeological landscape is indeed consistent with the historical sequence derived from the ethnohistoric traditions. Although only the Houmafakalele burial mound has been directly radiocarbon dated to the seventeenth century, the distribution of Tongan-style burial and *sia heu lupe* mounds on geologically recent portions of the island (i.e., those exposed by tectonic uplift) strongly implies that these sites date to the last few centuries of the Niuatoputapu sequence. This is precisely the kind of settlement landscape that would be predicted in the case of conquest and political domination. Whereas there is no indication in the archaeological record of an earlier emphasis on monument construction, there was evidently a sudden proliferation of mounds in the final decades prior to the historic period. All of these are of Tongan style, as distinct, for example, from Samoan or Fijian monument sites.

The settlement pattern interpretation outlined at the end of chapter 3, however, suggests the presence of about 12 territorial groups—each presumably headed by a chiefly line—on the island in the protohistoric era. Only one of these can have been associated with the foreign Ma'atu lineage, and based on both archaeological and ethnohistoric criteria this was the land unit centered at Vaipoa, where the most impressive burial monuments, such as the Tofi'a Mound (Site NT-22), are situated. What then of the other 11 radial land units? It seems most plausible that these reflect local lineages which, while politically subordinate to Ma'atu (and in turn, to the Tu'i Tonga and Tu'i Ha'atakalaua in Tongatapu), continued to function as land-holding groups, each marked by its own burial cluster and pigeon-snaring mounds. The vestigial remnant of this system of local chiefly lineages is presumably the various minor *hou'eiki* titles (e.g., Telai, Lapuka, Vivili), that still exist on Niuatoputapu, but which are no longer associated with discrete territorial units. (Instead, the island is today divided into three *tofi'a* or estates, two held by the King and the noble Tangipa respectively, and a now vacant one formerly held by Ma'atu.) This settlement pattern is consonant with our understanding that the political subjugation of Niuatoputapu was achieved by the superposition of a dominant Tongan lineage (Ma'atu) onto the previously existing autochthonous political structure. These local lineages continued to exist, and to occupy their traditional lands, presumably owing obeisance, tribute, and martial support to the Ma'atu, who in turn represented the island to the dual paramounts in Tongatapu.

If this interpretation of the Niuatoputapu settlement landscape is indeed historically correct, we should be able to test it through further excavation and dating of monument sites not only on Niuatoputapu, but on other islands subjected to similar conquest during the late protohistoric Tongan expansion. The best candidate is certainly 'Uvea, which ethnohistoric sources suggest came under Tongan domination at the same time as Niuatoputapu. The initial settlement pattern work on 'Uvea of Kirch (1975a, 1976) and of Frimigacci et al. (1984) has confirmed the presence of distinctly Tongan-style field monuments, including faced burial mounds and classic *sia heu lupe*. As noted earlier, the tomb at Atavalu excavated by Frimigacci et al. is remarkably similar in both construction and interment style to Houmafakalele III; we must await radiocarbon dating of this or other 'Uvean sites, however, to confirm that the construction of such distinctly Tongan monuments also dates to the sixteenth and seventeenth centuries.

* * *

Though but a small and in many respects insignificant island amongst the larger and more famous archipelagoes of Polynesia, Niuatoputapu encompasses within its long prehistory virtually all of the significant cultural developments critical to a historical understanding of Polynesia as a cultural region. The island was settled by early Lapita voyagers who first colonized the western fringes of Polynesia at the close of the second millennium B.C. The breakdown of the Lapita exchange network and the development of a distinct Ancestral Polynesian culture are clearly evidenced in the Niuatoputapu sequence. The gradual transformation of the island into a largely anthropogenic landscape, and the development of a terrestrial production system, mirror changes that occurred on other islands throughout the region. Finally, the appearance in late prehistory of the monumental signals of political hierarchy—in this case through the forceful intrusion of a conquering polity—mark the evolution of socio-political complexity for which Polynesia has been so anthropologically scrutinized. Thus, while the prehistory of Niuatoputapu is in its minutiae historically unique, in its broader patterns it encapsulates much that is characteristic of the whole of Polynesia.

REFERENCES CITED

Akimichi, T. 1978. The ecological aspect of Lau (Solomon Islands) ethnoichthyology. *Journal of the Polynesian Society* 87:301–26.

Anderson, A. J. 1978. Archaeological explorations on 'Ata Island, Tonga. *Royal Society of New Zealand Bulletin* 17:1–21.

Bagnis, R., P. Mazellier, J. Bennett, and E. Christian. 1972. *Fishes of Polynesia.* Papeete: Editions du Pacifique.

Ball, S. C. 1933. *Jungle Fowls from Pacific Islands.* B.P. Bishop Museum Bulletin 108. Honolulu.

Barnett, G.L. 1978. *A Manual for the Identification of Fish Bones.* Canberra: Australian National University.

Barrau, J. 1961. *Subsistence Agriculture in Polynesia and Micronesia.* B.P. Bishop Museum Bulletin 223. Honolulu.

_____. 1963. *Plants and the Migrations of Pacific Peoples.* Bishop Museum Press, Honolulu.

_____. 1965a. Histoire et préhistoire horticoles de l'Océanie tropical. *Journal de la Société des Océanistes* 21:55–78.

_____. 1965b. L'humide et le sec: An essay on ethnobiological adaptation to contrastive environments in the Indo-Pacific area. *Journal of the Polynesian Society* 74:329–346.

Barrera, W., Jr., and P.V. Kirch. 1973. Basaltic glass artifacts from Hawaii: Their dating and prehistoric uses. *Journal of the Polynesian Society* 82(2): 176–87.

Beaglehole, J.C., ed. 1967. *The Journals of Captain James Cook on His Voyages of Discovery.* Vol. 3, *The Voyage of the Resolution and Discovery.* 1776-1780. Hakluyt Society, extra series no. 36. Cambridge, England: Cambridge University Press.

_____. 1969. *The Journals of Captain James Cook on His Voyages of Discovery.* Vol. 2, *The Voyage of Resolution and Adventure. 1772-1775.* Hakluyt Society, extra series no. 35. Cambridge, England: Cambridge University Press.

Bellwood, P.S. 1979. Settlement patterns. In J. Jennings, ed, *The Prehistory of Polynesia,* pp. 308–22. Cambridge, Mass.: Harvard University Press.

Bennett, M.A. 1974. *Basic Ceramic Analysis.* Eastern New Mexico University Contributions in Anthropology 6(1). Portales.

Best, S. 1981. Excavations at Site VL 21/5 Naigani Island, Fiji: A Preliminary Report. Department of Anthropology, University of Auckland, New Zealand.

_____. 1984. Lakeba: The prehistory of a Fijian island. Ph.D. Diss., Department of Anthropology, University of Auckland, New Zealand.

Biggs, B. 1965. Direct and indirect inheritance in Rotuman. *Lingua* 14:383–445.

_____. 1971. The languages of Polynesia. In T.A. Sebeok, ed., *Current Trends in Linguistics* 8(1):466–505. The Hague: Mouton.

Biggs, B., D.S. Walsh, and J. Waqa. 1970. *Proto-Polynesian Reconstructions with English to Proto-Polynesian Finder List.* Department of Anthropology, University of Auckland, New Zealand. Working Papers in Anthropology, Archaeology, Linguistics, and Maori Studies.

Binford, L.R. 1983. *In Pursuit of the Past.* London: Thames and Hudson.

Birks, L. 1973. *Archaeological Excavations at Sigatoka Dune Site, Fiji.* Fiji Museum Bulletin 1. Suva.

Birks, L., and H. Birks. 1968. Adzes from excavations at Sigatoka, Fiji. *Archaeology and Physical Anthropology in Oceania* 3(2):105–15.

_____. 1972. Stone artifacts from Tonga and Fiji. *Asian Perspectives* 15(1):93–96.

Bloom, A.L. 1974. Holocene sea level and tectonics in the Southwest Pacific. *Geological Society of America, Abstracts with Programs* 6(7):658.

Borrie, W.D., R. Firth, and J. Spillius. 1957. The population of Tikopia, 1929 and 1952. *Population Studies* 10:229–52.

Boserup, E. 1965. *The Conditions of Agricultural Growth: The Economics of Agrarian Change under Population Pressure.* London: Allen and Unwin.

Bott, E. 1982. *Tongan Society at the Time of Captain Cook's Visits: Discussions with Her Majesty Queen Salote Tupou.* Polynesian Society Memoir 44. Wellington, New Zealand.

Brookfield, H.C. 1972. Intensification and disintensification in Pacific agriculture: A theoretical approach. *Pacific Viewpoint* 13(1):30–48.

Buck, P.H. (Te Rangi Hiroa). 1930. *Samoan Material Culture.* B.P. Bishop Museum Bulletin 75. Honolulu.

Burrows, E.G. 1936. *Ethnology of Futuna.* B.P. Bishop Museum Bulletin 138. Honolulu.

____. 1937. *Ethnology of 'Uvea.* B.P. Bishop Museum Bulletin 145. Honolulu.

____. 1939. *Western Polynesia: A Study in Cultural Differentiation.* Ethnological Studies 7. Gothenburg.

Cameron, A.M. 1976. Toxicity of coral reef fishes. In O.A. Jones and R. Endean, eds., *Biology and Geology of Coral Reefs,* vol. 3, pp. 155–76. New York: Academic Press.

Campbell, S.F. 1983. Attaining rank: A classification of shell valuables. In J.W. Leach and E. Leach, eds., *The Kula: New Perspectives on Massim Exchange,* pp. 229–48. Cambridge England: Cambridge University Press.

Carrington, H., ed. 1948. *The Discovery of Tahiti* (Journal of H.M.S. Dolfin in 1766-68). Hakluyt Society, second series, no. 98. London.

Cassels, R. 1984. Faunal extinction and prehistoric man in New Zealand and the Pacific islands. In P.S. Martin and R.G. Kline, eds., *Quaternary Extinctions,* pp. 741–67. Tucson: University of Arizona Press.

Chappell, J. 1982. Sea levels and sediments: Some features of the context of coastal archaeological sites in the tropics. *Archaeology in Oceania* 17:69–78.

Chappell, J., and B.G. Thom. 1977. Sea levels and coasts. In J. Allen, J. Golson, and R. Jones, ed., *Sunda and Sahul,* pp. 275–91. London: Academic Press.

Chase, C.G. 1971. Tectonic history of the Fiji Plateau. *Geological Society of America Bulletin* 82:3087–3110.

Christensen, C.C., and P.V. Kirch. 1981. Non-marine molluscs from archaeological sites on Tikopia, Solomon Islands. *Pacific Science* 35:75–88.

_____. 1986. Non marine molluscs and ecological change at Barbers Point, O'ahu, Hawai'i. *Occasional Papers, Bernice P. Bishop Museum* 26:52-80.

Clark, P., and F. Evans. 1954. Distance to nearest neighbor as a measure of spatial relationships in populations. *Ecology* 35(4):445–453.

Cleghorn, P.L. 1984. An historical review of Polynesian stone adze studies. *Journal of the Polynesian Society* 93:399–420.

Coleman, P.J., ed. 1973. *The Western Pacific: Island Arcs, Marginal Seas, Geochemistry.* University of Western Australia Press.

Collocott, E.E.V. 1972. *Ko E Ta'u 'e Teau.* London: William Clowes and Sons. (Published for Siasi Wesiliana Tau'ataina 'o Tonga).

Cordell, L.S. 1984. *Prehistory of the Southwest.* Orlando: Academic Press.

Cox, P.A. 1980. Masi and tanu 'eli: Ancient Polynesian technologies for the preservation and concealment of food. *Pacific Tropical Botanical Garden Bulletin* 10(4):81–93.

Craib, J.L. 1977. A typological investigation of Western Micronesian adzes. Master's thesis, Department of Anthropology, California State University, Long Beach.

Davidson, J.M. 1969a. Archaeological excavations in two burial mounds at 'Atele, Tongatapu. *Records of the Auckland Institute and Museum* 6(4-6):251-286.

____. 1969b. Excavation of a coastal midden deposit, Su-Lo-1. In R.C. Green and J.W. Davidson, eds., *Archaeology in Western Samoa,* vol. 1, pp. 224–52. Auckland Institute and Museum Bulletin 7.

____. 1971a. *Archaeology on Nukuoro Atoll.* Auckland Institute and Museum Bulletin 9.

____. 1971b. Preliminary report on an archaeological survey of the Vava'u Group, Tonga. In R. Fraser, ed., *Cook Bicentenary Expedition in the Southwestern Pacific,* pp. 29-40. Royal Society New Zealand Bulletin 8.

____. 1979. Samoa and Tonga. In J. Jennings, ed., *The Prehistory of Polynesia,* pp. 82-109. Cambridge, Mass.: Harvard University Press.

____. 1984. *The Prehistory of New Zealand.* Auckland: Longman Paul.

Dickinson, W.R. 1974. Sand tempers in sherds from Niuatoputapu and elsewhere in Tonga. *Journal of the Polynesian Society* 83:342–45.

Donovan, L.J. 1973. A study of the decorative system of the Lapita potters in Reefs and Santa Cruz Islands. Master's thesis, Department of Anthropology, University of Auckland, New Zealand.

Duff, R. 1959. Neolithic adzes of Eastern Polynesia. In J.D. Freeman and W.R. Geddes, eds., *Anthropology in the South Seas,* pp. 121–47. New Plymouth, New Zealand.

Dunnell, R.C. 1986. Five decades of American archaeology. In D.J. Meltzer, D.D. Fowler, and J.A. Sabloff, eds., *American Archaeology Past and Future,* pp. 3–49. Washington, D.C.: Smithsonian Institution Press.

Dye, T.S. 1980. The linguistic position of Niuafo'ou. *Journal of the Polynesian Society* 89(3):349–57.

_____. 1983. Fish and fishing on Niuatoputapu, Tonga. *Oceania* 53:242-71.

Dye, T. and P.V. Kirch. 1980. End-of-fieldwork progress report, archaeological survey of Arno Atoll, Marshall Islands. Dept. of Anthropology, Ms. No. 121080. B.P. Bishop Museum, Honolulu.

Elbert, S.H. 1953. Internal relationships of Polynesian languages and dialects. *Southwestern Journal of Anthropology* 9:147–73.

Emory, K.P. 1968. East Polynesian relationships as revealed through adzes. In I. Yawata and Y.H. Sinoto, eds., *Prehistoric Culture in Oceania*, pp. 151–69. Honolulu: Bishop Museum Press.

Ewart, A., and W.B. Bryan. 1973. The petrology and geochemistry of the Tongan Islands. In P.J. Coleman, ed., *The Western Pacific: Island Arcs, Marginal Seas, Geochemistry*, pp. 503–22. University of Western Australia Press.

Fairbridge, R.W. 1961. Eustatic changes in sea level. In L. Ahrens, F. Press, K. Rankama, and S. Runcorn, eds., *Physics and Chemistry of the Earth*, vol. 4, pp. 99–185. New York: Pergamon Press.

Figueroa, G., and E. Sanchez. 1965. Adzes from certain islands of Eastern Polynesia. In T. Heyerdahl and E. Ferdon, Jr., eds., *Reports of the Norwegian Archaeological Expedition to Easter Island and the East Pacific*, vol. 2, pp. 169–254. Monographs of the School of American Research no. 24, pt. 2. Santa Fe.

Firth, R. 1936. *We, The Tikopia*. London: George Allen and Unwin.

____. 1939. *Primitive Polynesian Economy*. London: George Routledge and Sons.

Folk, R.L. 1974. *Petrology of Sedimentary Rocks*. Hemphill Publishing Co., Austin, Texas.

Fosberg, F.R. 1963. Disturbance in island ecosystems. In J.L. Gressitt, ed., *Pacific Basin Biogeography*, pp. 557–61. Honolulu: Bishop Museum Press.

Fowler, H.W. 1955. *Archaeological Fishbones Collected by E.W. Gifford in Fiji*. B.P. Bishop Museum Bulletin 214. Honolulu.

____. 1959. *Fishes of Fiji*. Suva: Government of Fiji.

French-Wright, R. 1983. Proto-Oceanic horticultural practices. Master's thesis, Department of Anthropology, University of Auckland, New Zealand.

Frimigacci, D., J.P. Siorat, and B. Vienne. 1984. Inventaire et fouille des sites archeologiques et ethnohistoriques de l'ile d'Uvea. Documents Provisoires, ORSTOM, Centre de Noumea.

Frost, E.L. 1979. Fiji. In J.D. Jennings, ed., *The Prehistory of Polynesia*, pp. 61–81. Cambridge, Mass.: Harvard University Press.

Garanger, J. 1972. *Archéologie des Nouvelles-Hébrides*. Publications de la Société des Oceanistes, no. 30. Paris.

Geraghty, P.A. 1983. *The History of the Fijian Languages*. Oceanic Linguistics Special Publication no. 19. Honolulu: University of Hawaii Press.

Gifford, E.W. 1924. *Tongan Myths and Tales*. B.P. Bishop Museum Bulletin 8. Honolulu.

_____. 1929. *Tongan Society*. B.P. Bishop Museum Bulletin 61. Honolulu.

_____. 1951. Archaeological excavations in Fiji. *University of California Anthropological Records* 13(3):189-288.

Gifford, E.W., and R. Shutler, Jr. 1956. Archaeological excavations in New Caledonia. *University of California Anthropological Records* 18(1): 1–148.

Gill, J., and M. Gorton. 1973. A proposed geological and geochemical history of Eastern Melanesia. In P.J. Coleman, ed., *The Western Pacific: Island Arcs, Marginal Seas, Geochemistry*, pp. 543–66. University of Western Australia Press.

Gillespie, R. and P. Swadling. 1979. Marine shells give reliable radiocarbon ages for middens. *Search* 10:92-93.

Goldman, B., and F.H. Talbot. 1976. Aspects of the ecology of coral reef fishes. In R. Endean, ed., *Biology and Geology of Coral Reefs*, vol. 3(2): 125–54.

Goldman, I. 1970. *Ancient Polynesian Society*. Chicago: University of Chicago Press.

Golson, J. 1957. Report to Tri-Institutional Pacific Program on archaeological field work in Tonga and Samoa. Auckland (mimeograph).

____. 1971. Lapita ware and its transformations. In R.C. Green and M. Kelly, eds., *Studies in Oceanic Culture History*, vol. 2, pp. 67–76. Pacific Anthropological Records 12. Honolulu: B.P. Bishop Museum.

Gould, R.A. 1980. *Living Archaeology*. Cambridge, England: Cambridge University Press.

Grace, G.W. 1959. *The Position of the Polynesian Languages Within the Austronesian Language Family*. Mem. 16, International Journal American Linguistics, Indiana University Publications in Anthropology and Linguistics Also B.P. Bishop Museum Spec. Publ. 46.

____. 1967. Effect of heterogeneity in the lexicostatistical test list: The case of Rotuman. In G.A. Highland et. al., eds., *Polynesian Culture History*, pp. 289–302. Honolulu: Bishop Museum Press.

Grayson, D.K. 1984. *Quantitative Zooarchaeology*. Orlando: Academic Press.

Green, D., and D.J. Cullen. 1973. The tectonic evolution of the Fiji region. In P.J. Coleman, ed., *The Western Pacific: Island Arcs, Marginal Seas, Geochemistry*, pp. 127-45. University of Western Australia Press.

Green, R.C. 1963. A suggested revision of the Fijian sequence. *Journal of the Polynesian Society* 72(3):235–260.

_____. 1966. Linguistic subgrouping within Polynesia: The implications for prehistoric settlement. *Journal of the Polynesian Society* 75(1):6-38.

_____. 1968. West Polynesian prehistory. In I. Yawata and Y. Sinoto, eds., *Prehistoric Culture in Oceania*, pp. 99-109. Honolulu: Bishop Museum Press.

_____. 1969. Excavations at VA-1, 1963–64. In R.C. Green and J.M. Davidson, eds., *Archaeology in Western Samoa*, vol. 1, pp. 114–37. Auckland Institute and Museum Bulletin 6.

_____. 1971. Evidence for the development of the early Polynesian adz kit. *New Zealand Archaeological Association Newsletter* 14(1):12–44.

_____. 1972a. Revision of the Tongan sequence. *Journal of the Polynesian Society* 81(1):79–86.

_____. 1972b. Aspects of the Neolithic in Oceania: Polynesia. In N. Barnard, ed., *Early Chinese Art and its Possible Influence in the Pacific Basin*, vol. 3, pp. 655–91. New York: Intercultural Arts Press.

_____. 1974a. Excavations of the prehistoric occupations of SU-SA-3. In R. Green and J. Davidson, eds., *Archaeology in Western Samoa*, vol. 2, pp. 108-54. Auckland Institute and Museum Bulletin 7.

_____. 1974b. A review of portable artifacts from Western Samoa. In R.C. Green and J. Davidson, eds., *Archaeology in Western Samoa*, vol. 2 pp. 245-75. Auckland Institute and Museum Bulletin 7.

_____. 1974c. Sites with Lapita pottery: Importing and voyaging. *Mankind* 9:253-59.

_____. 1976. Lapita sites in the Santa Cruz group. In R.C. Green and M. Cresswell, eds., *Southeast Solomon Islands Cultural History*, pp. 245–65. Royal Society of New Zealand Bulletin 11.

_____. 1978. *New Sites with Lapita Pottery and their Implications for an Understanding of the Settlement of the Western Pacific*. Department of Anthropology, University of Auckland, New Zealand. Working Papers in Anthropology, Archaeology, Linguistics, and Maori Studies no. 51.

_____. 1979. Lapita. In J. Jennings, ed., *The Prehistory of Polynesia*, pp. 27-60. Cambridge, Mass.: Harvard University Press.

_____. 1981. Location of the Polynesian homeland: A continuing problem. In J. Hollyman and A. Pawley, eds., *Studies in Pacific Languages and Cultures in Honor of Bruce Biggs*, pp. 133–58. Auckland: Linguistic Society of New Zealand.

_____. 1986. Lapita fishing: The evidence of Site SE-RF-2 from the Main Reef Islands, Santa Cruz Group, Solomons. In A. Anderson, ed., *Traditional fishing in the Pacific*, pp. 119–35. Pacific Anthropological Records 37.

Green, R.C., and J.M. Davidson, eds. 1969a. *Archaeology in Western Samoa*, vol. 1. Auckland Institute and Museum Bulletin 6.

_____. 1969b. Description and classification of Samoan adzes. In R.C. Green and J.M. Davidson, eds., *Archaeology in Western Samoa*, vol. 1, pp. 21–32. Auckland Institute and Museum Bulletin 6.

_____. 1974. *Archaeology in Western Samoa*, vol. 2. Auckland Institute and Museum Bulletin 7.

Green, R.C. and H. G. Richards. 1975. Lapita pottery and a lower sea level in western Samoa. *Pacific Science* 29(4):309-15.

Groube, L.M. 1967. Models in prehistory: A consideration of the New Zealand evidence. *Archaeology and Physical Anthropology in Oceania* 2:1–27.

_____. 1971. Tonga, Lapita pottery, and Polynesian origins. *Journal of the Polynesian Society* 80:278–316.

Guiart, J. 1963. Un état palatial Océanien: l'Empire maritime des Tui Tonga. Appendix to *Structure de la Chefferie en Mélanésie du Sud*. Travaux et Mémoires de l'Institut d'Ethnologie, vol. 66. Paris.

Gunson, N. 1977. The coming of foreigners. In N. Rutherford, ed., *Friendly Islands: A History of Tonga*, pp. 90-113. Melbourne: Oxford University Press.

Hage, P. 1977. Centrality in the Kula Ring. *Journal of the Polynesian Society* 86:27–36.

Hage, P., and F. Harary. 1983. *Structural Models in Anthropology*. Cambridge, England: Cambridge University Press.

_____. (in press.) *Exchange in Oceania*.

Hedrick, J. n.d. Archaeological investigation of Malo prehistory: Lapita settlement strategy in the northern New Hebrides. Draft ms. of Ph.D. Diss., University of Pennsylvania.

Hodder, I., and C. Orton. 1976. *Spatial Analysis in Archaeology*. Cambridge, England: Cambridge University Press.

Hoffmeister, J. E. 1932. *Geology of Eua, Tonga*. B.P. Bishop Museum Bulletin 96. Honolulu.

Holmer, R.N. 1980. Samoan ceramic analysis. In J.D. Jennings and R.N. Holmer, eds., *Archaeological Excavations in Western Samoa*. Pacific Anthropological Records 32. Honolulu: B.P. Bishop Museum.

Howells, W. 1973. *The Pacific Islanders*. New York: Charles Scribner's Sons.

Hughes, P., G. Hope, M. Latham, and M. Brookfield. 1979. Prehistoric man-induced degradation of the Lakeba landscape: Evidence from two inland swamps. In H. Brookfield, ed., *Lakeba:*

Environmental Change, Population Dynamics, and Resource Use, pp. 93–110. UNESCO, Paris.

Hunt, T. 1980. Toward Fiji's past: Archaeological research on southwestern Viti Levu. Master's thesis, Department of Anthropology, University of Auckland, New Zealand.

_____. 1981. New evidence for early horticulture in Fiji. *Journal of the Polynesian Society* 90:259–69.

_____. 1986. Conceptual and substantive issues in Fijian prehistory. In P.V. Kirch, ed., *Island Societies: Archaeological Approaches to Evolution and Transformation*, pp. 20–32. Cambridge, England: Cambridge University Press.

Hunt, T. and P.V. Kirch. in press. An archaeological survey of the Manu'a Islands, American Samoa. *Journal of the Polynesian Society.*

Irwin, G. 1983. Chieftainship, Kula, and trade in Massim prehistory. In J.W. Leach and E. Leach, eds., *The Kula: New Perspectives on Massi Exchange*, pp. 29–72. Cambridge, England: Cambridge University Press.

_____. 1985. *The Emergence of Mailu.* Terra Australis 10. Canberra: The Australian National University.

Janetski, J. 1976. Dietary remains from Jane's Camp—a midden site. In J. Jennings et al., *Excavations on Upou, Western Samoa*, pp. 75-82. Pacific Anthropological Records 25. Honolulu: B.P. Bishop Museum.

_____. 1980. Analysis of dietary remains from Potusa and Falemoa. In J. Jennings and R.N. Holmer, eds., *Archaeological Excavation in Western Samoa*, pp. 117-22. Pacific Anthropological Records 32. B.P. Bishop Museum. Honolulu.

Jennings, J., ed. 1979. *The Prehistory of Polynesia.* Cambridge, Mass.: Harvard University Press.

Jennings, J. and R.N. Holmer. 1980. *Archaeological Excavations in Western Samoa.* Pacific Anthropological Records 32. Honolulu: B.P. Bishop Museum.

Jennings, J., R. Holmer, and G. Jackmond. 1982. Samoan village patterns: Four examples. *Journal of the Polynesian Society* 91:81-102.

Jennings, J., R. Holmer, J. Janetski, and H. Smith. 1976. *Excavations on Upolu, Western Samoa.* Pacific Anthropological Records 25. Honolulu: B.P. Bishop Museum.

Johnson, G. 1977. Aspects of regional analysis in archaeology. *Annual Review of Anthropology* 6:479–508.

Jordan, D.S. and A. Seale. 1906. *The Fishes of Samoa.* U.S. Bureau of Fisheries Bulletin 25:175–455.

Kaeppler, A.L. 1971a. Rank in Tonga. *Ethnology* 10(2):174-93.

_____. 1971b. Eighteenth century Tonga: New interpretations of Tongan society and material culture at the time of Captain Cook. *Man* 6(2): 204–20.

_____. 1973. Pottery sherds from Tungua, Ha'apai. *Journal of the Polynesian Society* 82:218–22.

_____. 1978. Exchange patterns in goods and spouses: Fiji, Tonga, and Samoa. *Mankind* 11(3):246–52.

Kay, R.M.A. 1984. Analysis of archaeological material from Naigani. Master's thesis, Department of Anthropology, University of Auckland, New Zealand.

Kern, R.A. 1948. The vocabularies of Jacob Le Maire. *Acta Orientalia* 20: 216–37.

Kirch, P.V. 1973. Prehistoric subsistence patterns in the northern Marquesas Islands, French Polynesia. *Archaeology and Physical Anthropology in Oceania* 8:24-40.

_____. 1975a. Cultural adaptation and ecology in Western Polynesia: An ethnoarchaeological study. Ph.D. Diss., Department of Anthropology, Yale University.

_____. 1975b. Halawa Valley in Hawaiian prehistory. In P.V. Kirch and M. Kelly, eds., *Prehistory and Ecology in a Windward Hawaiian Valley: Halawa Valley, Molokai.* Pacific Anthropological Records 24. Honolulu.

_____. 1976. Ethno-archaeological investigations in Futuna and 'Uvea (Western Polynesia): A preliminary report. *Journal of the Polynesian Society* 85(1):27–69.

_____. 1977. Ethnoarchaeological investigations on Niuatoputapu, Tonga (Western Polynesia): A preliminary report to the National Science Foundation. Dept. of Anthropology, B.P. Bishop Museum, Honolulu.

_____. 1978a. Indigenous agriculture on 'Uvea (Western Polynesia). *Economic Botany* 32(2):157–81.

_____. 1978b. The Lapitoid Period in West Polynesia: Excavations and Survey in Niuatoputapu, Tonga. *Journal of Field Archaeology* 5(1):1-13.

_____. 1979. Subsistence and ecology. In J. Jennings, ed., *The Prehistory of Polynesia*, pp. 286–307. Cambridge, Mass.: Harvard University Press.

_____. 1980a. Burial structures and societal ranking in Vava'u, Tonga. *Journal of the Polynesian Society* 89(3):291–308.

_____. 1980b. Polynesian prehistory: Cultural adaptation in island ecosystems. *American Scientist* 68(1):39–48.

_____. 1981. Lapitoid settlements of Futuna and Alofi, Western Polynesia. *Archaeology in Oceania* 16:127–43.

_____. 1982a. Advances in Polynesian prehistory: Three decades in review. In F. Wendorf and A.E. Close, eds., *Advances in World Archaeology*, vol. 1, pp. 51–97. New York: Academic Press.

_____. 1982b. A revision of the Anuta sequence. *Journal of the Polynesian Society* 91:245–54.

_____. 1983a. An archaeological exploration of Vanikoro, Santa Cruz Islands, Eastern Melanesia. *New Zealand Journal of Archaeology* 5:69–113.

_____. 1983b. Man's role in modifying tropical and subtropical Polynesian ecosystems. *Archaeology in Oceania* 18:26-31.

_____. 1984a. *The Evolution of the Polynesian Chiefdoms*. New Studies in Archaeology. Cambridge, England: Cambridge University Press.

_____. 1984b. The Polynesian Outliers: Continuity, change, and replacement. *Journal of Pacific History* 19:224–38.

_____. 1985. *Feathered Gods and Fishhooks: An Introduction to Hawaiian Archaeology and Prehistory*. Honolulu: University of Hawaii Press.

_____. 1986. Exchange systems and inter-island contact in the transformation of an island society: The Tikopia case. In P.V. Kirch, ed., *Island Societies: Archaeological Approaches to Evolution and Transformation*, pp. 33-41. Cambridge, England: Cambridge University Press.

_____. 1987. Lapita and Oceanic cultural origins: excavations in the Mussau Islands, Bismarck Archipelago, 1985. *Journal of Field Archaeology* 14:163-80.

_____. (in press.) Long-distance exchange and island colonization: The Lapita case. *Norwegian Archaeological Review*.

Kirch, P.V. and C.C. Christensen. in press. Extinct achatinellid snails from Easter Island: biogeographic, ecological, and archaeological implications. *Burke Museum Contributions in Anthropology and Natural History*.

Kirch, P.V. and T.S. Dye. 1979. Ethnoarchaeology and the development of Polynesian fishing strategies. *Journal of the Polynesian Society* 88(1):53–76.

Kirch, P.V. and R.C. Green. 1987. History, phylogeny, and evolution in Polynesia. *Current Anthropology* 28:431-56.

Kirch, P.V. and P.H. Rosendahl. 1973. Archaeological investigation of Anuta. In D.E. Yen and G. Gordon, eds., *Anuta: A Polynesian Outlier in the Solomon Islands*, pp. 25–108. Pacific Anthropological Records 21. Honolulu: B.P. Bishop Museum.

_____. 1976. Early Anutan settlement and the position of Anuta in the prehistory of the Southwest Pacific. In R.C. Green and M. Cresswell, eds., *Southeast Solomon Islands Cultural History*, pp. 223-44. Royal Society of New Zealand Bulletin 11.

Kirch, P.V. and D.E. Yen. 1982. *Tikopia: The Prehistory and Ecology of a Polynesian Outlier*. B.P. Bishop Museum Bulletin 238. Honolulu.

Klein, J., J.C. Lerman, P.E. Damon, and E.K. Ralph. 1982. Calibration of radiocarbon dates: Tables based on the consensus data of the workshop on calibrating the radiocarbon time scale. *Radiocarbon* 24(2):103–50.

La Pérouse, J.F. de G. de. 1799. *Voyage Round the World, Performed in the Years 1785, 1786, 1787 & 1788, by the Boussole and Astrolabe*, Biblioteca Australiana no. 28. New York: Da Capro Press (reprint).

Ladd, H.S. 1934. *Geology of Viti Levu, Fiji*. B.P. Bishop Museum Bulletin 119. Honolulu.

Law, G. 1984. Archaeological carbon dating using marine shell—the New Zealand experience. Paper presented at the New Zealand Archaeological Association Conference, Oamaru.

Leach, B.F. and G. Ward. 1981. *Archaeology on Kapingamarangi Atoll*. Otago: Privately Published.

McCoy, P.C. 1982. Manufacturing technology. In P.V. Kirch and D.E. Yen, *Tikopia: The Prehistory and Ecology of a Polynesian Outlier*, B.P. Bishop Museum Bulletin 238, pp. 261-269. Honolulu.

McKern, W.C. 1929. *The Archaeology of Tonga*. B.P. Bishop Museum Bulletin 60. Honolulu.

Mahina, 'O. 1986. Religion, politics, and the Tu'i Tonga empire. Master's thesis, Department of Anthropology, University of Auckland, New Zealand.

Malinowski, B. 1922. *Argonauts of the Western Pacific*. London: George Routledge & Sons.

Martens, J.H.C. 1939. Beaches. In P.D. Trask, ed., *Recent Marine Sediments*, pp. 207–18. London: Thomas Murby and Co.

Martin, J. 1820. *An Account of the Natives of the Tonga Islands...Arranged from the Extensive Communications of Mr. William Mariner*. 1st American Edition, Boston: Charles Ewer.

Mayr, E. 1945. *Birds of the Southwest Pacific*. New York: MacMillan Co.

Mead, S.M., L. Birks, H. Birks, and E. Shaw. 1973. *The Lapita Style of Fiji and its Associations*. Polynesian Society Memoir 38. Wellington.

Meehan, B. 1982. *Shell Bed to Shell Midden*. Canberra: Australian Institute of Aboriginal Studies.

Merrill, E.D. 1945. *Plant Life of the Pacific World*. New York: MacMillan Co.

Meyer, O. 1909. Funde Prähistorischer Töpferei und Steinmesser auf Vuatom, Bismarck Archipel. *Anthropos* 4:251–2, 1093–5.

Moratto, M.J. 1984. *California Archaeology.* Orlando: Academic Press.

Morgenstein, M., and T.J. Riley. 1974. Hydration-rind dating of basaltic glass: A new method for archaeological chronologies. *Asian Perspectives* 17(2):145–59.

Morgenstein, M., and P. Rosendahl. 1976. Basaltic glass hydration dating in Hawaii. In R.E. Taylor, ed., *Advances in Obsidian Glass Studies: Archaeological and Geochemical Perspectives,* pp. 141–64. New Jersey: Noyes Press.

Munro, I.S.R. 1967. *The Fishes of New Guinea.* Port Moresby: Department of Agriculture, Stock, and Fisheries.

Nance, J.D. 1981. Statistical fact and archaeological faith: Two models in small-sites sampling. *Journal of Field Archaeology* 8(2):151–65.

Nie, N., C. Hull, J. Jenkins, K. Steinbrenner, and D. Bent. 1975. *SPSS: Statistical Package for the Social Sciences.* New York: McGraw-Hill.

Olson, L. 1983. Hawaiian volcanic glass applied 'dating' and 'sourcing': Archaeological context. In J.T. Clark and P.V. Kirch, eds., *Archaeological Investigations of the Mudlane-Waimea-Kawaihae Road Corridor, Island of Hawai'i: An Interdisciplinary Study of an Environmental Transect.* Department of Anthropology Report 83–1. Honolulu: B.P. Bishop Museum.

Olson, S.L., and H.F. James. 1984. The role of Polynesians in the extinction of the avifauna of the Hawaiian Islands. In P.S. Martin and R.G. Kline, eds., *Quarternary Extinctions,* pp. 768–80. Tucson: University of Arizona Press.

Parry, J.T. 1977. *Ring-Ditch Fortifications in the Rewa Delta, Fiji.* Fiji Museum Bulletin 3. Suva.

_____. 1981. *Ring-Ditch Fortifications in the Navua Delta, Fiji.* Fiji Museum Bulletin 7. Suva.

Pawley, A. 1966. Polynesian languages: A subgrouping based on shared innovations in morphology. *Journal of the Polynesian Society* 75(1):39–64.

_____. 1967. The relationships of Polynesian Outlier languages. *Journal of the Polynesian Society* 76:259–96.

_____. 1972. On the internal relationships of eastern Oceanic languages. In R.C. Green and M. Kelly, eds., *Studies in Oceanic Culture History,* vol. 3, pp. 1–142. Pacific Anthropological Records 13. Honolulu: B.P. Bishop Museum Press.

_____. 1979. *New Evidence on the Position of Rotuman.* Working Papers in Anthropology no. 56. University of Auckland, New Zealand.

Pawley, A., and T. Sayaba. 1971. Fijian dialect divisions: Eastern and Western. *Journal of the Polynesian Society* 80.

Plog, F. 1973. Diachronic anthropology. In C.L. Redman, ed., *Research and Theory in Current Archeology,* pp. 181–98. New York: John Wiley and Sons.

Poulsen, J. 1964. Preliminary report on pottery finds in Tonga. *Asian Perspectives* 8:184–95.

_____. 1967. A contribution to the prehistory of the Tongan Islands. Ph.D. Diss., Department of Anthropology, Australian National University, Canberra.

_____. 1968. Archaeological excavations on Tongatapu. In I. Yawata and Y.H. Sinoto, eds., *Prehistoric Culture in Oceania,* pp. 85–92. Honolulu: B.P. Bishop Museum Press.

_____. 1970. Shell artifacts in Oceania: Their distribution and significance. In R.C. Green and M. Kelly, eds., *Studies in Oceanic Culture History,* vol. 1, pp. 33–46. Pacific Anthropological Records 11. Honolulu: Bishop Museum Press.

_____. 1976. The chronology of early Tongan prehistory and the Lapita ware. In J. Garanger, ed., *La Préhistoire Océanienne,* pp. 223–50. IX Congrés, Union Internationale des Science Préhistorique et Protohistoriques, CNRS, Nice.

_____. 1977. Archaeology and prehistory. In N. Rutherford, ed., *Friendly Islands: A History of Tonga,* pp. 4–26. Melbourne: Oxford University Press.

_____. 1983. The chronology of early Tongan prehistory and the Lapita ware. *Journal de la Société des Océanistes* 76:46–56.

Redman, C.L. 1974. *Archaeological Sampling Strategies.* Addison-Wesley Module in Anthropology no. 55.

Richards, P.W. 1952. *The Tropical Rain Forest.* Cambridge: Cambridge University Press.

Rogers, G.A. 1973. *Report on Archaeological Survey in Niuatoputapu Island, Tonga.* Working Papers in Anthropology, Archaeology, Linguistics, and Maori Studies no. 28. Department of Anthropology, University of Auckland, New Zealand.

_____. 1974. Archaeological discoveries on Niuatoputapu Island, Tonga. *Journal of the Polynesian Society* 83(3):308–48.

_____. 1975. Kai and kava in Niuatoputapu: Social relations, ideologies and contexts in a rural Tongan community. Ph.D. Thesis, Auckland University, New Zealand.

Rouse, I. and J.M. Cruxent. 1963. *Venezuelan Archaeology.* New Haven: Yale University Press.

Sahlins, M.D. 1958. *Social Stratification in Polynesia.* Seattle: American Ethnological Society.

_____. 1981. The stranger-king, or Dumézil among the Fijians. *Journal of Pacific History* 16:107–32.

_____. 1985. *Islands of History.* Chicago: University of Chicago Press.

St. John, H. 1977. The flora of Niuatoputapu Island, Tonga. *Phytologia* 36:374–90.

Schouten, W. 1619. *A Wonderful Voyage Round About the World.* New York: De Capo Press (reprint, 1968).

Schultz, L.P. 1958. *Review of the Parrotfish Family Scaridae.* U.S. National Museum Bulletin 214. Washington, D.C.

Sclater, J.G., J.W. Hawkins, J. Mammerick, and C.G. Chase. 1972. Crustal extension between the Tonga and Lau ridges: petrologic and geophysical evidence. *Geological Society of America Bulletin* 83:505–18.

Shutler, R. Jr. and J. Marck. 1975. On the dispersal of the Austronesian horticulturalists. *Archaeology and Physical Anthropology in Oceania* 10(2):81–113.

Shutler, R. Jr. and M.E. Shutler. 1975. *Oceanic Prehistory.* Menlo Park: Cummings Publishing Co.

Sinoto, Y.H. and P.C. McCoy. 1975. Report on the preliminary excavation of an early habitation site on Huahine, Society Islands. *Journal de la Société des Océanistes* 47:143–86.

Sneath, P.H.A., and R.R. Sokal. 1973. *Numerical Taxonomy.* San Francisco: W.H. Freeman and Co.

Spriggs, M. 1981. Vegetable kingdoms: Taro irrigation and Pacific prehistory. Ph.D. Diss., Department of Anthropology, Australian National University.

_____. 1986. Landscape, land use and political transformation in southern Melanesia. In P.V. Kirch, ed., *Island Societies: Archaeological Approaches to Evolution and Transformation,* pp. 6–19. Cambridge University Press.

Steadman, D.W. 1985. Fossil Birds from Mangaia, Southern Cook Islands. *British Ornithology Club Bulletin* 105:58–66.

Steadman, D.W. and P.V. Kirch. in prep. Bird remains from archaeological sites on Tikopia and Anuta.

Steadman, D.W. and S.L. Olson. 1985. Bird remains from an archaeological site on Henderson Island, South Pacific: Man-caused extinctions on an 'uninhabited' island. *Proceedings U.S. National Academy of Sciences* 82:6191–95.

Steadman, D.W. and M.C. Zarriello. in press. Two new species of parrots (Aves: Psittacidae) from archaeological sites in the Marquesas Islands. *Proceedings of the Biological Society of Washington.*

Stearns, H.T. 1944. Geology of the Samoan Islands. *Geological Society of America Bulletin* 56:1279–1332.

_____. 1945. Eustatic shore lines in the Pacific. *Geological Society America Bulletin* 56:1071–78.

Stone, E.L. Jr. 1951. The soils of Arno Atoll, Marshall Islands. *Atoll Research Bulletin* 5. Washington, D.C.: Pacific Science Board.

Stuiver, M. 1984. Radiocarbon timescale calibration. *Quarterly Review of Archaeology* 5(1):8-9.

Stuiver, M. and H. A. Polach. 1977. Reporting of ^{14}C data. *Radiocarbon* 19:355–63.

Suggs, R.C. 1961. *Archaeology of Nuku Hiva, Marquesas Islands, French Polynesia.* Anthropological Papers, American Museum of Natural History 49(1).

Tate, G.H.H. 1951. *The rodents of Australia and New Guinea.* American Museum of Natural History Bulletin 97(4):187–430.

Taylor, F.W., and A.L. Bloom. 1975. Pleistocene tectonics and sea level fluctuations in Tonga and Fiji. *Geological Society of America, Abstracts with Programs* 7(7):1292.

_____. 1977. Coral reefs on tectonic blocks, Tonga Island arc. *Proceedings Third International Coral Reef Symposium,* pp. 275–81. University of Miami.

Taylor, R.C. 1973. *An Atlas of Pacific Islands Rainfall.* Hawaii Institute of Geophysics, Data Report no. 25. Honolulu: University of Hawaii.

Terrell, J. 1986. *Prehistory in the Pacific Islands.* Cambridge, England: Cambridge University Press.

Tinker, S.W. 1978. *Fishes of Hawaii.* Honolulu: Hawaiian Service, Inc.

Trotter, M., and G.C. Gleser. 1958. A re-evaluation of estimation of stature based on measurements of stature taken during life and of long bones after death. *American Journal of Physical Anthropology* 16:79–124.

van Balgooy, M.M.J. 1960. Preliminary plant geographical analysis of the Pacific as based on the distribution of Phanerogam genera. *Blumea* 10:384–431.

Villiers, J.A.J. de, trans. 1906. *The East and West Indian Mirror, Being an Account of...the Australian Navigations of Jacob le Maire.* Hakluyt Society, ser. 2, no. 18. Cambridge, England: Cambridge University Press.

Visher, G.S. 1969. Grain size distributions and depositional processes. *Journal of Sedimentary Petrology* 39:1074-1106.

Visher, S.S. 1925. *Tropical Cyclones of the Pacific.* B.P. Bishop Museum Bulletin 20. Honolulu.

Ward, G.K. 1974a. An investigation of the source of the "obsidian" flakes from two Samoan sites. In R.C. Green and J. Davidson, eds., *Archaeology on Western Samoa,* vol. 2, pp. 167–69. Auckland Institute and Museum Bulletin 7.

_____. 1974b. Source of obsidian from Niuatoputapu sites. *Journal of the Polynesian Society* 83:345.

Ward, G.K., and I.E. Smith. 1974. Characterization of chert sources as an aid to the identification of patterns of trade, Southeast Solomon Islands. *Mankind* 9(4):281–6.

Williamson, R.W. 1924. *The Social and Political Systems of Central Polynesia.* 3 vols. Cambridge, England: Cambridge University Press.

Wilson, J. 1799. *A Missionary Voyage to the Southern Pacific Ocean Performed in the Years 1796, 1797, 1798 in the Ship Duff....* London: T. Chapman.

Yen, D.E. 1971. The development of agriculture in Oceania. In R.C. Green and M. Kelly, eds., *Studies in Oceanic Culture History,* vol. 2. Pacific Anthropological Records 12. Honolulu: B.P. Bishop Museum Press.

_____. 1973a. The origins of Oceanic agriculture. *Archaeology and Physical Anthropology in Oceania* 8:68–85.

_____. 1973b. Agriculture in Anutan subsistence. In D.E. Yen and J. Gordon, eds., *Anuta: A Polynesian Outlier in the Solomon Islands,* pp. 112–49. Pacific Anthropological Records 21. Honolulu: B.P. Bishop Museum Press.

_____. 1975. Indigenous food processing in Oceania. In M. Arnott, ed., *Gastronomy: The Anthropology of Food and Food Habits,* pp. 147–68. Chicago: Aldine.

_____. n.d. (1986) Lapita, among other things, a tribute to Jack Golson. Paper delivered at the Lapita Homeland Project Workshop, May 28, 1986, at the Australian Museum, Sydney.

Yuncker, T.G., 1959. *Plants of Tonga.* B.P. Bishop Museum Bulletin 220. Honolulu.

APPENDIX A

ARCHAEOLOGICAL SITES OF NIUATOPUTAPU ISLAND

SITE NO.	NAME/DESCRIPTION	CLASS	BIOTOPE	REMARKS
NT- 1	Esi 'o Panuve	4	V	
2	Alokivakaloa	4	V	
3	Esi 'o Pilolevu	4	IVA	
4	Mata ki 'Uvea	8	V	
5	Mata ki Ha'amoa	8	V	
6	Siamanafa	6	IVA	
7	Sia ko Finetengalelei	9	II	
8	Ha'afo'ou	9	IVA	
9	Haufakalaki	6	II	
10	Nofoatoa	8	II	
11	Motu I	7	IVA	
12	Motu II	7	IVA	
13	Motu III	7	IVA	
14	Kolo	7	II	
15	Tokelau	7	II	
16-19	------------ GAP ------------			
20	Tu'atangiketatau	12	IVA	
21	Olosenga'Falepouahi	12	IVA	
22	Tofi'a	12	IVA	
23	Langi 'o Seketoa (?)	12	IVA	
24	Langi 'o Ma'atu Sioeli Kiivalu	11	IVA	
25	Angihoa	12	IVA	
26	Failoto	11	IVA	
27	Faakikava	11	IVA	
28	Funga'ana I	12	IVA	
29	Funga'ana II	12	IVA	
30	Hihifo I	10	IVA	
31	Tofi'a I	12	IVA	

SITE NO.	NAME/DESCRIPTION	CLASS	BIOTOPE	REMARKS
NT- 32	Falehau I	11	IVA	
33	Falehau II	11	IVA	
34	Falehau III	11	IVA	
35	Loto'aa I	12	IVA	
36	Loto'aa II	11	IVA	
37	Ve'elangi III	11	IVA	
38	Sisipalaeva'e	—	IVA	Destroyed
39	- - - - - - - Unassigned Number - - - - - - -			
40	Atatuka I	11	IVA/B	
41	Atatuka II	9	V	
42	Atatuka III	11	V	
43-49	- - - - - - - - - - GAP - - - - - - - - - -			
50	Houmafakalele I	11	IVA	
51	Houmafakalele II	7	IVA	
52	Houmafakalele III	12	V	Excavated
53	Vaivai	11	IVA	
54	Houmafakalele IV	11	V	
55	Houmafakalele V	11	V	Excavated
56-69	- - - - - - - - - - GAP - - - - - - - - - -			
70	Makafaakimuli	14	II	
71	Paamaka	3	I	
72	Soopii	3	I	
73	Ve'etoki	3	I	
74	Finekata	14	IVA	
75	Tukupeau	14	VI	
76	Falehuufanga	14	IVA	
77	Funga'ana Quarry	13	IVA	
78	Avalua	—	III (?)	Probably natural
79	Loto'aa III	—	III/IVA	Natural; old shoreline
80-89	- - - - - - - - - - GAP - - - - - - - - - -			
90	Lolokoka	1	III	Excavated
91	Ha'afisi	1	III	Excavated
92	Tu'akolo-Nahau	1	III	Excavated
93	Pome'e	1	III	Excavated
94	Falehau	1	III	
95	Matavai	1	III	
96	Tokelau	1	III	
97	Faka'ahotaha	1	III	
98	Lolopipi	1	III	
99	Fanakava	1	III	
100	Loto'aa	1	III	Excavated
101	Ve'elangi II	16	IVA	
102	Taumaahina	16	IVA	
103	Peitolahi	16	IVA	See also NT-195
104	Nukufotu	16	IVA	See also NT-155
105	Taputangi	16	IVA	
106	Matavai	16	IVA	
107	Kalevalio	16	IVA	
108	Haufolau	16	IVA	
109	Vaipoa	16	IVA	
110	Matavai Village	Site Complex	III/IVA	Excavated
111	Toma	Site Complex	V	
112	Vaipoa Church	1	III/IVA	Excavated
113	Holoiafu	1	III	Excavated

SITE NO.	NAME/DESCRIPTION	CLASS	BIOTOPE	REMARKS
NT- 114	Talitoka	12	IVA	
115	Lauliki Settlement	2/15	II	
116	Lolokoka	11	IVA	
117	Faka'alofa	3	I	
118	Fungafo'imoa	6 (?)	I	
119	Fungamuihelu	6	I	
120	Faka'ahotaha Quarry	13	IVA	
121	Hihifo	6	III	
122	Peak above Vaipoa	—	I	Coral paving
123	Falehau	6	IVA	
124	Falehau	5	IVA	
125	Niutoua (Ngesii)	2	IVA	Excavated
126	Ngesii	12	IVA	
127	Hihifo Quarried Slab	13	VI	
128	Hihifo	12	III	
129	Tu'afonua	1	III	Excavated
130	Faka'ahotaha	11	V	
131	Faka'ahotaha	11	V	
132	Faka'ahotaha	11	V	
133	Faka'ahotaha	5 (?)	III	
134	Ha'ale'a	—	I	Coral paving
135	Ha'ale'a	15	I	
136	Mafa Slopes	15	II	
137	Hala Lapaha	3	II	
138	Sia near Matavai	8	IVA	
139	Funga'ana	9	IVA	Excavated
140	Hala Lapaha	3	II	
141	Hala Lapaha	—	II	Pit/depression
142	Sia	9	II	
143	Funga'ana	11	V	
144	Funga'ana	11	V	
145	Funga'ana	11	V	
146	Funga'ana	9	IVA	
147	Funga'ana	9	IVA	
148	Matavai	5	III	
149	Hihifo	9	IVA	
150	Hihifo	6/1	III	Excavated
151	Mound near Matavai	6	IVB	
152	Mound near Matavai	6	IVB	
153	Terrace above Pome'e	3	II	
154	Mound near Loto'aa	5 (?)	III	
155	Matavai (Nukufotu)	12	IVA	
156	Mafa	3	I	
157	Hihifo	11	IVA	
158	Vaipoa Inland	3/15	II	
159	Vaipoa Inland	3/15	II	
160	Vaipoa Inland	3/15	II	
161	Vaipoa Inland	15	II	
162	Vaipoa Inland	1	II/III	
163	Hihifo Transect	1/2	III/IVA	Excavated
164	Houmafakalele	11	V	
165	Houmafakalele	11	V	
166	Houmafakalele	11	V	
167	Houmafakalele	11	V	

SITE NO.	NAME/DESCRIPTION	CLASS	BIOTOPE	REMARKS
NT- 168	Houmafakalele	11	V	
169	Houmafakalele	11	V	
170	Houmafakalele	11	V	
171	Sia near Mata Sites	9	V	
172	Motu	11	IVA	
173	Taumaahina	12	IVA	
174	Taumaahina	12	IVA	
175	Taumaahina	12	IVA	
176	Angihoa	12	IVA	
177	Ve'elangi I	12	IVA	
178	Fakapaia	9	IVA	
179	Ve'elolo I	7	V	
180	Ve'elolo II	9	V	
181	Loto'aa	11	IVA	
182	Loto'aa	10	III	
183	Pottery Site/Terrace	1	II	
184	Atatuka	11	V	
185	Atatuka	11	V	
186	Atatuka	11	V	
187	Atatuka	11	V	
188	Fisikuohele	10 (?)	IVA	
189	Vaipoa	11	IVA	
190	Tou'one, Vaipoa	11	IVA	
191	Maa pits, Hala Lapaha	15	II	
192	Terrace, Hala Lapaha	3	II	
193	Terrace, maa pits, Hala Lapaha	3/15	II	
194	Terraces	3	II	
195	Peitolahi	12	IVA	
196	Hihifo	11	IVA	

APPENDIX B

TEMPER SANDS IN SHERDS FROM NIUATOPUTAPU EXCAVATIONS IN TONGA

by W. R. Dickinson

EIGHTEEN SHERDS COLLECTED by P.V. Kirch on Niuatoputapu in Tonga were examined in thin section and compared with 36 other Tongan sherds examined previously for Davidson, Poulsen, Rogers, Shutler, and Sinoto from Niuatoputapu (9), Vava'u (3), Ha'apai (14), and Tongatapu (10). All fall within the Tongan spectrum of calcareous, ferromagnesian, and pumiceous or lithic tempers described previously (Dickinson 1974a). Table 1 indicates the temper type present in each sherd examined, and table 2 shows the modal composition of each temper type identified. On petrographic grounds alone, no specific sources for the various related temper types can be suggested. All are andesitic arc tempers suitable for derivation from an active volcanic chain like that which forms the bedrock islands of Tonga. The prevalence of the same grain types, though in varying proportions, from all the Tongan sites sampled to date suggests that the sands represent aggregates of various kinds collected from beaches, ravines, and pyroclastic accumulations within Tonga.

Grain Types

The tempers in the Kirch sherds from Niuatoputapu are volcanic sands of simple mineralogy except for some that contain admixtures of calcareous sand representing shelly detritus from fringing reefs. All are moderately to well sorted, but the degree of rounding varies. The dominant grain types are (a) volcanic rock fragments, commonly glassy and pumiceous, and (b) crystals of pyroxene and plagioclase, which are the common phenocryst minerals in Tongan volcanic rocks. Both clinopyroxene and orthopyroxene occur, although the latter is distinctly less abundant. Subordinate opaque iron oxides are ubiquitous as well, and rare quartz grains are also present.

The volcanic rock fragments in sherds from Niuatoputapu are typically glass-rich and pumiceous, commonly with markedly stretched vesicles that form a planar fabric within the grains. The volcanic rock fragments in sherds from Tongatapu, Ha'apai, and Vava'u are mainly microcrystalline varieties. However, some glassy pumiceous grains similar to those in sherds from Niuatoputapu also occur in selected sherds from the other Tongan sites.

Calcareous Tempers

Three (3) of the sherds (see table 1) contain well sorted and subrounded beach (?) sands in which calcareous grains of reef detritus are dominant (see table 2). One other sherd (see table 1) contains a related calcareous ferromagnesian temper (Calc-FM) in which pyroxene is the dominant grain type. The tempers in these four sherds from the Kirch collection on Niuatoputapu are closely comparable to similar calcareous and ferromagnesian tempers in four analogous sherds from the earlier Rogers collection on Niuatoputapu (Dickinson, 1974a). The volcanic rock fragments in these varieties of calcareous temper sand are mostly microcrystalline types lacking the

TABLE 1

CORRELATION OF ARTIFACT COLLECTION NUMBER (PVK) AND THIN-SECTION SLIDE NUMBER (WRD) FOR SELECTED SHERDS OF VARIOUS TEMPER TYPES EXCAVATED ON NIUATOPUTAPU, TONGA

ARTIFACT NUMBER	SLIDE NUMBER	TEMPER TYPE
NT-90-A25I-5	42-1	Calcareous
NT-90-YY25II-2	42-2	Pumiceous
NT-90-YY25II-3	42-3	Placer
NT-90-YY25III-8	42-4	Calc-FM*
NT-90-YY26I-4	42-5	Calcareous
NT-90-ZZ25I-7	42-6	Calcareous
NT-93-60-1	42-7	Pumiceous**
BT-93-89-3	42-8	Crystal-Lithic
NT-93-90-20	42-9	Crystal-Lithic
NT-93-100-1	42-10	Pumiceous
NT-93110-6	42-11	Pumiceous
NT-93-110-7	42-12	Pumiceous
NT-100-218-5	42-13	Pumiceous
NT-100-218-6	42-14	Crystal-Lithic
NT-100-218-7	42-15	Crystal-Lithic
NT-100-218-8	42-16	Pumiceous
NT-100-220-5	42-17	Placer
NT-100-230-5	42-18	Pumiceous

* Calc-FM signifies calcareous ferromagnesian (see text)
** Fully 90% of grains are volcanic rock fragments, mostly pumiceous types

pumiceous structures so widespread in other Niuatoputapu sherds. Origins elsewhere in Tonga may well be indicated, but similar calcareous ferromagnesian tempers are present alike in selected sherds from Tongatapu, Ha'apai, and Vava'u. Consequently, no specific source can be isolated. Moreover, the mingling of ferromagnesian volcanic sands and calcareous reefal sands may well be a process that is duplicated in a number of places scattered throughout Tonga.

Pumiceous Tempers

Eight (8) of the sherds, the largest number, contain lithic sands in which glassy volcanic rock fragments, mainly with pumiceous textures, are dominant (see tables 1, 2). This temper type is the most abundant in the Rogers collection as well as in the Kirch collection from Niuatoputapu. It seems likely that this sand represents some common kind of ash or reworked ash available locally on Niuatoputapu or on nearby Tafahi.

Crystal-Lithic Tempers

Four other sherds contain crystal-lithic tempers (tables 1, 2) in which pyroxene and plagioclase grains are present in proportions subequal to those of the pumiceous volcanic rock fragments. The higher content of mineral grains in the crystal-lithic sands can be attributed to additional winnowing of the normal pumiceous sands. The crystal-lithic temper is thus merely a variant of the presumably indigenous Niuatoputapu (—Tafahi?) temper suite.

Placer Tempers

Two of the sherds contain sands for which even more marked winnowing produced a placer concentration of iron oxide grains (table 1, 2). Except for their higher content of opaques, the placer tempers are thus similar in mineralogy to the pumiceous and crystal-lithic tempers.

Discussion

Two-thirds to three-quarters of the sherds examined in thin section from the Kirch and Rogers collections on Niuatoputapu contain pumiceous, crystal-lithic, or placer variants of a presumably indigenous Niuatoputapu (—Tafahi?) temper suite. The diagnostic signature of the temper type is the abundance of glassy volcanic rock fragments having a pale brown or tan color in thin section and the microvesicular structure of pumiceous ash. The remainder of the Niuatoputapu sherds contain a spectrum of generally related calcareous and calcareous ferromagnesian tempers of uncertain origin or origins, either from sites nearby or elsewhere within Tonga. Both sets of sherds contain temper sands of andesitic arc type whose most likely origin was within Tonga; known Fijian and Samoan tempers are distinctly different (Dickinson, 1969, 1971, 1973, 1974b, 1976).

TABLE 2

APPROXIMATE COMPOSITIONS OF NIUATOPUTAPU TEMPER TYPES OR VARIANTS IN ESTIMATED FREQUENCY PERCENTAGE BASED ON COUNTS OF 100 TO 200 SAND GRAINS PER SHERD

GRAIN TYPE	CALCAREOUS	CALC-FM	PUMICEOUS*	CRYSTAL-LITHIC	PLACER
(No. of Sherds)	(3)	(1)	(7)	(4)	(2)
Calcareous	65-75	10	—	—	—
Volcanic Rock Fragments	10-15	10-15	50-75	30-40	30-40
Pyroxene	10	60	10-30	30-40	20-30
Plagioclase (& minor quartz)	2-5	10-15	10-20	25-35	15-20
Opaque Iron Oxides	2-5	5	2-5	2-5	20

* Rare calcareous grains also present.

REFERENCES CITED

Dickinson, W.R. 1969. Temper sands in prehistoric potsherds from Vailele and Falefa. Report 19. In R.C. Green and Davidson, J.M., eds., *Archaeology in Western Samoa*, vol. 1, pp. 271-273. Auckland Institute and Museum Bulletin 6.

_____. 1971. Petrography of some sand tempers in prehistoric pottery from Viti Levu, Fiji. *Fiji Museum Records*, 1(5):107-121 (Sigatoka Research Project Misc. Pap. No. 2).

_____. 1973. Sand temper in prehistoric potsherds from the Singatoka Dunes, Viti Levu, Fiji. In L. Birks, *Archaeological Excavations at Sigatoka Dune Site, Fiji*, pp. 69-72. Fiji Museum Bulletin 1. Suva.

_____. 1974a. Sand tempers in sherds from Niuatoputapu and elsewhere in Tonga. *Journal of the Polynesian Society* 83:342-345.

_____. 1974b. Temper sands in sherds from Mulifanua and comparison with similar tempers at Vailele and Sasoa'a (Falefa), Report 35. In R.C. Green and J.M. Davidson, eds., *Archaeology in Western Samoa*, vol. 2, pp. 179-170. Auckland Institute and Museum Bulletin 7.

_____. 1976. Mineralogy and petrology of sand tempers in sherds from the ferry berth site, Paradise site, and Jane's Camp. In J.D. Jennings, R.N. Holmer, J.C. Janetski, and J.L. Smith, *Excavations on Upolu, Western Samoa*, pp. 99-103. Pacific Anthropological Records 25. Honolulu: B.P. Bishop Museum.

APPENDIX C

ARCHAEOLOGICAL INVESTIGATIONS ON TAFAHI ISLAND

by Tom Dye

TAFAHI ISLAND, A YOUTHFUL VOLCANIC CONE, stands just over 7 km from the northern tip of Niuatoputapu Island. In outline the island resembles a triangle with rounded corners, the apex of which points to the NNW. From south to north the island measures 2.75 km, with a maximum width in the south of only 1.175 km, and an area of just 333 ha (Wood 1978:108). The island's summit, at a height of 560 m, is reached at the caldera rim near the SW corner of the island. Slopes along the west side descend precipitously from the caldera rim and are cut by steep-sided ravines that carry immense boulders when flooded with rain. Along the north, east and south sides similarly steep slopes are broken by a narrow sill of more gently sloping land between 100 and 250 m elevation, and it is upon this sill that the Tafahi people build their homes and plant their gardens.

At the north end of the island the sill is at its broadest and most gently sloping, extending nearly to the sea. The island's only village, Kolokakala, is located here today. Along the entire east side of the island and most of the south side as well, the sill is truncated by steep cliffs and access to the coast is extremely difficult. Only at Olovalu, near the SW end of the sill do the slopes lessen somewhat, so that one can walk with relative ease to the sea.

Tafahi's surface is almost invariably rocky and the active work of erosion is everywhere apparent. The trail leading from Kolokakala to the prime garden lands of the sill is uneven and strewn with immense boulders, so that any form of wheeled transport is impossible. Subsistence crops and the narcotic *kava (Piper methysticum),* grown primarily for export, are transported to town on the backs of small horses, or more frequently suspended from the ends of a pole balanced on a shoulder *(ha'amo)* and carried back. This is difficult labor, even with a relatively light load, and the reputation for hard work that Tafahi men have in Tonga is well earned.

Just as Tafahi's rugged face makes work on land difficult, so her narrow, wave-swept fringing reefs make the usual Tongan forms of shallow-water fishing treacherous. Along the south and southwest coasts these reefs provide so little protection that beaches are composed of coral cobbles and boulders, but elsewhere clean white sand and gravel beaches are common. Outboard motorboats gain access to the shore through one of two small channels on the northern end of the western coast, the larger and safer of which was blasted within the last few years by a construction crew from New Zealand. Both channels are narrow and treacherous in all but the calmest seas. For much of the year the preferred fishing strategy, that of angling with a handline from a boat just outside the reef, is impossible due to high seas which block passage through the channels.

The archaeological survey and excavation results reported here are based on two periods of fieldwork on Tafahi totalling ten working days. The first fieldwork period, from November 27 to December 3, 1976 was devoted entirely to survey. The author is indebted to Paulo Faka'osi for invaluable assistance during this phase of fieldwork. The second period, from March 9 to 13, 1984 was devoted to excavation of a pottery-bearing site at Fatuloa, and further surface collection of pottery sherds. The twin aims of this fieldwork period were to collect sufficient pottery to place the early occupation of the island within the pottery sequence established for Niuatoputapu Island, and to test for the presence of pottery deposits similar to those excavated at sites NT-90, -93, and -100. During this phase the author was assisted by Greg McManus, Sione Holikimafua Hoa, Salesi Limoni, and Kolio 'Afa. Much of this report was written in Tonga, and the author owes a great debt to Sione and Piula Hoa and Sione Falani, whose care and attention made report preparation possible. Finally, neither period of fieldwork would have taken place without the encouragement and guidance of Patrick Kirch, who suggested that the author explore Tafahi in the first place.

SURVEY

Survey results reported here are designed to serve as a general guide to the prehistoric sites of Tafahi Island. Future work on the island will hopefully show them to be incomplete and deficient in detail, but given the small size of the island and the intimacy with which its residents know the land, it is doubtful whether any serious gaps remain. Survey techniques were designed for speed rather than extreme precision. Sites were located by compass triangulation where possible, or more commonly through a combination of azimuth from some known point and dead reckoning. To make up for loss of mapping each site without a local name has been named after the land unit *('api)* in which it is located, and the name of the tenant in 1984 is given. These data should aid future attempts to relocate the sites described below. Sites are located in figure 1 and listed in table 1.

Habitation Sites

Oral history records a time when settlement covered a wider area than it does today. Whether this indicates a population greater than the 47 reported in 1931 (Wood 1978:108), or the 265 censused in 1976 (Kingdom of Tonga, n.d.), or merely reflects a change in settlement pattern is unknown. Given the considerable constraints to productive agriculture imposed by the island's small size and steep slopes, and the paucity of productive fishing reefs, it is doubtful that the prehistoric population ever exceeded its present level for long periods of time. Apart from Kolokakala, which has been settled for as long as anyone can remember, two places are pointed out as former settlement sites *(nofo'anga).* The first of these (Site 1) represents an uphill extension of the present village to a place known as Mata ki 'Uvea. The entire area from Kolokakala to Mata ki 'Uvea has been much disturbed by cultivation, so that only segments of rock alignments and scattered patches of coral gravel and pebbles *(patapata)* indicate a past use of the area different from that of today. The remnant rock alignments are constructed of volcanic cobble and boulder slabs, 10 to 15 cm thick, set end-to-end on their long edges. No corners were found from which the original length of alignments could be measured. Informants also claimed that the area had been used as a

TABLE 1

SITE NAMES, TYPES, AND LOCATIONS OF STRUCTURAL FEATURES ON TAFAHI ISLAND

SITE NO.	SITE NAME	SITE TYPE	GRID COORDINATES
1	Mata ki 'Uvea	habitation/burial complex	HC 518 456
2	Faletoli'a	*'esi, fa'itoka*	HC 520 454
3	No name	*'esi*	HC 524 454
4	Sia keli	*sia*	HC 527 542
5	'Auhangamea	*fa'itoka*	HC 532 442
6	'One'atea I	*fa'itoka*	HC 527 456
7	'One'atea II	*'esi*	HC 528 455
8	Fakahifonga	platform	HC 531 439
9	Kolotau, Fungapiu	fortress/*fa'itoka*	HC 524 446
10	Manuvai	*sia*	HC 525 457

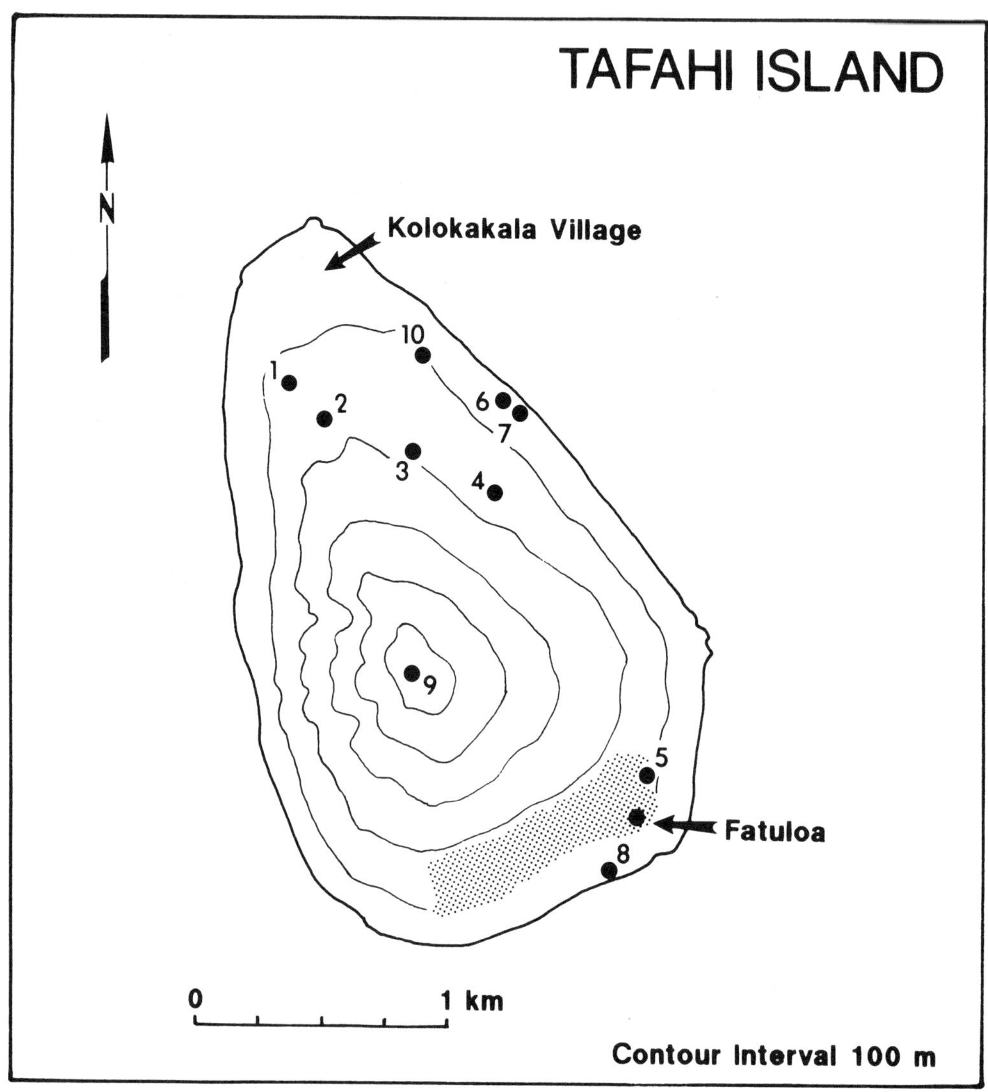

Figure 1. Map of Tafahi Island, showing the locations of archaeological sites. Stippled area indicates the extent of the pottery zone.

burial ground, and given that slab alignments and *patapata* are features of both house sites and graves, it is not possible to state with certainty the function of any particular site. It seems reasonable to suppose that both house sites and graves are found in the area.

The second area of past habitation recalled by oral tradition is located on the sill at the island's SE corner. Like Mata ki 'Uvea the sill here is frequently cultivated and remnants of features which may have been sites are now badly disturbed. They generally appear today as small patches of dispersed coral *patapata* made soft and rotten through dissolution by rainwater and the acidity of the island's volcanic soils. *Patapata* patches were encountered sparsely distributed throughout the sill, generally on small, fairly level areas *(lauua)* cleared of volcanic rock. No attempt was made to locate these features precisely. Due to the probability that this broad area contains several discrete site clusters it was not assigned a site number.

A third habitation site, though somewhat specialized, is Kolotau (Site 9), a fortress located at the island's summit. The site is fortified by a combination of natural and man-made features. To the west the summit is bounded by sheer cliffs, difficult to ascend and easily defended. Defensive earthworks take advantage of this situation with a ditch up to 2 m deep and 2 m wide that encircles the summit and abuts the cliff on either side of the site at a level about 100 m below the summit. This ditch, now much eroded and collapsed in places, is still quite striking and if combined with a stout wooden palisade on its uphill side, like other Tongan *kolotau* (Martin 1981:79, 80; McKern 1929:80-1), would certainly have proved a formidable barrier. No vestiges of a palisade remain, however, and the interior of Kolotau yields no evidence of extended habitation or extensive modification.

Mounds and Platforms

McKern (1929:10) proposed a five-fold classification of Tongan mounds and platforms based primarily on functional considerations, but with certain structural correlates. McKern's classification is summarized in Table 2.

Though open to criticism (Davidson 1969:279 ff), the classification serves as a useful point of departure. As with any other classification based on orally transmitted categories, terms and their referents are subject to change over time and space. Discrepancies between McKern's classification and classifications now elicited from Tongans in various parts of the Kingdom point to certain terminological and semantic changes taking place in the Tongan language. This discussion points to the probable nature of some of these changes and discusses the limitations of the classification with regard to the data collected on Tafahi's mounds and platforms.

The distinction noted by McKern between mounds with a flat surface and mounds with a central depression is widely used in Tonga today to distinguish *'esi* (chiefly resting places) from *sia heu lupe* (pigeon snaring mounds). But, as McKern (1929:13, 19) himself realized, informants are not always consistent in their classification of these structures and there is no guarantee that, once constructed, a mound's function could not change. A further complication encountered when trying to apply the distinction between *'esi* and *sia heu lupe* in the field is that Tongans today often use the unmarked generic term *sia* to refer to mounds in general, without implying a particular form or function. If McKern's classification were to be followed strictly these *sia* would have to be considered unclassified mounds, despite the fact that to informants the term *sia* contrasts with mounds used for burial, the generic term for which is *fa'toka*. In the descriptions below, *sia* refers to unfaced mounds with or without central depressions, and stands in a relationship of inclusion to the more specific terms *'esi* and *sia heu lupe*.

TABLE 2

McKERN'S CLASSIFICATION OF MOUNDS AND PLATFORMS

CLASS	FUNCTION	STRUCTURAL CORRELATES
I. *'Esi* mound A. Circular B. Rectangular	I. Chiefly resting place	I. Faced with stone or timber; flat or slightly sloping surface
II. Pigeon mounds A. Type I B. Type II	II. Site of chiefly pigeon-snaring	II. Raised area with central depression A. Stone faced; lined central pit B. Unfaced; shallow central depression
III. House platform	III. Foundation for house construction	III. Stone door sill
IV. Grave mounds A. *Tanu'anga* B. *Fa'itoka*	IV. Burial A. Commoner B. Chiefly family and retainers	IV. Raised area A. Small; earth or sand B. Large; interior stone vault
C. *Langi*	C. Tu'i Tonga family	C. Rectangular platform faced with dressed stone; stepped or unstepped; one or more internal stone vaults
V. Unclassified mounds		

McKern says little about house platforms in *Archaeology of Tonga*. The problems faced when trying to distinguish disturbed house platforms from grave sites on the basis of surface remains is noted above. This is a problem that will need a solution when the archaeology of Tonga's recent past comes into its own.

Finally, the Tongan classification of grave mounds presented by McKern appears to be falling victim to changes in the social order. Though informants can still be found who will independently verify McKern's information, the majority of Tongans today use the terms *tanu'anga* and *fa'itoka* as virtual synonyms when referring to grave sites. In present usage the main distinction between the terms is that *fa'itoka* refers only to human graves, whereas *tanu'anga* can be used to refer more generally to a place where something (anything) is buried. The result of this is that informant testimony to the effect that a certain feature is a *fa'itoka* does not necessarily imply that the feature was used to inter a chief and his retinue (Davidson 1969:282), but instead refers to the fact that the feature was used for human burial. This apparent weakening of the distinction between chiefly (not royal) and commoner graves most likely has as its basis Tonga's 1862 Edict of Emancipation, which strictly curtailed the despotic control previously exercised by chiefs over commoners (see Latukefu 1975:33-5).

'Esi, Chiefly Resting Places

Three *'esi* were recorded on Tafahi.

Site 2, feature 1; Faletoli'a, Catholic Church garden

A nearly circular structure, varying between 20 and 22.5 m in diameter, constructed of volcanic boulders and cobbles to a maximum height of just over 2 m. The platform surface has been filled with soil and is generally free of rock. Near the middle of the platform is a very slightly raised rectangular area, approximately 8 x 7 m, with remnants of a limestone slab facing and coral *patapata* which, though distributed thinly over the entire platform, appears to be concentrated within the rectangular area. This interior platform is an unusual feature for a chiefly resting place and was not recorded by McKern for other *'esi* in Tonga. There is, however, no guarantee that the *'esi* and the interior platform are contemporaneous, nor that the site ever functioned as a chiefly resting place. The site has been badly disturbed by cultivation activities over its entire surface and by the removal of cobbles and boulders from the platform to construct a wall that marks the present boundary of the Catholic Church garden.

Site 3, No name, 'api 'o 'Eneasi Folau

An oddly shaped platform constructed of volcanic boulders and cobbles piled atop a natural rock outcrop, the shape of the outcrop perhaps determining the shape of the platform. Maximum plan dimensions are approximately 17 m N-S and 18 m E-W, with a maximum height on the northern, downslope side of 5 m. Wall heights diminish progressively upslope to a height of one meter on the western wall and .75 m on the eastern. The platform's surface is soil-covered and relatively free of stones. No interior features were noted.

Site 7, 'One'atea II, 'api 'o Masalu

A rectangular volcanic boulder and cobble faced terrace that abuts the talus slope at the back of a narrow coastal plain, about 20 m above the high tide line. The terrace measures 18 m x 6.5 m and stands 0.75 m high along its seaward face. The surface is sandy soil nearly free of stones and lacking interior features. The ends of the terrace have been broken down by vegetation growth but the site is in otherwise good condition.

Sia, Mounds

Site 4, Sia keli, 'api 'o Kilione Vaka

An earthen mound 22 x 14 m in plan, with a central depression about 50 cm deep measuring 4.5 x 3 m. The site is now cut by the main trail from Kolokakala to the gardens of the sill, and where the trail crosses the edges of the mound volcanic rocks are exposed, suggesting a possible boulder facing for the mound. If the mound were ever faced however, only one other small boulder remains exposed to view, and it is likely that the mound was never faced.

Site 10, Manuvai, 'api 'o Saia Malamala

A terrace situated near the edge of a cliff east of Kolokakala which holds a commanding view of the ocean. The terrace is faced on the north and west sides by a volcanic boulder wall that reaches a height of 2 m. The wall diminishes in height as it approaches the uphill slope to the south, creating a level surface for the terrace. The eastern portion of the retaining wall is broken down, making the extent of the feature difficult to determine. The top of the *sia* is covered with a rich humic soil. There is no coral *patapata* and no remnant of a central depression.

According to local tradition, when pigeons fly to Tafahi from Samoa they alight at Manuvai. As they are extremely tired from their long flight they make easy prey. The site is noteworthy in that it is faced and lacks a central depression. If McKern's classification were followed it would be necessary to class this site as an *'esi*. Informants, however, were unanimous and quite specific about the function of the site. It is possible that the site had more than one function. The fine view and cool breeze at Manuvai would certainly recommend it as a chiefly resting place *('esi)*.

Fa'itoka, Burial Mounds

Site 2, Feature 2, Faletoli'a, 'api 'oe Siasi Katolika

Located immediately upslope from Site 2, Feature 1 is a raised area of mixed coralline beach sand and volcanic soil about 25 x 10 m in extent and identified by informants as a *fa'itoka*. This information was verified by the presence on the ground surface of many bone fragments, including a single intact human vertebra. The entire *fa'itoka* has been churned up by repeated cultivation and now is in a very poor state of preservation.

Site 5, 'Auhangamea, 'api 'o Finetoupalangi

An area of scattered coral *patapata* of undetermined extent and lacking any surface structural features. A single piece of human cranium was found on the surface, suggesting use of the area as a burial ground. The area is now gardened intensively.

Site 6, 'One'atea I, 'api 'o Masalu

A two-stepped terrace built among the boulders of the talus on the inland edge of a narrow coastal plain. The first step is bounded by a 17 m long coral and volcanic boulder and cobble facing that varies in height between 0.5 and 1.0 m. The inner step, about 0.2 m high, defines an area 5 x 3.5 m, and is constructed of beach rock boulder slabs set on edge end-to-end. The beach rock slabs show no obvious quarrying marks.

This site is said to be the resting place of a Samoan woman, Nikola Afa, and her child. Nikola was pregnant at the time of her arrival on Tafahi and asked that both she and her child be buried at this spot so that they could look to their homeland in the afterlife.

Site 9, Feature 2, Fungapiu

A small earthen mound, 3.5 x 2.5 m, located at the island's peak. The mound stands about 50 cm high and is encircled by a ditch 50 cm wide and between 25 and 50 cm deep. Coral *patapata* is scattered over the surface of the mound.

UNCLASSIFIED SITE

Site 8, Fakahifonga

A terrace, 13 x 9 m in plan, located at the base of the talus slope on the coastal plain. The facing wall, up to 2 m wide is built upon four massive volcanic boulders to a maximum height of 3 m. Construction materials include volcanic boulders and numerous coral boulders collected from the coral boulder and cobble beach that fronts the site. The platform surface is covered with coral *patapata*. The site is in good condition, except for the southeastern corner, which has slumped. Informants did not know the function of this site, though the presence of the coral *patapata* on the surface suggests a *fa'itoka*.

POTTERY BEARING SITES

Prehistoric earthenware pottery, similar to that found in profusion on the north coast of Niuatoputapu Island was found thinly scattered over two broad areas of Tafahi Island.

The first area, at the present village of Kolokakala, was first recognized in the late 1960s by Paulo Faka'osi, a Tafahi resident who recovered a single potsherd at 'Ahao on the SE outskirts of the village. Pottery at Kolokakala was found primarily in the erosion channels that scar the village, but also on the surface of dwelling terraces where erosion is at a minimum. In no case was pottery found in the face of an erosion cut, or in any other location that would indicate the presence of a primary deposit, so the source of the pottery found on the surface is still unknown. A search of the bush uphill from the village in 1976 failed to turn up a single surface sherd.

This unfortunate situation is to be expected, however, for the land in Kolokakala has been extensively worked and reworked through erosion and terracing for house platforms. If, as seems probable, settlement during the era of pottery manufacture was on the site of Kolokakala village, then the more than 1,000 years since pottery manufacture's demise must have witnessed the complete turnover of the village soil and consequent destruction of primary pottery deposits.

The second area at which pottery was found stretches from 'Auhangamea to Olovalu on the sill along the island's south side. Pottery sherds were found here widely distributed over the surface, but seemingly concentrated on the numerous small flats that break the island's rocky slopes. In 1976, when this distribution was first noted, two explanations seemed equally probable. The first was that the small flat areas observed today are fairly permanent features of the island

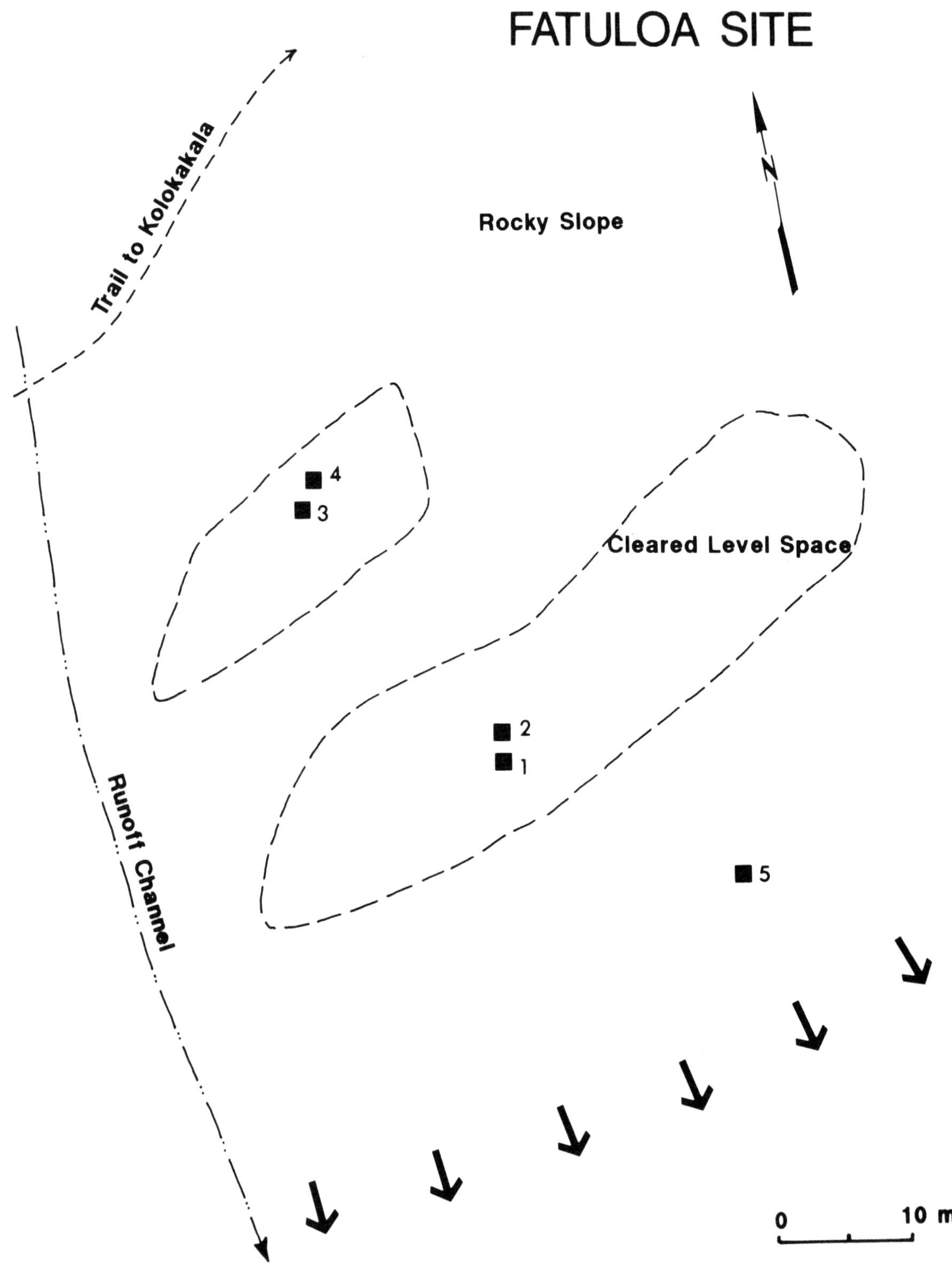

Figure 2. Plan of the Fatuloa site, showing the locations of test pits 1-5.

landscape, whose high concentration of surface pottery was due to their being loci of primary pottery deposition. The second was that the flat areas, as areas of deposition in a landscape dominated by erosion, serve as temporary "reservoirs" for pottery as it makes its way downslope. The two explanations are not mutually exclusive, but clearly if Tafahi were to contribute significantly to an understanding of the early prehistory of Tonga's northern islands intact primary deposits would have to be found and excavated. A primary aim of the 1984 research was to discover, through limited test excavations of an area with a high concentration of surface sherds, the relative contribution of primary deposition to the distribution of pottery observed today.

EXCAVATION

The area chosen for excavation is in the land district of Fatuloa, within the gardens of Hanitele Hui, a Tafahi resident (see figure 2). Fatuloa, like other areas on the island's narrow SE sill, is dominated by steep slopes strewn with volcanic boulders and cobbles. Fatuloa differs from most other areas in having a relatively large flat area immediately inland of the coastal cliffs. In 1984 this flat area had been planted to *'ufi (Dioscorea* sp.), but caterpillars had killed nearly the entire garden, leaving the ground surface exposed and easily surveyed. Surface survey revealed a high concentration of sherds on this large flat and on the relatively gentle slope leading to the cliff edge, with a markedly sparser distribution of sherds on the small flat above and on the rocky slopes leading up to the trail.

Five 1 m^2 test pits were excavated to sterile subsoil following standard archaeological practice, with soil sifted through 0.25 inch mesh screen to facilitate recovery of small artifacts. Test pits 1 and 2 were placed near the middle of the large flat. Test pits 3 and 4 were excavated on the small flat immediately above, and test pit 5 was excavated on the slope leading to the cliff edge (see map).

Stratigraphic profiles of test pits 1-4 were similar and may be described together. In these pits a single layer of black (5YR 2.5/1, moist) loam, 38 to 75 cm thick, with a fine crumb structure overlay a strong brown (7.5YR 4/5) clay subsoil with numerous saprolitic pebbles. The contact between the two layers was abrupt except where disturbed by roots and digging for gardening. Scattered throughout the black loam soil are numerous volcanic pebbles, and in test pits 1 and 2 on the large flat, many potsherds, flakes of volcanic glass and fine-grained rock were recovered.

The stratigraphy of test pit 5 differs in that the boundary between the two layers is gradual. Numerous sherds, volcanic glass flakes and fine-grained rocks were found within the dark loam and extended through the gradual boundary between the two layers.

In all cases the strong brown subsoil proved to be devoid of cultural material.

Two features, both excavated into the strong brown subsoil of test pit 3 were noted (see figure 3). Feature 1,

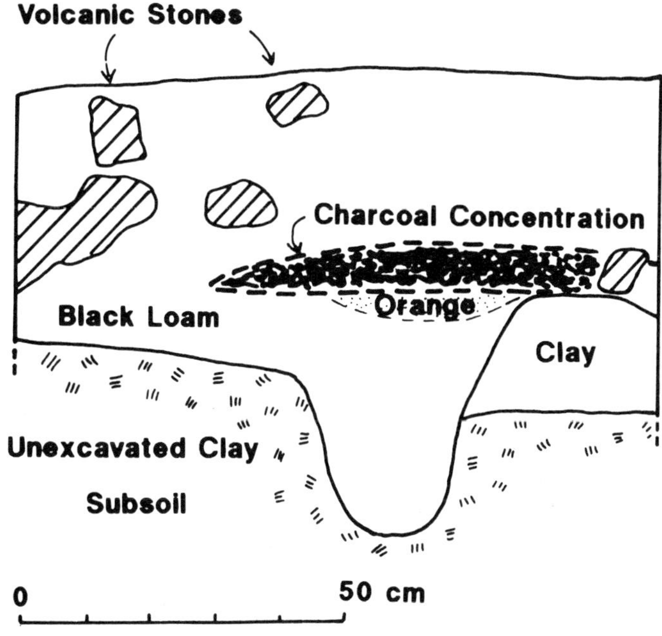

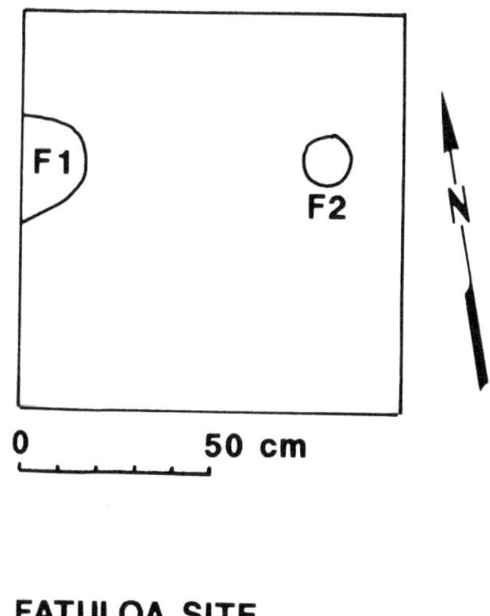

Figure 3. Plan and profile of the east face of Test Pit 3, Fatuloa.

TABLE 3

GENERAL SUMMARY OF COLLECTIONS MADE DURING THE 1984 FIELD SEASON FROM TAFAHI ISLAND

LOCATION NAME	POTTERY			LITHICS		SHELL*	CORAL (GM)
	SHERDS (N)	RIMS (N)	WEIGHT (GM)	F.G. ROCK (N)	VOLC. GLASS (N)		
Kilikili	61	2	240	3	2	—	—
Fatuloa (surface)	256	7	680	7	13	—	—
'Auhangamea	12	1	70	4	1	—	—
Olovalu	6	0	40	0	0	—	—
Kolokakala	3	0	26	16	3	—	—
Fatuloa (excavated)							
Pit 1	190	2	370	3	33	P	70
Pit 2	145	1	313	0	16	P	112
Pit 3	7	0	12	1	3	A	226
Pit 4	3	1	4	0	4	A	1
Pit 5, I	136	2	275	3	19	P	0
Pit 5, II	11	1	37	0	3	P	0
TOTALS	830	17	2067	37	97		409

* P = Present, A = Absent

partially excavated in the western edge of the pit, is a nearly circular depression 25 cm in diameter and 19 cm deep filled with Layer I loam soil. Immediately above the feature, in the west face of the pit is a lens of black, charcoal rich soil, c. 8 cm thick that caps a small pocket of orange soils apparently oxidized during the burning that produced the black lens.

Feature 12 is a circular pit 12 cm in diameter, dug some 30 cm into the Layer II subsoil. The walls of the pit are firm and straight.

In addition to these features a large quantity of coral pebbles was recovered from the south half of the pit.

An interpretation of Features 1 and 2 and the concentration of coral pebbles is that pit 3 was placed at the edge of a buried house platform, the two features representing the remains of post holes and the coral pebbles a portion of the house floor. But with the extremely limited exposure this interpretation is little more than conjecture, and other interpretations, which do not posit a relationship between the feature and the coral pebbles may not be excluded.

ARTIFACT COLLECTIONS

Collections made during the 1984 field season are summarized in table 3 and are described briefly here. More complete descriptions of the adzes collected will be published elsewhere.

The total collection of 830 potsherds comprises 807 plain body sherds, 17 rimsherds, four carinated body sherds, and two fragments of a probable pot handle. None of the sherds exhibits the dentate stamped decoration characteristic of Lapita pottery. With the exception of a single rimsherd collected from the surface at Fatuloa (TO-Tf-fa-S78) with a probable everted orientation, all rims are very nearly vertically oriented. Due to the small size of most sherds, estimates of metrical characteristics of the pots from which they derived are usually impossible. Rough estimates from four rims suggest pots with orifice diameters of 12, 16, 20 and 24 cm.

The fine-grained rock collected includes unmodified flakes, polished flakes, and complete and partial adzes.

The six complete and nearly complete adzes exhibit a range of cross-sections and appear to be manufactured from at least two distinct rock types. Sources for either rock type are unknown to Tafahi residents and searches along the sill and in the major valleys of the west coast failed to yield a possible source. Visually similar rocks were collected eroding from the base of Mafa Ridge on Niuatoputapu, at a location suggested by Tafahi and Niuatoputapu residents. Work in progress is designed to characterize the fine-grained Niuatoputapu rocks for use in a comparative reference collection and to posit a source for the adze rocks collected on Tafahi. The results of this work will appear elsewhere.

The volcanic glass found distributed over most of the island has its source at Tefitomaka, where nodules of glass are embedded in tuff. Most of the glassy nodules are altered and soft, but with a bit of searching fresh nodules up to the size of a chicken egg may be found. Similar tuff outcrops behind Vaipoa village on Niuatoputapu yield glassy nodules as well, but given the convenient local source it seems likely that volcanic glass found on Tafahi derives from Tefitomaka.

The small amounts of marine shell collected during excavation at Fatuloa are from *Turbo, Tridacna,* and *Trochus* spp. All were heavily weathered due to contact with the acidic garden soils.

INTERPRETATION

Surface survey reveals that the two most habitable areas of rugged Tafahi Island were settled at least by the Polynesian Plain Ware period. The possibility of earlier settlement during Lapita times, difficult to disprove under the best of circumstances, seems unlikely. Settlement appears to have been dispersed, in contrast to the present nucleated pattern. Given the coincidence of pottery distribution with garden lands it is reasonable to conjecture a pattern of individual households placed here and there among active and fallow swidden gardens. Whether settlement was permanent, or represents intermittent use of the island by Niuatoputapu residents can not be determined on the basis of the data at hand.

Excavation data reinforce the general impression derived from the island's steep slopes and active erosion that sites capable of yielding information comparable to that yielded by sites NT-90, -93, and -100 are absent on Tafahi. While the features uncovered in test pit 3 at Fatuloa indicate that structural remains may persist for some period in the face of erosion and repeated digging for gardens, it seems unlikely that these features belong to the pottery making period. The temptation to see these features as analogous to those uncovered at Lolokoka is tempered by the contrast that at Fatuloa the features were not accompanied by potsherds that had escaped the ravages of the gardener's digging tools. Tafahi Island holds little promise for future explorations of the region's pottery-making period.

REFERENCES

Davidson, J. 1969. Archaeological excavations in two burial mounds at 'Atele, Tongatapu. *Records of the Auckland Institute and Museum* 6: 251-86.

Kingdom of Tonga. n.d. *Census of Population and Housing, 1976*. Nuku'alofa.

Latukefu, S. 1975. *The Tongan Constitution: A Brief History to Celebrate its Centenary*. Nuku'alofa, Tonga Traditions Committee.

Martin, J. 1981. *Tonga Islands: William Mariners Account*. 4th ed. Neiafu, Tonga: Vava'u Press.

McKern, W. C. 1929. *Archaeology of Tonga*. Bernice P. Bishop Museum Bulletin 60. Honolulu.

Wood, A.H. 1978. *History and Geography of Tonga*. Canberra, Kalia Press. Originally published 1932.

PATRICK V. KIRCH, Director of the Burke Museum in Seattle from 1984 through 1988 and Professor of Anthropology at the University of California at Berkeley, has conducted extensive archaeological research in the Pacific islands. Kirch, who received his Ph.D. from Yale University in 1975, has led archaeological expeditions to Tonga, Samoa, the Solomon Islands, Papua New Guinea, and several Micronesian islands. He has also done extensive work in Hawaii, where for a period of ten years he was a staff member of the B.P. Bishop Museum. His more recent works include *Feathered Gods and Fishhooks: An Introduction to Hawaiian Archaeology and Prehistory* (1985, University of Hawaii Press, Honolulu), *The Evolution of the Polynesian Chiefdoms* (1984, New Studies in Archaeology, Cambridge University Press, Cambridge), and *Tikopia: The Prehistory and Ecology of a Polynesian Outlier* (1982, B.P. Bishop Museum Bulletin 238, Honolulu).

Burke Museum

ISBN 0-929598-01-6

Brother Francis presents

The Story of Imelda Lambertini

The Patroness of First Holy Communicants

A COLORING STORYBOOK

The Stor
Imelda Laml

as seen on the D

Brother Francis: The Bı

Illustrations by: HERALD ENTERTAINMENT, INC.
Visit our Brother Francis series website at: www.brotherfrancisonline.com
Printed in the United States of America
First Printing: February 2012
ISBN: 978-0-9838096-5-4